THE COMPLETE PLAYS

CHRISTOPHER MARLOWE (b. 1564) was the eldest son of Canterbury shoemaker John Marlowe, and his wife, Katherine. He was elected to the King's School Canterbury at the age of fourteen, and within two years had secured a scholarship which took him to Corpus Christi College, Cambridge, where he was supposedly destined for a career in the Anglican Church. He successfully completed his BA examinations in 1584, and continued his studies as a candidate for the MA. During this period his absences from Cambridge stirred rumours that he was about to flee to the Catholic seminary at Rheims in France. In 1587 the Privy Council took the unusual step of persuading the University authorities to grant Marlowe his MA since he had been employed 'in matters touching the benefit of his country'; this has fuelled speculation that he was working as a government agent.

Marlowe probably began his writing career at Cambridge, composing translations of Ovid's *Amores*, and Lucan's *Pharsalia*, as well as producing *Dido, Queen of Carthage* for the Children of the Chapel in 1586 (possibly co-written with Thomas Nashe). In 1587–8 he acquired his reputation as one of the leading new talents on the London stage with *Tamburlaine the Great*. His finest play, *Doctor Faustus*, was written in 1588–9, and was followed by *The Jew of Malta* (*c.* 1590), *Edward the Second* and *The Massacre at Paris* (both *c.* 1592). The erotic epyllion *Hero and Leander* was probably written in 1592–3 when the plague forced the theatres to close.

Throughout this period, Marlowe was frequently in trouble with the authorities, though for his actions and not his playwriting. He and the poet Thomas Watson were briefly imprisoned in September 1589 for their involvement in the death of William Bradley; in 1592 Marlowe was deported from Flushing, Holland, having been implicated in a counterfeiting scheme. He acquired a dangerous reputation as an atheist, and the following year he was summoned to appear before the Privy Council on charges of blasphemy, arising from evidence provided by Thomas Kyd, the author of the hugely popular play *The Spanish Tragedy*.

Several days later, on 30 May 1593, Christopher Marlowe was fatally stabbed in Deptford.

FRANK ROMANY was educated at Magdalen College, Oxford, where he also taught for some years. He was until September 2003 Lecturer and Tutor in English at St John's College, Oxford. He has published on Shakespeare and is at work on a book on John Milton.

ROBERT LINDSEY is the Associate Editor of the journal *Medieval and Renaissance Drama in England*. He has edited Marlowe's *Edward the Second* and has completed a new edition of the plays of John Webster. He is a lecturer in Classical Acting at the Central School of Speech and Drama, London.

CHRISTOPHER MARLOWE

The Complete Plays

Edited by FRANK ROMANY
and ROBERT LINDSEY

PENGUIN BOOKS

PENGUIN BOOKS

Published by the Penguin Group

Penguin Books Ltd, 80 Strand, London WC2R ORL, England

Penguin Group (USA) Inc., 375 Hudson Street, New York, New York 10014, USA

Penguin Books Australia Ltd, 250 Camberwell Road, Camberwell, Victoria 3124, Australia

Penguin Books Canada Ltd, 10 Alcorn Avenue, Toronto, Ontario, Canada M4V 3B2

Penguin Books India (P) Ltd, 11, Community Centre, Panchsheel Park, New Delhi – 110 017, India

Penguin Books (NZ) Ltd, Cnr Rosedale and Airborne Roads, Albany, Auckland, New Zealand

Penguin Books (South Africa) (Pty) Ltd, 24 Sturdee Avenue, Rosebank 2196, South Africa

Penguin Books Ltd, Registered Offices: 80 Strand, London WC2R ORL, England

www.penguin.com

First published 2003

11

Set in 10.25/12.25 pt PostScript Adobe Sabon
Typeset by Rowland Phototypesetting Ltd, Bury St Edmunds, Suffolk
Printed in England by Clays Ltd, St Ives plc

ISBN-13: 978-0-140-43633-4

www.greenpenguin.co.uk

Penguin Books is committed to a sustainable future
for our business, our readers and our planet.
The book in your hands is made from paper
certified by the Forest Stewardship Council.

Contents

Preface

This is an edition of the seven plays which modern scholarship has convincingly attributed to Marlowe. The texts have been edited from the earliest printed editions and are fully modernized. Although it has become fashionable to print two versions of *Doctor Faustus* (the A- and B-texts), we have included only the A-text, in the belief that the B-text is for the most part a later, post-Marlovian adaptation of the play, the inclusion of which would have made this already large volume unwieldy for its readers. The text of *Doctor Faustus* is discussed in more detail in the Notes, while general editorial procedures are explained in the Note on the Texts.

Individual English words which are unfamiliar, obsolete or obscure are, as far as possible, explained in the Glossary (G); allusions to named people and places in the List of Mythological, Historical and Geographical Names (N). These provide core information only (such as the essential meanings of words and the outlines of myths). For further help with the understanding of the texts, the reader is referred to the Notes. Each play has a headnote dealing with matters such as the date, sources and interpretation of the play, followed by more detailed notes on the text. These deal with individual words in cases where fuller discussion is required than is possible in (G), or where the reader might not realize that an unfamiliar Elizabethan meaning is intended ('false friends'), or where Marlowe's usage is idiosyncratic; with the meaning of larger sense-units; with matters of theatrical and literary interpretation; and with the specific local pertinence of mythological and historical allusions. The Notes also record substantive emendations to the text, and include translations, as literal as possible, of passages in languages other than English.

This edition is a close collaboration between the editors, but readers may wish to know that the texts have been prepared by Robert Lindsey, while Frank Romany is principally responsible for the Introduction and Notes. Both editors wish to express their gratitude to Monica Schmoller for her patient work as copy-editor, and to the British Library and the Folger Shakespeare Library for their permission to reproduce manuscript materials in their collections.

Chronology

1564 *26 February*: Christopher, son of John Marlowe, a shoe-maker, and his wife Katherine, baptized at St George the Martyr, Canterbury.

1579 Awarded scholarship at the King's School Canterbury (where he had perhaps received his earlier education).

1580 *December*: Earliest recorded residence at Corpus Christi College, Cambridge.

1581–7 Parker Scholar at Corpus Christi.

1584 Petitions for BA degree.

1585–6 Some absences from Cambridge.

1586? *Dido, Queen of Carthage*, perhaps co-written with Thomas Nashe.

1587 *July*: MA, after certification from the Privy Council that rumours that Marlowe intended to leave England for Rheims, home of an English Catholic seminary, were untrue, and that he had done the queen 'good service'.

1587–8 *Tamburlaine the Great* Parts One and Two performed in London.

1588? At work on translations of Ovid's *Amores*, published as *All Ovid's Elegies*, and of Book One of Lucan's epic *Pharsalia* (*De Bello Civile*), published as *Lucan's First Book*.

1588–9 Earlier possible date of composition of *Doctor Faustus*.

1589 *18 September*: Imprisoned in Newgate on suspicion of murder after William Bradley, a little-known figure with a history of violence, is killed in a fight with Marlowe and his friend the poet Thomas Watson.

3 December: Appears before justices and is discharged.

1590 Perhaps acting as a courier in France.

?Writes *The Jew of Malta*.

1591 Shares lodgings with the dramatist Thomas Kyd.

1592 *26 January*: Deported from Flushing, Holland, after Richard Baines, convert from Catholicism and intelligence agent, implicates him in a counterfeiting scheme.

9 May: Bound over to keep the peace after a brawl with constables in Shoreditch.

?Writes *Edward the Second* and *The Massacre at Paris*.

1592–3 Theatres closed because of plague. Possible composition of erotic narrative poem *Hero and Leander*. Later possible date of composition of *Doctor Faustus*.

1593 *18 May*: Privy Council issues warrant for his arrest, at the house of Thomas Walsingham, Marlowe's patron, in Kent or elsewhere, after Kyd claims that supposedly heretical papers found in his rooms belong to Marlowe.

20 May: Answers warrant and appears before Privy Council.

30 May: Murdered apparently in self-defence by Ingram Frizer, servant of Walsingham, in Deptford.

1 June: Buried at St Nicholas church, Deptford.

?*2 June*: Baines accuses Marlowe of numerous blasphemies.

28 June: Frizer pardoned.

Introduction

It is not easy to account for the power of Marlowe's plays.* They are unevenly written, not always well constructed, and some survive only in mangled and unreliable texts. Yet an obscure, even dark, imaginative energy is released in them – in the victories of Tamburlaine, in Faustus' encounters with the demonic, in the irreverence of Barabas and in the humiliation of Edward. At bottom, this energy is religious. Elizabethan playwrights were not allowed to handle sacred subjects, but their greatest plays often depend on the feeling of a sacred power gone dark. Marlowe's plays of power and helplessness are filled with the energy of the sacred and its desecration.

He was apparently destined for the Church. Born and brought up in Canterbury, the ancient spiritual capital of England, he went up to Corpus Christi College, Cambridge, on a scholarship designed to educate boys for the ministry. In 1587 the university authorities considered withholding his MA (he was rumoured to be about to defect to the Catholic seminary at Rheims), until the Privy Council intervened to point out that in his absences from Cambridge he had done the queen 'good service' – a phrase usually taken to mean spying – 'and deserved to be rewarded for his faithful dealing'.[1] He got his MA, but instead of taking holy orders began writing plays for the London theatres, disreputable places – at least in the eyes of the godly – which were under constant attack as dens of iniquity. Marlowe's association with learning continued to be important to him: as late as

*New readers are advised that this Introduction and the Commentary make details of the plot explicit.

1592, when he was deported from Holland for his part in a counterfeiting scheme, he was still 'by his profession [i.e., by his own account] a scholar'.[2] But his learning was turned to distinctly heterodox ends: he translated Ovid's *Amores*, erotic poems that verged on pornography in Elizabethan eyes (they were published surreptitiously as *All Ovid's Elegies*, the title emphasizing the fact that they were unexpurgated); and he acquired a dangerous reputation for atheism. The sometime Cambridge don, Gabriel Harvey, called him 'a Lucian', associating him with the Greek satirist notorious for mocking the gods.[3] His religious views were under investigation at the time of his violent death in 1593. One Richard Cholmeley claimed to have been 'converted' by him and alleged that 'Marlowe is able to show more sound reasons for atheism than any divine in England is able to give to prove divinity and that Marlowe told him that he hath read the atheist lecture to Sir Walter Ralegh and others.'[4]

This learned heterodoxy has obvious relevance to the plays: Dr Faustus, having 'commenced' (1.3) and been 'graced' (Prologue, 17) like a Cambridge graduate, is a scholar who punningly bids 'Divinity, adieu!' (1.50) and makes a pact with the devil; and Machevil, in the prologue to *The Jew of Malta*, has to stop himself delivering an atheist lecture to the audience. More importantly, Marlowe's learning gets into the very fabric of his astonishing poetry. Consider his most famous lines, Faustus' address to the shade of Helen of Troy:

> Was this the face that launched a thousand ships
> And burnt the topless towers of Ilium?
> Sweet Helen, make me immortal with a kiss.
> Her lips sucks forth my soul. See where it flies!
> Come, Helen, come, give me my soul again.
> Here will I dwell, for heaven be in these lips,
> And all is dross that is not Helena.
> I will be Paris, and for love of thee
> Instead of Troy shall Wittenberg be sacked,
> And I will combat with weak Menelaus,
> And wear thy colours on my plumèd crest.

Yea, I will wound Achilles in the heel
And then return to Helen for a kiss.
O, thou art fairer than the evening air,
Clad in the beauty of a thousand stars.
Brighter art thou than flaming Jupiter
When he appeared to hapless Semele,
More lovely than the monarch of the sky
In wanton Arethusa's azured arms;
And none but thou shalt be my paramour. (13.90–109)

This hymn of sexual desire conceals learned ironies in its dense classical allusions. The opening questions come from Lucian's *Dialogues of the Dead*, in which a visitor to the underworld, seeing Helen's no-longer-recognizable skull, asks: 'And is this what those thousand ships sailed for from all over Greece? Is this why all those Greeks and barbarians were killed? And all those cities sacked?'⁵ Marlowe turns this into part of an oddly humanistic sexual fantasy, the necrophiliac equivalent of the scholar's desire to revive the classical past. Faustus has earlier produced Helen as an erotic after-dinner show for his scholars; now, to take his mind off his imminent damnation, he becomes her lover, repeatedly kissing her and crooning her name. Helen haunted Marlowe's imagination. What fascinated him was the destructiveness of her beauty: men died and cities burned for it. And to complete the fantasy of being a modern Paris, strutting in triumph over the heroes of antiquity, Faustus includes the destruction of his own city: 'Instead of Troy shall Wittenberg be sacked'. The later mythological allusions are similarly fraught with dangerous beauty. 'Hapless Semele' would admit the god's sexual approach only if he came in all his glory; she was consumed by his lightning. Yet the 'thousand stars', their number matching the ships, are alight with natural beauty (starlight often ignites Marlowe's poetry), and the eye catches the flash of sunlight on water in the otherwise unknown conjunction of the sun-god Apollo and the liquefied Arethusa. Moreover, the beauty of these heavenly bodies – uncertainly gods or planets – is male beauty, and the uncertainty in Faustus' imagining of ravishment plays back over the speech as a whole. The initial question – *was* this the face? – is only half-rhetorical: this is not Helen but a boy-actor and, more darkly, a succubus (an evil spirit in female form) who 'sucks forth [his] soul' in ways that are indistinguishably erotic and terrifying.

The self-destructive desire in these lines is a central preoccupation of all Marlowe's plays. *Dido, Queen of Carthage*, possibly the earliest and perhaps co-written with his younger Cambridge contemporary Thomas Nashe, is an adaptation of Virgil's narrative in the *Aeneid* of Dido's tragic passion for the Trojan exile Aeneas. It was performed, its title-page tells us, by the boy-actors of the Chapel Children's company. These two aspects of the play – its closeness to the most prestigious of Latin texts and its performance by boys – are in tension throughout the action. On the one hand, it is a learned play, full of direct translations of Virgil's most famous lines: when Aeneas asks his divine mother, disguised as a huntress, 'But what may I, fair virgin, call your name' (1.1.188), he is translating Virgil's '*o quàm te memorem virgo?*'; his speeches describing the fall and burning of Troy are bravura versions of the great narrative of *Aeneid* II; and at key moments of Act 5, the play simply quotes Virgil's Latin directly. On the other hand, the action is frequently mock-heroic, the *Aeneid* in falsetto voices. The opening scene sets the tone, beginning not with grand heterosexual passion but with the pederastic Jupiter '*dandling* GANYMEDE *upon his knee*' (0.2SD). The ambivalence of the posture, an erotic game with a child, is present too in the opening line in his sexual invitation ('Come, gentle Ganymede, and play with me'); and the Ganymede to whom the god's bribes are offered is detectably a tarty, petulant Elizabethan page-boy. This scene is not in Virgil. It owes much to Lucian, and fits well the horrified description of the boy-actors' repertoire in *The Children of the Chapel Stripped and Whipped* (1569): 'Even in her Majesty's chapel do these pretty upstart youths profane the Lord's day by the lascivious writhing of their tender limbs, and gorgeous decking of their apparel, in feigning bawdy fables gathered from the idolatrous heathen poets.'[6] Jupiter's sexual wheedling – an extended version of Marlowe's famous lyric 'The Passionate

Shepherd to his Love' ('Come live with me, and be my love')[7] –
is the first of many such invitations. Marlowe multiplies and
complicates the love-affairs, and his characters express their
desires in ways that are persistently and disturbingly linked with
children. The principal changes to Virgil are in the boy-parts
of Ascanius and Cupid. Venus abducts Ascanius with sticky
promises of 'sugar-almonds, sweet conserves, / A silver girdle
and a golden purse' (2.1.305–6) so that Cupid can take his place
and cause Dido to fall for Aeneas. When she does, she offers
('Conditionally that thou wilt stay with me') to refit his ships
with erotically luxurious

> tackling made of rivelled gold,
> Wound on the barks of odoriferous trees;
> Oars of massy ivory, full of holes,
> Through which the water shall delight to play (3.1.113, 115–18)

and promises Achates a sailor-suit that will allure the nymphs
and mermaids, 'So that Aeneas may but stay with me' (132).
Everyone is turned on, including the old Nurse, who invites
Cupid to her

> orchard that hath store of plums,
> Brown almonds, services, ripe figs, and dates,
> Dewberries, apples, yellow oranges . . . (4.5.4–6)

The cumulative effect is to drive the play away from epic and
towards comedy – the comedy of John Lyly, whose *Gallathea*
(1583–5), also written for boy-actors, makes much of the havoc
wreaked by Cupid in disguise.

Yet *Dido* is tragedy, not comedy, a generically labile play in
which love is funny but dangerous, its menace signalled by
constant reminders of Helen and the fall of Troy. When Cupid
snuggles up to Dido and sings a song on her knee in order to get
close enough to touch her with his infatuating golden arrow,
the dialogue itself glitters ominously:

DIDO
   . . . tell me where learn'dst thou this pretty song?
CUPID
   My cousin Helen taught it me in Troy. (3.1.27–8)

To keep Aeneas, Dido is even prepared to copy 'that ticing strumpet' (2.1.300):

> So thou wouldst prove as true as Paris did,
> Would, as fair Troy was, Carthage might be sacked
> And I be called a second Helena! (5.1.146–8)

Dramatic irony works here much as it does in Shakespeare's *Troilus and Cressida*: Aeneas won't be true, but will leave in the ships Dido has given him; and Carthage, of course, will be sacked in the wars with Rome which she calls down at the end of the play. Fire is everywhere – even the most woodenly Elizabethan line, 'Gentle Achates, reach the tinder-box' (1.1.166), has a spark in it – and the flames of love at once recall the firing of Troy and point forward to the fire in which Dido immolates herself. Dido's funeral pyre, fuelled by the tokens of Aeneas' love, is both a solemn sacrifice and a faintly comic hecatomb. Its arch solemnity is typical of the play as a whole; like the rest of the play, its erotic and ironic force are still underrated.

Tamburlaine the Great was Marlowe's first big hit. Written for adult players, it too is a striking instance of Renaissance neo-classicism. This may surprise us in a history-play about a fourteenth-century Asiatic conqueror, but part of Tamburlaine's significance to the Elizabethans was the coincidence of his conquests with the European Renaissance: 'During [his] reign began the restitution of learning and of the arts.'[8] Hence the hero praises his wife by claiming that if Zenocrate had lived

> before the siege of Troy,
> Helen, whose beauty summoned Greece to arms
> And drew a thousand ships to Tenedos,
> Had not been named in Homer's *Iliads*. (Part Two, 2.4.86–9)

Tamburlaine's poetry of wealth and power – what Ben Jonson called 'Marlowe's mighty line'[9] – has in fact less affinity with Homer than with the war-poetry of Lucan's *Pharsalia* (Marlowe translated its first book, and Tamburlaine alludes in Part One 3.3 to the battle that gives the poem its title). Jonson more sourly complained of the plays' 'scenical strutting, and furious vociferation',[10] and modern audiences also sometimes feel wearied by what can seem a formless action driven on by rant.

But *Tamburlaine* is not one play, but two. Part One, which its original running-title called *The Conquests of Tamburlaine the Scythian Shepherd*, is about the unstoppable rise of its hero from poverty and obscurity to 'The sweet fruition of an earthly crown' (2.6.69). It has an exceptionally clear five-act structure (roughly one per conquest), and its action was originally diversified by comic scenes which the printer cut because he thought them 'a great disgrace to so honorable and stately a history' ('To the Gentlemen Readers', 16–17). Nonetheless, it begins with comic bathos: Persia, whose past kings 'triumphed over Afric, and the bounds / Of Europe' (1.1.9–10) is now ruled by the effete Mycetes; in the first scene, the crown passes with comic rapidity to his ambitious brother Cosroe, who promises the rebels they will 'triumph over many provinces' (173). Into this power-vacuum, in Acts 1 and 2, comes Tamburlaine, a passionate shepherd – Marlowe emphasizes his humble origins, just as he exaggerates Aeneas' destitution in *Dido* – whose invitation to love ('Disdains Zenocrate to live with me? . . .', 1.2.82–105) is an astonishing offer of barbaric splendour. He even uses the display of his treasure as a military tactic. He briefly supports Cosroe, until the usurper unintentionally fuels his desire to 'ride in triumph through Persepolis', then turns on 'this triumphing king' (2.5.49, 87) and, at the end of Act 2, hymning 'aspiring minds' (2.6.60) over Cosroe's expiring body, he plucks the crown from his corpse and puts it on. Thereafter, each act ends with a coronation.

We *see* few battles. Instead the play feels like a triumphal pageant, and the idea of the Roman triumph is deep in its structure. Roman triumphal processions were celebrations of

victory, elaborate street-theatre which displayed the trium-
phator's glory in plundered spoils and the marching bodies of
enslaved captives. Their fascination for Renaissance artists is
apparent in Petrarch's allegorical *Trionfi* (1356–74); in Edmund
Spenser's *The Faerie Queene* (1590–96); and most memorably
in Mantegna's *Triumphs of Caesar* (1486–92), now at
Hampton Court and well known in the sixteenth century
through reproduction in woodcuts and engravings. *Tamburlaine*'s catalogues of names, its exhibitions of wealth and its
stage-pageantry bring the triumph to the London stage.

Yet Tamburlaine's triumphs over his enemies increasingly
seem the ceremonious exultations of sadism. The defeated Bajazeth is put in a cage and 'in triumph drawn' (4.2.86); Tamburlaine, who has felt the 'thirst of reign and sweetness of a crown'
(2.6.52), feasts while his prisoner starves, and torments him
with the strange confection of '*a second course of crowns*'
(4.4.110SD). Zenocrate, herself part of the spoils of war, is
increasingly used to register the horror of Tamburlaine's atrocities. Her pity for his victims prompts his one soliloquy ('Ah,
fair Zenocrate, divine Zenocrate . . .', 5.1.135–90); but it is a
rapturous contemplation of her suffering beauty – her crying
excites him – as a force *almost* powerful enough to restrain him.
The whole play ponders the connection of beauty and pain in
his question, 'What is beauty, saith my sufferings, then?' (1.160).
Its ending is disconcerting. Zenocrate has drawn the traditional
warnings about 'fickle empery' and 'earthly pomp' (1.352–3)
from the fall of Bajazeth and his wife; now, with their corpses
and her sometime fiancé's still on stage, she is enthroned and
crowned. This extraordinary tableau has been compared to the
amoral triumph of the lovers at the end of Monteverdi's opera
L'Incoronazione di Poppea (1642).[11] It is at once an emblem of
victory and a warning of the brutality and transience of power.

To some, Part Two seems just more of the same. But the
effect may be deliberate. The hero is a murderous automaton,
compulsively repeating what the play's running-title calls *The
Bloody Conquests of Mighty Tamburlaine*. And there are differences. Tamburlaine is offstage for most of the first two acts. He
is older; his conquests are now an empire; attention shifts to

some extent to his heirs and a new generation of antagonists. The play opens on the banks of the Danube, where the Muslim world meets Christendom, and is set against a backdrop of geopolitical conflicts. (Tellingly, the ringing place-names are now more precise: Marlowe was using an atlas.[12]) The conflicts are at once religious and territorial, and the play is not on the Christian side. The perfidious Christians are overrun by a pious Muslim who calls on Christ; the God he reveres is one 'that sits on high and never sleeps, / Nor in one place is circumscriptible' (2.2.49–50). Beyond the vast Asiatic spaces over which the action is fought out, there is a vaster spiritual dimension.

Tamburlaine too is seen against this background. His conquests continue, but are now vulnerable to irony. Callapine escapes his captivity by seducing his gaoler with an offer of a crown that parodies Tamburlaine's invitations to power; his idle and cowardly son is a damaging mockery of his killer-ethic; and, most importantly, he is helpless in the face of Zenocrate's death: his frustrated rant about invading Heaven and Hell to win her back is deflated by Theridamas's realism: 'She is dead, / And all this raging cannot make her live' (2.4.119–20). Hitherto invulnerable, his wounding his own arm to teach his sons courage is also the self-mutilation of blocked grief. He cannot even bury her body, but drags it with him, burning towns as perverse monuments to her memory. There are more victories, but they are circumscribed by the increasingly persistent references to Heaven, Hell and death.

A nuclear scientist, watching the first atomic bomb explode, grimly applied to himself the words of a great Hindu god: 'I am become Death, the destroyer of worlds.'[13] Tamburlaine too identifies with death, and his terrible chariot drawn by captive kings belongs in the traditional Triumph of Death. The idea of earthly conquest is still strong towards the end of the play – in Babylon, where earlier conquerors 'Have rode in triumph, triumphs Tamburlaine' (5.1.70) – but his march to Samarkand is cut short by his own death. Yet even here, Marlowe avoids conventional Christian moralizing. His final illness begins just after he has burned the Koran, an act which could be interpreted as a fatal defiance of divine power, except that he burns it in the

name of God ('For he is God alone, and none but he', 5.1.201).
And in the last scene, the crown with which he invests his son is
the sign of a purely secular power. The play remains studiedly
ambiguous about the religious meaning, if any, of 'Tamburlaine,
the scourge of God' (5.3.248).

Of Marlowe's own religious views, nothing certain can be
known. The closest we come is the dubious record of 'his damnable judgement of religion, and scorn of God's word' preserved
in the 'note' Richard Baines delivered to the Privy Council
close to the time of Marlowe's death. Baines was a hostile and
unreliable witness (he had been apprehended with Marlowe for
counterfeiting in Holland; each accused the other of intending
to desert to the Catholic enemy), and his note is an informer's
delation. But it is the nearest thing we have to evidence and is
reprinted at the end of this Introduction. The opinions it contains are clever and provocative. The religion of Moses was
magical trickery, designed, like all religion, 'only to keep men
in awe'. The New Testament is 'filthily written', its mysteries
sexual scandals. The most entertaining blasphemy – 'That
St John the Evangelist was bedfellow to Christ and leaned always
in his bosom, and that he used him [note the ambiguity of the
pronouns] as the sinners of Sodoma' – sounds like an accusation
until you read the disarming sequel: 'That all they that love not
tobacco and boys were fools.'

More important, perhaps, to an understanding of the place
of religion in Marlowe's plays is the context of Counter-
Reformation Europe. 'Atheism' in the sixteenth century did not
preclude belief in God. It was what you accused someone else
of. The unity of Christendom, at once political and religious,
was split by a confessional division which turned each side's
deepest spiritual convictions to derision. For Protestants, Catholicism was a murderous conspiracy to uphold the hegemony
of Spain and the papacy; in Catholic eyes, Protestants were
merely seditious heretics. Much of continental Europe was
involved in religious wars. Marlowe knew this world – he had
been in France as well as in Holland[14] – and it colours the
mockeries and solemnities of the plays.

It is literally the setting of *The Massacre at Paris*, which dramatizes the St Bartholomew's Day Massacre (1572) and its aftermath. The play opens with an ecumenical marriage, but within moments the cast is divided by the key ritual that separated Catholics from Protestants: the Catholics go to mass 'to honour this solemnity' (which Catherine de Medici promises – aside – to 'dissolve with blood and cruelty', 1.24–5), leaving the Protestants to express their satisfaction at the discomfiture of the Catholic leader the duke of Guise, and their hope of making the 'Gospel flourish in this land' (56). Guise is a monster of politic atheism – 'My policy hath framed religion. / Religion: *O Diabole!*' (2.62–3) – who engineers the massacre to further his own ambition for the crown. The killing is done with grim sacrilegious humour which 'reproduces with remarkable accuracy forms of ritualized violence peculiar to the French religious wars':[15] Guise kills a preacher with a mockery of a Protestant sermon (' "Dearly beloved brother" – thus 'tis written. *He stabs him*', 7.5); church-bells sound throughout. The play is virulently anti-Catholic; but, although the text in which it survives is too poor to make certain judgements, its satire seems also to cover the anti-Guisard backlash which follows. Anjou, who has gleefully joined in the killing, becomes king and coolly orders the deaths of the Catholic leaders, only to be slain himself by a treacherous friar. His death allows the Protestant Navarre to gain the throne; but one cannot be sure how complacently an Elizabethan audience would have heard the king's dying call on his minion to 'slice the Catholics' (24.99), nor Navarre's promise to continue the cycle of violence through revenge. The play's very 'orthodoxy' is disquieting.

In a sense, this is also true of *Doctor Faustus*. A dark Morality, the play 'tells the world-story of a man who, seeking for all knowledge, pledged his soul to the devil, only to find the misery of a hopeless repentance in this world and damnation in the world to come'.[16] Marlowe's play should not be confused with later developments of the Faust-legend ('the world-story'): it is a dramatization of the anonymous German *Faustbook*, which has been called 'at once a cautionary tale and a book of marvels, a jest-book and a theological tract'.[17] Many of the play's least critically popular scenes are necessary, famous parts of the story

Marlowe took from the *Faustbook*, a distinctive product of
post-Reformation Germany, with its anxieties about magic and
religion, knowledge and salvation. This is the world in which
the play, especially in its opening scenes, is quite precisely set:
the unheroic, academic world of Wittenberg, Luther's own university, evoked by the technical language of 'scholarism' (Prologue, 16) and theology which the characters speak. Faustus'
ambitions too are localized: the desire to 'be as cunning as
Agrippa' (1.119) alludes ironically to Henry Cornelius Agrippa
of Nettesheim, who explored the practice of learned magic in
one book (*De Occulta Philosophia*, 1510, published 1533), and
then renounced the follies of learning in another (*De Vanitate
Scientiarum*, 1531); Faustus' wish to 'chase the Prince of Parma
from our land' (1.95) makes him a contemporary of Spain's
wars in Northern Europe.

Faustus dreams of 'omnipotence' and hopes 'All things that
move between the quiet poles [of the universe] / Shall be at my
command' (1.56, 58–9); instead, he becomes, like Mephistopheles, 'servant to great Lucifer' (3.41) and a stage-conjuror of
a type familiar from other Elizabethan plays (such as the heroes
of Robert Greene's *Friar Bacon and Friar Bungay* or Anthony
Munday's *John a Kent and John a Cumber*, both c. 1589). The
story told in Marlowe's play, in fact, is well on the way to its
'degeneration' in the next two centuries into the popular media
of ballads, farces and puppet shows – the last being the form
in which Goethe first knew it. Yet it is also a spectacle of
damnation.

This makes it all the more disturbing that we do not know
quite what we are seeing. Consider Faustus' first speech, his
survey of the arts and decision to practise magic. The spatial
setting, with Faustus turning the pages of books '*in his study*'
(1.0SD), is exact. But is this happening in real time? Are we
actually watching him make his fatal decision, or is the speech
a symbolic condensation of a longer process? Is this the speech
of a presenter in a Morality play, or of a character in a tragedy?
The soliloquy bespeaks a character with an acute inner subjectivity (Faustus names himself obsessively throughout the play),
but one who still receives the ministrations of good and evil

angels. The action here, like the play as a whole, is fascinatingly poised between older and still evolving dramatic forms.

There are comparable – fearful – uncertainties in Faustus' encounters with the devil. Mephistopheles is a new kind of devil, quiet, melancholy, menacing in the very honesty with which he explains his coming 'to get [Faustus'] glorious soul'. And he brings a new, spatially disquieting Hell with him in his own 'fainting soul': 'Why, this is hell, nor am I out of it.' At first he comes as a familiar 'Devil'; later, he always accompanies Faustus in the guise of 'an old Franciscan friar' (3.50, 84, 78, 23SD, 26). Since Faustus wears the robes and cross of a Doctor of Divinity ('a divine in show', 1.3), the stage is occupied – apparently – by two religious figures, both of whom (since Faustus bargains to 'be a spirit in form and substance', 5.97) are in fact evil spirits. Wagner's mock-academic question about his master – 'is not he *corpus naturale*?' (2.20–21) – thus has disturbing ironic force. What we see onstage may not be all that is there. Hence the stories of early performances of the play being disrupted by real devils: there is always the danger that a real spirit might answer the actor's summons. *Doctor Faustus* is a spiritual tragedy, a play centred on what cannot be staged, the invisible, immortal soul. Part of what is so disturbing about the pact that consigns in his own blood Faustus' soul to the devil is the ontological uncertainty over how exactly such material, corporeal forms, can bind the immaterial soul. Is it, in fact, the pact that damns Faustus? What does it mean to sell one's soul? Faustus gains no new knowledge: Mephistopheles's answers to his cosmological questions are freshman truisms, and Faustus is stupidly blind to the evidence of his own senses:

FAUSTUS Come, I think hell's a fable.

. . .

MEPHISTOPHELES
    But, Faustus, I am an instance to prove the contrary,
    For I am damnèd and am now in hell. (5.129, 138–9)

Faustus lives for twenty-four years after he signs the pact, but in some sense he is already damned.

A witty student once remarked that the play has 'a beginning, a muddle, and an end',[18] and Marlowe may not have written all its middle scenes. But there is a terrible bathos in Faustus' adventures. His journeys seem aimless; time is uncertain (the chronology shifts uneasily to the reign of Charles V) and empty, structured only by episodes of trickery. Elizabethan audiences probably enjoyed Faustus' pope-baiting as a liberating defiance of an exploded religious solemnity. Yet there is something troubling here. Magic, in sixteenth-century eyes, was an inverted religion, and, when Faustus and Mephistopheles are anathematized, though they '*beat the* FRIARS, *and fling fireworks among them*' (8.99SD), they do also leave. It is not quite clear how much spiritual power the old religion still commands.

The clowning scenes too seem confused and irrelevant. One of their functions is parodic. Wagner is a sorcerer's apprentice whose taking Robin the Clown into his service reflects ironically on Faustus' ambiguous master–servant relationship with Mephistopheles. Faustus experiences his longings as appetites to be glutted, and thinks the pageant of the Seven Deadly Sins 'feeds [his] soul' (7.163): Hazlitt called it 'a hunger and thirst after unrighteousness'.[19] The Clown's hunger is comparable ('he would give his soul to the devil for a shoulder of mutton', 4.8–9), but more safely comic. The devils Robin and Rafe conjure up (remember that in the main plot Mephistopheles is free not to answer Faustus' summons) are as familiar as their lice. There is never a sense that their souls are in danger, the clowns are safe with these devils: they are the devils you know, and they play by the older rules. When Mephistopheles punishes them by turning them into animals, they look forward to satisfying their humble appetites: Robin will 'get nuts and apples enow' as an ape; Rafe's head, as a dog, 'will never be out of the pottage pot' (9.49, 51). Faustus' jokey adventures, by contrast, are pointless distractions from the appalling reality of his damnation, and, as the 'fatal time' draws closer, they are full of grim anticipation: 'What, dost think I am a horse-doctor?' he mockingly asks the Horse-courser, who later pulls off his leg in innocent anticipation of Mephistopheles's threats to dismember him; and then immediately reels to a sudden apprehension of despair: 'What art thou, Faustus, but a man condemned to die?' (11.30, 27–8, 29). The play's middle scenes accord with a contradictory Elizabethan aesthetic, violently juxtaposing the serious and the comic.

Its final scenes are highly concentrated. With Faustus' return to Wittenberg, space and time contract, and Marlowe exploits the audience's consciousness of the approaching end. Body and soul are again prominent. 'Belly-cheer' at the scholars' feast and lust for Helen 'glut the longing of [his] heart's desire' (13.6, 82), but we are watching a man lose his soul. The good and evil angels no longer appear, their allegorical contest replaced by one between Helen and Mephistopheles and the mysterious Old Man who suddenly materializes with each of Helen's appearances and calls on Faustus to repent. Helen takes both his soul and his bodily substance: Faustus is committing the sin of demoniality, carnal intercourse with an evil spirit (one of the play's editors thought this his unforgivable sin).[20] The Old Man draws attention to other body fluids, calling on Faustus to 'drop blood, and mingle it with tears' (13.39) in a highly corporeal appeal to the redeemer whose blood Faustus will see streaming 'in the firmament' in his last hour. Instead, Faustus again uses it to sign away his soul. The bodily and the spiritual are interfused. Faustus has taken a 'surfeit of deadly sin that hath damned both body and soul', and when he finds himself unable to pray – 'I would lift up my hands, but see, they hold them, they hold them' (14.75, 11–12, 31–2) – it is all the more disturbing that 'they' are not, to our eyes, there.

When the Old Man dies, his body tormented but his soul untouched, he walks off the stage into another world ('Hence, hell! For hence I fly unto my God', 13.118), and we are made acutely aware of that other world at the end of the play. As in the first scene, Faustus is alone in his study; but he 'sees' Heaven and Hell. Time 'really' passes in this scene's 'one bare hour' – the clock strikes it – and beyond it, 'perpetually' (14.63, 64), stretches damnation. Faustus' monologue is a frenzied attempt to stop the cosmic clock, but his magic is useless: 'The stars move still, time runs, the clock will strike, / The devil will come, and Faustus must be damned' (14.72–3). His punishment approaches with the inexorability of a natural law. His body does not 'turn to air', nor his soul 'into little waterdrops' (14.113, 115). The devils come and lead him out of sight.

His fall is as inevitable as the law of gravity. God seems not to act at all – perhaps the most fearful thing to its first audiences. In ancient tragedy, the gods destroy a mortal who offends them with his pride (*hubris*). Marlowe's application of this tragic model to the damnation of Faustus is not reassuring to a Christian audience.

'Pythagoras' *metempsychosis*' (14.104), the transmigration of the soul, offers no escape in the harshly orthodox world of *Doctor Faustus*. At the start of *The Jew of Malta*, the soul of Machevil (Machiavelli's post-mortem name spells out his immorality as clearly as his claiming to 'count religion but a childish toy', Prologue, 14), having transmigrated through the body of the duke of Guise, arrives to 'present' (Prologue, 30) Barabas, who sits in his counting-house, like Faustus in his study, counting his wealth – 'Infinite riches in a little room' (1.1.37). Thereafter, the soul is irrelevant to the material world of a play filled with jewels and gold. Malta itself is a little room, cramped and urban, a fortified Mediterranean island which draws Turks, Christians and Jews alike, all blown in by 'The wind that bloweth all the world besides: / Desire of gold' (3.5.3–4). Religious differences here are harshly ethnic, territorial, not moral. The Knights of Malta sanctimoniously confiscate Barabas's wealth to buy off the Turks, and most of the action is taken up with his vengeance against Ferneze for this judicial theft. The play is largely a satire on Christian venality and hypocrisy. There is little poetry: 'The Passionate Shepherd' reappears in parody-form in the mangled mythologies of the runaway slave Ithamore's invitation to the prostitute Bellamira:

> I'll be thy Jason, thou my golden fleece;
> . . .
> Thou in those groves, by Dis above,
> Shalt live with me and be my love. (4.2.93, 100–101)

The language is dominated by obliquities, puns and asides. It is a revenge-tragedy that tips over into farce, 'the farce of the old English comic humour', in T. S. Eliot's inescapable formulation, 'terribly serious even savage comic humour'.[21]

Barabas entirely dominates the plot, and he is something other than a vulgar anti-Semitic stereotype: he is a stereotype, a monster, in the making. Alone when he first appears, Barabas is consistently isolated. He feels no more solidarity with his fellow Jews than with 'these swine-eating Christians, / (Unchosen nation, never circumcised . . .)' (2.3.7–8), and is unmoved by the Turkish threat: 'Nay, let 'em combat, conquer, and kill all, / So they spare me, my daughter, and my wealth' (1.1.150–51). But the provisos make him vulnerable. Robbed of his wealth and his house, he becomes further desocialized. His soliloquies and snarling asides, besides being brilliant comic devices, are also the verbal tics of a man talking principally to himself. The complex satirical functions of his interactions are especially clear in 2.3, in which he lures his daughter's two Christian suitors, Lodowick and Mathias, into a murderous rivalry to be avenged on Lodowick's father. Barabas covers his asides to the audience with some invented Jewish ritual:

> 'Tis a custom held with us
> That, when we speak with gentiles like to you,
> We turn into the air to purge ourselves;
> For unto us the promise doth belong. (2.3.45–8)

This enactment of Jewish separateness maliciously parodies the Christian fantasy of the *foetor Judaicus*, the 'Jewish stench' supposedly given off by menstruating Jewish men, and neatly captures the mutual hostility of the two religions.[22] Later in the scene, a respectable Christian matron conveniently illustrates the usual prejudice: 'Converse not with him, he is cast off from heaven' (3.161). But this apartheid masks a secret commerce. Both groups, after all, have come to buy people at a Christian-run slave-market; the 'diamond' Barabas discusses with Lodowick is his daughter. But in the complicated equivocations it is not clear Lodowick knows they are talking about Abigall. The puns are Barabas's private joke.

Something odd happens to him in this scene. Many readers complain that his famous 'confession' to Ithamore, a compound of familiar anti-Semitic fantasy – 'As for myself, I walk abroad a-nights / And kill sick people groaning under walls' (3.177–8) – is both ethically and aesthetically offensive. Why should so secretive a character blurt out the truth? Is this earlier career not implausible? Exactly. As he talks with his newly purchased *alter ego* ('we are villains both. / Both circumcisèd, we hate Christians both', 3.217–18), we watch Barabas being dehumanized, *becoming* the anti-Semitic mask he wears ('O brave, master, I worship your nose for this!', 3.176). From now on, he is alienated even from Abigall – eventually, he kills her – and creates a mock-family by promising, falsely, to adopt Ithamore as his heir. There is a huge comic relish in his murder of a whole convent along with his daughter in an act of poisonous charity, and as his murderousness gets funnier, it gets steadily less and less human, as in his response to the passing bells that sound for the nuns (compare the bells in *The Massacre at Paris*):

> There is no music to a Christian's knell.
> How sweet the bells ring, now the nuns are dead,
> That sound at other times like tinkers' pans! (4.1.1–3)

He suffers a further symbolic loss of identity when he goes to poison Ithamore disguised as a French lutanist. And when he 'dies', his dehumanization is completed by having his corpse thrown out over the city-walls like rubbish.

Those who deplore this un-charactering of Barabas also feel the play tails off in its later acts into unmotivated intrigue. Certainly, *The Jew of Malta* is Marlowe's only play to make such extensive use of intrigue, and its characters share Barabas's delight in 'crossbiting' (4.3.13): Ithamore wonders,

> Why, was there ever seen such villainy,
> So neatly plotted and so well performed?
> Both held in hand, and flatly both beguiled? (3.3.1–3)

This delight in symmetry is present in individual scenes – Shakespeare found the germ of *Romeo and Juliet*'s balcony-scene in the antithetically constructed 2.1 – and in the plot at large. For the ending brings Barabas full circle. In the opening scenes, he had recognized the exclusion of the Jews from political power, and was content not only to leave such power to Christian 'policy' (1.1.138), but to relish his own separation from the 'polity'. At the end, when he is made governor, he rashly forgets Ferneze's unscrupulousness, and is therefore caught in his own trap, dropped into the burning cauldron he has prepared for the Turks. If this has the too-neat symmetry of poetic justice, it also makes Ferneze's closing *Te Deum* seem all the more ironic.

Edward the Second too is markedly symmetrical. In charting the king's decline, from his coronation to abjection and murder, the play also frames the rise and fall of his lover Gaveston, in the first half, and, in the second, the rise and fall of his enemy Mortimer. Looked at more closely, its symmetries are those of irreconcilable conflict, the civil war that breaks out to the cries,

WARWICK
  Saint George for England and the barons' right!
EDWARD
  Saint George for England and King Edward's right! (12.35–6)

This pattern of verbal contest is everywhere. Characters measure lines like swords:

MORTIMER
  Why should you love him whom the world hates so?
EDWARD
  Because he loves me more than all the world. (4.76–7)

The barons' hatred of Edward's love is less homophobia than class-antagonism. Gaveston is an upstart on whom the king showers favours at the expense of the old nobility. From his first appearance, he is a Marlovian overreacher, who, while Edward loves him, thinks himself

> as great
> As Caesar riding in the Roman street
> With captive kings at his triumphant car. (1.171–3)

Unlike *Tamburlaine*, however, or Shakespeare's history-plays, *Edward the Second* is strikingly unceremonious. 'Triumphs' here often mean 'idle triumphs, masques, lascivious shows' (6.156), erotic courtly entertainments of the kind with which Gaveston intends to manipulate 'the pliant king' (1.52), lavish tournaments without the substance of military power. Edward and Gaveston's love looks like a hopeless fantasy in the face of the barons' armed muscle:

EDWARD
  Lay hands on that traitor Mortimer!
MORTIMER SENIOR
  Lay hands on that traitor Gaveston!
    [*They seize* GAVESTON.]
KENT
  Is this the duty that you owe your king?
WARWICK
  We know our duties. Let him know his peers. (4.20–23)

This manhandling is symptomatic. In this brutally pragmatic world, physical proximity, bodily intimacy, is the key to political influence. Gaveston is exiled and returned; Edward embraces him and pushes Isabel his queen aside. The first half of the action is literally fought out over the possession of Gaveston's body, 'That, like the Greekish strumpet [Helen], trained to arms / And bloody wars so many valiant knights' (9.15–16). When the barons get hold of him, they bundle him round the stage and the country, and then treacherously cut off his head. Beheadings and references to beheadings are unnervingly abundant. They point forward to the play's final tableau, in which Mortimer's head is placed on top of the coffin of the recently murdered king, whose own death – on a bed, with a red-hot spit forced up into his bowels – is an obscene parody of sexual penetration.

The middle scenes are confusing, filled with sudden shifts

of allegiance and unexpected reversals of fortune. Mortimer emerges as a full-blown Machiavellian and seduces the queen, who changes from wronged wife into her more historically traditional role of 'she-wolf of France'. But the biggest changes are in Edward. Almost imperceptibly, as he is separated from Gaveston, his affections are transferred to the younger Spencer, to whom he is introduced, pointedly, on Gaveston's wedding-day, and with whom, rather than with Gaveston, he flees from Tynemouth. More importantly, he is now a pathetic victim, and it is his body that is moved passively about the stage. The people change but the roles remain the same, and the characters are increasingly aware of traditional patternings that give shape to the action. Mortimer's ascendancy is a familiar affair: Edward is his prisoner and he keeps control of the prince by physically abducting him from his uncle; Kent is dispatched in the usual way:

EDWARD III
  My lord, he is my uncle and shall live.
MORTIMER
  My lord, he is your enemy and shall die. (24.90–1)

Appropriately, Mortimer envisions his own career in the traditional, secular terms of the wheel of Fortune (26.59–63).

But there is something more eerie in the counterpointed scenes of Edward's fall. Disguised in a monk's habit and surrounded by other cowled figures, the king begins to contemplate his decline as an instance of the medieval genre of the Falls of Princes, his language too becoming momentarily archaic: 'Whilom I was, powerful and full of pomp' (20.13). A play which opened with a fantasy of Renaissance courtly shows ('Italian masques by night', 1.54) is becoming medieval. Its action fills with obscure atavistic menace. The mower who betrays Edward is only 'A gloomy fellow in a mead below' (20.29) – but he is a Reaper, a figure of death touched in to the landscape. 'The day grows old' (20.85) in the most ordinary sense, but the diurnal references are oddly insistent about the coming of night, and the emphasis returns when the king, plunged into darkness in the closing scenes, tries, like Faustus, to hold back the end of the day:

> Stand still, you watches of the element;
> All times and seasons, rest you at a stay,
> That Edward may be still fair England's king.
> But day's bright beams doth vanish fast away,
> And needs I must resign my wishèd crown. (21.66–70)

His head brought low by uncrowning and unmanned by shaving, his deconsecrated body immersed in excrement and murderously violated through the anus, Edward's torments are physically appalling symbolic degradations. They suggest the torments of the damned, and his murderer is a kind of devil. 'Lightborne' is a version of 'Lucifer', and he shares the name with a fallen angel in the Chester Mystery plays. The closing scenes of this least providential of history-plays are full of a hellish fear that is made the worse by being so resolutely unreligious.

Modern criticism, concentrating on Marlowe's 'subversiveness', sometimes makes him sound like Joe Orton in doublet and hose. To some Elizabethans, he was something more dangerous. Richard Baines's testimony against Marlowe includes the pious wish that 'all men in Christianity ought to endeavour that the mouth of so dangerous a member may be stopped'. Speculation continues that, when Marlowe was killed in Deptford in May 1593, that is exactly what happened.[23]

Notes

1. Quoted by Frederick S. Boas, *Christopher Marlowe, A Biographical and Critical Study* (Oxford, 1940), p. 22.
2. R. B. Wernham, 'Christopher Marlowe at Flushing', *English Historical Review* 91 (1976), pp. 344–5.
3. Gabriel Harvey, *A New Letter of Notable Contents* (1593), sig. D^r.
4. British Library MS Harley 6848 fols. 190–91.
5. Lucian, *Selected Works*, tr. Bryan P. Reardon (Indianapolis, 1965), p. 34.

6. Quoted by Thomas Warton, *History of English Poetry* (1774–81), ed. W. C. Hazlitt (1871), IV, 217. The original is now lost, and it is possible that this is a forgery, but the sentiment was commonplace.

7. Christopher Marlowe, *The Complete Poems and Translations*, ed. Stephen Orgel (Harmondsworth, 1971), p. 211.

8. Louis Le Roy, *Of the Interchangeable Course, or Variety of Things*, tr. Robert Apsley (1594), sig. A4^r. Tamburlaine is in effect the hero of Le Roy's book: see fols. 107^v–109^v and 119^v–120^r.

9. 'To the Memory of My Beloved, the Author, Mr William Shakespeare: And What He Hath Left Us' (30), *The Complete Poems*, ed. George Parfitt (Harmondsworth, 1975), p. 263.

10. *Discoveries* 963–4, in *Complete Poems*, ed. Parfitt, p. 398.

11. Emrys Jones, 'Into the Open', *Essays in Criticism* 33 (1983), p. 344.

12. Ethel Seaton, 'Marlowe's Map', *Essays and Studies* 10 (1924), pp. 13–35.

13. Jack Rummel, *Robert Oppenheimer, Dark Prince* (Oxford, 1992), p. 11. Oppenheimer was recalling the words of Siva to Arjuna, *Baghavad-Gita* 10.

14. Philip Henderson, 'Marlowe as a Messenger', *Times Literary Supplement*, 12 June 1953, p. 381.

15. Julia Briggs, 'Marlowe's *Massacre at Paris*: A Reconsideration', *Review of English Studies* n.s. 34 (1983), p. 259.

16. Felix E. Schelling, *English Drama* (London, 1914), p. 68.

17. Harry Levin, *Christopher Marlowe: The Overreacher* (London, 1954), p. 131.

18. Reported by Roma Gill, ' "Such Conceits as Clownage Keeps in Pay": Comedy in *Dr Faustus*', in *The Fool and the Trickster: Studies in Honour of Enid Welsford*, ed. Paul V. A. Williams (Cambridge, 1979), p. 56.

19. *Lectures on the Age of Elizabeth* (1820), repr. in *Marlowe, 'Dr Faustus': A Casebook*, ed. John Jump (London, 1969), p. 27.

20. W. W. Greg, 'The Damnation of Faustus', *Modern Language Review* 61 (1946), repr. in Jump, *Casebook*, pp. 71–88.

21. T. S. Eliot, *Selected Essays* (London, 1951), p. 105.

22. Cf. Wilbur Sanders, *The Dramatist and the Received Idea: Studies in the Plays of Marlowe and Shakespeare* (Cambridge, 1968), p. 42.

23. See Charles Nicholl, *The Reckoning: The Murder of Christopher Marlowe* (London, 1992).

'The Baines Note' (text in British Library
MS Harley 6848, ff. 185–6)

A note containing the opinion of one Christopher Marly concerning his damnable judgement of religion, and scorn of God's word.

That the Indians and many authors of antiquity have assuredly written of above sixteen thousand years agone, whereas Adam is proved to have lived within six thousand years.

He affirmeth that Moses was but a juggler and that one Hariot, being Sir W[alter] Ralegh's man, can do more than he.

That Moses made the Jews to travel forty years in the wilderness, (which journey might have been done in less than one year) ere they came to the promised land to th'intent that those who were privy to most of his subtleties might perish and so an everlasting superstition remain in the hearts of the people.

That the first beginning of religion was only to keep men in awe.

That it was an easy matter for Moses being brought up in all the arts of the Egyptians to abuse the Jews being a rude and gross people.

That Christ was a bastard and his mother dishonest.

That he was the son of a carpenter, and that if the Jews among whom he was born did crucify him they best knew him and whence he came.

That Christ deserved better to die than Barabbas and that the Jews made a good choice, though Barabbas were both a thief and a murderer.

That if there be any God or any good religion, then it is in the Papists because the service of God is performed with more ceremonies, as elevation of the mass, organs, singing men, shaven crowns & etc. That all Protestants are hypocritical asses.

That if he were put to write a new religion, he would undertake both a more excellent and admirable method, and that all the New Testament is filthily written.

That the woman of Samaria and her sister were whores and that Christ knew them dishonestly.

That St John the Evangelist was bedfellow to Christ and

leaned always in his bosom, that he used him as the sinners of Sodoma.

That all they that love not tobacco and boys were fools.

That all the apostles were fishermen and base fellows neither of wit nor worth, that Paul only had wit but he was a timorous fellow in bidding men to be subject to magistrates against his conscience.

That he had as good right to coin as the Queen of England, and that he was acquainted with one Poley, a prisoner in Newgate, who hath great skill in mixture of metals, and having learned some things of him he meant through help of a cunning stamp-maker to coin French crowns, pistolets and English shillings.

That if Christ would have instituted the sacrament with more ceremonial reverence it would have been had in more admiration, that it would have been much better being administered in a tobacco pipe.

That the angel Gabriel was bawd to the Holy Ghost, because he brought the salutation to Mary.

That one Ric[hard] Cholmley hath confessed that he was persuaded by Marlowe's reasons to become an atheist.

These things, with many other, shall by good and honest witness be approved to be his opinions and common speeches, and that this Marlowe doth not only hold them himself, but almost into every company he cometh he persuades men to atheism willing them not to be afeard of bugbears and hobgoblins, and utterly scorning both God and his ministers as I, Richard Baines, will justify and approve both by mine oath and the testimony of many honest men, and almost all men with whom he hath conversed any time will testify the same, and as I think all men in Christianity ought to endeavour that the mouth of so dangerous a member may be stopped; he saith likewise that he hath quoted a number of contrarieties out of the Scripture which he hath given to some great men who in convenient time shall be named. When these things shall be called in question the witness shall be produced.

Richard Baines

Further Reading

C. L. Barber, *Creating Elizabethan Tragedy: The Theater of Marlowe and Kyd*, ed. Richard P. Wheeler (Chicago, 1988).

Emily C. Bartels, *Spectacles of Strangeness: Imperialism, Alienation and Marlowe* (Philadelphia, 1993).

Lawrence Danson, 'Christopher Marlowe: The Questioner', *English Literary Renaissance* 12 (1982), pp. 3–29.

Kenneth Friedenreich, Roma Gill and Constance B. Kuriyama (eds.), *'A Poet and a Filthy Play-Maker': New Essays on Christopher Marlowe* (New York, 1988).

Darryll Grantley and Peter Roberts (eds.), *Christopher Marlowe and English Renaissance Culture* (Aldershot, 1996).

Stephen J. Greenblatt, 'Marlowe and the Will to Absolute Play', *Renaissance Self-Fashioning: From More to Shakespeare* (Chicago and London, 1980), pp. 193–221.

Michael Hattaway, *Elizabethan Popular Theatre: Plays in Performance* (London, 1982).

Alvin Kernan (ed.), *Two Renaissance Mythmakers: Christopher Marlowe and Ben Jonson*, Selected Papers from the English Institute, 1975–6, new series no. 1 (Baltimore, 1977).

Constance Brown Kuriyama, *Hammer or Anvil: Psychological Patterns in Christopher Marlowe's Plays* (New Brunswick, 1980).

——, *Christopher Marlowe: A Renaissance Life* (Ithaca, NY, and London, 2002).

Harry Levin, *Christopher Marlowe: The Overreacher* (London, 1954).

Arthur Lindley, 'The Unbeing of the Overreacher: Proteanism

and the Marlovian Hero', *Modern Language Review* 84 (1989), pp. 1–17.

Wilbur Sanders, *The Dramatist and the Received Idea: Studies in the Plays of Marlowe and Shakespeare* (Cambridge, 1968).

Ethel Seaton, 'Fresh Sources for Marlowe', *Review of English Studies* 5 (1929), pp. 385–401.

Vivien Thomas and William Tydeman (eds.), *Christopher Marlowe: The Plays and their Sources* (London, 1994).

Judith Weil, *Christopher Marlowe: Merlin's Prophet* (Cambridge, 1977).

DIDO, QUEEN OF CARTHAGE

Standard Modern Edition

H. J. Oliver (ed.), *Dido Queen of Carthage and The Massacre at Paris*, Revels Plays (Manchester, 1968).

Criticism

Jackson I. Cope, 'Marlowe's *Dido* and the Titillating Children', *English Literary Renaissance* 4 (1974), pp. 315–25.

Brian Gibbons, '"Unstable Proteus": *The Tragedy of Dido Queen of Carthage*', in *Christopher Marlowe*, ed. Brian Morris (London, 1968).

Roma Gill, 'Marlowe's Virgil: *Dido Queene of Carthage*', *Review of English Studies* n.s. 28 (1977), pp. 141–55.

Margo Hendricks, 'Managing the Barbarian: *The Tragedy of Dido Queen of Carthage*', *Renaissance Drama* 23 (1992), pp. 165–88.

Malcolm Kelsall, *Christopher Marlowe* (Leiden, 1981), ch. 3.

Mary E. Smith, 'Staging Marlowe's *Dido Queene of Carthage*', *Studies in English Literature 1500–1900* 17 (1977), pp. 177–90.

TAMBURLAINE

Standard Modern Editions

J. S. Cunningham (ed.), *Tamburlaine the Great*, Revels Plays (Manchester, 1981).

David Fuller (ed.), *Tamburlaine Parts 1 and 2*, Complete Works, vol. 5 (Oxford, 1998).

John Jump (ed.), *Tamburlaine the Great* (London, 1967).

Criticism

C. L. Barber, *Creating Elizabethan Tragedy: The Theater of Marlowe and Kyd*, ed. Richard P. Wheeler (Chicago, 1988), 45–86.

David Daiches, 'Language and Action in Marlowe's *Tamburlaine*', *More Literary Essays* (Edinburgh, 1968), pp. 42–69.

Helen Gardner, 'The Second Part of *Tamburlaine the Great*', *Modern Language Review* 37 (1942), pp. 18–24.

John Gillies, 'Marlowe, the Timur myth, and the Motives of Geography', in *Playing the Globe: Genre and Geography in English Renaissance Drama*, ed. John Gillies and Virginia Mason Vaughan (Madison, Wis., and London, 1998), pp. 203–29.

Ethel Seaton, 'Marlowe's Map', *Essays and Studies* 10 (1924), pp. 13–35.

Eugene M. Waith, *The Herculean Hero in Marlowe, Chapman, Shakespeare and Dryden* (New York and London, 1962).

——, 'Marlowe and the Jades of Asia', *Studies in English Literature* 5 (1965), pp. 229–45.

Richard Wilson, 'Visible Bullets: *Tamburlaine the Great* and Ivan the Terrible', *English Literary History* 62 (1995), pp. 47–68.

THE JEW OF MALTA

Standard Modern Edition

N. W. Bawcutt (ed.), *The Jew of Malta*, Revels Plays (Manchester, 1978).

Criticism

Howard S. Babb, ' "Policy" in Marlowe's *The Jew of Malta*', *English Literary History* 24 (1957), pp. 85–94.

Thomas Cartelli, 'Shakespeare's Merchant, Marlowe's Jew: The Problem of Cultural Difference', *Shakespeare Studies* 20 (1987), pp. 255–68.

Coburn Freer, 'Lies and Lying in *The Jew of Malta*', in Kenneth Friedenreich et al. (eds.), *'A Poet and a Filthy Play-Maker': New Essays on Christopher Marlowe* (New York, 1988), pp. 143–65.

Stephen J. Greenblatt, 'Marlowe, Marx, and Anti-Semitism', in his *Learning to Curse: Essays in Early Modern Culture* (Chicago and London, 1990), pp. 40–58.

G. K. Hunter, 'The Theology of *The Jew of Malta*', *Journal of the Warburg and Courtauld Institutes* 27 (1964), pp. 211–40.

Ian McAdam, 'Carnal Identity in *The Jew of Malta*', *English Literary Renaissance* 26 (1996), pp. 46–74.

Catherine Minshull, 'Marlowe's "Sound Machevill"', *Renaissance Drama* n.s. 13 (1982).

Wilbur Sanders, *The Dramatist and the Received Idea: Studies in the Plays of Marlowe and Shakespeare* (Cambridge, 1968), ch. 3

DOCTOR FAUSTUS

Standard Modern Editions

David Bevington and Eric Rasmussen (eds.), *Doctor Faustus. A- and B-Texts (1604, 1616)*, Revels Plays (Manchester, 1993).

—— (eds.), *Dr Faustus and Other Plays* (Oxford, 1995).

Criticism

C. L. Barber, 'The Form of Faustus' Fortunes Good or Bad', *Tulane Drama Review* 8 (1964), pp. 92–119; repr. in his *Creating Elizabethan Tragedy: The Theater of Marlowe and Kyd*, ed. Richard P. Wheeler (Chicago, 1988), pp. 87–130.

Max Bluestone, '*Libido Speculandi*: Doctrine and Dramaturgy in Contemporary Interpretations of Marlowe's *Doctor Faustus*', in *Reinterpretations of Elizabethan Drama. Selected Papers from the English Institute*, ed. Norman Rabkin (New York, 1969), pp. 33–88.

Roma Gill, ' "Such Conceits as Clownage Keeps in Pay": Comedy in *Doctor Faustus*', in *The Fool and the Trickster: Studies in Honour of Enid Welsford*, ed. Paul V. A. Williams (Cambridge, 1979), pp. 55–63.

Michael Hattaway, 'The Theology of Marlowe's *Doctor Faustus*', *Renaissance Drama* n.s. 3 (1970), pp. 51–78.

J. H. Jones (ed.), *The English Faust Book* (Cambridge, 1994).

John Jump (ed.), *Marlowe, 'Doctor Faustus': A Casebook* (London, 1969).

Harry Levin, *Christopher Marlowe: The Overreacher*, ch. 5.

Gareth Roberts, 'Necromantic Books: Christopher Marlowe, *Doctor Faustus* and Agrippa of Nettesheim', in *Christopher Marlowe and English Renaissance Culture*, ed. Darryll Grantley and Peter Roberts (Aldershot, 1996), pp. 148–71.

Wilbur Sanders, *The Dramatist and the Received Idea: Studies in the Plays of Marlowe and Shakespeare* (Cambridge, 1968), chs. 10–12.

Edward A. Snow, 'Marlowe's *Doctor Faustus* and the Ends of Desire', in *Two Renaissance Mythmakers: Christopher Marlowe and Ben Jonson*, Selected Papers of the English Institute, ed. Alvin Kernan (Baltimore, 1977), pp. 70–110.

EDWARD THE SECOND

Standard Modern Editions

Charles R. Forker (ed.), *Edward the Second*, Revels Plays (Manchester, 1994).

Roma Gill (ed.), *Edward II* (Oxford, 1967).

Richard Rowland (ed.), *Edward II*, Complete Works, vol. 3 (Oxford, 1994).

Martin Wiggins and Robert Lindsey (eds.), *Edward the Second* (London, 1997).

Suggested Further Reading

Debra Belt, 'Anti-theatricalism and Rhetoric in Marlowe's *Edward II*', *English Literary History* 21 (1991), pp. 134–60.

Gregory W. Bredbeck, *Sodomy and Interpretation: Marlowe to Milton* (Ithaca, NY, 1991).

Thomas F. Cartelli, *Marlowe, Shakespeare, and the Economy of Theatrical Experience* (Philadelphia, 1991).

Robert Fricker, 'The Dramatic Structure of *Edward II*', *English Studies* 34 (1953), pp. 128–44.

Michael Hattaway, *Elizabethan Popular Theatre: Plays in Performance* (London, 1982), pp. 141–59.

Clifford Leech, 'Marlowe's *Edward II*: Power and Suffering', *Critical Quarterly* 1 (1959), pp. 181–96.

J. F. McElroy, 'Repetition, Contrariety and Individualization in *Edward II*', *Studies in English Literature 1500–1900* 24 (1984), pp. 205–24.

THE MASSACRE AT PARIS

Standard Modern Editions

H. J. Oliver (ed.), *Dido Queen of Carthage and The Massacre at Paris*, Revels Plays (Manchester, 1968).

Edward J. Esche (ed.), *The Massacre at Paris*, Complete Works, vol. 5 (Oxford, 1998).

Suggested Further Reading

Julia Briggs, 'Marlowe's *Massacre at Paris*: A Reconsideration',
Review of English Studies n.s. 34 (1983), pp. 257–78.

Richard Hillman, *Shakespeare, Marlowe and the Politics of France* (Basingstoke, 2002), pp. 72–112.

Andrew M. Kirk, 'Marlowe and the Disordered Face of French History', *Studies in English Literature* 35 (1995), pp. 193–213.

Paul H. Kocher, 'François Hotman and Marlowe's *The Massacre at Paris*', *PMLA* 56 (1941), pp. 349–68.

——, 'Contemporary Pamphlet Backgrounds for Marlowe's *The Massacre at Paris*', *Modern Language Quarterly* 8 (1947), pp. 157–73, 309–18.

David Potter, 'Marlowe's *Massacre at Paris* and the Reputation of Henri III of France', in *Christopher Marlowe and English Renaissance Culture*, ed. Darryll Grantley and Peter Roberts (Aldershot, 1996), pp. 148–71.

Judith Weil, *Christopher Marlowe: Merlin's Prophet* (Cambridge, 1977).

A Note on the Texts

The texts in this volume have been freshly edited from the earliest printed editions of Marlowe's plays. The spellings, punctuation, speech-prefixes, stage directions and lineation preserved in the original editions have been silently modernized in accordance with the particular needs of each text, given that Marlowe's plays were subject to the diverse conventions of printers. We have undertaken these modernizations conservatively, and have not sought to impose an arbitrary consistency across the volume: the grand rhetorical speeches of *Tamburlaine*, for example, require a different presentation from that demanded by the rapid conversational exchanges of *The Jew of Malta*. Elizabethan compositors' punctuation does not necessarily respect the sense-units of the original. Richard Jones's printing of *Tamburlaine the Great*, for example, contains many verse lines ending with full stops which affect the intelligibility of the text. We have freely repunctuated with the aim of making the syntactic structure as clear as possible for the modern reader.

Elizabethan spellings have been modernized, so 'mushrump', 'centronel' and 'vild' become 'mushroom', 'sentinel' and 'vile'. All '-ed' endings have been standardized, so 'serv'd' becomes 'served' and 'returnd' becomes 'returned'. Syllabic '-ed' endings have been marked '-èd'. Contractions in the original have been retained but in their modern form, so 'swolne' and 'tane' become 'swoll'n' and 'ta'en'. We have followed the original lineation of the copy-texts, except when it is evident that verse has been mistakenly printed as prose and vice versa. These alterations have not been noted. Substantive changes to the wording of the original texts, on the other hand, have been recorded with some discussion in the Notes.

Printing-house errors such as turned letters, misplaced and transposed type and obvious cases of missing type have been silently corrected. Where 'and' is used, meaning 'if', we have silently adopted the modern form, 'an'. The abbreviations 'Mr' and 'S.' have been expanded to 'Master' and 'Saint', respectively. All numbers in the copy-texts have also been expanded, so '24' becomes 'four and twenty'.

Speech-prefixes and character names have been standardized throughout in accordance with the designations given in the Dramatis Personae. Where no act-division is present in the original text (*Doctor Faustus*, *Edward the Second* and *The Massacre at Paris*), the text has been sub-divided into scenes only. Foreign languages have been corrected throughout, and are translated in the Notes. We have regularized the Latin except in the case of *Doctor Faustus*, where some incorrect usages seem to have comic, or other, significance.

We have been sparing in the use of editorial stage-directions, which are enclosed in square brackets; these are added to clarify rather than prescribe the stage action. Where possible, we have reproduced the original positioning of stage-directions as set in the copy-texts, but in some cases, it has made better sense to move those stage-directions which do not correspond with the stage action implied by the text. A number of 'late entries' in the copy-text have therefore been repositioned to indicate when a character is most likely to enter the stage.

DIDO, QUEEN OF CARTHAGE

[Dramatis Personae

JUPITER

GANYMEDE

MERCURY, *or* HERMES

VENUS

AENEAS

ASCANIUS, *Aeneas's son*

ACHATES

ILIONEUS

CLOANTHUS

SERGESTUS

IARBAS, *King of Gaetulia*

DIDO

ANNA, *her sister*

CUPID

JUNO

A LORD

NURSE

ATTENDANTS]

ACT 1

Scene 1

Here the curtains drawn; there is discovered JUPITER *dandling* GANYMEDE *upon his knee, and* MERCURY *lying asleep.*

JUPITER

Come, gentle Ganymede, and play with me:
I love thee well, say Juno what she will.

GANYMEDE

I am much better for your worthless love
That will not shield me from her shrewish blows!
Today, whenas I filled into your cups
And held the cloth of pleasance whiles you drank,
She reached me such a rap for that I spilled
As made the blood run down about mine ears.

JUPITER

What? Dares she strike the darling of my thoughts?
By Saturn's soul and this earth-threat'ning hair,   10
That, shaken thrice, makes nature's buildings quake,
I vow, if she but once frown on thee more,
To hang her meteor-like 'twixt heaven and earth
And bind her hand and foot with golden cords,
As once I did for harming Hercules!

GANYMEDE

Might I but see that pretty sport a-foot,
O, how would I with Helen's brother laugh,
And bring the gods to wonder at the game!
Sweet Jupiter, if e'er I pleased thine eye,

20   Or seemèd fair, walled-in with eagle's wings,
        Grace my immortal beauty with this boon,
        And I will spend my time in thy bright arms.
JUPITER
        What is't, sweet wag, I should deny thy youth,
        Whose face reflects such pleasure to mine eyes
        As I, exhaled with thy fire-darting beams,
        Have oft driven back the horses of the night,
        Whenas they would have haled thee from my sight?
        Sit on my knee and call for thy content,
        Control proud fate and cut the thread of time.
30   Why, are not all the gods at thy command,
        And heaven and earth the bounds of thy delight?
        Vulcan shall dance to make thee laughing sport,
        And my nine daughters sing when thou art sad;
        From Juno's bird I'll pluck her spotted pride
        To make thee fans wherewith to cool thy face;
        And Venus' swans shall shed their silver down
        To sweeten out the slumbers of thy bed;
        Hermes no more shall show the world his wings,
        If that thy fancy in his feathers dwell,
40   But, as this one, I'll tear them all from him,
            [*Plucks feather*]
        Do thou but say, 'their colour pleaseth me'.
        Hold here, my little love! [*Gives jewels.*] These linkèd gems
        My Juno wore upon her marriage-day,
        Put thou about thy neck, my own sweet heart,
        And trick thy arms and shoulders with my theft.
GANYMEDE
        I would have a jewel for mine ear,
        And a fine brooch to put in my hat,
        And then I'll hug with you an hundred times.
JUPITER
        And shall have, Ganymede, if thou wilt be my love.
            Enter VENUS.
VENUS
50   Ay, this is it! You can sit toying there
        And playing with that female wanton boy

Whiles my Aeneas wanders on the seas
And rests a prey to every billow's pride.
Juno, false Juno, in her chariot's pomp,
Drawn through the heavens by steeds of Boreas' brood,
Made Hebe to direct her airy wheels
Into the windy country of the clouds,
Where, finding Aeolus entrenched with storms
And guarded with a thousand grisly ghosts,
She humbly did beseech him for our bane,   60
And charged him drown my son with all his train.
Then gan the winds break ope their brazen doors,
And all Aeolia to be up in arms;
Poor Troy must now be sacked upon the sea,
And Neptune's waves be envious men of war;
Epeus' horse, to Etna's hill transformed,
Preparèd stands to wrack their wooden walls,
And Aeolus, like Agamemnon, sounds
The surges, his fierce soldiers, to the spoil.
See how the night, Ulysses-like, comes forth,   70
And intercepts the day as Dolon erst!
Ay me! The stars, surprised, like Rhesus' steeds
Are drawn by darkness forth Astraeus' tents.
What shall I do to save thee, my sweet boy,
Whenas the waves do threat our crystal world,
And Proteus, raising hills of floods on high,
Intends ere long to sport him in the sky?
False Jupiter, reward'st thou virtue so?
What? Is not piety exempt from woe?
Then die, Aeneas, in thine innocence,   80
Since that religion hath no recompense.

JUPITER
Content thee, Cytherea, in thy care,
Since thy Aeneas' wand'ring fate is firm,
Whose weary limbs shall shortly make repose
In those fair walls I promised him of yore.
But first in blood must his good fortune bud
Before he be the lord of Turnus' town,
Or force her smile that hitherto hath frowned.

Three winters shall he with the Rutiles war,
90   And in the end subdue them with his sword,
And full three summers likewise shall he waste
In managing those fierce barbarian minds;
Which once performed, poor Troy, so long suppressed,
From forth her ashes shall advance her head,
And flourish once again that erst was dead.
But bright Ascanius, beauty's better work,
Who with the sun divides one radiant shape,
Shall build his throne amidst those starry towers
That earth-born Atlas groaning underprops;
100   No bounds but heaven shall bound his empery,
Whose azured gates, enchased with his name,
Shall make the morning haste her grey uprise
To feed her eyes with his engraven fame.
Thus in stout Hector's race three hundred years
The Roman sceptre royal shall remain,
Till that a princess-priest, conceived by Mars,
Shall yield to dignity a double birth,
Who will eternise Troy in their attempts.

VENUS
How may I credit these thy flattering terms,
110   When yet both sea and sands beset their ships,
And Phoebus, as in Stygian pools, refrains
To taint his tresses in the Tyrrhene main?

JUPITER
I will take order for that presently.
Hermes, awake, and haste to Neptune's realm;
Whereas the wind-god, warring now with fate,
Besiege the offspring of our kingly loins,
Charge him from me to turn his stormy powers
And fetter them in Vulcan's sturdy brass,
That durst thus proudly wrong our kinsman's peace.
                                        [*Exit* MERCURY.]
120   Venus, farewell, thy son shall be our care.
Come, Ganymede, we must about this gear.
                        Exeunt JUPITER *with* GANYMEDE.

VENUS

    Disquiet seas, lay down your swelling looks,
    And court Aeneas with your calmy cheer,
    Whose beauteous burden well might make you proud,
    Had not the heavens, conceived with hell-born clouds,
    Veiled his resplendent glory from your view.
    For my sake pity him, Oceanus,
    That erstwhile issued from thy wat'ry loins,
    And had my being from thy bubbling froth.
    Triton, I know, hath filled his trump with Troy,   130
    And therefore will take pity on his toil,
    And call both Thetis and Cymodoce
    To succour him in this extremity.

      Enter AENEAS *with* ASCANIUS [*and* ACHATES], *with one*
      or two more.

    What, do I see my son now come on shore?
    Venus, how art thou compassed with content,
    The while thine eyes attract their sought-for joys!
    Great Jupiter, still honoured mayst thou be
    For this so friendly aid in time of need!
    Here in this bush disguisèd will I stand,
    Whiles my Aeneas spends himself in plaints,   140
    And heaven and earth with his unrest acquaints.

      [VENUS *stands aside.*]

AENEAS

    You sons of care, companions of my course,
    Priam's misfortune follows us by sea,
    And Helen's rape doth haunt ye at the heels.
    How many dangers have we overpassed!
    Both barking Scylla and the sounding rocks,
    The Cyclops' shelves and grim Ceraunia's seat
    Have you o'ergone, and yet remain alive!
    Pluck up your hearts, since fate still rests our friend,
    And changing heavens may those good days return   150
    Which Pergama did vaunt in all her pride.

ACHATES

    Brave Prince of Troy, thou only art our god,
    That by thy virtues free'st us from annoy,

And makes our hopes survive to coming joys.
Do thou but smile and cloudy heaven will clear,
Whose night and day descendeth from thy brows.
Though we be now in extreme misery
And rest the map of weather-beaten woe,
Yet shall the agèd sun shed forth his hair
160   To make us live unto our former heat,
And every beast the forest doth send forth
Bequeath her young ones to our scanted food.

ASCANIUS
Father, I faint. Good father, give me meat.

AENEAS
Alas, sweet boy, thou must be still a while
Till we have fire to dress the meat we killed.
Gentle Achates, reach the tinder-box,
That we may make a fire to warm us with
And roast our new-found victuals on this shore.
    [AENEAS *kindles a flame.*]

VENUS [*aside*]
See what strange arts necessity finds out!
170   How near, my sweet Aeneas, art thou driven!

AENEAS
Hold, take this candle and go light a fire;
You shall have leaves and windfall boughs enow
Near to these woods to roast your meat withal.
Ascanius, go and dry thy drenchèd limbs,
Whiles I with my Achates rove abroad
To know what coast the wind hath driven us on,
Or whether men or beasts inhabit it.
                        [*Exeunt* ASCANIUS *and others.*]

ACHATES
The air is pleasant, and the soil most fit
For cities and society's supports;
180   Yet much I marvel that I cannot find
No steps of men imprinted in the earth.

VENUS [*aside*]
Now is the time for me to play my part.
[*To them*] Ho, young men, saw you, as you came,

Any of all my sisters wand'ring here,
Having a quiver girded to her side
And clothèd in a spotted leopard's skin?

AENEAS

I neither saw nor heard of any such.
But what may I, fair virgin, call your name,
Whose looks set forth no mortal form to view,
Nor speech bewrays aught human in thy birth?   190
Thou art a goddess that delud'st our eyes
And shrouds thy beauty in this borrowed shape.
But whether thou the sun's bright sister be,
Or one of chaste Diana's fellow nymphs,
Live happy in the height of all content
And lighten our extremes with this one boon,
As to instruct us under what good heaven
We breathe as now, and what this world is called
On which by tempests' fury we are cast.
Tell us, O tell us, that are ignorant,   200
And this right hand shall make thy altars crack
With mountain-heaps of milk-white sacrifice.

VENUS

Such honour, stranger, do I not affect.
It is the use for Tyrian maids to wear
Their bow and quiver in this modest sort
And suit themselves in purple for the nonce,
That they may trip more lightly o'er the lawns
And overtake the tuskèd boar in chase.
Bùt for the land whereof thou dost enquire,
It is the Punic kingdom, rich and strong,   210
Adjoining on Agenor's stately town,
The kingly seat of southern Libya,
Whereas Sidonian Dido rules as queen.
But what are you that ask of me these things?
Whence may you come, or whither will you go?

AENEAS

Of Troy am I, Aeneas is my name,
Who, driven by war from forth my native world,
Put sails to sea to seek out Italy,

And my divine descent from sceptred Jove.
220 With twice twelve Phrygian ships I ploughed the deep,
And made that way my mother Venus led;
But of them all, scarce seven do anchor safe,
And they so wracked and weltered by the waves
As every tide tilts 'twixt their oaken sides;
And all of them, unburdened of their load,
Are ballasted with billows' wat'ry weight.
But hapless I, God wot, poor and unknown,
Do trace these Libyan deserts all despised,
Exiled forth Europe and wide Asia both,
230 And have not any coverture but heaven.

VENUS
Fortune hath favoured thee, whate'er thou be,
In sending thee unto this courteous coast.
A' God's name on, and haste thee to the court
Where Dido will receive ye with her smiles;
And for thy ships, which thou supposest lost,
Not one of them hath perished in the storm,
But are arrivèd safe not far from hence.
And so I leave thee to thy fortune's lot,
Wishing good luck unto thy wand'ring steps.

                                                                    Exit.

AENEAS
240 Achates, 'tis my mother that is fled,
I know her by the movings of her feet.
Stay, gentle Venus, fly not from thy son!
Too cruel, why wilt thou forsake me thus?
Or in these shades deceiv'st mine eyes so oft?
Why talk we not together hand in hand,
And tell our griefs in more familiar terms?
But thou art gone and leav'st me here alone,
To dull the air with my discursive moan.

                                                                    Exeunt.

Scene 2

Enter ILIONEUS *and* CLOANTHUS [*with* SERGESTUS *and*
IARBAS].

ILIONEUS
Follow, ye Trojans, follow this brave lord,
And plain to him the sum of your distress.

IARBAS
Why, what are you, or wherefore do you sue?

ILIONEUS
Wretches of Troy, envièd of the winds,
That crave such favour at your honour's feet
As poor distressèd misery may plead;
Save, save, O save our ships from cruel fire,
That do complain the wounds of thousand waves,
And spare our lives whom every spite pursues.
We come not, we, to wrong your Libyan gods,   10
Or steal your household lares from their shrines;
Our hands are not prepared to lawless spoil,
Nor armèd to offend in any kind.
Such force is far from our unweaponed thoughts,
Whose fading weal, of victory forsook,
Forbids all hope to harbour near our hearts.

IARBAS
But tell me, Trojans – Trojans if you be –
Unto what fruitful quarters were ye bound
Before that Boreas buckled with your sails?

CLOANTHUS
There is a place, Hesperia termed by us,   20
An ancient empire, famousèd for arms,
And fertile in fair Ceres' furrowed wealth,
Which now we call Italia, of his name
That in such peace long time did rule the same.
Thither made we
When suddenly gloomy Orion rose
And led our ships into the shallow sands,
Whereas the southern wind with brackish breath,

Dispersed them all amongst the wrackful rocks.
30   From thence a few of us escaped to land;
The rest, we fear, are folded in the floods.
IARBAS
Brave men-at-arms, abandon fruitless fears
Since Carthage knows to entertain distress.
SERGESTUS
Ay, but the barbarous sort do threat our ships,
And will not let us lodge upon the sands:
In multitudes they swarm unto the shore,
And from the first earth interdict our feet.
IARBAS
Myself will see they shall not trouble ye.
Your men and you shall banquet in our court,
40   And every Trojan be as welcome here
As Jupiter to silly Baucis' house.
Come in with me, I'll bring you to my queen,
Who shall confirm my words with further deeds.
SERGESTUS
Thanks, gentle lord, for such unlooked-for grace.
Might we but once more see Aeneas' face,
Then would we hope to quite such friendly turns
As shall surpass the wonder of our speech.

                                                    [*Exeunt.*]

ACT 2

Enter AENEAS, ACHATES, *and* ASCANIUS [*and others*].

AENEAS

Where am I now? These should be Carthage walls.

ACHATES

Why stands my sweet Aeneas thus amazed?

AENEAS

O my Achates, Theban Niobe,
Who for her sons' death wept out life and breath,
And, dry with grief, was turned into a stone,
Had not such passions in her head as I.
Methinks that town there should be Troy, yon Ida's hill,
There Xanthus' stream, because here's Priamus,
And when I know it is not, then I die.

ACHATES

And in this humour is Achates too.   10
I cannot choose but fall upon my knees
And kiss his hand. O, where is Hecuba?
Here she was wont to sit; but, saving air,
Is nothing here, and what is this but stone?

AENEAS

O, yet this stone doth make Aeneas weep!
And would my prayers, as Pygmalion's did,
Could give it life, that under his conduct
We might sail back to Troy and be revenged
On these hard-hearted Grecians which rejoice

20   That nothing now is left of Priamus!
      O, Priamus is left, and this is he!
      Come, come aboard, pursue the hateful Greeks!
ACHATES
      What means Aeneas?
AENEAS
      Achates, though mine eyes say this is stone,
      Yet thinks my mind that this is Priamus;
      And when my grievèd heart sighs and says no,
      Then would it leap out to give Priam life.
      O were I not at all, so thou mightst be!
      Achates, see, King Priam wags his hand!
30   He is alive, Troy is not overcome!
ACHATES
      Thy mind, Aeneas, that would have it so,
      Deludes thy eyesight. Priamus is dead.
AENEAS
      Ah, Troy is sacked, and Priamus is dead,
      And why should poor Aeneas be alive?
ASCANIUS
      Sweet father, leave to weep. This is not he,
      For, were it Priam, he would smile on me.
ACHATES
      Aeneas, see, here come the citizens.
      Leave to lament, lest they laugh at our fears.
            Enter CLOANTHUS, SERGESTUS, ILIONEUS [*and others*].
AENEAS
      Lords of this town, or whatsoever style
40   Belongs unto your name, vouchsafe of ruth
      To tell us who inhabits this fair town,
      What kind of people and who governs them;
      For we are strangers driven on this shore,
      And scarcely know within what clime we are.
ILIONEUS
      I hear Aeneas' voice but see him not,
      For none of these can be our general.
ACHATES
      Like Ilioneus speaks this nobleman,

But Ilioneus goes not in such robes.

SERGESTUS
You are Achates, or I deceived.

ACHATES
Aeneas, see, Sergestus or his ghost!   50

ILIONEUS
He names Aeneas, let us kiss his feet.

CLOANTHUS
It is our captain! See, Ascanius!

SERGESTUS
Live long Aeneas and Ascanius!

AENEAS
Achates, speak, for I am overjoyed.

ACHATES
O Ilioneus, art thou yet alive?

ILIONEUS
Blest be the time I see Achates' face!

CLOANTHUS
Why turns Aeneas from his trusty friends?

AENEAS
Sergestus, Ilioneus and the rest,
Your sight amazed me. O, what destinies
Have brought my sweet companions in such plight?   60
O tell me, for I long to be resolved!

ILIONEUS
Lovely Aeneas, these are Carthage walls,
And here Queen Dido wears th'imperial crown,
Who for Troy's sake hath entertained us all
And clad us in these wealthy robes we wear.
Oft hath she asked us under whom we served,
And when we told her, she would weep for grief,
Thinking the sea had swallowed up thy ships;
And now she sees thee, how will she rejoice!

SERGESTUS
See where her servitors pass through the hall   70
Bearing a banquet. Dido is not far.

ILIONEUS
Look where she comes. Aeneas, view her well.

AENEAS

Well may I view her, but she sees not me.

    Enter DIDO [*with* ANNA *and* IARBAS] *and her train.*

DIDO

What stranger art thou that dost eye me thus?

AENEAS

Sometime I was a Trojan, mighty queen,

But Troy is not. What shall I say I am?

ILIONEUS

Renownèd Dido, 'tis our general,

Warlike Aeneas.

DIDO

Warlike Aeneas, and in these base robes?

80 Go fetch the garment which Sichaeus ware.

Brave Prince, welcome to Carthage and to me,

Both happy that Aeneas is our guest.

Sit in this chair and banquet with a queen;

Aeneas is Aeneas, were he clad

In weeds as bad as ever Irus ware.

AENEAS

This is no seat for one that's comfortless.

May it please your grace to let Aeneas wait:

For though my birth be great, my fortune's mean,

Too mean to be companion to a queen.

DIDO

90 Thy fortune may be greater than thy birth.

Sit down, Aeneas, sit in Dido's place,

And if this be thy son, as I suppose,

Here let him sit. Be merry, lovely child.

AENEAS

This place beseems me not. O pardon me!

DIDO

I'll have it so. Aeneas, be content.

ASCANIUS

Madam, you shall be my mother.

DIDO

And so I will, sweet child. [*To* AENEAS] Be merry, man;

Here's to thy better fortune and good stars.
[*She raises a toast.*]

AENEAS

In all humility I thank your grace.

DIDO

Remember who thou art. Speak like thyself;   100
Humility belongs to common grooms.

AENEAS

And who so miserable as Aeneas is?

DIDO

Lies it in Dido's hands to make thee blest,
Then be assured thou art not miserable.

AENEAS

O Priamus! O Troy! O Hecuba!

DIDO

May I entreat thee to discourse at large,
And truly too, how Troy was overcome?
For many tales go of that city's fall,
And scarcely do agree upon one point.
Some say Antenor did betray the town,   110
Others report 'twas Sinon's perjury;
But all in this, that Troy is overcome,
And Priam dead. Yet how, we hear no news.

AENEAS

A woeful tale bids Dido to unfold,
Whose memory, like pale death's stony mace,
Beats forth my senses from this troubled soul,
And makes Aeneas sink at Dido's feet.

DIDO

What, faints Aeneas to remember Troy,
In whose defence he fought so valiantly?
Look up and speak.   120

AENEAS

Then speak, Aeneas, with Achilles' tongue,
And, Dido, and you Carthaginian peers,
Hear me, but yet with Myrmidons' harsh ears,
Daily inured to broils and massacres,

Lest you be moved too much with my sad tale.
The Grecian soldiers, tired with ten years' war,
Began to cry, 'Let us unto our ships,
Troy is invincible, why stay we here?'
With whose outcries Atrides being appalled,
130   Summoned the captains to his princely tent,
Who, looking on the scars we Trojans gave,
Seeing the number of their men decreased,
And the remainder weak and out of heart,
Gave up their voices to dislodge the camp,
And so in troops all marched to Tenedos;
Where when they came, Ulysses on the sand
Assayed with honey words to turn them back;
And as he spoke to further his intent,
The winds did drive huge billows to the shore,
140   And heaven was darkened with tempestuous clouds.
Then he alleged the gods would have them stay,
And prophesied Troy should be overcome;
And therewithal he called false Sinon forth,
A man compact of craft and perjury,
Whose ticing tongue was made of Hermes' pipe,
To force a hundred watchful eyes to sleep;
And him, Epeus having made the horse,
With sacrificing wreaths upon his head,
Ulysses sent to our unhappy town,
150   Who, grovelling in the mire of Xanthus' banks,
His hands bound at his back, and both his eyes
Turned up to heaven, as one resolved to die,
Our Phrygian shepherds haled within the gates
And brought unto the court of Priamus,
To whom he used action so pitiful,
Looks so remorseful, vows so forcible,
As therewithal the old man overcome,
Kissed him, embraced him, and unloosed his bands,
And then – O Dido, pardon me!

DIDO
160   Nay, leave not here, resolve me of the rest.

AENEAS

O, th'enchanting words of that base slave
Made him to think Epeus' pine-tree horse
A sacrifice t'appease Minerva's wrath;
The rather, for that one Laocoön,
Breaking a spear upon his hollow breast,
Was with two wingèd serpents stung to death.
Whereat aghast, we were commanded straight
With reverence to draw it into Troy;
In which unhappy work was I employed:
These hands did help to hale it to the gates,   170
Through which it could not enter, 'twas so huge.
O, had it never entered, Troy had stood!
But Priamus, impatient of delay,
Enforced a wide breach in that rampired wall,
Which thousand battering-rams could never pierce,
And so came in this fatal instrument,
At whose accursèd feet, as overjoyed,
We banqueted, till, overcome with wine,
Some surfeited, and others soundly slept.
Which Sinon viewing, caused the Greekish spies   180
To haste to Tenedos and tell the camp;
Then he unlocked the horse, and suddenly
From out his entrails Neoptolemus,
Setting his spear upon the ground, leapt forth,
And after him a thousand Grecians more,
In whose stern faces shined the quenchless fire
That after burnt the pride of Asia.
By this, the camp was come unto the walls,
And through the breach did march into the streets,
Where, meeting with the rest, 'Kill, kill!' they cried.   190
Frighted with this confusèd noise, I rose,
And looking from a turret might behold
Young infants swimming in their parents' blood,
Headless carcasses pilèd up in heaps,
Virgins half-dead, dragged by their golden hair
And with main force flung on a ring of pikes,

Old men with swords thrust through their agèd sides,
Kneeling for mercy to a Greekish lad,
Who with steel pole-axes dashed out their brains.
200   Then buckled I mine armour, drew my sword,
And thinking to go down, came Hector's ghost,
With ashy visage, bluish sulphur eyes,
His arms torn from his shoulders, and his breast
Furrowed with wounds, and – that which made me weep –
Thongs at his heels, by which Achilles' horse
Drew him in triumph through the Greekish camp,
Burst from the earth, crying, 'Aeneas, fly!
Troy is a-fire, the Grecians have the town!'

DIDO
O Hector, who weeps not to hear thy name?

AENEAS
210   Yet flung I forth and, desperate of my life,
Ran in the thickest throngs, and with this sword
Sent many of their savage ghosts to hell.
At last came Pyrrhus, fell and full of ire,
His harness dropping blood, and on his spear
The mangled head of Priam's youngest son,
And after him his band of Myrmidons,
With balls of wildfire in their murdering paws,
Which made the funeral flame that burnt fair Troy;
All which hemmed me about, crying, 'This is he!'

DIDO
220   Ah, how could poor Aeneas 'scape their hands?

AENEAS
My mother, Venus, jealous of my health,
Conveyed me from their crooked nets and bands;
So I escaped the furious Pyrrhus' wrath,
Who then ran to the palace of the king,
And at Jove's altar finding Priamus,
About whose withered neck hung Hecuba,
Folding his hand in hers, and jointly both
Beating their breasts and falling on the ground,
He, with his falchion's point raised up at once,
230   And with Megaera's eyes, stared in their face,

Threat'ning a thousand deaths at every glance.
To whom the agèd king thus trembling spoke:
'Achilles' son, remember what I was:
Father of fifty sons, but they are slain,
Lord of my fortune, but my fortune's turned,
King of this city, but my Troy is fired,
And now am neither father, lord, nor king.
Yet who so wretched but desires to live?
O let me live, great Neoptolemus!'
Not moved at all, but smiling at his tears,   240
This butcher, whilst his hands were yet held up,
Treading upon his breast, struck off his hands.

DIDO

O end, Aeneas! I can hear no more.

AENEAS

At which the frantic queen leaped on his face,
And in his eyelids hanging by the nails,
A little while prolonged her husband's life.
At last the soldiers pulled her by the heels
And swung her howling in the empty air,
Which sent an echo to the wounded king;
Whereat he lifted up his bed-rid limbs,   250
And would have grappled with Achilles' son,
Forgetting both his want of strength and hands:
Which he disdaining whisked his sword about,
And with the wind thereof the king fell down.
Then from the navel to the throat at once
He ripped old Priam, at whose latter gasp
Jove's marble statue gan to bend the brow
As loathing Pyrrhus for this wicked act.
Yet he, undaunted, took his father's flag
And dipped it in the old king's chill cold blood,   260
And then in triumph ran into the streets,
Through which he could not pass for slaughtered men;
So, leaning on his sword, he stood stone still,
Viewing the fire wherewith rich Ilion burnt.
By this, I got my father on my back,
This young boy in mine arms, and by the hand

Led fair Creusa, my beloved wife;
When thou, Achates, with thy sword mad'st way,
And we were round-environed with the Greeks.
270 O there I lost my wife, and had not we
Fought manfully, I had not told this tale.
Yet manhood would not serve; of force we fled,
And as we went unto our ships, thou knowest
We saw Cassandra sprawling in the streets,
Whom Ajax ravished in Diana's fane,
Her cheeks swoll'n with sighs, her hair all rent,
Whom I took up to bear unto our ships.
But suddenly the Grecians followed us,
And I, alas, was forced to let her lie.
280 Then got we to our ships and, being aboard,
Polyxena cried out, 'Aeneas, stay!
The Greeks pursue me, stay and take me in!'
Moved with her voice, I leapt into the sea,
Thinking to bear her on my back aboard,
For all our ships were launched into the deep,
And as I swum, she, standing on the shore,
Was by the cruel Myrmidons surprised
And after by that Pyrrhus sacrificed.

DIDO
I die with melting ruth; Aeneas, leave!
ANNA
290 O, what became of agèd Hecuba?
IARBAS
How got Aeneas to the fleet again?
DIDO
But how 'scaped Helen, she that caused this war?
AENEAS
Achates, speak, sorrow hath tired me quite.
ACHATES
What happened to the queen we cannot show;
We hear they led her captive into Greece.
As for Aeneas, he swum quickly back,
And Helena betrayed Deiphobus,
Her lover after Alexander died,

And so was reconciled to Menelaus.

DIDO

O had that ticing strumpet ne'er been born!   300
Trojan, thy ruthful tale hath made me sad.
Come, let us think upon some pleasing sport,
To rid me from these melancholy thoughts.

Exeunt [except ASCANIUS].
Enter VENUS *[with* CUPID] *at another door, and takes*
ASCANIUS *by the sleeve.*

VENUS

Fair child, stay thou with Dido's waiting-maid,
I'll give thee sugar-almonds, sweet conserves,
A silver girdle and a golden purse,
And this young prince shall be thy playfellow.

ASCANIUS

Are you Queen Dido's son?

CUPID

Ay, and my mother gave me this fine bow.

ASCANIUS

Shall I have such a quiver and a bow?   310

VENUS

Such bow, such quiver, and such golden shafts,
Will Dido give to sweet Ascanius.
For Dido's sake I take thee in my arms
And stick these spangled feathers in thy hat;
Eat comfits in mine arms, and I will sing.
Now is he fast asleep, and in this grove,
Amongst green brakes, I'll lay Ascanius,
And strew him with sweet-smelling violets,
Blushing roses, purple hyacinth;
These milk-white doves shall be his sentinels,   320
Who, if that any seek to do him hurt,
Will quickly fly to Cytherea's fist.
Now, Cupid, turn thee to Ascanius' shape,
And go to Dido, who, instead of him,
Will set thee on her lap and play with thee;
Then touch her white breast with this arrow head,
That she may dote upon Aeneas' love,

And by that means repair his broken ships,
Victual his soldiers, give him wealthy gifts,
330   And he at last depart to Italy,
Or else in Carthage make his kingly throne.

CUPID

I will, fair mother, and so play my part
As every touch shall wound Queen Dido's heart.

[*Exit.*]

VENUS

Sleep, my sweet nephew, in these cooling shades,
Free from the murmur of these running streams,
The cry of beasts, the rattling of the winds,
Or whisking of these leaves. All shall be still,
And nothing interrupt thy quiet sleep
Till I return and take thee hence again.

Exit.

ACT 3

Scene 1

Enter CUPID *alone* [*disguised as* ASCANIUS].

CUPID
    Now, Cupid, cause the Carthaginian queen
    To be enamoured of thy brother's looks;
    Convey this golden arrow in thy sleeve,
    Lest she imagine thou art Venus' son;
    And when she strokes thee softly on the head,
    Then shall I touch her breast and conquer her.
        Enter IARBAS, ANNA *and* DIDO.

IARBAS
    How long, fair Dido, shall I pine for thee?
    'Tis not enough that thou dost grant me love,
    But that I may enjoy what I desire:
    That love is childish which consists in words.   10

DIDO
    Iarbas, know that thou of all my wooers –
    And yet have I had many mightier kings –
    Hast had the greatest favours I could give.
    I fear me Dido hath been counted light
    In being too familiar with Iarbas,
    Albeit the gods do know no wanton thought
    Had ever residence in Dido's breast.

IARBAS
    But Dido is the favour I request.

DIDO
    Fear not, Iarbas, Dido may be thine.

ANNA

20   Look, sister, how Aeneas' little son
    Plays with your garments and embraceth you.

CUPID

    No, Dido will not take me in her arms,
    I shall not be her son, she loves me not.

DIDO

    Weep not, sweet boy, thou shalt be Dido's son.
    Sit in my lap and let me hear thee sing.
      [CUPID *sings*.]
    No more, my child. Now talk another while,
    And tell me where learn'dst thou this pretty song?

CUPID

    My cousin Helen taught it me in Troy.

DIDO

    How lovely is Ascanius when he smiles!

CUPID

30   Will Dido let me hang about her neck?

DIDO

    Ay, wag, and give thee leave to kiss her too.

CUPID

    What will you give me? Now I'll have this fan.

DIDO

    Take it, Ascanius, for thy father's sake.

IARBAS

    Come, Dido, leave Ascanius! Let us walk!

DIDO

    Go thou away, Ascanius shall stay.

IARBAS

    Ungentle queen, is this thy love to me?

DIDO

    O stay, Iarbas, and I'll go with thee.

CUPID

    And if my mother go, I'll follow her.

DIDO [*to* IARBAS]

    Why stay'st thou here? Thou art no love of mine.

IARBAS

40   Iarbas, die, seeing she abandons thee!

DIDO
  No, live Iarbas; what hast thou deserved,
  That I should say 'Thou art no love of mine'?
  Something thou hast deserved. Away, I say!
  Depart from Carthage! Come not in my sight!

IARBAS
  Am I not king of rich Gaetulia?

DIDO
  Iarbas, pardon me, and stay a while.

CUPID
  Mother, look here.

DIDO
  What tell'st thou me of rich Gaetulia?
  Am not I queen of Libya? Then depart!

IARBAS
  I go to feed the humour of my love,   50
  Yet not from Carthage for a thousand worlds.

DIDO
  Iarbas!

IARBAS Doth Dido call me back?

DIDO
  No, but I charge thee never look on me.

IARBAS
  Then pull out both mine eyes, or let me die.

                                      Exit IARBAS.

ANNA
  Wherefore doth Dido bid Iarbas go?

DIDO
  Because his loathsome sight offends mine eye,
  And in my thoughts is shrined another love.
  O Anna, didst thou know how sweet love were,
  Full soon wouldst thou abjure this single life.

ANNA
  Poor soul, I know too well the sour of love.   60
  [*Aside*] O that Iarbas could but fancy me!

DIDO
  Is not Aeneas fair and beautiful?

ANNA

    Yes, and Iarbas foul and favourless.

DIDO

    Is he not eloquent in all his speech?

ANNA

    Yes, and Iarbas rude and rustical.

DIDO

    Name not Iarbas! But, sweet Anna, say,
    Is not Aeneas worthy Dido's love?

ANNA

    O sister, were you empress of the world,
    Aeneas well deserves to be your love;
70   So lovely is he that where'er he goes
    The people swarm to gaze him in the face.

DIDO

    But tell them none shall gaze on him but I,
    Lest their gross eye-beams taint my lover's cheeks.
    Anna, good sister Anna, go for him,
    Lest with these sweet thoughts I melt clean away.

ANNA

    Then, sister, you'll abjure Iarbas' love?

DIDO

    Yet must I hear that loathsome name again?
    Run for Aeneas, or I'll fly to him.

Exit ANNA.

CUPID

    You shall not hurt my father when he comes.

DIDO

80   No, for thy sake I'll love thy father well.
    O dull-conceited Dido, that till now
    Didst never think Aeneas beautiful!
    But now, for quittance of this oversight,
    I'll make me bracelets of his golden hair;
    His glistering eyes shall be my looking-glass,
    His lips an altar, where I'll offer up
    As many kisses as the sea hath sands.
    Instead of music I will hear him speak,
    His looks shall be my only library;

And thou, Aeneas, Dido's treasury,   90
In whose fair bosom I will lock more wealth
Than twenty thousand Indias can afford.
O, here he comes! Love, love, give Dido leave
To be more modest than her thoughts admit,
Lest I be made a wonder to the world.
　　[*Enter* AENEAS, ACHATES, SERGESTUS, ILIONEUS *and*
　　CLOANTHUS.]
Achates, how doth Carthage please your lord?

ACHATES
That will Aeneas show your majesty.

DIDO
Aeneas, art thou there?

AENEAS
I understand your highness sent for me.

DIDO
No, but now thou art here, tell me, in sooth,   100
In what might Dido highly pleasure thee?

AENEAS
So much have I received at Dido's hands
As, without blushing, I can ask no more.
Yet, Queen of Afric, are my ships unrigged,
My sails all rent in sunder with the wind,
My oars broken and my tackling lost,
Yea, all my navy split with rocks and shelves;
Nor stern nor anchor have our maimèd fleet;
Our masts the furious winds struck overboard:
Which piteous wants if Dido will supply,   110
We will account her author of our lives.

DIDO
Aeneas, I'll repair thy Trojan ships,
Conditionally that thou wilt stay with me,
And let Achates sail to Italy.
I'll give thee tackling made of rivelled gold,
Wound on the barks of odoriferous trees;
Oars of massy ivory, full of holes,
Through which the water shall delight to play.
Thy anchors shall be hewed from crystal rocks,

120   Which if thou lose shall shine above the waves;
The masts whereon thy swelling sails shall hang,
Hollow pyramides of silver plate;
The sails of folded lawn, where shall be wrought
The wars of Troy, but not Troy's overthrow;
For ballast, empty Dido's treasury,
Take what ye will, but leave Aeneas here.
Achates, thou shalt be so manly clad
As sea-born nymphs shall swarm about thy ships,
And wanton mermaids court thee with sweet songs,
130   Flinging in favours of more sovereign worth
Than Thetis hangs about Apollo's neck,
So that Aeneas may but stay with me.

AENEAS
Wherefore would Dido have Aeneas stay?

DIDO
To war against my bordering enemies.
Aeneas, think not Dido is in love;
For if that any man could conquer me,
I had been wedded ere Aeneas came.
See where the pictures of my suitors hang;
And are not these as fair as fair may be?
    [*Showing pictures.*]

ACHATES
140   I saw this man at Troy, ere Troy was sacked.

AENEAS
I this in Greece when Paris stole fair Helen.

ILIONEUS
This man and I were at Olympus games.

SERGESTUS
I know this face, he is a Persian born.
I travelled with him to Aetolia.

CLOANTHUS
And I in Athens with this gentleman,
Unless I be deceived, disputed once.

DIDO
But speak, Aeneas, know you none of these?

AENEAS
  No, madam, but it seems that these are kings.
DIDO
  All these and others which I never saw
  Have been most urgent suitors for my love;   150
  Some came in person, others sent their legates;
  Yet none obtained me. I am free from all,
  [*aside*] And yet, God knows, entangled unto one.
  This was an orator, and thought by words
  To compass me, but yet he was deceived;
  And this a Spartan courtier, vain and wild,
  But his fantastic humours pleased not me;
  This was Alcion, a musician,
  But played he ne'er so sweet, I let him go;
  This was the wealthy king of Thessaly,   160
  But I had gold enough and cast him off;
  This, Meleager's son, a warlike prince,
  But weapons 'gree not with my tender years;
  The rest are such as all the world well knows,
  Yet now I swear, by heaven and him I love,
  I was as far from love as they from hate.
AENEAS
  O happy shall he be whom Dido loves!
DIDO
  Then never say that thou art miserable,
  Because it may be thou shalt be my love.
  Yet boast not of it, for I love thee not.   170
  And yet I hate thee not. [*Aside*] O, if I speak,
  I shall betray myself. [*To* AENEAS] Aeneas, speak!
  We two will go a-hunting in the woods,
  But not so much for thee – thou art but one –
  As for Achates and his followers.
                                                Exeunt.

Scene 2

Enter JUNO *to* ASCANIUS *asleep*.

JUNO
Here lies my hate, Aeneas' cursed brat,
The boy wherein false Destiny delights,
The heir of Fame, the favourite of the Fates,
That ugly imp that shall outwear my wrath,
And wrong my deity with high disgrace.
But I will take another order now,
And raze th'eternal register of time;
Troy shall no more call him her second hope,
Nor Venus triumph in his tender youth;
For here, in spite of heaven, I'll murder him,
And feed infection with his let-out life.
Say, Paris, now shall Venus have the ball?
Say, vengeance, now shall her Ascanius die?
O no! God wot, I cannot watch my time,
Nor quit good turns with double fee down told!
Tut, I am simple, without mind to hurt,
And have no gall at all to grieve my foes;
But lustful Jove and his adulterous child
Shall find it written on confusion's front,
That only Juno rules in Rhamnus town.
    Enter VENUS.

VENUS
What should this mean? My doves are back returned,
Who warn me of such danger prest at hand
To harm my sweet Ascanius' lovely life.
Juno, my mortal foe, what make you here?
Avaunt, old witch, and trouble not my wits!

JUNO
Fie, Venus, that such causeless words of wrath
Should e'er defile so fair a mouth as thine!
Are not we both sprung of celestial race,
And banquet as two sisters with the gods?
Why is it, then, displeasure should disjoin

Whom kindred and acquaintance co-unites?
VENUS
  Out, hateful hag! Thou wouldst have slain my son
  Had not my doves discovered thy intent;
  But I will tear thy eyes from forth thy head,
  And feast the birds with their blood-shotten balls,
  If thou but lay thy fingers on my boy.
JUNO
  Is this, then, all the thanks that I shall have
  For saving him from snakes' and serpents' stings,
  That would have killed him sleeping as he lay?
  What though I was offended with thy son   40
  And wrought him mickle woe on sea and land,
  When, for the hate of Trojan Ganymede,
  That was advancèd by my Hebe's shame,
  And Paris' judgement of the heavenly ball,
  I mustered all the winds unto his wrack
  And urged each element to his annoy?
  Yet now I do repent me of his ruth,
  And wish that I had never wronged him so.
  Bootless I saw it was to war with fate,
  That hath so many unresisted friends: 50
  Wherefore I changed my counsel with the time,
  And planted love where envy erst had sprung.
VENUS
  Sister of Jove, if that thy love be such
  As these protestations do paint forth,
  We two as friends one fortune will divide.
  Cupid shall lay his arrows in thy lap,
  And to a sceptre change his golden shafts;
  Fancy and modesty shall live as mates,
  And thy fair peacocks by my pigeons perch.
  Love my Aeneas, and desire is thine;   60
  The day, the night, my swans, my sweets, are thine.
JUNO
  More than melodious are these words to me,
  That overcloy my soul with their content.
  Venus, sweet Venus, how may I deserve

Such amorous favours at thy beauteous hand?
But that thou mayst more easily perceive
How highly I do prize this amity,
Hark to a motion of eternal league,
Which I will make in quittance of thy love:
70   Thy son, thou know'st, with Dido now remains,
And feeds his eyes with favours of her court;
She likewise in admiring spends her time
And cannot talk nor think of aught but him.
Why should not they then join in marriage
And bring forth mighty kings to Carthage town,
Whom casualty of sea hath made such friends?
And, Venus, let there be a match confirmed
Betwixt these two, whose loves are so alike,
And both our deities, conjoined in one,
80   Shall chain felicity unto their throne.

VENUS

Well could I like this reconcilement's means,
But much I fear my son will ne'er consent,
Whose armèd soul, already on the sea,
Darts forth her light to Lavinia's shore.

JUNO

Fair Queen of Love, I will divorce these doubts,
And find the way to weary such fond thoughts:
This day they both a-hunting forth will ride
Into these woods adjoining to these walls,
When, in the midst of all their gamesome sports,
90   I'll make the clouds dissolve their wat'ry works
And drench Silvanus' dwellings with their showers;
Then in one cave the queen and he shall meet,
And interchangeably discourse their thoughts,
Whose short conclusion will seal up their hearts
Unto the purpose which we now propound.

VENUS

Sister, I see you savour of my wiles;
Be it as you will have it for this once.
Meantime, Ascanius shall be my charge,

Whom I will bear to Ida in mine arms,
And couch him in Adonis' purple down.   100

                                        Exeunt.

Scene 3

Enter DIDO, AENEAS, ANNA, IARBAS, ACHATES, [CUPID
dressed as ASCANIUS,] *and* FOLLOWERS.

DIDO
  Aeneas, think not but I honour thee
  That thus in person go with thee to hunt.
  My princely robes, thou seest, are laid aside,
  Whose glittering pomp Diana's shrouds supplies;
  All fellows now, disposed alike to sport:
  The woods are wide, and we have store of game.
  Fair Trojan, hold my golden bow a while,
  Until I gird my quiver to my side.
  Lords, go before. We two must talk alone.
                              [*Exeunt* FOLLOWERS.]

IARBAS [*aside*]
  Ungentle, can she wrong Iarbas so?   10
  I'll die before a stranger have that grace.
  'We two will talk alone' – what words be these?

DIDO
  What makes Iarbas here of all the rest?
  We could have gone without your company.

AENEAS
  But love and duty led him on perhaps
  To press beyond acceptance to your sight.

IARBAS
  Why, man of Troy, do I offend thine eyes?
  Or art thou grieved thy betters press so nigh?

DIDO
  How now, Gaetulian, are ye grown so brave
  To challenge us with your comparisons?   20

Peasant, go seek companions like thyself,
And meddle not with any that I love.
Aeneas, be not moved at what he says,
For otherwhile he will be out of joint.

IARBAS

Women may wrong by privilege of love;
But should that man of men, Dido except,
Have taunted me in these opprobrious terms,
I would have either drunk his dying blood,
Or else I would have given my life in gage!

DIDO

30   Huntsmen, why pitch you not your toils apace,
And rouse the light-foot deer from forth their lair?

ANNA

Sister, see, see Ascanius in his pomp,
Bearing his hunt-spear bravely in his hand!

DIDO

Yea, little son, are you so forward now?

CUPID

Ay, mother, I shall one day be a man
And better able unto other arms;
Meantime these wanton weapons serve my war,
Which I will break betwixt a lion's jaws.

DIDO

What, dar'st thou look a lion in the face?

CUPID

40   Ay, and outface him too, do what he can!

ANNA

How like his father speaketh he in all!

AENEAS

And mought I live to see him sack rich Thebes,
And load his spear with Grecian princes' heads,
Then would I wish me with Anchises' tomb,
And dead to honour that hath brought me up.

IARBAS

And might I live to see thee shipped away,
And hoist aloft on Neptune's hideous hills,
Then would I wish me in fair Dido's arms,

And dead to scorn that hath pursued me so.

AENEAS

Stout friend, Achates, dost thou know this wood?   50

ACHATES

As I remember, here you shot the deer
That saved your famished soldiers' lives from death,
When first you set your foot upon the shore,
And here we met fair Venus, virgin-like,
Bearing her bow and quiver at her back.

AENEAS

O, how these irksome labours now delight
And overjoy my thoughts with their escape!
Who would not undergo all kind of toil
To be well stored with such a winter's tale?

DIDO

Aeneas, leave these dumps and let's away,   60
Some to the mountains, some unto the soil,
You to the valleys, [*to* IARBAS] thou unto the house.

                    [*Exeunt;* IARBAS *remains*].

IARBAS

Ay, this it is which wounds me to the death,
To see a Phrygian, forfeit to the sea,
Preferred before a man of majesty.
O love! O hate! O cruel women's hearts,
That imitate the moon in every change
And, like the planets, ever love to range!
What shall I do, thus wrongèd with disdain?
Revenge me on Aeneas or on her?   70
On her? Fond man, that were to war 'gainst heaven,
And with one shaft provoke ten thousand darts.
This Trojan's end will be thy envy's aim,
Whose blood will reconcile thee to content
And make love drunken with thy sweet desire.
But Dido, that now holdeth him so dear,
Will die with very tidings of his death;
But time will discontinue her content
And mould her mind unto new fancy's shapes.
O God of heaven, turn the hand of fate   80

Unto that happy day of my delight!
And then – what then? Iarbas shall but love.
So doth he now, though not with equal gain:
That resteth in the rival of thy pain,
Who ne'er will cease to soar till he be slain.

Exit.

Scene 4

The storm. Enter AENEAS *and* DIDO *in the cave at several times.*

DIDO
Aeneas!
AENEAS   Dido!
DIDO
Tell me, dear love, how found you out this cave?
AENEAS
By chance, sweet queen, as Mars and Venus met.
DIDO
Why, that was in a net, where we are loose,
And yet I am not free. O would I were!
AENEAS
Why, what is it that Dido may desire
And not obtain, be it in human power?
DIDO
The thing that I will die before I ask,
And yet desire to have before I die.
AENEAS
10   It is not aught Aeneas may achieve?
DIDO
Aeneas? No, although his eyes do pierce.
AENEAS
What, hath Iarbas angered her in aught?
And will she be avengèd on his life?
DIDO
Not angered me, except in ang'ring thee.

AENEAS

Who, then, of all so cruel may he be
That should detain thy eye in his defects?

DIDO

The man that I do eye where'er I am,
Whose amorous face, like Paean, sparkles fire,
Whenas he butts his beams on Flora's bed.
Prometheus hath put on Cupid's shape,   20
And I must perish in his burning arms.
Aeneas, O Aeneas, quench these flames!

AENEAS

What ails my queen? Is she fall'n sick of late?

DIDO

Not sick, my love, but sick I must conceal
The torment that it boots me not reveal.
And yet I'll speak, and yet I'll hold my peace;
Do shame her worst, I will disclose my grief.
Aeneas, thou art he – what did I say?
Something it was that now I have forgot.

AENEAS

What means fair Dido by this doubtful speech?   30

DIDO

Nay, nothing. But Aeneas loves me not.

AENEAS

Aeneas' thoughts dare not ascend so high
As Dido's heart, which monarchs might not scale.

DIDO

It was because I saw no king like thee,
Whose golden crown might balance my content;
But now that I have found what to affect,
I follow one that loveth fame for me,
And rather had seem fair to Sirens' eyes
Than to the Carthage queen that dies for him.

AENEAS

If that your majesty can look so low   40
As my despisèd worths, that shun all praise,
With this my hand I give to you my heart,
And vow by all the gods of hospitality,

By heaven and earth, and my fair brother's bow,
By Paphos, Capys, and the purple sea
From whence my radiant mother did descend,
And by this sword that saved me from the Greeks,
Never to leave these new-uprearèd walls
Whiles Dido lives and rules in Juno's town,
50   Never to like or love any but her!

DIDO

What more than Delian music do I hear,
That calls my soul from forth his living seat
To move unto the measures of delight?
Kind clouds that sent forth such a courteous storm
As made disdain to fly to fancy's lap!
Stout love, in mine arms make thy Italy,
Whose crown and kingdom rests at thy command.
'Sichaeus', not 'Aeneas', be thou called;
The 'King of Carthage', not 'Anchises' son'.
60   Hold, take these jewels at thy lover's hand,
These golden bracelets and this wedding-ring,
Wherewith my husband wooed me yet a maid,
And be thou King of Libya, by my gift.

Exeunt to the cave.

ACT 4

Scene 1

Enter ACHATES, [CUPID *dressed as*] ASCANIUS, IARBAS,
and ANNA.

ACHATES
Did ever men see such a sudden storm,
Or day so clear so suddenly o'ercast?

IARBAS
I think some fell enchantress dwelleth here
That can call them forth whenas she please,
And dive into black tempests' treasury
Whenas she means to mask the world with clouds.

ANNA
In all my life I never knew the like.
It hailed, it snowed, it light'nèd, all at once.

ACHATES
I think it was the devils' revelling night,
There was such hurly-burly in the heavens;   10
Doubtless Apollo's axle-tree is cracked,
Or aged Atlas' shoulder out of joint,
The motion was so over-violent.

IARBAS
In all this coil, where have ye left the queen?

CUPID
Nay, where's my warlike father, can you tell?
    [*Enter* DIDO *and* AENEAS.]

ANNA
Behold where both of them come forth the cave.

IARBAS [*aside*]
   Come forth the cave? Can heaven endure this sight?
   Iarbas, curse that unrevenging Jove,
   Whose flinty darts slept in Typhoeus' den
20   Whiles these adulterers surfeited with sin.
   Nature, why mad'st me not some poisonous beast,
   That with the sharpness of my edgèd sting
   I might have staked them both unto the earth,
   Whil'st they were sporting in this darksome cave?

AENEAS
   The air is clear and southern winds are whist.
   Come, Dido, let us hasten to the town,
   Since gloomy Aeolus doth cease to frown.

DIDO
   Achates and Ascanius, well met.

AENEAS
   Fair Anna, how escaped you from the shower?

ANNA
30   As others did, by running to the wood.

DIDO
   But where were you, Iarbas, all this while?

IARBAS
   Not with Aeneas in the ugly cave.

DIDO
   I see Aeneas sticketh in your mind,
   But I will soon put by that stumbling-block,
   And quell those hopes that thus employ your cares.

Exeunt.

Scene 2

Enter IARBAS *to sacrifice.*

IARBAS
   Come, servants, come; bring forth the sacrifice,
   That I may pacify that gloomy Jove
   Whose empty altars have enlarged our ills.

[*Enter* SERVANTS *with the sacrifice, then exeunt.*]
Eternal Jove, great master of the clouds,
Father of gladness and all frolic thoughts,
That with thy gloomy hand corrects the heaven
When airy creatures war amongst themselves,
Hear, hear, O hear Iarbas' plaining prayers
Whose hideous echoes make the welkin howl
And all the woods 'Eliza' to resound!   10
The woman that thou willed us entertain,
Where, straying in our borders up and down,
She craved a hide of ground to build a town,
With whom we did divide both laws and land
And all the fruits that plenty else sends forth,
Scorning our loves and royal marriage-rites,
Yields up her beauty to a stranger's bed,
Who, having wrought her shame, is straightway fled.
Now, if thou be'st a pitying god of power,
On whom ruth and compassion ever waits,   20
Redress these wrongs and warn him to his ships,
That now afflicts me with his flattering eyes.
     Enter ANNA.
ANNA
    How now, Iarbas, at your prayers so hard?
IARBAS
    Ay, Anna, is there aught you would with me?
ANNA
    Nay, no such weighty business of import
    But may be slacked until another time.
    Yet, if you would partake with me the cause
    Of this devotion that detaineth you,
    I would be thankful for such courtesy.
IARBAS
    Anna, against this Trojan do I pray,   30
    Who seeks to rob me of thy sister's love
    And dive into her heart by coloured looks.
ANNA
    Alas, poor king, that labours so in vain
    For her that so delighteth in thy pain!

Be ruled by me and seek some other love,
Whose yielding heart may yield thee more relief.

IARBAS

Mine eye is fixed where fancy cannot start.
O leave me, leave me to my silent thoughts
That register the numbers of my ruth,
40 And I will either move the thoughtless flint
Or drop out both mine eyes in drizzling tears,
Before my sorrow's tide have any stint.

ANNA

I will not leave Iarbas, whom I love,
In this delight of dying pensiveness.
Away with Dido! Anna be thy song,
Anna, that doth admire thee more than heaven!

IARBAS

I may nor will list to such loathsome change
That intercepts the course of my desire.
Servants, come fetch these empty vessels here,
50 For I will fly from these alluring eyes
That do pursue my peace where'er it goes.

Exit.

ANNA

Iarbas, stay, loving Iarbas, stay,
For I have honey to present thee with!
Hard-hearted, wilt not deign to hear me speak?
I'll follow thee with outcries ne'er the less
And strew thy walks with my dishevelled hair.

Exit.

Scene 3

Enter AENEAS *alone.*

AENEAS

Carthage, my friendly host, adieu,
Since destiny doth call me from the shore.
Hermes this night, descending in a dream,

Hath summoned me to fruitful Italy;
Jove wills it so, my mother wills it so;
Let my Phoenissa grant, and then I go.
Grant she or no, Aeneas must away,
Whose golden fortunes, clogged with courtly ease,
Cannot ascend to fame's immortal house
Or banquet in bright honour's burnished hall,   10
Till he hath furrowed Neptune's glassy fields
And cut a passage through his topless hills.
Achates, come forth! Sergestus, Ilioneus,
Cloanthus, haste away! Aeneas calls!
    Enter ACHATES, CLOANTHUS, SERGESTUS, *and* ILIONEUS.

ACHATES
What wills our lord, or wherefore did he call?

AENEAS
The dreams, brave mates, that did beset my bed,
When sleep but newly had embraced the night,
Commands me leave these unrenownèd realms,
Whereas nobility abhors to stay,
And none but base Aeneas will abide.   20
Aboard, aboard, since Fates do bid aboard
And slice the sea with sable-coloured ships,
On whom the nimble winds may all day wait
And follow them as footmen through the deep!
Yet Dido casts her eyes like anchors out
To stay my fleet from loosing forth the bay.
'Come back, come back!' I hear her cry afar,
'And let me link thy body to my lips,
That, tied together by the striving tongues,
We may as one sail into Italy!'   30

ACHATES
Banish that ticing dame from forth your mouth
And follow your foreseeing stars in all.
This is no life for men-at-arms to live,
Where dalliance doth consume a soldier's strength
And wanton motions of alluring eyes
Effeminate our minds inured to war.

ILIONEUS
    Why, let us build a city of our own,
    And not stand lingering here for amorous looks.
    Will Dido raise old Priam forth his grave
40 And build the town again the Greeks did burn?
    No, no, she cares not how we sink or swim,
    So she may have Aeneas in her arms.
CLOANTHUS
    To Italy, sweet friends, to Italy!
    We will not stay a minute longer here.
AENEAS
    Trojans, aboard, and I will follow you.

                    [*Exeunt* TROJANS; AENEAS *remains.*]

    I fain would go, yet beauty calls me back.
    To leave her so and not once say farewell
    Were to transgress against all laws of love;
    But if I use such ceremonious thanks
50 As parting friends accustom on the shore,
    Her silver arms will coll me round about
    And tears of pearl cry, 'Stay, Aeneas, stay!'
    Each word she says will then contain a crown,
    And every speech be ended with a kiss.
    I may not dure this female drudgery,
    To sea, Aeneas, find out Italy!

                                                    Exit.

                        Scene 4

            Enter DIDO *and* ANNA.
DIDO
    O Anna, run unto the water side,
    They say Aeneas' men are going aboard;
    It may be he will steal away with them.
    Stay not to answer me! Run, Anna, run!

                                        [*Exit* ANNA.]

    O foolish Trojans that would steal from hence

And not let Dido understand their drift!
I would have given Achates store of gold,
And Ilioneus gum and Libyan spice;
The common soldiers rich embroidered coats
And silver whistles to control the winds,   10
Which Circe sent Sichaeus when he lived;
Unworthy are they of a queen's reward.
See where they come; how might I do to chide?
    Enter ANNA, *with* AENEAS, ACHATES, ILIONEUS,
    SERGESTUS [*and* ATTENDANTS].

ANNA
'Twas time to run. Aeneas had been gone;
The sails were hoising up and he aboard.

DIDO
Is this thy love to me?

AENEAS
O princely Dido, give me leave to speak;
I went to take my farewell of Achates.

DIDO
How haps Achates bid me not farewell?

ACHATES
Because I feared your grace would keep me here.   20

DIDO
To rid thee of that doubt, aboard again;
I charge thee put to sea and stay not here.

ACHATES
Then let Aeneas go aboard with us.

DIDO
Get you aboard, Aeneas means to stay.

AENEAS
The sea is rough, the winds blow to the shore.

DIDO
O false Aeneas, now the sea is rough,
But when you were aboard 'twas calm enough!
Thou and Achates meant to sail away.

AENEAS
Hath not the Carthage Queen mine only son?
Thinks Dido I will go and leave him here?   30

DIDO

Aeneas, pardon me, for I forgot
That young Ascanius lay with me this night.
Love made me jealous, but, to make amends,
Wear the imperial crown of Libya,
Sway thou the Punic sceptre in my stead,
And punish me, Aeneas, for this crime.
　　[DIDO *gives* AENEAS *the crown and sceptre.*]

AENEAS

This kiss shall be fair Dido's punishment.

DIDO

O, how a crown becomes Aeneas' head!
Stay here, Aeneas, and command as king.

AENEAS

40　How vain am I to wear this diadem
And bear this golden sceptre in my hand!
A burgonet of steel and not a crown,
A sword and not a sceptre fits Aeneas.

DIDO

O, keep them still, and let me gaze my fill.
Now looks Aeneas like immortal Jove;
O, where is Ganymede to hold his cup
And Mercury to fly for what he calls?
Ten thousand Cupids hover in the air
And fan it in Aeneas' lovely face!
50　O that the clouds were here wherein thou fled'st,
That thou and I unseen might sport ourselves!
Heavens, envious of our joys, is waxen pale,
And when we whisper, then the stars fall down
To be partakers of our honey talk.

AENEAS

O Dido, patroness of all our lives,
When I leave thee, death be my punishment!
Swell, raging seas, frown, wayward Destinies;
Blow winds, threaten, ye rocks and sandy shelves!
This is the harbour that Aeneas seeks,
60　Let's see what tempests can annoy me now.

DIDO

Not all the world can take thee from mine arms.
Aeneas may command as many Moors
As in the sea are little water drops.
And now, to make experience of my love,
Fair sister Anna, lead my lover forth
And, seated on my jennet, let him ride
As Dido's husband through the Punic streets,
And will my guard, with Mauritanian darts,
To wait upon him as their sovereign lord.

ANNA

What if the citizens repine thereat?   70

DIDO

Those that dislike what Dido gives in charge,
Command my guard to slay for their offence.
Shall vulgar peasants storm at what I do?
The ground is mine that gives them sustenance,
The air wherein they breathe, the water, fire,
All that they have, their lands, their goods, their lives;
And I, the goddess of all these, command
Aeneas ride as Carthaginian king.

ACHATES

Aeneas, for his parentage, deserves
As large a kingdom as is Libya.   80

AENEAS

Ay, and unless the Destinies be false,
I shall be planted in as rich a land.

DIDO

Speak of no other land, this land is thine,
Dido is thine; henceforth I'll call thee lord.
    [To ANNA]
 Do as I bid thee, sister, lead the way,
And from a turret I'll behold my love.

AENEAS

Then here in me shall flourish Priam's race,
And thou and I, Achates, for revenge
For Troy, for Priam, for his fifty sons,

90   Our kinsmen's loves and thousand guiltless souls
     Will lead an host against the hateful Greeks
     And fire proud Lacedaemon o'er their heads.

                    Exit [AENEAS, *with the* TROJANS].

DIDO
     Speaks not Aeneas like a conqueror?
     O blessèd tempests that did drive him in!
     O happy sand that made him run aground!
     Henceforth you shall be our Carthage gods.
     Ay, but it may be he will leave my love
     And seek a foreign land called Italy.
     O that I had a charm to keep the winds
100 Within the closure of a golden ball,
     Or that the Tyrrhene Sea were in mine arms
     That he might suffer shipwreck on my breast
     As oft as he attempts to hoist up sail!
     I must prevent him, wishing will not serve.
     Go, bid my nurse take young Ascanius
     And bear him in the country to her house;
     Aeneas will not go without his son.
     Yet, lest he should, for I am full of fear,
     Bring me his oars, his tackling, and his sails.

                         [*Exeunt* ATTENDANTS.]

110 What if I sink his ships? O, he'll frown!
     Better he frown than I should die for grief.
     I cannot see him frown, it may not be.
     Armies of foes resolved to win this town,
     Or impious traitors vowed to have my life,
     Affright me not: only Aeneas' frown
     Is that which terrifies poor Dido's heart.
     Not bloody spears, appearing in the air,
     Presage the downfall of my empery,
     Nor blazing comets threatens Dido's death:
120 It is Aeneas' frown that ends my days.
     If he forsake me not, I never die,
     For in his looks I see eternity,
     And he'll make me immortal with a kiss.

Enter a LORD [*with* ATTENDANTS *carrying oars, tackling and sails*].

LORD

Your nurse is gone with young Ascanius,
And here's Aeneas' tackling, oars, and sails.

DIDO

Are these the sails that, in despite of me,
Packed with the winds to bear Aeneas hence?
I'll hang ye in the chamber where I lie.
Drive, if you can, my house to Italy:
I'll set the casement open, that the winds   130
May enter in and once again conspire
Against the life of me, poor Carthage queen;
But, though he go, he stays in Carthage still,
And let rich Carthage fleet upon the seas,
So I may have Aeneas in mine arms.
Is this the wood that grew in Carthage plains,
And would be toiling in the watery billows
To rob their mistress of her Trojan guest?
O cursèd tree, hadst thou but wit or sense
To measure how I prize Aeneas' love,   140
Thou wouldst have leapt from out the sailors' hands
And told me that Aeneas meant to go!
And yet I blame thee not, thou art but wood.
The water, which our poets term a nymph,
Why did it suffer thee to touch her breast
And shrunk not back, knowing my love was there?
The water is an element, no nymph.
Why should I blame Aeneas for his flight?
O Dido, blame not him, but break his oars,
These were the instruments that launched him forth.   150
There's not so much as this base tackling too
But dares to heap up sorrow to my heart.
Was it not you that hoisèd up these sails?
Why burst you not and they fell in the seas?
For this will Dido tie ye full of knots,
And shear ye all asunder with her hands.

Now serve to chastise shipboys for their faults,
Ye shall no more offend the Carthage queen.
Now let him hang my favours on his masts
160   And see if those will serve instead of sails;
For tackling, let him take the chains of gold
Which I bestowed upon his followers;
Instead of oars, let him use his hands
And swim to Italy. I'll keep these sure;
Come, bear them in.

                                        Exeunt.

Scene 5

Enter the NURSE, *with* CUPID *for* ASCANIUS.

NURSE
My Lord Ascanius, ye must go with me.
CUPID
Whither must I go? I'll stay with my mother.
NURSE
No, thou shalt go with me unto my house.
I have an orchard that hath store of plums,
Brown almonds, services, ripe figs, and dates,
Dewberries, apples, yellow oranges;
A garden where are bee-hives full of honey,
Musk-roses and a thousand sort of flowers,
And in the midst doth run a silver stream,
10   Where thou shalt see the red-gilled fishes leap,
White swans, and many lovely water-fowls.
Now speak, Ascanius, will ye go or no?
CUPID
Come, come, I'll go; how far hence is your house?
NURSE
But hereby, child; we shall get thither straight.
CUPID
Nurse, I am weary; will you carry me?

NURSE
  Ay, so you'll dwell with me and call me mother.

CUPID
  So you'll love me, I care not if I do.

NURSE
  That I might live to see this boy a man!
  How prettily he laughs! Go, ye wag,
  You'll be a twigger when you come to age.   20
  Say Dido what she will, I am not old;
  I'll be no more a widow, I am young;
  I'll have a husband, or else a lover.

CUPID A husband, and no teeth?

NURSE
  O what mean I to have such foolish thoughts!
  Foolish is love, a toy. O sacred love,
  If there be any heaven in earth, 'tis love,
  Especially in women of our years.
  Blush, blush for shame, why shouldst thou think of love?
  A grave and not a lover fits thy age.   30
  A grave? Why? I may live a hundred years:
  Fourscore is but a girl's age, love is sweet.
  My veins are withered and my sinews dry,
  Why do I think of love, now I should die?

CUPID Come, nurse.

NURSE
  Well, if he come a-wooing, he shall speed:
  O how unwise was I to say him nay!

                                 Exeunt.

ACT 5

Enter AENEAS, *with a paper in his hand, drawing the platform of the city; with him* ACHATES, CLOANTHUS, [SERGESTUS] *and* ILIONEUS.

AENEAS
Triumph, my mates, our travels are at end.
Here will Aeneas build a statelier Troy
Than that which grim Atrides overthrew.
Carthage shall vaunt her petty walls no more,
For I will grace them with a fairer frame
And clad her in a crystal livery
Wherein the day may evermore delight;
From golden India Ganges will I fetch,
Whose wealthy streams may wait upon her towers,
And triple-wise entrench her round about;
The sun from Egypt shall rich odours bring,
Wherewith his burning beams, like labouring bees
That load their thighs with Hybla's honey's spoils,
Shall here unburden their exhaled sweets,
And plant our pleasant suburbs with her fumes.

ACHATES
What length or breadth shall this brave town contain?

AENEAS
Not past four thousand paces at the most.

ILIONEUS
But what shall it be called? 'Troy', as before?

AENEAS

That have I not determined with myself.

CLOANTHUS

Let it be termed 'Aenea', by your name.   20

SERGESTUS

Rather 'Ascania', by your little son.

AENEAS

Nay, I will have it called 'Anchisaeon',
Of my old father's name.

   Enter HERMES *with* ASCANIUS.

HERMES

Aeneas, stay, Jove's herald bids thee stay.

AENEAS

Whom do I see? Jove's wingèd messenger?
Welcome to Carthage new-erected town.

HERMES

Why, cousin, stand you building cities here
And beautifying the empire of this queen
While Italy is clean out of thy mind?
Too too forgetful of thine own affairs,   30
Why wilt thou so betray thy son's good hap?
The king of gods sent me from highest heaven
To sound this angry message in thine ears:
Vain man, what monarchy expect'st thou here?
Or with what thought sleep'st thou in Libya shore?
If that all glory hath forsaken thee
And thou despise the praise of such attempts,
Yet think upon Ascanius' prophecy,
And young Iulus' more than thousand years,
Whom I have brought from Ida where he slept   40
And bore young Cupid unto Cyprus isle.

AENEAS

This was my mother that beguiled the queen
And made me take my brother for my son.
No marvel, Dido, though thou be in love,
That daily dandlest Cupid in thy arms!
Welcome, sweet child, where hast thou been this long?

ASCANIUS

Eating sweet comfits with Queen Dido's maid,
Who ever since hath lulled me in her arms.

AENEAS

Sergestus, bear him hence unto our ships,
50   Lest Dido, spying him, keep him for a pledge.

> [*Exit* SERGESTUS *with* ASCANIUS.]

HERMES

Spend'st thou thy time about this little boy
And giv'st not ear unto the charge I bring?
I tell thee thou must straight to Italy,
Or else abide the wrath of frowning Jove.

> [*Exit.*]

AENEAS

How should I put into the raging deep,
Who have no sails nor tackling for my ships?
What, would the gods have me, Deucalion-like,
Float up and down where'er the billows drive?
Though she repaired my fleet and gave me ships,
60   Yet hath she ta'en away my oars and masts
And left me neither sail nor stern aboard.

> *Enter to them* IARBAS.

IARBAS

How now, Aeneas, sad? What means these dumps?

AENEAS

Iarbas, I am clean besides myself.
Jove hath heaped on me such a desperate charge,
Which neither art nor reason may achieve,
Nor I devise by what means to contrive.

IARBAS

As how, I pray? May I entreat you tell?

AENEAS

With speed he bids me sail to Italy,
Whenas I want both rigging for my fleet
70   And also furniture for these my men.

IARBAS

If that be all, then cheer thy drooping looks,
For I will furnish thee with such supplies.

Let some of those thy followers go with me
And they shall have what thing soe'er thou need'st.

AENEAS

Thanks, good Iarbas, for thy friendly aid;
Achates and the rest shall wait on thee
Whilst I rest thankful for this courtesy.

Exit IARBAS *and* AENEAS' *train.*

Now will I haste unto Lavinian shore,
And raise a new foundation to old Troy.
Witness the gods, and witness heaven and earth,   80
How loath I am to leave these Libyan bounds,
But that eternal Jupiter commands!

Enter DIDO *to* AENEAS.

DIDO [*aside*]

I fear I saw Aeneas' little son
Led by Achates to the Trojan fleet;
If it be so, his father means to fly.
But here he is; now, Dido, try thy wit.
Aeneas, wherefore go thy men aboard?
Why are thy ships new-rigged? Or to what end,
Launched from the haven, lie they in the road?
Pardon me, though I ask; love makes me ask.   90

AENEAS

O pardon me if I resolve thee why!
Aeneas will not feign with his dear love.
I must from hence; this day, swift Mercury,
When I was laying a platform for these walls,
Sent from his father Jove, appeared to me,
And in his name rebuked me bitterly
For lingering here, neglecting Italy.

DIDO

But yet Aeneas will not leave his love.

AENEAS

I am commanded by immortal Jove
To leave this town and pass to Italy,   100
And therefore must of force.

DIDO

These words proceed not from Aeneas' heart.

AENEAS

    Not from my heart, for I can hardly go.

    And yet I may not stay. Dido, farewell!

DIDO

    Farewell? Is this the mends for Dido's love?

    Do Trojans use to quit their lovers thus?

    Fare well may Dido, so Aeneas stay;

    I die if my Aeneas say farewell.

AENEAS

    Then let me go and never say farewell.

DIDO

110   'Let me go'; 'farewell'; 'I must from hence':

    These words are poison to poor Dido's soul.

    O speak like my Aeneas, like my love!

    Why look'st thou toward the sea? The time hath been

    When Dido's beauty chained thine eyes to her.

    Am I less fair than when thou sawest me first?

    O then, Aeneas, 'tis for grief of thee!

    Say thou wilt stay in Carthage with thy queen,

    And Dido's beauty will return again.

    Aeneas, say, how canst thou take thy leave?

120   Wilt thou kiss Dido? O, thy lips have sworn

    To stay with Dido! Canst thou take her hand?

    Thy hand and mine have plighted mutual faith!

    Therefore, unkind Aeneas, must thou say

    'Then let me go and never say farewell'?

AENEAS

    O Queen of Carthage, wert thou ugly-black,

    Aeneas could not choose but hold thee dear.

    Yet must he not gainsay the gods' behest.

DIDO

    The gods? What gods be those that seek my death?

    Wherein have I offended Jupiter

130   That he should take Aeneas from mine arms?

    O no, the gods weigh not what lovers do;

    It is Aeneas calls Aeneas hence,

    And woeful Dido, by these blubbered cheeks,

    By this right hand and by our spousal rites

Desires Aeneas to remain with her.
Si bene quid de te merui, fuit aut tibi quidquam
Dulce meum, miserere domus labentis, et istam
Oro, si quis adhuc precibus locus, exue mentem.

AENEAS

Desine meque tuis incendere teque querelis,
Italiam non sponte sequor.   140

DIDO

Hast thou forgot how many neighbour kings
Were up in arms for making thee my love?
How Carthage did rebel, Iarbas storm,
And all the world calls me a second Helen,
For being entangled by a stranger's looks?
So thou wouldst prove as true as Paris did,
Would, as fair Troy was, Carthage might be sacked
And I be called a second Helena!
Had I a son by thee, the grief were less,
That I might see Aeneas in his face.   150
Now if thou goest, what canst thou leave behind
But rather will augment than ease my woe?

AENEAS

In vain, my love, thou spend'st thy fainting breath,
If words might move me, I were overcome.

DIDO

And wilt thou not be moved with Dido's words?
Thy mother was no goddess, perjured man,
Nor Dardanus the author of thy stock;
But thou art sprung from Scythian Caucasus,
And tigers of Hercynia gave thee suck.
Ah, foolish Dido, to forbear this long!   160
Wast thou not wracked upon this Libyan shore,
And cam'st to Dido like a fisher swain?
Repaired not I thy ships, made thee a king,
And all thy needy followers noblemen?
O serpent that came creeping from the shore,
And I for pity harboured in my bosom,
Wilt thou now slay me with thy venomed sting
And hiss at Dido for preserving thee?

Go, go, and spare not. Seek out Italy;
170   I hope that that which love forbids me do,
The rocks and sea-gulfs will perform at large,
And thou shalt perish in the billows' ways
To whom poor Dido doth bequeath revenge.
Ay, traitor, and the waves shall cast thee up,
Where thou and false Achates first set foot;
Which if it chance, I'll give ye burial,
And weep upon your lifeless carcasses,
Though thou nor he will pity me a whit.
Why star'st thou in my face? If thou wilt stay,
180   Leap in mine arms, mine arms are open wide.
If not, turn from me, and I'll turn from thee;
For though thou hast the heart to say farewell,
I have not power to stay thee.

                          [*Exit* AENEAS.]
                Is he gone?
Ay, but he'll come again, he cannot go.
He loves me too too well to serve me so.
Yet he that in my sight would not relent
Will, being absent, be obdurate still.
By this is he got to the water-side;
And see, the sailors take him by the hand,
190   But he shrinks back, and now, rememb'ring me,
Returns amain: welcome, welcome, my love!
But where's Aeneas? Ah, he's gone, he's gone!
    [*Enter* ANNA.]

ANNA
What means my sister thus to rave and cry?
DIDO
O Anna, my Aeneas is aboard
And, leaving me, will sail to Italy!
Once didst thou go and he came back again;
Now bring him back and thou shalt be a queen,
And I will live a private life with him.
ANNA Wicked Aeneas!
DIDO
200   Call him not wicked, sister, speak him fair,

And look upon him with a mermaid's eye;
Tell him, I never vowed at Aulis' gulf
The desolation of his native Troy,
Nor sent a thousand ships unto the walls,
Nor ever violated faith to him;
Request him gently, Anna, to return;
I crave but this, he stay a tide or two,
That I may learn to bear it patiently;
If he depart thus suddenly, I die.
Run, Anna, run! Stay not to answer me!   210

ANNA

I go, fair sister; heavens grant good success!

Exit.

Enter the NURSE.

NURSE

O Dido, your little son Ascanius
Is gone! He lay with me last night
And in the morning he was stol'n from me;
I think some fairies have beguiled me.

DIDO

O cursèd hag and false dissembling wretch
That slayest me with thy harsh and hellish tale!
Thou for some petty gift hast let him go,
And I am thus deluded of my boy.
Away with her to prison presently!   220
    [*Enter* ATTENDANTS.]
Traitoress too keen and cursed sorceress!

NURSE

I know not what you mean by treason, I,
I am as true as any one of yours.

Exeunt [ATTENDANTS *with*] *the* NURSE.

DIDO

Away with her, suffer her not to speak.
My sister comes. I like not her sad looks.
    Enter ANNA.

ANNA

Before I came, Aeneas was aboard,
And, spying me, hoist up the sails amain;

But I cried out, 'Aeneas, false Aeneas, stay!'
Then gan he wag his hand, which, yet held up,
230   Made me suppose he would have heard me speak.
Then gan they drive into the ocean,
Which when I viewed, I cried, 'Aeneas, stay!
Dido, fair Dido wills Aeneas stay!'
Yet he, whose heart's of adamant or flint,
My tears nor plaints could mollify a whit.
Then carelessly I rent my hair for grief,
Which seen to all, though he beheld me not,
They gan to move him to redress my ruth,
And stay a while to hear what I could say;
240   But he, clapped under hatches, sailed away.

DIDO
O Anna, Anna, I will follow him!

ANNA
How can ye go when he hath all your fleet?

DIDO
I'll frame me wings of wax like Icarus,
And o'er his ships will soar unto the sun,
That they may melt and I fall in his arms;
Or else I'll make a prayer unto the waves
That I may swim to him like Triton's niece.
O Anna, fetch Arion's harp,
That I may tice a dolphin to the shore
250   And ride upon his back unto my love!
Look, sister, look, lovely Aeneas' ships!
See, see, the billows heave him up to heaven,
And now down falls the keels into the deep.
O sister, sister, take away the rocks,
They'll break his ships! O Proteus, Neptune, Jove,
Save, save Aeneas, Dido's liefest love!
Now is he come on shore, safe without hurt;
But see, Achates wills him put to sea,
And all the sailors merry-make for joy,
260   But he, rememb'ring me, shrinks back again.
See where he comes. Welcome, welcome, my love!

ANNA

    Ah sister, leave these idle fantasies.

    Sweet sister, cease; remember who you are.

DIDO

    Dido I am, unless I be deceived,

    And must I rave thus for a runagate?

    Must I make ships for him to sail away?

    Nothing can bear me to him but a ship,

    And he hath all my fleet. What shall I do,

    But die in fury of this oversight?

    Ay, I must be the murderer of myself: 270

    No, but I am not; yet I will be straight.

    Anna, be glad; now have I found a mean

    To rid me from these thoughts of lunacy:

    Not far from hence

    There is a woman famousèd for arts,

    Daughter unto the nymphs Hesperides,

    Who willed me sacrifice his ticing relics.

    Go, Anna, bid my servants bring me fire.

                                   Exit ANNA.

    Enter IARBAS.

IARBAS

    How long will Dido mourn a stranger's flight

    That hath dishonoured her and Carthage both?   280

    How long shall I with grief consume my days

    And reap no guerdon for my truest love?

DIDO

    Iarbas, talk not of Aeneas, let him go.

    [*Enter* ATTENDANTS *with wood and torches, and exeunt.*]

    Lay to thy hands and help me make a fire

    That shall consume all that this stranger left;

    For I intend a private sacrifice

    To cure my mind that melts for unkind love.

IARBAS

    But afterwards will Dido grant me love?

DIDO

    Ay, ay, Iarbas, after this is done,

290   None in the world shall have my love but thou.
           [DIDO *and* IARBAS *build a fire*.]
       So, leave me now, let none approach this place.

                                              Exit IARBAS.

       Now, Dido, with these relics burn thyself,
       And make Aeneas famous through the world
       For perjury and slaughter of a queen.
       Here lie the sword that in the darksome cave
       He drew and swore by to be true to me:
       Thou shalt burn first, thy crime is worse than his.
       Here lie the garment which I clothed him in
       When first he came on shore: perish thou too.
300   These letters, lines, and perjured papers all
       Shall burn to cinders in this precious flame.
       And now, ye gods that guide the starry frame
       And order all things at your high dispose,
       Grant, though the traitors land in Italy,
       They may be still tormented with unrest,
       And from mine ashes let a conqueror rise,
       That may revenge this treason to a queen
       By ploughing up his countries with the sword!
       Betwixt this land and that be never league;
310   *Litora litoribus contraria, fluctibus undas*
       Imprecor; arma armis; pugnent ipsique nepotes:
       Live, false Aeneas! Truest Dido dies;
       Sic, sic iuvat ire sub umbras.
           [*Throws herself onto the fire.*]
           Enter Anna.

   ANNA
       O help, Iarbas! Dido in these flames
       Hath burnt herself! Ay me, unhappy me!
           Enter IARBAS *running.*

   IARBAS
       Cursèd Iarbas, die to expiate
       The grief that tires upon thine inward soul!
       Dido, I come to thee: ay me, Aeneas!
           [*Kills himself.*]

ANNA
    What can my tears or cries prevail me now?
    Dido is dead, Iarbas slain, Iarbas, my dear love!   320
    O sweet Iarbas, Anna's sole delight,
    What fatal Destiny envies me thus
    To see my sweet Iarbas slay himself?
    But Anna now shall honour thee in death
    And mix her blood with thine; this shall I do
    That gods and men may pity this my death
    And rue our ends, senseless of life or breath.
    Now, sweet Iarbas, stay! I come to thee!
      [*Kills herself.*]

TAMBURLAINE
THE GREAT,
PART ONE

[Dramatis Personae

THE PROLOGUE
MYCETES, *King of Persia*
COSROE, *his brother*
MEANDER
THERIDAMAS
ORTYGIUS
CENEUS
MENAPHON
TAMBURLAINE
ZENOCRATE, *daughter to the Sultan of Egypt*
TECHELLES
USUMCASANE
MAGNETES
AGYDAS
LORDS
SOLDIERS
A SPY
A MESSENGER
BAJAZETH, *Emperor of Turkey*
KING OF FEZ
KING OF MOROCCO
KING OF ARGIER
BASSOES
ANIPPE, *maid to Zenocrate*
ZABINA, *wife to Bajazeth*
EBEA, *maid to Zabina*
THE SULTAN OF EGYPT
CAPOLIN, *an Egyptian*

ALCIDAMAS, *King of Arabia*
GOVERNOR OF DAMASCUS
CITIZENS
FOUR VIRGINS
PHILEMUS
MOORS
ATTENDANTS]

TO THE GENTLEMEN READERS AND OTHERS THAT TAKE PLEASURE IN READING HISTORIES

Gentlemen and courteous readers whosoever: I have here published in print for your sakes, the two tragical discourses of the Scythian shepherd Tamburlaine, that became so great a conqueror and so mighty a monarch. My hope is, that they will be now no less acceptable unto you to read after your serious affairs and studies than they have been, lately, delightful for many of you to see, when the same were showed in London upon stages. I have purposely omitted and left out some fond and frivolous jestures, digressing and, in my poor opinion, far unmeet for the matter, which I thought might 10 seem more tedious unto the wise than any way else to be regarded – though, haply, they have been of some vain conceited fondlings greatly gaped at, what times they were showed upon the stage in their graced deformities. Nevertheless, now to be mixtured in print with such matter of worth, it would prove a great disgrace to so honourable and stately a history. Great folly were it in me to commend unto your wisdoms, either the eloquence of the author that writ them, or the worthiness of the matter itself; I therefore leave unto your learned censures both the one and the other, and myself 20 the poor printer of them unto your most courteous and favourable protection: which if you vouchsafe to accept, you shall evermore bind me to employ what travail and service I can to the advancing and pleasuring of your excellent degree.

Yours, most humble at commandment,

R. J.

Printer.

[*Enter*] *the* PROLOGUE.

PROLOGUE

From jigging veins of rhyming mother-wits
And such conceits as clownage keeps in pay,
We'll lead you to the stately tent of war,
Where you shall hear the Scythian Tamburlaine
5   Threat'ning the world with high astounding terms
And scourging kingdoms with his conquering sword.
View but his picture in this tragic glass,
And then applaud his fortunes as you please.

[*Exit.*]

ACT 1

[*Enter*] MYCETES, COSROE, MEANDER, THERIDAMAS,
ORTYGIUS, CENEUS, [MENAPHON,] *with others.*

MYCETES
  Brother Cosroe, I find myself aggrieved,
  Yet insufficient to express the same,
  For it requires a great and thund'ring speech.
  Good brother, tell the cause unto my lords,
  I know you have a better wit than I.

COSROE
  Unhappy Persia, that in former age
  Hast been the seat of mighty conquerors
  That in their prowess and their policies
  Have triumphed over Afric, and the bounds
  Of Europe where the sun dares scarce appear   10
  For freezing meteors and congealèd cold –
  Now to be ruled and governed by a man
  At whose birthday Cynthia with Saturn joined,
  And Jove, the sun, and Mercury denied
  To shed their influence in his fickle brain!
  Now Turks and Tartars shake their swords at thee,
  Meaning to mangle all thy provinces.

MYCETES
  Brother, I see your meaning well enough,
  And through your planets I perceive you think
  I am not wise enough to be a king.   20
  But I refer me to my noblemen

That know my wit and can be witnesses.
I might command you to be slain for this,
Meander, might I not?

MEANDER

Not for so small a fault, my sovereign lord.

MYCETES

I mean it not, but yet I know I might.
Yet live, yea, live, Mycetes wills it so.
Meander, thou my faithful counsellor,
Declare the cause of my conceivèd grief,
30   Which is, God knows, about that Tamburlaine,
That like a fox in midst of harvest time
Doth prey upon my flocks of passengers,
And, as I hear, doth mean to pull my plumes.
Therefore 'tis good and meet for to be wise.

MEANDER

Oft have I heard your majesty complain
Of Tamburlaine, that sturdy Scythian thief,
That robs your merchants of Persepolis
Trading by land unto the Western Isles,
And in your confines with his lawless train
40   Daily commits incivil outrages,
Hoping, misled by dreaming prophecies,
To reign in Asia and with barbarous arms
To make himself the monarch of the East.
But ere he march in Asia or display
His vagrant ensign in the Persian fields,
Your grace hath taken order by Theridamas,
Charged with a thousand horse, to apprehend
And bring him captive to your highness' throne.

MYCETES

Full true thou speak'st, and like thyself, my lord,
50   Whom I may term a Damon for thy love.
Therefore 'tis best, if so it like you all,
To send my thousand horse incontinent
To apprehend that paltry Scythian.
How like you this, my honourable lords?
Is it not a kingly resolution?

COSROE
  It cannot choose, because it comes from you.
MYCETES
  Then hear thy charge, valiant Theridamas,
  The chiefest captain of Mycetes' host,
  The hope of Persia, and the very legs
  Whereon our state doth lean, as on a staff   60
  That holds us up and foils our neighbour foes:
  Thou shalt be leader of this thousand horse,
  Whose foaming gall with rage and high disdain
  Have sworn the death of wicked Tamburlaine.
  Go frowning forth, but come thou smiling home,
  As did Sir Paris with the Grecian dame.
  Return with speed! Time passeth swift away.
  Our life is frail, and we may die today.

THERIDAMAS
  Before the moon renew her borrowed light,
  Doubt not, my lord and gracious sovereign,   70
  But Tamburlaine and that Tartarian rout
  Shall either perish by our warlike hands
  Or plead for mercy at your highness' feet.

MYCETES
  Go, stout Theridamas, thy words are swords,
  And with thy looks thou conqu'rest all thy foes.
  I long to see thee back return from thence,
  That I may view these milk-white steeds of mine
  All loaden with the heads of killèd men,
  And from their knees even to their hoofs below
  Besmeared with blood, that makes a dainty show.   80

THERIDAMAS
  Then now, my lord, I humbly take my leave.

                              Exit [THERIDAMAS].

MYCETES
  Theridamas, farewell ten thousand times!
  Ah, Menaphon, why stayest thou thus behind
  When other men press forward for renown?
  Go, Menaphon, go into Scythia,
  And foot by foot follow Theridamas.

COSROE

    Nay, pray you, let him stay; a greater task

    Fits Menaphon than warring with a thief.

    Create him prorex of Assyria,

90   That he may win the Babylonians' hearts,

    Which will revolt from Persian government

    Unless they have a wiser king than you.

MYCETES

    'Unless they have a wiser king than you'!

    These are his words, Meander, set them down.

COSROE

    And add this to them, that all Asia

    Lament to see the folly of their king.

MYCETES

    Well, here I swear by this my royal seat –

COSROE

    You may do well to kiss it, then.

MYCETES

    Embossed with silk as best beseems my state,

100   To be revenged for these contemptuous words.

    O, where is duty and allegiance now?

    Fled to the Caspian or the ocean main?

    What, shall I call thee brother? No, a foe,

    Monster of nature, shame unto thy stock,

    That dar'st presume thy sovereign for to mock.

    Meander, come. I am abused, Meander.

                  Exit [*with* MEANDER *and others*].

                   COSROE *and* MENAPHON *remain*.

MENAPHON

    How now, my lord, what, mated and amazed

    To hear the king thus threaten like himself?

COSROE

    Ah, Menaphon, I pass not for his threats.

110   The plot is laid by Persian noblemen

    And captains of the Median garrisons

    To crown me emperor of Asia.

    But this it is that does excruciate

    The very substance of my vexèd soul:

To see our neighbours, that were wont to quake
And tremble at the Persian monarch's name,
Now sits and laughs our regiment to scorn;
And – that which might resolve me into tears –
Men from the farthest equinoctial line
Have swarmed in troops into the Eastern Inde,   120
Lading their ships with gold and precious stones,
And made their spoils from all our provinces.

MENAPHON
This should entreat your highness to rejoice,
Since Fortune gives you opportunity
To gain the title of a conqueror
By curing of this maimèd empery.
Afric and Europe bordering on your land
And continent to your dominions,
How easily may you with a mighty host
Pass into Graecia, as did Cyrus once,   130
And cause them to withdraw their forces home
Lest you subdue the pride of Christendom!
    [*A trumpet sounds.*]

COSROE
But, Menaphon, what means this trumpet's sound?

MENAPHON
Behold, my lord, Ortygius and the rest,
Bringing the crown to make you emperor.
    Enter ORTYGIUS *and* CENEUS, *bearing a crown, with
    others.*

ORTYGIUS
Magnificent and mighty prince Cosroe,
We, in the name of other Persian states
And commons of this mighty monarchy,
Present thee with th'imperial diadem.

CENEUS
The warlike soldiers and the gentlemen   140
That heretofore have filled Persepolis
With Afric captains taken in the field,
Whose ransom made them march in coats of gold
With costly jewels hanging at their ears

And shining stones upon their lofty crests,
Now living idle in the wallèd towns,
Wanting both pay and martial discipline,
Begin in troops to threaten civil war
And openly exclaim against the king.
150   Therefore, to stay all sudden mutinies,
We will invest your highness emperor,
Whereat the soldiers will conceive more joy
Than did the Macedonians at the spoil
Of great Darius and his wealthy host.

COSROE

Well, since I see the state of Persia droop
And languish in my brother's government,
I willingly receive th'imperial crown
And vow to wear it for my country's good,
In spite of them shall malice my estate.

ORTYGIUS [*crowning* COSROE]
160   And in assurance of desired success
We here do crown thee monarch of the East,
Emperor of Asia and of Persia,
Great lord of Media and Armenia,
Duke of Assyria and Albania,
Mesopotamia and of Parthia,
East India and the late-discovered isles,
Chief lord of all the wide vast Euxine Sea
And of the ever-raging Caspian lake.
Long live Cosroë, mighty emperor!

COSROE

170   And Jove may never let me longer live
Than I may seek to gratify your love
And cause the soldiers that thus honour me
To triumph over many provinces!
By whose desires of discipline in arms
I doubt not shortly but to reign sole king,
And with the army of Theridamas,
Whither we presently will fly, my lords,
To rest secure against my brother's force.

ORTYGIUS

We knew, my lord, before we brought the crown,
Intending your investion so near   180
The residence of your despisèd brother,
The lords would not be too exasperate
To injure or suppress your worthy title.
Or if they would, there are in readiness
Ten thousand horse to carry you from hence
In spite of all suspected enemies.

COSROE

I know it well, my lord, and thank you all.

ORTYGIUS

Sound up the trumpets, then. God save the king!
    [*The trumpets sound.*]   *Exeunt.*

Scene 2

[*Enter*] TAMBURLAINE, *leading* ZENOCRATE; TECHELLES,
USUMCASANE, *other* LORDS, [MAGNETES *and* AGYDAS,]
and SOLDIERS *loaden with treasure.*

TAMBURLAINE

Come, lady, let not this appal your thoughts.
The jewels and the treasure we have ta'en
Shall be reserved, and you in better state
Than if you were arrived in Syria,
Even in the circle of your father's arms,
The mighty Sultan of Egyptia.

ZENOCRATE

Ah, shepherd, pity my distressèd plight,
If, as thou seem'st, thou art so mean a man,
And seek not to enrich thy followers
By lawless rapine from a silly maid   10
Who, travelling with these Median lords
To Memphis, from my uncle's country of Media,
Where all my youth I have been governèd,

Have passed the army of the mighty Turk,
Bearing his privy signet and his hand
To safe conduct us thorough Africa.

MAGNETES

And, since we have arrived in Scythia,
Besides rich presents from the puissant Cham
We have his highness' letters to command
20   Aid and assistance if we stand in need.

TAMBURLAINE

But now you see these letters and commands
Are countermanded by a greater man,
And through my provinces you must expect
Letters of conduct from my mightiness
If you intend to keep your treasure safe.
But since I love to live at liberty,
As easily may you get the Sultan's crown
As any prizes out of my precinct;
For they are friends that help to wean my state
30   Till men and kingdoms help to strengthen it,
And must maintain my life exempt from servitude.
But tell me, madam, is your grace betrothed?

ZENOCRATE

I am, my lord, for so you do import.

TAMBURLAINE

I am a lord, for so my deeds shall prove,
And yet a shepherd by my parentage.
But, lady, this fair face and heavenly hue
Must grace his bed that conquers Asia
And means to be a terror to the world,
Measuring the limits of his empery
40   By east and west as Phoebus doth his course.
Lie here, ye weeds that I disdain to wear!
    [*He removes his shepherd's cloak.*]
This complete armour and this curtle-axe
Are adjuncts more beseeming Tamburlaine.
And, madam, whatsoever you esteem
Of this success and loss unvaluèd,
Both may invest you empress of the East,

And these that seem but silly country swains
May have the leading of so great an host
As with their weight shall make the mountains quake,
Even as when windy exhalations,   50
Fighting for passage, tilt within the earth.

TECHELLES
As princely lions when they rouse themselves,
Stretching their paws and threat'ning herds of beasts,
So in his armour looketh Tamburlaine.
Methinks I see kings kneeling at his feet,
And he with frowning brows and fiery looks
Spurning their crowns from off their captive heads.

USUMCASANE
And making thee and me, Techelles, kings,
That even to death will follow Tamburlaine.

TAMBURLAINE
Nobly resolved, sweet friends and followers.   60
These lords, perhaps, do scorn our estimates,
And think we prattle with distempered spirits;
But since they measure our deserts so mean
That in conceit bear empires on our spears,
Affecting thoughts coequal with the clouds,
They shall be kept our forcèd followers
Till with their eyes they view us emperors.

ZENOCRATE
The gods, defenders of the innocent,
Will never prosper your intended drifts
That thus oppress poor friendless passengers.   70
Therefore at least admit us liberty,
Even as thou hop'st to be eternizèd
By living Asia's mighty emperor.

AGYDAS
I hope our lady's treasure and our own
May serve for ransom to our liberties.
Return our mules and empty camels back,
That we may travel into Syria,
Where her betrothèd, Lord Alcidamus,
Expects th'arrival of her highness' person.

MAGNETES

80   And wheresoever we repose ourselves
        We will report but well of Tamburlaine.

TAMBURLAINE

        Disdains Zenocrate to live with me?
        Or you, my lords, to be my followers?
        Think you I weigh this treasure more than you?
        Not all the gold in India's wealthy arms
        Shall buy the meanest soldier in my train.
        Zenocrate, lovelier than the love of Jove,
        Brighter than is the silver Rhodope,
        Fairer than whitest snow on Scythian hills,
90   Thy person is more worth to Tamburlaine
        Than the possession of the Persian crown,
        Which gracious stars have promised at my birth.
        A hundred Tartars shall attend on thee,
        Mounted on steeds swifter than Pegasus;
        Thy garments shall be made of Median silk,
        Enchased with precious jewels of mine own,
        More rich and valurous than Zenocrate's;
        With milk-white harts upon an ivory sled
        Thou shalt be drawn amidst the frozen pools
100   And scale the icy mountains' lofty tops,
        Which with thy beauty will be soon resolved;
        My martial prizes, with five hundred men,
        Won on the fifty-headed Volga's waves,
        Shall all we offer to Zenocrate,
        And then myself to fair Zenocrate.

TECHELLES [to TAMBURLAINE]

        What now? In love?

TAMBURLAINE

        Techelles, women must be flatterèd.
        But this is she with whom I am in love.
                Enter a SOLDIER.

SOLDIER

        News, news!

TAMBURLAINE

110   How now, what's the matter?

SOLDIER

A thousand Persian horsemen are at hand,
Sent from the king to overcome us all.

TAMBURLAINE

How now, my lords of Egypt and Zenocrate?
Now must your jewels be restored again
And I that triumphed so be overcome.
How say you, lordings, is not this your hope?

AGYDAS

We hope yourself will willingly restore them.

TAMBURLAINE

Such hope, such fortune, have the thousand horse.
Soft ye, my lords and sweet Zenocrate:
You must be forcèd from me ere you go.   120
A thousand horsemen! We, five hundred foot!
An odds too great for us to stand against.
But are they rich? And is their armour good?

SOLDIER

Their plumèd helms are wrought with beaten gold,
Their swords enamelled, and about their necks
Hangs massy chains of gold down to the waist,
In every part exceeding brave and rich.

TAMBURLAINE

Then shall we fight courageously with them;
Or look you I should play the orator?

TECHELLES

No. Cowards and faint-hearted runaways   130
Look for orations when the foe is near.
Our swords shall play the orators for us.

USUMCASANE

Come, let us meet them at the mountain top,
And with a sudden and an hot alarm
Drive all their horses headlong down the hill.

TECHELLES

Come, let us march.

TAMBURLAINE

Stay, Techelles, ask a parley first.
        The SOLDIERS [*of* TAMBURLAINE] *enter.*

Open the mails, yet guard the treasure sure.
Lay out our golden wedges to the view,
140   That their reflections may amaze the Persians.
     [*The* SOLDIERS *lay out the gold bars.*]
And look we friendly on them when they come,
But if they offer word or violence
We'll fight five hundred men-at-arms to one
Before we part with our possession.
And 'gainst the general we will lift our swords
And either lance his greedy thirsting throat
Or take him prisoner, and his chain shall serve
For manacles till he be ransomed home.

TECHELLES
I hear them come. Shall we encounter them?

TAMBURLAINE
150   Keep all your standings, and not stir a foot.
Myself will bide the danger of the brunt.
     Enter THERIDAMAS *with others.*

THERIDAMAS
Where is this Scythian Tamburlaine?

TAMBURLAINE
Whom seek'st thou, Persian? I am Tamburlaine.

THERIDAMAS [*aside*]
Tamburlaine?
A Scythian shepherd, so embellishèd
With nature's pride and richest furniture?
His looks do menace heaven and dare the gods,
His fiery eyes are fixed upon the earth,
As if he now devised some stratagem,
160   Or meant to pierce Avernus' darksome vaults
And pull the triple-headed dog from hell.

TAMBURLAINE [*to* TECHELLES]
Noble and mild this Persian seems to be,
If outward habit judge the inward man.

TECHELLES [*to* TAMBURLAINE]
His deep affections make him passionate.

TAMBURLAINE [*to* TECHELLES]
With what a majesty he rears his looks!

[*To* THERIDAMAS]
In thee, thou valiant man of Persia,
I see the folly of thy emperor.
Art thou but captain of a thousand horse,
That by characters graven in thy brows
And by thy martial face and stout aspect   170
Deserv'st to have the leading of an host?
Forsake thy king, and do but join with me,
And we will triumph over all the world.
I hold the Fates bound fast in iron chains
And with my hand turn Fortune's wheel about,
And sooner shall the sun fall from his sphere
Than Tamburlaine be slain or overcome.
Draw forth thy sword, thou mighty man-at-arms,
Intending but to raze my charmèd skin,
And Jove himself will stretch his hand from heaven   180
To ward the blow and shield me safe from harm.
See how he rains down heaps of gold in showers
As if he meant to give my soldiers pay!
    [*He points to the gold bars.*]
And, as a sure and grounded argument
That I shall be the monarch of the East,
He sends this Sultan's daughter, rich and brave,
To be my queen and portly emperess.
If thou wilt stay with me, renownèd man,
And lead thy thousand horse with my conduct,
Besides thy share of this Egyptian prize,   190
Those thousand horse shall sweat with martial spoil
Of conquered kingdoms and of cities sacked.
Both we will walk upon the lofty clifts,
And Christian merchants that with Russian stems
Plough up huge furrows in the Caspian Sea
Shall vail to us as lords of all the lake.
Both we will reign as consuls of the earth,
And mighty kings shall be our senators.
Jove sometime maskèd in a shepherd's weed,
And by those steps that he hath scaled the heavens   200
May we become immortal like the gods.

Join with me now in this my mean estate
(I call it mean, because, being yet obscure,
The nations far removed admire me not),
And when my name and honour shall be spread
As far as Boreas claps his brazen wings
Or fair Boötes sends his cheerful light,
Then shalt thou be competitor with me
And sit with Tamburlaine in all his majesty.

THERIDAMAS
210   Not Hermes, prolocutor to the gods,
Could use persuasions more pathetical.

TAMBURLAINE
Nor are Apollo's oracles more true
Than thou shalt find my vaunts substantial.

TECHELLES
We are his friends, and if the Persian king
Should offer present dukedoms to our state,
We think it loss to make exchange for that
We are assured of by our friend's success.

USUMCASANE
And kingdoms at the least we all expect,
Besides the honour in assurèd conquests
220   Where kings shall crouch unto our conquering swords
And hosts of soldiers stand amazed at us,
When with their fearful tongues they shall confess,
'These are the men that all the world admires.'

THERIDAMAS
What strong enchantments tice my yielding soul?
Are these resolvèd noble Scythians?
But shall I prove a traitor to my king?

TAMBURLAINE
No, but the trusty friend of Tamburlaine.

THERIDAMAS
Won with thy words and conquered with thy looks,
I yield myself, my men, and horse to thee,
230   To be partaker of thy good or ill
As long as life maintains Theridamas.

TAMBURLAINE
  Theridamas, my friend, take here my hand,
  Which is as much as if I swore by heaven
  And called the gods to witness of my vow.
  Thus shall my heart be still combined with thine
  Until our bodies turn to elements
  And both our souls aspire celestial thrones.
  Techelles and Casane, welcome him.

TECHELLES
  Welcome, renownèd Persian, to us all!

USUMCASANE
  Long may Theridamas remain with us!   240

TAMBURLAINE
  These are my friends, in whom I more rejoice
  Than doth the king of Persia in his crown.
  And by the love of Pylades and Orestes,
  Whose statues we adore in Scythia,
  Thyself and them shall never part from me
  Before I crown you kings in Asia.
  Make much of them, gentle Theridamas,
  And they will never leave thee till the death.

THERIDAMAS
  Nor thee nor them, thrice-noble Tamburlaine,
  Shall want my heart to be with gladness pierced   250
  To do you honour and security.

TAMBURLAINE
  A thousand thanks, worthy Theridamas.
  And now, fair madam, and my noble lords,
  If you will willingly remain with me
  You shall have honours as your merits be –
  Or else you shall be forced with slavery.

AGYDAS
  We yield unto thee, happy Tamburlaine.

TAMBURLAINE
  For you, then, madam, I am out of doubt.

ZENOCRATE
  I must be pleased perforce, wretched Zenocrate!

                                        Exeunt.

ACT 2

Scene 1

[*Enter*] COSROE, MENAPHON, ORTYGIUS, CENEUS, *with
other* SOLDIERS.

COSROE
    Thus far are we towards Theridamas
    And valiant Tamburlaine, the man of fame,
    The man that in the forehead of his fortune
    Bears figures of renown and miracle.
    But tell me, that hast seen him, Menaphon,
    What stature wields he, and what personage?
MENAPHON
    Of stature tall, and straightly fashionèd,
    Like his desire, lift upwards and divine;
    So large of limbs, his joints so strongly knit,
10   Such breadth of shoulders as might mainly bear
    Old Atlas' burden. 'Twixt his manly pitch,
    A pearl more worth than all the world is placed,
    Wherein by curious sovereignty of art
    Are fixed his piercing instruments of sight,
    Whose fiery circles bear encompassèd
    A heaven of heavenly bodies in their spheres
    That guides his steps and actions to the throne
    Where honour sits invested royally;
    Pale of complexion, wrought in him with passion,
20   Thirsting with sovereignty, with love of arms.
    His lofty brows in folds do figure death,
    And in their smoothness amity and life.

About them hangs a knot of amber hair
Wrappèd in curls, as fierce Achilles' was,
On which the breath of heaven delights to play,
Making it dance with wanton majesty.
His arms and fingers long and sinewy,
Betokening valour and excess of strength;
In every part proportioned like the man
Should make the world subdued to Tamburlaine.   30

COSROE
Well hast thou portrayed in thy terms of life
The face and personage of a wondrous man.
Nature doth strive with Fortune and his stars
To make him famous in accomplished worth,
And well his merits show him to be made
His fortune's master and the king of men,
That could persuade at such a sudden pinch,
With reasons of his valour and his life,
A thousand sworn and overmatching foes.
Then, when our powers in points of swords are joined   40
And closed in compass of the killing bullet,
Though strait the passage and the port be made
That leads to palace of my brother's life,
Proud is his fortune if we pierce it not.
And when the princely Persian diadem
Shall overweigh his weary witless head
And fall like mellowed fruit, with shakes of death,
In fair Persia noble Tamburlaine
Shall be my regent and remain as king.

ORTYGIUS
In happy hour we have set the crown   50
Upon your kingly head, that seeks our honour
In joining with the man ordained by heaven
To further every action to the best.

CENEUS
He that with shepherds and a little spoil
Durst, in disdain of wrong and tyranny,
Defend his freedom 'gainst a monarchy,
What will he do supported by a king,

Leading a troop of gentlemen and lords,
And stuffed with treasure for his highest thoughts?

COSROE

60   And such shall wait on worthy Tamburlaine.
Our army will be forty thousand strong
When Tamburlaine and brave Theridamas
Have met us by the river Araris,
And all conjoined to meet the witless king
That now is marching near to Parthia,
And with unwilling soldiers faintly armed,
To seek revenge on me and Tamburlaine –
To whom, sweet Menaphon, direct me straight.

MENAPHON

I will, my lord.

                                   Exeunt.

Scene 2

[*Enter*] MYCETES, MEANDER, *with other* LORDS *and*
SOLDIERS.

MYCETES

Come, my Meander, let us to this gear.
I tell you true, my heart is swoll'n with wrath
On this same thievish villain Tamburlaine,
And of that false Cosroe, my traitorous brother.
Would it not grieve a king to be so abused
And have a thousand horsemen ta'en away?
And, which is worst, to have his diadem
Sought for by such scald knaves as love him not?
I think it would. Well then, by heavens I swear,

10   Aurora shall not peep out of her doors
But I will have Cosroë by the head
And kill proud Tamburlaine with point of sword.
Tell you the rest, Meander, I have said.

MEANDER

Then, having passed Armenian deserts now,

And pitched our tents under the Georgian hills,
Whose tops are covered with Tartarian thieves
That lie in ambush waiting for a prey,
What should we do but bid them battle straight
And rid the world of those detested troops,
Lest, if we let them linger here a while,   20
They gather strength by power of fresh supplies?
This country swarms with vile outrageous men
That live by rapine and by lawless spoil,
Fit soldiers for the wicked Tamburlaine.
And he that could with gifts and promises
Inveigle him that led a thousand horse
And make him false his faith unto his king
Will quickly win such as are like himself.
Therefore cheer up your minds, prepare to fight.
He that can take or slaughter Tamburlaine   30
Shall rule the province of Albania.
Who brings that traitor's head, Theridamas',
Shall have a government in Media,
Beside the spoil of him and all his train.
But if Cosroë (as our spials say,
And as we know) remains with Tamburlaine,
His highness' pleasure is that he should live
And be reclaimed with princely lenity.
    [*Enter a* SPY.]
SPY
An hundred horsemen of my company,
Scouting abroad upon these champian plains,   40
Have viewed the army of the Scythians,
Which make reports it far exceeds the king's.
MEANDER
Suppose they be in number infinite,
Yet being void of martial discipline,
All running headlong after greedy spoils
And more regarding gain than victory,
Like to the cruel brothers of the earth
Sprung of the teeth of dragons venomous,
Their careless swords shall lance their fellows' throats

50   And make us triumph in their overthrow.
MYCETES
        Was there such brethren, sweet Meander, say,
        That sprung of teeth of dragons venomous?
MEANDER
        So poets say, my lord.
MYCETES
        And 'tis a pretty toy to be a poet.
        Well, well, Meander, thou art deeply read,
        And having thee I have a jewel sure.
        Go on, my lord, and give your charge, I say,
        Thy wit will make us conquerors today.
MEANDER
        Then, noble soldiers, to entrap these thieves
60   That live confounded in disordered troops,
        If wealth or riches may prevail with them,
        We have our camels laden all with gold
        Which you that be but common soldiers
        Shall fling in every corner of the field,
        And while the base-born Tartars take it up,
        You, fighting more for honour than for gold,
        Shall massacre those greedy-minded slaves;
        And when their scattered army is subdued
        And you march on their slaughtered carcasses,
70   Share equally the gold that bought their lives
        And live like gentlemen in Persia.
        Strike up the drum, and march courageously!
        Fortune herself doth sit upon our crests.
MYCETES
        He tells you true, my masters, so he does.
        Drums, why sound ye not when Meander speaks?
        [*Strike drums.*]   *Exeunt.*

Scene 3

[*Enter*] COSROE, TAMBURLAINE, THERIDAMAS,
TECHELLES, USUMCASANE, ORTYGIUS, *with others*.

COSROE
Now, worthy Tamburlaine, have I reposed
In thy approvèd fortunes all my hope.
What think'st thou, man, shall come of our attempts?
For even as from assurèd oracle,
I take thy doom for satisfaction.

TAMBURLAINE
And so mistake you not a whit, my lord,
For fates and oracles of heaven have sworn
To royalize the deeds of Tamburlaine,
And make them blest that share in his attempts.
And doubt you not but, if you favour me   10
And let my fortunes and my valour sway
To some direction in your martial deeds,
The world will strive with hosts of men-at-arms
To swarm unto the ensign I support.
The host of Xerxes, which by fame is said
To drink the mighty Parthian Araris,
Was but a handful to that we will have.
Our quivering lances shaking in the air
And bullets like Jove's dreadful thunderbolts,
Enrolled in flames and fiery smouldering mists,   20
Shall threat the gods more than Cyclopian wars;
And with our sun-bright armour as we march
We'll chase the stars from heaven and dim their eyes
That stand and muse at our admirèd arms.

THERIDAMAS [*to* COSROE]
You see, my lord, what working words he hath.
But when you see his actions top his speech,
Your speech will stay, or so extol his worth
As I shall be commended and excused
For turning my poor charge to his direction.

30   And these his two renownèd friends, my lord,
     Would make one thrust and strive to be retained
     In such a great degree of amity.

TECHELLES
     With duty and with amity we yield
     Our utmost service to the fair Cosroe.

COSROE
     Which I esteem as portion of my crown.
     Usumcasane and Techelles both,
     When she that rules in Rhamnus' golden gates
     And makes a passage for all prosperous arms
     Shall make me solely emperor of Asia,
40   Then shall your meeds and valours be advanced
     To rooms of honour and nobility.

TAMBURLAINE
     Then haste, Cosroë, to be king alone,
     That I with these my friends and all my men
     May triumph in our long-expected fate.
     The king your brother is now hard at hand.
     Meet with the fool, and rid your royal shoulders
     Of such a burden as outweighs the sands
     And all the craggy rocks of Caspia.
          [*Enter a* MESSENGER.]

MESSENGER
     My lord, we have discovered the enemy
50   Ready to charge you with a mighty army.

COSROE
     Come, Tamburlaine, now whet thy wingèd sword
     And lift thy lofty arm into the clouds,
     That it may reach the king of Persia's crown
     And set it safe on my victorious head.

TAMBURLAINE [*brandishing his sword*]
     See where it is, the keenest curtle-axe
     That e'er made passage thorough Persian arms.
     These are the wings shall make it fly as swift
     As doth the lightning or the breath of heaven,
     And kill as sure as it swiftly flies.

COSROE
Thy words assure me of kind success.   60
Go, valiant soldier, go before, and charge
The fainting army of that foolish king.

TAMBURLAINE
Usumcasane and Techelles, come.
We are enough to scare the enemy,
And more than needs to make an emperor.

                                        [*Exeunt.*]

[*Scene 4*]

[*Enter the armies*] *to the battle* [*and exeunt*], *and* MYCETES
*comes out alone with his crown in his hand, offering to
hide it.*

MYCETES
Accurst be he that first invented war!
They knew not, ah, they knew not, simple men,
How those were hit by pelting cannon shot
Stand staggering like a quivering aspen leaf
Fearing the force of Boreas' boist'rous blasts!
In what a lamentable case were I
If nature had not given me wisdom's lore!
For kings are clouts that every man shoots at,
Our crown the pin that thousands seek to cleave.
Therefore in policy I think it good   10
To hide it close – a goodly stratagem,
And far from any man that is a fool.
So shall not I be known, or if I be,
They cannot take away my crown from me.
Here will I hide it in this simple hole.
          Enter TAMBURLAINE.

TAMBURLAINE
What, fearful coward, straggling from the camp,
When kings themselves are present in the field?

MYCETES
  Thou liest.

TAMBURLAINE Base villain, dar'st thou give the lie?

MYCETES
  Away, I am the king. Go, touch me not.
20 Thou break'st the law of arms unless thou kneel
  And cry me, 'Mercy, noble king!'

TAMBURLAINE
  Are you the witty king of Persia?

MYCETES
  Ay, marry, am I. Have you any suit to me?

TAMBURLAINE
  I would entreat you to speak but three wise words.

MYCETES
  So I can, when I see my time.

TAMBURLAINE [*seizing the crown*] Is this your crown?

MYCETES Ay, didst thou ever see a fairer?

TAMBURLAINE You will not sell it, will ye?

MYCETES Such another word, and I will have thee executed.
30 Come, give it me.

TAMBURLAINE No, I took it prisoner.

MYCETES You lie, I gave it you.

TAMBURLAINE Then 'tis mine.

MYCETES No, I mean I let you keep it.

TAMBURLAINE Well, I mean you shall have it again.
    [*Giving the crown*]
  Here, take it for a while. I lend it thee
  Till I may see thee hemmed with armèd men.
  Then shalt thou see me pull it from thy head.
  Thou art no match for mighty Tamburlaine.
                        [*Exit* TAMBURLAINE.]

MYCETES
40 O gods, is this Tamburlaine the thief?
  I marvel much he stole it not away.
    Sound trumpets to the battle, and he runs in.

[Scene 5]

[*Enter*] COSROE [*crowned*], TAMBURLAINE,
THERIDAMAS, MENAPHON, MEANDER, ORTYGIUS,
TECHELLES, USUMCASANE, *with others.*

TAMBURLAINE [*presenting* COSROE *with* MYCETES'*s crown*]
  Hold thee, Cosroe, wear two imperial crowns.
  Think thee invested now as royally,
  Even by the mighty hand of Tamburlaine,
  As if as many kings as could encompass thee
  With greatest pomp had crowned thee emperor.

COSROE
  So do I, thrice-renownèd man-at-arms,
  And none shall keep the crown but Tamburlaine.
  Thee do I make my regent of Persia
  And general lieutenant of my armies.
  Meander, you that were our brother's guide   10
  And chiefest counsellor in all his acts,
  Since he is yielded to the stroke of war,
  On your submission we with thanks excuse
  And give you equal place in our affairs.

MEANDER [*kneeling*]
  Most happy emperor, in humblest terms
  I vow my service to your majesty,
  With utmost virtue of my faith and duty.

COSROE
  Thanks, good Meander. [MEANDER *rises.*]
                      Then, Cosroë, reign,
  And govern Persia in her former pomp.
  Now send embassage to thy neighbour kings   20
  And let them know the Persian king is changed
  From one that knew not what a king should do
  To one that can command what 'longs thereto.
  And now we will to fair Persepolis
  With twenty thousand expert soldiers.
  The lords and captains of my brother's camp
  With little slaughter take Meander's course

And gladly yield them to my gracious rule.
Ortygius and Menaphon, my trusty friends,
30   Now will I gratify your former good
And grace your calling with a greater sway.

ORTYGIUS

And as we ever aimed at your behoof
And sought your state all honour it deserved,
So will we with our powers and our lives
Endeavour to preserve and prosper it.

COSROE

I will not thank thee, sweet Ortygius;
Better replies shall prove my purposes.
And now, Lord Tamburlaine, my brother's camp
I leave to thee and to Theridamas,
40   To follow me to fair Persepolis.
Then will we march to all those Indian mines
My witless brother to the Christians lost,
And ransom them with fame and usury.
And till thou overtake me, Tamburlaine,
Staying to order all the scattered troops,
Farewell, lord regent and his happy friends!
I long to sit upon my brother's throne.

MENAPHON

Your majesty shall shortly have your wish,
And ride in triumph through Persepolis.

>   *Exeunt;* TAMBURLAINE, TECHELLES, THERIDAMAS,
>   USUMCASANE *remain.*

TAMBURLAINE

50   'And ride in triumph through Persepolis'!
Is it not brave to be a king, Techelles?
Usumcasane and Theridamas,
Is it not passing brave to be a king,
And ride in triumph through Persepolis?

TECHELLES

O my lord, 'tis sweet and full of pomp.

USUMCASANE

To be a king is half to be a god.

THERIDAMAS

    A god is not so glorious as a king.

    I think the pleasure they enjoy in heaven

    Cannot compare with kingly joys in earth:

    To wear a crown enchased with pearl and gold,   60

    Whose virtues carry with it life and death;

    To ask, and have; command, and be obeyed;

    When looks breed love, with looks to gain the prize,

    Such power attractive shines in princes' eyes.

TAMBURLAINE

    Why, say, Theridamas, wilt thou be a king?

THERIDAMAS

    Nay, though I praise it, I can live without it.

TAMBURLAINE

    What says my other friends? Will you be kings?

TECHELLES

    Ay, if I could, with all my heart, my lord.

TAMBURLAINE

    Why, that's well said, Techelles. So would I,

    And so would you, my masters, would you not?   70

USUMCASANE

    What then, my lord?

TAMBURLAINE

    Why then, Casane, shall we wish for aught

    The world affords in greatest novelty,

    And rest attemptless, faint and destitute?

    Methinks we should not; I am strongly moved

    That if I should desire the Persian crown

    I could attain it with a wondrous ease.

    And would not all our soldiers soon consent

    If we should aim at such a dignity?

THERIDAMAS

    I know they would with our persuasions.   80

TAMBURLAINE

    Why then, Theridamas, I'll first essay

    To get the Persian kingdom to myself;

    Then thou for Parthia, they for Scythia and Media.

And if I prosper, all shall be as sure
As if the Turk, the Pope, Afric, and Greece
Came creeping to us with their crowns apace.

TECHELLES
Then shall we send to this triumphing king
And bid him battle for his novel crown?

USUMCASANE
Nay, quickly then, before his room be hot.

TAMBURLAINE
90   'Twill prove a pretty jest, in faith, my friends.

THERIDAMAS
A jest, to charge on twenty thousand men?
I judge the purchase more important far.

TAMBURLAINE
Judge by thyself, Theridamas, not me,
For presently Techelles here shall haste
To bid him battle ere he pass too far,
And lose more labour than the gain will quite.
Then shalt thou see the Scythian Tamburlaine
Make but a jest to win the Persian crown.
Techelles, take a thousand horse with thee
100   And bid him turn him back to war with us
That only made him king to make us sport.
We will not steal upon him cowardly,
But give him warning and more warriors.
Haste thee, Techelles. We will follow thee.

                                        [*Exit* TECHELLES.]

What saith Theridamas?

THERIDAMAS   Go on, for me.

                                              Exeunt.

Scene 6

[*Enter*] COSROE, MEANDER, ORTYGIUS, MENAPHON, *with other* SOLDIERS.

COSROE

What means this devilish shepherd to aspire
With such a giantly presumption,
To cast up hills against the face of heaven
And dare the force of angry Jupiter?
But as he thrust them underneath the hills
And pressed out fire from their burning jaws,
So will I send this monstrous slave to hell,
Where flames shall ever feed upon his soul.

MEANDER

Some powers divine, or else infernal, mixed
Their angry seeds at his conception;   10
For he was never sprung of human race,
Since with the spirit of his fearful pride,
He dares so doubtlessly resolve of rule,
And by profession be ambitious.

ORTYGIUS

What god, or fiend, or spirit of the earth,
Or monster turnèd to a manly shape,
Or of what mould or mettle he be made,
What star or state soever govern him,
Let us put on our meet encount'ring minds,
And, in detesting such a devilish thief,   20
In love of honour and defence of right
Be armed against the hate of such a foe,
Whether from earth, or hell, or heaven he grow.

COSROE

Nobly resolved, my good Ortygius.
And since we all have sucked one wholesome air,
And with the same proportion of elements
Resolve, I hope we are resembled,
Vowing our loves to equal death and life.
Let's cheer our soldiers to encounter him,

30   That grievous image of ingratitude,
        That fiery thirster after sovereignty,
        And burn him in the fury of that flame
        That none can quench but blood and empery.
        Resolve, my lords and loving soldiers, now
        To save your king and country from decay.
        Then strike up drum! [*Strike drum.*]
                                And all the stars that make
        The loathsome circle of my dated life,
        Direct my weapon to his barbarous heart
        That thus opposeth him against the gods,
40   And scorns the powers that govern Persia!

                                        [*Exeunt.*]
        Enter [*the armies*] *to the battle, and after the battle
        enter* COSROE *wounded,* THERIDAMAS, TAMBURLAINE,
        TECHELLES, USUMCASANE, *with others.*

COSROE
        Barbarous and bloody Tamburlaine,
        Thus to deprive me of my crown and life!
        Treacherous and false Theridamas,
        Even at the morning of my happy state,
        Scarce being seated in my royal throne,
        To work my downfall and untimely end!
        An uncouth pain torments my grievèd soul,
        And death arrests the organ of my voice,
        Who, ent'ring at the breach thy sword hath made,
50   Sacks every vein and artier of my heart.
        Bloody and insatiate Tamburlaine!

TAMBURLAINE
        The thirst of reign and sweetness of a crown,
        That caused the eldest son of heavenly Ops
        To thrust his doting father from his chair
        And place himself in th'empyreal heaven,
        Moved me to manage arms against thy state.
        What better precedent than mighty Jove?
        Nature, that framed us of four elements
        Warring within our breasts for regiment,
60   Doth teach us all to have aspiring minds.

Our souls, whose faculties can comprehend
The wondrous architecture of the world
And measure every wand'ring planet's course,
Still climbing after knowledge infinite
And always moving as the restless spheres,
Wills us to wear ourselves and never rest
Until we reach the ripest fruit of all,
That perfect bliss and sole felicity,
The sweet fruition of an earthly crown.

THERIDAMAS
And that made me to join with Tamburlaine,   70
For he is gross and like the massy earth
That moves not upwards nor by princely deeds
Doth mean to soar above the highest sort.

TECHELLES
And that made us, the friends of Tamburlaine,
To lift our swords against the Persian king.

USUMCASANE
For as when Jove did thrust old Saturn down,
Neptune and Dis gained each of them a crown,
So do we hope to reign in Asia
If Tamburlaine be placed in Persia.

COSROE
The strangest men that ever nature made!   80
I know not how to take their tyrannies.
My bloodless body waxeth chill and cold,
And with my blood my life slides through my wound.
My soul begins to take her flight to hell,
And summons all my senses to depart.
The heat and moisture, which did feed each other,
For want of nourishment to feed them both,
Is dry and cold, and now doth ghastly death
With greedy talons gripe my bleeding heart,
And like a harpy tires on my life.   90
Theridamas and Tamburlaine, I die,
And fearful vengeance light upon you both!
    [*He dies.*]
    He [TAMBURLAINE] *takes the crown and puts it on.*

TAMBURLAINE
  Not all the curses which the Furies breathe
  Shall make me leave so rich a prize as this.
  Theridamas, Techelles, and the rest,
  Who think you now is King of Persia?
ALL Tamburlaine! Tamburlaine!
TAMBURLAINE
  Though Mars himself, the angry god of arms,
  And all the earthly potentates conspire
  To dispossess me of this diadem,
  Yet will I wear it in despite of them
  As great commander of this eastern world,
  If you but say that Tamburlaine shall reign.
ALL
  Long live Tamburlaine, and reign in Asia!
TAMBURLAINE
  So, now it is more surer on my head
  Than if the gods had held a parliament
  And all pronounced me King of Persia.

                                              [*Exeunt.*]

ACT 3

Scene 1

[*Enter*] BAJAZETH, *the* KINGS OF FEZ, MOROCCO, *and*
ARGIER, [BASSOES,] *with others in great pomp.*

BAJAZETH
  Great kings of Barbary, and my portly bassoes,
  We hear the Tartars and the eastern thieves,
  Under the conduct of one Tamburlaine,
  Presume a bickering with your emperor,
  And thinks to rouse us from our dreadful siege
  Of the famous Grecian Constantinople.
  You know our army is invincible;
  As many circumcisèd Turks we have
  And warlike bands of Christians renied
  As hath the ocean or the Terrene Sea   10
  Small drops of water when the moon begins
  To join in one her semicircled horns.
  Yet would we not be braved with foreign power,
  Nor raise our siege before the Grecians yield,
  Or breathless lie before the city walls.
FEZ
  Renownèd emperor and mighty general,
  What if you sent the bassoes of your guard
  To charge him to remain in Asia,
  Or else to threaten death and deadly arms
  As from the mouth of mighty Bajazeth?   20
BAJAZETH
  Hie thee, my basso, fast to Persia.

Tell him thy lord the Turkish emperor,
Dread lord of Afric, Europe, and Asia,
Great king and conqueror of Graecia,
The ocean Terrene, and the coal-black sea,
The high and highest monarch of the world,
Wills and commands (for say not I entreat)
Not once to set his foot in Africa
Or spread his colours in Graecia,
30   Lest he incur the fury of my wrath.
Tell him I am content to take a truce
Because I hear he bears a valiant mind.
But if, presuming on his silly power,
He be so mad to manage arms with me,
Then stay thou with him; say I bid thee so.
And if before the sun have measured heaven
With triple circuit thou regreet us not,
We mean to take his morning's next arise
For messenger he will not be reclaimed,
40   And mean to fetch thee in despite of him.
BASSO
Most great and puissant monarch of the earth,
Your basso will accomplish your behest
And show your pleasure to the Persian,
As fits the legate of the stately Turk.

Exit BASSO.

ARGIER
They say he is the King of Persia;
But if he dare attempt to stir your siege,
'Twere requisite he should be ten times more,
For all flesh quakes at your magnificence.
BAJAZETH
True, Argier, and tremble at my looks.
MOROCCO
50   The spring is hindered by your smothering host,
For neither rain can fall upon the earth,
Nor sun reflex his virtuous beams thereon,
The ground is mantled with such multitudes.

BAJAZETH
    All this is true as holy Mahomet,
    And all the trees are blasted with our breaths.
FEZ
    What thinks your greatness best to be achieved
    In pursuit of the city's overthrow?
BAJAZETH
    I will the captive pioners of Argier
    Cut off the water that by leaden pipes
    Runs to the city from the mountain Carnon;   60
    Two thousand horse shall forage up and down,
    That no relief or succour come by land;
    And all the sea my galleys countermand.
    Then shall our footmen lie within the trench,
    And with their cannons mouthed like Orcus' gulf
    Batter the walls, and we will enter in;
    And thus the Grecians shall be conquerèd.

                                                  Exeunt.

Scene 2

    [*Enter*] AGYDAS, ZENOCRATE, ANIPPE, *with others.*
AGYDAS
    Madam Zenocrate, may I presume
    To know the cause of these unquiet fits
    That work such trouble to your wonted rest?
    'Tis more than pity such a heavenly face
    Should by heart's sorrow wax so wan and pale,
    When your offensive rape by Tamburlaine
    (Which of your whole displeasures should be most)
    Hath seemed to be digested long ago.
ZENOCRATE
    Although it be digested long ago,
    As his exceeding favours have deserved,   10
    And might content the queen of heaven as well

As it hath changed my first-conceived disdain,
Yet, since, a farther passion feeds my thoughts
With ceaseless and disconsolate conceits,
Which dyes my looks so lifeless as they are
And might, if my extremes had full events,
Make me the ghastly counterfeit of death.

AGYDAS

Eternal heaven sooner be dissolved,
And all that pierceth Phoebe's silver eye,
20   Before such hap fall to Zenocrate!

ZENOCRATE

Ah, life and soul still hover in his breast
And leave my body senseless as the earth,
Or else unite you to his life and soul,
That I may live and die with Tamburlaine!

Enter [from behind] TAMBURLAINE *with* TECHELLES *and
others.*

AGYDAS

With Tamburlaine? Ah, fair Zenocrate,
Let not a man so vile and barbarous,
That holds you from your father in despite
And keeps you from the honours of a queen,
Being supposed his worthless concubine,
30   Be honoured with your love but for necessity.
So now the mighty Sultan hears of you,
Your highness needs not doubt but in short time
He will, with Tamburlaine's destruction,
Redeem you from this deadly servitude.

ZENOCRATE

Agydas, leave to wound me with these words,
And speak of Tamburlaine as he deserves.
The entertainment we have had of him
Is far from villainy or servitude,
And might in noble minds be counted princely.

AGYDAS

40   How can you fancy one that looks so fierce,
Only disposed to martial stratagems?
Who, when he shall embrace you in his arms,

Will tell how many thousand men he slew,
And when you look for amorous discourse
Will rattle forth his facts of war and blood,
Too harsh a subject for your dainty ears.

ZENOCRATE
As looks the sun through Nilus' flowing stream,
Or when the morning holds him in her arms,
So looks my lordly love, fair Tamburlaine;
His talk much sweeter than the Muses' song   50
They sung for honour 'gainst Pierides,
Or when Minerva did with Neptune strive;
And higher would I rear my estimate
Than Juno, sister to the highest god,
If I were matched with mighty Tamburlaine.

AGYDAS
Yet be not so inconstant in your love,
But let the young Arabian live in hope
After your rescue to enjoy his choice.
You see, though first the King of Persia,
Being a shepherd, seemed to love you much,   60
Now in his majesty he leaves those looks,
Those words of favour, and those comfortings,
And gives no more than common courtesies.

ZENOCRATE
Thence rise the tears that so distain my cheeks,
Fearing his love through my unworthiness.

   TAMBURLAINE *goes to her, and takes her away lovingly by*
   the hand, looking wrathfully on AGYDAS, *and says nothing.*
                                       [*Exeunt.* AGYDAS *remains.*]

AGYDAS
Betrayed by fortune and suspicious love,
Threatened with frowning wrath and jealousy,
Surprised with fear of hideous revenge,
I stand aghast, but most astonièd
To see his choler shut in secret thoughts   70
And wrapped in silence of his angry soul.
Upon his brows was portrayed ugly death,
And in his eyes the fury of his heart,

That shine as comets, menacing revenge,
And casts a pale complexion on his cheeks.
As when the seaman sees the Hyades
Gather an army of Cimmerian clouds
(Auster and Aquilon, with wingèd steeds
All sweating, tilt about the watery heavens
80   With shivering spears enforcing thunderclaps,
And from their shields strike flames of lightning),
All fearful folds his sails, and sounds the main,
Lifting his prayers to the heavens for aid
Against the terror of the winds and waves,
So fares Agydas for the late-felt frowns
That sent a tempest to my daunted thoughts
And makes my soul divine her overthrow.
     Enter TECHELLES *with a naked dagger.*
TECHELLES [*giving the dagger*]
See you, Agydas, how the king salutes you.
He bids you prophesy what it imports.
                                    Exit [TECHELLES].

AGYDAS
90   I prophesied before, and now I prove,
The killing frowns of jealousy and love.
He needed not with words confirm my fear,
For words are vain where working tools present
The naked action of my threatened end.
It says, Agydas, thou shalt surely die,
And of extremities elect the least:
More honour and less pain it may procure
To die by this resolvèd hand of thine
Than stay the torments he and heaven have sworn.
100   Then haste, Agydas, and prevent the plagues
Which thy prolongèd fates may draw on thee.
Go wander free from fear of tyrant's rage,
Removèd from the torments and the hell
Wherewith he may excruciate thy soul,
And let Agydas by Agydas die,
And with this stab slumber eternally.
     [*Stabs himself.*]

[*Enter* TECHELLES *and* USUMCASCANE.]

TECHELLES

Usumcasane, see how right the man
Hath hit the meaning of my lord the king.

USUMCASANE

Faith, and, Techelles, it was manly done;
And since he was so wise and honourable,   110
Let us afford him now the bearing hence
And crave his triple-worthy burial.

TECHELLES

Agreed, Casane. We will honour him.

[*Exeunt, bearing the body.*]

Scene 3

[*Enter*] TAMBURLAINE, TECHELLES, USUMCASANE,
THERIDAMAS, BASSO, ZENOCRATE, [ANIPPE,] *with others*
[*with a throne*].

TAMBURLAINE

Basso, by this thy lord and master knows
I mean to meet him in Bithynia.
See how he comes! Tush, Turks are full of brags
And menace more than they can well perform.
He meet me in the field and fetch thee hence!
Alas, poor Turk, his fortune is too weak
T'encounter with the strength of Tamburlaine.
View well my camp, and speak indifferently:
Do not my captains and my soldiers look
As if they meant to conquer Africa?   10

BASSO

Your men are valiant, but their number few,
And cannot terrify his mighty host.
My lord, the great commander of the world,
Besides fifteen contributory kings,
Hath now in arms ten thousand janizaries
Mounted on lusty Mauritanian steeds,

Brought to the war by men of Tripoli;
Two hundred thousand footmen that have served
In two set battles fought in Graecia;
20 And for the expedition of this war,
If he think good, can from his garrisons
Withdraw as many more to follow him.

TECHELLES
The more he brings, the greater is the spoil;
For, when they perish by our warlike hands,
We mean to seat our footmen on their steeds
And rifle all those stately janizars.

TAMBURLAINE
But will those kings accompany your lord?

BASSO
Such as his highness please, but some must stay
To rule the provinces he late subdued.

TAMBURLAINE [*to his followers*]
30 Then fight courageously, their crowns are yours.
This hand shall set them on your conquering heads
That made me emperor of Asia.

USUMCASANE
Let him bring millions infinite of men,
Unpeopling western Africa and Greece,
Yet we assure us of the victory.

THERIDAMAS
Even he, that in a trice vanquished two kings
More mighty than the Turkish emperor,
Shall rouse him out of Europe and pursue
His scattered army till they yield or die.

TAMBURLAINE
40 Well said, Theridamas! Speak in that mood,
For 'will' and 'shall' best fitteth Tamburlaine,
Whose smiling stars gives him assurèd hope
Of martial triumph ere he meet his foes.
I that am termed the scourge and wrath of God,
The only fear and terror of the world,
Will first subdue the Turk and then enlarge
Those Christian captives which you keep as slaves,

Burdening their bodies with your heavy chains,
And feeding them with thin and slender fare,
That naked row about the Terrene Sea,   50
And when they chance to breathe and rest a space,
Are punished with bastones so grievously
That they lie panting on the galley's side
And strive for life at every stroke they give.
These are the cruel pirates of Argier,
That damnèd train, the scum of Africa,
Inhabited with straggling runagates,
That make quick havoc of the Christian blood.
But, as I live, that town shall curse the time
That Tamburlaine set foot in Africa.   60

Enter BAJAZETH *with his* BASSOES [*with a throne,*] *and*
contributory KINGS [OF FEZ, MOROCCO *and* ARGIER;
ZABINA *and* EBEA].

BAJAZETH
Bassoes and janizaries of my guard,
Attend upon the person of your lord,
The greatest potentate of Africa.

TAMBURLAINE
Techelles and the rest, prepare your swords.
I mean t'encounter with that Bajazeth.

BAJAZETH
Kings of Fez, Moroccus, and Argier,
He calls me Bajazeth, whom you call lord!
Note the presumption of this Scythian slave.
I tell thee, villain, those that lead my horse
Have to their names titles of dignity;   70
And dar'st thou bluntly call me Bajazeth?

TAMBURLAINE
And know thou, Turk, that those which lead my horse
Shall lead thee captive thorough Africa;
And dar'st thou bluntly call me Tamburlaine?

BAJAZETH
By Mahomet my kinsman's sepulchre,
And by the holy Alcoran I swear
He shall be made a chaste and lustless eunuch,

    And in my sarell tend my concubines,
    And all his captains that thus stoutly stand
80   Shall draw the chariot of my emperess,
    Whom I have brought to see their overthrow.

TAMBURLAINE
    By this my sword that conquered Persia,
    Thy fall shall make me famous through the world.
    I will not tell thee how I'll handle thee,
    But every common soldier of my camp
    Shall smile to see thy miserable state.

FEZ [*to* BAJAZETH]
    What means the mighty Turkish emperor
    To talk with one so base as Tamburlaine?

MOROCCO
    Ye Moors and valiant men of Barbary,
90   How can ye suffer these indignities?

ARGIER
    Leave words and let them feel your lances' points,
    Which glided through the bowels of the Greeks.

BAJAZETH
    Well said, my stout contributory kings!
    Your threefold army and my hugy host
    Shall swallow up these base-born Persians.

TECHELLES
    Puissant, renowned, and mighty Tamburlaine,
    Why stay we thus prolonging all their lives?

THERIDAMAS
    I long to see those crowns won by our swords,
    That we may reign as kings of Africa.

USUMCASANE
100 What coward would not fight for such a prize?

TAMBURLAINE
    Fight all courageously, and be you kings!
    I speak it, and my words are oracles.

BAJAZETH
    Zabina, mother of three braver boys
    Than Hercules, that in his infancy
    Did pash the jaws of serpents venomous,

Whose hands are made to gripe a warlike lance,
Their shoulders broad, for complete armour fit,
Their limbs more large and of a bigger size
Than all the brats y-sprung from Typhon's loins,
Who, when they come unto their father's age,   110
Will batter turrets with their manly fists:
Sit here upon this royal chair of state
And on thy head wear my imperial crown,
Until I bring this sturdy Tamburlaine
And all his captains bound in captive chains.

ZABINA
Such good success happen to Bajazeth!

TAMBURLAINE
Zenocrate, the loveliest maid alive,
Fairer than rocks of pearl and precious stone,
The only paragon of Tamburlaine,
Whose eyes are brighter than the lamps of heaven,   120
And speech more pleasant than sweet harmony,
That with thy looks canst clear the darkened sky
And calm the rage of thund'ring Jupiter:
Sit down by her, adornèd with my crown,
As if thou wert the empress of the world.
Stir not, Zenocrate, until thou see
Me march victoriously with all my men,
Triumphing over him and these his kings,
Which I will bring as vassals to thy feet.
Till then, take thou my crown, vaunt of my worth,   130
And manage words with her as we will arms.

ZENOCRATE
And may my love, the King of Persia,
Return with victory and free from wound!

BAJAZETH
Now shalt thou feel the force of Turkish arms
Which lately made all Europe quake for fear.
I have of Turks, Arabians, Moors, and Jews,
Enough to cover all Bithynia.
Let thousands die, their slaughtered carcasses
Shall serve for walls and bulwarks to the rest;

140   And as the heads of Hydra, so my power,
       Subdued, shall stand as mighty as before.
       If they should yield their necks unto the sword,
       Thy soldiers' arms could not endure to strike
       So many blows as I have heads for thee.
       Thou knowest not, foolish-hardy Tamburlaine,
       What 'tis to meet me in the open field,
       That leave no ground for thee to march upon.

TAMBURLAINE
       Our conquering swords shall marshal us the way
       We use to march upon the slaughtered foe,
150   Trampling their bowels with our horses' hoofs –
       Brave horses, bred on the white Tartarian hills.
       My camp is like to Julius Caesar's host,
       That never fought but had the victory;
       Nor in Pharsalia was there such hot war
       As these my followers willingly would have.
       Legions of spirits fleeting in the air,
       Direct our bullets and our weapons' points,
       And make our strokes to wound the senseless air;
       And when she sees our bloody colours spread,
160   Then Victory begins to take her flight,
       Resting herself upon my milk-white tent.
       But come, my lords, to weapons let us fall!
       The field is ours, the Turk, his wife, and all.
                              Exit [TAMBURLAINE,] *with his followers.*

BAJAZETH
       Come, kings and bassoes, let us glut our swords
       That thirst to drink the feeble Persians' blood!
                              Exit [BAJAZETH,] *with his followers.*

ZABINA
       Base concubine, must thou be placed by me
       That am the empress of the mighty Turk?

ZENOCRATE
       Disdainful Turkess and unreverend boss,
       Call'st thou me concubine, that am betrothed
170   Unto the great and mighty Tamburlaine?

ZABINA

  To Tamburlaine, the great Tartarian thief!

ZENOCRATE

  Thou wilt repent these lavish words of thine
  When thy great basso-master and thyself
  Must plead for mercy at his kingly feet,
  And sue to me to be your advocates.

ZABINA

  And sue to thee? I tell thee, shameless girl,
  Thou shalt be laundress to my waiting-maid.
  How lik'st thou her, Ebea? Will she serve?

EBEA

  Madam, she thinks perhaps she is too fine.
  But I shall turn her into other weeds,   180
  And make her dainty fingers fall to work.

ZENOCRATE

  Hear'st thou, Anippe, how thy drudge doth talk,
  And how my slave, her mistress, menaceth?
  Both, for their sauciness, shall be employed
  To dress the common soldiers' meat and drink,
  For we will scorn they should come near ourselves.

ANIPPE

  Yet sometimes let your highness send for them
  To do the work my chambermaid disdains.

  They sound [to] the battle within, and stay.

ZENOCRATE

  Ye gods and powers that govern Persia
  And made my lordly love her worthy king,   190
  Now strengthen him against the Turkish Bajazeth,
  And let his foes, like flocks of fearful roes
  Pursued by hunters, fly his angry looks,
  That I may see him issue conqueror.

ZABINA

  Now, Mahomet, solicit God himself,
  And make him rain down murdering shot from heaven
  To dash the Scythians' brains, and strike them dead
  That dare to manage arms with him

That offered jewels to thy sacred shrine
200   When first he warred against the Christians.
    [*They sound*] *to the battle again.*

ZENOCRATE

By this the Turks lie welt'ring in their blood,
And Tamburlaine is lord of Africa.

ZABINA

Thou art deceived, I heard the trumpets sound
As when my emperor overthrew the Greeks
And led them captive into Africa.
Straight will I use thee as thy pride deserves;
Prepare thyself to live and die my slave.

ZENOCRATE

If Mahomet should come from heaven and swear
My royal lord is slain or conquerèd,
210   Yet should he not persuade me otherwise
But that he lives and will be conqueror.
    BAJAZETH *flies* [*across the stage*], *and he* [TAMBURLAINE]
    pursues him [*offstage*]. *The battle short, and they* [*re-*]*enter*
    [*fighting*]. BAJAZETH *is overcome.*

TAMBURLAINE

Now, king of bassoes, who is conqueror?

BAJAZETH

Thou, by the fortune of this damnèd soil.

TAMBURLAINE

Where are your stout contributory kings?
    Enter TECHELLES, THERIDAMAS, USUMCASANE.

TECHELLES

We have their crowns; their bodies strew the field.

TAMBURLAINE

Each man a crown? Why, kingly fought, i'faith.
Deliver them into my treasury.
    [TECHELLES, THERIDAMAS *and* USUMCASANE *hand over*
    the crowns.]

ZENOCRATE

Now let me offer to my gracious lord
His royal crown again, so highly won.

TAMBURLAINE

   Nay, take the Turkish crown from her, Zenocrate,   220
   And crown me emperor of Africa.

ZABINA

   No, Tamburlaine, though now thou gat the best,
   Thou shalt not yet be lord of Africa.

THERIDAMAS [*to* ZABINA]

   Give her the crown, Turkess, you were best.
     He takes it from her and gives it ZENOCRATE.

ZABINA

   Injurious villains, thieves, runagates!
   How dare you thus abuse my majesty?

THERIDAMAS

   Here, madam, you are empress, she is none.

TAMBURLAINE [*as* ZENOCRATE *crowns him*]

   Not now, Theridamas, her time is past.
   The pillars that have bolstered up those terms
   Are fall'n in clusters at my conquering feet.   230

ZABINA

   Though he be prisoner, he may be ransomed.

TAMBURLAINE

   Not all the world shall ransom Bajazeth.

BAJAZETH

   Ah, fair Zabina, we have lost the field,
   And never had the Turkish emperor
   So great a foil by any foreign foe.
   Now will the Christian miscreants be glad,
   Ringing with joy their superstitious bells,
   And making bonfires for my overthrow.
   But ere I die, those foul idolaters
   Shall make me bonfires with their filthy bones;   240
   For, though the glory of this day be lost,
   Afric and Greece have garrisons enough
   To make me sovereign of the earth again.

TAMBURLAINE

   Those wallèd garrisons will I subdue,
   And write myself great lord of Africa.

So from the east unto the furthest west
Shall Tamburlaine extend his puissant arm.
The galleys and those pilling brigantines,
That yearly sail to the Venetian gulf,
250   And hover in the straits for Christians' wrack,
Shall lie at anchor in the isle Asant
Until the Persian fleet and men-of-war,
Sailing along the oriental sea,
Have fetched about the Indian continent,
Even from Persepolis to Mexico,
And thence unto the Straits of Jubalter,
Where they shall meet and join their force in one,
Keeping in awe the Bay of Portingale
And all the ocean by the British shore.
260   And by this means I'll win the world at last.

BAJAZETH

Yet set a ransom on me, Tamburlaine.

TAMBURLAINE

What, think'st thou Tamburlaine esteems thy gold?
I'll make the kings of India, ere I die,
Offer their mines, to sue for peace, to me,
And dig for treasure to appease my wrath.
Come, bind them both, and one lead in the Turk.
The Turkess let my love's maid lead away.
    They bind them.

BAJAZETH

Ah, villains, dare ye touch my sacred arms?
O Mahomet, O sleepy Mahomet!

ZABINA

270   O cursèd Mahomet, that makest us thus
The slaves to Scythians rude and barbarous!

TAMBURLAINE

Come, bring them in, and for this happy conquest
Triumph, and solemnize a martial feast.

                                            Exeunt.

ACT 4

[*Enter the*] SULTAN OF EGYPT *with three or four* LORDS,
CAPOLIN [*and a* MESSENGER].

SULTAN
  Awake, ye men of Memphis! Hear the clang
  Of Scythian trumpets! Hear the basilisks
  That, roaring, shake Damascus' turrets down!
  The rogue of Volga holds Zenocrate,
  The Sultan's daughter, for his concubine,
  And with a troop of thieves and vagabonds
  Hath spread his colours to our high disgrace,
  While you faint-hearted base Egyptians
  Lie slumbering on the flow'ry banks of Nile,
  As crocodiles that unaffrighted rest   10
  While thund'ring cannons rattle on their skins.

MESSENGER
  Nay, mighty Sultan, did your greatness see
  The frowning looks of fiery Tamburlaine,
  That with his terror and imperious eyes
  Commands the hearts of his associates,
  It might amaze your royal majesty.

SULTAN
  Villain, I tell thee, were that Tamburlaine
  As monstrous as Gorgon, prince of hell,
  The Sultan would not start a foot from him.
  But speak, what power hath he?

MESSENGER   Mighty lord,   20

Three hundred thousand men in armour clad
Upon their prancing steeds, disdainfully
With wanton paces trampling on the ground;
Five hundred thousand footmen threat'ning shot,
Shaking their swords, their spears, and iron bills,
Environing their standard round, that stood
As bristle-pointed as a thorny wood.
Their warlike engines and munition
Exceed the forces of their martial men.

SULTAN

30   Nay, could their numbers countervail the stars,
Or ever-drizzling drops of April showers,
Or withered leaves that Autumn shaketh down,
Yet would the Sultan by his conquering power
So scatter and consume them in his rage
That not a man should live to rue their fall.

CAPOLIN

So might your highness, had you time to sort
Your fighting men and raise your royal host.
But Tamburlaine by expedition
Advantage takes of your unreadiness.

SULTAN

40   Let him take all th'advantages he can.
Were all the world conspired to fight for him,
Nay, were he devil – as he is no man –
Yet in revenge of fair Zenocrate,
Whom he detaineth in despite of us,
This arm should send him down to Erebus
To shroud his shame in darkness of the night.

MESSENGER

Pleaseth your mightiness to understand,
His resolution far exceedeth all.
The first day when he pitcheth down his tents,
50   White is their hue, and on his silver crest
A snowy feather spangled white he bears,
To signify the mildness of his mind
That, satiate with spoil, refuseth blood.
But when Aurora mounts the second time,

As red as scarlet is his furniture;
Then must his kindled wrath be quenched with blood,
Not sparing any that can manage arms.
But if these threats move not submission,
Black are his colours, black pavilion,
His spear, his shield, his horse, his armour, plumes,   60
And jetty feathers menace death and hell.
Without respect of sex, degree, or age,
He razeth all his foes with fire and sword.

SULTAN
Merciless villain, peasant ignorant
Of lawful arms or martial discipline!
Pillage and murder are his usual trades;
The slave usurps the glorious name of war.
See, Capolin, the fair Arabian king,
That hath been disappointed by this slave
Of my fair daughter and his princely love,   70
May have fresh warning to go war with us
And be revenged for her disparagement.

                                                    [*Exeunt.*]

Scene 2

[*A throne is brought on. Enter*] TAMBURLAINE [*all in
white*], TECHELLES, THERIDAMAS, USUMCASANE,
ZENOCRATE, ANIPPE, *two* MOORS *drawing* BAJAZETH
in his cage, and his wife [ZABINA] *following him.*

TAMBURLAINE Bring out my footstool.

    They take him [BAJAZETH] *out of the cage.*

BAJAZETH
Ye holy priests of heavenly Mahomet,
That, sacrificing, slice and cut your flesh,
Staining his altars with your purple blood,
Make heaven to frown, and every fixèd star
To suck up poison from the moorish fens
And pour it in this glorious tyrant's throat!

TAMBURLAINE

The chiefest God, first mover of that sphere
Enchased with thousands ever-shining lamps,
10   Will sooner burn the glorious frame of heaven
Than it should so conspire my overthrow.
But, villain, thou that wishest this to me,
Fall prostrate on the low, disdainful earth
And be the footstool of great Tamburlaine,
That I may rise into my royal throne.

BAJAZETH

First shalt thou rip my bowels with thy sword
And sacrifice my heart to death and hell
Before I yield to such a slavery.

TAMBURLAINE

Base villain, vassal, slave to Tamburlaine,
20   Unworthy to embrace or touch the ground
That bears the honour of my royal weight,
Stoop, villain, stoop, stoop, for so he bids
That may command thee piecemeal to be torn
Or scattered like the lofty cedar trees
Struck with the voice of thund'ring Jupiter.

BAJAZETH

Then, as I look down to the damnèd fiends,
Fiends, look on me, and, thou dread god of hell,
With ebon sceptre strike this hateful earth
And make it swallow both of us at once!
        He [TAMBURLAINE] *gets up upon him* [BAJAZETH] *to his*
        chair.

TAMBURLAINE

30   Now clear the triple region of the air,
And let the majesty of heaven behold
Their scourge and terror tread on emperors.
Smile, stars that reigned at my nativity,
And dim the brightness of their neighbour lamps!
Disdain to borrow light of Cynthia.
For I, the chiefest lamp of all the earth,
First rising in the east with mild aspect

But fixèd now in the meridian line,
Will send up fire to your turning spheres
And cause the sun to borrow light of you.   40
My sword struck fire from his coat of steel
Even in Bithynia, when I took this Turk,
As when a fiery exhalation
Wrapped in the bowels of a freezing cloud,
Fighting for passage, makes the welkin crack,
And casts a flash of lightning to the earth.
But ere I march to wealthy Persia
Or leave Damascus and th'Egyptian fields,
As was the fame of Clymene's brainsick son
That almost brent the axletree of heaven,   50
So shall our swords, our lances, and our shot
Fill all the air with fiery meteors.
Then, when the sky shall wax as red as blood,
It shall be said I made it red myself,
To make me think of naught but blood and war.

ZABINA

Unworthy king, that by thy cruelty
Unlawfully usurp'st the Persian seat,
Dar'st thou, that never saw an emperor
Before thou met my husband in the field,
Being thy captive, thus abuse his state,   60
Keeping his kingly body in a cage
That roofs of gold and sun-bright palaces
Should have prepared to entertain his grace,
And treading him beneath thy loathsome feet
Whose feet the kings of Africa have kissed?

TECHELLES [to TAMBURLAINE]

You must devise some torment worse, my lord,
To make these captives rein their lavish tongues.

TAMBURLAINE

Zenocrate, look better to your slave.

ZENOCRATE

She is my handmaid's slave, and she shall look
That these abuses flow not from her tongue.   70

Chide her, Anippe.

ANIPPE [to ZABINA]

Let these be warnings for you, then, my slave,
How you abuse the person of the king,
Or else I swear to have you whipped stark naked.

BAJAZETH

Great Tamburlaine, great in my overthrow,
Ambitious pride shall make thee fall as low
For treading on the back of Bajazeth,
That should be horsèd on four mighty kings.

TAMBURLAINE

Thy names and titles and thy dignities
80   Are fled from Bajazeth and remain with me,
That will maintain it 'gainst a world of kings.
Put him in again.

[*They put* BAJAZETH *into the cage.*]

BAJAZETH

Is this a place for mighty Bajazeth?
Confusion light on him that helps thee thus!

TAMBURLAINE

There, whiles he lives, shall Bajazeth be kept,
And where I go be thus in triumph drawn;
And thou, his wife, shalt feed him with the scraps
My servitors shall bring thee from my board.
For he that gives him other food than this
90   Shall sit by him and starve to death himself.
This is my mind, and I will have it so.
Not all the kings and emperors of the earth,
If they would lay their crowns before my feet,
Shall ransom him or take him from his cage.
The ages that shall talk of Tamburlaine,
Even from this day to Plato's wondrous year,
Shall talk how I have handled Bajazeth.
These Moors that drew him from Bithynia
To fair Damascus, where we now remain,
100 Shall lead him with us wheresoe'er we go.
Techelles and my loving followers,
Now may we see Damascus' lofty towers,

Like to the shadows of Pyramides
That with their beauties graced the Memphian fields.
The golden statue of their feathered bird
That spreads her wings upon the city walls
Shall not defend it from our battering shot.
The townsmen mask in silk and cloth of gold,
And every house is as a treasury.
The men, the treasure, and the town is ours.   110

THERIDAMAS
Your tents of white now pitched before the gates,
And gentle flags of amity displayed,
I doubt not but the governor will yield,
Offering Damascus to your majesty.

TAMBURLAINE
So shall he have his life, and all the rest.
But if he stay until the bloody flag
Be once advanced on my vermilion tent,
He dies, and those that kept us out so long.
And when they see me march in black array,
With mournful streamers hanging down their heads,   120
Were in that city all the world contained,
Not one should 'scape, but perish by our swords.

ZENOCRATE
Yet would you have some pity for my sake,
Because it is my country's, and my father's.

TAMBURLAINE
Not for the world, Zenocrate, if I have sworn.
Come, bring in the Turk.

                                           Exeunt.

Scene 3

[*Enter the*] SULTAN, [*the* KING OF] ARABIA, CAPOLIN,
with streaming colours, and SOLDIERS.

SULTAN
Methinks we march as Meleager did,

Environèd with brave Argolian knights,
To chase the savage Calydonian boar;
Or Cephalus with lusty Theban youths,
Against the wolf that angry Themis sent
To waste and spoil the sweet Aonian fields.
A monster of five hundred thousand heads,
Compact of rapine, piracy, and spoil,
The scum of men, the hate and scourge of God,
Raves in Egyptia and annoyeth us.
My lord, it is the bloody Tamburlaine,
A sturdy felon and a base-bred thief
By murder raisèd to the Persian crown,
That dares control us in our territories.
To tame the pride of this presumptuous beast,
Join your Arabians with the Sultan's power;
Let us unite our royal bands in one
And hasten to remove Damascus' siege.
It is a blemish to the majesty
And high estate of mighty emperors
That such a base, usurping vagabond
Should brave a king or wear a princely crown.

ARABIA

Renownèd Sultan, have ye lately heard
The overthrow of mighty Bajazeth
About the confines of Bithynia?
The slavery wherewith he persecutes
The noble Turk and his great emperess?

SULTAN

I have, and sorrow for his bad success.
But, noble lord of great Arabia,
Be so persuaded that the Sultan is
No more dismayed with tidings of his fall,
Than in the haven when the pilot stands
And views a stranger's ship rent in the winds,
And shiverèd against a craggy rock.
Yet, in compassion of his wretched state,
A sacred vow to heaven and him I make,
Confirming it with Ibis' holy name,

That Tamburlaine shall rue the day, the hour,
Wherein he wrought such ignominious wrong
Unto the hallowed person of a prince,   40
Or kept the fair Zenocrate so long
As concubine, I fear, to feed his lust.

ARABIA

Let grief and fury hasten on revenge!
Let Tamburlaine for his offences feel
Such plagues as heaven and we can pour on him.
I long to break my spear upon his crest
And prove the weight of his victorious arm,
For Fame, I fear, hath been too prodigal
In sounding through the world his partial praise.

SULTAN

Capolin, hast thou surveyed our powers?   50

CAPOLIN

Great emperors of Egypt and Arabia,
The number of your hosts united is
A hundred and fifty thousand horse,
Two hundred thousand foot, brave men-at-arms,
Courageous and full of hardiness,
As frolic as the hunters in the chase
Of savage beasts amid the desert woods.

ARABIA

My mind presageth fortunate success.
And, Tamburlaine, my spirit doth foresee
The utter ruin of thy men and thee.   60

SULTAN

Then rear your standards! Let your sounding drums
Direct our soldiers to Damascus' walls.
Now, Tamburlaine, the mighty Sultan comes
And leads with him the great Arabian king
To dim thy baseness and obscurity,
Famous for nothing but for theft and spoil,
To raze and scatter thy inglorious crew
Of Scythians and slavish Persians.
    [*Sound drums.*]   *Exeunt.*

Scene 4

The banquet [is brought on], and to it cometh TAM-
BURLAINE *all in scarlet,* [ZENOCRATE,] THERIDAMAS,
TECHELLES, USUMCASANE, *the* TURK [BAJAZETH, *drawn
in his cage,* ZABINA,] *with others.*

TAMBURLAINE
   Now hang our bloody colours by Damascus,
   Reflexing hues of blood upon their heads
   While they walk quivering on their city walls,
   Half dead for fear before they feel my wrath.
   Then let us freely banquet and carouse
   Full bowls of wine unto the god of war,
   That means to fill your helmets full of gold
   And make Damascus' spoils as rich to you
   As was to Jason Colchis' golden fleece.
10   And now, Bajazeth, hast thou any stomach?

BAJAZETH Ay, such a stomach, cruel Tamburlaine, as I could
   willingly feed upon thy blood-raw heart.

TAMBURLAINE Nay, thine own is easier to come by; pluck out
   that, and 'twill serve thee and thy wife. Well, Zenocrate,
   Techelles, and the rest, fall to your victuals.

BAJAZETH
   Fall to, and never may your meat digest!
   Ye Furies, that can mask invisible,
   Dive to the bottom of Avernus' pool,
   And in your hands bring hellish poison up
20   And squeeze it in the cup of Tamburlaine!
   Or, wingèd snakes of Lerna, cast your stings,
   And leave your venoms in this tyrant's dish!

ZABINA
   And may this banquet prove as ominous
   As Procne's to th'adulterous Thracian king
   That fed upon the substance of his child!

ZENOCRATE My lord, how can you suffer these outrageous
   curses by these slaves of yours?

TAMBURLAINE
  To let them see, divine Zenocrate,
  I glory in the curses of my foes,
  Having the power from the empyreal heaven   30
  To turn them all upon their proper heads.

TECHELLES I pray you, give them leave, madam. This speech is
  a goodly refreshing to them.

THERIDAMAS But if his highness would let them be fed, it would
  do them more good.

TAMBURLAINE [*to* BAJAZETH] Sirrah, why fall you not to? Are
  you so daintily brought up you cannot eat your own flesh?

BAJAZETH
  First, legions of devils shall tear thee in pieces.

USUMCASANE
  Villain, knowest thou to whom thou speakest?

TAMBURLAINE O, let him alone. Here, eat, sir. Take it from my   40
  sword's point, or I'll thrust it to thy heart.

  He [BAJAZETH] *takes it and stamps upon it.*

THERIDAMAS He stamps it under his feet, my lord.

TAMBURLAINE [*to* BAJAZETH] Take it up, villain, and eat it, or
  I will make thee slice the brawns of thy arms into carbonadoes
  and eat them.

USUMCASANE Nay, 'twere better he killed his wife, and then
  she shall be sure not to be starved, and he be provided for a
  month's victual beforehand.

TAMBURLAINE [*to* BAJAZETH] Here is my dagger; dispatch her
  while she is fat, for if she live but a while longer, she will fall   50
  into a consumption with fretting, and then she will not be
  worth the eating.

THERIDAMAS [*to* TECHELLES] Dost thou think that Mahomet
  will suffer this?

TECHELLES 'Tis like he will, when he cannot let it.

TAMBURLAINE [*to* BAJAZETH] Go to, fall to your meat. What,
  not a bit? Belike he hath not been watered today. Give him
  some drink.

  They give him water to drink, and he flings it on the ground.
  Fast, and welcome, sir, while hunger make you eat. How

60   now, Zenocrate, doth not the Turk and his wife make a
     goodly show at a banquet?

ZENOCRATE Yes, my lord.

THERIDAMAS Methinks 'tis a great deal better than a consort
     of music.

TAMBURLAINE Yet music would do well to cheer up Zenocrate.
     [*To* ZENOCRATE] Pray thee, tell: why art thou so sad? If thou
     wilt have a song, the Turk shall strain his voice. But why is it?

ZENOCRATE
     My lord, to see my father's town besieged,
     The country wasted where myself was born,
70   How can it but afflict my very soul?
     If any love remain in you, my lord,
     Or if my love unto your majesty
     May merit favour at your highness' hands,
     Then raise your siege from fair Damascus' walls
     And with my father take a friendly truce.

TAMBURLAINE
     Zenocrate, were Egypt Jove's own land,
     Yet would I with my sword make Jove to stoop.
     I will confute those blind geographers
     That make a triple region in the world,
80   Excluding regions which I mean to trace,
     And with this pen reduce them to a map,
     Calling the provinces, cities, and towns
     After my name and thine, Zenocrate.
     Here at Damascus will I make the point
     That shall begin the perpendicular.
     And wouldst thou have me buy thy father's love
     With such a loss? Tell me, Zenocrate.

ZENOCRATE
     Honour still wait on happy Tamburlaine!
     Yet give me leave to plead for him, my lord.

TAMBURLAINE
90   Content thyself. His person shall be safe,
     And all the friends of fair Zenocrate,
     If with their lives they will be pleased to yield
     Or may be forced to make me emperor;

For Egypt and Arabia must be mine.
  [*To* BAJAZETH]
Feed, you slave; thou may'st think thyself happy to be fed
from my trencher.

BAJAZETH
My empty stomach, full of idle heat,
Draws bloody humours from my feeble parts,
Preserving life by hasting cruel death.
My veins are pale, my sinews hard and dry,   100
My joints benumbed. Unless I eat, I die.

ZABINA Eat, Bajazeth. Let us live in spite of them, looking some
happy power will pity and enlarge us.

TAMBURLAINE [*offering* BAJAZETH *an empty plate*] Here,
Turk, wilt thou have a clean trencher?

BAJAZETH Ay, tyrant, and more meat.

TAMBURLAINE Soft, sir, you must be dieted; too much eating
will make you surfeit.

THERIDAMAS [*to* TAMBURLAINE] So it would, my lord,
specially having so small a walk and so little exercise.   110
  Enter a second course of crowns.

TAMBURLAINE Theridamas, Techelles, and Casane, here are
the cates you desire to finger, are they not?

THERIDAMAS Ay, my lord, but none save kings must feed with
these.

TECHELLES 'Tis enough for us to see them and for Tamburlaine
only to enjoy them.

TAMBURLAINE [*raising a toast*] Well, here is now to the Sultan
of Egypt, the King of Arabia, and the Governor of Damascus.
Now take these three crowns, and pledge me, my contributory
kings. [*He presents the crowns.*] I crown you here, Therid-   120
amas, King of Argier; Techelles, King of Fez; and Usumcasane,
King of Moroccus. How say you to this, Turk? These are not
your contributory kings.

BAJAZETH
Nor shall they long be thine, I warrant them.

TAMBURLAINE
Kings of Argier, Moroccus, and of Fez,
You that have marched with happy Tamburlaine

As far as from the frozen plage of heaven
Unto the wat'ry morning's ruddy bower
And thence by land unto the torrid zone,
130 Deserve these titles I endow you with
By valour and by magnanimity.
Your births shall be no blemish to your fame,
For virtue is the fount whence honour springs,
And they are worthy she investeth kings.

THERIDAMAS

And since your highness hath so well vouchsafed,
If we deserve them not with higher meeds
Than erst our states and actions have retained,
Take them away again and make us slaves.

TAMBURLAINE

Well said, Theridamas! When holy Fates
140 Shall 'stablish me in strong Egyptia,
We mean to travel to th'Antarctic Pole,
Conquering the people underneath our feet,
And be renowned as never emperors were.
Zenocrate, I will not crown thee yet,
Until with greater honours I be graced.

                                                        [*Exeunt.*]

ACT 5

Scene 1

[Enter] *the* GOVERNOR OF DAMASCUS, *with three or four*
CITIZENS, *and four* VIRGINS *with branches of laurel in
their hands.*

GOVERNOR
Still doth this man, or rather god of war,
Batter our walls and beat our turrets down;
And to resist with longer stubbornness
Or hope of rescue from the Sultan's power
Were but to bring our wilful overthrow
And make us desperate of our threatened lives.
We see his tents have now been alterèd
With terrors to the last and cruell'st hue;
His coal-black colours everywhere advanced
Threaten our city with a general spoil;   10
And if we should with common rites of arms
Offer our safeties to his clemency,
I fear the custom proper to his sword,
Which he observes as parcel of his fame,
Intending so to terrify the world,
By any innovation or remorse
Will never be dispensed with till our deaths.
Therefore, for these our harmless virgins' sakes,
Whose honours and whose lives rely on him,
Let us have hope that their unspotted prayers,   20
Their blubbered cheeks, and hearty humble moans
Will melt his fury into some remorse,

And use us like a loving conqueror.
FIRST VIRGIN
　　If humble suits or imprecations,
　　Uttered with tears of wretchedness and blood
　　Shed from the heads and hearts of all our sex –
　　Some made your wives, and some your children –
　　Might have entreated your obdurate breasts
　　To entertain some care of our securities
30　　Whiles only danger beat upon our walls,
　　These more than dangerous warrants of our death
　　Had never been erected as they be,
　　Nor you depend on such weak helps as we.
GOVERNOR
　　Well, lovely virgins, think our country's care,
　　Our love of honour, loath to be enthralled
　　To foreign powers and rough imperious yokes,
　　Would not with too much cowardice or fear,
　　Before all hope of rescue were denied,
　　Submit yourselves and us to servitude.
40　　Therefore, in that your safeties and our own,
　　Your honours, liberties, and lives, were weighed
　　In equal care and balance with our own,
　　Endure as we the malice of our stars,
　　The wrath of Tamburlaine and power of wars;
　　Or be the means the overweighing heavens
　　Have kept to qualify these hot extremes,
　　And bring us pardon in your cheerful looks.
SECOND VIRGIN
　　Then here, before the majesty of heaven
　　And holy patrons of Egyptia,
50　　With knees and hearts submissive we entreat
　　Grace to our words and pity to our looks,
　　That this device may prove propitious,
　　And through the eyes and ears of Tamburlaine
　　Convey events of mercy to his heart.
　　Grant that these signs of victory we yield
　　May bind the temples of his conquering head
　　To hide the folded furrows of his brows,

And shadow his displeasèd countenance
With happy looks of ruth and lenity.
Leave us, my lord, and loving countrymen;   60
What simple virgins may persuade, we will.

GOVERNOR

Farewell, sweet virgins, on whose safe return
Depends our city, liberty, and lives!

Exeunt [all except the VIRGINS. *Enter]* TAMBURLAINE,
TECHELLES, THERIDAMAS, USUMCASANE, *with others;*
TAMBURLAINE *all in black, and very melancholy.*

TAMBURLAINE

What, are the turtles frayed out of their nests?
Alas, poor fools, must you be first shall feel
The sworn destruction of Damascus?
They know my custom. Could they not as well
Have sent ye out when first my milk-white flags
Through which sweet mercy threw her gentle beams,
Reflexing them on your disdainful eyes,   70
As now when fury and incensèd hate
Flings slaughtering terror from my coal-black tents
And tells for truth submissions comes too late?

FIRST VIRGIN

Most happy king and emperor of the earth,
Image of honour and nobility,
For whom the powers divine have made the world
And on whose throne the holy Graces sit,
In whose sweet person is comprised the sum
Of nature's skill and heavenly majesty:
Pity our plights, O, pity poor Damascus!   80
Pity old age, within whose silver hairs
Honour and reverence evermore have reigned!
Pity the marriage bed, where many a lord,
In prime and glory of his loving joy,
Embraceth now with tears of ruth and blood
The jealous body of his fearful wife,
Whose cheeks and hearts – so punished with conceit
To think thy puissant never-stayèd arm
Will part their bodies and prevent their souls

90   From heavens of comfort yet their age might bear –
        Now wax all pale and withered to the death,
        As well for grief our ruthless governor
        Have thus refused the mercy of thy hand
        (Whose sceptre angels kiss and Furies dread)
        As for their liberties, their loves, or lives.
        O then, for these, and such as we ourselves,
        For us, for infants, and for all our bloods,
        That never nourished thought against thy rule,
        Pity, O, pity, sacred emperor,
100   The prostrate service of this wretched town;
        And take in sign thereof this gilded wreath
        Whereto each man of rule hath given his hand
        And wished, as worthy subjects, happy means
        To be investors of thy royal brows,
        Even with the true Egyptian diadem.
            [*She offers a laurel wreath.*]

TAMBURLAINE
        Virgins, in vain ye labour to prevent
        That which mine honour swears shall be performed.
        Behold my sword – what see you at the point?

VIRGINS
        Nothing but fear and fatal steel, my lord.

TAMBURLAINE
110   Your fearful minds are thick and misty, then,
        For there sits Death, there sits imperious Death,
        Keeping his circuit by the slicing edge.
        But I am pleased you shall not see him there;
        He now is seated on my horsemen's spears,
        And on their points his fleshless body feeds.
        Techelles, straight go charge a few of them
        To charge these dames, and show my servant Death,
        Sitting in scarlet on their armèd spears.

VIRGINS
        O, pity us!

TAMBURLAINE
120   Away with them, I say, and show them Death.
            They [TECHELLES *and others*] *take them away.*

I will not spare these proud Egyptians,
Nor change my martial observations
For all the wealth of Gihon's golden waves,
Or for the love of Venus, would she leave
The angry god of arms and lie with me.
They have refused the offer of their lives,
And know my customs are as peremptory
As wrathful planets, death, or destiny.
    Enter TECHELLES.
What, have your horsemen shown the virgins Death?

TECHELLES
They have, my lord, and on Damascus' walls   130
Have hoisted up their slaughtered carcasses.

TAMBURLAINE
A sight as baneful to their souls, I think,
As are Thessalian drugs or mithridate.
But go, my lords, put the rest to the sword.
                        Exeunt; [TAMBURLAINE *remains*].
Ah, fair Zenocrate, divine Zenocrate!
Fair is too foul an epithet for thee
That, in thy passion for thy country's love
And fear to see thy kingly father's harm,
With hair dishevelled wip'st thy watery cheeks,
And like to Flora in her morning's pride,   140
Shaking her silver tresses in the air,
Rain'st on the earth resolvèd pearl in showers
And sprinklest sapphires on thy shining face
Where Beauty, mother to the Muses, sits
And comments volumes with her ivory pen,
Taking instructions from thy flowing eyes –
Eyes, when that Ebena steps to heaven
In silence of thy solemn evening's walk,
Making the mantle of the richest night,
The moon, the planets, and the meteors, light.   150
There angels in their crystal armours fight
A doubtful battle with my tempted thoughts
For Egypt's freedom and the Sultan's life –
His life that so consumes Zenocrate,

Whose sorrows lay more siege unto my soul
Than all my army to Damascus' walls;
And neither Persians' sovereign nor the Turk
Troubled my senses with conceit of foil
So much by much as doth Zenocrate.
160   What is beauty, saith my sufferings, then?
If all the pens that ever poets held
Had fed the feeling of their masters' thoughts,
And every sweetness that inspired their hearts,
Their minds and muses on admirèd themes;
If all the heavenly quintessence they still
From their immortal flowers of poesy,
Wherein as in a mirror we perceive
The highest reaches of a human wit;
If these had made one poem's period,
170   And all combined in beauty's worthiness,
Yet should there hover in their restless heads,
One thought, one grace, one wonder at the least,
Which into words no virtue can digest.
But how unseemly is it for my sex,
My discipline of arms and chivalry,
My nature, and the terror of my name,
To harbour thoughts effeminate and faint!
Save only that in beauty's just applause,
With whose instinct the soul of man is touched,
180   And every warrior that is rapt with love
Of fame, of valour, and of victory,
Must needs have beauty beat on his conceits,
I thus conceiving and subduing, both,
That which hath stopped the tempest of the gods,
Even from the fiery spangled veil of heaven,
To feel the lovely warmth of shepherds' flames
And march in cottages of strewèd weeds,
Shall give the world to note, for all my birth,
That virtue solely is the sum of glory
190   And fashions men with true nobility.
Who's within there?
        Enter two or three [ATTENDANTS].

Hath Bajazeth been fed today?
ATTENDANT Ay, my lord.
TAMBURLAINE Bring him forth, and let us know if the town be
  ransacked.

                              [*Exeunt* ATTENDANTS.]
    Enter TECHELLES, THERIDAMAS, USUMCASANE, *and
    others.*

TECHELLES
  The town is ours, my lord, and fresh supply
  Of conquest and of spoil is offered us.

TAMBURLAINE
  That's well, Techelles, what's the news?

TECHELLES
  The Sultan and the Arabian king together,
  March on us with such eager violence   200
  As if there were no way but one with us.

TAMBURLAINE
  No more there is not, I warrant thee, Techelles.
    They bring in the TURK [BAJAZETH, *in his cage, followed
    by* ZABINA].

THERIDAMAS
  We know the victory is ours, my lord.
  But let us save the reverend Sultan's life
  For fair Zenocrate that so laments his state.

TAMBURLAINE
  That will we chiefly see unto, Theridamas,
  For sweet Zenocrate, whose worthiness
  Deserves a conquest over every heart.
  And now, my footstool, if I lose the field,
  You hope of liberty and restitution.   210
  Here let him stay, my masters, from the tents,
  Till we have made us ready for the field.
  Pray for us, Bajazeth, we are going.

                    Exeunt. [BAJAZETH *and* ZABINA *remain.*]

BAJAZETH
  Go, never to return with victory!
  Millions of men encompass thee about
  And gore thy body with as many wounds!

Sharp, forkèd arrows light upon thy horse!
Furies from the black Cocytus lake
Break up the earth, and with their firebrands
220   Enforce thee run upon the baneful pikes!
Volleys of shot pierce through thy charmèd skin,
And every bullet dipped in poisoned drugs!
Or roaring cannons sever all thy joints,
Making thee mount as high as eagles soar!

ZABINA

Let all the swords and lances in the field
Stick in his breast as in their proper rooms!
At every pore let blood come dropping forth,
That ling'ring pains may massacre his heart
And madness send his damnèd soul to hell!

BAJAZETH

230   Ah, fair Zabina, we may curse his power,
The heavens may frown, the earth for anger quake,
But such a star hath influence in his sword
As rules the skies, and countermands the gods
More than Cimmerian Styx or Destiny.
And then shall we in this detested guise,
With shame, with hunger, and with horror aye
Griping our bowels with retorquèd thoughts,
And have no hope to end our ecstasies.

ZABINA

Then is there left no Mahomet, no God,
240   No fiend, no Fortune, nor no hope of end
To our infamous, monstrous slaveries?
Gape, earth, and let the fiends infernal view
A hell as hopeless and as full of fear
As are the blasted banks of Erebus,
Where shaking ghosts with ever-howling groans
Hover about the ugly ferryman
To get a passage to Elysium!
Why should we live, O, wretches, beggars, slaves,
Why live we, Bajazeth, and build up nests
250   So high within the region of the air,
By living long in this oppression,

That all the world will see and laugh to scorn
The former triumphs of our mightiness
In this obscure infernal servitude?

BAJAZETH

O life more loathsome to my vexèd thoughts
Than noisome parbreak of the Stygian snakes
Which fills the nooks of hell with standing air,
Infecting all the ghosts with cureless griefs!
O dreary engines of my loathèd sight
That sees my crown, my honour, and my name   260
Thrust under yoke and thraldom of a thief,
Why feed ye still on day's accursèd beams
And sink not quite into my tortured soul?
You see my wife, my queen and emperess,
Brought up and proppèd by the hand of fame,
Queen of fifteen contributory queens,
Now thrown to rooms of black abjection,
Smearèd with blots of basest drudgery,
And villeiness to shame, disdain, and misery.
Accursèd Bajazeth, whose words of ruth,   270
That would with pity cheer Zabina's heart
And make our souls resolve in ceaseless tears,
Sharp hunger bites upon and gripes the root
From whence the issues of my thoughts do break.
O poor Zabina, O my queen, my queen,
Fetch me some water for my burning breast,
To cool and comfort me with longer date,
That, in the shortened sequel of my life,
I may pour forth my soul into thine arms
With words of love, whose moaning intercourse   280
Hath hitherto been stayed with wrath and hate
Of our expressless, banned inflictions.

ZABINA

Sweet Bajazeth, I will prolong thy life
As long as any blood or spark of breath
Can quench or cool the torments of my grief.

She goes out.

BAJAZETH

Now, Bajazeth, abridge thy baneful days
And beat thy brains out of thy conquered head,
Since other means are all forbidden me
That may be ministers of my decay.
290 O highest lamp of ever-living Jove,
Accursèd day, infected with my griefs,
Hide now thy stainèd face in endless night
And shut the windows of the lightsome heavens!
Let ugly Darkness with her rusty coach,
Engirt with tempests wrapped in pitchy clouds,
Smother the earth with never-fading mists,
And let her horses from their nostrils breathe
Rebellious winds and dreadful thunderclaps,
That in this terror Tamburlaine may live,
300 And my pined soul, resolved in liquid air,
May still excruciate his tormented thoughts!
Then let the stony dart of senseless cold
Pierce through the centre of my withered heart
And make a passage for my loathèd life!
   He brains himself against the cage.
   Enter ZABINA.

ZABINA

What do mine eyes behold? My husband dead!
His skull all riven in twain, his brains dashed out!
The brains of Bajazeth, my lord and sovereign!
O Bajazeth, my husband and my lord,
O Bajazeth, O Turk, O emperor – give him his liquor? Not I.
310 Bring milk and fire, and my blood I bring him again; tear me
in pieces, give me the sword with a ball of wildfire upon it.
Down with him, down with him! Go to my child. Away,
away, away! Ah, save that infant, save him, save him! I, even
I, speak to her. The sun was down. Streamers white, red,
black, here, here, here. Fling the meat in his face. Tamburlaine, Tamburlaine! Let the soldiers be buried. Hell, death,
Tamburlaine, hell! Make ready my coach, my chair, my
jewels. I come, I come, I come!
   She runs against the cage and brains herself.

[*Enter*] ZENOCRATE *with* ANIPPE.

ZENOCRATE

    Wretched Zenocrate, that livest to see
    Damascus' walls dyed with Egyptian blood,   320
    Thy father's subjects and thy countrymen,
    Thy streets strewed with dissevered joints of men
    And wounded bodies gasping yet for life,
    But most accurst to see the sun-bright troop
    Of heavenly virgins and unspotted maids,
    Whose looks might make the angry god of arms
    To break his sword and mildly treat of love,
    On horsemen's lances to be hoisted up
    And guiltlessly endure a cruel death!
    For every fell and stout Tartarian steed,   330
    That stamped on others with their thund'ring hoofs,
    When all their riders charged their quivering spears,
    Began to check the ground and rein themselves,
    Gazing upon the beauty of their looks.
    Ah, Tamburlaine, wert thou the cause of this,
    That term'st Zenocrate thy dearest love,
    Whose lives were dearer to Zenocrate
    Than her own life, or aught save thine own love?
    [*She sees the bodies of* BAJAZETH *and* ZABINA.]
    But see, another bloody spectacle!
    Ah, wretched eyes, the enemies of my heart,   340
    How are ye glutted with these grievous objects,
    And tell my soul more tales of bleeding ruth!
    See, see, Anippe, if they breathe or no.

ANIPPE

    No breath, nor sense, nor motion in them both.
    Ah, madam, this their slavery hath enforced,
    And ruthless cruelty of Tamburlaine.

ZENOCRATE

    Earth, cast up fountains from thy entrails,
    And wet thy cheeks for their untimely deaths;
    Shake with their weight in sign of fear and grief;
    Blush, heaven, that gave them honour at their birth,   350
    And let them die a death so barbarous!

Those that are proud of fickle empery
And place their chiefest good in earthly pomp,
Behold the Turk and his great emperess!
Ah, Tamburlaine my love, sweet Tamburlaine,
That fight'st for sceptres and for slippery crowns,
Behold the Turk and his great emperess!
Thou that in conduct of thy happy stars,
Sleep'st every night with conquest on thy brows,
360   And yet wouldst shun the wavering turns of war,
In fear and feeling of the like distress,
Behold the Turk and his great emperess!
Ah, mighty Jove and holy Mahomet,
Pardon my love, O, pardon his contempt
Of earthly fortune and respect of pity,
And let not conquest ruthlessly pursued
Be equally against his life incensed
In this great Turk and hapless emperess!
And pardon me that was not moved with ruth
370   To see them live so long in misery.
Ah, what may chance to thee, Zenocrate?

ANIPPE

Madam, content yourself, and be resolved
Your love hath Fortune so at his command
That she shall stay, and turn her wheel no more
As long as life maintains his mighty arm
That fights for honour to adorn your head.
    Enter [PHILEMUS,] *a messenger.*

ZENOCRATE

What other heavy news now brings Philemus?

PHILEMUS

Madam, your father and th'Arabian king,
The first affecter of your excellence,
380   Comes now as Turnus 'gainst Aeneas did,
Armèd with lance into th'Egyptian fields,
Ready for battle 'gainst my lord the king.

ZENOCRATE

Now shame and duty, love and fear, presents
A thousand sorrows to my martyred soul.

Whom should I wish the fatal victory,
When my poor pleasures are divided thus
And racked by duty from my cursèd heart?
My father and my first betrothèd love
Must fight against my life and present love,
Wherein the change I use condemns my faith   390
And makes my deeds infamous through the world.
But as the gods, to end the Trojans' toil,
Prevented Turnus of Lavinia
And fatally enriched Aeneas' love,
So, for a final issue to my griefs,
To pacify my country and my love,
Must Tamburlaine, by their resistless powers,
With virtue of a gentle victory
Conclude a league of honour to my hope;
Then, as the powers divine have preordained,   400
With happy safety of my father's life
Send like defence of fair Arabia.
> *They sound to the battle, and* TAMBURLAINE *enjoys the*
> *victory. After,* [*the* KING OF] ARABIA *enters wounded.*

ARABIA

What cursèd power guides the murdering hands
Of this infamous tyrant's soldiers,
That no escape may save their enemies,
Nor fortune keep themselves from victory?
Lie down, Arabia, wounded to the death,
And let Zenocrate's fair eyes behold
That, as for her thou bear'st these wretched arms,
Even so for her thou diest in these arms,   410
Leaving thy blood for witness of thy love.

ZENOCRATE

Too dear a witness for such love, my lord.
Behold Zenocrate, the cursèd object
Whose fortunes never masterèd her griefs!
Behold her wounded in conceit for thee,
As much as thy fair body is for me.

ARABIA

Then shall I die with full contented heart,

Having beheld divine Zenocrate,
Whose sight with joy would take away my life,
420   As now it bringeth sweetness to my wound,
If I had not been wounded as I am.
Ah, that the deadly pangs I suffer now
Would lend an hour's licence to my tongue
To make discourse of some sweet accidents
Have chanced thy merits in this worthless bondage,
And that I might be privy to the state
Of thy deserved contentment and thy love!
But, making now a virtue of thy sight
To drive all sorrow from my fainting soul,
430   Since death denies me further cause of joy,
Deprived of care, my heart with comfort dies,
Since thy desirèd hand shall close mine eyes.
    [*He dies.*]
    Enter TAMBURLAINE *leading the* SULTAN; TECHELLES,
    THERIDAMAS, USUMCASANE [*bearing a crown for*
    ZENOCRATE], *with others.*

TAMBURLAINE
Come, happy father of Zenocrate,
A title higher than thy Sultan's name.
Though my right hand have thus enthrallèd thee,
Thy princely daughter here shall set thee free;
She that hath calmed the fury of my sword,
Which had ere this been bathed in streams of blood
As vast and deep as Euphrates or Nile.

ZENOCRATE
440   O, sight thrice welcome to my joyful soul,
To see the king my father issue safe
From dangerous battle of my conquering love!

SULTAN
Well met, my only dear Zenocrate,
Though with the loss of Egypt and my crown.

TAMBURLAINE
'Twas I, my lord, that gat the victory.
And therefore grieve not at your overthrow,
Since I shall render all into your hands

And add more strength to your dominions
Than ever yet confirmed th'Egyptian crown.
The god of war resigns his room to me,   450
Meaning to make me general of the world.
Jove, viewing me in arms, looks pale and wan,
Fearing my power should pull him from his throne.
Where'er I come, the Fatal Sisters sweat,
And grisly Death, by running to and fro
To do their ceaseless homage to my sword;
And here in Afric, where it seldom rains,
Since I arrived with my triumphant host
Have swelling clouds, drawn from wide gasping wounds,
Been oft resolved in bloody purple showers –   460
A meteor that might terrify the earth
And make it quake at every drop it drinks.
Millions of souls sit on the banks of Styx,
Waiting the back return of Charon's boat;
Hell and Elysium swarm with ghosts of men
That I have sent from sundry foughten fields
To spread my fame through hell and up to heaven.
And see, my lord, a sight of strange import:
Emperors and kings lie breathless at my feet.
The Turk and his great empress, as it seems,   470
Left to themselves while we were at the fight,
Have desperately dispatched their slavish lives.
With them Arabia too hath left his life –
All sights of power to grace my victory.
And such are objects fit for Tamburlaine,
Wherein as in a mirror may be seen
His honour, that consists in shedding blood
When men presume to manage arms with him.

SULTAN

Mighty hath God and Mahomet made thy hand,
Renownèd Tamburlaine, to whom all kings   480
Of force must yield their crowns and emperies.
And I am pleased with this my overthrow
If, as beseems a person of thy state,
Thou hast with honour used Zenocrate.

TAMBURLAINE
Her state and person wants no pomp, you see;
And for all blot of foul inchastity,
I record heaven, her heavenly self is clear.
Then let me find no further time to grace
Her princely temples with the Persian crown;
490   But here these kings, that on my fortunes wait,
And have been crowned for provèd worthiness
Even by this hand that shall establish them,
Shall now, adjoining all their hands with mine,
Invest her here my queen of Persia.
What saith the noble Sultan and Zenocrate?

SULTAN
I yield with thanks and protestations
Of endless honour to thee for her love.

TAMBURLAINE
Then doubt I not but fair Zenocrate
Will soon consent to satisfy us both.

ZENOCRATE
500   Else should I much forget myself, my lord.

THERIDAMAS
Then let us set the crown upon her head,
That long hath lingered for so high a seat.

TECHELLES
My hand is ready to perform the deed,
For now her marriage time shall work us rest.

USUMCASANE
And here's the crown, my lord. Help set it on.

TAMBURLAINE
Then sit thou down, divine Zenocrate.
And here we crown thee queen of Persia
And all the kingdoms and dominions
That late the power of Tamburlaine subdued.
510   As Juno, when the giants were suppressed,
That darted mountains at her brother Jove,
So looks my love, shadowing in her brows
Triumphs and trophies for my victories;
Or, as Latona's daughter, bent to arms,

Adding more courage to my conquering mind.
To gratify thee, sweet Zenocrate,
Egyptians, Moors, and men of Asia,
From Barbary unto the Western Indie,
Shall pay a yearly tribute to thy sire,
And from the bounds of Afric to the banks   520
Of Ganges shall his mighty arm extend.
And now, my lords and loving followers,
That purchased kingdoms by your martial deeds,
Cast off your armour, put on scarlet robes,
Mount up your royal places of estate,
Environèd with troops of noble men,
And there make laws to rule your provinces.
Hang up your weapons on Alcides' post,
For Tamburlaine takes truce with all the world.
    [*To* ZENOCRATE]
Thy first betrothèd love, Arabia,   530
Shall we with honour, as beseems, entomb,
With this great Turk and his fair emperess.
Then after all these solemn exequies,
We will our celebrated rites of marriage solemnize.
                                            [*Exeunt.*]

TAMBURLAINE
THE GREAT,
PART TWO

[Dramatis Personae

THE PROLOGUE
ORCANES, *King of Natolia*
GAZELLUS, *Viceroy of Byron*
URIBASSA, *a Natolian lord*
SIGISMOND, *King of Hungary*
FREDERICK, *lord of Buda*
BALDWIN, *lord of Bohemia*
CALLAPINE, *son to Bajazeth, and prisoner to Tamburlaine*
ALMEDA, *his keeper*
TAMBURLAINE, *King of Persia*
ZENOCRATE, *wife to Tamburlaine*
CALYPHAS ⎫
AMYRAS ⎬ *Tamburlaine's sons*
CELEBINUS ⎭
THERIDAMAS, *King of Argier*
TECHELLES, *King of Fez*
USUMCASANE, *King of Morocco*
A MESSENGER
THREE PHYSICIANS
KING OF TREBIZOND
KING OF SORIA
KING OF JERUSALEM
SOLDIERS
PIONERS
A CAPTAIN OF BALSERA
OLYMPIA, *wife to the Captain of Balsera*
THE CAPTAIN'S SON
PERDICAS, *companion to Calyphas*

TURKISH CONCUBINES
GOVERNOR OF BABYLON
MAXIMUS
CITIZENS
KING OF AMASIA
A CAPTAIN
ATTENDANTS]

[*Enter*] *the* PROLOGUE.

PROLOGUE

The general welcome Tamburlaine received
When he arrivèd last upon our stage
Hath made our poet pen his second part,
Where death cuts off the progress of his pomp
And murd'rous Fates throws all his triumphs down.   5
But what became of fair Zenocrate,
And with how many cities' sacrifice
He celebrated her sad funeral,
Himself in presence shall unfold at large.

                                                [*Exit.*]

ACT 1

Scene 1

[*Enter*] ORCANES *King of Natolia,* GAZELLUS *viceroy of Byron,* URIBASSA, *and their train, with drums and trumpets.*

ORCANES
Egregious viceroys of these eastern parts,
Placed by the issue of great Bajazeth,
And sacred lord, the mighty Callapine,
Who lives in Egypt prisoner to that slave
Which kept his father in an iron cage:
Now have we marched from fair Natolia
Two hundred leagues, and on Danubius' banks
Our warlike host in complete armour rest,
Where Sigismond the king of Hungary
10   Should meet our person to conclude a truce.
What, shall we parley with the Christian,
Or cross the stream and meet him in the field?

GAZELLUS
King of Natolia, let us treat of peace.
We all are glutted with the Christians' blood,
And have a greater foe to fight against:
Proud Tamburlaine, that now in Asia
Near Guyron's head doth set his conquering feet,
And means to fire Turkey as he goes.
'Gainst him, my lord, must you address your power.

URIBASSA
20   Besides, King Sigismond hath brought from Christendom

More than his camp of stout Hungarians,
Slavonians, Almains, rutters, Muffs, and Danes,
That with the halberd, lance, and murdering axe
Will hazard that we might with surety hold.

ORCANES

Though from the shortest northern parallel,
Vast Gruntland, compassed with the frozen sea,
Inhabited with tall and sturdy men,
Giants as big as hugy Polypheme,
Millions of soldiers cut the Arctic line,
Bringing the strength of Europe to these arms,   30
Our Turkey blades shall glide through all their throats
And make this champian mead a bloody fen.
Danubius' stream, that runs to Trebizond,
Shall carry wrapped within his scarlet waves,
As martial presents to our friends at home,
The slaughtered bodies of these Christians.
The Terrene main, wherein Danubius falls,
Shall by this battle be the bloody sea.
The wand'ring sailors of proud Italy
Shall meet those Christians fleeting with the tide,   40
Beating in heaps against their argosies,
And make fair Europe, mounted on her bull,
Trapped with the wealth and riches of the world,
Alight and wear a woeful mourning weed.

GAZELLUS

Yet, stout Orcanes, prorex of the world,
Since Tamburlaine hath mustered all his men,
Marching from Cairon northward with his camp
To Alexandria and the frontier towns,
Meaning to make a conquest of our land,
'Tis requisite to parley for a peace   50
With Sigismond the King of Hungary,
And save our forces for the hot assaults
Proud Tamburlaine intends Natolia.

ORCANES

Viceroy of Byron, wisely hast thou said.
My realm, the centre of our empery,

Once lost, all Turkey would be overthrown,
And for that cause the Christians shall have peace.
Slavonians, Almains, rutters, Muffs, and Danes,
Fear not Orcanes, but great Tamburlaine –
60   Nor he, but Fortune that hath made him great.
We have revolted Grecians, Albanese,
Sicilians, Jews, Arabians, Turks, and Moors,
Natolians, Sorians, black Egyptians,
Illyrians, Thracians, and Bithynians,
Enough to swallow forceless Sigismond,
Yet scarce enough t'encounter Tamburlaine.
He brings a world of people to the field.
From Scythia to the oriental plage
Of India, where raging Lantchidol
70   Beats on the regions with his boisterous blows,
That never seaman yet discoverèd,
All Asia is in arms with Tamburlaine.
Even from the midst of fiery Cancer's tropic
To Amazonia under Capricorn,
And thence as far as Archipelago,
All Afric is in arms with Tamburlaine.
Therefore, viceroys, the Christians must have peace.

> [*Enter*] SIGISMOND, FREDERICK, BALDWIN, *and their*
> *train, with drums and trumpets.*

SIGISMOND

Orcanes, as our legates promised thee,
We with our peers have crossed Danubius' stream
80   To treat of friendly peace or deadly war.
Take which thou wilt, for as the Romans used,
I here present thee with a naked sword.

> [*He presents his sword.*]

Wilt thou have war, then shake this blade at me;
If peace, restore it to my hands again,
And I will sheathe it to confirm the same.

ORCANES

Stay, Sigismond. Forgett'st thou I am he
That with the cannon shook Vienna walls
And made it dance upon the continent,

As when the massy substance of the earth
Quiver about the axletree of heaven?   90
Forgett'st thou that I sent a shower of darts,
Mingled with powdered shot and feathered steel,
So thick upon the blink-eyed burghers' heads,
That thou thyself, then County Palatine,
The king of Boheme, and the Austric duke
Sent heralds out, which basely on their knees
In all your names desired a truce of me?
Forgett'st thou that, to have me raise my siege,
Wagons of gold were set before my tent,
Stamped with the princely fowl that in her wings   100
Carries the fearful thunderbolts of Jove?
How canst thou think of this and offer war?

SIGISMOND
Vienna was besieged, and I was there,
Then County Palatine, but now a king,
And what we did was in extremity.
But now, Orcanes, view my royal host
That hides these plains, and seems as vast and wide
As doth the desert of Arabia
To those that stand on Baghdad's lofty tower,
Or as the ocean to the traveller   110
That rests upon the snowy Apennines;
And tell me whether I should stoop so low,
Or treat of peace with the Natolian king.

GAZELLUS
Kings of Natolia and of Hungary,
We came from Turkey to confirm a league,
And not to dare each other to the field.
A friendly parley might become ye both.

FREDERICK
And we from Europe to the same intent,
Which if your general refuse or scorn,
Our tents are pitched, our men stand in array,   120
Ready to charge you ere you stir your feet.

ORCANES
So prest are we. But yet if Sigismond

Speak as a friend and stand not upon terms,
Here is his sword; let peace be ratified
On these conditions specified before,
Drawn with advice of our ambassadors.

SIGISMOND

Then here I sheathe it, and give thee my hand
Never to draw it out or manage arms
Against thyself or thy confederates,
130   But, whilst I live, will be at truce with thee.

ORCANES

But, Sigismond, confirm it with an oath
And swear in sight of heaven and by thy Christ.

SIGISMOND

By Him that made the world and saved my soul,
The son of God and issue of a maid,
Sweet Jesus Christ, I solemnly protest
And vow to keep this peace inviolable.

ORCANES

By sacred Mahomet, the friend of God,
Whose holy Alcoran remains with us,
Whose glorious body, when he left the world,
140   Closed in a coffin, mounted up the air
And hung on stately Mecca's temple roof,
I swear to keep this truce inviolable;
Of whose conditions and our solemn oaths
Signed with our hands, each shall retain a scroll
As memorable witness of our league.
Now, Sigismond, if any Christian king
Encroach upon the confines of thy realm,
Send word Orcanes of Natolia
Confirmed this league beyond Danubius' stream,
150   And they will, trembling, sound a quick retreat,
So am I feared among all nations.

SIGISMOND

If any heathen potentate or king
Invade Natolia, Sigismond will send
A hundred thousand horse trained to the war
And backed by stout lancers of Germany,

The strength and sinews of th'imperial seat.

ORCANES

I thank thee, Sigismond; but when I war,
All Asia Minor, Africa, and Greece,
Follow my standard and my thund'ring drums.
Come, let us go and banquet in our tents.   160
I will dispatch chief of my army hence
To fair Natolia and to Trebizond,
To stay my coming 'gainst proud Tamburlaine.
Friend Sigismond, and peers of Hungary,
Come banquet and carouse with us a while
And then depart we to our territories.

Exeunt.

Scene 2

[*Enter*] CALLAPINE *with* ALMEDA, *his keeper.*

CALLAPINE

Sweet Almeda, pity the ruthful plight
Of Callapine, the son of Bajazeth,
Born to be monarch of the western world,
Yet here detained by cruel Tamburlaine.

ALMEDA

My lord, I pity it, and with my heart
Wish your release. But he whose wrath is death,
My sovereign lord, renownèd Tamburlaine,
Forbids you further liberty than this.

CALLAPINE

Ah, were I now but half so eloquent
To paint in words what I'll perform in deeds,   10
I know thou wouldst depart from hence with me.

ALMEDA

Not for all Afric. Therefore move me not.

CALLAPINE

Yet hear me speak, my gentle Almeda.

ALMEDA
　　No speech to that end, by your favour, sir.
CALLAPINE
　　By Cairo runs –
ALMEDA
　　No talk of running, I tell you, sir.
CALLAPINE
　　A little further, gentle Almeda.
ALMEDA
　　Well, sir, what of this?
CALLAPINE
　　By Cairo runs to Alexandria Bay

20　Darote's streams, wherein at anchor lies
　　A Turkish galley of my royal fleet,
　　Waiting my coming to the river side,
　　Hoping by some means I shall be released,
　　Which, when I come aboard, will hoist up sail
　　And soon put forth into the Terrene Sea,
　　Where 'twixt the isles of Cyprus and of Crete
　　We quickly may in Turkish seas arrive.
　　Then shalt thou see a hundred kings and more,
　　Upon their knees, all bid me welcome home.

30　Amongst so many crowns of burnished gold
　　Choose which thou wilt; all are at thy command.
　　A thousand galleys manned with Christian slaves
　　I freely give thee, which shall cut the Straits
　　And bring armadoes from the coasts of Spain,
　　Fraughted with gold of rich America.
　　The Grecian virgins shall attend on thee,
　　Skilful in music and in amorous lays,
　　As fair as was Pygmalion's ivory girl,
　　Or lovely Io metamorphosèd.

40　With naked negroes shall thy coach be drawn,
　　And as thou rid'st in triumph through the streets,
　　The pavement underneath thy chariot wheels
　　With Turkey carpets shall be coverèd,
　　And cloth of arras hung about the walls,
　　Fit objects for thy princely eye to pierce.

A hundred bassoes, clothed in crimson silk,
Shall ride before thee on Barbarian steeds,
And when thou goest, a golden canopy
Enchased with precious stones which shine as bright
As that fair veil that covers all the world,   50
When Phoebus, leaping from his hemisphere,
Descendeth downward to th'Antipodes –
And more than this, for all I cannot tell.

ALMEDA

How far hence lies the galley, say you?

CALLAPINE

Sweet Almeda, scarce half a league from hence.

ALMEDA

But need we not be spied going aboard?

CALLAPINE

Betwixt the hollow hanging of a hill
And crooked bending of a craggy rock,
The sails wrapped up, the mast and tacklings down,
She lies so close that none can find her out.   60

ALMEDA I like that well. But tell me, my lord, if I should let you
go, would you be as good as your word? Shall I be made a
king for my labour?

CALLAPINE

As I am Callapine the emperor,
And by the hand of Mahomet, I swear
Thou shalt be crowned a king and be my mate.

ALMEDA

Then here I swear, as I am Almeda,
Your keeper under Tamburlaine the Great –
For that's the style and title I have yet –
Although he sent a thousand armèd men   70
To intercept this haughty enterprise,
Yet would I venture to conduct your grace
And die before I brought you back again.

CALLAPINE

Thanks, gentle Almeda. Then let us haste,
Lest time be past and, ling'ring, let us both.

ALMEDA
　　When you will, my lord. I am ready.
CALLAPINE
　　Even straight. And farewell, cursèd Tamburlaine!
　　Now go I to revenge my father's death.

　　　　　　　　　　　　　　　　　　　　　Exeunt.

Scene 3

[*Enter*] TAMBURLAINE *with* ZENOCRATE, *and his three sons,* CALYPHAS, AMYRAS, *and* CELEBINUS, *with drums and trumpets.* [*A throne is brought on.*]

TAMBURLAINE
　　Now, bright Zenocrate, the world's fair eye,
　　Whose beams illuminate the lamps of heaven,
　　Whose cheerful looks do clear the cloudy air
　　And clothe it in a crystal livery,
　　Now rest thee here on fair Larissa plains,
　　Where Egypt and the Turkish empire parts,
　　Between thy sons that shall be emperors
　　And every one commander of a world.
ZENOCRATE
　　Sweet Tamburlaine, when wilt thou leave these arms
10　And save thy sacred person free from scathe
　　And dangerous chances of the wrathful war?
TAMBURLAINE
　　When heaven shall cease to move on both the poles,
　　And when the ground whereon my soldiers march
　　Shall rise aloft and touch the hornèd moon,
　　And not before, my sweet Zenocrate.
　　Sit up and rest thee like a lovely queen.
　　So, now she sits in pomp and majesty,
　　When these my sons, more precious in mine eyes
　　Than all the wealthy kingdoms I subdued,
20　Placed by her side, look on their mother's face.
　　But yet methinks their looks are amorous,

Not martial as the sons of Tamburlaine;
Water and air, being symbolized in one,
Argue their want of courage and of wit;
Their hair as white as milk and soft as down,
Which should be like the quills of porcupines,
As black as jet, and hard as iron or steel,
Bewrays they are too dainty for the wars.
Their fingers made to quaver on a lute,
Their arms to hang about a lady's neck,   30
Their legs to dance and caper in the air,
Would make me think them bastards, not my sons,
But that I know they issued from thy womb,
That never looked on man but Tamburlaine.

ZENOCRATE

My gracious lord, they have their mother's looks,
But when they list, their conquering father's heart.
This lovely boy, the youngest of the three,
Not long ago bestrid a Scythian steed,
Trotting the ring and tilting at a glove,
Which when he tainted with his slender rod,   40
He reined him straight and made him so curvet
As I cried out for fear he should have fall'n.

TAMBURLAINE [*to* CELEBINUS]

Well done, my boy, thou shalt have shield and lance,
Armour of proof, horse, helm, and curtle-axe,
And I will teach thee how to charge thy foe
And harmless run among the deadly pikes.
If thou wilt love the wars and follow me,
Thou shalt be made a king and reign with me,
Keeping in iron cages emperors.
If thou exceed thy elder brothers' worth   50
And shine in complete virtue more than they,
Thou shalt be king before them, and thy seed
Shall issue crownèd from their mother's womb.

CELEBINUS

Yes, father, you shall see me, if I live,
Have under me as many kings as you
And march with such a multitude of men

As all the world shall tremble at their view.

TAMBURLAINE

These words assure me, boy, thou art my son.
When I am old and cannot manage arms,
60   Be thou the scourge and terror of the world.

AMYRAS

Why may not I, my lord, as well as he,
Be termed the scourge and terror of the world?

TAMBURLAINE

Be all a scourge and terror to the world,
Or else you are not sons of Tamburlaine.

CALYPHAS

But while my brothers follow arms, my lord,
Let me accompany my gracious mother.
They are enough to conquer all the world,
And you have won enough for me to keep.

TAMBURLAINE

Bastardly boy, sprung from some coward's loins
70   And not the issue of great Tamburlaine,
Of all the provinces I have subdued,
Thou shalt not have a foot, unless thou bear
A mind courageous and invincible.
For he shall wear the crown of Persia
Whose head hath deepest scars, whose breast most wounds,
Which, being wroth, sends lightning from his eyes,
And in the furrows of his frowning brows
Harbours revenge, war, death, and cruelty.
For in a field, whose superficies
80   Is covered with a liquid purple veil
And sprinkled with the brains of slaughtered men,
My royal chair of state shall be advanced,
And he that means to place himself therein
Must armèd wade up to the chin in blood.

ZENOCRATE

My lord, such speeches to our princely sons
Dismays their minds before they come to prove
The wounding troubles angry war affords.

CELEBINUS

No, madam, these are speeches fit for us.
For if his chair were in a sea of blood,
I would prepare a ship and sail to it   90
Ere I would lose the title of a king.

AMYRAS

And I would strive to swim through pools of blood
Or make a bridge of murdered carcasses,
Whose arches should be framed with bones of Turks,
Ere I would lose the title of a king.

TAMBURLAINE

Well, lovely boys, you shall be emperors both,
Stretching your conquering arms from east to west.
    [*To* CALYPHAS]
And, sirrah, if you mean to wear a crown,
When we shall meet the Turkish deputy
And all his viceroys, snatch it from his head,   100
And cleave his pericranion with thy sword.

CALYPHAS

If any man will hold him, I will strike,
And cleave him to the channel with my sword.

TAMBURLAINE

Hold him and cleave him, too, or I'll cleave thee,
For we will march against them presently.
Theridamas, Techelles, and Casane
Promised to meet me on Larissa plains
With hosts apiece against this Turkish crew,
For I have sworn by sacred Mahomet
To make it parcel of my empery.   110
The trumpets sound, Zenocrate. They come.
    Enter THERIDAMAS *and his train, with drums and*
    trumpets.
Welcome, Theridamas, King of Argier!

THERIDAMAS

My lord, the great and mighty Tamburlaine,
Arch-monarch of the world, I offer here
My crown, myself, and all the power I have,

In all affection at thy kingly feet.
[*He presents his crown to* TAMBURLAINE.]
TAMBURLAINE
Thanks, good Theridamas.
THERIDAMAS
Under my colours march ten thousand Greeks,
And of Argier and Afric's frontier towns
120   Twice twenty thousand valiant men-at-arms,
All which have sworn to sack Natolia.
Five hundred brigantines are under sail,
Meet for your service on the sea, my lord,
That, launching from Argier to Tripoli,
Will quickly ride before Natolia
And batter down the castles on the shore.
TAMBURLAINE
Well said, Argier. Receive thy crown again.
[*He returns* THERIDAMAS's *crown.*]
Enter TECHELLES *and* USUMCASANE *together.*
Kings of Moroccus and of Fez, welcome.
USUMCASANE [*presenting his crown to* TAMBURLAINE]
Magnificent and peerless Tamburlaine,
130   I and my neighbour King of Fez have brought,
To aid thee in this Turkish expedition,
A hundred thousand expert soldiers.
From Azamor to Tunis near the sea
Is Barbary unpeopled for thy sake,
And all the men in armour under me,
Which with my crown I gladly offer thee.
TAMBURLAINE [*returning* USUMCASANE's *crown*]
Thanks, King of Moroccus. Take your crown again.
TECHELLES [*presenting his crown to* TAMBURLAINE]
And, mighty Tamburlaine, our earthly god,
Whose looks make this inferior world to quake,
140   I here present thee with the crown of Fez
And with an host of Moors trained to the war,
Whose coal-black faces make their foes retire
And quake for fear, as if infernal Jove,
Meaning to aid thee in these Turkish arms,

Should pierce the black circumference of hell
With ugly Furies bearing fiery flags
And millions of his strong tormenting spirits.
From strong Tesella unto Biledull
All Barbary is unpeopled for thy sake.

TAMBURLAINE [*returning* TECHELLES'*s crown*]
Thanks, King of Fez. Take here thy crown again.   150
Your presence, loving friends and fellow kings,
Makes me to surfeit in conceiving joy.
If all the crystal gates of Jove's high court
Were opened wide, and I might enter in
To see the state and majesty of heaven,
It could not more delight me than your sight.
Now will we banquet on these plains a while
And after march to Turkey with our camp,
In number more than are the drops that fall
When Boreas rents a thousand swelling clouds;   160
And proud Orcanes of Natolia
With all his viceroys shall be so afraid
That though the stones, as at Deucalion's flood,
Were turned to men, he should be overcome.
Such lavish will I make of Turkish blood
That Jove shall send his wingèd messenger
To bid me sheathe my sword and leave the field.
The sun, unable to sustain the sight,
Shall hide his head in Thetis' watery lap
And leave his steeds to fair Boötes' charge;   170
For half the world shall perish in this fight.
But now, my friends, let me examine ye.
How have ye spent your absent time from me?

USUMCASANE
My lord, our men of Barbary have marched
Four hundred miles with armour on their backs
And lain in leaguer fifteen months and more.
For since we left you at the Sultan's court,
We have subdued the southern Guallatia
And all the land unto the coast of Spain.
We kept the narrow Strait of Gibraltar,   180

And made Canarea call us kings and lords,
Yet never did they recreate themselves
Or cease one day from war and hot alarms;
And therefore let them rest a while, my lord.

TAMBURLAINE

They shall, Casane, and 'tis time, i'faith.

TECHELLES

And I have marched along the river Nile
To Machda, where the mighty Christian priest
Called John the Great, sits in a milk-white robe,
Whose triple mitre I did take by force
190 And made him swear obedience to my crown.
From thence unto Cazates did I march,
Where Amazonians met me in the field,
With whom, being women, I vouchsafed a league;
And with my power did march to Zanzibar,
The western part of Afric, where I viewed
The Ethiopian sea, rivers and lakes,
But neither man nor child in all the land.
Therefore I took my course to Manico,
Where, unresisted, I removed my camp;
200 And by the coast of Byather at last
I came to Cubar, where the negroes dwell,
And, conquering that, made haste to Nubia.
There, having sacked Borno, the kingly seat,
I took the king and led him bound in chains
Unto Damasco, where I stayed before.

TAMBURLAINE

Well done, Techelles. What saith Theridamas?

THERIDAMAS

I left the confines and the bounds of Afric
And made a voyage into Europe,
Where by the river Tyros I subdued
210 Stoka, Podalia, and Codemia,
Then crossed the sea and came to Oblia,
And Nigra Silva, where the devils dance,
Which in despite of them I set on fire.
From thence I crossed the gulf called by the name

Mare Maggiore of th'inhabitants.
Yet shall my soldiers make no period
Until Natolia kneel before your feet.

TAMBURLAINE

Then will we triumph, banquet, and carouse;
Cooks shall have pensions to provide us cates
And glut us with the dainties of the world.   220
Lachryma Christi and Calabrian wines
Shall common soldiers drink in quaffing bowls –
Ay, liquid gold when we have conquered him,
Mingled with coral and with orient pearl.
Come, let us banquet and carouse the whiles.

Exeunt.

ACT 2

Scene 1

[*Enter*] SIGISMOND, FREDERICK, BALDWIN, *with their
train.*

SIGISMOND

Now say, my lords of Buda and Bohemia,
What motion is it that inflames your thoughts
And stirs your valours to such sudden arms?

FREDERICK

Your majesty remembers, I am sure,
What cruel slaughter of our Christian bloods
These heathenish Turks and pagans lately made
Betwixt the city Zula and Danubius,
How through the midst of Varna and Bulgaria
And almost to the very walls of Rome

10   They have, not long since, massacred our camp.
It resteth now, then, that your majesty
Take all advantages of time and power,
And work revenge upon these infidels.
Your highness knows for Tamburlaine's repair –
That strikes a terror to all Turkish hearts –
Natolia hath dismissed the greatest part
Of all his army, pitched against our power
Betwixt Cutheia and Orminius' mount,
And sent them marching up to Belgasar,

20   Acantha, Antioch, and Caesaria,
To aid the kings of Soria and Jerusalem.
Now then, my lord, advantage take hereof,

And issue suddenly upon the rest,
That, in the fortune of their overthrow,
We may discourage all the pagan troop
That dare attempt to war with Christians.

SIGISMOND

But calls not, then, your grace to memory
The league we lately made with King Orcanes,
Confirmed by oath and articles of peace,
And calling Christ for record of our truths?   30
This should be treachery and violence
Against the grace of our profession.

BALDWIN

No whit, my lord. For with such infidels,
In whom no faith nor true religion rests,
We are not bound to those accomplishments
The holy laws of Christendom enjoin;
But as the faith which they profanely plight
Is not by necessary policy
To be esteemed assurance for ourselves,
So what we vow to them should not infringe   40
Our liberty of arms and victory.

SIGISMOND

Though I confess the oaths they undertake
Breed little strength to our security,
Yet those infirmities that thus defame
Their faiths, their honours, and their religion
Should not give us presumption to the like.
Our faiths are sound and must be consummate,
Religious, righteous, and inviolate.

FREDERICK

Assure your grace, 'tis superstition
To stand so strictly on dispensive faith.   50
And should we lose the opportunity
That God hath given to venge our Christians' death
And scourge their foul blasphemous paganism?
As fell to Saul, to Balaam, and the rest
That would not kill and curse at God's command,
So surely will the vengeance of the Highest,

And jealous anger of His fearful arm,
Be poured with rigour on our sinful heads
If we neglect this offered victory.

SIGISMOND

60   Then arm, my lords, and issue suddenly,
Giving commandment to our general host
With expedition to assail the pagan
And take the victory our God hath given.

Exeunt.

Scene 2

[*Enter*] ORCANES, GAZELLUS, URIBASSA, *with their train.*

ORCANES

Gazellus, Uribassa, and the rest,
Now will we march from proud Orminius' mount
To fair Natolia, where our neighbour kings
Expect our power and our royal presence,
T'encounter with the cruel Tamburlaine
That nigh Larissa sways a mighty host
And with the thunder of his martial tools
Makes earthquakes in the hearts of men and heaven.

GAZELLUS

And now come we to make his sinews shake
10   With greater power than erst his pride hath felt.
An hundred kings by scores will bid him arms,
And hundred thousands subjects to each score –
Which, if a shower of wounding thunderbolts
Should break out of the bowels of the clouds
And fall as thick as hail upon our heads
In partial aid of that proud Scythian,
Yet should our courages and steelèd crests
And numbers more than infinite of men
Be able to withstand and conquer him.

URIBASSA

   Methinks I see how glad the Christian king   20
   Is made for joy of your admitted truce,
   That could not but before be terrified
   With unacquainted power of our host.
     Enter a MESSENGER.

MESSENGER

   Arm, dread sovereign, and my noble lords!
   The treacherous army of the Christians,
   Taking advantage of your slender power,
   Comes marching on us and determines straight
   To bid us battle for our dearest lives.

ORCANES

   Traitors, villains, damnèd Christians!
   Have I not here the articles of peace   30
   And solemn covenants we have both confirmed,
   He by his Christ and I by Mahomet?

GAZELLUS

   Hell and confusion light upon their heads
   That with such treason seek our overthrow
   And cares so little for their prophet, Christ!

ORCANES

   Can there be such deceit in Christians,
   Or treason in the fleshly heart of man,
   Whose shape is figure of the highest god?
   Then if there be a Christ, as Christians say
   (But in their deeds deny him for their Christ),   40
   If he be son to everliving Jove
   And hath the power of his outstretched arm,
   If he be jealous of his name and honour
   As is our holy prophet Mahomet,
   Take here these papers as our sacrifice
   And witness of thy servant's perjury!
    [*He burns the articles of peace.*]
   Open, thou shining veil of Cynthia,
   And make a passage from the empyreal heaven,
   That He that sits on high and never sleeps,

50   Nor in one place is circumscriptible,
        But everywhere fills every continent
        With strange infusion of his sacred vigour,
        May in his endless power and purity
        Behold and venge this traitor's perjury!
        Thou Christ, that art esteemed omnipotent,
        If thou wilt prove thyself a perfect God
        Worthy the worship of all faithful hearts,
        Be now revenged upon this traitor's soul,
        And make the power I have left behind
60   (Too little to defend our guiltless lives)
        Sufficient to discomfort and confound
        The trustless force of those false Christians.
        To arms, my lords! On Christ still let us cry.
        If there be Christ, we shall have victory.

                                                        [*Exeunt.*]

[Scene 3]

        Sound to the battle, and SIGISMOND *comes out wounded.*
SIGISMOND
        Discomfited is all the Christian host,
        And God hath thundered vengeance from on high
        For my accurst and hateful perjury.
        O just and dreadful punisher of sin,
        Let the dishonour of the pains I feel
        In this my mortal well-deservèd wound
        End all my penance in my sudden death,
        And let this death, wherein to sin I die,
        Conceive a second life in endless mercy!
            [*He dies.*]
            Enter ORCANES, GAZELLUS, URIBASSA, *with others.*
ORCANES
10   Now lie the Christians bathing in their bloods,
        And Christ or Mahomet hath been my friend.

GAZELLUS
    See here the perjured traitor, Hungary,
    Bloody and breathless for his villainy.
ORCANES
    Now shall his barbarous body be a prey
    To beasts and fowls, and all the winds shall breathe
    Through shady leaves of every senseless tree
    Murmurs and hisses for his heinous sin.
    Now scalds his soul in the Tartarian streams
    And feeds upon the baneful tree of hell,
    That Zoacum, that fruit of bitterness,   20
    That in the midst of fire is engraft,
    Yet flourisheth as Flora in her pride,
    With apples like the heads of damnèd fiends.
    The devils there in chains of quenchless flame
    Shall lead his soul through Orcus' burning gulf
    From pain to pain, whose change shall never end.
    What sayest thou yet, Gazellus, to his foil,
    Which we referred to justice of his Christ
    And to His power, which here appears as full
    As rays of Cynthia to the clearest sight?   30
GAZELLUS
    'Tis but the fortune of the wars, my lord,
    Whose power is often proved a miracle.
ORCANES
    Yet in my thoughts shall Christ be honourèd,
    Not doing Mahomet an injury,
    Whose power had share in this our victory.
    And since this miscreant hath disgraced his faith
    And died a traitor both to heaven and earth,
    We will both watch and ward shall keep his trunk
    Amidst these plains for fowls to prey upon.
    Go, Uribassa, give it straight in charge.   40
URIBASSA I will, my lord.
            Exit URIBASSA [*and* SOLDIERS, *with the body*].
ORCANES
    And now, Gazellus, let us haste and meet

Our army, and our brother of Jerusalem,
Of Soria, Trebizond, and Amasia,
And happily, with full Natolian bowls
Of Greekish wine, now let us celebrate
Our happy conquest and his angry fate.

Exeunt.

Scene 4

The arras is drawn, and ZENOCRATE *lies in her bed of state,* TAMBURLAINE *sitting by her; three* PHYSICIANS *about her bed, tempering potions.* THERIDAMAS, TECHELLES, USUMCASANE, *and the three* SONS [CALYPHAS, AMYRAS, CELEBINUS].

TAMBURLAINE
Black is the beauty of the brightest day!
The golden ball of heaven's eternal fire,
That danced with glory on the silver waves,
Now wants the fuel that inflamed his beams,
And all with faintness and for foul disgrace
He binds his temples with a frowning cloud,
Ready to darken earth with endless night.
Zenocrate, that gave him light and life,
Whose eyes shot fire from their ivory bowers
10   And tempered every soul with lively heat,
Now by the malice of the angry skies,
Whose jealousy admits no second mate,
Draws in the comfort of her latest breath,
All dazzled with the hellish mists of death.
Now walk the angels on the walls of heaven,
As sentinels to warn th'immortal souls
To entertain divine Zenocrate.
Apollo, Cynthia, and the ceaseless lamps
That gently looked upon this loathsome earth
20   Shine downwards now no more, but deck the heavens
To entertain divine Zenocrate.

The crystal springs whose taste illuminates
Refinèd eyes with an eternal sight,
Like trièd silver, runs through Paradise
To entertain divine Zenocrate.
The cherubins and holy seraphins
That sing and play before the King of Kings,
Use all their voices and their instruments
To entertain divine Zenocrate.
And in this sweet and curious harmony,   30
The god that tunes this music to our souls
Holds out his hand in highest majesty
To entertain divine Zenocrate.
Then let some holy trance convey my thoughts
Up to the place of th'empyreal heaven,
That this my life may be as short to me
As are the days of sweet Zenocrate.
Physicians, will no physic do her good?

PHYSICIAN
My lord, your majesty shall soon perceive;
An if she pass this fit, the worst is past.   40

TAMBURLAINE
Tell me, how fares my fair Zenocrate?

ZENOCRATE
I fare, my lord, as other empresses,
That, when this frail and transitory flesh
Hath sucked the measure of that vital air
That feeds the body with his dated health,
Wanes with enforced and necessary change.

TAMBURLAINE
May never such a change transform my love,
In whose sweet being I repose my life,
Whose heavenly presence, beautified with health,
Gives light to Phoebus and the fixèd stars,   50
Whose absence makes the sun and moon as dark
As when, opposed in one diameter,
Their spheres are mounted on the serpent's head,
Or else descended to his winding train.
Live still, my love, and so conserve my life,

Or, dying, be the author of my death.
ZENOCRATE
Live still, my lord, O, let my sovereign live,
And sooner let the fiery element
Dissolve and make your kingdom in the sky
60   Than this base earth should shroud your majesty!
For, should I but suspect your death by mine,
The comfort of my future happiness
And hope to meet your highness in the heavens,
Turned to despair, would break my wretched breast,
And fury would confound my present rest.
But let me die, my love, yet let me die,
With love and patience let your true love die.
Your grief and fury hurts my second life.
Yet let me kiss my lord before I die,
70   And let me die with kissing of my lord.
But since my life is lengthened yet a while,
Let me take leave of these my loving sons
And of my lords, whose true nobility
Have merited my latest memory.
Sweet sons, farewell! In death resemble me,
And in your lives your father's excellency.
Some music, and my fit will cease, my lord.
     They call [for] music.
TAMBURLAINE
Proud fury and intolerable fit,
That dares torment the body of my love
80   And scourge the scourge of the immortal God!
Now are those spheres where Cupid used to sit,
Wounding the world with wonder and with love,
Sadly supplied with pale and ghastly death
Whose darts do pierce the centre of my soul.
Her sacred beauty hath enchanted heaven,
And, had she lived before the siege of Troy,
Helen, whose beauty summoned Greece to arms
And drew a thousand ships to Tenedos,
Had not been named in Homer's *Iliads*;
90   Her name had been in every line he wrote.

Or, had those wanton poets, for whose birth
Old Rome was proud, but gazed a while on her,
Nor Lesbia nor Corinna had been named;
Zenocrate had been the argument
Of every epigram or elegy.
    The music sounds, and she dies.
What, is she dead? Techelles, draw thy sword,
And wound the earth, that it may cleave in twain,
And we descend into th'infernal vaults
To hale the Fatal Sisters by the hair
And throw them in the triple moat of hell   100
For taking hence my fair Zenocrate.
Casane and Theridamas, to arms!
Raise cavalieros higher than the clouds,
And with the cannon break the frame of heaven,
Batter the shining palace of the sun
And shiver all the starry firmament,
For amorous Jove hath snatched my love from hence,
Meaning to make her stately queen of heaven.
What god soever holds thee in his arms,
Giving thee nectar and ambrosia,   110
Behold me here, divine Zenocrate,
Raving, impatient, desperate, and mad,
Breaking my steelèd lance with which I burst
The rusty beams of Janus' temple doors,
Letting out death and tyrannizing war
To march with me under this bloody flag;
And if thou pitiest Tamburlaine the Great,
Come down from heaven and live with me again!

THERIDAMAS
    Ah, good my lord, be patient. She is dead,
    And all this raging cannot make her live.   120
    If words might serve, our voice hath rent the air,
    If tears, our eyes have watered all the earth,
    If grief, our murdered hearts have strained forth blood.
    Nothing prevails, for she is dead, my lord.

TAMBURLAINE
    'For she is dead'! Thy words do pierce my soul.

Ah, sweet Theridamas, say so no more.
Though she be dead, yet let me think she lives
And feed my mind that dies for want of her.
Where'er her soul be, thou shalt stay with me,
Embalmed with cassia, ambergris, and myrrh,
Not lapped in lead but in a sheet of gold;
And till I die thou shalt not be interred.
Then in as rich a tomb as Mausolus',
We both will rest and have one epitaph
Writ in as many several languages
As I have conquered kingdoms with my sword.
This cursèd town will I consume with fire
Because this place bereft me of my love.
The houses, burnt, will look as if they mourned,
And here will I set up her stature
And march about it with my mourning camp,
Drooping and pining for Zenocrate.

The arras is drawn. [*Exeunt.*]

ACT 3

Scene 1

Enter the kings of TREBIZOND *and* SORIA, *one bringing a sword, and another a sceptre; next,* [ORCANES, *King of*] *Natolia and* [*the King of*] JERUSALEM *with the imperial crown; after,* CALLAPINE, *and after him other* LORDS [*and* ALMEDA]. ORCANES *and* JERUSALEM *crown him* [CALLAPINE,] *and the other give him the sceptre.*

ORCANES Callapinus Cyricelibes, otherwise Cybelius, son and successive heir to the late mighty emperor Bajazeth, by the aid of God and his friend Mahomet emperor of Natolia, Jerusalem, Trebizond, Soria, Amasia, Thracia, Illyria, Carmonia, and all the hundred and thirty kingdoms late contributory to his mighty father: long live Callapinus, emperor of Turkey!

CALLAPINE
Thrice worthy kings of Natolia, and the rest,
I will requite your royal gratitudes
With all the benefits my empire yields.   10
And, were the sinews of th'imperial seat
So knit and strengthened as when Bajazeth,
My royal lord and father, filled the throne,
Whose cursèd fate hath so dismembered it,
Then should you see this thief of Scythia,
This proud usurping king of Persia,
Do us such honour and supremacy,
Bearing the vengeance of our father's wrongs,
As all the world should blot our dignities

20   Out of the book of base-born infamies.
         And now I doubt not but your royal cares
         Hath so provided for this cursèd foe
         That, since the heir of mighty Bajazeth,
         (An emperor so honoured for his virtues)
         Revives the spirit of true Turkish hearts
         In grievous memory of his father's shame,
         We shall not need to nourish any doubt
         But that proud Fortune, who hath followed long
         The martial sword of mighty Tamburlaine,
30   Will not retain her old inconstancy,
         And raise our honours to as high a pitch
         In this our strong and fortunate encounter.
         For so hath heaven provided my escape
         From all the cruelty my soul sustained,
         By this my friendly keeper's happy means,
         That Jove, surcharged with pity of our wrongs,
         Will pour it down in showers on our heads,
         Scourging the pride of cursèd Tamburlaine.

ORCANES
         I have a hundred thousand men in arms,
40   Some that, in conquest of the perjured Christian,
         Being a handful to a mighty host,
         Think them in number yet sufficient
         To drink the river Nile or Euphrates,
         And, for their power, enow to win the world.

JERUSALEM
         And I as many from Jerusalem,
         Judaea, Gaza, and Scalonia's bounds,
         That on Mount Sinai with their ensigns spread,
         Look like the parti-coloured clouds of heaven
         That show fair weather to the neighbour morn.

TREBIZOND
50   And I as many bring from Trebizond,
         Chio, Famastro, and Amasia,
         All bord'ring on the Mare-Major Sea,
         Riso, Sancina, and the bordering towns
         That touch the end of famous Euphrates,

Whose courages are kindled with the flames
The cursèd Scythian sets on all their towns,
And vow to burn the villain's cruel heart.

SORIA

From Soria with seventy thousand strong,
Ta'en from Aleppo, Soldino, Tripoli,
And so unto my city of Damasco,   60
I march to meet and aid my neighbour kings,
All which will join against this Tamburlaine
And bring him captive to your highness' feet.

ORCANES

Our battle, then, in martial manner pitched,
According to our ancient use, shall bear
The figure of the semicircled moon,
Whose horns shall sprinkle through the tainted air
The poisoned brains of this proud Scythian.

CALLAPINE

Well then, my noble lords, for this my friend
That freed me from the bondage of my foe,   70
I think it requisite and honourable
To keep my promise and to make him king,
That is a gentleman, I know, at least.

ALMEDA

That's no matter, sir, for being a king,
For Tamburlaine came up of nothing.

JERUSALEM

Your majesty may choose some 'pointed time,
Performing all your promise to the full.
'Tis nought for your majesty to give a kingdom.

CALLAPINE

Then will I shortly keep my promise, Almeda.

ALMEDA

Why, I thank your majesty.   80

Exeunt.

Scene 2

[*Enter*] TAMBURLAINE *with* USUMCASANE, *and his three*
SONS [CALYPHAS, AMYRAS, CELEBINUS]; *four* [SOL-
DIERS] *bearing the hearse of* ZENOCRATE, *and the drums*
sounding a doleful march, the town burning.

TAMBURLAINE
So, burn the turrets of this cursèd town.
Flame to the highest region of the air
And kindle heaps of exhalations
That, being fiery meteors, may presage
Death and destruction to th'inhabitants;
Over my zenith hang a blazing star
That may endure till heaven be dissolved,
Fed with the fresh supply of earthly dregs,
Threat'ning a death and famine to this land!
10   Flying dragons, lightning, fearful thunderclaps,
Singe these fair plains, and make them seem as black
As is the island where the Furies mask
Compassed with Lethe, Styx, and Phlegethon,
Because my dear Zenocrate is dead!

CALYPHAS
This pillar placed in memory of her,
Where in Arabian, Hebrew, Greek, is writ:
'This town, being burnt by Tamburlaine the Great,
Forbids the world to build it up again.'

AMYRAS
And here this mournful streamer shall be placed,
20   Wrought with the Persian and Egyptian arms
To signify she was a princess born
And wife unto the monarch of the East.

CELEBINUS
And here this table, as a register
Of all her virtues and perfections.

TAMBURLAINE
And here the picture of Zenocrate
To show her beauty which the world admired –

Sweet picture of divine Zenocrate
That, hanging here, will draw the gods from heaven
And cause the stars fixed in the southern arc,
Whose lovely faces never any viewed   30
That have not passed the centre's latitude,
As pilgrims travel to our hemisphere
Only to gaze upon Zenocrate.
Thou shalt not beautify Larissa plains,
But keep within the circle of mine arms!
At every town and castle I besiege
Thou shalt be set upon my royal tent,
And when I meet an army in the field,
Those looks will shed such influence in my camp
As if Bellona, goddess of the war,   40
Threw naked swords and sulphur balls of fire
Upon the heads of all our enemies.
And now, my lords, advance your spears again.
Sorrow no more, my sweet Casane, now.
Boys, leave to mourn. This town shall ever mourn,
Being burnt to cinders for your mother's death.

CALYPHAS
If I had wept a sea of tears for her,
It would not ease the sorrow I sustain.

AMYRAS
As is that town, so is my heart consumed
With grief and sorrow for my mother's death.   50

CELEBINUS
My mother's death hath mortified my mind,
And sorrow stops the passage of my speech.

TAMBURLAINE
But now, my boys, leave off, and list to me
That mean to teach you rudiments of war.
I'll have you learn to sleep upon the ground,
March in your armour thorough watery fens,
Sustain the scorching heat and freezing cold,
Hunger and thirst – right adjuncts of the war;
And after this to scale a castle wall,
Besiege a fort, to undermine a town,   60

And make whole cities caper in the air.
Then next, the way to fortify your men,
In champian grounds what figure serves you best;
For which the quinque-angle form is meet,
Because the corners there may fall more flat
Whereas the fort may fittest be assailed,
And sharpest where th'assault is desperate.
The ditches must be deep, the counterscarps
Narrow and steep, the walls made high and broad,
70   The bulwarks and the rampires large and strong,
With cavalieros and thick counterforts,
And room within to lodge six thousand men.
It must have privy ditches, countermines,
And secret issuings to defend the ditch,
It must have high argins and covered ways
To keep the bulwark fronts from battery,
And parapets to hide the musketeers,
Casemates to place the great artillery,
And store of ordnance, that from every flank
80   May scour the outward curtains of the fort,
Dismount the cannon of the adverse part,
Murder the foe, and save the walls from breach.
When this is learned for service on the land,
By plain and easy demonstration
I'll teach you how to make the water mount,
That you may dry-foot march through lakes and pools,
Deep rivers, havens, creeks, and little seas,
And make a fortress in the raging waves,
Fenced with the concave of a monstrous rock,
90   Invincible by nature of the place.
When this is done, then are ye soldiers,
And worthy sons of Tamburlaine the Great.

CALYPHAS
My lord, but this is dangerous to be done.
We may be slain or wounded ere we learn.

TAMBURLAINE
Villain, art thou the son of Tamburlaine
And fear'st to die, or with a curtle-axe

To hew thy flesh and make a gaping wound?
Hast thou beheld a peal of ordnance strike
A ring of pikes, mingled with shot and horse,
Whose shattered limbs, being tossed as high as heaven,   100
Hang in the air as thick as sunny motes,
And canst thou, coward, stand in fear of death?
Hast thou not seen my horsemen charge the foe,
Shot through the arms, cut overthwart the hands,
Dyeing their lances with their streaming blood,
And yet at night carouse within my tent,
Filling their empty veins with airy wine
That, being concocted, turns to crimson blood,
And wilt thou shun the field for fear of wounds?
View me, thy father, that hath conquered kings   110
And with his host marched round about the earth
Quite void of scars and clear from any wound,
That by the wars lost not a dram of blood,
And see him lance his flesh to teach you all.
    He cuts his arm.
A wound is nothing, be it ne'er so deep;
Blood is the god of war's rich livery.
Now look I like a soldier, and this wound
As great a grace and majesty to me
As if a chair of gold enamellèd,
Enchased with diamonds, sapphires, rubies,   120
And fairest pearl of wealthy India,
Were mounted here under a canopy,
And I sat down, clothed with the massy robe
That late adorned the Afric potentate
Whom I brought bound unto Damascus' walls.
Come, boys, and with your fingers search my wound
And in my blood wash all your hands at once,
While I sit smiling to behold the sight.
    [*They probe his wound with their fingers.*]
Now, my boys, what think you of a wound?
CALYPHAS I know not what I should think of it. Methinks 'tis   130
    a pitiful sight.
CELEBINUS 'Tis nothing. Give me a wound, father.

AMYRAS And me another, my lord.

TAMBURLAINE [*to* CELEBINUS] Come, sirrah, give me your
arm.

CELEBINUS Here, father, cut it bravely as you did your own.

TAMBURLAINE
It shall suffice thou dar'st abide a wound.
My boy, thou shalt not lose a drop of blood
Before we meet the army of the Turk.
140 But then run desperate through the thickest throngs,
Dreadless of blows, of bloody wounds and death.
And let the burning of Larissa walls,
My speech of war, and this my wound you see,
Teach you, my boys, to bear courageous minds
Fit for the followers of great Tamburlaine.
Usumcasane, now come let us march
Towards Techelles and Theridamas,
That we have sent before to fire the towns,
The towers and cities of these hateful Turks,
150 And hunt that coward, faint-heart runaway,
With that accursèd traitor Almeda,
Till fire and sword have found them at a bay.

USUMCASANE
I long to pierce his bowels with my sword,
That hath betrayed my gracious sovereign,
That curst and damnèd traitor Almeda.

TAMBURLAINE
Then let us see if coward Callapine
Dare levy arms against our puissance,
That we may tread upon his captive neck
And treble all his father's slaveries.

                                                    Exeunt.

Scene 3

[*Enter*] TECHELLES, THERIDAMAS, *and their train*
[SOLDIERS *and* PIONERS].

THERIDAMAS
  Thus have we marched northward from Tamburlaine
  Unto the frontier point of Soria;
  And this is Balsera, their chiefest hold,
  Wherein is all the treasure of the land.

TECHELLES
  Then let us bring our light artillery,
  Minions, falc'nets, and sakers, to the trench,
  Filling the ditches with the walls' wide breach,
  And enter in to seize upon the gold.
  How say ye, soldiers, shall we not?

SOLDIERS
  Yes, my lord, yes! Come, let's about it.   10

THERIDAMAS
  But stay a while. Summon a parley, drum.
  It may be they will yield it quietly,
  Knowing two kings, the friends to Tamburlaine,
  Stand at the walls with such a mighty power.
    [*Drums*] *summon the battle.*
    [*Enter above*] CAPTAIN *with his wife* [OLYMPIA] *and*
    SON.

CAPTAIN
  What require you, my masters?

THERIDAMAS
  Captain, that thou yield up thy hold to us.

CAPTAIN
  To you? Why, do you think me weary of it?

TECHELLES
  Nay, captain, thou art weary of thy life
  If thou withstand the friends of Tamburlaine.

THERIDAMAS
  These pioners of Argier in Africa,   20
  Even in the cannon's face shall raise a hill

Of earth and faggots higher than thy fort,
And over thy argins and covered ways
Shall play upon the bulwarks of thy hold
Volleys of ordnance till the breach be made
That with his ruin fills up all the trench;
And when we enter in, not heaven itself
Shall ransom thee, thy wife, and family.

TECHELLES

Captain, these Moors shall cut the leaden pipes
30   That bring fresh water to thy men and thee,
And lie in trench before thy castle walls,
That no supply of victual shall come in,
Nor any issue forth but they shall die.
And therefore, captain, yield it quietly.

CAPTAIN

Were you, that are the friends of Tamburlaine,
Brothers to holy Mahomet himself,
I would not yield it. Therefore do your worst.
Raise mounts, batter, entrench, and undermine,
Cut off the water, all convoys that can,
40   Yet I am resolute. And so, farewell,

                                              [*Exeunt above.*]

THERIDAMAS

Pioners, away! And where I stuck the stake
Entrench with those dimensions I prescribed.
Cast up the earth towards the castle wall,
Which, till it may defend you, labour low,
And few or none shall perish by their shot.

PIONERS We will, my lord.

                                    Exeunt [PIONERS].

TECHELLES

A hundred horse shall scout about the plains
To spy what force comes to relieve the hold.
Both we, Theridamas, will entrench our men,
50   And with the Jacob's staff measure the height
And distance of the castle from the trench,
That we may know if our artillery
Will carry full point-blank unto their walls.

THERIDAMAS

    Then see the bringing of our ordinance
    Along the trench into the battery,
    Where we will have gabions of six foot broad
    To save our cannoneers from musket shot,
    Betwixt which shall our ordnance thunder forth,
    And with the breach's fall, smoke, fire, and dust,
    The crack, the echo, and the soldiers' cry,   60
    Make deaf the air and dim the crystal sky.

TECHELLES

    Trumpets and drums, alarum presently!
    And, soldiers, play the men. The hold is yours!

                                                 [Exeunt.]

[*Scene 4*]

Enter the CAPTAIN *with his wife* [OLYMPIA] *and* SON.

OLYMPIA

    Come, good my lord, and let us haste from hence
    Along the cave that leads beyond the foe.
    No hope is left to save this conquered hold.

CAPTAIN

    A deadly bullet gliding through my side
    Lies heavy on my heart. I cannot live.
    I feel my liver pierced, and all my veins
    That there begin and nourish every part
    Mangled and torn, and all my entrails bathed
    In blood that straineth from their orifex.
    Farewell, sweet wife! Sweet son, farewell! I die.   10
      [He dies.]

OLYMPIA

    Death, whither art thou gone, that both we live?
    Come back again, sweet Death, and strike us both!
    One minute end our days, and one sepulchre
    Contain our bodies! Death, why com'st thou not?
      [She draws a knife.]

Well, this must be the messenger for thee.
Now, ugly Death, stretch out thy sable wings,
And carry both our souls where his remains.
Tell me, sweet boy, art thou content to die?
These barbarous Scythians, full of cruelty,
20 And Moors in whom was never pity found,
Will hew us piecemeal, put us to the wheel,
Or else invent some torture worse than that.
Therefore, die by thy loving mother's hand,
Who gently now will lance thy ivory throat
And quickly rid thee both of pain and life.

SON

Mother, dispatch me, or I'll kill myself.
For think ye I can live, and see him dead?
Give me your knife, good mother, or strike home.
The Scythians shall not tyrannize on me.
30 Sweet mother, strike, that I may meet my father!
  She stabs him.

OLYMPIA

Ah, sacred Mahomet, if this be sin,
Entreat a pardon of the God of heaven,
And purge my soul before it come to thee!
  [*She burns the bodies.*] *Enter* THERIDAMAS, TECHELLES,
  and all their train. [OLYMPIA *tries to kill herself.*]

THERIDAMAS

How now, madam, what are you doing?

OLYMPIA

Killing myself, as I have done my son,
Whose body with his father's I have burnt,
Lest cruel Scythians should dismember him.

TECHELLES

'Twas bravely done, and like a soldier's wife.
Thou shalt with us to Tamburlaine the Great,
40 Who, when he hears how resolute thou wert,
Will match thee with a viceroy or a king.

OLYMPIA

My lord deceased was dearer unto me
Than any viceroy, king, or emperor,

And for his sake here will I end my days.

THERIDAMAS

But lady, go with us to Tamburlaine,
And thou shalt see a man greater than Mahomet,
In whose high looks is much more majesty
Than from the concave superficies
Of Jove's vast palace, the empyreal orb,
Unto the shining bower where Cynthia sits   50
Like lovely Thetis in a crystal robe;
That treadeth Fortune underneath his feet
And makes the mighty god of arms his slave;
On whom Death and the Fatal Sisters wait
With naked swords and scarlet liveries;
Before whom, mounted on a lion's back,
Rhamnusia bears a helmet full of blood
And strews the way with brains of slaughtered men;
By whose proud side the ugly Furies run,
Hearkening when he shall bid them plague the world;   60
Over whose zenith, clothed in windy air
And eagle's wings joined to her feathered breast,
Fame hovereth, sounding of her golden trump,
That to the adverse poles of that straight line
Which measureth the glorious frame of heaven
The name of mighty Tamburlaine is spread –
And him, fair lady, shall thy eyes behold.
Come.

OLYMPIA [*kneeling*]

Take pity of a lady's ruthful tears,
That humbly craves upon her knees to stay   70
And cast her body in the burning flame
That feeds upon her son's and husband's flesh.

TECHELLES

Madam, sooner shall fire consume us both
Than scorch a face so beautiful as this,
In frame of which Nature hath showed more skill
Than when she gave eternal chaos form,
Drawing from it the shining lamps of heaven.

THERIDAMAS

    Madam, I am so far in love with you

    That you must go with us. No remedy.

OLYMPIA

80   Then carry me I care not where you will,

    And let the end of this my fatal journey

    Be likewise end to my accursèd life.

TECHELLES

    No madam, but the beginning of your joy.

    Come willingly, therefore.

THERIDAMAS

    Soldiers, now let us meet the general,

    Who by this time is at Natolia,

    Ready to charge the army of the Turk.

    The gold, the silver, and the pearl ye got

    Rifling this fort, divide in equal shares.

90   This lady shall have twice so much again

    Out of the coffers of our treasury.

Exeunt.

Scene 5

[*Enter*] CALLAPINE, ORCANES, JERUSALEM, TREBIZOND, SORIA, ALMEDA, *with their train.* [*To them a* MESSENGER.]

MESSENGER

    Renownèd emperor, mighty Callapine,

    God's great lieutenant over all the world,

    Here at Aleppo with an host of men

    Lies Tamburlaine, this king of Persia –

    In number more than are the quivering leaves

    Of Ida's forest, where your highness' hounds

    With open cry pursues the wounded stag –

    Who means to girt Natolia's walls with siege,

    Fire the town, and overrun the land.

CALLAPINE
   My royal army is as great as his,   10
   That from the bounds of Phrygia to the sea
   Which washeth Cyprus with his brinish waves,
   Covers the hills, the valleys, and the plains.
   Viceroys and peers of Turkey, play the men!
   Whet all your swords to mangle Tamburlaine,
   His sons, his captains, and his followers.
   By Mahomet, not one of them shall live!
   The field wherein this battle shall be fought
   For ever term the Persians' sepulchre
   In memory of this our victory.   20
ORCANES
   Now he that calls himself the scourge of Jove,
   The emperor of the world, and earthly god,
   Shall end the warlike progress he intends
   And travel headlong to the lake of hell
   Where legions of devils, knowing he must die
   Here in Natolia by your highness' hands,
   All brandishing their brands of quenchless fire,
   Stretching their monstrous paws, grin with their teeth
   And guard the gates to entertain his soul.
CALLAPINE
   Tell me, viceroys, the number of your men,   30
   And what our army royal is esteemed.
JERUSALEM
   From Palestina and Jerusalem,
   Of Hebrews three score thousand fighting men
   Are come since last we showed your majesty.
ORCANES
   So from Arabia desert, and the bounds
   Of that sweet land whose brave metropolis
   Re-edified the fair Semiramis,
   Came forty thousand warlike foot and horse
   Since last we numbered to your majesty.
TREBIZOND
   From Trebizond in Asia the Less,   40

Naturalized Turks and stout Bithynians
Came to my bands full fifty thousand more
That, fighting, knows not what retreat doth mean,
Nor e'er return but with the victory,
Since last we numbered to your majesty.

SORIA

Of Sorians from Halla is repaired,
And neighbour cities of your highness' land,
Ten thousand horse and thirty thousand foot
Since last we numbered to your majesty;
50   So that the army royal is esteemed
Six hundred thousand valiant fighting men.

CALLAPINE

Then welcome, Tamburlaine, unto thy death.
Come, puissant viceroys, let us to the field –
The Persians' sepulchre – and sacrifice
Mountains of breathless men to Mahomet,
Who now with Jove opens the firmament
To see the slaughter of our enemies.

    [*Enter*] TAMBURLAINE *with his three* SONS [CALYPHAS,
    AMYRAS, CELEBINUS], USUMCASANE, *with other*
    [SOLDIERS].

TAMBURLAINE

How now, Casane? See, a knot of kings,
Sitting as if they were a-telling riddles.

USUMCASANE

60   My lord, your presence makes them pale and wan.
Poor souls, they look as if their deaths were near.

TAMBURLAINE

Why, so he is, Casane. I am here.
But yet I'll save their lives and make them slaves.
Ye petty kings of Turkey, I am come
As Hector did into the Grecian camp
To overdare the pride of Graecia
And set his warlike person to the view
Of fierce Achilles, rival of his fame.
I do you honour in the simile;
70   For if I should, as Hector did Achilles

(The worthiest knight that ever brandished sword)
Challenge in combat any of you all,
I see how fearfully ye would refuse
And fly my glove as from a scorpion.

ORCANES
Now thou art fearful of thy army's strength,
Thou wouldst with overmatch of person fight.
But, shepherd's issue, baseborn Tamburlaine,
Think of thy end. This sword shall lance thy throat.

TAMBURLAINE
Villain, the shepherd's issue, at whose birth
Heaven did afford a gracious aspect   80
And joined those stars that shall be opposite
Even till the dissolution of the world,
And never meant to make a conqueror
So famous as is mighty Tamburlaine,
Shall so torment thee and that Callapine
That like a roguish runaway suborned
That villain there, that slave, that Turkish dog,
To false his service to his sovereign,
As ye shall curse the birth of Tamburlaine.

CALLAPINE
Rail not, proud Scythian, I shall now revenge   90
My father's vile abuses and mine own.

JERUSALEM
By Mahomet, he shall be tied in chains,
Rowing with Christians in a brigantine
About the Grecian isles to rob and spoil,
And turn him to his ancient trade again.
Methinks the slave should make a lusty thief.

CALLAPINE
Nay, when the battle ends, all we will meet
And sit in council to invent some pain
That most may vex his body and his soul.

TAMBURLAINE Sirrah Callapine, I'll hang a clog about your   100
neck for running away again. You shall not trouble me thus
to come and fetch you.
But as for you, viceroy, you shall have bits

And, harnessed like my horses, draw my coach,
And, when ye stay, be lashed with whips of wire.
I'll have you learn to feed on provender,
And in a stable lie upon the planks.

ORCANES
But, Tamburlaine, first thou shalt kneel to us
And humbly crave a pardon for thy life.

TREBIZOND
110 The common soldiers of our mighty host
Shall bring thee bound unto the general's tent.

SORIA
And all have jointly sworn thy cruel death,
Or bind thee in eternal torment's wrath.

TAMBURLAINE Well, sirs, diet yourselves. You know I shall
have occasion shortly to journey you.

CELEBINUS
See, father, how Almeda the gaoler looks upon us!

TAMBURLAINE [*to* ALMEDA]
Villain, traitor, damnèd fugitive,
I'll make thee wish the earth had swallowed thee.
See'st thou not death within my wrathful looks?
120 Go, villain, cast thee headlong from a rock,
Or rip thy bowels and rend out thy heart
T'appease my wrath, or else I'll torture thee,
Searing thy hateful flesh with burning irons
And drops of scalding lead, while all thy joints
Be racked and beat asunder with the wheel.
For, if thou livest, not any element
Shall shroud thee from the wrath of Tamburlaine.

CALLAPINE
Well, in despite of thee he shall be king.
Come, Almeda, receive this crown of me.
130 I here invest thee king of Ariadan,
Bordering on Mare Rosso near to Mecca.
        [CALLAPINE *offers* ALMEDA *a crown.*]

ORCANES [*to* ALMEDA] What, take it, man!

ALMEDA [*to* TAMBURLAINE] Good my lord, let me take it.

CALLAPINE [*to* ALMEDA] Dost thou ask him leave? Here, take it.

TAMBURLAINE [*to* ALMEDA] Go to, sirrah, take your crown, and make up the half dozen.

    [ALMEDA *takes the crown.*]

So, sirrah, now you are a king you must give arms.

ORCANES [*to* TAMBURLAINE] So he shall, and wear thy head in his scutcheon.   140

TAMBURLAINE No, let him hang a bunch of keys on his standard, to put him in remembrance he was a gaoler, that, when I take him, I may knock out his brains with them, and lock you in the stable when you shall come sweating from my chariot.

TREBIZOND Away! Let us to the field, that the villain may be slain.

TAMBURLAINE [*to a* SOLDIER] Sirrah, prepare whips, and bring my chariot to my tent. For as soon as the battle is done, I'll ride in triumph through the camp.   150

    Enter THERIDAMAS, TECHELLES, *and their train.*

How now, ye petty kings, lo, here are bugs
Will make the hair stand upright on your heads
And cast your crowns in slavery at their feet.
Welcome, Theridamas and Techelles both.
See ye this rout, and know ye this same king?

THERIDAMAS
Ay, my lord, he was Callapine's keeper.

TAMBURLAINE Well, now you see he is a king, look to him, Theridamas, when we are fighting, lest he hide his crown as the foolish King of Persia did.

SORIA No, Tamburlaine, he shall not be put to that exigent, I 160
warrant thee.

TAMBURLAINE
You know not, sir.
But now, my followers and my loving friends,
Fight as you ever did, like conquerors.
The glory of this happy day is yours.
My stern aspect shall make fair Victory,

Hovering betwixt our armies, light on me,
Loaden with laurel wreaths to crown us all.

TECHELLES

I smile to think how, when the field is fought
170   And rich Natolia ours, our men shall sweat
With carrying pearl and treasure on their backs.

TAMBURLAINE

You shall be princes all immediately.
Come fight, ye Turks, or yield us victory.

ORCANES

No, we will meet thee, slavish Tamburlaine.

Exeunt.

ACT 4

Alarm. AMYRAS *and* CELEBINUS *issue from the tent where*
CALYPHAS *sits asleep.*

AMYRAS
   Now in their glories shine the golden crowns
   Of these proud Turks, much like so many suns
   That half dismay the majesty of heaven.
   Now, brother, follow we our father's sword
   That flies with fury swifter than our thoughts
   And cuts down armies with his conquering wings.

CELEBINUS
   Call forth our lazy brother from the tent,
   For, if my father miss him in the field,
   Wrath kindled in the furnace of his breast
   Will send a deadly lightning to his heart.   10

AMYRAS [*calling into the tent*]
   Brother, ho! What, given so much to sleep
   You cannot leave it when our enemies' drums
   And rattling cannons thunder in our ears
   Our proper ruin and our father's foil?

CALYPHAS
   Away, ye fools! My father needs not me,
   Nor you, in faith, but that you will be thought
   More childish-valorous than manly-wise.
   If half our camp should sit and sleep with me,
   My father were enough to scare the foe.
   You do dishonour to his majesty   20

To think our helps will do him any good.

AMYRAS

What, dar'st thou then be absent from the fight,
Knowing my father hates thy cowardice
And oft hath warned thee to be still in field,
When he himself amidst the thickest troops
Beats down our foes to flesh our taintless swords?

CALYPHAS

I know, sir, what it is to kill a man.
It works remorse of conscience in me.
I take no pleasure to be murderous,
30   Nor care for blood when wine will quench my thirst.

CELEBINUS

O cowardly boy! Fie, for shame, come forth.
Thou dost dishonour manhood and thy house.

CALYPHAS

Go, go, tall stripling, fight you for us both,
And take my other toward brother here,
For person like to prove a second Mars.
'Twill please my mind as well to hear both you
Have won a heap of honour in the field
And left your slender carcasses behind
As if I lay with you for company.

AMYRAS

40   You will not go, then?

CALYPHAS

You say true.

AMYRAS

Were all the lofty mounts of Zona Mundi
That fill the midst of farthest Tartary
Turned into pearl and proffered for my stay,
I would not bide the fury of my father
When, made a victor in these haughty arms,
He comes and finds his sons have had no shares
In all the honours he proposed for us.

CALYPHAS

Take you the honour, I will take my ease;
50   My wisdom shall excuse my cowardice.

I go into the field before I need?
> *Alarm, and* AMYRAS *and* CELEBINUS *run in.*
The bullets fly at random where they list,
And, should I go and kill a thousand men,
I were as soon rewarded with a shot,
And sooner far than he that never fights.
And, should I go and do nor harm nor good,
I might have harm, which all the good I have,
Joined with my father's crown, would never cure.
I'll to cards. Perdicas!
> [*Enter* PERDICAS.]

PERDICAS Here, my lord.   60

CALYPHAS Come, thou and I will go to cards to drive away the
time.

PERDICAS Content, my lord. But what shall we play for?

CALYPHAS Who shall kiss the fairest of the Turks' concubines
first, when my father hath conquered them.

PERDICAS Agreed, i'faith.
> *They play* [*in the open tent*].

CALYPHAS They say I am a coward, Perdicas, and I fear as little
their *taratantaras*, their swords, or their cannons as I do a
naked lady in a net of gold, and, for fear I should be afraid,
would put it off and come to bed with me.   70

PERDICAS Such a fear, my lord, would never make ye retire.

CALYPHAS I would my father would let me be put in the front
of such a battle once, to try my valour.
> *Alarm.*
What a coil they keep! I believe there will be some hurt done
anon amongst them.
> *Enter* TAMBURLAINE, THERIDAMAS, TECHELLES,
> USUMCASANE, AMYRAS, CELEBINUS, *leading the Turkish*
> *kings* [ORCANES *of Natolia,* JERUSALEM, TREBIZOND,
> SORIA; *and* SOLDIERS].

TAMBURLAINE
See now, ye slaves, my children stoops your pride
And leads your glories sheep-like to the sword.
Bring them, my boys, and tell me if the wars
Be not a life that may illustrate gods,

80   And tickle not your spirits with desire
        Still to be trained in arms and chivalry?
AMYRAS
        Shall we let go these kings again, my lord,
        To gather greater numbers 'gainst our power,
        That they may say it is not chance doth this
        But matchless strength and magnanimity?
TAMBURLAINE
        No, no, Amyras, tempt not Fortune so.
        Cherish thy valour still with fresh supplies,
        And glut it not with stale and daunted foes.
        But where's this coward – villain, not my son,
90   But traitor to my name and majesty?
            He goes in [the tent] and brings him [CALYPHAS] *out.*
        Image of sloth and picture of a slave,
        The obloquy and scorn of my renown,
        How may my heart, thus firèd with mine eyes,
        Wounded with shame and killed with discontent,
        Shroud any thought may hold my striving hands
        From martial justice on thy wretched soul?
THERIDAMAS
        Yet pardon him, I pray your majesty.
TECHELLES AND USUMCASANE
        Let all of us entreat your highness' pardon.
            [*They kneel.*]
TAMBURLAINE
        Stand up, ye base, unworthy soldiers!
100   Know ye not yet the argument of arms?
AMYRAS
        Good my lord, let him be forgiven for once,
        And we will force him to the field hereafter.
TAMBURLAINE
        Stand up, my boys, and I will teach ye arms
        And what the jealousy of wars must do.
        O Samarcanda, where I breathèd first
        And joyed the fire of this martial flesh,
        Blush, blush, fair city, at thine honour's foil
        And shame of nature, which Jaertis' stream,

Embracing thee with deepest of his love,
Can never wash from thy distainèd brows!   110
Here, Jove, receive his fainting soul again –
    [*He stabs* CALYPHAS.]
A form not meet to give that subject essence
Whose matter is the flesh of Tamburlaine,
Wherein an incorporeal spirit moves,
Made of the mould whereof thyself consists,
Which makes me valiant, proud, ambitious,
Ready to levy power against thy throne,
That I might move the turning spheres of heaven;
For earth and all this airy region
Cannot contain the state of Tamburlaine.   120
By Mahomet, thy mighty friend, I swear,
In sending to my issue such a soul,
Created of the massy dregs of earth,
The scum and tartar of the elements,
Wherein was neither courage, strength, or wit,
But folly, sloth, and damnèd idleness,
Thou hast procured a greater enemy
Than he that darted mountains at thy head,
Shaking the burden mighty Atlas bears,
Whereat thou, trembling, hidd'st thee in the air,   130
Clothed with a pitchy cloud for being seen.
And now, ye cankered curs of Asia,
That will not see the strength of Tamburlaine
Although it shine as brightly as the sun,
Now you shall feel the strength of Tamburlaine,
And by the state of his supremacy
Approve the difference 'twixt himself and you.

ORCANES
    Thou showest the difference 'twixt ourselves and thee,
    In this thy barbarous damnèd tyranny.

JERUSALEM
    Thy victories are grown so violent   140
    That shortly heaven, filled with the meteors
    Of blood and fire thy tyrannies have made,
    Will pour down blood and fire on thy head,

    Whose scalding drops will pierce thy seething brains
    And with our bloods revenge our bloods on thee.
TAMBURLAINE
    Villains, these terrors and these tyrannies,
    (If tyrannies war's justice ye repute)
    I execute, enjoined me from above,
    To scourge the pride of such as heaven abhors;
150   Nor am I made arch-monarch of the world,
    Crowned and invested by the hand of Jove,
    For deeds of bounty or nobility.
    But since I exercise a greater name,
    The scourge of God and terror of the world,
    I must apply myself to fit those terms,
    In war, in blood, in death, in cruelty,
    And plague such peasants as resist in me
    The power of heaven's eternal majesty.
    Theridamas, Techelles, and Casane,
160   Ransack the tents and the pavilions
    Of these proud Turks, and take their concubines.
    Make them bury this effeminate brat,
    For not a common soldier shall defile
    His manly fingers with so faint a boy.
    Then bring those Turkish harlots to my tent,
    And I'll dispose them as it likes me best.
    Meanwhile, take him in.
SOLDIERS We will, my lord.
            [*Exeunt* SOLDIERS *with the body of* CALYPHAS.]
JERUSALEM
    O damnèd monster, nay, a fiend of hell,
170   Whose cruelties are not so harsh as thine,
    Nor yet imposed with such a bitter hate!
ORCANES
    Revenge it, Rhadamanth and Aeacus,
    And let your hates, extended in his pains,
    Expel the hate wherewith he pains our souls!
TREBIZOND
    May never day give virtue to his eyes,
    Whose sight, composed of fury and of fire,

Doth send such stern affections to his heart!

SORIA

May never spirit, vein, or artier feed
The cursèd substance of that cruel heart,
But, wanting moisture and remorseful blood,   180
Dry up with anger and consume with heat!

TAMBURLAINE

Well, bark, ye dogs. I'll bridle all your tongues
And bind them close with bits of burnished steel
Down to the channels of your hateful throats,
And with the pains my rigour shall inflict,
I'll make ye roar, that earth may echo forth
The far-resounding torments ye sustain,
As when an herd of lusty Cimbrian bulls
Run mourning round about the females' miss,
And, stung with fury of their following,   190
Fill all the air with troublous bellowing.
I will, with engines never exercised,
Conquer, sack, and utterly consume
Your cities and your golden palaces,
And with the flames that beat against the clouds,
Incense the heavens and make the stars to melt,
As if they were the tears of Mahomet
For hot consumption of his country's pride.
And, till by vision or by speech I hear
Immortal Jove say 'Cease, my Tamburlaine',   200
I will persist a terror to the world,
Making the meteors that, like armèd men,
Are seen to march upon the towers of heaven,
Run tilting round about the firmament,
And break their burning lances in the air
For honour of my wondrous victories.
Come, bring them in to our pavilion.

                                                    Exeunt.

Scene 2

[Enter] OLYMPIA *alone.*

OLYMPIA

Distressed Olympia, whose weeping eyes
Since thy arrival here beheld no sun,
But, closed within the compass of a tent,
Hath stained thy cheeks and made thee look like death,
Devise some means to rid thee of thy life
Rather than yield to his detested suit
Whose drift is only to dishonour thee.
And since this earth, dewed with thy brinish tears,
Affords no herbs whose taste may poison thee,
10   Nor yet this air, beat often with thy sighs,
Contagious smells and vapours to infect thee,
Nor thy close cave a sword to murder thee,
Let this invention be the instrument.

Enter THERIDAMAS.

THERIDAMAS

Well met, Olympia. I sought thee in my tent,
But, when I saw the place obscure and dark
Which with thy beauty thou wast wont to light,
Enraged, I ran about the fields for thee,
Supposing amorous Jove had sent his son,
The wingèd Hermes, to convey thee hence.
20   But now I find thee, and that fear is past.
Tell me, Olympia, wilt thou grant my suit?

OLYMPIA

My lord and husband's death, with my sweet son's,
With whom I buried all affections
Save grief and sorrow, which torment my heart,
Forbids my mind to entertain a thought
That tends to love, but meditate on death –
A fitter subject for a pensive soul.

THERIDAMAS

Olympia, pity him in whom thy looks
Have greater operation and more force

Than Cynthia's in the watery wilderness,   30
For with thy view my joys are at the full,
And ebb again as thou depart'st from me.

OLYMPIA

Ah, pity me, my lord, and draw your sword,
Making a passage for my troubled soul,
Which beats against this prison to get out
And meet my husband and my loving son.

THERIDAMAS

Nothing but still thy husband and thy son?
Leave this, my love, and listen more to me.
Thou shalt be stately queen of fair Argier,
And, clothed in costly cloth of massy gold,   40
Upon the marble turrets of my court
Sit like to Venus in her chair of state,
Commanding all thy princely eye desires;
And I will cast off arms and sit with thee,
Spending my life in sweet discourse of love.

OLYMPIA

No such discourse is pleasant in mine ears
But that where every period ends with death
And every line begins with death again.
I cannot love to be an emperess.

THERIDAMAS

Nay, lady, then if nothing will prevail,   50
I'll use some other means to make you yield.
Such is the sudden fury of my love,
I must and will be pleased, and you shall yield.
Come to the tent again.

OLYMPIA

Stay, good my lord! And, will you save my honour,
I'll give your grace a present of such price
As all the world cannot afford the like.

THERIDAMAS What is it?

OLYMPIA

An ointment which a cunning alchemist
Distillèd from the purest balsamum   60
And simplest extracts of all minerals,

In which the essential form of marble stone,
Tempered by science metaphysical
And spells of magic from the mouths of spirits,
With which if you but 'noint your tender skin,
Nor pistol, sword, nor lance can pierce your flesh.

THERIDAMAS

Why, madam, think ye to mock me thus palpably?

OLYMPIA

To prove it, I will 'noint my naked throat,
Which when you stab, look on your weapon's point,
70   And you shall see't rebated with the blow.

THERIDAMAS

Why gave you not your husband some of it,
If you loved him, and it so precious?

OLYMPIA

My purpose was, my lord, to spend it so,
But was prevented by his sudden end.
And for a present easy proof hereof,
That I dissemble not, try it on me.

THERIDAMAS

I will, Olympia, and will keep it for
The richest present of this eastern world.
    She anoints her throat.

OLYMPIA

Now stab, my lord, and mark your weapon's point,
80   That will be blunted if the blow be great.

THERIDAMAS [*stabs her throat*]

Here then, Olympia.
What, have I slain her? Villain, stab thyself!
Cut off this arm that murderèd my love,
In whom the learned rabbis of this age
Might find as many wondrous miracles
As in the theoria of the world!
Now hell is fairer than Elysium;
A greater lamp than that bright eye of heaven
From whence the stars do borrow all their light
90   Wanders about the black circumference,
And now the damnèd souls are free from pain,

For every Fury gazeth on her looks.
Infernal Dis is courting of my love,
Inventing masques and stately shows for her,
Opening the doors of his rich treasury
To entertain this queen of chastity,
Whose body shall be tombed with all the pomp
The treasure of my kingdom may afford.

Exit, taking her away.

Scene 3

[*Enter*] TAMBURLAINE, *drawn in his chariot by* [*the kings of*] TREBIZOND *and* SORIA *with bits in their mouths, reins in his left hand, in his right hand a whip, with which he scourgeth them.* TECHELLES, THERIDAMAS, USUMCASANE, AMYRAS, CELEBINUS; [ORCANES, *King of*] *Natolia and* [*the King of*] JERUSALEM *led by with five or six common* SOLDIERS.

TAMBURLAINE

Holla, ye pampered jades of Asia!
What, can ye draw but twenty miles a day
And have so proud a chariot at your heels
And such a coachman as great Tamburlaine,
But from Asphaltis, where I conquered you,
To Byron here where thus I honour you?
The horse that guide the golden eye of heaven
And blow the morning from their nostrils,
Making their fiery gait above the clouds,
Are not so honoured in their governor   10
As you, ye slaves, in mighty Tamburlaine.
The headstrong jades of Thrace Alcides tamed,
That King Aegeus fed with human flesh
And made so wanton that they knew their strengths,
Were not subdued with valour more divine
Than you by this unconquered arm of mine.
To make you fierce, and fit my appetite,

You shall be fed with flesh as raw as blood
And drink in pails the strongest muscadel.
20   If you can live with it, then live, and draw
My chariot swifter than the racking clouds.
If not, then die like beasts and fit for nought
But perches for the black and fatal ravens.
Thus am I right the scourge of highest Jove,
And see the figure of my dignity
By which I hold my name and majesty.

AMYRAS
Let me have coach, my lord, that I may ride
And thus be drawn with these two idle kings.

TAMBURLAINE
Thy youth forbids such ease, my kingly boy.
30   They shall tomorrow draw my chariot
While these their fellow kings may be refreshed.

ORCANES
O thou that swayest the region under earth,
And art a king as absolute as Jove,
Come as thou didst in fruitful Sicily,
Surveying all the glories of the land!
And as thou took'st the fair Proserpina,
Joying the fruit of Ceres' garden plot,
For love, for honour, and to make her queen,
So for just hate, for shame, and to subdue
40   This proud contemner of thy dreadful power,
Come once in fury and survey his pride,
Haling him headlong to the lowest hell!

THERIDAMAS [to TAMBURLAINE]
Your majesty must get some bits for these,
To bridle their contemptuous cursing tongues
That like unruly never-broken jades
Break through the hedges of their hateful mouths
And pass their fixèd bounds exceedingly.

TECHELLES
Nay, we will break the hedges of their mouths
And pull their kicking colts out of their pastures.

USUMCASANE

    Your majesty already hath devised   50

    A mean as fit as may be to restrain

    These coltish coach-horse tongues from blasphemy.

       [CELEBINUS *bridles* ORCANES.]

CELEBINUS

    How like you that, sir king? Why speak you not?

JERUSALEM

    Ah, cruel brat, sprung from a tyrant's loins,

    How like his cursèd father he begins

    To practise taunts and bitter tyrannies!

TAMBURLAINE

    Ay, Turk, I tell thee, this same boy is he

    That must, advanced in higher pomp than this,

    Rifle the kingdoms I shall leave unsacked

    If Jove, esteeming me too good for earth,   60

    Raise me to match the fair Aldebaran

    Above the threefold astracism of heaven

    Before I conquer all the triple world.

    Now fetch me out the Turkish concubines.

    I will prefer them for the funeral

    They have bestowed on my abortive son.

       The CONCUBINES *are brought in.*

    Where are my common soldiers now that fought

    So lion-like upon Asphaltis' plains?

SOLDIERS Here, my lord.

TAMBURLAINE

    Hold ye, tall soldiers. Take ye queens apiece,   70

    (I mean such queens as were kings' concubines.)

    Take them. Divide them and their jewels too,

    And let them equally serve all your turns.

SOLDIERS We thank your majesty.

TAMBURLAINE

    Brawl not, I warn you, for your lechery,

    For every man that so offends shall die.

ORCANES

    Injurious tyrant, wilt thou so defame

The hateful fortunes of thy victory
To exercise upon such guiltless dames
80   The violence of thy common soldiers' lust?
TAMBURLAINE
Live content, then, ye slaves, and meet not me
With troops of harlots at your slothful heels.
CONCUBINES
O, pity us, my lord, and save our honours!
TAMBURLAINE
Are ye not gone, ye villains, with your spoils?
                    They [SOLDIERS] *run away with the* LADIES.
JERUSALEM
O, merciless, infernal cruelty!
TAMBURLAINE
'Save your honours'! 'Twere but time indeed,
Lost long before you knew what honour meant.
THERIDAMAS
It seems they meant to conquer us, my lord,
And make us jesting pageants for their trulls.
TAMBURLAINE
90   And now themselves shall make our pageant,
And common soldiers jest with all their trulls.
Let them take pleasure soundly in their spoils
Till we prepare our march to Babylon,
Whither we next make expedition.
TECHELLES
Let us not be idle, then, my lord,
But presently be prest to conquer it.
TAMBURLAINE
We will, Techelles. Forward, then, ye jades!
Now crouch, ye kings of greatest Asia,
And tremble when ye hear this scourge will come
100   That whips down cities and controlleth crowns,
Adding their wealth and treasure to my store.
The Euxine Sea north to Natolia,
The Terrene west, the Caspian north-north-east,
And on the south Sinus Arabicus,
Shall all be loaden with the martial spoils

We will convey with us to Persia.
Then shall my native city Samarcanda
And crystal waves of fresh Jaertis' stream,
The pride and beauty of her princely seat,
Be famous through the furthest continents;   110
For there my palace royal shall be placed,
Whose shining turrets shall dismay the heavens
And cast the fame of Ilion's tower to hell.
Thorough the streets with troops of conquered kings
I'll ride in golden armour like the sun,
And in my helm a triple plume shall spring,
Spangled with diamonds dancing in the air,
To note me emperor of the threefold world,
Like to an almond tree y-mounted high
Upon the lofty and celestial mount   120
Of ever-green Selinus, quaintly decked
With blooms more white than Erycina's brows,
Whose tender blossoms tremble every one
At every little breath that thorough heaven is blown.
Then in my coach, like Saturn's royal son,
Mounted his shining chariot gilt with fire,
And drawn with princely eagles through the path
Paved with bright crystal and enchased with stars,
When all the gods stand gazing at his pomp,
So will I ride through Samarcanda streets,   130
Until my soul, dissevered from this flesh,
Shall mount the milk-white way and meet him there.
To Babylon, my lords, to Babylon!

                                                                Exeunt.

ACT 5

Scene 1

Enter the GOVERNOR OF BABYLON *upon the walls with* [MAXIMUS *and*] *others.*

GOVERNOR

What saith Maximus?

MAXIMUS

My lord, the breach the enemy hath made
Gives such assurance of our overthrow
That little hope is left to save our lives,
Or hold our city from the conqueror's hands.
Then hang out flags, my lord, of humble truce,
And satisfy the people's general prayers
That Tamburlaine's intolerable wrath
May be suppressed by our submission.

GOVERNOR

10   Villain, respects thou more thy slavish life
Than honour of thy country or thy name?
Is not my life and state as dear to me,
The city and my native country's weal,
As any thing of price with thy conceit?
Have we not hope, for all our battered walls,
To live secure and keep his forces out,
When this our famous lake of Limnasphaltis
Makes walls afresh with every thing that falls
Into the liquid substance of his stream,
20   More strong than are the gates of death or hell?
What faintness should dismay our courages

When we are thus defenced against our foe
And have no terror but his threat'ning looks?
   Enter another [CITIZEN *above*], *kneeling to the*
   GOVERNOR.

FIRST CITIZEN
My lord, if ever you did deed of ruth
And now will work a refuge to our lives,
Offer submission, hang up flags of truce,
That Tamburlaine may pity our distress
And use us like a loving conqueror.
Though this be held his last day's dreadful siege
Wherein he spareth neither man nor child,   30
Yet are there Christians of Georgia here,
Whose state he ever pitied and relieved,
Will get his pardon if your grace would send.

GOVERNOR
How is my soul environèd,
And this eternized city Babylon
Filled with a pack of faint-heart fugitives
That thus entreat their shame and servitude!
   [*Enter another* CITIZEN *above, kneeling to the*
   GOVERNOR.]

SECOND CITIZEN
My lord, if ever you will win our hearts,
Yield up the town, save our wives and children!
For I will cast myself from off these walls,   40
Or die some death of quickest violence
Before I bide the wrath of Tamburlaine.

GOVERNOR
Villains, cowards, traitors to our state!
Fall to the earth and pierce the pit of hell,
That legions of tormenting spirits may vex
Your slavish bosoms with continual pains!
I care not, nor the town will never yield
As long as any life is in my breast.
   Enter THERIDAMAS *and* TECHELLES, *with other*
   SOLDIERS.

THERIDAMAS

    Thou desperate governor of Babylon,

50   To save thy life, and us a little labour,

    Yield speedily the city to our hands,

    Or else be sure thou shalt be forced with pains

    More exquisite than ever traitor felt.

GOVERNOR

    Tyrant, I turn the traitor in thy throat,

    And will defend it in despite of thee.

    Call up the soldiers to defend these walls.

TECHELLES

    Yield, foolish governor. We offer more

    Than ever yet we did to such proud slaves

    As durst resist us till our third day's siege.

60   Thou seest us prest to give the last assault,

    And that shall bide no more regard of parley.

GOVERNOR

    Assault and spare not. We will never yield.

      Alarm, and they scale the walls. [*Exeunt* CITIZENS *and*
      GOVERNOR *above, followed in by* THERIDAMAS,
      TECHELLES, *and their* SOLDIERS.] *Enter* TAMBURLAINE
      [*all in black, drawn in his chariot by the kings of*
      TREBIZOND *and* SORIA], *with* USUMCASANE, AMYRAS,
      and CELEBINUS, *with others; the two spare kings*
      [ORCANES *of Natolia, and* JERUSALEM].

TAMBURLAINE

    The stately buildings of fair Babylon,

    Whose lofty pillars, higher than the clouds,

    Were wont to guide the seaman in the deep,

    Being carried thither by the cannon's force,

    Now fill the mouth of Limnasphaltis' lake

    And make a bridge unto the battered walls.

    Where Belus, Ninus, and great Alexander

70   Have rode in triumph, triumphs Tamburlaine,

    Whose chariot wheels have burst th'Assyrians' bones,

    Drawn with these kings on heaps of carcasses.

    Now in the place where fair Semiramis,

Courted by kings and peers of Asia,
Hath trod the measures, do my soldiers march;
And in the streets, where brave Assyrian dames
Have rid in pomp like rich Saturnia,
With furious words and frowning visages
My horsemen brandish their unruly blades.
    Enter [below] THERIDAMAS *and* TECHELLES, *bringing the*
    GOVERNOR OF BABYLON.
Who have ye there, my lords?   80

THERIDAMAS

The sturdy governor of Babylon,
That made us all the labour for the town
And used such slender reck'ning of your majesty.

TAMBURLAINE

Go bind the villain. He shall hang in chains
Upon the ruins of this conquered town.
Sirrah, the view of our vermilion tents,
Which threatened more than if the region
Next underneath the element of fire
Were full of comets and of blazing stars
Whose flaming trains should reach down to the earth,   90
Could not affright you; no, nor I myself,
The wrathful messenger of mighty Jove,
That with his sword hath quailed all earthly kings,
Could not persuade you to submission,
But still the ports were shut. Villain, I say,
Should I but touch the rusty gates of hell,
The triple-headed Cerberus would howl
And wake black Jove to crouch and kneel to me;
But I have sent volleys of shot to you,
Yet could not enter till the breach was made.   100

GOVERNOR

Nor, if my body could have stopped the breach,
Shouldst thou have entered, cruel Tamburlaine.
'Tis not thy bloody tents can make me yield,
Nor yet thyself, the anger of the Highest,
For, though thy cannon shook the city walls,

My heart did never quake, or courage faint.

TAMBURLAINE

Well, now I'll make it quake. Go draw him up.
Hang him in chains upon the city walls,
And let my soldiers shoot the slave to death.

GOVERNOR

110   Vile monster, born of some infernal hag,
And sent from hell to tyrannize on earth,
Do all thy worst. Nor death, nor Tamburlaine,
Torture, or pain can daunt my dreadless mind.

TAMBURLAINE

Up with him, then; his body shall be scarred.

GOVERNOR

But Tamburlaine, in Limnasphaltis' lake
There lies more gold than Babylon is worth,
Which when the city was besieged I hid.
Save but my life, and I will give it thee.

TAMBURLAINE

Then, for all your valour, you would save your life?
120   Whereabout lies it?

GOVERNOR

Under a hollow bank, right opposite
Against the western gate of Babylon.

TAMBURLAINE

Go thither, some of you, and take his gold.

                                [Exeunt SOLDIERS.]

The rest, forward with execution!
Away with him hence, let him speak no more.
I think I make your courage something quail.

               [Exit GOVERNOR, *led away by* SOLDIERS.]

When this is done, we'll march from Babylon
And make our greatest haste to Persia.
These jades are broken-winded and half tired;
130   Unharness them, and let me have fresh horse.

      [SOLDIERS *unharness* TREBIZOND *and* SORIA.]

So, now their best is done to honour me,
Take them and hang them both up presently.

TREBIZOND
  Vile tyrant, barbarous, bloody Tamburlaine!
TAMBURLAINE Take them away, Theridamas. See them dis-
  patched.
THERIDAMAS I will, my lord.
      [*Exit* THERIDAMAS *with the kings of* TREBIZOND *and*
                                                    SORIA.]
TAMBURLAINE
  Come, Asian viceroys, to your tasks a while,
  And take such fortune as your fellows felt.
ORCANES
  First let thy Scythian horse tear both our limbs,
  Rather than we should draw thy chariot,   140
  And like base slaves abject our princely minds
  To vile and ignominious servitude.
JERUSALEM
  Rather lend me thy weapon, Tamburlaine,
  That I may sheathe it in this breast of mine.
  A thousand deaths could not torment our hearts
  More than the thought of this doth vex our souls.
AMYRAS
  They will talk still, my lord, if you do not bridle them.
TAMBURLAINE
  Bridle them, and let me to my coach.
      They bridle them. [*The* GOVERNOR OF BABYLON *is hung
      up in chains. Re-enter* THERIDAMAS. TAMBURLAINE
      mounts his chariot.]
AMYRAS
  See now, my lord, how brave the captain hangs!
TAMBURLAINE
  'Tis brave indeed, my boy. Well done!   150
  Shoot first, my lord, and then the rest shall follow.
THERIDAMAS
  Then have at him to begin withal.
      THERIDAMAS *shoots* [*the* GOVERNOR].
GOVERNOR
  Yet save my life, and let this wound appease

The mortal fury of great Tamburlaine.

TAMBURLAINE

No, though Asphaltis' lake were liquid gold
And offered me as ransom for thy life,
Yet shouldst thou die. Shoot at him all at once.
   They shoot.
So, now he hangs like Baghdad's governor,
Having as many bullets in his flesh

160   As there be breaches in her battered wall.
Go now and bind the burghers hand and foot,
And cast them headlong in the city's lake;
Tartars and Persians shall inhabit there,
And, to command the city, I will build
A citadel, that all Assyria,
Which hath been subject to the Persian king,
Shall pay me tribute for, in Babylon.

TECHELLES

What shall be done with their wives and children, my lord?

TAMBURLAINE

Techelles, drown them all, man, woman, and child.

170   Leave not a Babylonian in the town.

TECHELLES

I will about it straight. Come, soldiers.
                    Exit [TECHELLES *with* SOLDIERS].

TAMBURLAINE

Now, Casane, where's the Turkish Alcoran,
And all the heaps of superstitious books
Found in the temples of that Mahomet
Whom I have thought a god? They shall be burnt.

USUMCASANE [*presenting the books*] Here they are, my lord.

TAMBURLAINE

Well said. Let there be a fire presently.
   [*They light a fire.*]
In vain, I see, men worship Mahomet.
My sword hath sent millions of Turks to hell,

180   Slew all his priests, his kinsmen, and his friends,
And yet I live untouched by Mahomet.
There is a God full of revenging wrath,

From whom the thunder and the lightning breaks,
Whose scourge I am, and him will I obey.
So, Casane, fling them in the fire.
   [*They burn the books.*]
Now, Mahomet, if thou have any power,
Come down thyself and work a miracle.
Thou art not worthy to be worshippèd
That suffers flames of fire to burn the writ
Wherein the sum of thy religion rests.   190
Why send'st thou not a furious whirlwind down
To blow thy Alcoran up to thy throne,
Where men report thou sitt'st by God himself,
Or vengeance on the head of Tamburlaine,
That shakes his sword against thy majesty
And spurns the abstracts of thy foolish laws?
Well, soldiers, Mahomet remains in hell;
He cannot hear the voice of Tamburlaine.
Seek out another godhead to adore,
The God that sits in heaven, if any god,   200
For he is God alone, and none but he.
   [*Re-enter* TECHELLES.]

TECHELLES
I have fulfilled your highness' will, my lord.
Thousands of men, drowned in Asphaltis' lake,
Have made the water swell above the banks,
And fishes, fed by human carcasses,
Amazed, swim up and down upon the waves
As when they swallow assafoetida,
Which makes them fleet aloft and gasp for air.

TAMBURLAINE
Well, then, my friendly lords, what now remains,
But that we leave sufficient garrison,   210
And presently depart to Persia
To triumph after all our victories?

THERIDAMAS
Ay, good my lord. Let us in haste to Persia,
And let this captain be removed the walls
To some high hill about the city here.

TAMBURLAINE
  Let it be so. About it, soldiers.
  But stay, I feel myself distempered suddenly.
TECHELLES
  What is it dares distemper Tamburlaine?
TAMBURLAINE
  Something, Techelles, but I know not what.
220 But forth, ye vassals! Whatsoe'er it be,
  Sickness or death can never conquer me.

Exeunt.

Scene 2

Enter CALLAPINE, [*the King of*] AMASIA, [*a* CAPTAIN,
SOLDIERS,] *with drums and trumpets.*

CALLAPINE
  King of Amasia, now our mighty host
  Marcheth in Asia Major, where the streams
  Of Euphrates and Tigris swiftly runs,
  And here may we behold great Babylon,
  Circled about with Limnasphaltis' lake,
  Where Tamburlaine with all his army lies,
  Which being faint and weary with the siege,
  We may lie ready to encounter him
  Before his host be full from Babylon,
10 And so revenge our latest grievous loss,
  If God or Mahomet send any aid.
AMASIA
  Doubt not, my lord, but we shall conquer him.
  The monster that hath drunk a sea of blood
  And yet gapes still for more to quench his thirst,
  Our Turkish swords shall headlong send to hell;
  And that vile carcass drawn by warlike kings,
  The fowls shall eat, for never sepulchre
  Shall grace that base-born tyrant Tamburlaine.

CALLAPINE
  When I record my parents' slavish life,
  Their cruel death, mine own captivity,   20
  My viceroys' bondage under Tamburlaine,
  Methinks I could sustain a thousand deaths
  To be revenged of all his villainy.
  Ah, sacred Mahomet! Thou that hast seen
  Millions of Turks perish by Tamburlaine,
  Kingdoms made waste, brave cities sacked and burnt,
  And but one host is left to honour thee,
  Aid thy obedient servant Callapine,
  And make him, after all these overthrows,
  To triumph over cursèd Tamburlaine!   30
AMASIA
  Fear not, my lord. I see great Mahomet
  Clothèd in purple clouds, and on his head
  A chaplet brighter than Apollo's crown,
  Marching about the air with armèd men
  To join with you against this Tamburlaine.
CAPTAIN
  Renownèd general, mighty Callapine,
  Though God himself and holy Mahomet
  Should come in person to resist your power,
  Yet might your mighty host encounter all
  And pull proud Tamburlaine upon his knees   40
  To sue for mercy at your highness' feet.
CALLAPINE
  Captain, the force of Tamburlaine is great,
  His fortune greater, and the victories
  Wherewith he hath so sore dismayed the world
  Are greatest to discourage all our drifts.
  Yet when the pride of Cynthia is at full
  She wanes again, and so shall his, I hope,
  For we have here the chief selected men
  Of twenty several kingdoms at the least.
  Nor ploughman, priest, nor merchant stays at home;   50
  All Turkey is in arms with Callapine,

And never will we sunder camps and arms
Before himself or his be conquerèd.
This is the time that must eternize me
For conquering the tyrant of the world.
Come, soldiers, let us lie in wait for him,
And if we find him absent from his camp
Or that it be rejoined again at full,
Assail it and be sure of victory.

Exeunt.

Scene 3

[*Enter*] THERIDAMAS, TECHELLES, USUMCASANE.

THERIDAMAS

Weep, heavens, and vanish into liquid tears!
Fall, stars that govern his nativity,
And summon all the shining lamps of heaven
To cast their bootless fires to the earth
And shed their feeble influence in the air!
Muffle your beauties with eternal clouds,
For hell and darkness pitch their pitchy tents,
And Death with armies of Cimmerian spirits
Gives battle 'gainst the heart of Tamburlaine.
10   Now, in defiance of that wonted love
Your sacred virtues poured upon his throne
And made his state an honour to the heavens,
These cowards invisibly assail his soul
And threaten conquest on our sovereign;
But if he die, your glories are disgraced,
Earth droops and says that hell in heaven is placed.

TECHELLES

O then, ye powers that sway eternal seats
And guide this massy substance of the earth,
If you retain desert of holiness,
20   As your supreme estates instruct our thoughts,

Be not inconstant, careless of your fame;
Bear not the burden of your enemies' joys,
Triumphing in his fall whom you advanced;
But as his birth, life, health, and majesty
Were strangely blest and governèd by heaven,
So honour, heaven, till heaven dissolvèd be,
His birth, his life, his health, and majesty.

USUMCASANE
Blush, heaven, to lose the honour of thy name,
To see thy footstool set upon thy head,
And let no baseness in thy haughty breast   30
Sustain a shame of such inexcellence,
To see the devils mount in angels' thrones
And angels dive into the pools of hell.
And though they think their painful date is out
And that their power is puissant as Jove's,
Which makes them manage arms against thy state,
Yet make them feel the strength of Tamburlaine,
Thy instrument and note of majesty,
Is greater far than they can thus subdue;
For if he die, thy glory is disgraced,   40
Earth droops and says that hell in heaven is placed.
    [Enter TAMBURLAINE *in his chariot, drawn by* ORCANES,
    King of Natolia and the King of JERUSALEM, *attended by*
    AMYRAS, CELEBINUS, *and* PHYSICIANS.]

TAMBURLAINE
What daring god torments my body thus
And seeks to conquer mighty Tamburlaine?
Shall sickness prove me now to be a man,
That have been termed the terror of the world?
Techelles and the rest, come take your swords
And threaten him whose hand afflicts my soul.
Come let us march against the powers of heaven
And set black streamers in the firmament
To signify the slaughter of the gods.   50
Ah, friends, what shall I do? I cannot stand.
Come, carry me to war against the gods,

That thus envy the health of Tamburlaine.

THERIDAMAS

Ah, good my lord, leave these impatient words,
Which add much danger to your malady.

TAMBURLAINE

Why shall I sit and languish in this pain?
No! Strike the drums, and, in revenge of this,
Come, let us charge our spears and pierce his breast
Whose shoulders bear the axis of the world,
60   That if I perish, heaven and earth may fade.
Theridamas, haste to the court of Jove.
Will him to send Apollo hither straight
To cure me, or I'll fetch him down myself.

TECHELLES

Sit still, my gracious lord. This grief will cease
And cannot last, it is so violent.

TAMBURLAINE

Not last, Techelles? No, for I shall die.
See where my slave, the ugly monster Death,
Shaking and quivering, pale and wan for fear,
Stands aiming at me with his murdering dart,
70   Who flies away at every glance I give,
And when I look away comes stealing on.
Villain, away, and hie thee to the field!
I and mine army come to load thy bark
With souls of thousand mangled carcasses.
Look where he goes! But see, he comes again
Because I stay. Techelles, let us march,
And weary Death with bearing souls to hell.

PHYSICIAN

Pleaseth your majesty to drink this potion,
Which will abate the fury of your fit
80   And cause some milder spirits govern you.

TAMBURLAINE

Tell me, what think you of my sickness now?

PHYSICIAN

I viewed your urine, and the hypostasis,

Thick and obscure, doth make your danger great;
Your veins are full of accidental heat,
Whereby the moisture of your blood is dried.
The humidum and calor, which some hold
Is not a parcel of the elements
But of a substance more divine and pure,
Is almost clean extinguishèd and spent,
Which, being the cause of life, imports your death.   90
Besides, my lord, this day is critical,
Dangerous to those whose crisis is as yours.
Your artiers, which alongst the veins convey
The lively spirits which the heart engenders,
Are parched and void of spirit, that the soul,
Wanting those organons by which it moves,
Cannot endure by argument of art.
Yet if your majesty may escape this day,
No doubt but you shall soon recover all.

TAMBURLAINE
Then will I comfort all my vital parts   100
And live in spite of Death above a day.

                                        Alarm within.

   [*Enter a* MESSENGER.]

MESSENGER My lord, young Callapine, that lately fled from
   your majesty, hath now gathered a fresh army, and, hearing
   your absence in the field, offers to set upon us presently.

TAMBURLAINE
See, my physicians, now, how Jove hath sent
A present medicine to recure my pain!
My looks shall make them fly, and, might I follow,
There should not one of all the villain's power
Live to give offer of another fight.

USUMCASANE
I joy, my lord, your highness is so strong,   110
That can endure so well your royal presence
Which only will dismay the enemy.

TAMBURLAINE
I know it well, Casane. Draw, you slaves!

In spite of Death I will go show my face.
Alarm. TAMBURLAINE *goes in [in his chariot], and comes
out again with all the rest.*

TAMBURLAINE

Thus are the villains, cowards, fled for fear,
Like summer's vapours vanished by the sun.
And could I but a while pursue the field,
That Callapine should be my slave again.
But I perceive my martial strength is spent;
120   In vain I strive and rail against those powers
That mean t'invest me in a higher throne,
As much too high for this disdainful earth.
Give me a map, then, let me see how much
Is left for me to conquer all the world,
That these my boys may finish all my wants.
        One brings a map.
Here I began to march towards Persia,
Along Armenia and the Caspian Sea,
And thence unto Bithynia, where I took
The Turk and his great empress prisoners;
130   Then marched I into Egypt and Arabia,
And here, not far from Alexandria,
Whereas the Terrene and the Red Sea meet,
Being distant less than full a hundred leagues,
I meant to cut a channel to them both,
That men might quickly sail to India.
From thence to Nubia, near Borno lake,
And so along the Ethiopian sea,
Cutting the tropic line of Capricorn,
I conquered all as far as Zanzibar.
140   Then by the northern part of Africa
I came at last to Graecia, and from thence
To Asia, where I stay against my will,
Which is from Scythia, where I first began,
Backward and forwards, near five thousand leagues.
Look here, my boys, see what a world of ground
Lies westward from the midst of Cancer's line
Unto the rising of this earthly globe,

Whereas the sun, declining from our sight,
Begins the day with our Antipodes;
And shall I die, and this unconquerèd?   150
Lo, here, my sons, are all the golden mines,
Inestimable drugs, and precious stones,
More worth than Asia and the world beside;
And from th'Antarctic Pole eastward behold
As much more land, which never was descried,
Wherein are rocks of pearl that shine as bright
As all the lamps that beautify the sky;
And shall I die, and this unconquerèd?
Here, lovely boys; [*giving them the map*]
                    what Death forbids my life,
That let your lives command in spite of Death.   160

AMYRAS

Alas, my lord, how should our bleeding hearts,
Wounded and broken with your highness' grief,
Retain a thought of joy or spark of life?
Your soul gives essence to our wretched subjects,
Whose matter is incorporate in your flesh.

CELEBINUS

Your pains do pierce our souls; no hope survives,
For by your life we entertain our lives.

TAMBURLAINE

But sons, this subject, not of force enough
To hold the fiery spirit it contains,
Must part, imparting his impressions   170
By equal portions into both your breasts;
My flesh, divided in your precious shapes,
Shall still retain my spirit though I die,
And live in all your seeds immortally.
Then now remove me, that I may resign
My place and proper title to my son.
  [*To* AMYRAS]
First take my scourge and my imperial crown,
And mount my royal chariot of estate,
That I may see thee crowned before I die.
Help me, my lords, to make my last remove.   180

[They help him into a chair.]

THERIDAMAS

    A woeful change, my lord, that daunts our thoughts
    More than the ruin of our proper souls.

TAMBURLAINE

    Sit up, my son. Let me see how well
    Thou wilt become thy father's majesty.
      They crown him.

AMYRAS

    With what a flinty bosom should I joy
    The breath of life and burden of my soul,
    If, not resolved into resolvèd pains,
    My body's mortifièd lineaments
    Should exercise the motions of my heart,
190   Pierced with the joy of any dignity!
    O father, if the unrelenting ears
    Of Death and hell be shut against my prayers,
    And that the spiteful influence of heaven
    Deny my soul fruition of her joy,
    How should I step or stir my hateful feet
    Against the inward powers of my heart,
    Leading a life that only strives to die,
    And plead in vain unpleasing sovereignty?

TAMBURLAINE

    Let not thy love exceed thine honour, son,
200   Nor bar thy mind that magnanimity
    That nobly must admit necessity.
    Sit up, my boy, and with those silken reins
    Bridle the steelèd stomachs of those jades.

THERIDAMAS *[to* AMYRAS*]*

    My lord, you must obey his majesty,
    Since fate commands, and proud necessity.

AMYRAS *[ascending the chariot]*

    Heavens witness me, with what a broken heart
    And damnèd spirit I ascend this seat,
    And send my soul, before my father die,
    His anguish and his burning agony!

TAMBURLAINE

   Now fetch the hearse of fair Zenocrate.   210
   Let it be placed by this my fatal chair
   And serve as parcel of my funeral.

                              [Exeunt some.]

USUMCASANE

   Then feels your majesty no sovereign ease,
   Nor may our hearts, all drowned in tears of blood,
   Joy any hope of your recovery?

TAMBURLAINE

   Casane, no. The monarch of the earth
   And eyeless monster that torments my soul
   Cannot behold the tears ye shed for me,
   And therefore still augments his cruelty.

TECHELLES

   Then let some god oppose his holy power   220
   Against the wrath and tyranny of Death,
   That his tear-thirsty and unquenchèd hate
   May be upon himself reverberate.

     They bring in the hearse [of ZENOCRATE].

TAMBURLAINE

   Now, eyes, enjoy your latest benefit,
   And when my soul hath virtue of your sight,
   Pierce through the coffin and the sheet of gold
   And glut your longings with a heaven of joy.
   So, reign, my son! Scourge and control those slaves,
   Guiding thy chariot with thy father's hand.
   As precious is the charge thou undertak'st   230
   As that which Clymene's brainsick son did guide,
   When wand'ring Phoebe's ivory cheeks were scorched,
   And all the earth, like Etna, breathing fire.
   Be warned by him, then; learn with awful eye
   To sway a throne as dangerous as his.
   For if thy body thrive not full of thoughts
   As pure and fiery as Phyteus' beams,
   The nature of these proud rebelling jades
   Will take Occasion by the slenderest hair,

240   And draw thee piecemeal like Hippolytus,
        Through rocks more steep and sharp than Caspian clifts.
        The nature of thy chariot will not bear
        A guide of baser temper than myself,
        More than heaven's coach the pride of Phaethon.
        Farewell, my boys; my dearest friends, farewell!
        My body feels, my soul doth weep to see
        Your sweet desires deprived of company;
        For Tamburlaine, the scourge of God, must die.
            [*He dies.*]

AMYRAS
        Meet heaven and earth, and here let all things end!
250   For earth hath spent the pride of all her fruit,
        And heaven consumed his choicest living fire.
        Let earth and heaven his timeless death deplore,
        For both their worths will equal him no more.

                                                    [*Exeunt.*]

THE JEW OF MALTA

[Dramatis Personae

MACHEVIL, *the Prologue*
BARABAS
TWO MERCHANTS
THREE JEWS
FERNEZE, *the Governor of Malta*
KNIGHTS OF MALTA
OFFICERS
CALLAPINE
BASHAWS
CALYMATH
ABIGALL, *Barabas's daughter*
FRIAR JACOMO
FRIAR BARNARDINE
AN ABBESS
TWO NUNS
MATHIAS, *Katherine's son*
LODOWICK, *Ferneze's son*
MARTIN DEL BOSCO, *Vice-admiral of Spain*
ITHAMORE, *a slave*
SLAVES
KATHERINE
BELLAMIRA, *a courtesan*
PILIA-BORZA
TURKISH JANIZARIES
A MESSENGER
CARPENTERS
SERVANTS
ATTENDANTS]

[THE
DEDICATORY
EPISTLE]

To My Worthy Friend, Master Thomas Hammon, of Gray's Inn, etc.

This play, composed by so worthy an author as Master
Marlowe, and the part of the Jew presented by so unimitable
an actor as Master Alleyn, being in this later age commended
to the stage, as I ushered it unto the court, and presented it
to the Cock-pit, with these prologues and epilogues here
inserted, so now being newly brought to the press, I was loath
it should be published without the ornament of an epistle,
making choice of you unto whom to devote it, than whom
(of all those gentlemen and acquaintance within the compass
of my long knowledge) there is none more able to tax ignor-   10
ance or attribute right to merit. Sir, you have been pleased to
grace some of mine own works with your courteous patronage. I hope this will not be the worse accepted because commended by me, over whom none can claim more power or
privilege than yourself. I had no better a New Year's gift to
present you with. Receive it therefore as a continuance of that
inviolable obligement by which he rests still engaged, who, as
he ever hath, shall always remain,

Tuissimus,
Thomas Heywood   20

THE PROLOGUE
SPOKEN AT COURT

Gracious and great, that we so boldly dare
('Mongst other plays that now in fashion are)
To present this, writ many years agone,
And in that age thought second unto none,
We humbly crave your pardon. We pursue
The story of a rich and famous Jew
Who lived in Malta. You shall find him still,
In all his projects, a sound Machevill;
And that's his character. He that hath passed
So many censures is now come at last
To have your princely ears. Grace you him; then
You crown the action and renown the pen.

10

THE PROLOGUE
TO THE STAGE,
AT THE COCK-PIT

We know not how our play may pass this stage,
But by the best of *poets in that age   *Marlowe
The *Malta Jew* had being, and was made,
And he then by the best of *actors played.   *Alleyn
In *Hero and Leander*, one did gain
A lasting memory; in *Tamburlaine*,
This *Jew*, with others many, th' other wan
The attribute of peerless, being a man
Whom we may rank with (doing no one wrong)
Proteus for shapes and Roscius for a tongue,   10
So could he speak, so vary; nor is't hate
To merit in *him who doth personate   *Perkins
Our Jew this day, nor is it his ambition
To exceed, or equal, being of condition
More modest. This is all that he intends,
And that, too, at the urgence of some friends:
To prove his best, and if none here gainsay it,
The part he hath studied, and intends to play it.

THE JEW OF MALTA
[PROLOGUE]

[*Enter*] MACHEVIL.

MACHEVIL

Albeit the world think Machevil is dead,
Yet was his soul but flown beyond the Alps,
And, now the Guise is dead, is come from France
To view this land and frolic with his friends.
To some perhaps my name is odious,
But such as love me guard me from their tongues,
And let them know that I am Machevil,
And weigh not men, and therefore not men's words.
Admired I am of those that hate me most.
10   Though some speak openly against my books,
Yet will they read me and thereby attain
To Peter's chair, and, when they cast me off,
Are poisoned by my climbing followers.
I count religion but a childish toy
And hold there is no sin but ignorance.
Birds of the air will tell of murders past!
I am ashamed to hear such fooleries.
Many will talk of title to a crown;
What right had Caesar to the empery?
20   Might first made kings, and laws were then most sure
When, like the Draco's, they were writ in blood.
Hence comes it that a strong-built citadel
Commands much more than letters can import;
Which maximé had Phalaris observed,
He'd never bellowed in a brazen bull
Of great ones' envy. O'th'poor petty wights,

Let me be envied and not pitièd!
But whither am I bound? I come not, I,
To read a lecture here in Britainy,
But to present the tragedy of a Jew,   30
Who smiles to see how full his bags are crammed,
Which money was not got without my means.
I crave but this: grace him as he deserves,
And let him not be entertained the worse
Because he favours me.

                                              [Exit.]

ACT 1

[*Scene 1*]

Enter BARABAS *in his counting-house, with heaps of gold before him.*

BARABAS

So that of thus much that return was made,
And, of the third part of the Persian ships,
There was the venture summed and satisfied.
As for those Samnites and the men of Uz,
That bought my Spanish oils and wines of Greece,
Here have I pursed their paltry silverlings.
Fie, what a trouble 'tis to count this trash!
Well fare the Arabians, who so richly pay
The things they traffic for with wedge of gold,
10   Whereof a man may easily in a day
Tell that which may maintain him all his life.
The needy groom that never fingered groat
Would make a miracle of thus much coin;
But he whose steel-barred coffers are crammed full,
And all his lifetime hath been tired,
Wearying his fingers' ends with telling it,
Would in his age be loath to labour so,
And for a pound to sweat himself to death.
Give me the merchants of the Indian mines,
20   That trade in metal of the purest mould;
The wealthy Moor, that in the eastern rocks
Without control can pick his riches up,
And in his house heap pearl like pebble-stones,

Receive them free, and sell them by the weight –
Bags of fiery opals, sapphires, amethysts,
Jacinths, hard topaz, grass-green emeralds,
Beauteous rubies, sparkling diamonds,
And seld-seen costly stones of so great price,
As one of them, indifferently rated,
And of a carat of this quantity,   30
May serve in peril of calamity
To ransom great kings from captivity.
This is the ware wherein consists my wealth;
And thus methinks should men of judgement frame
Their means of traffic from the vulgar trade,
And as their wealth increaseth, so enclose
Infinite riches in a little room.
But now, how stands the wind?
Into what corner peers my halcyon's bill?
Ha, to the east? Yes. See, how stands the vanes?   40
East and by south. Why then, I hope my ships
I sent for Egypt and the bordering isles
Are gotten up by Nilus' winding banks;
Mine argosy from Alexandria,
Loaden with spice and silks, now under sail,
Are smoothly gliding down by Candy shore
To Malta, through our Mediterranean Sea.
But who comes here?
      Enter [FIRST] MERCHANT.
                              How now?
FIRST MERCHANT   Barabas,
Thy ships are safe, riding in Malta road;
And all the merchants with other merchandise   50
Are safe arrived, and have sent me to know
Whether yourself will come and custom them.
BARABAS
The ships are safe, thou say'st, and richly fraught?
FIRST MERCHANT
They are.
BARABAS   Why then, go bid them come ashore
And bring with them their bills of entry.

I hope our credit in the custom-house
Will serve as well as I were present there.
Go send 'em threescore camels, thirty mules,
And twenty wagons to bring up the ware.
60   But art thou master in a ship of mine,
And is thy credit not enough for that?

FIRST MERCHANT
The very custom barely comes to more
Than many merchants of the town are worth,
And therefore far exceeds my credit, sir.

BARABAS
Go tell 'em the Jew of Malta sent thee, man.
Tush, who amongst 'em knows not Barabas?

FIRST MERCHANT I go.

BARABAS
So then, there's somewhat come.
Sirrah, which of my ships art thou master of?

FIRST MERCHANT
Of the *Speranza*, sir.

70   BARABAS   And saw'st thou not
Mine argosy at Alexandria?
Thou couldst not come from Egypt or by Caire,
But at the entry there into the sea,
Where Nilus pays his tribute to the main,
Thou needs must sail by Alexandria.

FIRST MERCHANT
I neither saw them nor inquired of them.
But this we heard some of our seamen say:
They wondered how you durst with so much wealth
Trust such a crazèd vessel, and so far.

BARABAS
80   Tush, they are wise! I know her and her strength.
But go, go thou thy ways; discharge thy ship,
And bid my factor bring his loading in.

                                    [*Exit* FIRST MERCHANT.]
And yet I wonder at this argosy.
        Enter a SECOND MERCHANT.

SECOND MERCHANT
  Thine argosy from Alexandria,
  Know, Barabas, doth ride in Malta road,
  Laden with riches and exceeding store
  Of Persian silks, of gold, and orient pearl.

BARABAS
  How chance you came not with those other ships
  That sailed by Egypt?

SECOND MERCHANT Sir, we saw 'em not.

BARABAS
  Belike they coasted round by Candy shore   90
  About their oils, or other businesses.
  But 'twas ill done of you to come so far
  Without the aid or conduct of their ships.

SECOND MERCHANT
  Sir, we were wafted by a Spanish fleet
  That never left us till within a league,
  That had the galleys of the Turk in chase.

BARABAS
  O, they were going up to Sicily. Well, go
  And bid the merchants and my men dispatch
  And come ashore, and see the fraught discharged.

SECOND MERCHANT I go.   100
                      Exit [SECOND MERCHANT].

BARABAS
  Thus trolls our fortune in by land and sea,
  And thus are we on every side enriched.
  These are the blessings promised to the Jews,
  And herein was old Abram's happiness.
  What more may heaven do for earthly man
  Than thus to pour out plenty in their laps,
  Ripping the bowels of the earth for them,
  Making the sea their servant, and the winds
  To drive their substance with successful blasts?
  Who hateth me but for my happiness?   110
  Or who is honoured now but for his wealth?
  Rather had I, a Jew, be hated thus

Than pitied in a Christian poverty;
For I can see no fruits in all their faith
But malice, falsehood, and excessive pride,
Which methinks fits not their profession.
Haply some hapless man hath conscience,
And for his conscience lives in beggary.
They say we are a scattered nation;
120   I cannot tell, but we have scambled up
More wealth by far than those that brag of faith.
There's Kirriah Jairim, the great Jew of Greece,
Obed in Bairseth, Nones in Portugal,
Myself in Malta, some in Italy,
Many in France, and wealthy every one –
Ay, wealthier far than any Christian.
I must confess we come not to be kings.
That's not our fault. Alas, our number's few,
And crowns come either by succession,
130   Or urged by force; and nothing violent,
Oft have I heard tell, can be permanent.
Give us a peaceful rule; make Christians kings,
That thirst so much for principality.
I have no charge, nor many children,
But one sole daughter, whom I hold as dear
As Agamemnon did his Iphigen;
And all I have is hers. But who comes here?
        Enter THREE JEWS.
FIRST JEW
    Tush, tell not me, 'twas done of policy.
SECOND JEW
    Come, therefore, let us go to Barabas,
140   For he can counsel best in these affairs;
    And here he comes
BARABAS   Why, how now, countrymen?
    Why flock you thus to me in multitudes?
    What accident's betided to the Jews?
FIRST JEW
    A fleet of warlike galleys, Barabas,
    Are come from Turkey, and lie in our road;

And they this day sit in the council-house
To entertain them and their embassy.

BARABAS

Why, let 'em come, so they come not to war;
Or let 'em war, so we be conquerors.
(*Aside*) Nay, let 'em combat, conquer, and kill all,   150
So they spare me, my daughter, and my wealth.

FIRST JEW

Were it for confirmation of a league,
They would not come in warlike manner thus.

SECOND JEW

I fear their coming will afflict us all.

BARABAS

Fond men, what dream you of their multitudes?
What need they treat of peace that are in league?
The Turks and those of Malta are in league.
Tut, tut, there is some other matter in't.

FIRST JEW

Why, Barabas, they come for peace or war.

BARABAS

Haply for neither, but to pass along   160
Towards Venice by the Adriatic Sea,
With whom they have attempted many times,
But never could effect their stratagem.

THIRD JEW

And very wisely said; it may be so.

SECOND JEW

But there's a meeting in the senate-house,
And all the Jews in Malta must be there.

BARABAS

Umh. All the Jews in Malta must be there?
Ay, like enough. Why then, let every man
Provide him, and be there for fashion sake.
If anything shall there concern our state,   170
Assure yourselves I'll look – (*aside*) unto myself.

FIRST JEW

I know you will. Well, brethren, let us go.

SECOND JEW

Let's take our leaves. Farewell, good Barabas.

BARABAS

Do so. Farewell, Zaareth, farewell, Temainte.

[*Exeunt the* THREE JEWS.]

And, Barabas, now search this secret out.
Summon thy senses; call thy wits together.
These silly men mistake the matter clean.
Long to the Turk did Malta contribute,
Which tribute – all in policy, I fear –
180   The Turks have let increase to such a sum
As all the wealth of Malta cannot pay,
And now by that advantage thinks, belike,
To seize upon the town. Ay, that he seeks.
Howe'er the world go, I'll make sure for one,
And seek in time to intercept the worst,
Warily guarding that which I ha' got.
Ego mihimet sum semper proximus.
Why, let 'em enter, let 'em take the town.

[*Exit.*]

[*Scene 2*]

Enter [FERNEZE] *Governor of Malta,* KNIGHTS, [*and*
OFFICERS], *met by* [CALLAPINE *and other*] BASHAWS *of
the Turk* [*and*] CALYMATH.

FERNEZE

Now, bashaws, what demand you at our hands?

CALLAPINE

Know, Knights of Malta, that we came from Rhodes,
From Cyprus, Candy, and those other isles
That lie betwixt the Mediterranean seas.

FERNEZE

What's Cyprus, Candy, and those other isles
To us, or Malta? What at our hands demand ye?

CALYMATH
  The ten years' tribute that remains unpaid.
FERNEZE
  Alas, my lord, the sum is over-great.
  I hope your highness will consider us.
CALYMATH
  I wish, grave governor, 'twere in my power   10
  To favour you, but 'tis my father's cause,
  Wherein I may not, nay, I dare not dally.
FERNEZE
  Then give us leave, great Selim Calymath.
      [FERNEZE *speaks to his* KNIGHTS.]
CALYMATH [*to his* BASHAWS]
  Stand all aside, and let the knights determine,
  And send to keep our galleys under sail,
  For happily we shall not tarry here.
      [*To* FERNEZE]
   Now, governor, how are you resolved?
FERNEZE
  Thus: since your hard conditions are such
  That you will needs have ten years' tribute past,
  We may have time to make collection   20
  Amongst the inhabitants of Malta for't.
CALLAPINE
  That's more than is in our commission.
CALYMATH
  What, Callapine, a little courtesy!
  Let's know their time; perhaps it is not long,
  And 'tis more kingly to obtain by peace
  Than to enforce conditions by constraint.
  What respite ask you, governor?
FERNEZE   But a month.
CALYMATH
  We grant a month, but see you keep your promise.
  Now launch our galleys back again to sea,
  Where we'll attend the respite you have ta'en,   30
  And for the money send our messenger.

Farewell, great governor, and brave Knights of Malta.

FERNEZE

And all good fortune wait on Calymath!

    Exeunt [CALYMATH, CALLAPINE *and other* BASHAWS].

Go, one, and call those Jews of Malta hither.

Were they not summoned to appear today?

OFFICER

They were, my lord, and here they come.

    Enter BARABAS *and* THREE JEWS.

FIRST KNIGHT

Have you determined what to say to them?

FERNEZE

Yes, give me leave; and Hebrews, now come near.

From the emperor of Turkey is arrived

40 Great Selim Calymath, his highness' son,

To levy of us ten years' tribute past.

Now then, here know that it concerneth us.

BARABAS

Then, good my lord, to keep your quiet still,

Your lordship shall do well to let them have it.

FERNEZE

Soft, Barabas, there's more 'longs to't than so.

To what this ten years' tribute will amount,

That we have cast, but cannot compass it

By reason of the wars, that robbed our store;

And therefore are we to request your aid.

BARABAS

50 Alas, my lord, we are no soldiers;

And what's our aid against so great a prince?

FIRST KNIGHT

Tut, Jew, we know thou art no soldier;

Thou art a merchant and a moneyed man,

And 'tis thy money, Barabas, we seek.

BARABAS

How, my lord, my money?

FERNEZE   Thine and the rest.

For, to be short, amongst you 't must be had.

FIRST JEW
  Alas, my lord, the most of us are poor!
FERNEZE
  Then let the rich increase your portions.
BARABAS
  Are strangers with your tribute to be taxed?
SECOND KNIGHT
  Have strangers leave with us to get their wealth?   60
  Then let them with us contribute.
BARABAS
  How, equally?
FERNEZE   No, Jew, like infidels.
  For through our sufferance of your hateful lives,
  Who stand accursèd in the sight of heaven,
  These taxes and afflictions are befall'n,
  And therefore thus we are determinèd.
  Read there the articles of our decrees.
OFFICER (*reads*) 'First, the tribute money of the Turks shall all
  be levied amongst the Jews, and each of them to pay one half
  of his estate.'   70
BARABAS
  How, half his estate? [*Aside*] I hope you mean not mine.
FERNEZE Read on.
OFFICER (*reads*) 'Secondly, he that denies to pay shall straight
  become a Christian.'
BARABAS
  How, a Christian? [*Aside*] Hum, what's here to do?
OFFICER (*reads*) 'Lastly, he that denies this shall absolutely lose
  all he has.'
ALL THREE JEWS O my lord, we will give half!
BARABAS
  O earth-mettled villains, and no Hebrews born!
  And will you basely thus submit yourselves   80
  To leave your goods to their arbitrament?
FERNEZE
  Why, Barabas, wilt thou be christenèd?
BARABAS
  No, governor, I will be no convertite.

FERNEZE

    Then pay thy half.

BARABAS

    Why, know you what you did by this device?
    Half of my substance is a city's wealth.
    Governor, it was not got so easily,
    Nor will I part so slightly therewithal.

FERNEZE

    Sir, half is the penalty of our decree.
90   Either pay that, or we will seize on all.

BARABAS

    Corpo di Dio! Stay, you shall have half.
    Let me be used but as my brethren are.

FERNEZE

    No, Jew, thou hast denied the articles,
    And now it cannot be recalled.

BARABAS

    Will you then steal my goods?
    Is theft the ground of your religion?

FERNEZE

    No, Jew, we take particularly thine
    To save the ruin of a multitude;
    And better one want for a common good
100   Than many perish for a private man.
    Yet, Barabas, we will not banish thee,
    But here in Malta, where thou got'st thy wealth,
    Live still; and, if thou canst, get more.

BARABAS

    Christians, what or how can I multiply?
    Of naught is nothing made.

FIRST KNIGHT

    From naught at first thou cam'st to little wealth,
    From little unto more, from more to most.
    If your first curse fall heavy on thy head
    And make thee poor and scorned of all the world,
110   'Tis not our fault, but thy inherent sin.

BARABAS

    What? Bring you scripture to confirm your wrongs?

Preach me not out of my possessions.
Some Jews are wicked, as all Christians are;
But say the tribe that I descended of
Were all in general cast away for sin,
Shall I be tried by their transgression?
The man that dealeth righteously shall live;
And which of you can charge me otherwise?

FERNEZE

Out, wretched Barabas,
Sham'st thou not thus to justify thyself,   120
As if we knew not thy profession?
If thou rely upon thy righteousness,
Be patient, and thy riches will increase.
Excess of wealth is cause of covetousness,
And covetousness, O, 'tis a monstrous sin.

BARABAS

Ay, but theft is worse. Tush, take not from me then,
For that is theft; and if you rob me thus,
I must be forced to steal and compass more.

FIRST KNIGHT

Grave governor, list not to his exclaims.
Convert his mansion to a nunnery;   130
His house will harbour many holy nuns.
      Enter OFFICERS.

FERNEZE

It shall be so. Now, officers, have you done?

OFFICER

Ay, my lord, we have seized upon the goods
And wares of Barabas, which, being valued,
Amount to more than all the wealth in Malta.
And of the other we have seizèd half.

FERNEZE

Then we'll take order for the residue.

BARABAS

Well then, my lord, say, are you satisfied?
You have my goods, my money, and my wealth,
My ships, my store, and all that I enjoyed;   140
And having all, you can request no more,

Unless your unrelenting flinty hearts
Suppress all pity in your stony breasts,
And now shall move you to bereave my life.

FERNEZE

No, Barabas, to stain our hands with blood
Is far from us and our profession.

BARABAS

Why, I esteem the injury far less
To take the lives of miserable men,
Than be the causers of their misery.
You have my wealth, the labour of my life,
The comfort of mine age, my children's hope;
And therefore ne'er distinguish of the wrong.

FERNEZE

Content thee, Barabas, thou hast naught but right.

BARABAS

Your extreme right does me exceeding wrong.
But take it to you, i'th'devil's name!

FERNEZE

Come, let us in, and gather of these goods
The money for this tribute of the Turk.

FIRST KNIGHT

'Tis necessary that be looked unto;
For if we break our day, we break the league,
And that will prove but simple policy.

                    Exeunt [FERNEZE, KNIGHTS *and* OFFICERS].

BARABAS

Ay, policy! That's their profession,
And not simplicity, as they suggest.
The plagues of Egypt, and the curse of heaven,
Earth's barrenness, and all men's hatred
Inflict upon them, thou great Primus Motor!
And here upon my knees, striking the earth,
I ban their souls to everlasting pains
And extreme tortures of the fiery deep,
That thus have dealt with me in my distress.

FIRST JEW

O, yet be patient, gentle Barabas.

BARABAS

   O silly brethren, born to see this day!
   Why stand you thus unmoved with my laments?
   Why weep you not to think upon my wrongs?
   Why pine not I and die in this distress?

FIRST JEW

   Why, Barabas, as hardly can we brook
   The cruel handling of ourselves in this.
   Thou seest they have taken half our goods.

BARABAS

   Why did you yield to their extortion?
   You were a multitude, and I but one,
   And of me only have they taken all.   180

FIRST JEW

   Yet, brother Barabas, remember Job.

BARABAS

   What tell you me of Job? I wot his wealth
   Was written thus: he had seven thousand sheep,
   Three thousand camels, and two hundred yoke
   Of labouring oxen, and five hundred
   She-asses; but for every one of those,
   Had they been valued at indifferent rate,
   I had at home, and in mine argosy
   And other ships that came from Egypt last,
   As much as would have bought his beasts and him,   190
   And yet have kept enough to live upon;
   So that not he, but I, may curse the day,
   Thy fatal birthday, forlorn Barabas,
   And henceforth wish for an eternal night,
   That clouds of darkness may enclose my flesh
   And hide these extreme sorrows from mine eyes.
   For only I have toiled to inherit here
   The months of vanity and loss of time,
   And painful nights have been appointed me.

SECOND JEW

   Good Barabas, be patient.

BARABAS   Ay, ay;   200
   Pray leave me in my patience. You that

Were ne'er possessed of wealth are pleased with want.
But give him liberty at least to mourn,
That in a field amidst his enemies,
Doth see his soldiers slain, himself disarmed,
And knows no means of his recovery.
Ay, let me sorrow for this sudden chance;
'Tis in the trouble of my spirit I speak.
Great injuries are not so soon forgot.

FIRST JEW
210   Come, let us leave him in his ireful mood.
Our words will but increase his ecstasy.

SECOND JEW
On, then. But trust me, 'tis a misery
To see a man in such affliction.
Farewell, Barabas.

Exeunt [*the* THREE JEWS].

BARABAS   Ay, fare you well.
See the simplicity of these base slaves,
Who, for the villains have no wit themselves,
Think me to be a senseless lump of clay
That will with every water wash to dirt.
No, Barabas is born to better chance,
220   And framed of finer mould than common men,
That measure naught but by the present time.
A reaching thought will search his deepest wits,
And cast with cunning for the time to come,
For evils are apt to happen every day.

Enter ABIGALL, *the Jew's daughter.*
But whither wends my beauteous Abigall?
O, what has made my lovely daughter sad?
What, woman, moan not for a little loss.
Thy father has enough in store for thee.

ABIGALL
Not for myself, but agèd Barabas,
230   Father, for thee lamenteth Abigall.
But I will learn to leave these fruitless tears,
And, urged thereto with my afflictions,
With fierce exclaims run to the senate-house,

And in the senate reprehend them all,
And rent their hearts with tearing of my hair,
Till they reduce the wrongs done to my father.

BARABAS

No, Abigall, things past recovery
Are hardly cured with exclamations.
Be silent, daughter; sufferance breeds ease,
And time may yield us an occasion   240
Which on the sudden cannot serve the turn.
Besides, my girl, think me not all so fond
As negligently to forgo so much
Without provision for thyself and me.
Ten thousand portagues, besides great pearls,
Rich, costly jewels, and stones infinite,
Fearing the worst of this before it fell,
I closely hid.

ABIGALL   Where, father?

BARABAS   In my house, my girl.

ABIGALL

Then shall they ne'er be seen of Barabas,
For they have seized upon thy house and wares.   250

BARABAS

But they will give me leave once more, I trow,
To go into my house.

ABIGALL   That may they not,
For there I left the governor placing nuns,
Displacing me; and of thy house they mean
To make a nunnery, where none but their own sect
Must enter in, men generally barred.

BARABAS

My gold, my gold, and all my wealth is gone!
You partial heavens, have I deserved this plague?
What, will you thus oppose me, luckless stars,
To make me desperate in my poverty,   260
And, knowing me impatient in distress,
Think me so mad as I will hang myself,
That I may vanish o'er the earth in air
And leave no memory that e'er I was?

No, I will live, nor loathe I this my life;
And since you leave me in the ocean thus
To sink or swim, and put me to my shifts,
I'll rouse my senses and awake myself.
Daughter, I have it! Thou perceiv'st the plight
270 Wherein these Christians have oppressèd me.
Be ruled by me, for in extremity
We ought to make bar of no policy.

ABIGALL
Father, whate'er it be, to injure them
That have so manifestly wrongèd us,
What will not Abigall attempt?

BARABAS   Why, so.
Then thus: thou told'st me they have turned my house
Into a nunnery, and some nuns are there.

ABIGALL
I did.

BARABAS Then, Abigall, there must my girl
Entreat the Abbess to be entertained.

ABIGALL
How, as a nun?

280 BARABAS   Ay, daughter, for religion
Hides many mischiefs from suspicion.

ABIGALL
Ay, but father, they will suspect me there.

BARABAS
Let 'em suspect, but be thou so precise
As they may think it done of holiness.
Entreat 'em fair, and give them friendly speech,
And seem to them as if thy sins were great,
Till thou hast gotten to be entertained.

ABIGALL
Thus, father, shall I much dissemble.

BARABAS   Tush,
As good dissemble that thou never mean'st
290 As first mean truth and then dissemble it.
A counterfeit profession is better

Than unseen hypocrisy.

ABIGALL

Well, father, say I be entertained,
What then shall follow?

BARABAS   This shall follow then:
There have I hid, close underneath the plank
That runs along the upper-chamber floor,
The gold and jewels which I kept for thee.
But here they come. Be cunning, Abigall.

ABIGALL

Then, father, go with me.

BARABAS   No, Abigall, in this
It is not necessary I be seen,   300
For I will seem offended with thee for't.
Be close, my girl, for this must fetch my gold.
    Enter two FRIARS [JACOMO *and* BARNARDINE] *and* [*an*
    ABBESS *and*] TWO NUNS.

FRIAR JACOMO

Sisters,
We now are almost at the new-made nunnery.

ABBESS

The better; for we love not to be seen.
'Tis thirty winters long since some of us
Did stray so far amongst the multitude.

FRIAR JACOMO

But, madam, this house
And waters of this new-made nunnery
Will much delight you.   310

ABBESS

It may be so. But who comes here?

ABIGALL [*comes forward*]

Grave Abbess, and you, happy virgins' guide,
Pity the state of a distressèd maid!

ABBESS

What art thou, daughter?

ABIGALL

The hopeless daughter of a hapless Jew,

The Jew of Malta, wretched Barabas,
Sometimes the owner of a goodly house
Which they have now turned to a nunnery.

ABBESS
Well, daughter, say, what is thy suit with us?

ABIGALL
320   Fearing the afflictions which my father feels
Proceed from sin or want of faith in us,
I'd pass away my life in penitence,
And be a novice in your nunnery,
To make atonement for my labouring soul.

FRIAR JACOMO [to BARNARDINE]
No doubt, brother, but this proceedeth of the spirit.

FRIAR BARNARDINE [to JACOMO]
Ay, and of a moving spirit too, brother. But come,
Let us entreat she may be entertained.

ABBESS
Well, daughter, we admit you for a nun.

ABIGALL
First let me as a novice learn to frame
330   My solitary life to your strait laws,
And let me lodge where I was wont to lie.
I do not doubt, by your divine precepts
And mine own industry, but to profit much.

BARABAS (aside)
As much, I hope, as all I hid is worth.

ABBESS
Come, daughter, follow us.

BARABAS [coming forward]
Why, how now, Abigall? What mak'st thou
Amongst these hateful Christians?

FRIAR JACOMO
Hinder her not, thou man of little faith,
For she has mortified herself.

BARABAS   How, mortified?

FRIAR JACOMO
340   And is admitted to the sisterhood.

BARABAS
  Child of perdition, and thy father's shame,
  What wilt thou do among these hateful fiends?
  I charge thee on my blessing that thou leave
  These devils and their damnèd heresy.
ABIGALL
  Father, give me –
BARABAS   Nay, back, Abigall!
  (*Whispers to her*) And think upon the jewels and the gold;
  The board is markèd thus [*makes the sign of the cross*]
                              that covers it.
  [*Aloud*] Away, accursèd, from thy father's sight!
FRIAR JACOMO
  Barabas, although thou art in misbelief
  And wilt not see thine own afflictions,   350
  Yet let thy daughter be no longer blind.
BARABAS
  Blind, friar? I reck not thy persuasions.
     [*Aside to* ABIGALL.]
  The board is markèd thus [*makes the sign of the cross*]
                              that covers it.
  [*Aloud*] For I had rather die than see her thus.
  Wilt thou forsake me too in my distress,
  Seducèd daughter? (*Aside to her*) Go, forget not.
  [*Aloud*] Becomes it Jews to be so credulous?
  (*Aside to her*) Tomorrow early I'll be at the door.
  [*Aloud*] No, come not at me! If thou wilt be damned,
  Forget me, see me not, and so begone.   360
  (*Aside [to her]*) Farewell. Remember tomorrow morning.
  [*Aloud*] Out, out, thou wretch!
                                    [*Exeunt separately.*]

[Scene 3]

Enter MATHIAS.

MATHIAS
Who's this? Fair Abigall, the rich Jew's daughter,
Become a nun? Her father's sudden fall
Has humbled her and brought her down to this.
Tut, she were fitter for a tale of love
Than to be tirèd out with orisons;
And better would she far become a bed,
Embracèd in a friendly lover's arms,
Than rise at midnight to a solemn mass.
        Enter LODOWICK.

LODOWICK
Why, how now, Don Mathias, in a dump?

MATHIAS
10 Believe me, noble Lodowick, I have seen
The strangest sight, in my opinion,
That ever I beheld.

LODOWICK   What was't, I prithee?

MATHIAS
A fair young maid, scarce fourteen years of age,
The sweetest flower in Cytherea's field,
Cropped from the pleasures of the fruitful earth,
And strangely metamorphized nun.

LODOWICK
But say, what was she?

MATHIAS   Why, the rich Jew's daughter.

LODOWICK
What, Barabas, whose goods were lately seized?
Is she so fair?

MATHIAS   And matchless beautiful,
20 As, had you seen her, 'twould have moved your heart,
Though countermured with walls of brass, to love,
Or at the least to pity.

LODOWICK
An if she be so fair as you report,

'Twere time well spent to go and visit her.
How say you, shall we?

MATHIAS
I must and will, sir, there's no remedy.

LODOWICK [*aside*]
And so will I too, or it shall go hard.
Farewell, Mathias.

MATHIAS   Farewell, Lodowick.

> *Exeunt* [*at different doors*].

ACT 2

[*Scene 1*]

Enter BARABAS, *with a light.*

BARABAS

Thus like the sad presaging raven that tolls
The sick man's passport in her hollow beak,
And in the shadow of the silent night
Doth shake contagion from her sable wings,
Vexed and tormented runs poor Barabas
With fatal curses towards these Christians.
The incertain pleasures of swift-footed time
Have ta'en their flight and left me in despair,
And of my former riches rests no more

10 But bare remembrance – like a soldier's scar,
That has no further comfort for his maim.
O Thou, that with a fiery pillar led'st
The sons of Israel through the dismal shades,
Light Abraham's offspring, and direct the hand
Of Abigall this night! Or let the day
Turn to eternal darkness after this.
No sleep can fasten on my watchful eyes,
Nor quiet enter my distempered thoughts,
Till I have answer of my Abigall.

Enter ABIGALL, *above [with gold and jewels]*.

ABIGALL

20 Now have I happily espied a time
To search the plank my father did appoint.
And here, behold, unseen, where I have found

The gold, the pearls, and jewels which he hid.

BARABAS

Now I remember those old women's words,
Who in my wealth would tell me winter's tales,
And speak of spirits and ghosts that glide by night
About the place where treasure hath been hid.
And now methinks that I am one of those,
For whilst I live here lives my soul's sole hope,
And when I die here shall my spirit walk.   30

ABIGALL

Now that my father's fortune were so good
As but to be about this happy place!
'Tis not so happy; yet when we parted last,
He said he would attend me in the morn.
Then, gentle sleep, where'er his body rests,
Give charge to Morpheus that he may dream
A golden dream, and of the sudden wake,
Come, and receive the treasure I have found.

BARABAS

Bueno para todos mi ganado no era.
As good go on as sit so sadly thus.   40
But stay, what star shines yonder in the east?
The lodestar of my life, if Abigall.
Who's there?

ABIGALL   Who's that?

BARABAS   Peace, Abigall, 'tis I.

ABIGALL

Then, father, here receive thy happiness.

BARABAS

Hast thou't?

ABIGALL   Here. (*Throws down bags*) Hast thou't?
There's more, and more, and more.

BARABAS   O my girl,
My gold, my fortune, my felicity,
Strength to my soul, death to mine enemy!
Welcome, the first beginner of my bliss!
O Abigall, Abigall, that I had thee here too!   50
Then my desires were fully satisfied.

But I will practise thy enlargement thence.
O girl, O gold, O beauty, O my bliss!
   (*Hugs his bags*)

ABIGALL

Father, it draweth towards midnight now,
And 'bout this time the nuns begin to wake;
To shun suspicion, therefore, let us part.

BARABAS

Farewell, my joy, and by my fingers take
A kiss from him that sends it from his soul.

                     [*Exit* ABIGALL *above.*]

Now, Phoebus, ope the eyelids of the day,
60   And for the raven wake the morning lark,
That I may hover with her in the air,
Singing o'er these, as she does o'er her young,
   [*sings*]
Hermoso placer de los dineros.

                                 Exit.

[*Scene 2*]

Enter FERNEZE, MARTIN DEL BOSCO, *the* KNIGHTS [*and* OFFICERS].

FERNEZE

Now, captain, tell us whither thou art bound?
Whence is thy ship that anchors in our road?
And why thou cam'st ashore without our leave?

DEL BOSCO

Governor of Malta, hither am I bound;
My ship, the *Flying Dragon*, is of Spain,
And so am I. Del Bosco is my name,
Vice-admiral unto the Catholic king.

FIRST KNIGHT [*to* FERNEZE]

'Tis true, my lord. Therefore entreat him well.

DEL BOSCO

Our fraught is Grecians, Turks, and Afric Moors.

For, late upon the coast of Corsica,   10
Because we vailed not to the Turkish fleet,
Their creeping galleys had us in the chase;
But suddenly the wind began to rise,
And then we luffed and tacked, and fought at ease.
Some have we fired, and many have we sunk,
But one amongst the rest became our prize.
The captain's slain, the rest remain our slaves,
Of whom we would make sale in Malta here.

FERNEZE

Martin del Bosco, I have heard of thee.
Welcome to Malta, and to all of us.   20
But to admit a sale of these thy Turks
We may not, nay, we dare not give consent,
By reason of a tributary league.

FIRST KNIGHT

Del Bosco, as thou lov'st and honour'st us,
Persuade our governor against the Turk.
This truce we have is but in hope of gold,
And with that sum he craves might we wage war.

DEL BOSCO

Will Knights of Malta be in league with Turks,
And buy it basely too for sums of gold?
My lord, remember that, to Europe's shame,   30
The Christian isle of Rhodes, from whence you came,
Was lately lost, and you were stated here
To be at deadly enmity with Turks.

FERNEZE

Captain, we know it, but our force is small.

DEL BOSCO

What is the sum that Calymath requires?

FERNEZE

A hundred thousand crowns.

DEL BOSCO

My lord and king hath title to this isle,
And he means quickly to expel them hence;
Therefore be ruled by me, and keep the gold.
I'll write unto his majesty for aid,   40

And not depart until I see you free.
FERNEZE
    On this condition shall thy Turks be sold.
    Go, officers, and set them straight in show.

                                    [*Exeunt* OFFICERS.]

    Bosco, thou shalt be Malta's general;
    We and our warlike knights will follow thee
    Against these barbarous, misbelieving Turks.
DEL BOSCO
    So shall you imitate those you succeed;
    For when their hideous force environed Rhodes,
    Small though the number was that kept the town,
50 They fought it out, and not a man survived
    To bring the hapless news to Christendom.
FERNEZE
    So will we fight it out. Come, let's away.
    Proud-daring Calymath, instead of gold,
    We'll send thee bullets wrapped in smoke and fire.
    Claim tribute where thou wilt, we are resolved,
    Honour is bought with blood and not with gold.

                                                Exeunt.

[*Scene 3*]

Enter OFFICERS *with* [ITHAMORE *and other*] SLAVES.
FIRST OFFICER
    This is the marketplace. Here let 'em stand.
    Fear not their sale, for they'll be quickly bought.
SECOND OFFICER
    Every one's price is written on his back,
    And so much must they yield or not be sold.
        Enter BARABAS.
FIRST OFFICER.
    Here comes the Jew. Had not his goods been seized,
    He'd give us present money for them all.

BARABAS [*aside*]
　In spite of these swine-eating Christians,
　(Unchosen nation, never circumcised,
　Such as, poor villains, were ne'er thought upon
　Till Titus and Vespasian conquered us)   10
　Am I become as wealthy as I was.
　They hoped my daughter would ha' been a nun,
　But she's at home, and I have bought a house
　As great and fair as is the governor's;
　And there in spite of Malta will I dwell,
　Having Ferneze's hand, whose heart I'll have –
　Ay, and his son's, too, or it shall go hard.
　I am not of the tribe of Levi, I,
　That can so soon forget an injury.
　We Jews can fawn like spaniels when we please,   20
　And when we grin, we bite; yet are our looks
　As innocent and harmless as a lamb's.
　I learned in Florence how to kiss my hand,
　Heave up my shoulders when they call me dog,
　And duck as low as any barefoot friar,
　Hoping to see them starve upon a stall,
　Or else be gathered for in our synagogue,
　That when the offering basin comes to me,
　Even for charity I may spit into't.
　Here comes Don Lodowick, the governor's son,   30
　One that I love for his good father's sake.
　　Enter LODOWICK.
LODOWICK
　I hear the wealthy Jew walkèd this way.
　I'll seek him out and so insinuate
　That I may have a sight of Abigall,
　For Don Mathias tells me she is fair.
BARABAS [*aside*] Now will I show myself to have more of the
　serpent than the dove – that is, more knave than fool.
LODOWICK Yond' walks the Jew. Now for fair Abigall.
BARABAS [*aside*] Ay, ay, no doubt but she's at your command.
LODOWICK Barabas, thou know'st I am the governor's son.   40
BARABAS I would you were his father too, sir; that's all the

harm I wish you. [*Aside*] The slave looks like a hog's cheek
new singed.

    [BARABAS *turns away*.]

LODOWICK

Whither walk'st thou, Barabas?

BARABAS

No further. 'Tis a custom held with us
That, when we speak with gentiles like to you,
We turn into the air to purge ourselves;
For unto us the promise doth belong.

LODOWICK

Well, Barabas, canst help me to a diamond?

BARABAS

50   O, sir, your father had my diamonds.
Yet I have one left that will serve your turn.
(*Aside*) I mean my daughter – but ere he shall have her,
I'll sacrifice her on a pile of wood.
I ha' the poison of the city for him,
And the white leprosy.

LODOWICK

What sparkle does it give without a foil?

BARABAS

The diamond that I talk of ne'er was foiled.
[*Aside*] But when he touches it, it will be foiled.
[*To him*] Lord Lodowick, it sparkles bright and fair.

LODOWICK

60   Is it square or pointed? Pray let me know.

BARABAS

Pointed it is, good sir – (*aside*) but not for you.

LODOWICK

I like it much the better.

BARABAS   So do I, too.

LODOWICK

How shows it by night?

BARABAS   Outshines Cynthia's rays.
(*Aside*) You'll like it better far a-nights than days.

LODOWICK

And what's the price?

BARABAS [*aside*]   Your life, an if you have it.
  [*To him*] O, my lord, we will not jar about the price; come
  to my house and I will give't your honour – (*aside*) with a
  vengeance.

LODOWICK
  No, Barabas, I will deserve it first.

BARABAS
  Good sir,   70
  Your father has deserved it at my hands,
  Who, of mere charity and Christian ruth,
  To bring me to religious purity,
  And as it were in catechizing sort,
  To make me mindful of my mortal sins,
  Against my will, and whether I would or no,
  Seized all I had, and thrust me out o' doors,
  And made my house a place for nuns most chaste.

LODOWICK
  No doubt your soul shall reap the fruit of it.

BARABAS
  Ay, but, my lord, the harvest is far off;   80
  And yet I know the prayers of those nuns
  And holy friars, having money for their pains,
  Are wondrous – (*aside*) and indeed do no man good.
  [*To him*] And seeing they are not idle, but still doing,
  'Tis likely they in time may reap some fruit –
  I mean in fullness of perfection.

LODOWICK
  Good Barabas, glance not at our holy nuns.

BARABAS
  No, but I do it through a burning zeal,
  (*aside*) Hoping ere long to set the house afire;
  For though they do a while increase and multiply,   90
  I'll have a saying to that nunnery.
  [*To him*] As for the diamond, sir, I told you of,
  Come home, and there's no price shall make us part,
  Even for your honourable father's sake.
  (*Aside*) It shall go hard but I will see your death.
  [*To him*] But now I must be gone to buy a slave.

LODOWICK
   And, Barabas, I'll bear thee company.

BARABAS Come then, here's the marketplace. What's the price
   of this slave? Two hundred crowns? Do the Turks weigh so
100   much?

FIRST OFFICER Sir, that's his price.

BARABAS
   What, can he steal, that you demand so much?
   Belike he has some new trick for a purse.
   An if he has, he is worth three hundred plates,
   So that, being bought, the town seal might be got
   To keep him for his lifetime from the gallows.
   The sessions day is critical to thieves,
   And few or none 'scape but by being purged.

LODOWICK Ratest thou this Moor but at two hundred plates?
110 FIRST OFFICER No more, my lord.

BARABAS Why should this Turk be dearer than that Moor?

FIRST OFFICER Because he is young and has more qualities.

BARABAS [to the Turkish SLAVE] What, hast the philosopher's
   stone? An thou hast, break my head with it; I'll forgive thee.

FIRST SLAVE No, sir, I can cut and shave.

BARABAS Let me see, sirrah. Are you not an old shaver?

FIRST SLAVE Alas, sir, I am a very youth.

BARABAS A youth? I'll buy you, and marry you to Lady Vanity
   if you do well.

120 FIRST SLAVE I will serve you, sir.

BARABAS Some wicked trick or other. It may be under colour
   of shaving thou'lt cut my throat for my goods. Tell me, hast
   thou thy health well?

FIRST SLAVE Ay, passing well.

BARABAS So much the worse; I must have one that's sickly, an't
   be but for sparing victuals. 'Tis not a stone of beef a day will
   maintain you in these chops. Let me see one that's somewhat
   leaner.

FIRST OFFICER [pointing to ITHAMORE] Here's a leaner. How
130 like you him?

BARABAS [to ITHAMORE] Where was thou born?

ITHAMORE In Thrace. Brought up in Arabia.

BARABAS
  So much the better. Thou art for my turn.
  An hundred crowns? I'll have him; there's the coin.
    [*Gives money.*]
FIRST OFFICER
  Then mark him, sir, and take him hence.
BARABAS [*aside*]
  Ay, mark him, you were best, for this is he
  That by my help shall do much villainy.
      [*To* LODOWICK]
  My lord, farewell.
  [*To* ITHAMORE] Come, sirrah, you are mine.
  [*To* LODOWICK] As for the diamond, it shall be yours.
  I pray, sir, be no stranger at my house;   140
  All that I have shall be at your command.
      Enter MATHIAS [*and his*] *Mother* [KATHERINE].
MATHIAS [*aside*]
  What makes the Jew and Lodowick so private?
  I fear me 'tis about fair Abigall.
                                        [*Exit* LODOWICK.]
BARABAS [*aside to* ITHAMORE]
  Yonder comes Don Mathias, let us stay.
  He loves my daughter, and she holds him dear,
  But I have sworn to frustrate both their hopes
  And be revenged upon the governor.
KATHERINE
  This Moor is comeliest, is he not? Speak, son.
MATHIAS
  No, this is the better, mother. View this well.
BARABAS [*aside to* MATHIAS]
  Seem not to know me here before your mother,   150
  Lest she mistrust the match that is in hand.
  When you have brought her home, come to my house.
  Think of me as thy father. Son, farewell.
MATHIAS [*aside to* BARABAS]
  But wherefore talked Don Lodowick with you?
BARABAS [*aside to* MATHIAS]
  Tush, man, we talked of diamonds, not of Abigall.

KATHERINE
Tell me, Mathias, is not that the Jew?
BARABAS [*aloud to* MATHIAS]
As for the comment on the Maccabees,
I have it, sir, and 'tis at your command.
MATHIAS [*to* KATHERINE]
Yes, madam, and my talk with him was
160   About the borrowing of a book or two.
KATHERINE
Converse not with him, he is cast off from heaven.
    [*To* OFFICER]
Thou hast thy crowns, fellow. Come, let's away.
MATHIAS Sirrah Jew, remember the book.
BARABAS Marry will I, sir.
            Exeunt [MATHIAS, KATHERINE *and a* SLAVE].
FIRST OFFICER
Come, I have made a reasonable market, let's away.
    [*Exeunt* OFFICERS *with the rest of the* SLAVES. BARABAS
                        and ITHAMORE *remain*.]
BARABAS
Now let me know thy name, and therewithal
Thy birth, condition, and profession.
ITHAMORE Faith, sir, my birth is but mean, my name's
Ithamore, my profession what you please.
BARABAS
170   Hast thou no trade? Then listen to my words,
And I will teach thee that shall stick by thee.
First, be thou void of these affections:
Compassion, love, vain hope, and heartless fear.
Be moved at nothing; see thou pity none,
But to thyself smile when the Christians moan.
ITHAMORE
O brave, master, I worship your nose for this!
BARABAS
As for myself, I walk abroad a-nights
And kill sick people groaning under walls;
Sometimes I go about and poison wells;
180   And now and then, to cherish Christian thieves,

I am content to lose some of my crowns,
That I may, walking in my gallery,
See 'em go pinioned along by my door.
Being young, I studied physic, and began
To practise first upon the Italian;
There I enriched the priests with burials,
And always kept the sexton's arms in ure
With digging graves and ringing dead men's knells.
And after that was I an engineer,
And in the wars 'twixt France and Germany,   190
Under pretence of helping Charles the Fifth,
Slew friend and enemy with my stratagems.
Then after that was I an usurer,
And with extorting, cozening, forfeiting,
And tricks belonging unto brokery,
I filled the gaols with bankrupts in a year,
And with young orphans planted hospitals,
And every moon made some or other mad,
And now and then one hang himself for grief,
Pinning upon his breast a long great scroll   200
How I with interest tormented him.
But mark how I am blest for plaguing them:
I have as much coin as will buy the town.
But tell me now, how hast thou spent thy time?

ITHAMORE
Faith, master,
In setting Christian villages on fire,
Chaining of eunuchs, binding galley slaves.
One time I was an ostler in an inn,
And in the night-time secretly would I steal
To travellers' chambers and there cut their throats.   210
Once at Jerusalem, where the pilgrims kneeled,
I strewèd powder on the marble stones,
And therewithal their knees would rankle so
That I have laughed a-good to see the cripples
Go limping home to Christendom on stilts.

BARABAS
Why, this is something. Make account of me

As of thy fellow; we are villains both.
Both circumcisèd, we hate Christians both.
Be true and secret, thou shalt want no gold.
220   But stand aside, here comes Don Lodowick.
        Enter LODOWICK.

LODOWICK
    O, Barabas, well met.
    Where is the diamond you told me of?

BARABAS
    I have it for you, sir; please you walk in with me.
    What ho, Abigall! Open the door, I say.
        Enter ABIGALL [*with letters*].

ABIGALL
    In good time, father, here are letters come
    From Ormus, and the post stays here within.

BARABAS
    Give me the letters. Daughter, do you hear?
    Entertain Lodowick, the governor's son,
    With all the courtesy you can afford –
230   (*Aside* [*to her*]) Provided that you keep your maidenhead.
    Use him as if he were a Philistine.
    Dissemble, swear, protest, vow to love him;
    He is not of the seed of Abraham.
    [*Aloud*] I am a little busy, sir, pray pardon me.
    Abigall, bid him welcome for my sake.

ABIGALL
    For your sake and his own he's welcome hither.

BARABAS
    Daughter, a word more. [*Aside to her*]
                                            Kiss him, speak him fair,
    And like a cunning Jew so cast about
    That ye be both made sure ere you come out.

ABIGALL [*aside to* BARABAS]
240   O, father, Don Mathias is my love!

BARABAS [*aside to her*]
    I know it; yet, I say, make love to him.
    Do, it is requisite it should be so.
    [*Aloud*] Nay, on my life, it is my factor's hand.

But go you in, I'll think upon the account.
> [*Exeunt* LODOWICK *and* ABIGALL.]

The account is made, for Lodowick dies.
My factor sends me word a merchant's fled
That owes me for a hundred tun of wine.
I weigh it thus much. I have wealth enough.
For now by this has he kissed Abigall,
And she vows love to him, and he to her.   250
As sure as heaven rained manna for the Jews,
So sure shall he and Don Mathias die.
His father was my chiefest enemy.
> *Enter* MATHIAS.

Whither goes Don Mathias? Stay a while.

MATHIAS
Whither but to my fair love Abigall?

BARABAS
Thou know'st, and heaven can witness it is true,
That I intend my daughter shall be thine.

MATHIAS
Ay, Barabas, or else thou wrong'st me much.

BARABAS [*pretending to weep*]
O, heaven forbid I should have such a thought!
Pardon me though I weep. The governor's son   260
Will, whether I will or no, have Abigall.
He sends her letters, bracelets, jewels, rings.

MATHIAS
Does she receive them?

BARABAS
She? No, Mathias, no, but sends them back,
And when he comes she locks herself up fast;
Yet through the keyhole will he talk to her,
While she runs to the window, looking out
When you should come and hale him from the door.

MATHIAS
O, treacherous Lodowick!

BARABAS
Even now, as I came home, he slipped me in,   270
And I am sure he is with Abigall.

MATHIAS [*drawing his sword*]
  I'll rouse him thence.

BARABAS
  Not for all Malta; therefore sheathe your sword.
  If you love me, no quarrels in my house.
  But steal you in, and seem to see him not.
  I'll give him such a warning ere he goes
  As he shall have small hopes of Abigall.
  Away, for here they come.

     Enter LODOWICK [*with*] ABIGALL.

MATHIAS
  What, hand in hand? I cannot suffer this.

BARABAS
280 Mathias, as thou lov'st me, not a word.

MATHIAS
  Well, let it pass. Another time shall serve.

                          Exit [MATHIAS].

LODOWICK
  Barabas, is not that the widow's son?

BARABAS
  Ay, and take heed, for he hath sworn your death.

LODOWICK
  My death? What, is the base-born peasant mad?

BARABAS
  No, no, but happily he stands in fear
  Of that which you, I think, ne'er dream upon:
  My daughter here, a paltry, silly girl.

LODOWICK
  Why, loves she Don Mathias?

BARABAS
  Doth she not with her smiling answer you?

ABIGALL [*aside*]
290 He has my heart, I smile against my will.

LODOWICK
  Barabas, thou know'st I have loved thy daughter long.

BARABAS
  And so has she done you, even from a child.

LODOWICK
And now I can no longer hold my mind.

BARABAS
Nor I the affection that I bear to you.

LODOWICK
This is thy diamond. Tell me, shall I have it?

BARABAS
Win it and wear it. It is yet unfoiled.
O, but I know your lordship would disdain
To marry with the daughter of a Jew;
And yet I'll give her many a golden cross,
With Christian posies round about the ring.   300

LODOWICK
'Tis not thy wealth, but her that I esteem,
Yet crave I thy consent.

BARABAS
And mine you have; yet let me talk to her.
    (*Aside* [*to* ABIGALL].)
This offspring of Cain, this Jebusite,
That never tasted of the Passover,
Nor e'er shall see the land of Canaan,
Nor our Messias that is yet to come,
This gentle maggot – Lodowick, I mean –
Must be deluded. Let him have thy hand,
But keep thy heart till Don Mathias comes.   310

ABIGALL
What, shall I be betrothed to Lodowick?

BARABAS
It is no sin to deceive a Christian,
For they themselves hold it a principle,
Faith is not to be held with heretics.
But all are heretics that are not Jews;
This follows well, and therefore, daughter, fear not.
[*To* LODOWICK] I have entreated her, and she will grant.

LODOWICK
Then, gentle Abigall, plight thy faith to me.

ABIGALL [*aside*]
I cannot choose, seeing my father bids.

320   [*Aloud*] Nothing but death shall part my love and me.

LODOWICK
Now have I that for which my soul hath longed.

BARABAS (*aside*)
So have not I, but yet I hope I shall.

ABIGALL [*aside*]
O wretched Abigall, what hast thou done?

LODOWICK
Why on the sudden is your colour changed?

ABIGALL
I know not; but farewell, I must be gone.

BARABAS [*to* ITHAMORE]
Stay her, but let her not speak one word more.

LODOWICK
Mute o' the sudden? Here's a sudden change.

BARABAS
O, muse not at it, 'tis the Hebrews' guise
That maidens new-betrothed should weep a while.
330   Trouble her not, sweet Lodowick, depart.
She is thy wife, and thou shalt be mine heir.

LODOWICK
O, is't the custom? Then I am resolved.
But rather let the brightsome heavens be dim,
And nature's beauty choke with stifling clouds,
Than my fair Abigall should frown on me.
    Enter MATHIAS.
There comes the villain. Now I'll be revenged.

BARABAS
Be quiet, Lodowick. It is enough
That I have made thee sure to Abigall.

LODOWICK Well, let him go.

                                    Exit [LODOWICK].

BARABAS [*to* MATHIAS]
340   Well, but for me, as you went in at doors
You had been stabbed; but not a word on't now.
Here must no speeches pass, nor swords be drawn.

MATHIAS
Suffer me, Barabas, but to follow him.

BARABAS
  No. So shall I, if any hurt be done,
  Be made an accessory of your deeds.
  Revenge it on him when you meet him next.

MATHIAS
  For this I'll have his heart.

BARABAS
  Do so. Lo, here I give thee Abigall.
    [BARABAS *brings them together*.]

MATHIAS
  What greater gift can poor Mathias have?
  Shall Lodowick rob me of so fair a love?   350
  My life is not so dear as Abigall.

BARABAS
  My heart misgives me, that, to cross your love,
  He's with your mother, therefore after him.

MATHIAS
  What, is he gone unto my mother?

BARABAS
  Nay, if you will, stay till she comes herself.

MATHIAS
  I cannot stay, for if my mother come,
  She'll die with grief.
                            Exit [MATHIAS].

ABIGALL
  I cannot take my leave of him for tears.
  Father, why have you thus incensed them both?

BARABAS
  What's that to thee?

ABIGALL   I'll make 'em friends again.   360

BARABAS
  You'll make 'em friends?
  Are there not Jews enow in Malta
  But thou must dote upon a Christian?

ABIGALL
  I will have Don Mathias, he is my love.

BARABAS
  Yes, you shall have him. [*To* ITHAMORE] Go put her in.

ITHAMORE Ay, I'll put her in.
   [*He forces* ABIGALL *into the house.*]
BARABAS
   Now tell me, Ithamore, how lik'st thou this?
ITHAMORE
   Faith, master, I think by this
   You purchase both their lives. Is it not so?
BARABAS
370   True; and it shall be cunningly performed.
ITHAMORE
   O, master, that I might have a hand in this!
BARABAS
   Ay, so thou shalt, 'tis thou must do the deed.
   [*Giving a letter*]
   Take this and bear it to Mathias straight,
   And tell him that it comes from Lodowick.
ITHAMORE 'Tis poisoned, is it not?
BARABAS
   No, no, and yet it might be done that way.
   It is a challenge feigned from Lodowick.
ITHAMORE
   Fear not; I'll so set his heart afire
   That he shall verily think it comes from him.
BARABAS
380   I cannot choose but like thy readiness.
   Yet be not rash, but do it cunningly.
ITHAMORE
   As I behave myself in this, employ me hereafter.
BARABAS
   Away, then.

                              Exit [ITHAMORE].

   So, now will I go in to Lodowick,
   And like a cunning spirit feign some lie,
   Till I have set 'em both at enmity.

                                      Exit.

ACT 3

[Scene 1]

Enter [BELLAMIRA,] *a Courtesan.*

BELLAMIRA
    Since this town was besieged, my gain grows cold.
    The time has been that but for one bare night
    A hundred ducats have been freely given;
    But now against my will I must be chaste.
    And yet I know my beauty doth not fail.
    From Venice merchants, and from Padua
    Were wont to come rare-witted gentlemen,
    Scholars, I mean, learnèd and liberal;
    And now, save Pilia-Borza, comes there none,
    And he is very seldom from my house.   10
    And here he comes.

        Enter PILIA-BORZA.

PILIA-BORZA Hold thee, wench, there's something for thee to
    spend.

        [*He gives her money from a bag.*]

BELLAMIRA
    'Tis silver; I disdain it.

PILIA-BORZA
    Ay, but the Jew has gold,
    And I will have it, or it shall go hard.

BELLAMIRA
    Tell me, how cam'st thou by this?

PILIA-BORZA Faith, walking the back lanes through the gardens
    I chanced to cast mine eye up to the Jew's counting-house,

20 where I saw some bags of money, and in the night I clambered
    up with my hooks, and as I was taking my choice, I heard a
    rumbling in the house; so I took only this and run my way.
    But here's the Jew's man.

    Enter ITHAMORE.

BELLAMIRA Hide the bag.

PILIA-BORZA Look not towards him, let's away. Zounds, what
  a looking thou keep'st! Thou'lt betray's anon.

                  [*Exeunt* BELLAMIRA *and* PILIA-BORZA.]

ITHAMORE O, the sweetest face that ever I beheld! I know she
  is a courtesan by her attire. Now would I give a hundred of
  the Jew's crowns that I had such a concubine.

30 Well, I have delivered the challenge in such sort,
    As meet they will, and fighting die. Brave sport!

                                    Exit.

[*Scene 2*]

    Enter MATHIAS.

MATHIAS
  This is the place. Now Abigall shall see
  Whether Mathias holds her dear or no.

    Enter LODOWICK, *reading.*

LODOWICK
  What, dares the villain write in such base terms?

MATHIAS [*to* LODOWICK]
  I did it, and revenge it if thou dar'st.

    [*They*] *fight. Enter* BARABAS *above.*

BARABAS
  O, bravely fought! And yet they thrust not home.
  Now, Lodowick! Now, Mathias! So.

    [*Both fall dead.*]

  So, now they have showed themselves to be tall fellows.

VOICES WITHIN Part 'em, part 'em!

BARABAS
  Ay, part 'em now they are dead. Farewell, farewell.

                            Exit [BARABAS].

Enter FERNEZE, KATHERINE [*and* ATTENDANTS].

FERNEZE

What sight is this? My Lodowick slain!   10
These arms of mine shall be thy sepulchre.

KATHERINE

Who is this? My son Mathias slain!

FERNEZE

O Lodowick, hadst thou perished by the Turk,
Wretched Ferneze might have venged thy death.

KATHERINE

Thy son slew mine, and I'll revenge his death.

FERNEZE

Look, Katherine, look, thy son gave mine these wounds.

KATHERINE

O, leave to grieve me! I am grieved enough.

FERNEZE

O, that my sighs could turn to lively breath,
And these my tears to blood, that he might live!

KATHERINE

Who made them enemies?   20

FERNEZE

I know not, and that grieves me most of all.

KATHERINE

My son loved thine.

FERNEZE   And so did Lodowick him.

KATHERINE

Lend me that weapon that did kill my son,
And it shall murder me.

FERNEZE

Nay, madam, stay. That weapon was my son's,
And on that rather should Ferneze die.

KATHERINE

Hold. Let's inquire the causers of their deaths,
That we may venge their blood upon their heads.

FERNEZE

Then take them up, and let them be interred
Within one sacred monument of stone,   30
Upon which altar I will offer up

My daily sacrifice of sighs and tears,
And with my prayers pierce impartial heavens,
Till they reveal the causers of our smarts,
Which forced their hands divide united hearts.
Come, Katherine, our losses equal are,
Then of true grief let us take equal share.

Exeunt [with the bodies].

[*Scene 3*]

Enter ITHAMORE.

ITHAMORE
Why, was there ever seen such villainy,
So neatly plotted and so well performed?
Both held in hand, and flatly both beguiled?

Enter ABIGALL.

ABIGALL Why, how now, Ithamore, why laugh'st thou so?
ITHAMORE O mistress, ha, ha, ha!
ABIGALL Why, what ail'st thou?
ITHAMORE O, my master!
ABIGALL Ha!
ITHAMORE O mistress, I have the bravest, gravest, secret, subtle,
10   bottle-nosed knave to my master that ever gentleman had.
ABIGALL Say, knave, why rail'st upon my father thus?
ITHAMORE O, my master has the bravest policy.
ABIGALL Wherein?
ITHAMORE Why, know you not?
ABIGALL Why, no.
ITHAMORE Know you not of Mathias' and Don Lodowick's
    disaster?
ABIGALL No, what was it?
ITHAMORE Why, the devil invented a challenge, my master
20   writ it, and I carried it, first to Lodowick and *imprimis* to
    Mathias.
    And then they met, and, as the story says,
    In doleful wise they ended both their days.

ABIGALL And was my father furtherer of their deaths?

ITHAMORE Am I Ithamore?

ABIGALL Yes.

ITHAMORE So sure did your father write, and I carry, the
challenge.

ABIGALL

  Well, Ithamore, let me request thee this:

  Go to the new-made nunnery, and inquire   30

  For any of the friars of Saint Jacques,

  And say I pray them come and speak with me.

ITHAMORE I pray, mistress, will you answer me to one question?

ABIGALL Well, sirrah, what is't?

ITHAMORE A very feeling one: have not the nuns fine sport with
the friars now and then?

ABIGALL Go to, sirrah sauce, is this your question? Get ye gone.

ITHAMORE I will forsooth, mistress.

                                Exit [ITHAMORE].

ABIGALL

  Hard-hearted father, unkind Barabas,

  Was this the pursuit of thy policy,   40

  To make me show them favour severally,

  That by my favour they should both be slain?

  Admit thou loved'st not Lodowick for his sire,

  Yet Don Mathias ne'er offended thee.

  But thou wert set upon extreme revenge,

  Because the prior dispossessed thee once,

  And couldst not venge it but upon his son,

  Nor on his son but by Mathias' means,

  Nor on Mathias but by murdering me.

  But I perceive there is no love on earth,   50

  Pity in Jews, nor piety in Turks.

  But here comes cursèd Ithamore with the friar.

    Enter ITHAMORE [*and*] FRIAR [JACOMO].

FRIAR JACOMO *Virgo, salve!*

ITHAMORE When, duck you?

ABIGALL

  Welcome, grave friar. Ithamore, begone.

                                  Exit [ITHAMORE].

Know, holy sir, I am bold to solicit thee.

FRIAR JACOMO Wherein?

ABIGALL

To get me be admitted for a nun.

FRIAR JACOMO

Why, Abigall, it is not yet long since

60   That I did labour thy admission,

And then thou didst not like that holy life.

ABIGALL

Then were my thoughts so frail and unconfirmed,

And I was chained to follies of the world;

But now experience, purchasèd with grief,

Has made me see the difference of things.

My sinful soul, alas, hath paced too long

The fatal labyrinth of misbelief,

Far from the Son that gives eternal life.

FRIAR JACOMO

Who taught thee this?

ABIGALL   The abbess of the house,

70   Whose zealous admonition I embrace.

O therefore, Jacomo, let me be one,

Although unworthy, of that sisterhood.

FRIAR JACOMO

Abigall, I will, but see thou change no more,

For that will be most heavy to thy soul.

ABIGALL

That was my father's fault.

FRIAR JACOMO   Thy father's? How?

ABIGALL

Nay, you shall pardon me. [*Aside*] O Barabas,

Though thou deservest hardly at my hands,

Yet never shall these lips bewray thy life.

FRIAR JACOMO

Come, shall we go?

ABIGALL   My duty waits on you.

                                              Exeunt.

[Scene 4]

Enter BARABAS, *reading a letter*.

BARABAS
What, Abigall become a nun again?
False and unkind! What, hast thou lost thy father,
And, all unknown and unconstrained of me,
Art thou again got to the nunnery?
Now here she writes, and wills me to repent.
Repentance? *Spurca!* What pretendeth this?
I fear she knows ('tis so) of my device
In Don Mathias' and Lodovico's deaths.
If so, 'tis time it be seen into,
For she that varies from me in belief   10
Gives great presumption that she loves me not,
Or, loving, doth dislike of something done.
   [*Enter* ITHAMORE.]
But who comes here? O Ithamore, come near.
Come near, my love, come near, thy master's life,
My trusty servant, nay, my second self!
For I have now no hope but even in thee,
And on that hope my happiness is built.
When saw'st thou Abigall?

ITHAMORE Today.

BARABAS With whom?   20

ITHAMORE A friar.

BARABAS A friar? False villain, he hath done the deed.

ITHAMORE How, sir?

BARABAS Why, made mine Abigall a nun.

ITHAMORE That's no lie, for she sent me for him.

BARABAS
O, unhappy day!
False, credulous, inconstant Abigall!
But let 'em go; and Ithamore, from hence
Ne'er shall she grieve me more with her disgrace;
Ne'er shall she live to inherit aught of mine,   30
Be blest of me, nor come within my gates,

But perish underneath my bitter curse,
Like Cain by Adam, for his brother's death.
ITHAMORE O, master!
BARABAS
   Ithamore, entreat not for her, I am moved,
   And she is hateful to my soul and me.
   And 'less thou yield to this that I entreat,
   I cannot think but that thou hat'st my life.
ITHAMORE Who, I, master? Why, I'll run to some rock and
40   throw myself headlong into the sea. Why, I'll do anything for
   your sweet sake.
BARABAS
   O trusty Ithamore, no servant, but my friend!
   I here adopt thee for mine only heir.
   All that I have is thine when I am dead,
   And, whilst I live, use half; spend as myself.
   Here, take my keys. I'll give 'em thee anon.
   Go buy thee garments. But thou shalt not want.
   Only know this, that thus thou art to do.
   But first go fetch me in the pot of rice
50   That for our supper stands upon the fire.
ITHAMORE [aside] I hold my head my master's hungry.
   [To him] I go, sir.

                                             Exit [ITHAMORE].
BARABAS
   Thus every villain ambles after wealth,
   Although he ne'er be richer than in hope.
   But husht.
         Enter ITHAMORE with the pot.
ITHAMORE Here 'tis, master.
BARABAS Well said, Ithamore.
   What, hast thou brought the ladle with thee too?
ITHAMORE Yes, sir; the proverb says, he that eats with the devil
60   had need of a long spoon. I have brought you a ladle.
BARABAS
   Very well, Ithamore, then now be secret,
   And for thy sake, whom I so dearly love,
   Now shalt thou see the death of Abigall,

That thou mayst freely live to be my heir.

ITHAMORE Why, master, will you poison her with a mess of
rice porridge? That will preserve life, make her round and
plump, and batten more than you are aware.

BARABAS
Ay, but Ithamore, seest thou this?
   [*He shows a poison.*]
It is a precious powder that I bought
Of an Italian in Ancona once,   70
Whose operation is to bind, infect,
And poison deeply, yet not appear
In forty hours after it is ta'en.

ITHAMORE How, master?

BARABAS
Thus, Ithamore:
This even they use in Malta here – 'tis called
Saint Jacques' Even – and then, I say, they use
To send their alms unto the nunneries.
Among the rest bear this and set it there.
There's a dark entry where they take it in,   80
Where they must neither see the messenger,
Nor make inquiry who hath sent it them.

ITHAMORE How so?

BARABAS
Belike there is some ceremony in't.
There, Ithamore, must thou go place this pot.
Stay, let me spice it first.

ITHAMORE Pray do, and let me help you, master. Pray let me
taste first.

BARABAS
Prithee do. [ITHAMORE *tastes.*] What say'st thou now?

ITHAMORE Troth, master, I'm loath such a pot of pottage   90
should be spoiled.

BARABAS [*adding poison*]
Peace, Ithamore, 'tis better so than spared.
Assure thyself thou shalt have broth by the eye.
My purse, my coffer, and myself is thine.

ITHAMORE Well, master, I go.

BARABAS

Stay, first let me stir it, Ithamore.
As fatal be it to her as the draught
Of which great Alexander drunk and died,
And with her let it work like Borgia's wine,
Whereof his sire, the Pope, was poisonèd!
In few, the blood of Hydra, Lerna's bane,
The juice of hebon, and Cocytus' breath,
And all the poisons of the Stygian pool,
Break from the fiery kingdom, and in this
Vomit your venom and envenom her
That like a fiend hath left her father thus!

ITHAMORE What a blessing has he given't! Was ever pot of rice
porridge so sauced? What shall I do with it?

BARABAS

O my sweet Ithamore, go set it down,
And come again so soon as thou hast done,
For I have other business for thee.

ITHAMORE Here's a drench to poison a whole stable of Flanders
mares! I'll carry't to the nuns with a powder.

BARABAS

And the horse-pestilence to boot. Away!

ITHAMORE I am gone.
Pay me my wages, for my work is done.

Exit [ITHAMORE, *with the pot*].

BARABAS

I'll pay thee with a vengeance, Ithamore.

Exit.

[*Scene 5*]

Enter FERNEZE, [MARTIN DEL] BOSCO, KNIGHTS, [*and*
CALLAPINE, *the*] *bashaw* [*with his train*].

FERNEZE

Welcome, great bashaws. How fares Calymath?
What wind drives you thus into Malta road?

CALLAPINE
  The wind that bloweth all the world besides:
  Desire of gold.
FERNEZE   Desire of gold, great sir?
  That's to be gotten in the Western Inde;
  In Malta are no golden minerals.
CALLAPINE
  To you of Malta thus saith Calymath:
  The time you took for respite is at hand,
  For the performance of your promise passed,
  And for the tribute-money I am sent.   10
FERNEZE
  Bashaw, in brief, shalt have no tribute here,
  Nor shall the heathens live upon our spoil.
  First will we raze the city walls ourselves,
  Lay waste the island, hew the temples down,
  And, shipping off our goods to Sicily,
  Open an entrance for the wasteful sea,
  Whose billows, beating the resistless banks,
  Shall overflow it with their refluence.
CALLAPINE
  Well, governor, since thou hast broke the league
  By flat denial of the promised tribute,   20
  Talk not of razing down your city walls,
  You shall not need trouble yourselves so far.
  For Selim Calymath shall come himself,
  And with brass bullets batter down your towers,
  And turn proud Malta to a wilderness
  For these intolerable wrongs of yours.
  And so farewell.
                          [*Exeunt* CALLAPINE *and his train.*]
FERNEZE
  Farewell.
  And now, you men of Malta, look about,
  And let's provide to welcome Calymath.   30
  Close your portcullis, charge your basilisks,
  And as you profitably take up arms,
  So now courageously encounter them;

For by this answer broken is the league,
And naught is to be looked for now but wars,
And naught to us more welcome is than wars.

Exeunt.

[Scene 6]

Enter [the] two FRIARS [JACOMO *and* BARNARDINE].

FRIAR JACOMO
O brother, brother, all the nuns are sick,
And physic will not help them! They must die.

FRIAR BARNARDINE
The abbess sent for me to be confessed.
O, what a sad confession will there be!

FRIAR JACOMO
And so did fair Maria send for me.
I'll to her lodging; hereabouts she lies.

Exit [FRIAR JACOMO].

Enter ABIGALL.

FRIAR BARNARDINE
What, all dead save only Abigall?

ABIGALL
And I shall die too, for I feel death coming.
Where is the friar that conversed with me?

FRIAR BARNARDINE
10   O, he is gone to see the other nuns.

ABIGALL
I sent for him, but seeing you are come,
Be you my ghostly father; and first know
That in this house I lived religiously,
Chaste, and devout, much sorrowing for my sins.
But ere I came –

FRIAR BARNARDINE What then?

ABIGALL
I did offend high heaven so grievously,
As I am almost desperate for my sins,

And one offence torments me more than all.
You knew Mathias and Don Lodowick?   20
FRIAR BARNARDINE Yes, what of them?
ABIGALL
My father did contract me to 'em both:
First to Don Lodowick, him I never loved.
Mathias was the man that I held dear,
And for his sake did I become a nun.
FRIAR BARNARDINE
So. Say, how was their end?
ABIGALL
Both, jealous of my love, envied each other,
And by my father's practice, which is there
Set down at large, the gallants were both slain.
    [*She gives him a paper.*]
FRIAR BARNARDINE O, monstrous villainy!   30
ABIGALL
To work my peace, this I confess to thee.
Reveal it not, for then my father dies.
FRIAR BARNARDINE
Know that confession must not be revealed,
The canon law forbids it, and the priest
That makes it known, being degraded first,
Shall be condemned and then sent to the fire.
ABIGALL
So I have heard; pray therefore keep it close.
Death seizeth on my heart. Ah, gentle friar,
Convert my father that he may be saved,
And witness that I die a Christian.   40
    [*She dies.*]
FRIAR BARNARDINE
Ay, and a virgin, too, that grieves me most.
But I must to the Jew and exclaim on him,
And make him stand in fear of me.
    Enter FRIAR [JACOMO].
FRIAR JACOMO
O brother, all the nuns are dead! Let's bury them.

FRIAR BARNARDINE
  First help to bury this, then go with me
  And help me to exclaim against the Jew.
FRIAR JACOMO Why? What has he done?
FRIAR BARNARDINE
  A thing that makes me tremble to unfold.
FRIAR JACOMO What, has he crucified a child?
FRIAR BARNARDINE
50 No, but a worse thing. 'Twas told me in shrift;
  Thou know'st 'tis death an if it be revealed.
  Come, let's away.

                        Exeunt [carrying ABIGALL'*s body*].

ACT 4

[Scene 1]

Enter BARABAS [*and*] ITHAMORE. *Bells within.*

BARABAS
    There is no music to a Christian's knell.
    How sweet the bells ring, now the nuns are dead,
    That sound at other times like tinkers' pans!
    I was afraid the poison had not wrought,
    Or, though it wrought, it would have done no good,
    For every year they swell, and yet they live.
    Now all are dead; not one remains alive.

ITHAMORE That's brave, master. But think you it will not be
    known?

BARABAS How can it, if we two be secret?   10

ITHAMORE For my part fear you not.

BARABAS I'd cut thy throat if I did.

ITHAMORE
    And reason, too.
    But here's a royal monast'ry hard by;
    Good master, let me poison all the monks.

BARABAS
    Thou shalt not need, for, now the nuns are dead,
    They'll die with grief.

ITHAMORE Do you not sorrow for your daughter's death?

BARABAS
    No, but I grieve because she lived so long.
    An Hebrew born, and would become a Christian!   20
    Cazzo, diabole!

Enter the two FRIARS [JACOMO *and* BARNARDINE].

ITHAMORE Look, look, master, here come two religious caterpillars.

BARABAS I smelt 'em ere they came.

ITHAMORE God-a-mercy, nose! Come, let's be gone.

FRIAR BARNARDINE
Stay, wicked Jew! Repent, I say, and stay.

FRIAR JACOMO
Thou hast offended, therefore must be damned.

BARABAS [*aside to* ITHAMORE]
I fear they know we sent the poisoned broth.

ITHAMORE [*aside to* BARABAS]
And so do I, master. Therefore speak 'em fair.

30 FRIAR BARNARDINE Barabas, thou hast –

FRIAR JACOMO Ay, that thou hast –

BARABAS True, I have money. What though I have?

FRIAR BARNARDINE Thou art a –

FRIAR JACOMO Ay, that thou art, a –

BARABAS What needs all this? I know I am a Jew.

FRIAR BARNARDINE Thy daughter –

FRIAR JACOMO Ay, thy daughter –

BARABAS O, speak not of her; then I die with grief.

FRIAR BARNARDINE Remember that –

40 FRIAR JACOMO Ay, remember that –

BARABAS I must needs say that I have been a great usurer.

FRIAR BARNARDINE Thou hast committed –

BARABAS Fornication? But that was in another country; and
besides, the wench is dead.

FRIAR BARNARDINE Ay, but Barabas, remember Mathias and
Don Lodowick.

BARABAS Why, what of them?

FRIAR BARNARDINE I will not say that by a forged challenge
they met.

BARABAS (*aside* [*to* ITHAMORE])

50 She has confessed, and we are both undone,
My bosom inmate! But I must dissemble.
[*To them*]
O holy friars, the burden of my sins

Lie heavy on my soul. Then pray you tell me,
Is't not too late now to turn Christian?
I have been zealous in the Jewish faith,
Hard-hearted to the poor, a covetous wretch,
That would for lucre's sake have sold my soul.
A hundred for a hundred I have ta'en,
And now for store of wealth may I compare
With all the Jews in Malta. But what is wealth?   60
I am a Jew, and therefore am I lost.
Would penance serve for this my sin,
I could afford to whip myself to death –

ITHAMORE [*aside*]
And so could I; but penance will not serve.

BARABAS
To fast, to pray, and wear a shirt of hair,
And on my knees creep to Jerusalem.
Cellars of wine and sollars full of wheat,
Warehouses stuffed with spices and with drugs,
Whole chests of gold, in bullion and in coin,
Besides I know not how much weight in pearl,   70
Orient and round, have I within my house;
At Alexandria, merchandise unsold.
But yesterday two ships went from this town,
Their voyage will be worth ten thousand crowns.
In Florence, Venice, Antwerp, London, Seville,
Frankfurt, Lubeck, Moscow, and where not,
Have I debts owing; and in most of these,
Great sums of money lying in the banco.
All this I'll give to some religious house,
So I may be baptized and live therein.   80

FRIAR JACOMO
O good Barabas, come to our house!

FRIAR BARNARDINE
O no, good Barabas, come to our house!
And Barabas, you know –

BARABAS
I know that I have highly sinned.
You shall convert me; you shall have all my wealth.

FRIAR JACOMO
O, Barabas, their laws are strict.

BARABAS
I know they are, and I will be with you.

FRIAR JACOMO
They wear no shirts, and they go barefoot too.

BARABAS
Then 'tis not for me; and I am resolved
90   You shall confess me and have all my goods.

FRIAR BARNARDINE
Good Barabas, come to me.

BARABAS
You see I answer him, and yet he stays.
Rid him away, and go you home with me.

FRIAR JACOMO
I'll be with you tonight.

BARABAS
Come to my house at one o'clock this night.

FRIAR JACOMO
You hear your answer, and you may be gone.

FRIAR BARNARDINE Why, go get you away.

FRIAR JACOMO I will not go for thee.

FRIAR BARNARDINE Not? Then I'll make thee, rogue.

100   FRIAR JACOMO How, dost call me rogue?
        [The FRIARS] fight.

ITHAMORE Part 'em, master, part 'em.

BARABAS
This is mere frailty. Brethren, be content.
Friar Barnardine, go you with Ithamore.
        [Aside to FRIAR BARNARDINE]
You know my mind, let me alone with him.

FRIAR JACOMO
Why does he go to thy house? Let him be gone.

BARABAS [aside to FRIAR JACOMO]
I'll give him something, and so stop his mouth.
                Exit [ITHAMORE with FRIAR BARNARDINE].
I never heard of any man but he
Maligned the order of the Jacobins.

But do you think that I believe his words?
Why, brother, you converted Abigall,   110
And I am bound in charity to requite it,
And so I will. O Jacomo, fail not, but come.

FRIAR JACOMO

But, Barabas, who shall be your godfathers?
For presently you shall be shrived.

BARABAS

Marry, the Turk shall be one of my godfathers.
But not a word to any of your convent.

FRIAR JACOMO

I warrant thee, Barabas.

                              Exit [FRIAR JACOMO].

BARABAS

So, now the fear is past, and I am safe,
For he that shrived her is within my house.
What if I murdered him ere Jacomo comes?   120
Now I have such a plot for both their lives,
As never Jew nor Christian knew the like.
One turned my daughter, therefore he shall die;
The other knows enough to have my life,
Therefore 'tis not requisite he should live.
But are not both these wise men to suppose
That I will leave my house, my goods, and all,
To fast and be well whipped? I'll none of that.
Now, Friar Barnardine, I come to you.
I'll feast you, lodge you, give you fair words,   130
And after that, I and my trusty Turk –
No more but so. It must and shall be done.

      Enter ITHAMORE.

Ithamore, tell me, is the friar asleep?

ITHAMORE

Yes, and I know not what the reason is,
Do what I can, he will not strip himself,
Nor go to bed, but sleeps in his own clothes.
I fear me he mistrusts what we intend.

BARABAS

No, 'tis an order which the friars use.

Yet if he knew our meanings, could he 'scape?

ITHAMORE

140   No, none can hear him, cry he ne'er so loud.

BARABAS

Why, true. Therefore did I place him there.
The other chambers open towards the street.

ITHAMORE

You loiter, master. Wherefore stay we thus?
O, how I long to see him shake his heels!

   [FRIAR BARNARDINE *is discovered asleep.*]

BARABAS

Come on, sirrah,
Off with your girdle, make a handsome noose.

   [*They secure the* FRIAR'*s belt around his neck.*]

Friar, awake!

FRIAR BARNARDINE

What, do you mean to strangle me?

ITHAMORE

Yes, 'cause you use to confess.

BARABAS

150   Blame not us but the proverb, 'Confess and be hanged.'
Pull hard!

FRIAR BARNARDINE

What, will you have my life?

BARABAS

Pull hard, I say! You would have had my goods.

ITHAMORE

Ay, and our lives too. Therefore, pull amain.

   [*They strangle him.*]

'Tis neatly done, sir. Here's no print at all.

BARABAS

Then is it as it should be. Take him up.

ITHAMORE Nay, master, be ruled by me a little. So, let him lean
upon his staff.

   [*He props up the body.*]

Excellent! He stands as if he were begging of bacon.

BARABAS

160   Who would not think but that this friar lived?

What time o' night is't now, sweet Ithamore?
ITHAMORE
    Towards one.
BARABAS
    Then will not Jacomo be long from hence.
        [*They hide themselves.*]
        Enter [FRIAR] JACOMO.
FRIAR JACOMO
    This is the hour
    Wherein I shall proceed. O happy hour,
    Wherein I shall convert an infidel
    And bring his gold into our treasury!
    But soft, is not this Barnardine? It is;
    And, understanding I should come this way,
    Stands here o' purpose, meaning me some wrong,   170
    And intercept my going to the Jew.
    Barnardine!
    Wilt thou not speak? Thou think'st I see thee not.
    Away, I'd wish thee, and let me go by.
    No, wilt thou not? Nay then, I'll force my way.
    And see, a staff stands ready for the purpose.
    As thou lik'st that, stop me another time.
        [FRIAR JACOMO *seizes* FRIAR BARNARDINE's *staff and*]
        strike[s] *him;* [BARNARDINE] *falls. Enter* BARABAS [*and*
        ITHAMORE *from hiding*].
BARABAS
    Why, how now, Jacomo, what hast thou done?
FRIAR JACOMO
    Why, stricken him that would have struck at me.
BARABAS Who is it? Barnadine? Now out, alas, he is slain!   180
ITHAMORE Ay, master, he's slain. Look how his brains drop
    out on's nose.
FRIAR JACOMO Good sirs, I have done't, but nobody knows it
    but you two, I may escape.
BARABAS So might my man and I hang with you for company.
ITHAMORE
    No, let us bear him to the magistrates.
        [*They seize* FRIAR JACOMO.]

FRIAR JACOMO
  Good Barabas, let me go.
BARABAS
  No, pardon me, the law must have his course.
  I must be forced to give in evidence
190 That, being importuned by this Barnardine
  To be a Christian, I shut him out,
  And there he sat. Now I, to keep my word,
  And give my goods and substance to your house,
  Was up thus early with intent to go
  Unto your friary, because you stayed.
ITHAMORE
  Fie upon 'em, master, will you turn Christian,
  When holy friars turn devils and murder one another?
BARABAS
  No, for this example I'll remain a Jew.
  Heaven bless me! What, a friar a murderer?
200 When shall you see a Jew commit the like?
ITHAMORE
  Why, a Turk could ha' done no more.
BARABAS
  Tomorrow is the sessions; you shall to it.
  Come, Ithamore, let's help to take him hence.
FRIAR JACOMO
  Villains, I am a sacred person, touch me not.
BARABAS
  The law shall touch you, we'll but lead you, we.
  'Las, I could weep at your calamity.
  Take in the staff too, for that must be shown;
  Law wills that each particular be known.

                                                        Exeunt.

[*Scene 2*]

Enter [BELLAMIRA *the*] *Courtesan and* PILIA-BORZA.

BELLAMIRA Pilia-Borza, didst thou meet with Ithamore?

PILIA-BORZA I did.

BELLAMIRA And didst thou deliver my letter?

PILIA-BORZA I did.

BELLAMIRA And what think'st thou, will he come?

PILIA-BORZA I think so, and yet I cannot tell, for at the reading
of the letter he looked like a man of another world.

BELLAMIRA Why so?

PILIA-BORZA That such a base slave as he should be saluted by
such a tall man as I am, from such a beautiful dame as you.   10

BELLAMIRA And what said he?

PILIA-BORZA Not a wise word, only gave me a nod, as who
should say, 'Is it even so?' And so I left him, being driven to
a nonplus at the critical aspect of my terrible countenance.

BELLAMIRA And where didst meet him?

PILIA-BORZA Upon mine own freehold, within forty foot of the
gallows, conning his neck-verse, I take it, looking of a friar's
execution, whom I saluted with an old hempen proverb,
'*Hodie tibi, cras mihi*', and so I left him to the mercy of the
hangman. But the exercise being done, see where he comes.   20

Enter ITHAMORE.

ITHAMORE I never knew a man take his death so patiently as
this friar. He was ready to leap off ere the halter was about
his neck, and when the hangman had put on his hempen
tippet he made such haste to his prayers as if he had had
another cure to serve. Well, go whither he will, I'll be none of
his followers in haste. And now I think on't, going to the
execution, a fellow met me with a muschatoes like a raven's
wing and a dagger with a hilt like a warming-pan, and he
gave me a letter from one Madam Bellamira, saluting me in
such sort as if he had meant to make clean my boots with his   30
lips; the effect was that I should come to her house. I wonder
what the reason is. It may be she sees more in me than I can
find in myself, for she writes further that she loves me ever

since she saw me, and who would not requite such love?
Here's her house, and here she comes, and now would I were
gone. I am not worthy to look upon her.

PILIA-BORZA This is the gentleman you writ to.

ITHAMORE [aside] 'Gentleman'! He flouts me. What gentry can
be in a poor Turk of tenpence? I'll be gone.

40 BELLAMIRA Is't not a sweet-faced youth, Pilia?

ITHAMORE [aside] Again, 'sweet youth'! [To PILIA-BORZA]
Did not you, sir, bring the sweet youth a letter?

PILIA-BORZA I did, sir, and from this gentlewoman, who, as
myself and the rest of the family, stand or fall at your service.

BELLAMIRA
Though woman's modesty should hale me back,
I can withhold no longer. Welcome, sweet love.
    [She kisses him.]

ITHAMORE [aside] Now am I clean, or rather foully, out of the
way.
    [He starts to leave.]

BELLAMIRA Whither so soon?

50 ITHAMORE [aside] I'll go steal some money from my master, to
make me handsome. [Aloud] Pray pardon me, I must go see
a ship discharged.

BELLAMIRA Canst thou be so unkind to leave me thus?

PILIA-BORZA An ye did but know how she loves you, sir!

ITHAMORE Nay, I care not how much she loves me. Sweet
Bellamira, would I had my master's wealth for thy sake.

PILIA-BORZA And you can have it, sir, an if you please.

ITHAMORE If 'twere above ground I could and would have it,
but he hides and buries it up as partridges do their eggs, under
60 the earth.

PILIA-BORZA And is't not possible to find it out?

ITHAMORE By no means possible.

BELLAMIRA [aside to PILIA-BORZA]
What shall we do with this base villain, then?

PILIA-BORZA [aside to BELLAMIRA]
Let me alone, do but you speak him fair.
    [To ITHAMORE]
But you know some secrets of the Jew,

Which if they were revealed would do him harm.

ITHAMORE Ay, and such as – Go to, no more, I'll make him
send me half he has, and glad he 'scapes so too. Pen and ink!
I'll write unto him; we'll have money straight.

PILIA-BORZA [*giving pen and ink*] Send for a hundred crowns   70
at least.

ITHAMORE Ten hundred thousand crowns. (*He writes*) 'Master
Barabas –'

PILIA-BORZA Write not so submissively, but threat'ning him.

ITHAMORE 'Sirrah Barabas, send me a hundred crowns.'

PILIA-BORZA Put in two hundred at least.

ITHAMORE 'I charge thee send me three hundred by this bearer,
and this shall be your warrant. If you do not, no more but
so.'

PILIA-BORZA Tell him you will confess.   80

ITHAMORE 'Otherwise I'll confess all.' Vanish, and return in a
twinkle.

PILIA-BORZA Let me alone. I'll use him in his kind.

                              [*Exit* PILIA-BORZA.]

ITHAMORE Hang him, Jew!

BELLAMIRA
Now, gentle Ithamore, lie in my lap.
Where are my maids? Provide a running banquet;
Send to the merchant, bid him bring me silks.
Shall Ithamore my love go in such rags?

ITHAMORE
And bid the jeweller come hither too.

BELLAMIRA
I have no husband, sweet, I'll marry thee.   90

ITHAMORE
Content, but we will leave this paltry land,
And sail from hence to Greece, to lovely Greece.
I'll be thy Jason, thou my golden fleece;
Where painted carpets o'er the meads are hurled,
And Bacchus' vineyards overspread the world,
Where woods and forests go in goodly green,
I'll be Adonis, thou shalt be Love's queen.
The meads, the orchards, and the primrose lanes,

Instead of sedge and reed, bear sugar-canes.
100   Thou in those groves, by Dis above,
Shalt live with me and be my love.

BELLAMIRA
Whither will I not go with gentle Ithamore?
   Enter PILIA-BORZA [*with a moneybag*].

ITHAMORE How now? Hast thou the gold?

PILIA-BORZA Yes.

ITHAMORE But came it freely? Did the cow give down her milk
freely?

PILIA-BORZA At reading of the letter, he stared and stamped,
and turned aside. I took him by the beard and looked upon
him thus, told him he were best to send it, then he hugged
110   and embraced me.

ITHAMORE Rather for fear than love.

PILIA-BORZA Then like a Jew he laughed and jeered, and told
me he loved me for your sake, and said what a faithful servant
you had been.

ITHAMORE The more villain he to keep me thus. Here's goodly
'parel, is there not?

PILIA-BORZA To conclude, he gave me ten crowns.

ITHAMORE But ten? I'll not leave him worth a grey groat. Give
me a ream of paper. We'll have a kingdom of gold for't.

120   PILIA-BORZA [*providing paper*] Write for five hundred
crowns.

ITHAMORE [*writing*] 'Sirrah Jew, as you love your life, send me
five hundred crowns, and give the bearer one hundred.' Tell
him I must have't.

PILIA-BORZA I warrant your worship shall have't.

ITHAMORE And if he ask why I demand so much, tell him I
scorn to write a line under a hundred crowns.

PILIA-BORZA You'd make a rich poet, sir. I am gone.

                                  Exit [PILIA-BORZA].

ITHAMORE
Take thou the money. Spend it for my sake.

BELLAMIRA
130   'Tis not thy money but thyself I weigh.
Thus Bellamira esteems of gold;

[*she throws it aside*]
But thus of thee.
   [*She*] *kiss*[*es*] *him.*
ITHAMORE [*aside*] That kiss again! She runs division of my lips.
  What an eye she casts on me! It twinkles like a star.
BELLAMIRA
  Come, my dear love, let's in and sleep together.
ITHAMORE O, that ten thousand nights were put in one, that
  we might sleep seven years together afore we wake!
BELLAMIRA
  Come, amorous wag, first banquet and then sleep.
                                 [*Exeunt.*]

[Scene 3]

Enter BARABAS, *reading a letter.*
BARABAS
  'Barabas, send me three hundred crowns.'
  Plain 'Barabas'? O, that wicked courtesan!
  He was not wont to call me 'Barabas'.
  'Or else I will confess.' Ay, there it goes.
  But if I get him, *coupe de gorge* for that.
  He sent a shaggy, tottered, staring slave
  That, when he speaks, draws out his grisly beard
  And winds it twice or thrice about his ear;
  Whose face has been a grindstone for men's swords,
  His hands are hacked, some fingers cut quite off;   10
  Who, when he speaks, grunts like a hog and looks
  Like one that is employed in catzerie
  And crossbiting – such a rogue
  As is the husband to a hundred whores.
  And I by him must send three hundred crowns!
  Well, my hope is he will not stay there still;
  And when he comes – O, that he were but here!
     Enter PILIA-BORZA.
PILIA-BORZA Jew, I must ha' more gold.

BARABAS Why, want'st thou any of thy tale?

20 PILIA-BORZA No; but three hundred will not serve his turn.

BARABAS Not serve his turn, sir?

PILIA-BORZA No, sir, and therefore I must have five hundred
    more.

BARABAS I'll rather –

PILIA-BORZA O, good words, sir, and send it, you were best;
    see, there's his letter.

    [*He presents* ITHAMORE'*s second letter.*]

BARABAS Might he not as well come as send? Pray bid him
    come and fetch it; what he writes for you, ye shall have
    straight.

30 PILIA-BORZA Ay, and the rest too, or else –

BARABAS [*aside*] I must make this villain away. [*To him*] Please
    you dine with me, sir, (*aside*) and you shall be most heartily
    poisoned.

PILIA-BORZA No, God-a-mercy. Shall I have these crowns?

BARABAS I cannot do it, I have lost my keys.

PILIA-BORZA O, if that be all, I can pick ope your locks.

BARABAS Or climb up to my counting-house window? You
    know my meaning.

PILIA-BORZA I know enough, and therefore talk not to me of

40 your counting-house. The gold! – or know, Jew, it is in my
    power to hang thee.

BARABAS [*aside*] I am betrayed.
        [*To him*]
    'Tis not five hundred crowns that I esteem,
    I am not moved at that. This angers me,
    That he who knows I love him as myself
    Should write in this imperious vein. Why, sir,
    You know I have no child, and unto whom
    Should I leave all but unto Ithamore?

PILIA-BORZA Here's many words but no crowns. The crowns!

BARABAS

50 Commend me to him, sir, most humbly,
    And unto your good mistress as unknown.

PILIA-BORZA Speak, shall I have 'em, sir?

BARABAS Sir, here they are. [*He gives money.*]

[*Aside*] O, that I should part with so much gold!
[*To him*] Here, take 'em, fellow, with as good a will –
[*Aside*] As I would see thee hanged.
[*To him*]   O, love stops my breath.
Never loved man servant as I do Ithamore.
PILIA-BORZA I know it, sir.
BARABAS
    Pray, when, sir, shall I see you at my house?
PILIA-BORZA Soon enough, to your cost, sir. Fare you well.   60
                                        Exit [PILIA-BORZA].
BARABAS
    Nay, to thine own cost, villain, if thou com'st.
    Was ever Jew tormented as I am?
    To have a shag-rag knave to come demand
    Three hundred crowns, and then five hundred crowns?
    Well, I must seek a means to rid 'em all,
    And presently, for in his villainy
    He will tell all he knows, and I shall die for't.
    I have it!
    I will in some disguise go see the slave,
    And how the villain revels with my gold.   70
                                                        Exit.

[Scene 4]

Enter [BELLAMIRA] *the Courtesan*, ITHAMORE, PILIA-
    BORZA [*and* SERVANTS *with wine*].
BELLAMIRA I'll pledge thee, love, and therefore drink it off.
ITHAMORE Say'st thou me so? Have at it! And do you hear?
    [*He whispers to her.*]
BELLAMIRA Go to, it shall be so.
ITHAMORE Of that condition I will drink it up. Here's to thee.
BELLAMIRA Nay, I'll have all or none.
ITHAMORE There, if thou lov'st me, do not leave a drop.
BELLAMIRA Love thee? Fill me three glasses!
ITHAMORE Three-and-fifty dozen I'll pledge thee.

PILIA-BORZA Knavely spoke, and like a knight at arms.

10 ITHAMORE Hey, *Rivo Castiliano!* A man's a man.

BELLAMIRA Now to the Jew.

ITHAMORE Ha, to the Jew! And send me money, you were best.

PILIA-BORZA What wouldst thou do if he should send thee none?

ITHAMORE Do? Nothing. But I know what I know. He's a murderer.

BELLAMIRA I had not thought he had been so brave a man.

ITHAMORE You knew Mathias and the governor's son? He and
20   I killed 'em both, and yet never touched 'em.

PILIA-BORZA O, bravely done!

ITHAMORE I carried the broth that poisoned the nuns, and he
     and I – snickle hand too fast – strangled a friar.

BELLAMIRA You two alone?

ITHAMORE We two, and 'twas never known, nor never shall be
     for me.

PILIA-BORZA [*aside to* BELLAMIRA]
     This shall with me unto the governor.

BELLAMIRA [*aside to* PILIA-BORZA]
     And fit it should; but first let's ha' more gold.
          [*To* ITHAMORE]
     Come, gentle Ithamore, lie in my lap.

ITHAMORE
30   Love me little, love me long. Let music rumble,
     Whilst I in thy incony lap do tumble.
          Enter BARABAS *with a lute, disguised.*

BELLAMIRA
     A French musician! Come, let's hear your skill.

BARABAS
     Must tuna my lute for sound, twang, twang, first.

ITHAMORE Wilt drink, Frenchman? Here's to thee with a – Pox
     on this drunken hiccup!

BARABAS Gramercy, monsieur.

BELLAMIRA Prithee, Pilia-Borza, bid the fiddler give me the
     posy in his hat there.

PILIA-BORZA Sirrah, you must give my mistress your posy.

BARABAS *A vôtre commandement, madame.*   40

   [*He presents a nosegay which they sniff.*]

BELLAMIRA
   How sweet, my Ithamore, the flowers smell!

ITHAMORE Like thy breath, sweetheart, no violet like 'em.

PILIA-BORZA Foh, methinks they stink like a hollyhock.

BARABAS [*aside*]
   So, now I am revenged upon 'em all.
   The scent thereof was death; I poisoned it.

ITHAMORE Play, fiddler, or I'll cut your cat's guts into chitterlings.

BARABAS *Pardonnez-moi*, be no in tune yet. [*He tunes.*] So now,
   now all be in.

ITHAMORE Give him a crown, and fill me out more wine.   50

PILIA-BORZA [*giving money*] There's two crowns for thee. Play.

BARABAS (*aside*) How liberally the villain gives me mine own
   gold!

   [*He plays the lute.*]

PILIA-BORZA Methinks he fingers very well.

BARABAS (*aside*) So did you when you stole my gold.

PILIA-BORZA How swift he runs!

BARABAS (*aside*) You run swifter when you threw my gold out
   of my window.

BELLAMIRA Musician, hast been in Malta long?

BARABAS Two, three, four month, madame.   60

ITHAMORE Dost not know a Jew, one Barabas?

BARABAS Very mush, monsieur. You no be his man?

PILIA-BORZA His man?

ITHAMORE I scorn the peasant. Tell him so.

BARABAS [*aside*] He knows it already.

ITHAMORE 'Tis a strange thing of that Jew: he lives upon pickled
   grasshoppers and sauced mushrooms.

BARABAS (*aside*) What a slave's this! The governor feeds not as
   I do.

ITHAMORE He never put on clean shirt since he was circum-   70
   cised.

BARABAS (*aside*) O, rascal! I change myself twice a day.

ITHAMORE The hat he wears, Judas left under the elder when
he hanged himself.

BARABAS (*aside*) 'Twas sent me for a present from the Great
Cham.

PILIA-BORZA A masty slave he is.

[BARABAS *starts to leave.*]

Whither now, fiddler?

BARABAS *Pardonnez-moi*, monsieur, me be no well.

Exit [BARABAS].

80   PILIA-BORZA Farewell, fiddler. One letter more to the Jew.

BELLAMIRA Prithee, sweet love, one more, and write it sharp.

ITHAMORE No, I'll send by word of mouth now. [*To* PILIA-
BORZA] Bid him deliver thee a thousand crowns, by the same
token that the nuns loved rice, that Friar Barnardine slept in
his own clothes – any of 'em will do it.

PILIA-BORZA Let me alone to urge it, now I know the meaning.

ITHAMORE

The meaning has a meaning. Come, let's in.

To undo a Jew is charity, and not sin.

Exeunt.

ACT 5

Enter [FERNEZE *the*] *Governor,* KNIGHTS, MARTIN DEL
BOSCO [*and* OFFICERS].

FERNEZE
Now, gentlemen, betake you to your arms,
And see that Malta be well fortified.
And it behoves you to be resolute,
For Calymath, having hovered here so long,
Will win the town or die before the walls.

FIRST KNIGHT
And die he shall, for we will never yield.
        Enter [BELLAMIRA *the*] *Courtesan* [*and*] PILIA-BORZA.

BELLAMIRA
O, bring us to the governor.

FERNEZE
Away with her! She is a courtesan.

BELLAMIRA
Whate'er I am, yet, governor, hear me speak.
I bring thee news by whom thy son was slain: 10
Mathias did it not, it was the Jew.

PILIA-BORZA Who, besides the slaughter of these gentlemen,
poisoned his own daughter and the nuns, strangled a friar,
and I know not what mischief beside.

FERNEZE
Had we but proof of this!

BELLAMIRA
Strong proof, my lord. His man's now at my lodging

That was his agent; he'll confess it all.

FERNEZE
Go fetch him straight.

                                        [*Exeunt* OFFICERS.]
                            I always feared that Jew.
    Enter BARABAS [*and*] ITHAMORE [*guarded by some*
    OFFICERS].

BARABAS
I'll go alone, dogs, do not hale me thus.

20 ITHAMORE Nor me neither. I cannot outrun you, constable. O,
    my belly!

BARABAS [*aside*]
One dram of powder more had made all sure.
What a damned slave was I!

FERNEZE
Make fires, heat irons, let the rack be fetched.

FIRST KNIGHT
Nay, stay, my lord, 't may be he will confess.

BARABAS
Confess? What mean you, lords, who should confess?

FERNEZE
Thou and thy Turk: 'twas you that slew my son.

ITHAMORE Guilty, my lord, I confess. Your son and Mathias
    were both contracted unto Abigall; he forged a counterfeit
30   challenge.

BARABAS Who carried that challenge?

ITHAMORE I carried it, I confess, but who writ it? Marry, even
    he that strangled Barnardine, poisoned the nuns, and his own
    daughter.

FERNEZE
Away with him! His sight is death to me.

BARABAS
For what? You men of Malta, hear me speak.
She is a courtesan, and he a thief,
And he my bondman. Let me have law,
For none of this can prejudice my life.

FERNEZE
40   Once more, away with him! You shall have law.

BARABAS
　Devils, do your worst, I'll live in spite of you.
　As these have spoke, so be it to their souls.
　[*Aside*] I hope the poisoned flowers will work anon.
　　　　　　Exeunt [OFFICERS *with* BARABAS, ITHAMORE,
　　　　BELLAMIRA *and* PILIA-BORZA]. *Enter* KATHERINE.

KATHERINE
　Was my Mathias murdered by the Jew?
　Ferneze, 'twas thy son that murdered him.

FERNEZE
　Be patient, gentle madam, it was he.
　He forged the daring challenge made them fight.

KATHERINE
　Where is the Jew? Where is that murderer?

FERNEZE
　In prison, till the law has passed on him.
　　　Enter [*an*] OFFICER.

OFFICER
　My lord, the courtesan and her man are dead;   50
　So is the Turk, and Barabas the Jew.

FERNEZE Dead?

OFFICER
　Dead, my lord, and here they bring his body.
　　　[*Enter* OFFICERS, *carrying* BARABAS *as dead*.]

DEL BOSCO
　This sudden death of his is very strange.

FERNEZE
　Wonder not at it, sir, the heavens are just.
　Their deaths were like their lives, then think not of 'em.
　Since they are dead, let them be buried.
　For the Jew's body, throw that o'er the walls,
　To be a prey for vultures and wild beasts.
　　　[OFFICERS *throw down the body*.]
　So, now away, and fortify the town.   60
　　　　　　　　　　Exeunt [; BARABAS *remains*].

BARABAS [*rising*]
　What, all alone? Well fare, sleepy drink!
　I'll be revengèd on this accursèd town,

For by my means Calymath shall enter in.
I'll help to slay their children and their wives,
To fire the churches, pull their houses down,
Take my goods too, and seize upon my lands.
I hope to see the governor a slave,
And, rowing in a galley, whipped to death.

    Enter CALYMATH, BASHAWS, [*and*] TURKS.

CALYMATH
Whom have we there, a spy?

BARABAS
70   Yes, my good lord, one that can spy a place
Where you may enter and surprise the town.
My name is Barabas, I am a Jew.

CALYMATH
Art thou that Jew whose goods we heard were sold
For tribute-money?

BARABAS   The very same, my lord;
And since that time they have hired a slave, my man,
To accuse me of a thousand villainies.
I was imprisoned, but escaped their hands.

CALYMATH
Didst break prison?

BARABAS
No, no,
80   I drank of poppy and cold mandrake juice,
And, being asleep, belike they thought me dead,
And threw me o'er the walls. So, or how else,
The Jew is here, and rests at your command.

CALYMATH
'Twas bravely done. But tell me, Barabas,
Canst thou, as thou reportest, make Malta ours?

BARABAS
Fear not, my lord, for here against the sluice
The rock is hollow and of purpose digged
To make a passage for the running streams
And common channels of the city.
90   Now, whilst you give assault unto the walls,

I'll lead five hundred soldiers through the vault,
And rise with them i'th'middle of the town,
Open the gates for you to enter in,
And by this means the city is your own.

CALYMATH
If this be true, I'll make thee governor.

BARABAS
And if it be not true, then let me die.

CALYMATH
Thou'st doomed thyself. Assault it presently.

Exeunt.

[Scene 2]

Alarms. Enter [CALYMATH,] TURKS, [*and*] BARABAS,
[*with*] FERNEZE *and* KNIGHTS *prisoners.*

CALYMATH
Now vail your pride, you captive Christians,
And kneel for mercy to your conquering foe.
Now where's the hope you had of haughty Spain?
Ferneze, speak. Had it not been much better
To keep thy promise than be thus surprised?

FERNEZE
What should I say? We are captives and must yield.

CALYMATH
Ay, villains, you must yield, and under Turkish yokes
Shall groaning bear the burden of our ire.
And, Barabas, as erst we promised thee,
For thy desert we make thee governor.   10
Use them at thy discretion.

BARABAS   Thanks, my lord.

FERNEZE
O, fatal day, to fall into the hands
Of such a traitor and unhallowed Jew!
What greater misery could heaven inflict?

CALYMATH
    'Tis our command; and Barabas, we give,
    To guard thy person, these our janizaries;
    Entreat them well, as we have usèd thee.
    And now, brave bashaws, come, we'll walk about
    The ruined town and see the wrack we made.
20   Farewell, brave Jew, farewell, great Barabas.

BARABAS
    May all good fortune follow Calymath!
                    Exeunt [CALYMATH *and* BASHAWS].
    And now, as entrance to our safety,
    To prison with the governor and these
    Captains, his consorts and confederates.

FERNEZE
    O villain, heaven will be revenged on thee!

BARABAS
    Away, no more! Let him not trouble me.
            Exeunt [TURKS *with* FERNEZE *and* KNIGHTS].
    Thus hast thou gotten, by thy policy,
    No simple place, no small authority.
    I now am governor of Malta. True,
30   But Malta hates me, and, in hating me,
    My life's in danger; and what boots it thee,
    Poor Barabas, to be the governor,
    Whenas thy life shall be at their command?
    No, Barabas, this must be looked into;
    And since by wrong thou got'st authority,
    Maintain it bravely by firm policy,
    At least unprofitably lose it not.
    For he that liveth in authority,
    And neither gets him friends nor fills his bags,
40   Lives like the ass that Aesop speaketh of,
    That labours with a load of bread and wine
    And leaves it off to snap on thistle tops.
    But Barabas will be more circumspect.
    Begin betimes; Occasion's bald behind;
    Slip not thine opportunity, for fear too late
    Thou seek'st for much but canst not compass it.

[*Calling offstage*]
Within, there!
    Enter FERNEZE, *with a* GUARD [*of* TURKISH JANIZARIES].
FERNEZE My lord?
BARABAS [*aside*]
  Ay, 'lord'; thus slaves will learn.
  [*To him*] Now, governor.
  [*To the* GUARD]   Stand by, there.
                               Wait within.   50
                              [*Exit* GUARD.]
  This is the reason that I sent for thee:
  Thou seest thy life and Malta's happiness
  Are at my arbitrament, and Barabas
  At his discretion may dispose of both.
  Now tell me, governor, and plainly too,
  What think'st thou shall become of it and thee?
FERNEZE
  This, Barabas: since things are in thy power,
  I see no reason but of Malta's wrack,
  Nor hope of thee but extreme cruelty,
  Nor fear I death, nor will I flatter thee.   60
BARABAS
  Governor, good words, be not so furious.
  'Tis not thy life which can avail me aught.
  Yet you do live, and live for me you shall;
  And as for Malta's ruin, think you not
  'Twere slender policy for Barabas
  To dispossess himself of such a place?
  For sith, as once you said, within this isle,
  In Malta here, that I have got my goods,
  And in this city still have had success,
  And now at length am grown your governor,   70
  Yourselves shall see it shall not be forgot.
  For, as a friend not known but in distress,
  I'll rear up Malta, now remediless.
FERNEZE
  Will Barabas recover Malta's loss?
  Will Barabas be good to Christians?

BARABAS

What wilt thou give me, governor, to procure
A dissolution of the slavish bands
Wherein the Turk hath yoked your land and you?
What will you give me if I render you
80   The life of Calymath, surprise his men,
And in an outhouse of the city shut
His soldiers till I have consumed 'em all with fire?
What will you give him that procureth this?

FERNEZE

Do but bring this to pass which thou pretendest,
Deal truly with us as thou intimatest,
And I will send amongst the citizens
And by my letters privately procure
Great sums of money for thy recompense.
Nay, more; do this, and live thou governor still.

BARABAS

90   Nay, do thou this, Ferneze, and be free.
Governor, I enlarge thee. Live with me,
Go walk about the city, see thy friends.
Tush, send not letters to 'em, go thyself,
And let me see what money thou canst make.
Here is my hand that I'll set Malta free.
And thus we cast it: to a solemn feast
I will invite young Selim Calymath,
Where be thou present only to perform
One stratagem that I'll impart to thee,
100 Wherein no danger shall betide thy life,
And I will warrant Malta free for ever.

FERNEZE

Here is my hand. Believe me, Barabas,
I will be there and do as thou desirest.
When is the time?

BARABAS   Governor, presently.
For Calymath, when he hath viewed the town,
Will take his leave and sail toward Ottoman.

FERNEZE

Then will I, Barabas, about this coin,
And bring it with me to thee in the evening.

BARABAS

   Do so, but fail not. Now farewell, Ferneze.

                                     [Exit FERNEZE.*]*

   And thus far roundly goes the business.   110

   Thus, loving neither, will I live with both,

   Making a profit of my policy;

   And he from whom my most advantage comes

   Shall be my friend.

   This is the life we Jews are used to lead,

   And reason, too, for Christians do the like.

   Well, now about effecting this device:

   First, to surprise great Selim's soldiers,

   And then to make provision for the feast,

   That at one instant all things may be done.   120

   My policy detests prevention.

   To what event my secret purpose drives,

   I know, and they shall witness with their lives.

                                         Exit.

[Scene 3]

Enter CALYMATH [*and*] BASHAWS.

CALYMATH

   Thus have we viewed the city, seen the sack,

   And caused the ruins to be new repaired,

   Which with our bombards' shot and basilisks

   We rent in sunder at our entry.

   And, now I see the situation,

   And how secure this conquered island stands

   Environed with the Mediterranean Sea,

   Strong countermured with other petty isles,

   And, toward Calabria, backed by Sicily

   (Where Syracusian Dionysius reigned),   10

   Two lofty turrets that command the town –

   I wonder how it could be conquered thus.

     Enter a MESSENGER.

MESSENGER
    From Barabas, Malta's governor, I bring
    A message unto mighty Calymath.
    Hearing his sovereign was bound for sea
    To sail to Turkey, to great Ottoman,
    He humbly would entreat your majesty
    To come and see his homely citadel
    And banquet with him ere thou leav'st the isle.

CALYMATH
20   To banquet with him in his citadel?
    I fear me, messenger, to feast my train
    Within a town of war so lately pillaged
    Will be too costly and too troublesome.
    Yet would I gladly visit Barabas,
    For well has Barabas deserved of us.

MESSENGER
    Selim, for that, thus saith the governor:
    That he hath in store a pearl so big,
    So precious, and withal so orient,
    As, be it valued but indifferently,
30   The price thereof will serve to entertain
    Selim and all his soldiers for a month.
    Therefore he humbly would entreat your highness
    Not to depart till he has feasted you.

CALYMATH
    I cannot feast my men in Malta walls,
    Except he place his tables in the streets.

MESSENGER
    Know, Selim, that there is a monastery
    Which standeth as an outhouse to the town.
    There will he banquet them, but thee at home,
    With all thy bashaws and brave followers.

CALYMATH
40   Well, tell the governor we grant his suit.
    We'll in this summer evening feast with him.

MESSENGER I shall, my lord.

                              Exit [MESSENGER].

CALYMATH

And now, bold bashaws, let us to our tents,
And meditate how we may grace us best
To solemnize our governor's great feast.

Exeunt.

[Scene 4]

Enter FERNEZE, KNIGHTS, [*and* MARTIN] DEL BOSCO.

FERNEZE

In this, my countrymen, be ruled by me:
Have special care that no man sally forth
Till you shall hear a culverin discharged
By him that bears the linstock, kindled thus;
Then issue out and come to rescue me,
For happily I shall be in distress,
Or you releasèd of this servitude.

FIRST KNIGHT

Rather than thus to live as Turkish thralls,
What will we not adventure?

FERNEZE

On then, begone.

FIRST KNIGHT   Farewell, grave governor.   10

[*Exeunt.*]

[Scene 5]

Enter [BARABAS] *with a hammer above, very busy,* [*and*
CARPENTERS].

BARABAS

How stand the cords? How hang these hinges, fast?
Are all the cranes and pulleys sure?

CARPENTER   All fast.

BARABAS

Leave nothing loose, all levelled to my mind.
Why, now I see that you have art indeed.
    [*He gives money.*]
There, carpenters, divide that gold amongst you.
Go swill in bowls of sack and muscadine;
Down to the cellar, taste of all my wines.

CARPENTER

We shall, my lord, and thank you.

                                    Exeunt [CARPENTERS].

BARABAS

And if you like them, drink your fill and die;
For, so I live, perish may all the world.
Now, Selim Calymath, return me word
That thou wilt come, and I am satisfied.
    Enter MESSENGER.
Now, sirrah, what, will he come?

MESSENGER

He will, and has commanded all his men
To come ashore and march through Malta streets,
That thou mayst feast them in thy citadel.

                                    [*Exit* MESSENGER.]

BARABAS

Then now are all things as my wish would have 'em.
There wanteth nothing but the governor's pelf –
    Enter FERNEZE [*to* BARABAS, *with a bag of money*].
And see, he brings it. Now, governor, the sum?

FERNEZE

With free consent, a hundred thousand pounds.

BARABAS

Pounds, say'st thou, governor? Well, since it is no more,
I'll satisfy myself with that; nay, keep it still,
For if I keep not promise, trust not me.
And, governor, now partake my policy:
First, for his army, they are sent before,
Entered the monastery, and underneath
In several places are field-pieces pitched,
Bombards, whole barrels full of gunpowder,

That on the sudden shall dissever it,
And batter all the stones about their ears,   30
Whence none can possibly escape alive.
Now, as for Calymath and his consorts,
Here have I made a dainty gallery,
The floor whereof, this cable being cut,
Doth fall asunder, so that it doth sink
Into a deep pit past recovery.
        [*He gives* FERNEZE *a knife.*]
Here, hold that knife, and when thou seest he comes,
And with his bashaws shall be blithely set,
A warning-piece shall be shot off from the tower
To give thee knowledge when to cut the cord   40
And fire the house. Say, will not this be brave?

FERNEZE
O, excellent! [*He offers the bag of money.*]
                Here, hold thee, Barabas.
I trust thy word. Take what I promised thee.

BARABAS
No, governor, I'll satisfy thee first.
Thou shalt not live in doubt of anything.
Stand close, for here they come. [FERNEZE *hides himself.*]
                        Why, is not this
A kingly kind of trade, to purchase towns
By treachery and sell 'em by deceit?
Now tell me, worldlings, underneath the sun
If greater falsehood ever has been done.   50
        Enter CALYMATH *and* BASHAWS.

CALYMATH
Come, my companion bashaws, see, I pray,
How busy Barabas is there above
To entertain us in his gallery.
Let us salute him. Save thee, Barabas!

BARABAS
Welcome, great Calymath.

FERNEZE [*aside*]
How the slave jeers at him!

BARABAS
    Will't please thee, mighty Selim Calymath,
    To ascend our homely stairs?
CALYMATH   Ay, Barabas.
    Come, bashaws, attend.
FERNEZE [*coming forward*]
                                            Stay, Calymath!
60   For I will show thee greater courtesy
    Than Barabas would have afforded thee.
FIRST KNIGHT [*within*]
    Sound a charge there!
        A charge [*sounded*], *the cable cut, a cauldron discovered*
        [*into which* BARABAS *falls*].
        [*Enter* MARTIN DEL BOSCO *and* KNIGHTS.]
CALYMATH
    How now, what means this?
BARABAS
    Help, help me, Christians, help!
FERNEZE
    See, Calymath, this was devised for thee.
CALYMATH
    Treason, treason! Bashaws, fly!
FERNEZE
    No, Selim, do not fly.
    See his end first, and fly then if thou canst.
BARABAS
    O, help me, Selim, help me, Christians!
70   Governor, why stand you all so pitiless?
FERNEZE
    Should I, in pity of thy plaints or thee,
    Accursèd Barabas, base Jew, relent?
    No, thus I'll see thy treachery repaid,
    But wish thou hadst behaved thee otherwise.
BARABAS
    You will not help me, then?
FERNEZE   No, villain, no.
BARABAS
    And, villains, know you cannot help me now.

Then, Barabas, breathe forth thy latest fate,
And in the fury of thy torments strive
To end thy life with resolution.
Know, governor, 'twas I that slew thy son;   80
I framed the challenge that did make them meet.
Know, Calymath, I aimed thy overthrow,
And had I but escaped this stratagem,
I would have brought confusion on you all,
Damned Christians, dogs, and Turkish infidels!
But now begins the extremity of heat
To pinch me with intolerable pangs.
Die, life! Fly, soul! Tongue, curse thy fill and die!
      [*He dies.*]

CALYMATH
Tell me, you Christians, what doth this portend?

FERNEZE
This train he laid to have entrapped thy life.   90
Now, Selim, note the unhallowed deeds of Jews:
Thus he determined to have handled thee,
But I have rather chose to save thy life.

CALYMATH
Was this the banquet he prepared for us?
Let's hence, lest further mischief be pretended.

FERNEZE
Nay, Selim, stay, for since we have thee here,
We will not let thee part so suddenly.
Besides, if we should let thee go, all's one,
For with thy galleys couldst thou not get hence
Without fresh men to rig and furnish them.   100

CALYMATH
Tush, governor, take thou no care for that.
My men are all aboard,
And do attend my coming there by this.

FERNEZE
Why, heard'st thou not the trumpet sound a charge?

CALYMATH
Yes, what of that?

FERNEZE   Why, then the house was fired,

Blown up, and all thy soldiers massacred.

CALYMATH

O, monstrous treason!

FERNEZE   A Jew's courtesy;
For he that did by treason work our fall,
By treason hath delivered thee to us.
Know, therefore, till thy father hath made good
The ruins done to Malta and to us,
Thou canst not part; for Malta shall be freed,
Or Selim ne'er return to Ottoman.

CALYMATH

Nay, rather, Christians, let me go to Turkey,
In person there to meditate your peace.
To keep me here will naught advantage you.

FERNEZE

Content thee, Calymath, here thou must stay,
And live in Malta prisoner; for, come all the world
To rescue thee, so will we guard us now,
As sooner shall they drink the ocean dry
Than conquer Malta or endanger us.
So, march away, and let due praise be given
Neither to fate nor fortune, but to heaven.

                                                    [*Exeunt.*]

EPILOGUE
[SPOKEN AT COURT]

It is our fear, dread sovereign, we have been
Too tedious; neither can 't be less than sin
To wrong your princely patience. If we have,
Thus low dejected, we your pardon crave;
And if aught here offend your ear or sight,   5
We only act, and speak, what others write.

EPILOGUE

In graving with Pygmalion to contend,
Or painting with Apelles, doubtless the end
Must be disgrace. Our actor did not so;
He only aimed to go, but not outgo.
Nor think that this day any prize was played;
Here were no bets at all, no wagers laid.
All the ambition that his mind doth swell
Is but to hear from you (by me) 'twas well.

DOCTOR FAUSTUS

[Dramatis Personae

THE CHORUS

DOCTOR JOHN FAUSTUS

WAGNER

GOOD ANGEL

EVIL ANGEL

VALDES

CORNELIUS

THREE SCHOLARS

MEPHISTOPHELES

ROBIN, *the Clown*

RAFE

LUCIFER

BEELZEBUB

PRIDE
COVETOUSNESS
WRATH
ENVY } *the Seven Deadly Sins*
GLUTTONY
SLOTH
LECHERY

THE POPE

THE CARDINAL OF LORRAINE

FRIARS

A VINTNER

THE EMPEROR OF GERMANY, *Charles V*

A KNIGHT

ALEXANDER THE GREAT } *Spirits*
HIS PARAMOUR

A HORSE-COURSER
THE DUKE OF VANHOLT
THE DUCHESS OF VANHOLT
HELEN OF TROY, *a Spirit*
AN OLD MAN
DEVILS
ATTENDANTS]

[PROLOGUE]

Enter CHORUS.

CHORUS

Not marching now in fields of Trasimene
Where Mars did mate the Carthaginians,
Nor sporting in the dalliance of love
In courts of kings where state is overturned,
Nor in the pomp of proud audacious deeds,
Intends our muse to vaunt his heavenly verse.
Only this, gentlemen: we must perform
The form of Faustus' fortunes, good or bad.
To patient judgements we appeal our plaud,
And speak for Faustus in his infancy.   10
Now is he born, his parents base of stock,
In Germany, within a town called Rhode.
Of riper years to Wittenberg he went,
Whereas his kinsmen chiefly brought him up.
So soon he profits in divinity,
The fruitful plot of scholarism graced,
That shortly he was graced with doctor's name,
Excelling all whose sweet delight disputes
In heavenly matters of theology,
Till, swoll'n with cunning of a self-conceit,   20
His waxen wings did mount above his reach,
And melting heavens conspired his overthrow.
For, falling to a devilish exercise,
And glutted more with learning's golden gifts,
He surfeits upon cursèd necromancy;

Nothing so sweet as magic is to him,
Which he prefers before his chiefest bliss.
And this the man that in his study sits.

Exit.

[Scene 1]

Enter FAUSTUS *in his study.*

FAUSTUS

    Settle thy studies, Faustus, and begin
    To sound the depth of that thou wilt profess.
    Having commenced, be a divine in show,
    Yet level at the end of every art,
    And live and die in Aristotle's works.
    Sweet *Analytics*, 'tis thou hast ravished me!
    [*He reads*] '*Bene disserere est finis logices.*'
    Is to dispute well logic's chiefest end?
    Affords this art no greater miracle?
    Then read no more, thou hast attained the end.   10
    A greater subject fitteth Faustus' wit.
    Bid *On kai me on* farewell. Galen, come!
    Seeing *ubi desinit philosophus, ibi incipit medicus*,
    Be a physician, Faustus. Heap up gold,
    And be eternized for some wondrous cure.
    [*He reads*] '*Summum bonum medicinae sanitas*':
    The end of physic is our body's health.
    Why Faustus, hast thou not attained that end?
    Is not thy common talk sound aphorisms?
    Are not thy bills hung up as monuments,   20
    Whereby whole cities have escaped the plague
    And thousand desp'rate maladies been eased?
    Yet art thou still but Faustus, and a man.
    Wouldst thou make man to live eternally,

Or, being dead, raise them to life again,
Then this profession were to be esteemed.
Physic, farewell. Where is Justinian?
[*He reads*] '*Si una eademque res legatur duobus,*
Alter rem, alter valorem rei', etc.

30   A pretty case of paltry legacies!
[*He reads*] '*Exhaereditare filium non potest pater nisi –*'
Such is the subject of the Institute
And universal body of the law,
His study fits a mercenary drudge
Who aims at nothing but external trash,
Too servile and illiberal for me.
When all is done, divinity is best.
Jerome's Bible, Faustus, view it well.
[*He reads*] '*Stipendium peccati mors est.*' Ha!

40   '*Stipendium*', etc.
The reward of sin is death. That's hard.
[*He reads*] '*Si peccasse negamus, fallimur*
Et nulla est in nobis veritas.'
If we say that we have no sin,
We deceive ourselves, and there's no truth in us.
Why then belike we must sin,
And so consequently die.
Ay, we must die an everlasting death.
What doctrine call you this? *Che serà, serà,*

50   What will be, shall be? Divinity, adieu!
    [*He picks up a book of magic.*]
These metaphysics of magicians
And necromantic books are heavenly,
Lines, circles, schemes, letters, and characters –
Ay, these are those that Faustus most desires.
O, what a world of profit and delight,
Of power, of honour, of omnipotence
Is promised to the studious artisan!
All things that move between the quiet poles
Shall be at my command. Emperors and kings

60   Are but obeyed in their several provinces,
Nor can they raise the wind or rend the clouds;

But his dominion that exceeds in this
Stretcheth as far as doth the mind of man.
A sound magician is a mighty god.
Here, Faustus, try thy brains to gain a deity.
Wagner!

    Enter WAGNER.

              Commend me to my dearest friends,
The German Valdes and Cornelius.
Request them earnestly to visit me.

WAGNER I will, sir.

                          Exit [WAGNER].

FAUSTUS

Their conference will be a greater help to me   70
Than all my labours, plod I ne'er so fast.

    Enter the GOOD ANGEL *and the* EVIL ANGEL.

GOOD ANGEL

O Faustus, lay that damnèd book aside
And gaze not on it, lest it tempt thy soul
And heap God's heavy wrath upon thy head!
Read, read the Scriptures. That is blasphemy.

EVIL ANGEL

Go forward, Faustus, in that famous art
Wherein all nature's treasury is contained.
Be thou on earth as Jove is in the sky,
Lord and commander of these elements.

                    Exeunt [ANGELS].

FAUSTUS

How am I glutted with conceit of this!   80
Shall I make spirits fetch me what I please,
Resolve me of all ambiguities,
Perform what desperate enterprise I will?
I'll have them fly to India for gold,
Ransack the ocean for orient pearl,
And search all corners of the new-found world
For pleasant fruits and princely delicates.
I'll have them read me strange philosophy
And tell the secrets of all foreign kings.
I'll have them wall all Germany with brass   90

And make swift Rhine circle fair Wittenberg.
I'll have them fill the public schools with silk,
Wherewith the students shall be bravely clad.
I'll levy soldiers with the coin they bring
And chase the Prince of Parma from our land,
And reign sole king of all our provinces;
Yea, stranger engines for the brunt of war
Than was the fiery keel at Antwerp's bridge
I'll make my servile spirits to invent.
100 Come, German Valdes and Cornelius,
And make me blest with your sage conference!
    Enter VALDES *and* CORNELIUS.
Valdes, sweet Valdes, and Cornelius,
Know that your words have won me at the last
To practise magic and concealèd arts –
Yet not your words only, but mine own fantasy,
That will receive no object, for my head
But ruminates on necromantic skill.
Philosophy is odious and obscure;
Both law and physic are for petty wits;
110 Divinity is basest of the three,
Unpleasant, harsh, contemptible, and vile.
'Tis magic, magic that hath ravished me.
Then, gentle friends, aid me in this attempt,
And I, that have with concise syllogisms
Gravelled the pastors of the German Church,
And made the flow'ring pride of Wittenberg
Swarm to my problems as the infernal spirits
On sweet Musaeus when he came to hell,
Will be as cunning as Agrippa was,
120 Whose shadows made all Europe honour him.
VALDES
Faustus, these books, thy wit, and our experience
Shall make all nations to canonize us.
As Indian Moors obey their Spanish lords,
So shall the subjects of every element
Be always serviceable to us three.
Like lions shall they guard us when we please,

Like Almain rutters with their horsemen's staves,
Or Lapland giants, trotting by our sides;
Sometimes like women, or unwedded maids,
Shadowing more beauty in their airy brows   130
Than in the white breasts of the Queen of Love.
From Venice shall they drag huge argosies,
And from America the golden fleece
That yearly stuffs old Philip's treasury,
If learnèd Faustus will be resolute.

FAUSTUS
Valdes, as resolute am I in this
As thou to live. Therefore object it not.

CORNELIUS
The miracles that magic will perform
Will make thee vow to study nothing else.
He that is grounded in astrology,   140
Enriched with tongues, well seen in minerals,
Hath all the principles magic doth require.
Then doubt not, Faustus, but to be renowned
And more frequented for this mystery
Than heretofore the Delphian oracle.
The spirits tell me they can dry the sea
And fetch the treasure of all foreign wracks –
Ay, all the wealth that our forefathers hid
Within the massy entrails of the earth.
Then tell me, Faustus, what shall we three want?   150

FAUSTUS
Nothing, Cornelius. O, this cheers my soul!
Come, show me some demonstrations magical,
That I may conjure in some lusty grove
And have these joys in full possession.

VALDES
Then haste thee to some solitary grove,
And bear wise Bacon's and Albanus' works,
The Hebrew Psalter, and New Testament;
And whatsoever else is requisite,
We will inform thee ere our conference cease.

CORNELIUS

160   Valdes, first let him know the words of art,
        And then, all other ceremonies learned,
        Faustus may try his cunning by himself.

VALDES

        First I'll instruct thee in the rudiments,
        And then wilt thou be perfecter than I.

FAUSTUS

        Then come and dine with me, and after meat
        We'll canvass every quiddity thereof,
        For ere I sleep I'll try what I can do.
        This night I'll conjure, though I die therefore.

                                                        Exeunt.

[*Scene 2*]

        Enter two SCHOLARS.

FIRST SCHOLAR I wonder what's become of Faustus, that was
        wont to make our schools ring with '*sic probo*'.

SECOND SCHOLAR That shall we know, for see, here comes his
        boy.

        Enter WAGNER, [*carrying wine*].

FIRST SCHOLAR How now, sirrah, where's thy master?

WAGNER God in heaven knows.

SECOND SCHOLAR Why, dost not thou know?

WAGNER Yes, I know, but that follows not.

FIRST SCHOLAR Go to, sirrah! Leave your jesting, and tell us
10   where he is.

WAGNER That follows not necessary by force of argument
        that you, being licentiate, should stand upon't. Therefore,
        acknowledge your error, and be attentive.

SECOND SCHOLAR Why, didst thou not say thou knew'st?

WAGNER Have you any witness on't?

FIRST SCHOLAR Yes, sirrah, I heard you.

WAGNER Ask my fellow if I be a thief.

SECOND SCHOLAR Well, you will not tell us.

WAGNER Yes, sir, I will tell you. Yet if you were not dunces, you would never ask me such a question. For is not he *corpus* 20 *naturale*? And is not that *mobile*? Then, wherefore should you ask me such a question? But that I am by nature phlegmatic, slow to wrath, and prone to lechery – to love, I would say – it were not for you to come within forty foot of the place of execution, although I do not doubt to see you both hanged the next sessions. Thus, having triumphed over you, I will set my countenance like a precisian and begin to speak thus: Truly, my dear brethren, my master is within at dinner with Valdes and Cornelius, as this wine, if it could speak, it would inform your worships. And so the Lord bless you, 30 preserve you, and keep you, my dear brethren, my dear brethren.

Exit [WAGNER].

FIRST SCHOLAR Nay, then, I fear he is fall'n into that damned art for which they two are infamous through the world.

SECOND SCHOLAR Were he a stranger, and not allied to me, yet should I grieve for him. But come, let us go and inform the Rector, and see if he, by his grave counsel, can reclaim him.

FIRST SCHOLAR O, but I fear me nothing can reclaim him.

SECOND SCHOLAR Yet let us try what we can do.   40

Exeunt.

[*Scene 3*]

Enter FAUSTUS *to conjure.*

FAUSTUS
   Now that the gloomy shadow of the earth,
   Longing to view Orion's drizzling look,
   Leaps from th'Antarctic world unto the sky
   And dims the welkin with her pitchy breath,
   Faustus, begin thine incantations,
   And try if devils will obey thy hest,
   Seeing thou hast prayed and sacrificed to them.

Within this circle is Jehovah's name,
Forward and backward anagrammatized,
10 The breviated names of holy saints,
Figures of every adjunct to the heavens,
And characters of signs and erring stars,
By which the spirits are enforced to rise.
Then fear not, Faustus, but be resolute,
And try the uttermost magic can perform.
Sint mihi dei Acherontis propitii! Valeat numen triplex
Jehovae! Ignei, aerii, aquatici, spiritus, salvete! Orientis
princeps, Beelzebub, inferni ardentis monarcha, et
Demogorgon, propitiamus vos, ut appareat et surgat
20 *Mephistopheles. Quid tu moraris? Per Jehovam, Gehennam,*
et consecratam aquam quam nunc spargo, signumque crucis
quod nunc facio, et per vota nostra, ipse nunc surgat nobis
dicatis Mephistopheles!

[FAUSTUS *sprinkles holy water and makes a sign of the*
cross.]
Enter a DEVIL [MEPHISTOPHELES].
I charge thee to return and change thy shape,
Thou art too ugly to attend on me.
Go, and return an old Franciscan friar,
That holy shape becomes a devil best.
                              Exit DEVIL [MEPHISTOPHELES].
I see there's virtue in my heavenly words.
Who would not be proficient in this art?
30 How pliant is this Mephistopheles,
Full of obedience and humility!
Such is the force of magic and my spells.
Now, Faustus, thou art conjurer laureate,
That canst command great Mephistopheles.
Quin redis, Mephistopheles, fratris imagine!
          Enter MEPHISTOPHELES [*dressed as a friar*].
MEPHISTOPHELES
Now, Faustus, what wouldst thou have me do?
FAUSTUS
I charge thee wait upon me whilst I live,
To do whatever Faustus shall command,

Be it to make the moon drop from her sphere,
Or the ocean to overwhelm the world.   40
MEPHISTOPHELES
I am a servant to great Lucifer
And may not follow thee without his leave.
No more than he commands must we perform.
FAUSTUS
Did not he charge thee to appear to me?
MEPHISTOPHELES
No, I came now hither of mine own accord.
FAUSTUS
Did not my conjuring speeches raise thee? Speak.
MEPHISTOPHELES
That was the cause, but yet *per accidens*.
For when we hear one rack the name of God,
Abjure the Scriptures and his Saviour Christ,
We fly in hope to get his glorious soul,   50
Nor will we come unless he use such means
Whereby he is in danger to be damned.
Therefore, the shortest cut for conjuring
Is stoutly to abjure the Trinity
And pray devoutly to the prince of hell.
FAUSTUS
So Faustus hath
Already done, and holds this principle:
There is no chief but only Beelzebub,
To whom Faustus doth dedicate himself.
This word 'damnation' terrifies not him,   60
For he confounds hell in Elysium.
His ghost be with the old philosophers!
But leaving these vain trifles of men's souls,
Tell me what is that Lucifer thy lord?
MEPHISTOPHELES
Arch-regent and commander of all spirits.
FAUSTUS
Was not that Lucifer an angel once?
MEPHISTOPHELES
Yes, Faustus, and most dearly loved of God.

FAUSTUS

How comes it then that he is prince of devils?

MEPHISTOPHELES

O, by aspiring pride and insolence,

70   For which God threw him from the face of heaven.

FAUSTUS

And what are you that live with Lucifer?

MEPHISTOPHELES

Unhappy spirits that fell with Lucifer,

Conspired against our God with Lucifer,

And are for ever damned with Lucifer.

FAUSTUS

Where are you damned?

MEPHISTOPHELES

In hell.

FAUSTUS

How comes it then that thou art out of hell?

MEPHISTOPHELES

Why, this is hell, nor am I out of it.

Think'st thou that I, who saw the face of God

80   And tasted the eternal joys of heaven,

Am not tormented with ten thousand hells

In being deprived of everlasting bliss?

O Faustus, leave these frivolous demands,

Which strike a terror to my fainting soul!

FAUSTUS

What, is great Mephistopheles so passionate

For being deprivèd of the joys of heaven?

Learn thou of Faustus manly fortitude,

And scorn those joys thou never shalt possess.

Go bear these tidings to great Lucifer:

90   Seeing Faustus hath incurred eternal death

By desp'rate thoughts against Jove's deity,

Say he surrenders up to him his soul,

So he will spare him four-and-twenty years,

Letting him live in all voluptuousness,

Having thee ever to attend on me,

To give me whatsoever I shall ask,

To tell me whatsoever I demand,
To slay mine enemies and aid my friends,
And always be obedient to my will.
Go and return to mighty Lucifer,   100
And meet me in my study at midnight,
And then resolve me of thy master's mind.

MEPHISTOPHELES I will, Faustus.

Exit [MEPHISTOPHELES].

FAUSTUS
Had I as many souls as there be stars,
I'd give them all for Mephistopheles.
By him I'll be great emperor of the world,
And make a bridge through the moving air
To pass the ocean with a band of men;
I'll join the hills that bind the Afric shore
And make that land continent to Spain,   110
And both contributory to my crown.
The emperor shall not live but by my leave,
Nor any potentate of Germany.
Now that I have obtained what I desire,
I'll live in speculation of this art
Till Mephistopheles return again.

Exit.

[Scene 4]

Enter WAGNER *and* [ROBIN] *the Clown.*

WAGNER Sirrah boy, come hither.

ROBIN How, 'boy'? 'Swounds, 'boy'! I hope you have seen
many boys with such pickedevants as I have. 'Boy', quotha?

WAGNER Tell me, sirrah, hast thou any comings in?

ROBIN Ay, and goings out too, you may see else.

WAGNER Alas, poor slave, see how poverty jesteth in his naked-
ness! The villain is bare and out of service, and so hungry that
I know he would give his soul to the devil for a shoulder of
mutton, though it were blood raw.

10   ROBIN How? My soul to the devil for a shoulder of mutton,
        though 'twere blood raw? Not so, good friend. By'r Lady, I
        had need have it well roasted, and good sauce to it, if I pay so
        dear.

     WAGNER Well, wilt thou serve me, and I'll make thee go like
        Qui mihi discipulus?

     ROBIN How, in verse?

     WAGNER No, sirrah, in beaten silk and stavesacre.

     ROBIN How, how, knave's acre? [*Aside*] Aye, I thought that
        was all the land his father left him. [*To* WAGNER] Do ye hear?
20   I would be sorry to rob you of your living.

     WAGNER Sirrah, I say in stavesacre.

     ROBIN Oho, oho, 'stavesacre'! Why then, belike, if I were your
        man, I should be full of vermin.

     WAGNER So thou shalt, whether thou beest with me or no. But
        sirrah, leave your jesting, and bind yourself presently unto
        me for seven years, or I'll turn all the lice about thee into
        familiars, and they shall tear thee in pieces.

     ROBIN Do you hear, sir? You may save that labour. They are
        too familiar with me already. 'Swounds, they are as bold with
30   my flesh as if they had paid for my meat and drink.

     WAGNER Well, do you hear, sirrah? [*Offering money*] Hold,
        take these guilders.

     ROBIN Gridirons? What be they?

     WAGNER Why, French crowns.

     ROBIN Mass, but for the name of French crowns a man were as
        good have as many English counters. And what should I do
        with these?

     WAGNER Why now, sirrah, thou art at an hour's warning when-
        soever or wheresoever the devil shall fetch thee.

40   ROBIN No, no, here, take your gridirons again.
        [*He hands him the money.*]

     WAGNER Truly, I'll none of them.

     ROBIN Truly, but you shall.

     WAGNER [*to the audience*] Bear witness I gave them him.

     ROBIN Bear witness I give them you again.

     WAGNER Well, I will cause two devils presently to fetch thee
        away. Baliol and Belcher!

ROBIN Let your Balio and your Belcher come here and I'll knock
them. They were never so knocked since they were devils. Say
I should kill one of them, what would folks say? 'Do ye see
yonder tall fellow in the round slop? He has killed the devil.'   50
So I should be called 'Kill devil' all the parish over.

Enter two DEVILS, *and* [ROBIN] *the Clown runs up and
down crying.*

WAGNER Baliol and Belcher! Spirits, away!

Exeunt [DEVILS].

ROBIN What, are they gone? A vengeance on them! They have
vile long nails. There was a he devil and a she devil. I'll tell
you how you shall know them: all he devils has horns, and
all she devils has clefts and cloven feet.

WAGNER Well, sirrah, follow me.

ROBIN But do you hear? If I should serve you, would you teach
me to raise up Banios and Belcheos?

WAGNER I will teach thee to turn thyself to anything, to a dog,   60
or a cat, or a mouse, or a rat, or anything.

ROBIN How? A Christian fellow to a dog or a cat, a mouse or
a rat? No, no, sir. If you turn me into anything, let it be in the
likeness of a little, pretty, frisking flea, that I may be here
and there and everywhere. O, I'll tickle the pretty wenches'
plackets! I'll be amongst them, i'faith!

WAGNER Well, sirrah, come.

ROBIN But do you hear, Wagner?

WAGNER How? Baliol and Belcher!

ROBIN O Lord, I pray sir, let Banio and Belcher go sleep.   70

WAGNER Villain, call me Master Wagner, and let thy left eye be
diametarily fixed upon my right heel, with *quasi vestigiis
nostris insistere.*

Exit [WAGNER].

ROBIN God forgive me, he speaks Dutch fustian. Well, I'll
follow him, I'll serve him, that's flat.

Exit.

[Scene 5]

Enter FAUSTUS *in his study.*

FAUSTUS

Now, Faustus, must thou needs be damned,
And canst thou not be saved.
What boots it then to think of God or heaven?
Away with such vain fancies and despair!
Despair in God and trust in Beelzebub.
Now go not backward. No, Faustus, be resolute.
Why waverest thou? O, something soundeth in mine ears:
'Abjure this magic, turn to God again!'
Ay, and Faustus will turn to God again.

10   To God? He loves thee not.
The god thou servest is thine own appetite,
Wherein is fixed the love of Beelzebub.
To him I'll build an altar and a church,
And offer lukewarm blood of new-born babes.

Enter GOOD ANGEL *and* EVIL [ANGEL].

GOOD ANGEL

Sweet Faustus, leave that execrable art.

FAUSTUS

Contrition, prayer, repentance – what of them?

GOOD ANGEL

O, they are means to bring thee unto heaven.

EVIL ANGEL

Rather illusions, fruits of lunacy,
That makes men foolish that do trust them most.

GOOD ANGEL

20   Sweet Faustus, think of heaven and heavenly things.

EVIL ANGEL

No, Faustus, think of honour and wealth.

Exeunt [ANGELS].

FAUSTUS

Of wealth?
Why, the seigniory of Emden shall be mine.
When Mephistopheles shall stand by me,

What god can hurt thee, Faustus? Thou art safe,
Cast no more doubts. Come, Mephistopheles,
And bring glad tidings from great Lucifer.
Is't not midnight? Come, Mephistopheles!
Veni, veni, Mephistophile!
  Enter MEPHISTOPHELES.
Now tell, what says Lucifer thy lord?   30

MEPHISTOPHELES
That I shall wait on Faustus whilst he lives,
So he will buy my service with his soul.

FAUSTUS
Already Faustus hath hazarded that for thee.

MEPHISTOPHELES
But, Faustus, thou must bequeath it solemnly
And write a deed of gift with thine own blood,
For that security craves great Lucifer.
If thou deny it, I will back to hell.

FAUSTUS Stay, Mephistopheles, and tell me, what good will my
soul do thy lord?

MEPHISTOPHELES Enlarge his kingdom.   40

FAUSTUS Is that the reason he tempts us thus?

MEPHISTOPHELES
Solamen miseris socios habuisse doloris.

FAUSTUS
Have you any pain, that tortures others?

MEPHISTOPHELES
As great as have the human souls of men.
But tell me, Faustus, shall I have thy soul?
And I will be thy slave, and wait on thee,
And give thee more than thou hast wit to ask.

FAUSTUS
Ay, Mephistopheles, I give it thee.

MEPHISTOPHELES
Then stab thine arm courageously,
And bind thy soul that at some certain day   50
Great Lucifer may claim it as his own,
And then be thou as great as Lucifer.

FAUSTUS [*cutting his arm*]
    Lo, Mephistopheles, for love of thee
    I cut mine arm, and with my proper blood
    Assure my soul to be great Lucifer's,
    Chief lord and regent of perpetual night.
    View here the blood that trickles from mine arm,
    And let it be propitious for my wish.
MEPHISTOPHELES But Faustus, thou must write it in manner
60   of a deed of gift.
FAUSTUS
    Ay, so I will. [*He writes.*] But Mephistopheles,
    My blood congeals, and I can write no more.
MEPHISTOPHELES
    I'll fetch thee fire to dissolve it straight.
                                    Exit [MEPHISTOPHELES].
FAUSTUS
    What might the staying of my blood portend?
    Is it unwilling I should write this bill?
    Why streams it not, that I may write afresh?
    'Faustus gives to thee his soul' – ah, there it stayed!
    Why shouldst thou not? Is not thy soul thine own?
    Then write again: 'Faustus gives to thee his soul.'
        Enter MEPHISTOPHELES *with a chafer of coals.*
MEPHISTOPHELES
70   Here's fire. Come Faustus, set it on.
FAUSTUS
    So. Now the blood begins to clear again.
    Now will I make an end immediately. [*He writes.*]
MEPHISTOPHELES [*aside*]
    O, what will not I do to obtain his soul?
FAUSTUS
    Consummatum est. This bill is ended,
    And Faustus hath bequeathed his soul to Lucifer.
    But what is this inscription on mine arm?
    '*Homo, fuge!*' Whither should I fly?
    If unto God, he'll throw thee down to hell.
    My senses are deceived; here's nothing writ.
80   I see it plain. Here in this place is writ

'*Homo, fuge!*' Yet shall not Faustus fly.

MEPHISTOPHELES [*aside*]

I'll fetch him somewhat to delight his mind.

Exit [MEPHISTOPHELES, *then re-*]*enter with* DEVILS,
giving crowns and rich apparel to FAUSTUS, *and dance
and then depart.*

FAUSTUS

Speak, Mephistopheles. What means this show?

MEPHISTOPHELES

Nothing, Faustus, but to delight thy mind withal
And to show thee what magic can perform.

FAUSTUS

But may I raise up spirits when I please?

MEPHISTOPHELES

Ay, Faustus, and do greater things than these.

FAUSTUS

Then there's enough for a thousand souls.
Here, Mephistopheles, receive this scroll,
A deed of gift of body and of soul –   90
But yet conditionally that thou perform
All articles prescribed between us both.

MEPHISTOPHELES

Faustus, I swear by hell and Lucifer
To effect all promises between us made.

FAUSTUS Then hear me read them.

'On these conditions following:

First, that Faustus may be a spirit in form and substance.

Secondly, that Mephistopheles shall be his servant, and at
his command.

Thirdly, that Mephistopheles shall do for him and bring   100
him whatsoever.

Fourthly, that he shall be in his chamber or house invisible.

Lastly, that he shall appear to the said John Faustus at all
times in what form or shape soever he please.

I, John Faustus of Wittenberg, Doctor, by these presents
do give both body and soul to Lucifer, Prince of the East,
and his minister Mephistopheles, and furthermore grant unto
them that, four-and-twenty years being expired, the articles

above written inviolate, full power to fetch or carry the said
John Faustus, body and soul, flesh, blood, or goods, into their
habitation wheresoever.

By me, John Faustus.'

MEPHISTOPHELES Speak, Faustus. Do you deliver this as your
deed?

FAUSTUS [*giving the deed*] Ay. Take it, and the devil give thee
good on't.

MEPHISTOPHELES Now, Faustus, ask what thou wilt.

FAUSTUS
First will I question with thee about hell.
Tell me, where is the place that men call hell?

MEPHISTOPHELES
Under the heavens.

FAUSTUS   Ay, but whereabout?

MEPHISTOPHELES
Within the bowels of these elements,
Where we are tortured and remain for ever.
Hell hath no limits, nor is circumscribed
In one self place, for where we are is hell,
And where hell is must we ever be.
And, to conclude, when all the world dissolves,
And every creature shall be purified,
All places shall be hell that is not heaven.

FAUSTUS Come, I think hell's a fable.

MEPHISTOPHELES
Ay, think so still, till experience change thy mind.

FAUSTUS
Why, think'st thou then that Faustus shall be damned?

MEPHISTOPHELES
Ay, of necessity, for here's the scroll
Wherein thou hast given thy soul to Lucifer.

FAUSTUS
Ay, and body too. But what of that?
Think'st thou that Faustus is so fond
To imagine that after this life there is any pain?
Tush, these are trifles and mere old wives' tales.

MEPHISTOPHELES
   But, Faustus, I am an instance to prove the contrary,
   For I am damnèd and am now in hell.
FAUSTUS How? Now in hell? Nay, an this be hell, I'll willingly   140
   be damned here. What? Walking, disputing, etc.? But leaving
   off this, let me have a wife, the fairest maid in Germany, for
   I am wanton and lascivious and cannot live without a wife.
MEPHISTOPHELES How, a wife? I prithee, Faustus, talk not of
   a wife.
FAUSTUS Nay, sweet Mephistopheles, fetch me one, for I will
   have one.
MEPHISTOPHELES Well, thou wilt have one. Sit there till I
   come. I'll fetch thee a wife, in the devil's name.
      [*Exit* MEPHISTOPHELES, *then re-]enter with a* DEVIL
      dressed like a woman, with fireworks.
MEPHISTOPHELES Tell, Faustus, how dost thou like thy wife?   150
FAUSTUS A plague on her for a hot whore!
MEPHISTOPHELES Tut, Faustus, marriage is but a ceremonial toy.
   If thou lovest me, think no more of it.
                                              [*Exit* DEVIL.]
   I'll cull thee out the fairest courtesans
   And bring them ev'ry morning to thy bed.
   She whom thine eye shall like, thy heart shall have,
   Be she as chaste as was Penelope,
   As wise as Saba, or as beautiful
   As was bright Lucifer before his fall.
      [*Presenting a book*]
   Hold, take this book. Peruse it thoroughly.   160
   The iterating of these lines brings gold;
   The framing of this circle on the ground
   Brings whirlwinds, tempests, thunder, and lightning.
   Pronounce this thrice devoutly to thyself,
   And men in armour shall appear to thee,
   Ready to execute what thou desir'st.
FAUSTUS Thanks, Mephistopheles. Yet fain would I have a
   book wherein I might behold all spells and incantations, that
   I might raise up spirits when I please.

170 MEPHISTOPHELES Here they are in this book. (*There turn to them*)

FAUSTUS Now would I have a book where I might see all characters and planets of the heavens, that I might know their motions and dispositions.

MEPHISTOPHELES Here they are too. (*Turn to them*)

FAUSTUS Nay, let me have one book more, and then I have done, wherein I might see all plants, herbs, and trees that grow upon the earth.

MEPHISTOPHELES Here they be.

FAUSTUS O, thou art deceived.

180 MEPHISTOPHELES Tut, I warrant thee. (*Turn to them*)

[*Exeunt.*]

[*Scene 6*]

Enter ROBIN *the ostler with a book in his hand.*

ROBIN O, this is admirable! Here I ha' stol'n one of Doctor Faustus' conjuring books, and, i'faith, I mean to search some circles for my own use. Now will I make all the maidens in our parish dance at my pleasure stark naked before me, and so by that means I shall see more than e'er I felt or saw yet.

Enter RAFE, *calling* ROBIN.

RAFE Robin, prithee, come away. There a gentleman tarries to have his horse, and he would have his things rubbed and made clean; he keeps such a chafing with my mistress about it, and she has sent me to look thee out. Prithee, come away.

10 ROBIN Keep out, keep out, or else you are blown up, you are dismembered, Rafe! Keep out, for I am about a roaring piece of work.

RAFE Come, what dost thou with that same book? Thou canst not read.

ROBIN Yes, my master and mistress shall find that I can read – he for his forehead, she for her private study. She's born to bear with me, or else my art fails.

RAFE Why, Robin, what book is that?

ROBIN What book? Why the most intolerable book for conjuring that e'er was invented by any brimstone devil.   20

RAFE Canst thou conjure with it?

ROBIN I can do all these things easily with it: first, I can make thee drunk with hippocras at any tavern in Europe for nothing. That's one of my conjuring works.

RAFE Our Master Parson says that's nothing.

ROBIN True, Rafe, and more, Rafe, if thou hast any mind to Nan Spit, our kitchen maid, then turn her and wind her to thy own use as often as thou wilt, and at midnight.

RAFE O brave Robin! Shall I have Nan Spit, and to mine own use? On that condition I'll feed thy devil with horse-bread as   30
long as he lives, of free cost.

ROBIN No more, sweet Rafe. Let's go and make clean our boots, which lie foul upon our hands, and then to our conjuring, in the devil's name.

Exeunt.

[*Scene 7*]

[*Enter* FAUSTUS *in his study, and* MEPHISTOPHELES.]

FAUSTUS

When I behold the heavens, then I repent
And curse thee, wicked Mephistopheles,
Because thou hast deprived me of those joys.

MEPHISTOPHELES

Why Faustus,
Think'st thou heaven is such a glorious thing?
I tell thee, 'tis not half so fair as thou
Or any man that breathes on earth.

FAUSTUS How provest thou that?

MEPHISTOPHELES

It was made for man, therefore is man more excellent.

FAUSTUS

If it were made for man, 'twas made for me.   10
I will renounce this magic and repent.

Enter GOOD ANGEL *and* EVIL ANGEL.

GOOD ANGEL

    Faustus, repent yet, God will pity thee.

EVIL ANGEL

    Thou art a spirit, God cannot pity thee.

FAUSTUS

    Who buzzeth in mine ears I am a spirit?

    Be I a devil, yet God may pity me;

    Ay, God will pity me if I repent.

EVIL ANGEL

    Ay, but Faustus never shall repent.

                         Exeunt [ANGELS].

FAUSTUS

    My heart's so hardened I cannot repent.

    Scarce can I name salvation, faith, or heaven,

20   But fearful echoes thunders in mine ears:

    'Faustus, thou art damned!' Then swords and knives,

    Poison, guns, halters, and envenomed steel

    Are laid before me to dispatch myself;

    And long ere this I should have slain myself

    Had not sweet pleasure conquered deep despair.

    Have not I made blind Homer sing to me

    Of Alexander's love and Oenone's death?

    And hath not he that built the walls of Thebes

    With ravishing sound of his melodious harp

30   Made music with my Mephistopheles?

    Why should I die, then, or basely despair?

    I am resolved Faustus shall ne'er repent.

    Come, Mephistopheles, let us dispute again

    And argue of divine astrology.

    Tell me, are there many heavens above the moon?

    Are all celestial bodies but one globe,

    As is the substance of this centric earth?

MEPHISTOPHELES

    As are the elements, such are the spheres,

    Mutually folded in each other's orb;

40   And, Faustus, all jointly move upon one axletree,

    Whose terminine is termed the world's wide pole.

Nor are the names of Saturn, Mars, or Jupiter
Feigned, but are erring stars.

FAUSTUS But tell me, have they all one motion, both *situ et tempore*?

MEPHISTOPHELES All jointly move from east to west in four-and-twenty hours upon the poles of the world, but differ in their motion upon the poles of the zodiac.

FAUSTUS
Tush, these slender trifles Wagner can decide.
Hath Mephistopheles no greater skill?   50
Who knows not the double motion of the planets?
The first is finished in a natural day,
The second thus, as Saturn in thirty years,
Jupiter in twelve, Mars in four, the sun, Venus, and Mercury
in a year, the moon in twenty-eight days. Tush, these are
freshmen's suppositions. But tell me, hath every sphere a
dominion or *intelligentia*?

MEPHISTOPHELES Ay.

FAUSTUS How many heavens or spheres are there?

MEPHISTOPHELES Nine: the seven planets, the firmament, and   60
the empyreal heaven.

FAUSTUS Well, resolve me in this question: why have we not conjunctions, oppositions, aspects, eclipses all at one time, but in some years we have more, in some less?

MEPHISTOPHELES *Per inaequalem motum respectu totius.*

FAUSTUS Well, I am answered. Tell me who made the world.

MEPHISTOPHELES I will not.

FAUSTUS Sweet Mephistopheles, tell me.

MEPHISTOPHELES Move me not, for I will not tell thee.

FAUSTUS Villain, have I not bound thee to tell me anything?   70

MEPHISTOPHELES Ay, that is not against our kingdom, but this is. Think thou on hell, Faustus, for thou art damned.

FAUSTUS Think, Faustus, upon God, that made the world.

MEPHISTOPHELES Remember this.

Exit [MEPHISTOPHELES].

FAUSTUS
Ay, go, accursèd spirit, to ugly hell!
'Tis thou hast damned distressèd Faustus' soul.

Is't not too late?

Enter GOOD ANGEL *and* EVIL [ANGEL].

EVIL ANGEL

Too late.

GOOD ANGEL

Never too late, if Faustus can repent.

EVIL ANGEL

80   If thou repent, devils shall tear thee in pieces.

GOOD ANGEL

Repent, and they shall never raze thy skin.

Exeunt [ANGELS].

FAUSTUS

Ah, Christ, my Saviour,

Seek to save distressèd Faustus' soul!

Enter LUCIFER, BEELZEBUB, *and* MEPHISTOPHELES.

LUCIFER

Christ cannot save thy soul, for he is just.

There's none but I have int'rest in the same.

FAUSTUS

O, who art thou that look'st so terrible?

LUCIFER

I am Lucifer,

And this is my companion prince in hell.

FAUSTUS

O Faustus, they are come to fetch away thy soul!

LUCIFER

90   We come to tell thee thou dost injure us.

Thou talk'st of Christ, contrary to thy promise.

Thou shouldst not think of God. Think of the devil,

And of his dame, too.

FAUSTUS

Nor will I henceforth. Pardon me in this,

And Faustus vows never to look to heaven,

Never to name God or to pray to him,

To burn his Scriptures, slay his ministers,

And make my spirits pull his churches down.

LUCIFER

Do so, and we will highly gratify thee.

Faustus, we are come from hell to show thee some pastime.   100
Sit down, and thou shalt see all the Seven Deadly Sins appear
in their proper shapes.

FAUSTUS That sight will be as pleasing unto me as paradise was
to Adam, the first day of his creation.

LUCIFER Talk not of paradise nor creation, but mark this show.
Talk of the devil, and nothing else. Come away!

Enter the SEVEN DEADLY SINS.

Now, Faustus, examine them of their several names and
dispositions.

FAUSTUS What art thou, the first?

PRIDE I am Pride. I disdain to have any parents. I am like to   110
Ovid's flea: I can creep into every corner of a wench. Sometimes like a periwig I sit upon her brow, or like a fan of
feathers I kiss her lips. Indeed I do. What do I not? But fie,
what a scent is here! I'll not speak another word except the
ground were perfumed and covered with cloth of arras.

FAUSTUS What art thou, the second?

COVETOUSNESS I am Covetousness, begotten of an old churl
in an old leathern bag; and might I have my wish, I would
desire that this house and all the people in it were turned
to gold, that I might lock you up in my good chest. O my   120
sweet gold!

FAUSTUS What art thou, the third?

WRATH I am Wrath. I had neither father nor mother. I leaped
out of a lion's mouth when I was scarce half an hour old, and
ever since I have run up and down the world with this case of
rapiers, wounding myself when I had nobody to fight withal.
I was born in hell, and look to it, for some of you shall be my
father.

FAUSTUS What art thou, the fourth?

ENVY I am Envy, begotten of a chimney-sweeper and an oyster-   130
wife. I cannot read, and therefore wish all books were
burnt. I am lean with seeing others eat. O, that there
would come a famine through all the world, that all might
die, and I live alone! Then thou shouldst see how fat I would
be. But must thou sit and I stand? Come down, with a vengeance!

FAUSTUS Away, envious rascal! What art thou, the fifth?

GLUTTONY Who, I, sir? I am Gluttony. My parents are all dead, and the devil a penny they have left me but a bare pension, and that is thirty meals a day, and ten bevers – a small trifle to suffice nature. O, I come of a royal parentage. My grandfather was a gammon of bacon, my grandmother a hogshead of claret wine. My godfathers were these: Peter Pickle-herring and Martin Martlemas-beef. O, but my godmother, she was a jolly gentlewoman, and well beloved in every good town and city; her name was Mistress Margery March-beer. Now, Faustus, thou hast heard all my progeny, wilt thou bid me to supper?

FAUSTUS No, I'll see thee hanged. Thou wilt eat up all my victuals.

GLUTTONY Then the devil choke thee!

FAUSTUS Choke thyself, glutton! What art thou, the sixth?

SLOTH I am Sloth. I was begotten on a sunny bank, where I have lain ever since, and you have done me great injury to bring me from thence. Let me be carried thither again by Gluttony and Lechery. I'll not speak another word for a king's ransom.

FAUSTUS What are you, Mistress Minx, the seventh and last?

LECHERY Who, I, sir? I am one that loves an inch of raw mutton better than an ell of fried stockfish, and the first letter of my name begins with Lechery.

LUCIFER Away, to hell, to hell!

Exeunt the SINS.

Now, Faustus, how dost thou like this?

FAUSTUS O, this feeds my soul!

LUCIFER Tut, Faustus, in hell is all manner of delight.

FAUSTUS O, might I see hell and return again, how happy were I then!

LUCIFER Thou shalt. I will send for thee at midnight. [*Presenting a book*] In meantime, take this book, peruse it throughly, and thou shalt turn thyself into what shape thou wilt.

FAUSTUS [*taking the book*] Great thanks, mighty Lucifer. This will I keep as chary as my life.

LUCIFER Farewell, Faustus, and think on the devil.

FAUSTUS Farewell, great Lucifer. Come, Mephistopheles.

Exeunt.

[*Chorus 2*]

Enter WAGNER *alone.*

WAGNER

Learnèd Faustus,
To know the secrets of astronomy
Graven in the book of Jove's high firmament,
Did mount himself to scale Olympus' top,
Being seated in a chariot burning bright,
Drawn by the strength of yoky dragons' necks.
He now is gone to prove cosmography,
And, as I guess, will first arrive at Rome
To see the Pope and manner of his court,
And take some part of holy Peter's feast   10
That to this day is highly solemnized.

Exit WAGNER.

[*Scene 8*]

Enter FAUSTUS *and* MEPHISTOPHELES.

FAUSTUS

Having now, my good Mephistopheles,
Passed with delight the stately town of Trier,
Environed round with airy mountain tops,
With walls of flint and deep entrenchèd lakes,
Not to be won by any conquering prince;
From Paris next, coasting the realm of France,
We saw the river Maine fall into Rhine,
Whose banks are set with groves of fruitful vines.

Then up to Naples, rich Campania,
10   Whose buildings, fair and gorgeous to the eye,
The streets straight forth and paved with finest brick,
Quarters the town in four equivalents,
There saw we learnèd Maro's golden tomb,
The way he cut an English mile in length
Thorough a rock of stone in one night's space.
From thence to Venice, Padua, and the rest,
In midst of which a sumptuous temple stands
That threats the stars with her aspiring top.
Thus hitherto hath Faustus spent his time.
20   But tell me now, what resting place is this?
Hast thou, as erst I did command,
Conducted me within the walls of Rome?

MEPHISTOPHELES Faustus, I have; and because we will not be
unprovided, I have taken up his holiness' privy chamber for
our use.

FAUSTUS I hope his holiness will bid us welcome.

MEPHISTOPHELES Tut, 'tis no matter, man, we'll be bold with
his good cheer.
And now, my Faustus, that thou mayst perceive
30   What Rome containeth to delight thee with,
Know that this city stands upon seven hills
That underprops the groundwork of the same.
Just through the midst runs flowing Tiber's stream,
With winding banks that cut it in two parts,
Over the which four stately bridges lean,
That makes safe passage to each part of Rome.
Upon the bridge called Ponte Angelo
Erected is a castle passing strong,
Within whose walls such store of ordnance are,
40   And double cannons, framed of carvèd brass,
As match the days within one complete year,
Besides the gates and high pyramides
Which Julius Caesar brought from Africa.

FAUSTUS
Now, by the kingdoms of infernal rule,
Of Styx, Acheron, and the fiery lake

Of ever-burning Phlegethon, I swear
That I do long to see the monuments
And situation of bright splendent Rome.
Come, therefore, let's away!

MEPHISTOPHELES

Nay, Faustus, stay. I know you'd fain see the Pope   50
And take some part of holy Peter's feast,
Where thou shalt see a troupe of bald-pate friars
Whose *summum bonum* is in belly cheer.

FAUSTUS

Well, I am content to compass then some sport,
And by their folly make us merriment.
Then charm me that I may be invisible, to do what I please
unseen of any whilst I stay in Rome.

MEPHISTOPHELES So, Faustus, now do what thou wilt, thou
shalt not be discerned.

> *Sound a sennet. Enter the* POPE *and the* CARDINAL OF
> LORRAINE *to the banquet, with* FRIARS *attending.*

POPE My lord of Lorraine, will't please you draw near?   60
FAUSTUS Fall to, and the devil choke you an you spare.
POPE How now, who's that which spake? Friars, look about.
FRIAR Here's nobody, if it like your holiness.
POPE [*presenting a dish*] My lord, here is a dainty dish was sent
me from the bishop of Milan.
FAUSTUS I thank you, sir. (*Snatch it*)
POPE How now, who's that which snatched the meat from me?
Will no man look? My lord, this dish was sent me from the
cardinal of Florence.
FAUSTUS [*snatching the dish*] You say true. I'll ha't.   70
POPE What, again? My lord, I'll drink to your grace.
FAUSTUS [*snatching the cup*] I'll pledge your grace.
LORRAINE My lord, it may be some ghost, newly crept out of
purgatory, come to beg a pardon of your holiness.
POPE It may be so. Friars, prepare a dirge to lay the fury of this
ghost. Once again, my lord, fall to.

> *The* POPE *crosseth himself.*

FAUSTUS

What, are you crossing of yourself?

Well, use that trick no more, I would advise you.

[*The* POPE] *cross*[*es himself*] *again.*

Well, there's a second time. Aware the third,
80   I give you fair warning.

[*The* POPE] *cross*[*es himself*] *again, and* FAUSTUS *hits him a box of the ear, and they all* [*except* FAUSTUS *and* MEPHISTOPHELES] *run away.*

Come on, Mephistopheles, what shall we do?

MEPHISTOPHELES Nay, I know not. We shall be cursed with bell, book, and candle.

FAUSTUS

How? Bell, book, and candle, candle, book, and bell,
Forward and backward, to curse Faustus to hell.
Anon you shall hear a hog grunt, a calf bleat, and an ass bray,
Because it is Saint Peter's holy day.

Enter all the FRIARS *to sing the dirge.*

FRIAR

Come, brethren, let's about our business with good devotion.

[*The* FRIARS] *sing this.*

Cursèd be he that stole away his holiness' meat from the table.
90   *Maledicat Dominus.*

Cursèd be he that struck his holiness a blow on the face.
    Maledicat Dominus.

Cursèd be he that took Friar Sandelo a blow on the pate.
    Maledicat Dominus.

Cursèd be he that disturbeth our holy dirge.
    Maledicat Dominus.

Cursèd be he that took away his holiness' wine.
    Maledicat Dominus.

Et omnes sancti. Amen.

[FAUSTUS *and* MEPHISTOPHELES] *beat the* FRIARS, *and fling fireworks among them, and so exeunt.*

[Scene 9]

Enter ROBIN *[with a conjuring book] and* RAFE *with a silver goblet.*

ROBIN Come, Rafe, did not I tell thee we were for ever made by this Doctor Faustus' book? *Ecce signum!* Here's a simple purchase for horse-keepers. Our horses shall eat no hay as long as this lasts.

Enter the VINTNER.

RAFE But Robin, here comes the vintner.

ROBIN Hush, I'll gull him supernaturally. Drawer, I hope all is paid. God be with you. Come, Rafe.

[They start to leave.]

VINTNER *[to* ROBIN*]* Soft, sir, a word with you. I must yet have a goblet paid from you ere you go.

ROBIN I, a goblet? Rafe, I, a goblet? I scorn you, and you are   10
but a etc. I, a goblet? Search me.

VINTNER I mean so, sir, with your favour.

[The VINTNER *searches* ROBIN.*]*

ROBIN How say you now?

VINTNER I must say somewhat to your fellow – you, sir.

RAFE Me, sir? Me, sir? Search your fill.

[He passes the goblet to ROBIN; *the* VINTNER *searches* RAFE.*]*

Now, sir, you may be ashamed to burden honest men with a matter of truth.

VINTNER Well, t'one of you hath this goblet about you.

ROBIN You lie, drawer, 'tis afore me. Sirrah, you, I'll teach ye to impeach honest men. Stand by. I'll scour you for a goblet.   20
Stand aside, you had best, I charge you in the name of Beelzebub.

[He passes the goblet to RAFE.*]*

Look to the goblet, Rafe.

VINTNER What mean you, sirrah?

ROBIN I'll tell you what I mean. (*He reads.*)
'*Sanctobulorum Periphrasticon!*' Nay, I'll tickle you, vintner.

Look to the goblet, Rafe. '*Polypragmos Belseborams fram-
anto pacostiphos tostu Mephistopheles!*' etc.
  Enter MEPHISTOPHELES, [*who*] *sets squibs at their backs;
  they run about. [Exit* MEPHISTOPHELES.]
VINTNER O, *nomine Domine*! What mean'st thou, Robin? Thou
30 hast no goblet.
  Enter to them MEPHISTOPHELES.
RAFE *Peccatum peccatorum!* Here's thy goblet, good vintner.
ROBIN *Misericordia pro nobis!* What shall we do? Good devil,
  forgive me now, I'll never rob thy library more.
MEPHISTOPHELES Vanish, villains! Th'one like an ape, another
  like a bear, the third an ass, for doing this enterprise.
                                                        [*Exit* VINTNER.]
  Monarch of hell, under whose black survey
  Great potentates do kneel with awful fear,
  Upon whose altars thousand souls do lie,
  How am I vexèd with these villains' charms!
40 From Constantinople am I hither come
  Only for pleasure of these damnèd slaves.
ROBIN How, from Constantinople? You have had a great jour-
  ney. Will you take sixpence in your purse to pay for your
  supper and be gone?
MEPHISTOPHELES Well, villains, for your presumption I trans-
  form thee [*to* ROBIN] into an ape and thee [*to* RAFE] into a
  dog. And so, begone!
                                              Exit [MEPHISTOPHELES].
ROBIN How, into an ape? That's brave. I'll have fine sport with
  the boys; I'll get nuts and apples enow.
50 RAFE And I must be a dog.
ROBIN I'faith, thy head will never be out of the pottage pot.
                                                              Exeunt.

[Chorus 3]

Enter CHORUS.

CHORUS
When Faustus had with pleasure ta'en the view
Of rarest things and royal courts of kings,
He stayed his course and so returnèd home,
Where such as bear his absence but with grief –
I mean his friends and nearest companions –
Did gratulate his safety with kind words.
And in their conference of what befell,
Touching his journey through the world and air,
They put forth questions of astrology,
Which Faustus answered with such learnèd skill   10
As they admired and wondered at his wit.
Now is his fame spread forth in every land;
Amongst the rest the emperor is one,
Carolus the Fifth, at whose palace now
Faustus is feasted 'mongst his noblemen.
What there he did in trial of his art
I leave untold, your eyes shall see performed.

Exit.

[Scene 10]

Enter EMPEROR [OF GERMANY], FAUSTUS, [MEPHISTO-
PHELES,] *and a* KNIGHT, *with* ATTENDANTS.

EMPEROR Master Doctor Faustus, I have heard strange report
of thy knowledge in the black art – how that none in my
empire, nor in the whole world, can compare with thee for
the rare effects of magic. They say thou hast a familiar spirit by
whom thou canst accomplish what thou list. This, therefore, is
my request: that thou let me see some proof of thy skill, that
mine eyes may be witnesses to confirm what mine ears have
heard reported; and here I swear to thee, by the honour of

      mine imperial crown, that whatever thou dost, thou shalt be
10   no ways prejudiced or endamaged.

KNIGHT (*aside*) I'faith, he looks much like a conjurer.

FAUSTUS My gracious sovereign, though I must confess myself
    far inferior to the report men have published, and nothing
    answerable to the honour of your imperial majesty, yet, for
    that love and duty binds me thereunto, I am content to do
    whatsoever your majesty shall command me.

EMPEROR
    Then, Doctor Faustus, mark what I shall say.
    As I was sometime solitary set
    Within my closet, sundry thoughts arose
20   About the honour of mine ancestors,
    How they had won by prowess such exploits,
    Got such riches, subdued so many kingdoms
    As we that do succeed or they that shall
    Hereafter possess our throne shall,
    I fear me, never attain to that degree
    Of high renown and great authority.
    Amongst which kings is Alexander the Great,
    Chief spectacle of the world's pre-eminence,
    The bright shining of whose glorious acts
30   Lightens the world with his reflecting beams,
    As when I hear but motion made of him,
    It grieves my soul I never saw the man.
    If, therefore, thou by cunning of thine art
    Canst raise this man from hollow vaults below
    Where lies entombed this famous conqueror,
    And bring with him his beauteous paramour,
    Both in their right shapes, gesture, and attire
    They used to wear during their time of life,
    Thou shalt both satisfy my just desire
40   And give me cause to praise thee whilst I live.

FAUSTUS My gracious lord, I am ready to accomplish your
    request, so far forth as by art and power of my spirit I am
    able to perform.

KNIGHT (*aside*) I'faith, that's just nothing at all.

FAUSTUS But if it like your grace, it is not in my ability to

present before your eyes the true substantial bodies of those
two deceased princes, which long since are consumed to dust.

KNIGHT (*aside*) Ay, marry, Master Doctor, now there's a sign
of grace in you, when you will confess the truth.

FAUSTUS But such spirits as can lively resemble Alexander and   50
his paramour shall appear before your grace in that manner
that they best lived in, in their most flourishing estate, which
I doubt not shall sufficiently content your imperial majesty.

EMPEROR Go to, Master Doctor. Let me see them presently.

KNIGHT Do you hear, Master Doctor? You bring Alexander
and his paramour before the emperor?

FAUSTUS How then, sir?

KNIGHT I'faith, that's as true as Diana turned me to a stag.

FAUSTUS No, sir, but when Actaeon died, he left the horns for
you.   60

[*Aside to* MEPHISTOPHELES] Mephistopheles, begone!

                                        Exit MEPHISTOPHELES.

KNIGHT Nay, an you go to conjuring, I'll be gone.

                                               Exit KNIGHT.

FAUSTUS [*aside*] I'll meet with you anon for interrupting me so.
Here they are, my gracious lord.

    Enter MEPHISTOPHELES *with* ALEXANDER *and his*
    PARAMOUR.

EMPEROR Master Doctor, I heard this lady while she lived had
a wart or mole in her neck. How shall I know whether it be
so or no?

FAUSTUS Your highness may boldly go and see.

    [*The* EMPEROR *examines them, and then*] *exeunt* ALEX-
    ANDER [*and his* PARAMOUR].

EMPEROR Sure these are no spirits, but the true substantial
bodies of those two deceased princes.   70

FAUSTUS Will't please your highness now to send for the knight
that was so pleasant with me here of late?

EMPEROR One of you call him forth.

             [*An* ATTENDANT *leaves to summon the* KNIGHT.]
    Enter the KNIGHT *with a pair of horns on his head.*

How now, sir knight? Why, I had thought thou hadst been
a bachelor, but now I see thou hast a wife, that not only

gives thee horns, but makes thee wear them. Feel on thy
head.

KNIGHT [*to* FAUSTUS]
Thou damnèd wretch and execrable dog,
Bred in the concave of some monstrous rock,
80   How dar'st thou thus abuse a gentleman?
Villain, I say, undo what thou hast done.

FAUSTUS
O, not so fast, sir. There's no haste but good.
Are you remembered how you crossed me in my conference
with the emperor? I think I have met with you for it.

EMPEROR Good Master Doctor, at my entreaty release him. He
hath done penance sufficient.

FAUSTUS My gracious lord, not so much for the injury he
offered me here in your presence, as to delight you with some
mirth, hath Faustus worthily requited this injurious knight;
90   which being all I desire, I am content to release him of
his horns; and, sir knight, hereafter speak well of scholars.
[*Aside to* MEPHISTOPHELES] Mephistopheles, transform him
straight. [*The horns are removed.*] Now, my good lord, having
done my duty, I humbly take my leave.

EMPEROR
Farewell, Master Doctor. Yet, ere you go,
Expect from me a bounteous reward.
                          Exeunt EMPEROR [, KNIGHT *and* ATTENDANTS].

FAUSTUS
Now, Mephistopheles, the restless course
That time doth run with calm and silent foot,
Short'ning my days and thread of vital life,
100   Calls for the payment of my latest years.
Therefore, sweet Mephistopheles, let us make haste
To Wittenberg.

MEPHISTOPHELES
What, will you go on horseback or on foot?

FAUSTUS
Nay, till I am past this fair and pleasant green,
I'll walk on foot.

[*Scene 11*]

Enter [*to them*] *a* HORSE-COURSER.

HORSE-COURSER I have been all this day seeking one Master
Fustian. Mass, see where he is. God save you, Master Doctor.

FAUSTUS What, Horse-courser! You are well met.

HORSE-COURSER [*offering money*] Do you hear, sir? I have
brought you forty dollars for your horse.

FAUSTUS I cannot sell him so. If thou lik'st him for fifty, take
him.

HORSE-COURSER Alas, sir, I have no more. [*To* MEPHIS-
TOPHELES] I pray you, speak for me.

MEPHISTOPHELES [*to* FAUSTUS] I pray you, let him have him;   10
he is an honest fellow, and he has a great charge, neither wife
nor child.

FAUSTUS Well, come, give me your money. [*He takes the money.*]
My boy will deliver him to you. But I must tell you one thing
before you have him: ride him not into the water, at any hand.

HORSE-COURSER Why, sir, will he not drink of all waters?

FAUSTUS O, yes, he will drink of all waters. But ride him not
into the water. Ride him over hedge, or ditch, or where thou
wilt, but not into the water.

HORSE-COURSER Well, sir. [*Aside*] Now am I made man for   20
ever. I'll not leave my horse for forty. If he had but the quality
of hey, ding, ding, hey, ding, ding, I'd make a brave living on
him; he has a buttock as slick as an eel. [*To* FAUSTUS] Well,
goodbye, sir. Your boy will deliver him me? But hark ye, sir,
if my horse be sick or ill at ease, if I bring his water to you,
you'll tell me what it is?

FAUSTUS Away, you villain! What, dost think I am a horse-
doctor?

Exit HORSE-COURSER.

What art thou, Faustus, but a man condemned to die?
Thy fatal time doth draw to final end.   30
Despair doth drive distrust unto my thoughts.
Confound these passions with a quiet sleep.
Tush! Christ did call the thief upon the cross;

Then rest thee, Faustus, quiet in conceit.

[FAUSTUS] *sleep[s] in his chair.*

Enter HORSE-COURSER *all wet, crying.*

HORSE-COURSER Alas, alas! 'Doctor' Fustian, quotha! Mass, Doctor Lopus was never such a doctor. H'as given me a purgation, h'as purged me of forty dollars. I shall never see them more. But yet, like an ass as I was, I would not be ruled by him, for he bade me I should ride him into no water. Now I, thinking my horse had had some rare quality that he would not have had me known of, I, like a venturous youth, rid him into the deep pond at the town's end. I was no sooner in the middle of the pond, but my horse vanished away and I sat upon a bottle of hay, never so near drowning in my life. But I'll seek out my doctor and have my forty dollars again, or I'll make it the dearest horse! O, yonder is his snipper-snapper. Do you hear? You, hey-pass, where's your master?

MEPHISTOPHELES Why, sir, what would you? You cannot speak with him.

HORSE-COURSER But I will speak with him.

MEPHISTOPHELES Why, he's fast asleep. Come some other time.

HORSE-COURSER I'll speak with him now, or I'll break his glass windows about his ears.

MEPHISTOPHELES I tell thee he has not slept this eight nights.

HORSE-COURSER An he have not slept this eight weeks, I'll speak with him.

MEPHISTOPHELES See where he is, fast asleep.

HORSE-COURSER Ay, this is he. God save ye, Master Doctor. Master Doctor, Master Doctor Fustian! Forty dollars, forty dollars for a bottle of hay!

MEPHISTOPHELES Why, thou seest he hears thee not.

HORSE-COURSER (*holler in his ear*) So-ho, ho! So-ho, ho! No, will you not wake? I'll make you wake ere I go.

[*The* HORSE-COURSER] *pull[s] him by the leg, and pull[s] it away.*

Alas, I am undone! What shall I do?

FAUSTUS O my leg, my leg! Help, Mephistopheles! Call the officers! My leg, my leg!

MEPHISTOPHELES Come, villain, to the constable.

HORSE-COURSER O Lord, sir, let me go, and I'll give you forty
dollars more.   70

MEPHISTOPHELES Where be they?

HORSE-COURSER I have none about me. Come to my hostry,
and I'll give them you.

MEPHISTOPHELES Begone, quickly.

                            HORSE-COURSER runs away.

FAUSTUS What, is he gone? Farewell, he! Faustus has his
leg again, and the horse-courser, I take it, a bottle of hay
for his labour. Well, this trick shall cost him forty dollars
more.

    Enter WAGNER.

How now, Wagner, what's the news with thee?

WAGNER Sir, the duke of Vanholt doth earnestly entreat your   80
company.

FAUSTUS The duke of Vanholt! An honourable gentleman, to
whom I must be no niggard of my cunning. Come, Mephistopheles, let's away to him.

                                          Exeunt.

[*Scene 12*]

[*Enter* FAUSTUS *with* MEPHISTOPHELES.] *Enter to them
the* DUKE [OF VANHOLT] *and the* DUCHESS. *The* DUKE
speaks.

DUKE Believe me, Master Doctor, this merriment hath much
pleased me.

FAUSTUS My gracious lord, I am glad it contents you so
well. But it may be, madam, you take no delight in this. I
have heard that great-bellied women do long for some
dainties or other. What is it, madam? Tell me, and you shall
have it.

DUCHESS Thanks, good Master Doctor. And, for I see your
courteous intent to pleasure me, I will not hide from you the
thing my heart desires; and were it now summer, as it is   10

January and the dead time of the winter, I would desire no
better meat than a dish of ripe grapes.

FAUSTUS Alas, madam, that's nothing. [*Aside to* MEPHISTO-
PHELES] Mephistopheles, begone!

Exit MEPHISTOPHELES.

Were it a greater thing than this, so it would content you, you
should have it.

Enter MEPHISTOPHELES *with the grapes.*

Here they be, madam. Will't please you taste on them?

[*The* DUCHESS *tastes the grapes.*]

DUKE Believe me, Master Doctor, this makes me wonder above
the rest, that, being in the dead time of winter and in the
month of January, how you should come by these grapes.

FAUSTUS If it like your grace, the year is divided into two circles
over the whole world, that when it is here winter with us, in
the contrary circle it is summer with them, as in India, Saba,
and farther countries in the East; and by means of a swift
spirit that I have, I had them brought hither, as ye see. How
do you like them, madam? Be they good?

DUCHESS Believe me, Master Doctor, they be the best grapes
that e'er I tasted in my life before.

FAUSTUS
I am glad they content you so, madam.

DUKE
Come, madam, let us in,
Where you must well reward this learnèd man
For the great kindness he hath showed to you.

DUCHESS
And so I will, my lord, and whilst I live
Rest beholding for this courtesy.

FAUSTUS I humbly thank your grace.

DUKE Come, Master Doctor, follow us and receive your reward.

Exeunt.

[Scene 13]

Enter WAGNER *alone.*

WAGNER

I think my master means to die shortly,
For he hath given to me all his goods.
And yet methinks, if that death were near,
He would not banquet and carouse and swill
Amongst the students, as even now he doth,
Who are at supper with such belly-cheer
As Wagner ne'er beheld in all his life.
See where they come. Belike the feast is ended.

[*Exit* WAGNER.]

Enter FAUSTUS *with two or three* SCHOLARS [*and* MEPHISTOPHELES].

FIRST SCHOLAR   Master Doctor Faustus, since our conference
about fair ladies – which was the beautifull'st in all the world   10
– we have determined with ourselves that Helen of Greece
was the admirablest lady that ever lived. Therefore, Master
Doctor, if you will do us that favour as to let us see that
peerless dame of Greece, whom all the world admires for
majesty, we should think ourselves much beholding unto you.

FAUSTUS

Gentlemen,
For that I know your friendship is unfeigned,
And Faustus' custom is not to deny
The just requests of those that wish him well,
You shall behold that peerless dame of Greece,   20
No otherways for pomp and majesty
Than when Sir Paris crossed the seas with her
And brought the spoils to rich Dardania.
Be silent then, for danger is in words.

Music sounds and HELEN *passeth over the stage.*

SECOND SCHOLAR

Too simple is my wit to tell her praise,
Whom all the world admires for majesty.

THIRD SCHOLAR

No marvel though the angry Greeks pursued
With ten years' war the rape of such a queen,
Whose heavenly beauty passeth all compare.

FIRST SCHOLAR

30   Since we have seen the pride of nature's works
And only paragon of excellence,
    Enter an OLD MAN.
Let us depart, and for this glorious deed
Happy and blest be Faustus evermore.

FAUSTUS

Gentlemen, farewell. The same I wish to you.
                           Exeunt SCHOLARS.

OLD MAN

Ah, Doctor Faustus, that I might prevail
To guide thy steps unto the way of life,
By which sweet path thou mayst attain the goal
That shall conduct thee to celestial rest!
Break heart, drop blood, and mingle it with tears,
40   Tears falling from repentant heaviness
Of thy most vile and loathsome filthiness,
The stench whereof corrupts the inward soul
With such flagitious crimes of heinous sins,
As no commiseration may expel
But mercy, Faustus, of thy Saviour sweet,
Whose blood alone must wash away thy guilt.

FAUSTUS

Where art thou, Faustus? Wretch, what hast thou done?
Damned art thou, Faustus, damned! Despair and die!
Hell calls for right, and with a roaring voice
50   Says, 'Faustus, come! Thine hour is come.'
    MEPHISTOPHELES *gives him a dagger.*
And Faustus will come to do thee right.
    [FAUSTUS *prepares to stab himself.*]

OLD MAN

Ah, stay, good Faustus, stay thy desperate steps!
I see an angel hovers o'er thy head,
And with a vial full of precious grace

Offers to pour the same into thy soul.
Then call for mercy and avoid despair.

FAUSTUS

Ah, my sweet friend, I feel thy words
To comfort my distressèd soul.
Leave me a while to ponder on my sins.

OLD MAN

I go, sweet Faustus, but with heavy cheer, 60
Fearing the ruin of thy hopeless soul.

[*Exit the* OLD MAN.]

FAUSTUS

Accursèd Faustus, where is mercy now?
I do repent, and yet I do despair.
Hell strives with grace for conquest in my breast.
What shall I do to shun the snares of death?

MEPHISTOPHELES

Thou traitor, Faustus, I arrest thy soul
For disobedience to my sovereign lord.
Revolt, or I'll in piecemeal tear thy flesh.

FAUSTUS

Sweet Mephistopheles, entreat thy lord
To pardon my unjust presumption, 70
And with my blood again I will confirm
My former vow I made to Lucifer.

MEPHISTOPHELES

Do it then quickly, with unfeignèd heart,
Lest greater danger do attend thy drift.

[FAUSTUS *cuts his arm and writes with his blood.*]

FAUSTUS

Torment, sweet friend, that base and crooked age
That durst dissuade me from thy Lucifer,
With greatest torments that our hell affords.

MEPHISTOPHELES

His faith is great. I cannot touch his soul.
But what I may afflict his body with
I will attempt, which is but little worth. 80

FAUSTUS

One thing, good servant, let me crave of thee

To glut the longing of my heart's desire:
That I might have unto my paramour
That heavenly Helen which I saw of late,
Whose sweet embracings may extinguish clean
These thoughts that do dissuade me from my vow,
And keep mine oath I made to Lucifer.

MEPHISTOPHELES
Faustus, this, or what else thou shalt desire,
Shall be performed in twinkling of an eye.
    Enter HELEN.

FAUSTUS
90   Was this the face that launched a thousand ships
And burnt the topless towers of Ilium?
Sweet Helen, make me immortal with a kiss.
    [*They kiss.*]
Her lips sucks forth my soul. See where it flies!
Come, Helen, come, give me my soul again.
    [*They kiss again.*]
Here will I dwell, for heaven be in these lips,
And all is dross that is not Helena.
    Enter OLD MAN.
I will be Paris, and for love of thee
Instead of Troy shall Wittenberg be sacked,
And I will combat with weak Menelaus,
100 And wear thy colours on my plumèd crest.
Yea, I will wound Achilles in the heel
And then return to Helen for a kiss.
O, thou art fairer than the evening air,
Clad in the beauty of a thousand stars.
Brighter art thou than flaming Jupiter
When he appeared to hapless Semele,
More lovely than the monarch of the sky
In wanton Arethusa's azured arms;
And none but thou shalt be my paramour.
    Exeunt [FAUSTUS *and* HELEN, *with* MEPHISTOPHELES].

OLD MAN
110 Accursèd Faustus, miserable man,
That from thy soul exclud'st the grace of heaven

And fliest the throne of His tribunal seat!
  Enter the DEVILS.
Satan begins to sift me with his pride.
As in this furnace God shall try my faith,
My faith, vile hell, shall triumph over thee.
Ambitious fiends, see how the heavens smiles
At your repulse and laughs your state to scorn!
Hence, hell! For hence I fly unto my God.

                                                        Exeunt.

[*Scene 14*]

  Enter FAUSTUS *with the* SCHOLARS.
FAUSTUS Ah, gentlemen!
FIRST SCHOLAR What ails Faustus?
FAUSTUS Ah, my sweet chamber-fellow! Had I lived with thee,
  then had I lived still, but now I die eternally. Look, comes he
  not? Comes he not?
  [*The* SCHOLARS *speak among themselves.*]
SECOND SCHOLAR What means Faustus?
THIRD SCHOLAR Belike he is grown into some sickness by being
  over-solitary.
FIRST SCHOLAR If it be so, we'll have physicians to cure him.
  [*To* FAUSTUS] 'Tis but a surfeit. Never fear, man.   10
FAUSTUS A surfeit of deadly sin that hath damned both body
  and soul.
SECOND SCHOLAR Yet, Faustus, look up to heaven. Remember
  God's mercies are infinite.
FAUSTUS But Faustus' offence can ne'er be pardoned. The serpent that tempted Eve may be saved, but not Faustus. Ah,
  gentlemen, hear me with patience, and tremble not at my
  speeches. Though my heart pants and quivers to remember
  that I have been a student here these thirty years, O, would I
  had never seen Wittenberg, never read book! And what   20
  wonders I have done, all Germany can witness, yea, all the
  world, for which Faustus hath lost both Germany and the

world, yea, heaven itself – heaven, the seat of God, the throne of the blessed, the kingdom of joy – and must remain in hell for ever. Hell, ah, hell for ever! Sweet friends, what shall become of Faustus, being in hell for ever?

THIRD SCHOLAR Yet, Faustus, call on God.

FAUSTUS On God, whom Faustus hath abjured? On God, whom Faustus hath blasphemed? Ah, my God, I would weep, but
30   the devil draws in my tears. Gush forth blood instead of tears, yea, life and soul. O, he stays my tongue! I would lift up my hands, but see, they hold them, they hold them.

ALL Who, Faustus?

FAUSTUS Lucifer and Mephistopheles. Ah, gentlemen! I gave them my soul for my cunning.

ALL God forbid!

FAUSTUS God forbade it indeed, but Faustus hath done it. For vain pleasure of four-and-twenty years hath Faustus lost eternal joy and felicity. I writ them a bill with mine own
40   blood. The date is expired, the time will come, and he will fetch me.

FIRST SCHOLAR Why did not Faustus tell us of this before, that divines might have prayed for thee?

FAUSTUS Oft have I thought to have done so, but the devil threatened to tear me in pieces if I named God, to fetch both body and soul if I once gave ear to divinity. And now 'tis too late. Gentlemen, away, lest you perish with me.

SECOND SCHOLAR O, what shall we do to save Faustus?

FAUSTUS Talk not of me, but save yourselves and depart.

50   THIRD SCHOLAR God will strengthen me. I will stay with Faustus.

FIRST SCHOLAR [to the THIRD SCHOLAR] Tempt not God, sweet friend, but let us into the next room and there pray for him.

FAUSTUS Ay, pray for me, pray for me! And what noise soever ye hear, come not unto me, for nothing can rescue me.

SECOND SCHOLAR Pray thou, and we will pray that God may have mercy upon thee.

FAUSTUS Gentlemen, farewell. If I live till morning, I'll visit
60   you; if not, Faustus is gone to hell.

ALL Faustus, farewell.

Exeunt SCHOLARS.

The clock strikes eleven.

FAUSTUS

Ah, Faustus,

Now hast thou but one bare hour to live,

And then thou must be damned perpetually.

Stand still, you ever-moving spheres of heaven,

That time may cease and midnight never come!

Fair nature's eye, rise, rise again, and make

Perpetual day, or let this hour be but

A year, a month, a week, a natural day,

That Faustus may repent and save his soul!   70

O lente, lente currite noctis equi!

The stars move still, time runs, the clock will strike,

The devil will come, and Faustus must be damned.

O, I'll leap up to my God! Who pulls me down?

See, see where Christ's blood streams in the firmament!

One drop would save my soul, half a drop. Ah, my Christ!

Ah, rend not my heart for naming of my Christ!

Yet will I call on him. O, spare me, Lucifer!

Where is it now? 'Tis gone; and see where God

Stretcheth out his arm and bends his ireful brows!   80

Mountains and hills, come, come and fall on me,

And hide me from the heavy wrath of God!

No, no!

Then will I headlong run into the earth.

Earth, gape! O, no, it will not harbour me.

You stars that reigned at my nativity,

Whose influence hath allotted death and hell,

Now draw up Faustus like a foggy mist

Into the entrails of yon labouring cloud,

That when you vomit forth into the air,   90

My limbs may issue from your smoky mouths,

So that my soul may but ascend to heaven.

The watch strikes.

Ah, half the hour is past!

'Twill all be past anon.

O God,
If thou wilt not have mercy on my soul,
Yet for Christ's sake, whose blood hath ransomed me,
Impose some end to my incessant pain.
Let Faustus live in hell a thousand years,
A hundred thousand, and at last be saved.
O, no end is limited to damnèd souls.
Why wert thou not a creature wanting soul?
Or why is this immortal that thou hast?
Ah, Pythagoras' *metempsychosis*, were that true,
This soul should fly from me and I be changed
Unto some brutish beast.
All beasts are happy, for, when they die,
Their souls are soon dissolved in elements,
But mine must live still to be plagued in hell.
Curst be the parents that engendered me!
No, Faustus, curse thyself. Curse Lucifer,
That hath deprived thee of the joys of heaven.
   The clock striketh twelve.
O, it strikes, it strikes! Now, body, turn to air,
Or Lucifer will bear thee quick to hell.
   Thunder and lightning.
O soul, be changed into little waterdrops,
And fall into the ocean, ne'er be found!
My God, my God, look not so fierce on me!
   Enter [LUCIFER, MEPHISTOPHELES, *and other*] DEVILS.
Adders and serpents, let me breathe a while!
Ugly hell, gape not. Come not, Lucifer!
I'll burn my books. Ah, Mephistopheles!
                 [*The* DEVILS] *exeunt with him.*

[EPILOGUE]

Enter CHORUS.

CHORUS
Cut is the branch that might have grown full straight,
And burnèd is Apollo's laurel bough
That sometime grew within this learnèd man.
Faustus is gone. Regard his hellish fall,
Whose fiendful fortune may exhort the wise   5
Only to wonder at unlawful things,
Whose deepness doth entice such forward wits
To practise more than heavenly power permits.

[*Exit.*]

Terminat hora diem; terminat author opus.

EDWARD THE SECOND

[Dramatis Personae

GAVESTON
THREE POOR MEN
KING EDWARD II
EARL OF LANCASTER
MORTIMER SENIOR
MORTIMER JUNIOR
EDMUND EARL OF KENT, *brother to King Edward II*
GUY EARL OF WARWICK
THE BISHOP OF COVENTRY
THE ARCHBISHOP OF CANTERBURY
QUEEN ISABELLA
EARL OF PEMBROKE
BEAUMONT, *the Clerk of the Crown*
SPENCER JUNIOR
BALDOCK
THE KING'S NIECE
A MESSENGER
TWO LADIES-IN-WAITING
JAMES
A HORSEBOY
EARL OF ARUNDEL
SPENCER SENIOR
PRINCE EDWARD, *later King Edward III*
LEVUNE
A HERALD
SIR JOHN OF HAINAULT
RICE ap HOWELL
THE MAYOR OF BRISTOL

AN ABBOT
MONKS
A MOWER
EARL OF LEICESTER
THE BISHOP OF WINCHESTER
SIR WILLIAM TRUSSELL
SIR THOMAS BERKELEY
MATREVIS
GURNEY
LIGHTBORNE
A CHAMPION
LORDS
SOLDIERS
GUARDS
ATTENDANTS]

[*Scene 1*]

Enter GAVESTON *reading on a letter that was brought him from the* KING.

GAVESTON

'My father is deceased; come, Gaveston,
And share the kingdom with thy dearest friend.'
Ah, words that make me surfeit with delight!
What greater bliss can hap to Gaveston
Than live and be the favourite of a king?
Sweet prince, I come; these, these thy amorous lines
Might have enforced me to have swum from France,
And like Leander gasped upon the sand,
So thou wouldst smile and take me in thy arms.
The sight of London to my exiled eyes   10
Is as Elysium to a new-come soul –
Not that I love the city or the men,
But that it harbours him I hold so dear,
The king, upon whose bosom let me die,
And with the world be still at enmity.
What need the arctic people love starlight,
To whom the sun shines both by day and night?
Farewell, base stooping to the lordly peers;
My knee shall bow to none but to the king.
As for the multitude, that are but sparks   20
Raked up in embers of their poverty,
Tanti! I'll fawn first on the wind
That glanceth at my lips and flieth away.

But how now, what are these?
Enter three POOR MEN.

POOR MEN Such as desire your worship's service.

GAVESTON What canst thou do?

FIRST POOR MAN I can ride.

GAVESTON But I have no horses. What art thou?

SECOND POOR MAN A traveller.

30 GAVESTON Let me see, thou wouldst do well to wait at my
trencher and tell me lies at dinner time, and, as I like your
discoursing, I'll have you. And what art thou?

THIRD POOR MAN A soldier, that hath served against the Scot.

GAVESTON
Why, there are hospitals for such as you.
I have no war, and therefore, sir, begone.

THIRD POOR MAN
Farewell, and perish by a soldier's hand,
That wouldst reward them with an hospital.

GAVESTON [*aside*]
Ay, ay, these words of his move me as much
As if a goose should play the porcupine

40 And dart her plumes, thinking to pierce my breast.
But yet it is no pain to speak men fair;
I'll flatter these and make them live in hope.
[*To them*]
You know that I came lately out of France,
And yet I have not viewed my lord the king;
If I speed well, I'll entertain you all.

POOR MEN We thank your worship.

GAVESTON
I have some business, leave me to myself.

POOR MEN We will wait here about the court.

GAVESTON
Do. These are not men for me.
Exeunt [POOR MEN].

50 I must have wanton poets, pleasant wits,
Musicians that with touching of a string
May draw the pliant king which way I please.
Music and poetry is his delight;

Therefore I'll have Italian masques by night,
Sweet speeches, comedies, and pleasing shows;
And in the day, when he shall walk abroad,
Like sylvan nymphs my pages shall be clad;
My men, like satyrs grazing on the lawns,
Shall with their goat feet dance an antic hay.
Sometime a lovely boy in Dian's shape,   60
With hair that gilds the water as it glides,
Crownets of pearl about his naked arms,
And in his sportful hands an olive tree
To hide those parts which men delight to see,
Shall bathe him in a spring, and there hard by,
One like Actaeon peeping through the grove
Shall by the angry goddess be transformed,
And running in the likeness of an hart,
By yelping hounds pulled down and seem to die.
Such things as these best please his majesty,   70
My lord. Here comes the king and the nobles
From the parliament. I'll stand aside.

> *Enter the* KING [EDWARD], LANCASTER, MORTIMER
> SENIOR, MORTIMER JUNIOR, EDMUND EARL OF KENT,
> GUY EARL OF WARWICK, *etc.*

EDWARD Lancaster!

LANCASTER My lord?

GAVESTON [*aside*]
That earl of Lancaster do I abhor.

EDWARD
Will you not grant me this? [*Aside*] In spite of them
I'll have my will, and these two Mortimers
That cross me thus shall know I am displeased.

MORTIMER SENIOR
If you love us, my lord, hate Gaveston.

GAVESTON [*aside*]
That villain Mortimer! I'll be his death.   80

MORTIMER [*to* EDWARD]
Mine uncle here, this earl, and I myself
Were sworn to your father at his death
That he should ne'er return into the realm;

And know, my lord, ere I will break my oath,
This sword of mine that should offend your foes
Shall sleep within the scabbard at thy need,
And underneath thy banners march who will,
For Mortimer will hang his armour up.

GAVESTON [*aside*] *Mort Dieu!*

EDWARD

90   Well Mortimer, I'll make thee rue these words.
Beseems it thee to contradict thy king?
Frown'st thou thereat, aspiring Lancaster?
The sword shall plane the furrows of thy brows
And hew these knees that now are grown so stiff.
I will have Gaveston, and you shall know
What danger 'tis to stand against your king.

GAVESTON [*aside*] Well done, Ned!

LANCASTER

My lord, why do you thus incense your peers,
That naturally would love and honour you
100   But for that base and obscure Gaveston?
Four earldoms have I besides Lancaster –
Derby, Salisbury, Lincoln, Leicester.
These will I sell to give my soldiers pay
Ere Gaveston shall stay within the realm.
Therefore, if he be come, expel him straight.

KENT

Barons and earls, your pride hath made me mute,
But now I'll speak, and to the proof, I hope.
I do remember in my father's days,
Lord Percy of the north, being highly moved,
110   Braved Mowbray in presence of the king,
For which, had not his highness loved him well,
He should have lost his head; but with his look
The undaunted spirit of Percy was appeased,
And Mowbray and he were reconciled;
Yet dare you brave the king unto his face.
Brother, revenge it, and let these their heads
Preach upon poles for trespass of their tongues.

WARWICK O, our heads!

EDWARD

Ay, yours, and therefore I would wish you grant.

WARWICK

Bridle thy anger, gentle Mortimer.   120

MORTIMER

I cannot, nor I will not; I must speak.

Cousin, our hands, I hope, shall fence our heads

And strike off his that makes you threaten us.

Come, uncle, let us leave the brainsick king

And henceforth parley with our naked swords.

MORTIMER SENIOR

Wiltshire hath men enough to save our heads.

WARWICK

All Warwickshire will love him for my sake.

LANCASTER

And northward, Gaveston hath many friends.

Adieu, my lord, and either change your mind

Or look to see the throne where you should sit   130

To float in blood, and at thy wanton head

The glozing head of thy base minion thrown.

Exeunt NOBLES. [KENT, KING EDWARD *and* GAVESTON

remain.]

EDWARD

I cannot brook these haughty menaces!

Am I a king and must be overruled?

Brother, display my ensigns in the field;

I'll bandy with the barons and the earls,

And either die or live with Gaveston.

GAVESTON [*coming forward*]

I can no longer keep me from my lord.

EDWARD

What, Gaveston, welcome! Kiss not my hand;

Embrace me, Gaveston, as I do thee.   140

[*They embrace.*]

Why shouldst thou kneel? Knowest thou not who I am?

Thy friend, thy self, another Gaveston.

Not Hylas was more mourned of Hercules
Than thou hast been of me since thy exile.

GAVESTON

And since I went from hence, no soul in hell
Hath felt more torment than poor Gaveston.

EDWARD

I know it. Brother, welcome home my friend.
Now let the treacherous Mortimers conspire,
And that high-minded earl of Lancaster;
150 I have my wish, in that I joy thy sight,
And sooner shall the sea o'erwhelm my land
Than bear the ship that shall transport thee hence.
I here create thee Lord High Chamberlain,
Chief Secretary to the state and me,
Earl of Cornwall, King and Lord of Man.

GAVESTON

My lord, these titles far exceed my worth.

KENT

Brother, the least of these may well suffice
For one of greater birth than Gaveston.

EDWARD

Cease, brother, for I cannot brook these words.
160 Thy worth, sweet friend, is far above my gifts,
Therefore, to equal it, receive my heart.
If for these dignities thou be envied,
I'll give thee more, for but to honour thee
Is Edward pleased with kingly regiment.
Fear'st thou thy person? Thou shalt have a guard.
Wants thou gold? Go to my treasury.
Wouldst thou be loved and feared? Receive my seal,
Save or condemn, and in our name command
Whatso thy mind affects or fancy likes.

GAVESTON

170 It shall suffice me to enjoy your love,
Which whiles I have, I think myself as great
As Caesar riding in the Roman street
With captive kings at his triumphant car.
    Enter the BISHOP OF COVENTRY.

EDWARD

Whither goes my lord of Coventry so fast?

COVENTRY

To celebrate your father's exequies.
But is that wicked Gaveston returned?

EDWARD

Ay, priest, and lives to be revenged on thee
That wert the only cause of his exile.

GAVESTON

'Tis true, and, but for reverence of these robes,
Thou shouldst not plod one foot beyond this place.   180

COVENTRY

I did no more than I was bound to do,
And, Gaveston, unless thou be reclaimed,
As then I did incense the Parliament,
So will I now, and thou shalt back to France.

GAVESTON

Saving your reverence, you must pardon me.
   [*He lays hold of him.*]

EDWARD

Throw off his golden mitre, rend his stole,
And in the channel christen him anew.

KENT

Ah, brother, lay not violent hands on him,
For he'll complain unto the see of Rome.

GAVESTON

Let him complain unto the see of hell,   190
I'll be revenged on him for my exile.

EDWARD

No, spare his life, but seize upon his goods;
Be thou lord bishop, and receive his rents,
And make him serve thee as thy chaplain.
I give him thee; here, use him as thou wilt.

GAVESTON

He shall to prison, and there die in bolts.

EDWARD

Ay, to the Tower, the Fleet, or where thou wilt.

COVENTRY
　　For this offence be thou accurst of God.
EDWARD [*calling to* ATTENDANTS]
　　Who's there? Convey this priest to the Tower.
200　COVENTRY True, true.
　　　　　　　　[*Exit the* BISHOP OF COVENTRY, *guarded.*]
EDWARD
　　But in the meantime, Gaveston, away,
　　And take possession of his house and goods.
　　Come follow me, and thou shalt have my guard
　　To see it done and bring thee safe again.
GAVESTON
　　What should a priest do with so fair a house?
　　A prison may beseem his holiness.
　　　　　　　　　　　　　　　　　　　　[*Exeunt.*]

[*Scene 2*]

Enter both the MORTIMERS, WARWICK, *and* LANCASTER.
WARWICK
　　'Tis true, the bishop is in the Tower,
　　And goods and body given to Gaveston.
LANCASTER
　　What, will they tyrannize upon the Church?
　　Ah, wicked king! Accursèd Gaveston!
　　This ground, which is corrupted with their steps,
　　Shall be their timeless sepulchre or mine.
MORTIMER
　　Well, let that peevish Frenchman guard him sure;
　　Unless his breast be sword-proof, he shall die.
MORTIMER SENIOR
　　How now, why droops the earl of Lancaster?
MORTIMER
10　Wherefore is Guy of Warwick discontent?
LANCASTER
　　That villain Gaveston is made an earl.

MORTIMER SENIOR An earl!

WARWICK

Ay, and besides, Lord Chamberlain of the realm,
And Secretary too, and Lord of Man.

MORTIMER SENIOR

We may not, nor we will not suffer this.

MORTIMER

Why post we not from hence to levy men?

LANCASTER

'My lord of Cornwall' now at every word!
And happy is the man whom he vouchsafes,
For vailing of his bonnet, one good look.
Thus, arm in arm, the king and he doth march;   20
Nay more, the guard upon his lordship waits,
And all the court begins to flatter him.

WARWICK

Thus leaning on the shoulder of the king,
He nods, and scorns, and smiles at those that pass.

MORTIMER SENIOR

Doth no man take exceptions at the slave?

LANCASTER

All stomach him, but none dare speak a word.

MORTIMER

Ah, that bewrays their baseness, Lancaster.
Were all the earls and barons of my mind,
We'd hale him from the bosom of the king,
And at the court-gate hang the peasant up,   30
Who, swoll'n with venom of ambitious pride,
Will be the ruin of the realm and us.

> Enter the [ARCH]BISHOP OF CANTERBURY [and an
> ATTENDANT].

WARWICK

Here comes my lord of Canterbury's grace.

LANCASTER

His countenance bewrays he is displeased.

CANTERBURY [to his ATTENDANT]

First were his sacred garments rent and torn,
Then laid they violent hands upon him, next

Himself imprisoned and his goods asseized.
This certify the Pope. Away, take horse.

                         [Exit ATTENDANT.]

LANCASTER [*to* CANTERBURY]
   My lord, will you take arms against the king?
CANTERBURY
40   What need I? God himself is up in arms
   When violence is offered to the Church.
MORTIMER
   Then will you join with us that be his peers
   To banish or behead that Gaveston?
CANTERBURY
   What else, my lords? For it concerns me near;
   The bishopric of Coventry is his.
     Enter the QUEEN.
MORTIMER
   Madam, whither walks your majesty so fast?
QUEEN
   Unto the forest, gentle Mortimer,
   To live in grief and baleful discontent,
   For now my lord the king regards me not,
50   But dotes upon the love of Gaveston.
   He claps his cheeks and hangs about his neck,
   Smiles in his face and whispers in his ears,
   And when I come he frowns, as who should say,
   'Go whither thou wilt, seeing I have Gaveston.'
MORTIMER SENIOR
   Is it not strange that he is thus bewitched?
MORTIMER
   Madam, return unto the court again.
   That sly, inveigling Frenchman we'll exile
   Or lose our lives; and yet ere that day come,
   The king shall lose his crown, for we have power,
60   And courage too, to be revenged at full.
CANTERBURY
   But yet lift not your swords against the king.
LANCASTER
   No, but we'll lift Gaveston from hence.

WARWICK
　And war must be the means, or he'll stay still.
QUEEN
　Then let him stay, for, rather than my lord
　Shall be oppressed by civil mutinies,
　I will endure a melancholy life,
　And let him frolic with his minion.
CANTERBURY
　My lords, to ease all this, but hear me speak.
　We and the rest that are his counsellors
　Will meet and with a general consent   70
　Confirm his banishment with our hands and seals.
LANCASTER
　What we confirm the king will frustrate.
MORTIMER
　Then may we lawfully revolt from him.
WARWICK
　But say, my lord, where shall this meeting be?
CANTERBURY At the New Temple.
MORTIMER Content.
CANTERBURY
　And in the meantime I'll entreat you all
　To cross to Lambeth and there stay with me.
LANCASTER Come then, let's away.
MORTIMER Madam, farewell.   80
QUEEN
　Farewell, sweet Mortimer, and for my sake
　Forbear to levy arms against the king.
MORTIMER
　Ay, if words will serve; if not, I must.

　　　　　　　　　　　　　　　　　　　　　　　　[*Exeunt.*]

[Scene 3]

Enter GAVESTON *and the* EARL OF KENT.

GAVESTON

Edmund, the mighty prince of Lancaster,
That hath more earldoms than an ass can bear,
And both the Mortimers, two goodly men,
With Guy of Warwick, that redoubted knight,
5 Are gone towards Lambeth. There let them remain.

Exeunt.

[Scene 4]

Enter NOBLES [LANCASTER, WARWICK, PEMBROKE,
MORTIMER SENIOR, MORTIMER JUNIOR *and the*
ARCHBISHOP OF CANTERBURY, *attended by* GUARDS].

LANCASTER [*presenting a document*]

Here is the form of Gaveston's exile.
May it please your lordship to subscribe your name.

CANTERBURY Give me the paper.

[*He signs the document.*]

LANCASTER

Quick, quick, my lord, I long to write my name.

WARWICK

But I long more to see him banished hence.

MORTIMER

The name of Mortimer shall fright the king,
Unless he be declined from that base peasant.

Enter the KING *and* GAVESTON [*and* KENT. *The* KING *sits
on the throne with* GAVESTON *at his side*].

EDWARD

What? Are you moved that Gaveston sits here?
It is our pleasure, we will have it so.

LANCASTER

10 Your grace doth well to place him by your side,

For nowhere else the new earl is so safe.

MORTIMER SENIOR

What man of noble birth can brook this sight?
Quam male conveniunt!
See what a scornful look the peasant casts.

PEMBROKE

Can kingly lions fawn on creeping ants?

WARWICK

Ignoble vassal, that like Phaethon
Aspir'st unto the guidance of the sun!

MORTIMER

Their downfall is at hand, their forces down;
We will not thus be faced and overpeered.

EDWARD

Lay hands on that traitor Mortimer!   20

MORTIMER SENIOR

Lay hands on that traitor Gaveston!
    [*They seize* GAVESTON.]

KENT

Is this the duty that you owe your king?

WARWICK

We know our duties. Let him know his peers.

EDWARD

Whither will you bear him? Stay, or ye shall die.

MORTIMER SENIOR

We are no traitors; therefore threaten not.

GAVESTON [*to the* KING]

No, threaten not, my lord, but pay them home.
Were I a king –

MORTIMER

Thou villain, wherefore talks thou of a king,
That hardly art a gentleman by birth?

EDWARD

Were he a peasant, being my minion,   30
I'll make the proudest of you stoop to him.

LANCASTER

My lord, you may not thus disparage us.
Away, I say, with hateful Gaveston!

MORTIMER SENIOR
   And with the earl of Kent that favours him.
                           [*Exeunt* KENT *and* GAVESTON, *guarded.*]
EDWARD
   Nay, then lay violent hands upon your king.
   Here, Mortimer, sit thou in Edward's throne;
   Warwick and Lancaster, wear you my crown.
   Was ever king thus overruled as I?
LANCASTER
   Learn then to rule us better, and the realm.
MORTIMER
40   What we have done, our heart-blood shall maintain.
WARWICK
   Think you that we can brook this upstart pride?
EDWARD
   Anger and wrathful fury stops my speech.
CANTERBURY
   Why are you moved? Be patient, my lord,
   And see what we your counsellors have done.
MORTIMER
   My lords, now let us all be resolute,
   And either have our wills or lose our lives.
EDWARD
   Meet you for this, proud overdaring peers?
   Ere my sweet Gaveston shall part from me,
   This isle shall fleet upon the ocean
50   And wander to the unfrequented Inde.
CANTERBURY
   You know that I am legate to the Pope.
   On your allegiance to the See of Rome,
   Subscribe as we have done to his exile.
                     [*They present the document to the* KING.]
MORTIMER [*to* CANTERBURY]
   Curse him if he refuse, and then may we
   Depose him and elect another king.
EDWARD
   Ay, there it goes, but yet I will not yield,
   Curse me, depose me, do the worst you can.

LANCASTER
　Then linger not, my lord, but do it straight.
CANTERBURY
　Remember how the bishop was abused.
　Either banish him that was the cause thereof,　　　　　60
　Or I will presently discharge these lords
　Of duty and allegiance due to thee.
EDWARD [aside]
　It boots me not to threat, I must speak fair.
　The legate of the Pope will be obeyed.
　　[To CANTERBURY]
　My lord, you shall be Chancellor of the realm,
　Thou, Lancaster, High Admiral of our fleet,
　Young Mortimer and his uncle shall be earls,
　And you, Lord Warwick, President of the North,
　　[to PEMBROKE]
　And thou of Wales. If this content you not,
　Make several kingdoms of this monarchy　　　　　　70
　And share it equally amongst you all,
　So I may have some nook or corner left
　To frolic with my dearest Gaveston.
CANTERBURY
　Nothing shall alter us, we are resolved.
LANCASTER Come, come, subscribe.
MORTIMER
　Why should you love him whom the world hates so?
EDWARD
　Because he loves me more than all the world.
　Ah, none but rude and savage-minded men
　Would seek the ruin of my Gaveston.
　You that be noble born should pity him.　　　　　　80
WARWICK
　You that are princely born should shake him off.
　For shame, subscribe, and let the lown depart.
MORTIMER SENIOR [to CANTERBURY]
　Urge him, my lord.
CANTERBURY
　Are you content to banish him the realm?

EDWARD
  I see I must, and therefore am content.
  Instead of ink, I'll write it with my tears.
      [*He writes.*]
MORTIMER
  The king is lovesick for his minion.
EDWARD
  'Tis done, and now, accursèd hand, fall off!
LANCASTER [*taking the document*]
  Give it me. I'll have it published in the streets.
MORTIMER
90 I'll see him presently dispatched away.
CANTERBURY
  Now is my heart at ease.
WARWICK   And so is mine.
PEMBROKE
  This will be good news to the common sort.
MORTIMER SENIOR
  Be it or no, he shall not linger here.
                                    Exeunt NOBLES.
EDWARD
  How fast they run to banish him I love!
  They would not stir, were it to do me good.
  Why should a king be subject to a priest?
  Proud Rome, that hatchest such imperial grooms,
  For these thy superstitious taper lights,
  Wherewith thy antichristian churches blaze,
100 I'll fire thy crazèd buildings and enforce
  The papal towers to kiss the lowly ground,
  With slaughtered priests make Tiber's channel swell,
  And banks raised higher with their sepulchres.
  As for the peers that back the clergy thus,
  If I be king, not one of them shall live.
      Enter GAVESTON.
GAVESTON
  My lord, I hear it whispered everywhere
  That I am banished and must fly the land.

EDWARD

>'Tis true, sweet Gaveston. O, were it false!
>The legate of the Pope will have it so,
>And thou must hence or I shall be deposed.   110
>But I will reign to be revenged of them;
>And therefore, sweet friend, take it patiently.
>Live where thou wilt, I'll send thee gold enough;
>And long thou shalt not stay, or, if thou dost,
>I'll come to thee; my love shall ne'er decline.

GAVESTON

>Is all my hope turned to this hell of grief?

EDWARD

>Rend not my heart with thy too-piercing words;
>Thou from this land, I from myself am banished.

GAVESTON

>To go from hence grieves not poor Gaveston,
>But to forsake you, in whose gracious looks   120
>The blessedness of Gaveston remains,
>For nowhere else seeks he felicity.

EDWARD

>And only this torments my wretched soul,
>That, whether I will or no, thou must depart.
>Be governor of Ireland in my stead,
>And there abide till fortune call thee home.
>Here, take my picture and let me wear thine.
> [*They exchange pictures.*]
>O, might I keep thee here as I do this,
>Happy were I, but now most miserable.

GAVESTON

>'Tis something to be pitied of a king.   130

EDWARD

>Thou shalt not hence; I'll hide thee, Gaveston.

GAVESTON

>I shall be found, and then 'twill grieve me more.

EDWARD

>Kind words and mutual talk makes our grief greater;
>Therefore with dumb embracement let us part.
> [*They embrace.* GAVESTON *starts to leave.*]

Stay, Gaveston, I cannot leave thee thus.

GAVESTON

For every look, my lord, drops down a tear;
Seeing I must go, do not renew my sorrow.

EDWARD

The time is little that thou hast to stay,
And therefore give me leave to look my fill.

140   But come, sweet friend, I'll bear thee on thy way.

GAVESTON The peers will frown.

EDWARD

I pass not for their anger. Come, let's go.
O, that we might as well return as go!

Enter EDMUND [, EARL OF KENT] *and* QUEEN ISABEL.

QUEEN Whither goes my lord?

EDWARD

Fawn not on me, French strumpet; get thee gone.

QUEEN

On whom but on my husband should I fawn?

GAVESTON

On Mortimer, with whom, ungentle queen –
I say no more; judge you the rest, my lord.

QUEEN

In saying this, thou wrong'st me, Gaveston.

150   Is't not enough that thou corrupts my lord
And art a bawd to his affections,
But thou must call mine honour thus in question?

GAVESTON

I mean not so, your grace must pardon me.

EDWARD

Thou art too familiar with that Mortimer,
And by thy means is Gaveston exiled;
But I would wish thee reconcile the lords,
Or thou shalt ne'er be reconciled to me.

QUEEN

Your highness knows it lies not in my power.

EDWARD

Away then, touch me not. Come, Gaveston.

QUEEN [*to* GAVESTON]
Villain, 'tis thou that robb'st me of my lord.   160
GAVESTON
Madam, 'tis you that rob me of my lord.
EDWARD
Speak not unto her, let her droop and pine.
QUEEN
Wherein, my lord, have I deserved these words?
Witness the tears that Isabella sheds,
Witness this heart that, sighing for thee, breaks,
How dear my lord is to poor Isabel.
EDWARD [*pushing her away*]
And witness heaven how dear thou art to me.
There weep, for, till my Gaveston be repealed,
Assure thyself thou com'st not in my sight.
                              Exeunt EDWARD *and* GAVESTON.
QUEEN
O, miserable and distressèd queen!   170
Would when I left sweet France and was embarked,
That charming Circes, walking on the waves,
Had changed my shape, or at the marriage day
The cup of Hymen had been full of poison,
Or with those arms that twined about my neck
I had been stifled and not lived to see
The king my lord thus to abandon me.
Like frantic Juno will I fill the earth
With ghastly murmur of my sighs and cries,
For never doted Jove on Ganymede   180
So much as he on cursèd Gaveston.
But that will more exasperate his wrath.
I must entreat him, I must speak him fair,
And be a means to call home Gaveston;
And yet he'll ever dote on Gaveston,
And so am I for ever miserable.
    Enter the NOBLES [LANCASTER, WARWICK, PEMBROKE,
    MORTIMER SENIOR *and* MORTIMER JUNIOR] *to the*
    QUEEN.

LANCASTER

Look where the sister of the King of France
Sits wringing of her hands and beats her breast.

WARWICK

The king, I fear, hath ill entreated her.

PEMBROKE

190   Hard is the heart that injures such a saint.

MORTIMER

I know 'tis long of Gaveston she weeps.

MORTIMER SENIOR

Why? He is gone.

MORTIMER [*to the* QUEEN]

                    Madam, how fares your grace?

QUEEN

Ah, Mortimer! Now breaks the king's hate forth,
And he confesseth that he loves me not.

MORTIMER

Cry quittance, madam, then, and love not him.

QUEEN

No, rather will I die a thousand deaths.
And yet I love in vain; he'll ne'er love me.

LANCASTER

Fear ye not, madam. Now his minion's gone,
His wanton humour will be quickly left.

QUEEN

200   O never, Lancaster! I am enjoined
To sue unto you all for his repeal;
This wills my lord, and this must I perform,
Or else be banished from his highness' presence.

LANCASTER

For his repeal, madam? He comes not back,
Unless the sea cast up his shipwrack body.

WARWICK

And to behold so sweet a sight as that
There's none here but would run his horse to death.

MORTIMER

But, madam, would you have us call him home?

QUEEN

   Ay, Mortimer, for till he be restored
   The angry king hath banished me the court;   210
   And therefore, as thou lovest and tend'rest me,
   Be thou my advocate unto these peers.

MORTIMER

   What, would ye have me plead for Gaveston?

MORTIMER SENIOR

   Plead for him he that will, I am resolved.

LANCASTER

   And so am I, my lord. Dissuade the queen.

QUEEN

   O Lancaster, let him dissuade the king,
   For 'tis against my will he should return.

WARWICK

   Then speak not for him; let the peasant go.

QUEEN

   'Tis for myself I speak, and not for him.

PEMBROKE

   No speaking will prevail, and therefore cease.   220

MORTIMER

   Fair queen, forbear to angle for the fish
   Which, being caught, strikes him that takes it dead –
   I mean that vile torpedo, Gaveston,
   That now, I hope, floats on the Irish seas.

QUEEN

   Sweet Mortimer, sit down by me a while,
   And I will tell thee reasons of such weight
   As thou wilt soon subscribe to his repeal.

MORTIMER

   It is impossible, but speak your mind.

QUEEN

   Then thus, but none shall hear it but ourselves.
     [*They talk apart.*]

LANCASTER

   My lords, albeit the queen win Mortimer,   230
   Will you be resolute and hold with me?

MORTIMER SENIOR

  Not I against my nephew.

PEMBROKE

  Fear not, the queen's words cannot alter him.

WARWICK

  No? Do but mark how earnestly she pleads.

LANCASTER

  And see how coldly his looks make denial.

WARWICK

  She smiles. Now, for my life, his mind is changed.

LANCASTER

  I'll rather lose his friendship, I, than grant.

MORTIMER [*returning to the* NOBLES]

  Well, of necessity it must be so.

  My lords, that I abhor base Gaveston,

240 I hope your honours make no question,

  And therefore, though I plead for his repeal,

  'Tis not for his sake but for our avail –

  Nay, for the realm's behoof and for the king's.

LANCASTER

  Fie, Mortimer, dishonour not thyself.

  Can this be true, 'twas good to banish him,

  And is this true, to call him home again?

  Such reasons make white black and dark night day.

MORTIMER

  My lord of Lancaster, mark the respect.

LANCASTER

  In no respect can contraries be true.

QUEEN

250 Yet, good my lord, hear what he can allege.

WARWICK

  All that he speaks is nothing; we are resolved.

MORTIMER

  Do you not wish that Gaveston were dead?

PEMBROKE I would he were.

MORTIMER

  Why then, my lord, give me but leave to speak.

MORTIMER SENIOR
But, nephew, do not play the sophister.
MORTIMER
This which I urge is of a burning zeal
To mend the king and do our country good.
Know you not Gaveston hath store of gold
Which may in Ireland purchase him such friends
As he will front the mightiest of us all?   260
And whereas he shall live and be beloved,
'Tis hard for us to work his overthrow.
WARWICK
Mark you but that, my lord of Lancaster.
MORTIMER
But were he here, detested as he is,
How easily might some base slave be suborned
To greet his lordship with a poniard,
And none so much as blame the murderer,
But rather praise him for that brave attempt,
And in the chronicle enrol his name
For purging of the realm of such a plague.   270
PEMBROKE He saith true.
LANCASTER
Ay, but how chance this was not done before?
MORTIMER
Because, my lords, it was not thought upon.
Nay, more, when he shall know it lies in us
To banish him and then to call him home,
'Twill make him vail the top-flag of his pride,
And fear to offend the meanest nobleman.
MORTIMER SENIOR
But how if he do not, nephew?
MORTIMER
Then may we with some colour rise in arms;
For, howsoever we have borne it out,   280
'Tis treason to be up against the king.
So shall we have the people of our side,
Which for his father's sake lean to the king

But cannot brook a night-grown mushroom,
Such a one as my lord of Cornwall is,
Should bear us down of the nobility.
And when the commons and the nobles join,
'Tis not the king can buckler Gaveston;
We'll pull him from the strongest hold he hath.

290 My lords, if to perform this I be slack,
Think me as base a groom as Gaveston.

LANCASTER
On that condition, Lancaster will grant.

WARWICK
And so will Pembroke and I.

MORTIMER SENIOR   And I.

MORTIMER
In this I count me highly gratified,
And Mortimer will rest at your command.

QUEEN
And when this favour Isabel forgets,
Then let her live abandoned and forlorn.
But see, in happy time, my lord the king,
Having brought the earl of Cornwall on his way,

300 Is new returned. This news will glad him much,
Yet not so much as me. I love him more
Than he can Gaveston. Would he loved me
But half so much, then were I treble blest.

        Enter KING EDWARD, mourning [and ATTENDANTS,
        including BEAUMONT, Clerk of the Crown].

EDWARD
He's gone, and for his absence thus I mourn.
Did never sorrow go so near my heart
As doth the want of my sweet Gaveston,
And, could my crown's revenue bring him back,
I would freely give it to his enemies,
And think I gained, having bought so dear a friend.

QUEEN [to the NOBLES]

310 Hark, how he harps upon his minion.

EDWARD
My heart is as an anvil unto sorrow,

Which beats upon it like the Cyclops' hammers,
And with the noise turns up my giddy brain
And makes me frantic for my Gaveston.
Ah, had some bloodless Fury rose from hell
And with my kingly sceptre struck me dead,
When I was forced to leave my Gaveston!

LANCASTER
Diablo! What passions call you these?

QUEEN [*to* EDWARD]
My gracious lord, I come to bring you news.

EDWARD
That you have parlèd with your Mortimer?   320

QUEEN
That Gaveston, my lord, shall be repealed.

EDWARD
Repealed! The news is too sweet to be true.

QUEEN
But will you love me if you find it so?

EDWARD
If it be so, what will not Edward do?

QUEEN
For Gaveston, but not for Isabel.

EDWARD
For thee, fair queen, if thou lovest Gaveston,
I'll hang a golden tongue about thy neck,
Seeing thou hast pleaded with so good success.

QUEEN
No other jewels hang about my neck
Than these, my lord, nor let me have more wealth   330
Than I may fetch from this rich treasury.
    [*They kiss.*]
O, how a kiss revives poor Isabel!

EDWARD
Once more receive my hand, and let this be
A second marriage 'twixt thyself and me.

QUEEN
And may it prove more happy than the first.
    [*The* NOBLES *kneel.*]

My gentle lord, bespeak these nobles fair,
That wait attendance for a gracious look,
And on their knees salute your majesty.

EDWARD

Courageous Lancaster, embrace thy king,
340   And, as gross vapours perish by the sun,
Even so let hatred with thy sovereign's smile.
Live thou with me as my companion.

LANCASTER

This salutation overjoys my heart.

EDWARD

Warwick shall be my chiefest counsellor;
These silver hairs will more adorn my court
Than gaudy silks or rich embroidery.
Chide me, sweet Warwick, if I go astray.

WARWICK

Slay me, my lord, when I offend your grace.

EDWARD

In solemn triumphs and in public shows
350   Pembroke shall bear the sword before the king.

PEMBROKE

And with this sword Pembroke will fight for you.

EDWARD

But wherefore walks young Mortimer aside?
Be thou commander of our royal fleet,
Or, if that lofty office like thee not,
I make thee here Lord Marshal of the realm.

MORTIMER

My lord, I'll marshal so your enemies
As England shall be quiet and you safe.

EDWARD

And as for you, Lord Mortimer of Chirk,
Whose great achievements in our foreign war
360   Deserves no common place nor mean reward,
Be you the general of the levied troops
That now are ready to assail the Scots.

MORTIMER SENIOR

In this your grace hath highly honoured me,

For with my nature war doth best agree.

QUEEN

Now is the King of England rich and strong,
Having the love of his renownèd peers.

EDWARD

Ay, Isabel, ne'er was my heart so light.
Clerk of the Crown, direct our warrant forth
For Gaveston to Ireland; Beaumont, fly
As fast as Iris or Jove's Mercury.   370

BEAUMONT

It shall be done, my gracious lord.

                                        [*Exit* BEAUMONT.]

EDWARD

Lord Mortimer, we leave you to your charge.
Now let us in and feast it royally.
Against our friend the earl of Cornwall comes,
We'll have a general tilt and tournament,
And then his marriage shall be solemnized,
For wot you not that I have made him sure
Unto our cousin, the earl of Gloucester's heir?

LANCASTER

Such news we hear, my lord.

EDWARD

That day, if not for him, yet for my sake,   380
Who in the triumph will be challenger,
Spare for no cost; we will requite your love.

WARWICK

In this, or aught, your highness shall command us.

EDWARD

Thanks, gentle Warwick. Come, let's in and revel.

                        Exeunt; the MORTIMERS *remain.*

MORTIMER SENIOR

Nephew, I must to Scotland; thou stayest here.
Leave now to oppose thyself against the king.
Thou seest by nature he is mild and calm,
And, seeing his mind so dotes on Gaveston,
Let him without controlment have his will.
The mightiest kings have had their minions: 390

Great Alexander loved Hephaestion,
The conquering Hercules for Hylas wept,
And for Patroclus stern Achilles drooped.
And not kings only, but the wisest men:
The Roman Tully loved Octavius,
Grave Socrates, wild Alcibiades.
Then let his grace, whose youth is flexible,
And promiseth as much as we can wish,
Freely enjoy that vain, light-headed earl,
400   For riper years will wean him from such toys.

MORTIMER

Uncle, his wanton humour grieves not me,
But this I scorn, that one so basely born
Should by his sovereign's favour grow so pert
And riot it with the treasure of the realm.
While soldiers mutiny for want of pay,
He wears a lord's revenue on his back,
And Midas-like he jets it in the court
With base outlandish cullions at his heels,
Whose proud fantastic liveries make such show
410   As if that Proteus, god of shapes, appeared.
I have not seen a dapper jack so brisk.
He wears a short Italian hooded cloak,
Larded with pearl, and in his Tuscan cap
A jewel of more value than the crown.
Whiles other walk below, the king and he
From out a window laugh at such as we,
And flout our train, and jest at our attire.
Uncle, 'tis this that makes me impatient.

MORTIMER SENIOR

But, nephew, now you see the king is changed.

MORTIMER

420   Then so am I, and live to do him service.
But whiles I have a sword, a hand, a heart,
I will not yield to any such upstart.
You know my mind. Come, uncle, let's away.

Exeunt.

[Scene 5]

Enter SPENCER [JUNIOR] *and* BALDOCK.

BALDOCK
Spencer,
Seeing that our lord th'earl of Gloucester's dead,
Which of the nobles dost thou mean to serve?

SPENCER
Not Mortimer, nor any of his side,
Because the king and he are enemies.
Baldock, learn this of me: a factious lord
Shall hardly do himself good, much less us,
But he that hath the favour of a king
May with one word advance us while we live.
The liberal earl of Cornwall is the man   10
On whose good fortune Spencer's hope depends.

BALDOCK
What, mean you then to be his follower?

SPENCER
No, his companion, for he loves me well,
And would have once preferred me to the king.

BALDOCK
But he is banished; there's small hope of him.

SPENCER
Ay, for a while. But, Baldock, mark the end:
A friend of mine told me in secrecy
That he's repealed and sent for back again,
And even now a post came from the court
With letters to our lady from the king,   20
And as she read, she smiled, which makes me think
It is about her lover Gaveston.

BALDOCK
'Tis like enough, for since he was exiled
She neither walks abroad nor comes in sight.
But I had thought the match had been broke off
And that his banishment had changed her mind.

SPENCER
　Our lady's first love is not wavering.
　My life for thine, she will have Gaveston.
BALDOCK
　Then hope I by her means to be preferred,
30　Having read unto her since she was a child.
SPENCER
　Then, Baldock, you must cast the scholar off
　And learn to court it like a gentleman.
　'Tis not a black coat and a little band,
　A velvet-caped cloak faced before with serge,
　And smelling to a nosegay all the day,
　Or holding of a napkin in your hand,
　Or saying a long grace at a table's end,
　Or making low legs to a nobleman,
　Or looking downward with your eyelids close,
40　And saying, 'Truly, an't may please your honour',
　Can get you any favour with great men;
　You must be proud, bold, pleasant, resolute,
　And now and then stab as occasion serves.
BALDOCK
　Spencer, thou knowest I hate such formal toys,
　And use them but of mere hypocrisy.
　Mine old lord, while he lived, was so precise
　That he would take exceptions at my buttons,
　And, being like pins' heads, blame me for the bigness,
　Which made me curate-like in mine attire,
50　Though inwardly licentious enough
　And apt for any kind of villainy.
　I am none of these common pedants, I,
　That cannot speak without '*propterea quod*'.
SPENCER
　But one of those that saith '*quandoquidem*'
　And hath a special gift to form a verb.
BALDOCK
　Leave off this jesting, here my lady comes.
　　　Enter the LADY [*the* KING'S NIECE, *with letters*].

NIECE [*to herself*]
  The grief for his exile was not so much
  As is the joy of his returning home.
  This letter came from my sweet Gaveston.
  What need'st thou, love, thus to excuse thyself?   60
  I know thou couldst not come and visit me.
    [*She reads.*]
  'I will not long be from thee, though I die.'
  This argues the entire love of my lord.
    [*She reads.*]
  'When I forsake thee, death seize on my heart.'
  But rest thee here where Gaveston shall sleep.
    [*She places the letter in her bosom.*]
  Now to the letter of my lord the king.
    [*She reads from another letter.*]
  He wills me to repair unto the court
  And meet my Gaveston. Why do I stay,
  Seeing that he talks thus of my marriage day?
  Who's there? Baldock?   70
  See that my coach be ready, I must hence.
BALDOCK It shall be done, madam.

                                                    Exit.

NIECE
  And meet me at the park pale presently.
  Spencer, stay you and bear me company,
  For I have joyful news to tell thee of:
  My lord of Cornwall is a-coming over
  And will be at the court as soon as we.
SPENCER
  I knew the king would have him home again.
NIECE
  If all things sort out as I hope they will,
  Thy service, Spencer, shall be thought upon.   80
SPENCER
  I humbly thank your ladyship.
NIECE
  Come, lead the way, I long till I am there.

                                            [*Exeunt.*]

[*Scene 6*]

Enter EDWARD, *the* QUEEN, LANCASTER, MORTIMER
[JUNIOR], WARWICK, PEMBROKE, KENT, ATTENDANTS.

EDWARD

 The wind is good, I wonder why he stays;
 I fear me he is wracked upon the sea.

QUEEN [*aside to* LANCASTER]

 Look, Lancaster, how passionate he is,
 And still his mind runs on his minion.

LANCASTER [*to the* KING] My lord –

EDWARD

 How now, what news? Is Gaveston arrived?

MORTIMER

 Nothing but 'Gaveston'! What means your grace?
 You have matters of more weight to think upon;
 The King of France sets foot in Normandy.

EDWARD

10 A trifle. We'll expel him when we please.
 But tell me, Mortimer, what's thy device
 Against the stately triumph we decreed?

MORTIMER

 A homely one, my lord, not worth the telling.

EDWARD Prithee let me know it.

MORTIMER

 But seeing you are so desirous, thus it is:
 A lofty cedar tree, fair flourishing,
 On whose top branches kingly eagles perch,
 And by the bark a canker creeps me up.
 And gets unto the highest bough of all.

20 The motto: *Aeque tandem.*

EDWARD

 And what is yours, my lord of Lancaster?

LANCASTER

 My lord, mine's more obscure than Mortimer's.
 Pliny reports there is a flying fish
 Which all the other fishes deadly hate,

And therefore, being pursued, it takes the air;
No sooner is it up, but there's a fowl
That seizeth it. This fish, my lord, I bear;
The motto this: *Undique mors est.*

EDWARD

Proud Mortimer! Ungentle Lancaster!
Is this the love you bear your sovereign?   30
Is this the fruit your reconcilement bears?
Can you in words make show of amity,
And in your shields display your rancorous minds?
What call you this but private libelling
Against the earl of Cornwall and my brother?

QUEEN

Sweet husband, be content, they all love you.

EDWARD

They love me not that hate my Gaveston.
I am that cedar. Shake me not too much.
    [*To the* NOBLES]
And you the eagles, soar ye ne'er so high,
I have the jesses that will pull you down,   40
And *Aeque tandem* shall that canker cry
Unto the proudest peer of Britainy.
    [*To* LANCASTER]
Though thou compar'st him to a flying fish,
And threatenest death whether he rise or fall,
'Tis not the hugest monster of the sea
Nor foulest harpy that shall swallow him.

MORTIMER [*to the* NOBLES]

If in his absence thus he favours him,
What will he do whenas he shall be present?

LANCASTER

That shall we see. Look where his lordship comes.
    Enter GAVESTON.

EDWARD

My Gaveston!   50
Welcome to Tynemouth, welcome to thy friend.
Thy absence made me droop and pine away;
For, as the lovers of fair Danaë,

When she was locked up in a brazen tower,
Desired her more and waxed outrageous,
So did it sure with me; and now thy sight
Is sweeter far than was thy parting hence
Bitter and irksome to my sobbing heart.

GAVESTON
Sweet lord and king, your speech preventeth mine,
60   Yet have I words left to express my joy.
The shepherd nipped with biting winter's rage
Frolics not more to see the painted spring
Than I do to behold your majesty.

EDWARD
Will none of you salute my Gaveston?

LANCASTER
Salute him? Yes. Welcome, Lord Chamberlain.

MORTIMER
Welcome is the good earl of Cornwall.

WARWICK
Welcome, Lord Governor of the Isle of Man.

PEMBROKE
Welcome, Master Secretary.

KENT
Brother, do you hear them?

EDWARD
70   Still will these earls and barons use me thus?

GAVESTON
My lord, I cannot brook these injuries.

QUEEN
Ay me, poor soul, when these begin to jar.

EDWARD [*to* GAVESTON]
Return it to their throats, I'll be thy warrant.

GAVESTON
Base leaden earls, that glory in your birth,
Go sit at home and eat your tenants' beef,
And come not here to scoff at Gaveston,
Whose mounting thoughts did never creep so low
As to bestow a look on such as you.

LANCASTER
    Yet I disdain not to do this for you.
       [*He draws his sword.* MORTIMER JUNIOR *and* GAVESTON
       also draw.]
EDWARD
    Treason, treason! Where's the traitor?   80
PEMBROKE Here, here.
EDWARD
    Convey hence Gaveston! They'll murder him.
GAVESTON [*to* MORTIMER JUNIOR]
    The life of thee shall salve this foul disgrace.
MORTIMER
    Villain, thy life, unless I miss mine aim.
       [*He wounds* GAVESTON.]
QUEEN
    Ah, furious Mortimer, what hast thou done?
MORTIMER
    No more than I would answer, were he slain.
                   [*Exit* GAVESTON, *attended*.]
EDWARD
    Yes, more than thou canst answer, though he live.
    Dear shall you both aby this riotous deed.
    Out of my presence! Come not near the court!
MORTIMER
    I'll not be barred the court for Gaveston.   90
LANCASTER
    We'll hale him by the ears unto the block.
EDWARD
    Look to your own heads, his is sure enough.
WARWICK
    Look to your own crown, if you back him thus.
KENT
    Warwick, these words do ill beseem thy years.
EDWARD
    Nay, all of them conspire to cross me thus;
    But if I live, I'll tread upon their heads
    That think with high looks thus to tread me down.

Come, Edmund, let's away and levy men.
'Tis war that must abate these barons' pride.
                    Exeunt the KING [, QUEEN, *and* KENT, *attended*].

WARWICK
100   Let's to our castles, for the king is moved.

MORTIMER
Moved may he be, and perish in his wrath!

LANCASTER
Cousin, it is no dealing with him now.
He means to make us stoop by force of arms,
And therefore let us jointly here protest
To prosecute that Gaveston to the death.

MORTIMER
By heaven, the abject villain shall not live.

WARWICK
I'll have his blood or die in seeking it.

PEMBROKE
The like oath Pembroke takes.

LANCASTER   And so doth Lancaster.
Now send our heralds to defy the king,
110   And make the people swear to put him down.
                    Enter a POST.

MORTIMER
Letters, from whence?

MESSENGER
From Scotland, my lord.
        [MORTIMER JUNIOR *takes the letter*.]

LANCASTER
Why, how now, cousin, how fares all our friends?

MORTIMER
My uncle's taken prisoner by the Scots.

LANCASTER
We'll have him ransomed, man; be of good cheer.

MORTIMER
They rate his ransom at five thousand pound.
Who should defray the money but the king,
Seeing he is taken prisoner in his wars?
I'll to the king.

LANCASTER
Do, cousin, and I'll bear thee company.   120
WARWICK
Meantime, my lord of Pembroke and myself
Will to Newcastle here and gather head.
MORTIMER
About it then, and we will follow you.
LANCASTER
Be resolute and full of secrecy.
WARWICK I warrant you.
          [*Exeunt all but* MORTIMER JUNIOR *and* LANCASTER.]
MORTIMER
Cousin, an if he will not ransom him,
I'll thunder such a peal into his ears
As never subject did unto his king.
LANCASTER Content, I'll bear my part. Holla! Who's there?
     [*Enter a* GUARD.]
MORTIMER Ay, marry, such a guard as this doth well.   130
LANCASTER Lead on the way.
GUARD Whither will your lordships?
MORTIMER Whither else but to the king?
GUARD His highness is disposed to be alone.
LANCASTER Why, so he may, but we will speak to him.
GUARD You may not in, my lord.
MORTIMER May we not?
     [*Enter the* KING *and* KENT.]
EDWARD
How now, what noise is this?
Who have we there? Is't you?
     [*He starts to leave.*]
MORTIMER
Nay, stay, my lord, I come to bring you news: 140
Mine uncle's taken prisoner by the Scots.
EDWARD Then ransom him.
LANCASTER
'Twas in your wars, you should ransom him.
MORTIMER
And you shall ransom him, or else.

KENT

    What, Mortimer, you will not threaten him?

EDWARD

    Quiet yourself. You shall have the broad seal
    To gather for him thoroughout the realm.

LANCASTER

    Your minion Gaveston hath taught you this.

MORTIMER

    My lord, the family of the Mortimers

150   Are not so poor but, would they sell their land,
    Would levy men enough to anger you.
    We never beg, but use such prayers as these.
      [*he grasps the hilt of his sword*]

EDWARD Shall I still be haunted thus?

MORTIMER

    Nay, now you are here alone, I'll speak my mind.

LANCASTER

    And so will I, and then, my lord, farewell.

MORTIMER

    The idle triumphs, masques, lascivious shows,
    And prodigal gifts bestowed on Gaveston
    Have drawn thy treasure dry and made thee weak,
    The murmuring commons overstretchèd hath.

LANCASTER

160   Look for rebellion, look to be deposed.
    Thy garrisons are beaten out of France,
    And lame and poor lie groaning at the gates.
    The wild O'Neill, with swarms of Irish kerns,
    Lives uncontrolled within the English pale.
    Unto the walls of York the Scots made road,
    And, unresisted, drave away rich spoils.

MORTIMER

    The haughty Dane commands the narrow seas,
    While in the harbour ride thy ships unrigged.

LANCASTER

    What foreign prince sends thee ambassadors?

MORTIMER

170   Who loves thee but a sort of flatterers?

LANCASTER

Thy gentle queen, sole sister to Valois,
Complains that thou hast left her all forlorn.

MORTIMER

Thy court is naked, being bereft of those
That makes a king seem glorious to the world:
I mean the peers, whom thou shouldst dearly love.
Libels are cast again thee in the street,
Ballads and rhymes made of thy overthrow.

LANCASTER

The northern borderers, seeing their houses burnt,
Their wives and children slain, run up and down,
Cursing the name of thee and Gaveston.   180

MORTIMER

When wert thou in the field with banner spread?
But once, and then thy soldiers marched like players,
With garish robes, not armour; and thyself,
Bedaubed with gold, rode laughing at the rest,
Nodding and shaking of thy spangled crest,
Where women's favours hung like labels down.

LANCASTER

And thereof came it that the fleering Scots,
To England's high disgrace, have made this jig:
    'Maids of England, sore may you mourn,
    For your lemans you have lost at Bannocksbourn,   190
        With a heave and a ho!
    What weeneth the king of England,
    So soon to have won Scotland?
        With a rumbelow.'

MORTIMER

Wigmore shall fly, to set my uncle free.

LANCASTER

And when 'tis gone, our swords shall purchase more.
If ye be moved, revenge it as you can.
Look next to see us with our ensigns spread.

                    Exeunt NOBLES [MORTIMER JUNIOR *and*
                                        LANCASTER].

EDWARD

My swelling heart for very anger breaks.
200   How oft have I been baited by these peers,
And dare not be revenged, for their power is great!
Yet shall the crowing of these cockerels
Affright a lion? Edward, unfold thy paws,
And let their lives' blood slake thy fury's hunger.
If I be cruel and grow tyrannous,
Now let them thank themselves, and rue too late.

KENT

My lord, I see your love to Gaveston
Will be the ruin of the realm and you,
For now the wrathful nobles threaten wars,
210   And therefore, brother, banish him for ever.

EDWARD

Art thou an enemy to my Gaveston?

KENT

Ay, and it grieves me that I favoured him.

EDWARD

Traitor, begone! Whine thou with Mortimer.

KENT

So will I, rather than with Gaveston.

EDWARD

Out of my sight, and trouble me no more.

KENT

No marvel though thou scorn thy noble peers,
When I thy brother am rejected thus.

EDWARD Away!

Exit [KENT].

Poor Gaveston, that hast no friend but me.
220   Do what they can, we'll live in Tynemouth here,
And, so I walk with him about the walls,
What care I though the earls begirt us round?
Here comes she that's cause of all these jars.

> *Enter the* QUEEN, *three* LADIES [(*the* KING'S NIECE *and*
> *two* LADIES-IN-WAITING), GAVESTON,] BALDOCK, *and*
> SPENCER [JUNIOR].

QUEEN
My lord, 'tis thought the earls are up in arms.

EDWARD
Ay, and 'tis likewise thought you favour him.

QUEEN
Thus do you still suspect me without cause.

NIECE
Sweet uncle, speak more kindly to the queen.

GAVESTON [*aside to* EDWARD]
My lord, dissemble with her, speak her fair.

EDWARD [*to the* QUEEN]
Pardon me, sweet, I forgot myself.

QUEEN
Your pardon is quickly got of Isabel.   230

EDWARD
The younger Mortimer is grown so brave
That to my face he threatens civil wars.

GAVESTON
Why do you not commit him to the Tower?

EDWARD
I dare not, for the people love him well.

GAVESTON
Why then, we'll have him privily made away.

EDWARD
Would Lancaster and he had both caroused
A bowl of poison to each other's health!
But let them go, and tell me what are these.

NIECE
Two of my father's servants whilst he lived.
May't please your grace to entertain them now?   240

EDWARD [*to* BALDOCK]
Tell me, where wast thou born? What is thine arms?

BALDOCK
My name is Baldock, and my gentry
I fetched from Oxford, not from heraldry.

EDWARD
The fitter art thou, Baldock, for my turn.
Wait on me, and I'll see thou shalt not want.

BALDOCK
    I humbly thank your majesty.
EDWARD [*pointing to* SPENCER JUNIOR]
    Knowest thou him, Gaveston?
GAVESTON   Ay, my lord,
    His name is Spencer; he is well allied.
    For my sake, let him wait upon your grace;
250   Scarce shall you find a man of more desert.
EDWARD
    Then, Spencer, wait upon me; for his sake
    I'll grace thee with a higher style ere long.
SPENCER
    No greater titles happen unto me
    Than to be favoured of your majesty.
EDWARD [*to his* NIECE]
    Cousin, this day shall be your marriage feast.
    And, Gaveston, think that I love thee well
    To wed thee to our niece, the only heir
    Unto the earl of Gloucester late deceased.
GAVESTON
    I know, my lord, many will stomach me,
260   But I respect neither their love nor hate.
EDWARD
    The headstrong barons shall not limit me;
    He that I list to favour shall be great.
    Come, let's away, and when the marriage ends,
    Have at the rebels and their complices.
                                              Exeunt.

[*Scene 7*]

    Enter LANCASTER, MORTIMER [JUNIOR], WARWICK,
    PEMBROKE, KENT.
KENT
    My lords, of love to this our native land
    I come to join with you and leave the king,

And in your quarrel and the realm's behoof
Will be the first that shall adventure life.

LANCASTER
I fear me you are sent of policy,
To undermine us with a show of love.

WARWICK
He is your brother, therefore have we cause
To cast the worst, and doubt of your revolt.

KENT
Mine honour shall be hostage of my truth.
If that will not suffice, farewell, my lords.   10

MORTIMER
Stay, Edmund. Never was Plantagenet
False of his word, and therefore trust we thee.

PEMBROKE
But what's the reason you should leave him now?

KENT
I have informed the earl of Lancaster.

LANCASTER
And it sufficeth. Now, my lords, know this,
That Gaveston is secretly arrived,
And here in Tynemouth frolics with the king.
Let us with these our followers scale the walls
And suddenly surprise them unawares.

MORTIMER
I'll give the onset.

WARWICK   And I'll follow thee.   20

MORTIMER
This tattered ensign of my ancestors,
Which swept the desert shore of that Dead Sea
Whereof we got the name of Mortimer,
Will I advance upon this castle walls.
Drums, strike alarum! Raise them from their sport,
And ring aloud the knell of Gaveston.

LANCASTER
None be so hardy as to touch the king,
But neither spare you Gaveston nor his friends.

                                              Exeunt.

[*Scene 8*]

[*Alarums.*] *Enter the* KING *and* SPENCER [JUNIOR].

EDWARD

O tell me, Spencer, where is Gaveston?

SPENCER

I fear me he is slain, my gracious lord.

EDWARD

No, here he comes. Now let them spoil and kill.

[*Enter*] *to them* GAVESTON, [*the* QUEEN, *the* KING'S NIECE
and LORDS].

Fly, fly, my lords! The earls have got the hold.

Take shipping and away to Scarborough;

Spencer and I will post away by land.

GAVESTON

O stay, my lord. They will not injure you.

EDWARD

I will not trust them, Gaveston. Away!

GAVESTON Farewell, my lord.

10   EDWARD Lady, farewell.

NIECE

Farewell, sweet uncle, till we meet again.

EDWARD

Farewell, sweet Gaveston, and farewell, niece.

QUEEN

No farewell to poor Isabel, thy queen?

EDWARD

Yes, yes, for Mortimer, your lover's sake.

Exeunt all; ISABELLA *remains.*

QUEEN

Heavens can witness I love none but you.

From my embracements thus he breaks away.

O, that mine arms could close this isle about,

That I might pull him to me where I would,

Or that these tears that drizzle from mine eyes

20   Had power to mollify his stony heart,

That when I had him we might never part!

Enter the BARONS [LANCASTER, WARWICK, MORTIMER
JUNIOR *and others*]. *Alarums.*

LANCASTER
  I wonder how he 'scaped.
MORTIMER   Who's this, the queen?
QUEEN
  Ay, Mortimer, the miserable queen,
  Whose pining heart her inward sighs have blasted,
  And body with continual mourning wasted.
  These hands are tired with haling of my lord
  From Gaveston, from wicked Gaveston,
  And all in vain, for when I speak him fair
  He turns away and smiles upon his minion.
MORTIMER
  Cease to lament, and tell us where's the king?   30
QUEEN
  What would you with the king? Is't him you seek?
LANCASTER
  No, madam, but that cursèd Gaveston.
  Far be it from the thought of Lancaster
  To offer violence to his sovereign;
  We would but rid the realm of Gaveston.
  Tell us where he remains, and he shall die.
QUEEN
  He's gone by water unto Scarborough;
  Pursue him quickly, and he cannot 'scape.
  The king hath left him, and his train is small.
WARWICK
  Forslow no time, sweet Lancaster, let's march.   40
MORTIMER
  How comes it that the king and he is parted?
QUEEN
  That this your army, going several ways,
  Might be of lesser force, and, with the power
  That he intendeth presently to raise,
  Be easily suppressed; and therefore begone.
MORTIMER
  Here in the river rides a Flemish hoy.

Let's all aboard and follow him amain.

LANCASTER

The wind that bears him hence will fill our sails.
Come, come, aboard. 'Tis but an hour's sailing.

MORTIMER

50   Madam, stay you within this castle here.

QUEEN

No, Mortimer, I'll to my lord the king.

MORTIMER

Nay, rather sail with us to Scarborough.

QUEEN

You know the king is so suspicious
As, if he hear I have but talked with you,
Mine honour will be called in question,
And therefore, gentle Mortimer, begone.

MORTIMER

Madam, I cannot stay to answer you,
But think of Mortimer as he deserves.

                    [*Exeunt all; the* QUEEN *remains.*]

QUEEN

So well hast thou deserved, sweet Mortimer,
60   As Isabel could live with thee for ever.
In vain I look for love at Edward's hand,
Whose eyes are fixed on none but Gaveston.
Yet once more I'll importune him with prayers.
If he be strange and not regard my words,
My son and I will over into France,
And to the king my brother there complain
How Gaveston hath robbed me of his love;
But yet I hope my sorrows will have end,
And Gaveston this blessèd day be slain.

                                        Exit.

[*Scene 9*]

Enter GAVESTON, *pursued.*

GAVESTON
Yet, lusty lords, I have escaped your hands,
Your threats, your 'larums, and your hot pursuits;
And though divorcèd from King Edward's eyes,
Yet liveth Piers of Gaveston unsurprised,
Breathing, in hope (*malgrado* all your beards,
That muster rebels thus against your king)
To see his royal sovereign once again.

Enter the NOBLES [WARWICK, LANCASTER, PEMBROKE,
MORTIMER JUNIOR, *with* SOLDIERS, JAMES, HORSEBOY,
and ATTENDANTS].

WARWICK
Upon him, soldiers! Take away his weapons.

MORTIMER
Thou proud disturber of thy country's peace,
Corrupter of thy king, cause of these broils,   10
Base flatterer, yield! And were it not for shame,
Shame and dishonour to a soldier's name,
Upon my weapon's point here shouldst thou fall,
And welter in thy gore.

LANCASTER   Monster of men,
That, like the Greekish strumpet, trained to arms
And bloody wars so many valiant knights,
Look for no other fortune, wretch, than death.
Kind Edward is not here to buckler thee.

WARWICK
Lancaster, why talk'st thou to the slave?
Go, soldiers, take him hence, for by my sword,   20
His head shall off. Gaveston, short warning
Shall serve thy turn; it is our country's cause
That here severely we will execute
Upon thy person. Hang him at a bough.

GAVESTON My lord!

WARWICK
  Soldiers, have him away.
  But, for thou wert the favourite of a king,
  Thou shalt have so much honour at our hands.
GAVESTON
  I thank you all, my lords. Then I perceive
30 That heading is one, and hanging is the other,
  And death is all.
      Enter EARL OF ARUNDEL.
LANCASTER
  How now, my lord of Arundel?
ARUNDEL
  My lords, King Edward greets you all by me.
WARWICK
  Arundel, say your message.
ARUNDEL   His majesty,
  Hearing that you had taken Gaveston,
  Entreateth you by me yet but he may
  See him before he dies, for why, he says,
  And sends you word, he knows that die he shall;
  And if you gratify his grace so far,
40 He will be mindful of the courtesy.
WARWICK
  How now?
GAVESTON   Renownèd Edward, how thy name
  Revives poor Gaveston!
WARWICK   No, it needeth not.
  Arundel, we will gratify the king
  In other matters; he must pardon us in this.
  Soldiers, away with him.
GAVESTON   Why, my lord of Warwick,
  Will not these delays beget my hopes?
  I know it, lords, it is this life you aim at;
  Yet grant King Edward this.
MORTIMER   Shalt thou appoint
  What we shall grant? Soldiers, away with him.
50 Thus we'll gratify the king:

We'll send his head by thee. Let him bestow
His tears on that, for that is all he gets
Of Gaveston, or else his senseless trunk.

LANCASTER

Not so, my lord, lest he bestow more cost
In burying him than he hath ever earned.

ARUNDEL

My lords, it is his majesty's request,
And, in the honour of a king, he swears
He will but talk with him and send him back.

WARWICK

When, can you tell? Arundel, no.
We wot, he that the care of realm remits   60
And drives his nobles to these exigents
For Gaveston will, if he seize him once,
Violate any promise to possess him.

ARUNDEL

Then if you will not trust his grace in keep,
My lords, I will be pledge for his return.

MORTIMER

It is honourable in thee to offer this,
But, for we know thou art a noble gentleman,
We will not wrong thee so
To make away a true man for a thief.

GAVESTON

How mean'st thou, Mortimer? That is over-base.   70

MORTIMER

Away, base groom, robber of king's renown!
Question with thy companions and thy mates.

PEMBROKE

My lord Mortimer, and you my lords each one,
To gratify the king's request therein
Touching the sending of this Gaveston,
Because his majesty so earnestly
Desires to see the man before his death,
I will upon mine honour undertake
To carry him and bring him back again,

80   Provided this: that you, my lord of Arundel,
      Will join with me.
      WARWICK   Pembroke, what wilt thou do?
      Cause yet more bloodshed? Is it not enough
      That we have taken him, but must we now
      Leave him on 'had-I-wist' and let him go?
      PEMBROKE
      My lords, I will not over-woo your honours,
      But, if you dare trust Pembroke with the prisoner,
      Upon mine oath, I will return him back.
      ARUNDEL
      My lord of Lancaster, what say you in this?
      LANCASTER
      Why, I say let him go on Pembroke's word.
      PEMBROKE
90   And you, lord Mortimer?
      MORTIMER
      How say you, my lord of Warwick?
      WARWICK
      Nay, do your pleasures. I know how 'twill prove.
      PEMBROKE
      Then give him me.
      GAVESTON   Sweet sovereign, yet I come
      To see thee ere I die.
      WARWICK [aside]   Yet not, perhaps,
      If Warwick's wit and policy prevail.
      MORTIMER
      My lord of Pembroke, we deliver him you;
      Return him on your honour. Sound, away!
                    Exeunt; PEMBROKE, ARUNDEL, GAVESTON, and
                         PEMBROKE'S MEN, four SOLDIERS remain.
      PEMBROKE [to ARUNDEL]
      My lord, you shall go with me.
      My house is not far hence, out of the way
100   A little, but our men shall go along.
      We that have pretty wenches to our wives,
      Sir, must not come so near and balk their lips.

ARUNDEL
  'Tis very kindly spoke, my lord of Pembroke.
  Your honour hath an adamant of power
  To draw a prince.
PEMBROKE   So, my lord. Come hither, James.
  I do commit this Gaveston to thee.
  Be thou this night his keeper; in the morning
  We will discharge thee of thy charge. Begone.
GAVESTON
  Unhappy Gaveston, whither goest thou now?

                    Exit [GAVESTON] *with* [JAMES *and*]
                              PEMBROKE's [*other*] *servants*.

HORSEBOY
  My lord, we'll quickly be at Cobham.   110

                                              Exeunt.

                        [*Scene 10*]

    Enter GAVESTON *mourning, and the* EARL OF PEMBROKE'S
    MEN [*with* JAMES *and four* SOLDIERS].
GAVESTON
  O treacherous Warwick, thus to wrong thy friend!
JAMES
  I see it is your life these arms pursue.
GAVESTON
  Weaponless must I fall, and die in bands?
  O, must this day be period of my life?
  Centre of all my bliss! An ye be men,
  Speed to the king.
    Enter WARWICK *and his company*.
WARWICK   My lord of Pembroke's men,
  Strive you no longer; I will have that Gaveston.
JAMES
  Your lordship doth dishonour to yourself
  And wrong our lord, your honourable friend.

WARWICK

10 No, James, it is my country's cause I follow.
Go, take the villain. [GAVESTON *is taken.*]
                              Soldiers, come away.
We'll make quick work.
    [*To* JAMES]   Commend me to your master,
My friend, and tell him that I watched it well.
    [*To* GAVESTON]
Come, let thy shadow parley with King Edward.

GAVESTON

Treacherous earl, shall I not see the king?

WARWICK

The king of heaven perhaps, no other king.
Away!

                    Exeunt WARWICK *and his men, with* GAVESTON.
                              JAMES *remains with the others.*

JAMES

Come, fellows, it booted not for us to strive.
We will in haste go certify our lord.

                                                        Exeunt.

[*Scene 11*]

    Enter KING EDWARD *and* SPENCER [JUNIOR *and*
    BALDOCK,] *with drums and fifes.*

EDWARD

I long to hear an answer from the barons
Touching my friend, my dearest Gaveston.
Ah, Spencer, not the riches of my realm
Can ransom him! Ah, he is marked to die.
I know the malice of the younger Mortimer,
Warwick I know is rough, and Lancaster
Inexorable, and I shall never see
My lovely Piers, my Gaveston again.
The barons overbear me with their pride.

SPENCER

    Were I King Edward, England's sovereign,   10
    Son to the lovely Eleanor of Spain,
    Great Edward Longshanks' issue, would I bear
    These braves, this rage, and suffer uncontrolled
    These barons thus to beard me in my land,
    In mine own realm? My lord, pardon my speech.
    Did you retain your father's magnanimity,
    Did you regard the honour of your name,
    You would not suffer thus your majesty
    Be counterbuffed of your nobility.
    Strike off their heads, and let them preach on poles.   20
    No doubt, such lessons they will teach the rest
    As, by their preachments, they will profit much
    And learn obedience to their lawful king.

EDWARD

    Yea, gentle Spencer, we have been too mild,
    Too kind to them, but now have drawn our sword,
    And if they send me not my Gaveston,
    We'll steel it on their crest and poll their tops.

BALDOCK

    This haught resolve becomes your majesty,
    Not to be tied to their affection,
    As though your highness were a schoolboy still,   30
    And must be awed and governed like a child.

    Enter HUGH SPENCER, *an old man, father to the young*
    SPENCER, *with his truncheon, and* SOLDIERS.

SPENCER SENIOR

    Long live my sovereign, the noble Edward,
    In peace triumphant, fortunate in wars!

EDWARD

    Welcome, old man. Com'st thou in Edward's aid?
    Then tell thy prince of whence and what thou art.

SPENCER SENIOR

    Lo, with a band of bowmen and of pikes,
    Brown bills and targeteers, four hundred strong,
    Sworn to defend King Edward's royal right,

I come in person to your majesty –
40   Spencer, the father of Hugh Spencer there,
Bound to your highness everlastingly
For favours done in him unto us all.

EDWARD
Thy father, Spencer?

SPENCER   True, an it like your grace,
That pours, in lieu of all your goodness shown,
His life, my lord, before your princely feet.

EDWARD
Welcome ten thousand times, old man, again.
Spencer, this love, this kindness to thy king
Argues thy noble mind and disposition.
Spencer, I here create thee earl of Wiltshire,
50   And daily will enrich thee with our favour,
That, as the sunshine, shall reflect o'er thee.
Beside, the more to manifest our love,
Because we hear Lord Bruce doth sell his land,
And that the Mortimers are in hand withal,
Thou shalt have crowns of us t'outbid the barons;
And, Spencer, spare them not, but lay it on.
Soldiers, a largess, and thrice welcome all!

SPENCER
My lord, here comes the queen.
        Enter the QUEEN [*with a letter*] *and her son* [PRINCE
        EDWARD], *and* LEVUNE, *a Frenchman.*

EDWARD   Madam, what news?

QUEEN
News of dishonour, lord, and discontent.
60   Our friend Levune, faithful and full of trust,
Informeth us, by letters and by words,
That Lord Valois our brother, King of France,
Because your highness hath been slack in homage,
Hath seizèd Normandy into his hands.
These be the letters, this the messenger.
        [*She shows the letter to* EDWARD.]

EDWARD
Welcome, Levune. Tush, Sib, if this be all,

Valois and I will soon be friends again.
But to my Gaveston: shall I never see,
Never behold thee now? Madam, in this matter
We will employ you and your little son;   70
You shall go parley with the King of France.
Boy, see you bear you bravely to the king,
And do your message with a majesty.

PRINCE

Commit not to my youth things of more weight
Than fits a prince so young as I to bear,
And fear not, lord and father, heaven's great beams
On Atlas' shoulder shall not lie more safe
Than shall your charge committed to my trust.

QUEEN

Ah, boy, this towardness makes thy mother fear
Thou art not marked to many days on earth.   80

EDWARD

Madam, we will that you with speed be shipped,
And this our son; Levune shall follow you
With all the haste we can despatch him hence.
Choose of our lords to bear you company,
And go in peace; leave us in wars at home.

QUEEN

Unnatural wars, where subjects brave their king;
God end them once! My lord, I take my leave
To make my preparation for France.

        [*Exeunt the* QUEEN *and* PRINCE EDWARD.]
    Enter LORD ARUNDEL.

EDWARD

What, Lord Arundel, dost thou come alone?

ARUNDEL

Yea, my good lord, for Gaveston is dead.   90

EDWARD

Ah, traitors! Have they put my friend to death?
Tell me, Arundel, died he ere thou cam'st,
Or didst thou see my friend to take his death?

ARUNDEL

Neither, my lord, for, as he was surprised,

Begirt with weapons and with enemies round,
I did your highness' message to them all,
Demanding him of them – entreating rather –
And said, upon the honour of my name,
That I would undertake to carry him
100   Unto your highness and to bring him back.

EDWARD
And tell me, would the rebels deny me that?

SPENCER
Proud recreants!

EDWARD   Yea, Spencer, traitors all.

ARUNDEL
I found them at the first inexorable.
The earl of Warwick would not bide the hearing,
Mortimer hardly, Pembroke and Lancaster
Spake least; and when they flatly had denied,
Refusing to receive me pledge for him,
The earl of Pembroke mildly thus bespake:
'My lords, because our sovereign sends for him,
110   And promiseth he shall be safe returned,
I will this undertake: to have him hence
And see him re-delivered to your hands.'

EDWARD
Well, and how fortunes that he came not?

SPENCER
Some treason or some villainy was cause.

ARUNDEL
The earl of Warwick seized him on his way;
For, being delivered unto Pembroke's men,
Their lord rode home, thinking his prisoner safe,
But ere he came, Warwick in ambush lay
And bare him to his death, and in a trench
120   Strake off his head, and marched unto the camp.

SPENCER
A bloody part, flatly against law of arms.

EDWARD
O, shall I speak, or shall I sigh and die?

SPENCER

> My lord, refer your vengeance to the sword
> Upon these barons; hearten up your men;
> Let them not unrevenged murder your friends.
> Advance your standard, Edward, in the field,
> And march to fire them from their starting-holes.
>   EDWARD *kneels and saith*

EDWARD

> By earth, the common mother of us all,
> By heaven, and all the moving orbs thereof,
> By this right hand, and by my father's sword,   130
> And all the honours 'longing to my crown,
> I will have heads and lives for him, as many
> As I have manors, castles, towns, and towers.
> Treacherous Warwick, traitorous Mortimer!
> If I be England's king, in lakes of gore
> Your headless trunks, your bodies will I trail,
> That you may drink your fill and quaff in blood,
> And stain my royal standard with the same,
> That so my bloody colours may suggest
> Remembrance of revenge immortally   140
> On your accursèd traitorous progeny,
> You villains that have slain my Gaveston.
>   [*He rises.*]
> And in this place of honour and of trust,
> Spencer, sweet Spencer, I adopt thee here,
> And merely of our love we do create thee
> Earl of Gloucester and Lord Chamberlain,
> Despite of times, despite of enemies.

SPENCER

> My lord, here is a messenger from the barons
> Desires access unto your majesty.

EDWARD Admit him near.   150

Enter the HERALD *from the* BARONS, *with his coat of arms.*

HERALD

> Long live King Edward, England's lawful lord!

EDWARD

> So wish not they, iwis, that sent thee hither.

Thou com'st from Mortimer and his complices.
A ranker rout of rebels never was.
Well, say thy message.

HERALD

The barons up in arms by me salute
Your highness with long life and happiness,
And bid me say, as plainer to your grace,
That if without effusion of blood
You will this grief have ease and remedy,
That from your princely person you remove
This Spencer, as a putrefying branch
That deads the royal vine whose golden leaves
Impale your princely head, your diadem,
Whose brightness such pernicious upstarts dim,
Say they, and lovingly advise your grace
To cherish virtue and nobility,
And have old servitors in high esteem,
And shake off smooth dissembling flatterers.
This granted, they, their honours, and their lives
Are to your highness vowed and consecrate.

SPENCER

Ah, traitors, will they still display their pride?

EDWARD

Away! Tarry no answer, but begone.
Rebels, will they appoint their sovereign
His sports, his pleasures, and his company?
Yet ere thou go, see how I do divorce
Spencer from me. (*Embrace* SPENCER.)
                         Now get thee to thy lords,
And tell them I will come to chastise them
For murdering Gaveston. Hie thee, get thee gone.
Edward with fire and sword follows at thy heels.
                                        [*Exit the* HERALD.]
My lords, perceive you how these rebels swell?
Soldiers, good hearts, defend your sovereign's right,
For now, even now, we march to make them stoop.
Away!

                                                   Exeunt.

[*Scene 12*]

Alarums, excursions, a great fight, and a retreat. Enter the KING, SPENCER *the father,* SPENCER *the son, and the noblemen of the King's side.*

EDWARD

Why do we sound retreat? Upon them, lords!
This day I shall pour vengeance with my sword
On those proud rebels that are up in arms
And do confront and countermand their king.

SPENCER

I doubt it not, my lord, right will prevail.

SPENCER SENIOR

'Tis not amiss, my liege, for either part
To breathe a while; our men, with sweat and dust
All choked well near, begin to faint for heat,
And this retire refresheth horse and man.

SPENCER Here come the rebels.   10

Enter the BARONS: MORTIMER [JUNIOR], LANCASTER, WARWICK, PEMBROKE, *with others.*

MORTIMER

Look, Lancaster,
Yonder is Edward among his flatterers.

LANCASTER

And there let him be,
Till he pay dearly for their company.

WARWICK

And shall, or Warwick's sword shall smite in vain.

EDWARD

What, rebels, do you shrink and sound retreat?

MORTIMER

No, Edward, no. Thy flatterers faint and fly.

LANCASTER

Thou'd best betimes forsake them and their trains,
For they'll betray thee, traitors as they are.

SPENCER

Traitor on thy face, rebellious Lancaster!   20

PEMBROKE
  Away, base upstart. Brav'st thou nobles thus?
SPENCER SENIOR
  A noble attempt and honourable deed
  Is it not, trow ye, to assemble aid
  And levy arms against your lawful king?
EDWARD
  For which ere long their heads shall satisfy,
  T'appease the wrath of their offended king.
MORTIMER
  Then, Edward, thou wilt fight it to the last,
  And rather bathe thy sword in subjects' blood
  Than banish that pernicious company?
EDWARD
30 Ay, traitors all, rather than thus be braved,
  Make England's civil towns huge heaps of stones,
  And ploughs to go about our palace gates.
WARWICK
  A desperate and unnatural resolution.
  Alarum! To the fight!
  Saint George for England and the barons' right!
EDWARD
  Saint George for England and King Edward's right!
                                   [*Alarums. Exeunt.*]

[*Scene 13*]

  Enter EDWARD [, *the* SPENCERS, LEVUNE *and* BALDOCK],
  with the BARONS [*and* KENT] *captives.*
EDWARD
  Now, lusty lords, now, not by chance of war,
  But justice of the quarrel and the cause,
  Vailed is your pride. Methinks you hang the heads,
  But we'll advance them, traitors. Now 'tis time
  To be avenged on you for all your braves

And for the murder of my dearest friend,
To whom right well you knew our soul was knit:
Good Piers of Gaveston, my sweet favourite.
Ah, rebels, recreants, you made him away!

KENT
Brother, in regard of thee and of thy land   10
Did they remove that flatterer from thy throne.

EDWARD
So, sir, you have spoke. Away, avoid our presence.

                                        [*Exit* KENT.]

Accursèd wretches, was't in regard of us,
When we had sent our messenger to request
He might be spared to come to speak with us,
And Pembroke undertook for his return,
That thou, proud Warwick, watched the prisoner,
Poor Piers, and headed him against law of arms?
For which thy head shall overlook the rest
As much as thou in rage outwent'st the rest.   20

WARWICK
Tyrant, I scorn thy threats and menaces.
'Tis but temporal that thou canst inflict.

LANCASTER
The worst is death, and better die to live
Than live in infamy under such a king.

EDWARD
Away with them, my lord of Winchester.
These lusty leaders, Warwick and Lancaster,
I charge you roundly: off with both their heads.
Away!

WARWICK
Farewell, vain world.

LANCASTER   Sweet Mortimer, farewell.

          [*Exeunt* WARWICK *and* LANCASTER, *guarded,*
                         led away by SPENCER SENIOR.]

MORTIMER
England, unkind to thy nobility,   30
Groan for this grief! Behold how thou art maimed.

EDWARD

Go take that haughty Mortimer to the Tower.
There see him safe bestowed, and, for the rest,
Do speedy execution on them all.
Begone!

MORTIMER

What, Mortimer, can ragged stony walls
Immure thy virtue that aspires to heaven?
No, Edward, England's scourge, it may not be;
Mortimer's hope surmounts his fortune far.

                              [*Exit* MORTIMER JUNIOR, *guarded.*]

EDWARD

40 Sound drums and trumpets! March with me, my friends.
Edward this day hath crowned him king anew.

                                                            Exit.

     [*Drums and trumpets sound.*] *Exeunt*; SPENCER JUNIOR,
     LEVUNE *and* BALDOCK *remain.*

SPENCER

Levune, the trust that we repose in thee
Begets the quiet of King Edward's land.
Therefore be gone in haste, and with advice
Bestow that treasure on the lords of France,
That therewith all enchanted, like the guard
That suffered Jove to pass in showers of gold
To Danaë, all aid may be denied
To Isabel the queen, that now in France
50 Makes friends, to cross the seas with her young son
And step into his father's regiment.

LEVUNE

That's it these barons and the subtle queen
Long levelled at.

BALDOCK   Yea, but, Levune, thou seest
These barons lay their heads on blocks together.
What they intend, the hangman frustrates clean.

LEVUNE

Have you no doubts, my lords. I'll clap so close
Among the lords of France with England's gold
That Isabel shall make her plaints in vain,

And France shall be obdurate with her tears.
SPENCER
Then make for France amain, Levune, away!   60
Proclaim King Edward's wars and victories.

Exeunt.

[*Scene 14*]

Enter EDMUND [*the* EARL OF KENT].
KENT
Fair blows the wind for France. Blow, gentle gale,
Till Edmund be arrived for England's good.
Nature, yield to my country's cause in this.
A brother, no, a butcher of thy friends,
Proud Edward, dost thou banish me thy presence?
But I'll to France, and cheer the wrongèd queen,
And certify what Edward's looseness is.
Unnatural king, to slaughter noble men
And cherish flatterers!
Mortimer, I stay thy sweet escape;   10
Stand gracious, gloomy night, to his device!
Enter MORTIMER [JUNIOR] *disguised.*
MORTIMER
Holla! Who walketh there? Is't you, my lord?
KENT
Mortimer, 'tis I.
But hath thy potion wrought so happily?
MORTIMER
It hath, my lord. The warders all asleep,
I thank them, gave me leave to pass in peace.
But hath your grace got shipping unto France?
KENT Fear it not.

Exeunt.

[Scene 15]

Enter the QUEEN *and her son* [PRINCE EDWARD].

QUEEN
Ah, boy, our friends do fail us all in France,
The lords are cruel, and the king unkind.
What shall we do?

PRINCE   Madam, return to England,
And please my father well, and then a fig
For all my uncle's friendship here in France.
I warrant you, I'll win his highness quickly;
'A loves me better than a thousand Spencers.

QUEEN
Ah, boy, thou art deceived, at least in this,
To think that we can yet be tuned together.
10 No, no, we jar too far. Unkind Valois,
Unhappy Isabel! When France rejects,
Whither, O, whither dost thou bend thy steps?
        Enter SIR JOHN OF HAINAULT.

SIR JOHN
Madam, what cheer?

QUEEN   Ah, good Sir John of Hainault,
Never so cheerless nor so far distressed.

SIR JOHN
I hear, sweet lady, of the king's unkindness.
But droop not, madam; noble minds contemn
Despair. Will your grace with me to Hainault,
And there stay time's advantage with your son?
How say you, my lord, will you go with your friends
20 And shake off all our fortunes equally?

PRINCE
So pleaseth the queen my mother, me it likes.
The King of England nor the court of France
Shall have me from my gracious mother's side
Till I be strong enough to break a staff,
And then have at the proudest Spencer's head.

SIR JOHN Well said, my lord.
QUEEN
  O, my sweet heart, how do I moan thy wrongs,
  Yet triumph in the hope of thee, my joy.
  Ah, sweet Sir John, even to the utmost verge
  Of Europe, or the shore of Tanaïs,   30
  Will we with thee to Hainault, so we will.
  The marquis is a noble gentleman;
  His grace, I dare presume, will welcome me.
  But who are these?
    Enter EDMUND [EARL OF KENT] *and* MORTIMER
    [JUNIOR].
KENT   Madam, long may you live,
  Much happier than your friends in England do.
QUEEN
  Lord Edmund and Lord Mortimer alive?
  Welcome to France.
    [*To* MORTIMER] The news was here, my lord,
  That you were dead, or very near your death.
MORTIMER
  Lady, the last was truest of the twain,
  But Mortimer, reserved for better hap,   40
  Hath shaken off the thraldom of the Tower,
    [*to* PRINCE EDWARD]
  And lives t'advance your standard, good my lord.
PRINCE
  How mean you, an the king my father lives?
  No, my lord Mortimer, not I, I trow.
QUEEN
  Not, son? Why not? I would it were no worse.
  But, gentle lords, friendless we are in France.
MORTIMER
  Monsieur le Grand, a noble friend of yours,
  Told us at our arrival all the news:
  How hard the nobles, how unkind the king
  Hath showed himself. But, madam, right makes room   50
  Where weapons want; and, though a many friends

Are made away – as Warwick, Lancaster,
And others of our party and faction –
Yet have we friends, assure your grace, in England
Would cast up caps and clap their hands for joy
To see us there appointed for our foes.

KENT

Would all were well, and Edward well reclaimed
For England's honour, peace, and quietness!

MORTIMER

But by the sword, my lord, it must be deserved.
60   The king will ne'er forsake his flatterers.

SIR JOHN

My lords of England, sith the ungentle king
Of France refuseth to give aid of arms
To this distressèd queen his sister here,
Go you with her to Hainault. Doubt ye not
We will find comfort, money, men, and friends
Ere long to bid the English king a base.
How say, young prince, what think you of the match?

PRINCE

I think King Edward will outrun us all.

QUEEN

Nay, son, not so, and you must not discourage
70   Your friends that are so forward in your aid.

KENT

Sir John of Hainault, pardon us, I pray.
These comforts that you give our woeful queen
Bind us in kindness all at your command.

QUEEN

Yea, gentle brother, and the God of heaven
Prosper your happy motion, good Sir John!

MORTIMER

This noble gentleman, forward in arms,
Was born, I see, to be our anchor-hold.
Sir John of Hainault, be it thy renown
That England's queen and nobles in distress
80   Have been by thee restored and comforted.

SIR JOHN

Madam, along, and you, my lord, with me,
That England's peers may Hainault's welcome see.

[*Exeunt.*]

[*Scene 16*]

Enter the KING, ARUNDEL, *the* TWO SPENCERS, *with
others.*

EDWARD

Thus after many threats of wrathful war
Triumpheth England's Edward with his friends;
And triumph Edward, with his friends uncontrolled.
My lord of Gloucester, do you hear the news?

SPENCER What news, my lord?

EDWARD

Why, man, they say there is great execution
Done through the realm. My lord of Arundel,
You have the note, have you not?

ARUNDEL

From the lieutenant of the Tower, my lord.

EDWARD

I pray let us see it. What have we there?   10
Read it, Spencer.

SPENCER [JUNIOR] *reads their names.*

Why so, they barked apace a month ago;
Now, on my life, they'll neither bark nor bite.
Now, sirs, the news from France. Gloucester, I trow
The lords of France love England's gold so well
As Isabella gets no aid from thence.
What now remains? Have you proclaimed, my lord,
Reward for them can bring in Mortimer?

SPENCER

My lord, we have, and if he be in England,
'A will be had ere long, I doubt it not.   20

EDWARD

    'If', dost thou say? Spencer, as true as death,

    He is in England's ground. Our port-masters

    Are not so careless of their king's command.

       Enter a POST [*with letters*].

    How now, what news with thee? From whence come

       these?

POST

    Letters, my lord, and tidings forth of France,

    To you, my lord of Gloucester, from Levune.

EDWARD Read.

      SPENCER [JUNIOR] *reads the letter*.

SPENCER 'My duty to your honour promised, etc. I have, accord-
    ing to instructions in that behalf, dealt with the King of France
30   his lords, and effected that the queen, all discontented and
    discomforted, is gone; whither, if you ask, with Sir John of
    Hainault, brother to the marquis, into Flanders. With them
    are gone Lord Edmund and the Lord Mortimer, having in
    their company divers of your nation and others; and, as
    constant report goeth, they intend to give King Edward battle
    in England sooner than he can look for them. This is all the
    news of import.

                      Your honour's in all service, Levune.'

EDWARD

    Ah, villains, hath that Mortimer escaped?

40   With him is Edmund gone associate?

    And will Sir John of Hainault lead the round?

    Welcome, a' God's name, madam, and your son.

    England shall welcome you and all your rout.

    Gallop apace, bright Phoebus, through the sky,

    And dusky night, in rusty iron car,

    Between you both shorten the time, I pray,

    That I may see that most desirèd day

    When we may meet these traitors in the field.

    Ah, nothing grieves me but my little boy

50   Is thus misled to countenance their ills.

    Come, friends, to Bristol, there to make us strong;

And, winds, as equal be to bring them in
As you injurious were to bear them forth.

[*Exeunt.*]

[*Scene 17*]

Enter the QUEEN, *her son* [PRINCE EDWARD], EDMUND
[EARL OF KENT], MORTIMER [JUNIOR], *and* SIR JOHN
[OF HAINAULT].

QUEEN
  Now, lords, our loving friends and countrymen,
  Welcome to England all with prosperous winds.
  Our kindest friends in Belgia have we left
  To cope with friends at home – a heavy case,
  When force to force is knit, and sword and glaive
  In civil broils makes kin and countrymen
  Slaughter themselves in others, and their sides
  With their own weapons gored. But what's the help?
  Misgoverned kings are cause of all this wrack,
  And, Edward, thou art one among them all   10
  Whose looseness hath betrayed thy land to spoil
  And made the channels overflow with blood.
  Of thine own people patron shouldst thou be,
  But thou –
MORTIMER Nay, madam, if you be a warrior,
  Yet must not grow so passionate in speeches.
  Lords, sith that we are by sufferance of heaven
  Arrived and armèd in this prince's right,
  Here for our country's cause swear we to him
  All homage, fealty, and forwardness;
  And, for the open wrongs and injuries   20
  Edward hath done to us, his queen, and land,
  We come in arms to wreck it with the sword,
  That England's queen in peace may repossess
  Her dignities and honours, and withal

We may remove these flatterers from the king
That havocs England's wealth and treasury.

SIR JOHN

Sound trumpets, my lord, and forward let us march.
Edward will think we come to flatter him.

KENT

I would he never had been flattered more.

[*Trumpets sound. Exeunt.*]

[*Scene 18*]

Enter the KING, BALDOCK, *and* SPENCER THE SON, *flying about the stage.*

SPENCER

Fly, fly, my lord! The queen is over-strong;
Her friends do multiply, and yours do fail.
Shape we our course to Ireland, there to breathe.

EDWARD

What, was I born to fly and run away,
5   And leave the Mortimers conquerors behind?
Give me my horse, and let's r'enforce our troops,
And in this bed of honour die with fame.

BALDOCK

O no, my lord, this princely resolution
Fits not the time. Away! We are pursued.

[*Exeunt.*]

[*Scene 19*]

[*Enter*] EDMUND [EARL OF KENT] *alone, with a sword and target.*

KENT

This way he fled, but I am come too late.
Edward, alas, my heart relents for thee.

Proud traitor, Mortimer, why dost thou chase
Thy lawful king, thy sovereign, with thy sword,
Vile wretch, and why hast thou, of all unkind,
Borne arms against thy brother and thy king?
Rain showers of vengeance on my cursèd head,
Thou God, to whom in justice it belongs
To punish this unnatural revolt!
Edward, this Mortimer aims at thy life;   10
O, fly him, then! But, Edmund, calm this rage.
Dissemble or thou diest, for Mortimer
And Isabel do kiss while they conspire;
And yet she bears a face of love, forsooth.
Fie on that love that hatcheth death and hate!
Edmund, away. Bristol to Longshanks' blood
Is false. Be not found single for suspect;
Proud Mortimer pries near into thy walks.
       Enter the QUEEN, MORTIMER [JUNIOR], *the young*
       PRINCE [EDWARD], *and* SIR JOHN OF HAINAULT.

QUEEN
Successful battles gives the God of kings
To them that fight in right and fear his wrath.   20
Since then successfully we have prevailed,
Thanks be heaven's great architect and you.
Ere farther we proceed, my noble lords,
We here create our well-belovèd son,
Of love and care unto his royal person,
Lord Warden of the realm; and sith the Fates
Have made his father so infortunate,
Deal you, my lords, in this, my loving lords,
As to your wisdoms fittest seems in all.

KENT
Madam, without offence if I may ask,   30
How will you deal with Edward in his fall?

PRINCE
Tell me, good uncle, what Edward do you mean?

KENT
Nephew, your father; I dare not call him king.

MORTIMER
  My lord of Kent, what needs these questions?
  'Tis not in her controlment, nor in ours,
  But as the realm and Parliament shall please,
  So shall your brother be disposèd of.
      [*Aside to the* QUEEN]
  I like not this relenting mood in Edmund.
  Madam, 'tis good to look to him betimes.
QUEEN [*to* MORTIMER JUNIOR]
40 My lord, the Mayor of Bristol knows our mind.
MORTIMER
  Yea, madam, and they 'scape not easily
  That fled the field.
QUEEN   Baldock is with the king;
  A goodly chancellor, is he not, my lord?
SIR JOHN
  So are the Spencers, the father and the son.
KENT [*aside*]
  This Edward is the ruin of the realm.
      Enter RICE ap HOWELL *and the* MAYOR OF BRISTOL, *with*
      SPENCER THE FATHER [*captive, and* GUARDS].
RICE ap HOWELL
  God save Queen Isabel and her princely son!
  Madam, the mayor and citizens of Bristol,
  In sign of love and duty to this presence,
  Present by me this traitor to the state:
50 Spencer, the father to that wanton Spencer
  That like the lawless Catiline of Rome
  Revelled in England's wealth and treasury.
QUEEN
  We thank you all.
MORTIMER   Your loving care in this
  Deserveth princely favours and rewards.
  But where's the king and the other Spencer fled?
RICE ap HOWELL
  Spencer the son, created earl of Gloucester,
  Is with that smooth-tongued scholar Baldock gone
  And shipped but late for Ireland with the king.

MORTIMER
  Some whirlwind fetch them back or sink them all!
  They shall be started thence, I doubt it not.   60
PRINCE
  Shall I not see the king my father yet?
KENT [aside]
   Unhappy Edward, chased from England's bounds!
SIR JOHN
  Madam, what resteth? Why stand ye in a muse?
QUEEN
  I rue my lord's ill fortune; but alas,
  Care of my country called me to this war.
MORTIMER
  Madam, have done with care and sad complaint;
  Your king hath wronged your country and himself,
  And we must seek to right it as we may.
  Meanwhile, have hence this rebel to the block.
      [To SPENCER SENIOR]
  Your lordship cannot privilege your head.   70
SPENCER SENIOR
  Rebel is he that fights against his prince;
  So fought not they that fought in Edward's right.
MORTIMER
  Take him away, he prates. [SPENCER SENIOR is led away.]
                    You, Rice ap Howell,
  Shall do good service to her majesty,
  Being of countenance in your country here,
  To follow these rebellious runagates.
  We in mean while, madam, must take advice
  How Baldock, Spencer, and their complices
  May in their fall be followed to their end.
                                        Exeunt.

[*Scene 20*]

Enter the ABBOT, MONKS, [KING] EDWARD, SPENCER [JUNIOR], *and* BALDOCK [*disguised as monks*].

ABBOT

Have you no doubt, my lord, have you no fear.
As silent and as careful will we be
To keep your royal person safe with us,
Free from suspect and fell invasion
Of such as have your majesty in chase,
Yourself – and those your chosen company –
As danger of this stormy time requires.

EDWARD

Father, thy face should harbour no deceit.
O, hadst thou ever been a king, thy heart,

10   Pierced deeply with sense of my distress,
Could not but take compassion of my state.
Stately and proud, in riches and in train,
Whilom I was, powerful and full of pomp;
But what is he whom rule and empery
Have not in life or death made miserable?
Come, Spencer, come, Baldock, come sit down by me;
Make trial now of that philosophy
That in our famous nurseries of arts
Thou sucked'st from Plato and from Aristotle.

20   Father, this life contemplative is heaven.
O, that I might this life in quiet lead!
But we, alas, are chased, and you my friends;
Your lives and my dishonour they pursue.
Yet, gentle monks, for treasure, gold, nor fee
Do you betray us and our company.

MONKS

Your grace may sit secure if none but we
Do wot of your abode.

SPENCER

Not one alive; but shrewdly I suspect
A gloomy fellow in a mead below.

'A gave a long look after us, my lord,   30
And all the land, I know, is up in arms –
Arms that pursue our lives with deadly hate.

BALDOCK

We were embarked for Ireland, wretched we,
With awkward winds and sore tempests driven,
To fall on shore and here to pine in fear
Of Mortimer and his confederates.

EDWARD

Mortimer! Who talks of Mortimer?
Who wounds me with the name of Mortimer,
That bloody man? Good father, on thy lap
Lay I this head, laden with mickle care.   40
O, might I never open these eyes again,
Never again lift up this drooping head,
O, never more lift up this dying heart!

SPENCER

Look up, my lord. Baldock, this drowsiness
Betides no good; here even we are betrayed.

    Enter, with Welsh hooks, [SOLDIERS,] RICE ap HOWELL,
    a MOWER, *and the* EARL OF LEICESTER.

MOWER

Upon my life, those be the men ye seek.

RICE ap HOWELL

Fellow, enough. My lord, I pray be short.
A fair commission warrants what we do.

LEICESTER [*aside*]

The queen's commission, urged by Mortimer.
What cannot gallant Mortimer with the queen?   50
Alas, see where he sits and hopes unseen
T'escape their hands that seek to reave his life.
Too true it is, *Quem dies vidit veniens superbum,*
Hunc dies vidit fugiens iacentem.
But, Leicester, leave to grow so passionate.
Spencer and Baldock, by no other names
I arrest you of high treason here.
Stand not on titles, but obey th'arrest;
'Tis in the name of Isabel the queen.

60   My lord, why droop you thus?
EDWARD
      O day, the last of all my bliss on earth,
      Centre of all misfortune! O my stars!
      Why do you lour unkindly on a king?
      Comes Leicester, then, in Isabella's name
      To take my life, my company from me?
      Here, man, rip up this panting breast of mine
      And take my heart in rescue of my friends.
RICE ap HOWELL
      Away with them.
SPENCER [*to* LEICESTER]
                            It may become thee yet
      To let us take our farewell of his grace.
ABBOT
70   My heart with pity earns to see this sight,
      A king to bear these words and proud commands.
EDWARD
      Spencer, ah, sweet Spencer, thus then must we part?
SPENCER
      We must, my lord; so will the angry heavens.
EDWARD
      Nay, so will hell and cruel Mortimer,
      The gentle heavens have not to do in this.
BALDOCK
      My lord, it is in vain to grieve or storm.
      Here humbly of your grace we take our leaves.
      Our lots are cast; I fear me, so is thine.
EDWARD
      In heaven we may, in earth never shall we meet.
80   And, Leicester, say, what shall become of us?
LEICESTER
      Your majesty must go to Killingworth.
EDWARD
      'Must'! 'Tis somewhat hard when kings must go.
LEICESTER
      Here is a litter ready for your grace
      That waits your pleasure, and the day grows old.

RICE ap HOWELL
 As good be gone as stay and be benighted.

EDWARD
 A litter hast thou? Lay me in a hearse,
 And to the gates of hell convey me hence;
 Let Pluto's bells ring out my fatal knell,
 And hags howl for my death at Charon's shore,
 For friends hath Edward none, but these, and these,   90
 And these must die under a tyrant's sword.

RICE ap HOWELL
 My lord, be going. Care not for these,
 For we shall see them shorter by the heads.

EDWARD
 Well, that shall be shall be. Part we must,
 Sweet Spencer, gentle Baldock, part we must.
  [*He discards his robes.*]
 Hence, feignèd weeds! Unfeignèd are my woes.
 Father, farewell. Leicester, thou stay'st for me,
 And go I must. Life, farewell, with my friends.
    Exeunt EDWARD [*guarded*] *and* LEICESTER.

SPENCER
 O, is he gone? Is noble Edward gone,
 Parted from hence, never to see us more?   100
 Rend, sphere of heaven, and fire, forsake thy orb;
 Earth melt to air! Gone is my sovereign,
 Gone, gone, alas, never to make return.

BALDOCK
 Spencer, I see our souls are fleeted hence;
 We are deprived the sunshine of our life.
 Make for a new life, man; throw up thy eyes
 And heart and hand to heaven's immortal throne;
 Pay nature's debt with cheerful countenance.
 Reduce we all our lessons unto this:
 To die, sweet Spencer, therefore live we all;   110
 Spencer, all live to die, and rise to fall.

RICE ap HOWELL Come, come, keep these preachments till you
 come to the place appointed. You, and such as you are, have
 made wise work in England. Will your lordships away?

MOWER
Your worship, I trust, will remember me?

RICE ap HOWELL Remember thee, fellow? What else? Follow
me to the town.

[*Exeunt, with* SPENCER JUNIOR *and* BALDOCK *guarded.*]

[*Scene 21*]

Enter the KING [*crowned*], LEICESTER, *with a* BISHOP
[OF WINCHESTER, *and* TRUSSELL] *for the crown,* [*with*
ATTENDANTS].

LEICESTER
Be patient, good my lord, cease to lament.
Imagine Killingworth Castle were your court,
And that you lay for pleasure here a space,
Not of compulsion or necessity.

EDWARD
Leicester, if gentle words might comfort me,
Thy speeches long ago had eased my sorrows,
For kind and loving hast thou always been.
The griefs of private men are soon allayed,
But not of kings. The forest deer, being struck,
10   Runs to an herb that closeth up the wounds,
But when the imperial lion's flesh is gored,
He rends and tears it with his wrathful paw,
And, highly scorning that the lowly earth
Should drink his blood, mounts up into the air;
And so it fares with me, whose dauntless mind
The ambitious Mortimer would seek to curb,
And that unnatural queen, false Isabel,
That thus hath pent and mewed me in a prison.
For such outrageous passions cloy my soul
20   As with the wings of rancour and disdain
Full often am I soaring up to heaven,
To plain me to the gods against them both;
But when I call to mind I am a king,

Methinks I should revenge me of the wrongs
That Mortimer and Isabel have done.
But what are kings, when regiment is gone,
But perfect shadows in a sunshine day?
My nobles rule, I bear the name of king;
I wear the crown but am controlled by them,
By Mortimer and my unconstant queen,   30
Who spots my nuptial bed with infamy,
Whilst I am lodged within this cave of care,
Where sorrow at my elbow still attends
To company my heart with sad laments
That bleeds within me for this strange exchange.
But tell me, must I now resign my crown
To make usurping Mortimer a king?

WINCHESTER
Your grace mistakes, it is for England's good
And princely Edward's right we crave the crown.

EDWARD
No, 'tis for Mortimer, not Edward's head,   40
For he's a lamb encompassèd by wolves
Which in a moment will abridge his life.
But if proud Mortimer do wear this crown,
Heavens turn it to a blaze of quenchless fire,
Or, like the snaky wreath of Tisiphon,
Engirt the temples of his hateful head!
So shall not England's vine be perishèd,
But Edward's name survives, though Edward dies.

LEICESTER
My lord, why waste you thus the time away?
They stay your answer. Will you yield your crown?   50

EDWARD
Ah, Leicester, weigh how hardly I can brook
To lose my crown and kingdom without cause,
To give ambitious Mortimer my right,
That like a mountain overwhelms my bliss,
In which extreme my mind here murdered is.
But what the heavens appoint, I must obey.
    [*He removes the crown.*]

Here, take my crown, the life of Edward too!
Two kings in England cannot reign at once.
But stay a while. Let me be king till night,
60 That I may gaze upon this glittering crown;
So shall my eyes receive their last content,
My head the latest honour due to it,
And jointly both yield up their wishèd right.
Continue ever, thou celestial sun;
Let never silent night possess this clime.
Stand still, you watches of the element;
All times and seasons, rest you at a stay,
That Edward may be still fair England's king.
But day's bright beams doth vanish fast away,
70 And needs I must resign my wishèd crown.
Inhuman creatures, nursed with tiger's milk,
Why gape you for your sovereign's overthrow?
My diadem, I mean, and guiltless life.
     [*He puts the crown back on.*]
See, monsters, see, I'll wear my crown again.
What, fear you not the fury of your king?
But, hapless Edward, thou art fondly led;
They pass not for thy frowns as late they did,
But seeks to make a new-elected king,
Which fills my mind with strange despairing thoughts,
80 Which thoughts are martyrèd with endless torments,
And in this torment comfort find I none
But that I feel the crown upon my head,
And therefore let me wear it yet a while.

TRUSSELL
     My lord, the Parliament must have present news,
     And therefore say, will you resign or no?
          The KING *rageth.*

EDWARD
     I'll not resign, but whilst I live –
     Traitors, begone, and join you with Mortimer!
     Elect, conspire, install, do what you will;
     Their blood and yours shall seal these treacheries.

WINCHESTER
    This answer we'll return, and so farewell.   90
      [WINCHESTER *and* TRUSSELL *move to leave.*]
LEICESTER [*to* EDWARD]
    Call them again, my lord, and speak them fair,
    For if they go the prince shall lose his right.
EDWARD
    Call thou them back. I have no power to speak.
LEICESTER [*to* WINCHESTER]
    My lord, the king is willing to resign.
WINCHESTER If he be not, let him choose.
EDWARD
    O, would I might! But heavens and earth conspire
    To make me miserable. Here, receive my crown.
      [*He offers them the crown.*]
    Receive it? No, these innocent hands of mine
    Shall not be guilty of so foul a crime.
    He of you all that most desires my blood,   100
    And will be called the murderer of a king,
    Take it. What, are you moved? Pity you me?
    Then send for unrelenting Mortimer,
    And Isabel, whose eyes, being turned to steel,
    Will sooner sparkle fire than shed a tear.
    Yet stay, for rather than I will look on them,
    Here, here. [*He gives up the crown.*]
                Now, sweet God of heaven,
    Make me despise this transitory pomp
    And sit for aye enthronizèd in heaven!
    Come, Death, and with thy fingers close my eyes,   110
    Or if I live, let me forget myself.
WINCHESTER My lord –
EDWARD
    Call me not lord. Away, out of my sight!
    Ah, pardon me, grief makes me lunatic.
    Let not that Mortimer protect my son;
    More safety is there in a tiger's jaws
    Than his embracements. Bear this to the queen,
      [*he gives a handkerchief*]

Wet with my tears and dried again with sighs;
If with the sight thereof she be not moved,
120 Return it back and dip it in my blood.
Commend me to my son, and bid him rule
Better than I. Yet how have I transgressed,
Unless it be with too much clemency?

TRUSSELL
And thus most humbly do we take our leave.

EDWARD
Farewell.
        [*Exeunt* BISHOP OF WINCHESTER *and* TRUSSELL.]
        I know the next news that they bring
Will be my death, and welcome shall it be;
To wretched men death is felicity.
    Enter BERKELEY [*giving* LEICESTER *a letter*].

LEICESTER
Another post. What news brings he?
    [*He reads the letter.*]

EDWARD
Such news as I expect. Come, Berkeley, come,
130 And tell thy message to my naked breast.

BERKELEY
My lord, think not a thought so villainous
Can harbour in a man of noble birth.
To do your highness service and devoir,
And save you from your foes, Berkeley would die.

LEICESTER
My lord, the council of the queen commands
That I resign my charge.

EDWARD
And who must keep me now? Must you, my lord?

BERKELEY
Ay, my most gracious lord, so 'tis decreed.
    [*He hands the letter to the* KING.]

EDWARD
By Mortimer, whose name is written here.
140 Well may I rend his name that rends my heart!
    [*He tears up the letter.*]

This poor revenge hath something eased my mind.
So may his limbs be torn, as is this paper!
Hear me, immortal Jove, and grant it too.

BERKELEY
Your grace must hence with me to Berkeley straight.

EDWARD
Whither you will, all places are alike,
And every earth is fit for burial.

LEICESTER [*to* BERKELEY]
Favour him, my lord, as much as lieth in you.

BERKELEY
Even so betide my soul as I use him.

EDWARD
Mine enemy hath pitied my estate,
And that's the cause that I am now removed.   150

BERKELEY
And thinks your grace that Berkeley will be cruel?

EDWARD
I know not, but of this am I assured:
That death ends all, and I can die but once.
Leicester, farewell.

LEICESTER
Not yet, my lord. I'll bear you on your way.

Exeunt.

[*Scene 22*]

Enter MORTIMER [JUNIOR] *and* QUEEN ISABEL.

MORTIMER
Fair Isabel, now have we our desire:
The proud corrupters of the light-brained king
Have done their homage to the lofty gallows,
And he himself lies in captivity.
Be ruled by me, and we will rule the realm.
In any case, take heed of childish fear,
For now we hold an old wolf by the ears

That, if he slip, will seize upon us both
And grip the sorer, being gripped himself.
10   Think therefore, madam, that imports us much
To erect your son with all the speed we may
And that I be Protector over him,
For our behoof will bear the greater sway
Whenas a king's name shall be under writ.

QUEEN

Sweet Mortimer, the life of Isabel,
Be thou persuaded that I love thee well;
And therefore, so the prince my son be safe,
Whom I esteem as dear as these mine eyes,
Conclude against his father what thou wilt
20   And I myself will willingly subscribe.

MORTIMER

First would I hear news that he were deposed,
And then let me alone to handle him.

    Enter MESSENGER [*with a letter, followed by the* BISHOP
    OF WINCHESTER *with the crown*].

Letters, from whence?

MESSENGER [*presenting the letter*]
                    From Killingworth, my lord.

QUEEN

How fares my lord the king?

MESSENGER

In health, madam, but full of pensiveness.

QUEEN

Alas, poor soul, would I could ease his grief.
Thanks, gentle Winchester.
[*To the* MESSENGER]   Sirrah, begone.

                      [*Exit* MESSENGER.]

WINCHESTER

The king hath willingly resigned his crown.

QUEEN

O happy news! Send for the prince my son.

WINCHESTER

30   Further, or this letter was sealed, Lord Berkeley came,
So that he now is gone from Killingworth,

And we have heard that Edmund laid a plot
To set his brother free. No more but so:
The lord of Berkeley is so pitiful
As Leicester that had charge of him before.

QUEEN
Then let some other be his guardian.

MORTIMER
Let me alone. Here is the privy seal.

> [*Exit the* BISHOP OF WINCHESTER.
>   MORTIMER *calls offstage.*]

Who's there? Call hither Gurney and Matrevis.
To dash the heavy-headed Edmund's drift,
Berkeley shall be discharged, the king removed,   40
And none but we shall know where he lieth.

QUEEN
But, Mortimer, as long as he survives,
What safety rests for us, or for my son?

MORTIMER
Speak, shall he presently be dispatched and die?

QUEEN
I would he were, so it were not by my means.

> *Enter* MATREVIS *and* GURNEY.

MORTIMER
Enough. Matrevis, write a letter presently
Unto the lord of Berkeley from ourself,
That he resign the king to thee and Gurney,
And when 'tis done we will subscribe our name.

MATREVIS
It shall be done, my lord.

MORTIMER   Gurney.

GURNEY   My lord.   50

MORTIMER
As thou intendest to rise by Mortimer,
Who now makes Fortune's wheel turn as he please,
Seek all the means thou canst to make him droop,
And neither give him kind word nor good look.

GURNEY I warrant you, my lord.

MORTIMER
    And this above the rest, because we hear
    That Edmund casts to work his liberty,
    Remove him still from place to place by night
    Till at the last he come to Killingworth
60   And then from thence to Berkeley back again;
    And by the way, to make him fret the more,
    Speak curstly to him, and in any case
    Let no man comfort him if he chance to weep,
    But amplify his grief with bitter words.

MATREVIS
    Fear not, my lord, we'll do as you command.

MORTIMER
    So now away. Post thitherwards amain.

QUEEN
    Whither goes this letter? To my lord the king?
    Commend me humbly to his majesty,
    And tell him that I labour all in vain
70   To ease his grief and work his liberty;
    And bear him this as witness of my love.
      [*She gives* MATREVIS *a ring.*]

MATREVIS I will, madam.

               Exeunt MATREVIS *and* GURNEY.
    ISABEL *and* MORTIMER *remain. Enter the young* PRINCE
    [EDWARD], *and the* EARL OF KENT *talking with him.*
    [MORTIMER *and the* QUEEN *speak apart.*]

MORTIMER
    Finely dissembled. Do so still, sweet queen.
    Here comes the young prince, with the Earl of Kent.

QUEEN
    Something he whispers in his childish ears.

MORTIMER
    If he have such access unto the prince,
    Our plots and stratagems will soon be dashed.

QUEEN
    Use Edmund friendly, as if all were well.

MORTIMER [*aloud to* KENT]
    How fares my honourable lord of Kent?

KENT

In health, sweet Mortimer. How fares your grace?   80

QUEEN

Well, if my lord your brother were enlarged.

KENT

I hear of late he hath deposed himself.

QUEEN The more my grief.

MORTIMER And mine.

KENT [*aside*] Ah, they do dissemble.

QUEEN

Sweet son, come hither. I must talk with thee.

[*She takes* PRINCE EDWARD *to one side.*]

MORTIMER [*to* KENT]

Thou being his uncle and the next of blood,

Do look to be Protector over the prince.

KENT

Not I, my lord. Who should protect the son

But she that gave him life, I mean the queen?   90

PRINCE

Mother, persuade me not to wear the crown.

Let him be king, I am too young to reign.

QUEEN

But be content, seeing it his highness' pleasure.

PRINCE

Let me but see him first, and then I will.

KENT Ay, do, sweet nephew.

QUEEN Brother, you know it is impossible.

PRINCE Why, is he dead?

QUEEN No, God forbid!

KENT

I would those words proceeded from your heart.

MORTIMER

Inconstant Edmund, dost thou favour him,   100

That wast a cause of his imprisonment?

KENT

The more cause have I now to make amends.

MORTIMER

I tell thee 'tis not meet that one so false

Should come about the person of a prince.
   [*To* PRINCE EDWARD]
My lord, he hath betrayed the king his brother,
And therefore trust him not.

PRINCE

But he repents and sorrows for it now.

QUEEN

Come, son, and go with this gentle lord and me.

PRINCE

With you I will, but not with Mortimer.

MORTIMER

110   Why, youngling, 'sdain'st thou so of Mortimer?
[*Seizing him*] Then I will carry thee by force away.

PRINCE

Help, uncle Kent! Mortimer will wrong me.
               [*Exit* MORTIMER JUNIOR *with the* PRINCE.]

QUEEN

Brother Edmund, strive not; we are his friends.
Isabel is nearer than the earl of Kent.

KENT

Sister, Edward is my charge. Redeem him.

QUEEN

Edward is my son, and I will keep him.
                       [*Exit the* QUEEN.]

KENT

Mortimer shall know that he hath wronged me.
Hence will I haste to Killingworth Castle,
And rescue agèd Edward from his foes,
120   To be revenged on Mortimer and thee.
                              Exit.

[*Scene 23*]

Enter MATREVIS *and* GURNEY *with the* KING [*and*
SOLDIERS, *with torches*].

MATREVIS
My lord, be not pensive, we are your friends.
Men are ordained to live in misery;
Therefore come. Dalliance dangereth our lives.
EDWARD
Friends, whither must unhappy Edward go?
Will hateful Mortimer appoint no rest?
Must I be vexèd like the nightly bird
Whose sight is loathsome to all wingèd fowls?
When will the fury of his mind assuage?
When will his heart be satisfied with blood?
If mine will serve, unbowel straight this breast   10
And give my heart to Isabel and him;
It is the chiefest mark they level at.
GURNEY
Not so, my liege. The queen hath given this charge
To keep your grace in safety.
Your passions make your dolours to increase.
EDWARD
This usage makes my misery increase.
But can my air of life continue long
When all my senses are annoyed with stench?
Within a dungeon England's king is kept,
Where I am starved for want of sustenance;   20
My daily diet is heart-breaking sobs
That almost rents the closet of my heart.
Thus lives old Edward, not relieved by any,
And so must die, though pitièd by many.
O, water, gentle friends, to cool my thirst
And clear my body from foul excrements!
    [*Ditch water is brought onstage.*]
MATREVIS
Here's channel water, as our charge is given.

Sit down, for we'll be barbers to your grace.

EDWARD

Traitors, away! What, will you murder me,

30   Or choke your sovereign with puddle water?

GURNEY

No, but wash your face and shave away your beard,

Lest you be known and so be rescuèd.

MATREVIS

Why strive you thus? Your labour is in vain.

EDWARD

The wren may strive against the lion's strength,

But all in vain, so vainly do I strive

To seek for mercy at a tyrant's hand.

> *They wash him with puddle water, and shave his beard*
> *away.*

Immortal powers, that knows the painful cares

That waits upon my poor distressèd soul,

O, level all your looks upon these daring men

40   That wrongs their liege and sovereign, England's king.

O Gaveston, it is for thee that I am wronged;

For me, both thou and both the Spencers died,

And for your sakes a thousand wrongs I'll take.

The Spencers' ghosts, wherever they remain,

Wish well to mine. Then, tush, for them I'll die.

MATREVIS

'Twixt theirs and yours shall be no enmity.

Come, come, away. Now put the torches out,

We'll enter in by darkness to Killingworth.

> [*They put out their torches.*]
> *Enter* EDMUND [EARL OF KENT].

GURNEY

How now, who comes there?

> [*They draw their swords.*]

MATREVIS

50   Guard the king sure, it is the earl of Kent.

EDWARD

O gentle brother, help to rescue me!

MATREVIS
Keep them asunder! Thrust in the king.

KENT
Soldiers, let me but talk to him one word.

GURNEY
Lay hands upon the earl for this assault.

KENT
Lay down your weapons, traitors. Yield the king.

MATREVIS
Edmund, yield thou thyself, or thou shalt die.
[KENT *is seized*.]

KENT
Base villains, wherefore do you grip me thus?

GURNEY [*to the* SOLDIERS]
Bind him and so convey him to the court.

KENT
Where is the court but here? Here is the king,
And I will visit him. Why stay you me?   60

MATREVIS
The court is where Lord Mortimer remains.
Thither shall your honour go, and so farewell.
            Exeunt MATREVIS *and* GURNEY *with the* KING.
        EDMUND [EARL OF KENT] *and the* SOLDIERS *remain*.

KENT
O, miserable is that commonweal
Where lords keep courts and kings are locked in prison!

SOLDIER
Wherefore stay we? On, sirs, to the court.

KENT
Ay, lead me whither you will, even to my death,
Seeing that my brother cannot be released.
                        Exeunt [, KENT *guarded*].

[*Scene 24*]

Enter MORTIMER [JUNIOR] *alone* [*with a letter*].

MORTIMER

The king must die, or Mortimer goes down.
The commons now begin to pity him;
Yet he that is the cause of Edward's death
Is sure to pay for it when his son is of age,
And therefore will I do it cunningly.
This letter, written by a friend of ours,
Contains his death, yet bids them save his life.
'*Edwardum occidere nolite timere, bonum est*',
'Fear not to kill the king, 'tis good he die.'
10   But read it thus, and that's another sense:
'*Edwardum occidere nolite, timere bonum est*',
'Kill not the king, 'tis good to fear the worst.'
Unpointed as it is, thus shall it go,
That, being dead, if it chance to be found,
Matrevis and the rest may bear the blame
And we be quit that caused it to be done.
Within this room is locked the messenger
That shall convey it and perform the rest,
And by a secret token that he bears
20   Shall he be murdered when the deed is done.
Lightborne, come forth.
          [*Enter* LIGHTBORNE.]
Art thou as resolute as thou wast?

LIGHTBORNE

What else, my lord? And far more resolute.

MORTIMER

And hast thou cast how to accomplish it?

LIGHTBORNE

Ay, ay, and none shall know which way he died.

MORTIMER

But at his looks, Lightborne, thou wilt relent.

LIGHTBORNE

Relent? Ha, ha! I use much to relent.

MORTIMER
  Well, do it bravely and be secret.
LIGHTBORNE
  You shall not need to give instructions;
  'Tis not the first time I have killed a man.
  I learned in Naples how to poison flowers,   30
  To strangle with a lawn thrust through the throat,
  To pierce the windpipe with a needle's point,
  Or, whilst one is asleep, to take a quill
  And blow a little powder in his ears,
  Or open his mouth and pour quicksilver down;
  But yet I have a braver way than these.
MORTIMER What's that?
LIGHTBORNE
  Nay, you shall pardon me, none shall know my tricks.
MORTIMER
  I care not how it is, so it be not spied.
      [*Giving the letter*]
  Deliver this to Gurney and Matrevis.   40
  At every ten miles' end thou hast a horse.
      [*Giving a token*]
  Take this. Away, and never see me more.
LIGHTBORNE No?
MORTIMER No,
  Unless thou bring me news of Edward's death.
LIGHTBORNE
  That will I quickly do. Farewell, my lord.
                                    [*Exit* LIGHTBORNE.]
MORTIMER
  The prince I rule, the queen do I command;
  And, with a lowly *congé* to the ground,
  The proudest lords salute me as I pass.
  I seal, I cancel, I do what I will.   50
  Feared am I more than loved. Let me be feared,
  And when I frown, make all the court look pale.
  I view the prince with Aristarchus' eyes,
  Whose looks were as a breeching to a boy.
  They thrust upon me the protectorship

And sue to me for that that I desire,
While at the council table, grave enough,
And not unlike a bashful Puritan,
First I complain of imbecility,
60   Saying it is *onus quam gravissimum*,
Till, being interrupted by my friends,
Suscepi that *provinciam*, as they term it,
And, to conclude, I am Protector now.
Now is all sure. The queen and Mortimer
Shall rule the realm, the king, and none rule us;
Mine enemies will I plague, my friends advance,
And what I list command, who dare control?
Maior sum quam cui possit fortuna nocere;
And that this be the coronation day
70   It pleaseth me and Isabel the queen.
        [*Trumpets sound offstage.*]
The trumpets sound. I must go take my place.
        Enter the young KING, [ARCH]BISHOP [OF CANTERBURY],
        CHAMPION, NOBLES, QUEEN [*and* ATTENDANTS].

CANTERBURY
Long live King Edward, by the grace of God,
King of England and Lord of Ireland!

CHAMPION
If any Christian, Heathen, Turk, or Jew
Dares but affirm that Edward's not true king,
And will avouch his saying with the sword,
I am the champion that will combat him.

MORTIMER None comes. Sound, trumpets!
        [*The trumpets sound.*]

EDWARD III Champion, here's to thee.

QUEEN
80   Lord Mortimer, now take him to your charge.
        Enter SOLDIERS *with the* EARL OF KENT *prisoner.*

MORTIMER
What traitor have we there, with blades and bills?

SOLDIER
Edmund, the earl of Kent.

EDWARD III   What hath he done?

SOLDIER

 'A would have taken the king away perforce

 As we were bringing him to Killingworth.

MORTIMER

 Did you attempt his rescue, Edmund? Speak.

KENT

 Mortimer, I did; he is our king,

 And thou compell'st this prince to wear the crown.

MORTIMER

 Strike off his head! He shall have martial law.

KENT

 Strike off my head? Base traitor, I defy thee.

EDWARD III [*to* MORTIMER JUNIOR]

 My lord, he is my uncle and shall live.   90

MORTIMER

 My lord, he is your enemy and shall die.

  [*The* SOLDIERS *seize* KENT.]

KENT Stay, villains!

EDWARD III

 Sweet mother, if I cannot pardon him,

 Entreat my Lord Protector for his life.

QUEEN

 Son, be content. I dare not speak a word.

EDWARD III

 Nor I, and yet methinks I should command;

 But seeing I cannot, I'll entreat for him.

 My lord, if you will let my uncle live,

 I will requite it when I come of age.

MORTIMER

 'Tis for your highness' good, and for the realm's. 100

  [*To* SOLDIERS]

 How often shall I bid you bear him hence?

KENT

 Art thou king? Must I die at thy command?

MORTIMER

 At our command. Once more, away with him.

KENT

 Let me but stay and speak; I will not go.

Either my brother or his son is king,
And none of both them thirst for Edmund's blood.
And therefore, soldiers, whither will you hale me?
  They hale EDMUND [EARL OF KENT] *away, and carry him*
  to be beheaded.

EDWARD III
  What safety may I look for at his hands
  If that my uncle shall be murdered thus?

QUEEN
110 Fear not, sweet boy, I'll guard thee from thy foes.
  Had Edmund lived, he would have sought thy death.
  Come, son, we'll ride a-hunting in the park.

EDWARD III
  And shall my uncle Edmund ride with us?

QUEEN
  He is a traitor. Think not on him. Come.

                                           Exeunt.

[*Scene 25*]

  Enter MATREVIS *and* GURNEY [*with lights. A bed is thrust*
  onstage].

MATREVIS
  Gurney, I wonder the king dies not,
  Being in a vault up to the knees in water
  To which the channels of the castle run,
  From whence a damp continually ariseth
  That were enough to poison any man –
  Much more a king brought up so tenderly.

GURNEY
  And so do I, Matrevis. Yesternight
  I opened but the door to throw him meat,
  And I was almost stifled with the savour.

MATREVIS
10 He hath a body able to endure
  More than we can inflict, and therefore now

Let us assail his mind another while.

GURNEY
Send for him out thence, and I will anger him.

MATREVIS
But stay, who's this?
   Enter LIGHTBORNE.

LIGHTBORNE [*giving them the letter*]
                    My Lord Protector greets you.
   [MATREVIS *and* GURNEY *read the letter.*]

GURNEY [*aside to* MATREVIS]
What's here? I know not how to conster it.

MATREVIS [*aside to* GURNEY]
Gurney, it was left unpointed for the nonce.
'*Edwardum occidere nolite timere*',
That's his meaning.

LIGHTBORNE [*showing the token*]
Know you this token? I must have the king.

MATREVIS
Ay, stay a while, thou shalt have answer straight.   20
[*Aside to* GURNEY] This villain's sent to make away the king.

GURNEY [*aside to* MATREVIS]
I thought as much.

MATREVIS [*aside to* GURNEY] And when the murder's done,
See how he must be handled for his labour:
'*Pereat iste*.' Let him have the king.
What else?
[*To* LIGHTBORNE] Here is the keys, this is the lake.
   [*He points to the door of* EDWARD's *dungeon.*]
Do as you are commanded by my lord.

LIGHTBORNE
I know what I must do. Get you away.
Yet be not far off, I shall need your help.
See that in the next room I have a fire,
And get me a spit, and let it be red hot.   30

MATREVIS Very well.

GURNEY Need you anything besides?

LIGHTBORNE What else? A table and a featherbed.

GURNEY That's all?

LIGHTBORNE Ay, ay, so; when I call you, bring it in.

MATREVIS Fear not you that.

GURNEY [*giving a light*]

Here's a light to go into the dungeon.

LIGHTBORNE So.

[*Exeunt* MATREVIS *and* GURNEY.]

Now must I about this gear. Ne'er was there any

40 So finely handled as this king shall be.

[LIGHTBORNE *opens the door to the dungeon.*]

Foh! Here's a place indeed, with all my heart.

[*Enter* KING EDWARD.]

EDWARD

Who's there? What light is that? Wherefore comes thou?

LIGHTBORNE

To comfort you and bring you joyful news.

EDWARD

Small comfort finds poor Edward in thy looks.

Villain, I know thou com'st to murder me.

LIGHTBORNE

To murder you, my most gracious lord?

Far is it from my heart to do you harm.

The queen sent me to see how you were used,

For she relents at this your misery.

50 And what eyes can refrain from shedding tears

To see a king in this most piteous state?

EDWARD

Weep'st thou already? List a while to me,

And then thy heart, were it as Gurney's is,

Or as Matrevis', hewn from the Caucasus,

Yet will it melt ere I have done my tale.

This dungeon where they keep me is the sink

Wherein the filth of all the castle falls.

LIGHTBORNE O, villains!

EDWARD

And there in mire and puddle have I stood

60 This ten days' space, and, lest that I should sleep,

One plays continually upon a drum.

They give me bread and water, being a king,
So that for want of sleep and sustenance
My mind's distempered and my body's numbed,
And whether I have limbs or no I know not.
O, would my blood dropped out from every vein
As doth this water from my tattered robes!
Tell Isabel the queen I looked not thus,
When for her sake I ran at tilt in France,
And there unhorsed the duke of Cleremont.   70

LIGHTBORNE

O, speak no more, my lord! This breaks my heart.
Lie on this bed and rest yourself a while.

EDWARD

These looks of thine can harbour nought but death;
I see my tragedy written in thy brows.
Yet stay a while; forbear thy bloody hand,
And let me see the stroke before it comes,
That, even then when I shall lose my life,
My mind may be more steadfast on my God.

LIGHTBORNE

What means your highness to mistrust me thus?

EDWARD

What means thou to dissemble with me thus?   80

LIGHTBORNE

These hands were never stained with innocent blood,
Nor shall they now be tainted with a king's.

EDWARD

Forgive my thought for having such a thought.
One jewel have I left; receive thou this.
    [*He gives a jewel.*]
Still fear I, and I know not what's the cause,
But every joint shakes as I give it thee.
O, if thou harbour'st murder in thy heart,
Let this gift change thy mind and save thy soul.
Know that I am a king. O, at that name
I feel a hell of grief. Where is my crown?   90
Gone, gone, and do I remain alive?

LIGHTBORNE
>You're overwatched, my lord. Lie down and rest.

EDWARD
>But that grief keeps me waking, I should sleep,
>For not these ten days have these eyes' lids closed;
>Now as I speak they fall, and yet with fear
>Open again. [LIGHTBORNE *sits on the bed*.]
>   O, wherefore sits thou here?

LIGHTBORNE
>If you mistrust me, I'll be gone, my lord.

EDWARD
>No, no, for if thou mean'st to murder me
>Thou wilt return again, and therefore stay.

100 LIGHTBORNE He sleeps.

EDWARD
>O, let me not die yet! Stay, O, stay a while!

LIGHTBORNE How now, my lord?

EDWARD
>Something still buzzeth in mine ears
>And tells me if I sleep I never wake;
>This fear is that which makes me tremble thus.
>And therefore tell me: wherefore art thou come?

LIGHTBORNE
>To rid thee of thy life. Matrevis, come!
>   [*Enter* MATREVIS *and* GURNEY.]

EDWARD
>I am too weak and feeble to resist.
>Assist me, sweet God, and receive my soul!

110 LIGHTBORNE Run for the table.

EDWARD
>O, spare me, or dispatch me in a trice!
>   [MATREVIS *and* GURNEY *bring in a table and a red-hot*
>   *spit*.]

LIGHTBORNE
>So, lay the table down, and stamp on it,
>But not too hard, lest that you bruise his body.
>   [EDWARD *dies*.]

MATREVIS

I fear me that this cry will raise the town,
And therefore let us take horse and away.

LIGHTBORNE

Tell me, sirs, was it not bravely done?

GURNEY

Excellent well. Take this for thy reward.
    Then GURNEY *stabs* LIGHTBORNE.
Come, let us cast the body in the moat,
And bear the king's to Mortimer, our lord.
Away!   120
                                        Exeunt [with the bodies].

[*Scene 26*]

Enter MORTIMER [JUNIOR] *and* MATREVIS [*at different
    doors*].

MORTIMER

Is't done, Matrevis, and the murderer dead?

MATREVIS

Ay, my good lord. I would it were undone.

MORTIMER

Matrevis, if thou now growest penitent,
I'll be thy ghostly father. Therefore choose
Whether thou wilt be secret in this
Or else die by the hand of Mortimer.

MATREVIS

Gurney, my lord, is fled, and will, I fear,
Betray us both; therefore let me fly.

MORTIMER Fly to the savages.

MATREVIS I humbly thank your honour.   10
                                        [*Exit* MATREVIS.]

MORTIMER

As for myself, I stand as Jove's huge tree,
And others are but shrubs compared to me;
All tremble at my name, and I fear none.
Let's see who dare impeach me for his death?

Enter the QUEEN.

QUEEN

Ah, Mortimer, the king my son hath news
His father's dead, and we have murdered him.

MORTIMER

What if he have? The king is yet a child.

QUEEN

Ay, ay, but he tears his hair, and wrings his hands,
And vows to be revenged upon us both.
20   Into the council chamber he is gone
To crave the aid and succour of his peers.
Ay me! See where he comes, and they with him.
Now, Mortimer, begins our tragedy.
      Enter the KING, *with the* LORDS [*and* ATTENDANTS].

FIRST LORD

Fear not, my lord. Know that you are a king.

EDWARD III [*to* MORTIMER JUNIOR]

Villain!

MORTIMER

How now, my lord?

EDWARD III

Think not that I am frighted with thy words.
My father's murdered through thy treachery,
And thou shalt die, and on his mournful hearse
30   Thy hateful and accursèd head shall lie,
To witness to the world that by thy means
His kingly body was too soon interred.

QUEEN

Weep not, sweet son.

EDWARD III

Forbid not me to weep. He was my father,
And, had you loved him half so well as I,
You could not bear his death thus patiently;
But you, I fear, conspired with Mortimer.

FIRST LORD [*to* MORTIMER JUNIOR]

Why speak you not unto my lord the king?

MORTIMER
    Because I think scorn to be accused.
    Who is the man dare say I murdered him?   40

EDWARD III
    Traitor, in me my loving father speaks
    And plainly saith 'twas thou that murdered'st him.

MORTIMER
    But hath your grace no other proof than this?

EDWARD III
    Yes, if this be the hand of Mortimer.
      [*He shows the letter.*]

MORTIMER [*aside*]
    False Gurney hath betrayed me and himself.

QUEEN [*aside*]
    I feared as much. Murder cannot be hid.

MORTIMER
    'Tis my hand. What gather you by this?

EDWARD III
    That thither thou didst send a murderer.

MORTIMER
    What murderer? Bring forth the man I sent.

EDWARD III
    Ah, Mortimer, thou knowest that he is slain,   50
    And so shalt thou be too. Why stays he here?
    Bring him unto a hurdle! Drag him forth,
    Hang him, I say, and set his quarters up,
    But bring his head back presently to me.

QUEEN
    For my sake, sweet son, pity Mortimer.

MORTIMER
    Madam, entreat not. I will rather die
    Than sue for life unto a paltry boy.

EDWARD III
    Hence with the traitor, with the murderer!

MORTIMER
    Base Fortune, now I see that in thy wheel
    There is a point to which when men aspire   60

They tumble headlong down. That point I touched,
And, seeing there was no place to mount up higher,
Why should I grieve at my declining fall?
Farewell, fair queen. Weep not for Mortimer,
That scorns the world, and as a traveller
Goes to discover countries yet unknown.

EDWARD III [*to his* LORDS *and* ATTENDANTS]
What, suffer you the traitor to delay?

> [*Exit* MORTIMER JUNIOR, *guarded, with the* FIRST
> LORD.]

QUEEN
As thou received'st thy life from me,
Spill not the blood of gentle Mortimer.

EDWARD III
70 This argues that you spilt my father's blood,
Else would you not entreat for Mortimer.

QUEEN
I spill his blood? No.

EDWARD III
Ay, madam, you, for so the rumour runs.

QUEEN
That rumour is untrue; for loving thee
Is this report raised on poor Isabel.

EDWARD III [*to his* LORDS]
I do not think her so unnatural.

SECOND LORD
My lord, I fear me it will prove too true.

EDWARD III
Mother, you are suspected for his death,
And therefore we commit you to the Tower
80 Till further trial may be made thereof.
If you be guilty, though I be your son,
Think not to find me slack or pitiful.

QUEEN
Nay, to my death, for too long have I lived
Whenas my son thinks to abridge my days.

EDWARD III [*weeping*]
Away with her! Her words enforce these tears,

And I shall pity her if she speak again.

QUEEN

Shall I not mourn for my belovèd lord,
And with the rest accompany him to his grave?

SECOND LORD

Thus, madam, 'tis the king's will you shall hence.

QUEEN

He hath forgotten me. Stay, I am his mother.   90

SECOND LORD

That boots not. Therefore, gentle madam, go.

QUEEN

Then come, sweet death, and rid me of this grief.

                [*Exit the* QUEEN, *attended.*
   Enter the FIRST LORD *with* MORTIMER'*s head.*]

FIRST LORD

My lord, here is the head of Mortimer.

EDWARD III

Go fetch my father's hearse, where it shall lie,
And bring my funeral robes. Accursèd head,
Could I have ruled thee then as I do now,
Thou hadst not hatched this monstrous treachery!
   [*Enter* ATTENDANTS *with hearse.*]
Here comes the hearse. Help me to mourn, my lords.
Sweet father, here unto thy murdered ghost
I offer up this wicked traitor's head;   100
And let these tears distilling from mine eyes,
Be witness of my grief and innocency!

                       [*Exeunt.*]

THE MASSACRE AT PARIS

[Dramatis Personae

KING CHARLES IX, *King of France*
CATHERINE, *the Queen-Mother of France*
KING OF NAVARRE, *later King Henry IV*
PRINCE OF CONDÉ, *cousin to Navarre*
THE LORD HIGH ADMIRAL
MARGARET, *Catherine's daughter, wife to Navarre*
DUKE OF GUISE
AN APOTHECARY
A SOLDIER
OLD QUEEN OF NAVARRE, *mother of Henry,*
King of Navarre
DUKE OF ANJOU, *Charles IX's brother, later King Henry III*
DUKE DUMAINE
COSSIN
THE ADMIRAL'S MAN
GONZAGO
RETES
MOUNTSORRELL
LOREINE, *a Protestant preacher*
SEROUNE'S WIFE
SEROUNE
RAMUS
TALEUS
TWO SCHOOLMASTERS
TWO LORDS OF POLAND
TWO SOLDIERS
CARDINAL OF LORRAINE
PROTESTANTS

EPERNOUN

PLESHÉ

DUKE JOYEUX

MUGEROUN

A CUTPURSE

DUCHESS OF GUISE

MAID *to the Duchess of Guise*

BARTUS

A MESSENGER

CAPTAIN OF THE GUARD

THREE MURDERERS

THE GUISE'S SON

A FRIAR

A SURGEON

AN ENGLISH AGENT

ATTENDANTS]

[Scene 1]

Enter CHARLES *the French King,* [CATHERINE] *the*
QUEEN-MOTHER, *the* KING OF NAVARRE, *the* PRINCE OF
CONDÉ, *the* LORD HIGH ADMIRAL, *and* [MARGARET] *the*
QUEEN OF NAVARRE, *with others.*

CHARLES
Prince of Navarre, my honourable brother,
Prince Condé, and my good Lord Admiral,
I wish this union and religious league,
Knit in these hands, thus joined in nuptial rites,
May not dissolve till death dissolve our lives,
And that the native sparks of princely love,
That kindled first this motion in our hearts,
May still be fuelled in our progeny.

NAVARRE
The many favours which your grace hath shown
From time to time, but specially in this,   10
Shall bind me ever to your highness' will,
In what queen-mother or your grace commands.

CATHERINE
Thanks, son Navarre, you see we love you well
That link you in marriage with our daughter here;
And, as you know, our difference in religion
Might be a means to cross you in your love.

CHARLES
Well, madam, let that rest.
And now, my lords, the marriage-rites performed,

We think it good to go and consummate
20   The rest with hearing of a holy mass.
Sister, I think yourself will bear us company.

MARGARET I will, my good lord.

CHARLES

The rest that will not go, my lords, may stay.
Come, mother, let us go to honour this solemnity.

CATHERINE [*aside*]

Which I'll dissolve with blood and cruelty.

> *Exeunt the* KING [CHARLES], *the* QUEEN-MOTHER, *and
> the* QUEEN OF NAVARRE [*with others*]; NAVARRE, *the*
> PRINCE OF CONDÉ, *and the* LORD HIGH ADMIRAL
> *remain.*

NAVARRE

Prince Condé, and my good Lord Admiral,
Now Guise may storm, but do us little hurt,
Having the king, queen-mother on our sides,
To stop the malice of his envious heart
30   That seeks to murder all the protestants.
Have you not heard of late how he decreed
If that the king had given consent thereto,
That all the protestants that are in Paris
Should have been murderèd the other night?

ADMIRAL

My lord, I marvel that th'aspiring Guise
Dares once adventure, without the king's consent,
To meddle or attempt such dangerous things.

CONDÉ

My lord, you need not marvel at the Guise,
For what he doth the Pope will ratify,
40   In murder, mischief, or in tyranny.

NAVARRE

But He that sits and rules above the clouds
Doth hear and see the prayers of the just,
And will revenge the blood of innocents
That Guise hath slain by treason of his heart,
And brought by murder to their timeless ends.

ADMIRAL
  My lord, but did you mark the Cardinal,
  The Guise's brother, and the Duke Dumaine,
  How they did storm at these your nuptial rites,
  Because the house of Bourbon now comes in
  And joins your lineage to the crown of France?   50
NAVARRE
  And that's the cause that Guise so frowns at us
  And beats his brains to catch us in his trap,
  Which he hath pitched within his deadly toil.
  Come, my lords, let's go to the church, and pray
  That God may still defend the right of France
  And make His Gospel flourish in this land.

                                                    Exeunt.

[*Scene 2*]

  Enter the DUKE OF GUISE.
GUISE
  If ever Hymen loured at marriage-rites,
  And had his altars decked with dusky lights;
  If ever sun stained heaven with bloody clouds,
  And made it look with terror on the world;
  If ever day were turned to ugly night,
  And night made semblance of the hue of hell;
  This day, this hour, this fatal night,
  Shall fully show the fury of them all.
  Apothecary!
      Enter the APOTHECARY.
APOTHECARY My lord?   10
GUISE
  Now shall I prove and guerdon to the full
  The love thou bear'st unto the house of Guise.
  Where are those perfumèd gloves which I sent
  To be poisonèd? Hast thou done them? Speak!

Will every savour breed a pang of death?
APOTHECARY
  See where they be, my good lord,
  And he that smells but to them dies.
GUISE
  Then thou remainest resolute?
APOTHECARY
  I am, my lord, in what your grace commands,
20 Till death.
GUISE
  Thanks, my good friend, I will requite thy love.
  Go, then, present them to the Queen Navarre;
  For she is that huge blemish in our eye
  That makes these upstart heresies in France.
  Be gone, my friend, present them to her straight.

                              Exit APOTHECARY.

  Soldier!
    Enter a SOLDIER.
SOLDIER My lord?
GUISE
  Now come thou forth and play thy tragic part.
  Stand in some window opening near the street,
30 And when thou see'st the Admiral ride by,
  Discharge thy musket and perform his death,
  And then I'll guerdon thee with store of crowns.
SOLDIER I will, my lord.

                                     Exit.

GUISE
  Now, Guise, begin those deep-engendered thoughts
  To burst abroad those never-dying flames
  Which cannot be extinguished but by blood.
  Oft have I levelled, and at last have learned
  That peril is the chiefest way to happiness,
  And resolution honour's fairest aim.
40 What glory is there in a common good
  That hangs for every peasant to achieve?
  That like I best that flies beyond my reach.

Set me to scale the high pyramides,
And thereon set the diadem of France;
I'll either rend it with my nails to naught,
Or mount the top with my aspiring wings,
Although my downfall be the deepest hell.
For this I wake, when others think I sleep,
For this I wait, that scorns attendance else,
For this, my quenchless thirst whereon I build,   50
Hath often pleaded kindred to the king.
For this, this head, this heart, this hand and sword,
Contrives, imagines, and fully executes
Matters of import aimed at by many,
Yet understood by none.
For this, hath heaven engendered me of earth,
For this, this earth sustains my body's weight,
And with this weight I'll counterpoise a crown,
Or with seditions weary all the world.
For this, from Spain the stately Catholics   60
Sends Indian gold to coin me French *écues*;
For this, have I a largess from the Pope,
A pension and a dispensation too;
And by that privilege to work upon,
My policy hath framed religion.
Religion: *O Diabole!*
Fie, I am ashamed, how ever that I seem,
To think a word of such a simple sound,
Of so great matter should be made the ground.
The gentle king, whose pleasure uncontrolled   70
Weak'neth his body and will waste his realm,
If I repair not what he ruinates –
Him, as a child, I daily win with words,
So that for proof he barely bears the name;
I execute, and he sustains the blame.
The mother queen works wonders for my sake,
And in my love entombs the hope of France,
Rifling the bowels of her treasury
To supply my wants and necessity.

80   Paris hath full five hundred colleges –
      As monasteries, priories, abbeys, and halls –
      Wherein are thirty thousand able men,
      Besides a thousand sturdy student Catholics;
      And more – of my knowledge, in one cloister keeps
      Five hundred fat Franciscan friars and priests.
      All this, and more, if more may be comprised,
      To bring the will of our desires to end.
      Then, Guise, since thou hast all the cards within thy hands
      To shuffle or cut, take this as surest thing:
90   That, right or wrong, thou deal thyself a king.
      Ay, but Navarre, Navarre, 'tis but a nook of France,
      Sufficient yet for such a petty king,
      That, with a rabblement of his heretics,
      Blinds Europe's eyes and troubleth our estate.
      Him will we –
            Pointing to his sword.
      But first let's follow those in France
      That hinder our possession to the crown.
      As Caesar to his soldiers, so say I:
      Those that hate me will I learn to loathe.
100   Give me a look that, when I bend the brows,
      Pale death may walk in furrows of my face,
      A hand that with a grasp may gripe the world,
      An ear to hear what my detractors say,
      A royal seat, a sceptre, and a crown;
      That those which do behold, they may become
      As men that stand and gaze against the sun.
      The plot is laid, and things shall come to pass
      Where resolution strives for victory.

                                                              Exit.

[*Scene 3*]

Enter the KING OF NAVARRE *and* QUEEN [MARGARET],
and his MOTHER QUEEN [*the* OLD QUEEN], *the* PRINCE
OF CONDÉ, *the* ADMIRAL, *and the* APOTHECARY *with the
gloves, and he gives them to the* OLD QUEEN.

APOTHECARY Madam, I beseech your grace to accept this
simple gift.

OLD QUEEN Thanks, my good friend. Hold, take thou this
reward.

APOTHECARY I humbly thank your majesty.

Exit APOTHECARY.

OLD QUEEN
Methinks the gloves have a very strong perfume,
The scent whereof doth make my head to ache.

NAVARRE
Doth not your grace know the man that gave them you?

OLD QUEEN
Not well, but do remember such a man.

ADMIRAL
Your grace was ill-advised to take them, then,   10
Considering of these dangerous times.

OLD QUEEN
Help, son Navarre, I am poisoned!

MARGARET
The heavens forbid your highness such mishap!

NAVARRE
The late suspicion of the duke of Guise
Might well have moved your highness to beware
How you did meddle with such dangerous gifts.

MARGARET
Too late it is, my lord, if that be true,
To blame her highness, but I hope it be
Only some natural passion makes her sick.

OLD QUEEN
O, no, sweet Margaret, the fatal poison   20

Works within my head; my brain-pan breaks,
My heart doth faint, I die!
   She dies.

NAVARRE
My mother poisoned here before my face!
O gracious God, what times are these?
O grant, sweet God, my days may end with hers,
That I with her may die and live again!

MARGARET
Let not this heavy chance, my dearest lord,
For whose effects my soul is massacred,
Infect thy gracious breast with fresh supply
30 To aggravate our sudden misery.

ADMIRAL
Come, my lords, let us bear her body hence,
And see it honoured with just solemnity.
   As they are going, the SOLDIER *dischargeth his musket at
   the* LORD ADMIRAL.

CONDÉ
What, are you hurt, my Lord High Admiral?

ADMIRAL
Ay, my good lord, shot through the arm.

NAVARRE We are betrayed! Come, my lords, and let us go tell
the king of this.

ADMIRAL
These are the cursed Guisians that do seek our death.
O, fatal was this marriage to us all.
   They bear away the [OLD] QUEEN *and go out.*

[Scene 4]

Enter the KING [CHARLES], [CATHERINE *the*] QUEEN-
MOTHER, *the* DUKE OF GUISE, DUKE ANJOU, DUKE
DUMAINE [, COSSIN *and* ATTENDANTS].

CATHERINE
My noble son, and princely duke of Guise,
Now have we got the fatal straggling deer
Within the compass of a deadly toil,
And as we late decreed we may perform.

CHARLES
Madam, it will be noted through the world
An action bloody and tyrannical –
Chiefly since under safety of our word
They justly challenge their protection.
Besides, my heart relents that noble men,
Only corrupted in religion,   10
Ladies of honour, knights, and gentlemen,
Should for their conscience taste such ruthless ends.

ANJOU
Though gentle minds should pity others' pains,
Yet will the wisest note their proper griefs,
And rather seek to scourge their enemies
Than be themselves base subjects to the whip.

GUISE
Methinks, my lord, Anjou hath well advised
Your highness to consider of the thing,
And rather choose to seek your country's good
Than pity or relieve these upstart heretics.   20

CATHERINE
I hope these reasons may serve my princely son
To have some care for fear of enemies.

CHARLES
Well, madam, I refer it to your majesty,
And to my nephew here, the duke of Guise:
What you determine, I will ratify.

CATHERINE
    Thanks to my princely son. Then tell me, Guise,
    What order will you set down for the massacre?
GUISE
    Thus, madam:
    They that shall be actors in this massacre
30   Shall wear white crosses on their burgonets,
    And tie white linen scarfs about their arms;
    He that wants these and is suspect of heresy,
    Shall die, be he king or emperor. Then I'll have
    A peal of ordinance shot from the tower,
    At which they all shall issue out and set the streets;
    And then, the watchword being given, a bell shall ring,
    Which when they hear, they shall begin to kill,
    And never cease until that bell shall cease;
    Then breathe a while.
        Enter the ADMIRAL'S MAN.
CHARLES
40   How now, fellow, what news?
MAN
    An it please your grace, the Lord High Admiral,
    Riding the streets, was traitorously shot,
    And most humble entreats your majesty
    To visit him sick in his bed.
CHARLES
    Messenger, tell him I will see him straight.
                        Exit [ADMIRAL'S MAN].
    What shall we do now with the Admiral?
CATHERINE
    Your majesty were best go visit him,
    And make a show as if all were well.
CHARLES
    Content, I will go visit the Admiral.
GUISE [*aside*]
50   And I will go take order for his death.
                                      Exit.

    Enter the ADMIRAL *in his bed.*

CHARLES
How fares it with my Lord High Admiral?
Hath he been hurt with villains in the street?
I vow and swear, as I am King of France,
To find and to repay the man with death,
With death delayed and torments never used,
That durst presume, for hope of any gain,
To hurt the noble man their sovereign loves.

ADMIRAL
Ah, my good lord, these are the Guisians
That seek to massacre our guiltless lives.

CHARLES
Assure yourself, my good Lord Admiral,   60
I deeply sorrow for your treacherous wrong,
And that I am not more secure myself
Than I am careful you should be preserved.
Cossin, take twenty of our strongest guard,
And under your direction see they keep
All treacherous violence from our noble friend,
Repaying all attempts with present death
Upon the cursèd breakers of our peace.
And so be patient, good Lord Admiral,
And every hour I will visit you.   70

ADMIRAL
I humbly thank your royal majesty.

                                          Exeunt.

[*Scene 5*]

Enter GUISE, ANJOU, DUMAINE, GONZAGO, RETES,
MOUNTSORRELL, *and* SOLDIERS *to the massacre.*

GUISE
Anjou, Dumaine, Gonzago, Retes, swear
By the argent crosses in your burgonets
To kill all that you suspect of heresy.

DUMAINE
 I swear by this to be unmerciful.
ANJOU
 I am disguised and none knows who I am,
 And therefore mean to murder all I meet.
GONZAGO
 And so will I.
RETES   And I.
GUISE
 Away, then, break into the Admiral's house.
RETES
 Ay, let the Admiral be first dispatched.
GUISE
10 The Admiral,
 Chief standard-bearer to the Lutherans,
 Shall in the entrance of this massacre
 Be murdered in his bed.
 Gonzago, conduct them thither, and then
 Beset his house, that not a man may live.
ANJOU
 That charge is mine. Switzers, keep you the streets;
 And at each corner shall the king's guard stand.
GONZAGO Come, sirs, follow me.
                    Exit GONZAGO *and others with him.*
ANJOU
 Cossin, the captain of the Admiral's guard,
20 Placed by my brother, will betray his lord.
 Now, Guise, shall Catholics flourish once again,
 The head being off, the members cannot stand.
RETES
 But look, my lord, there's some in the Admiral's house.
     Enter [GONZAGO *and others*] *into the* ADMIRAL's *house,
     and he in his bed.*
ANJOU
 In lucky time; come, let us keep this lane
 And slay his servants that shall issue out.
GONZAGO Where is the Admiral?

ADMIRAL O, let me pray before I die!

GONZAGO Then pray unto our Lady; kiss this cross.
    Stab him.

ADMIRAL O God, forgive my sins!
    [*Dies.*]

GUISE Gonzago, what, is he dead?   30

GONZAGO Ay, my lord.

GUISE Then throw him down.
    [*The body of the* ADMIRAL *is thrown down.*]

ANJOU Now, cousin, view him well; it may be it is some other
    and he escaped.

GUISE
    Cousin, 'tis he, I know him by his look.
    See where my soldier shot him through the arm;
    He missed him near, but we have struck him now.
    Ah, base Shatillian and degenerate,
    Chief standard-bearer to the Lutherans,
    Thus in despite of thy religion   40
    The duke of Guise stamps on thy lifeless bulk!

ANJOU
    Away with him! Cut off his head and hands,
    And send them for a present to the Pope;
    And when this just revenge is finished,
    Unto Mount Faucon will we drag his corse,
    And he that living hated so the cross,
    Shall, being dead, be hanged thereon in chains.

GUISE
    Anjou, Gonzago, Retes, if that you three
    Will be as resolute as I and Dumaine,
    There shall not be a Huguenot breathe in France.   50

ANJOU
    I swear by this cross, we'll not be partial,
    But slay as many as we can come near.

GUISE
    Mountsorrell, go shoot the ordnance off,
    That they which have already set the street
    May know their watchword, then toll the bell,

And so let's forward to the massacre.
MOUNTSORRELL I will, my lord.

Exit MOUNTSORRELL.

GUISE And now, my lords, let us closely to our business.
ANJOU Anjou will follow thee.
60   DUMAINE And so will Dumaine.
      The ordinance being shot off, the bell tolls.
GUISE Come, then, let's away.

Exeunt.

[Scene 6]

The GUISE *enters again, with all the rest, with their swords
drawn, chasing the* PROTESTANTS.
GUISE *Tue, tue, tue!*
      Let none escape. Murder the Huguenots.
ANJOU Kill them, kill them!

Exeunt.

[Scene 7]

Enter LOREINE, *running; the* GUISE *and the rest pursuing
him.*
GUISE
      Loreine, Loreine, follow Loreine! Sirrah,
      Are you a preacher of these heresies?
LOREINE
      I am a preacher of the word of God,
      And thou a traitor to thy soul and Him.
GUISE
5   'Dearly beloved brother' – thus 'tis written.
      He stabs him [and LOREINE *dies].*
ANJOU
      Stay, my lord, let me begin the psalm.

GUISE
  Come, drag him away, and throw him in a ditch.

                                                              Exeunt.

[*Scene 8*]

  Enter MOUNTSORRELL *and knocks at* SEROUNE's *door.*
SEROUNE'S WIFE [*within*] Who is that which knocks there?
MOUNTSORRELL Mountsorrell, from the duke of Guise.
SEROUNE'S WIFE [*within*] Husband, come down, here's one
  would speak with you from the duke of Guise.
  Enter SEROUNE.
SEROUNE To speak with me, from such a man as he?
MOUNTSORRELL Ay, ay, for this, Seroune, and thou shalt ha't.
  Showing his dagger.
SEROUNE O, let me pray before I take my death.
MOUNTSORRELL Dispatch then, quickly.
SEROUNE O Christ, my saviour!
MOUNTSORRELL Christ, villain? Why dar'st thou to presume   10
  to call on Christ, without the intercession of some saint?
  Sanctus Jacobus, he was my saint; pray to him.
SEROUNE O, let me pray unto my God.
MOUNTSORRELL Then take this with you.
                                                      Stab him. Exit.

[*Scene 9*]

  Enter RAMUS *in his study.*
RAMUS
  What fearful cries comes from the river Seine
  That frights poor Ramus sitting at his book?
  I fear the Guisians have passed the bridge,
  And mean once more to menace me.
  Enter TALEUS.

TALEUS
   Fly, Ramus, fly, if thou wilt save thy life.
RAMUS
   Tell me, Taleus, wherefore should I fly?
TALEUS
   The Guisians are
   Hard at thy door, and mean to murder us.
   Hark, hark, they come. I'll leap out at the window.
10 RAMUS Sweet Taleus, stay.
           Enter GONZAGO *and* RETES.
GONZAGO Who goes there?
RETES 'Tis Taleus, Ramus' bedfellow.
GONZAGO What art thou?
TALEUS I am as Ramus is – a Christian.
RETES O, let him go, he is a Catholic.
                                                    Exit TALEUS.

GONZAGO
   Come Ramus, more gold, or thou shalt have the stab.
RAMUS
   Alas, I am a scholar, how should I have gold?
   All that I have is but my stipend from the king,
   Which is no sooner received but it is spent.
           Enter the GUISE *and* ANJOU [*with* DUMAINE, MOUNT-
           SORRELL *and* SOLDIERS].
20 ANJOU Who have you there?
RETES 'Tis Ramus, the king's Professor of Logic.
GUISE Stab him.
RAMUS
   O, good my lord, wherein hath Ramus been so offencious?
GUISE
   Marry, sir, in having a smack in all,
   And yet didst never sound anything to the depth.
   Was it not thou that scoff'dst the *Organon*,
   And said it was a heap of vanities?
   He that will be a flat dichotomist,
   And seen in nothing but epitomes,
30 Is in your judgement thought a learnèd man;
   And he, forsooth, must go and preach in Germany,

Excepting against doctors' axioms,
And *ipse dixi* with this quiddity,
Argumentum testimonii est inartificiale.
To contradict which, I say: Ramus shall die.
How answer you that? Your *nego argumentum*
Cannot serve, sirrah. Kill him.

RAMUS

O, good my lord, let me but speak a word.

ANJOU Well, say on.

RAMUS

Not for my life do I desire this pause,   40
But in my latter hour to purge myself,
In that I know the things that I have wrote,
Which, as I hear, one Scheckius takes it ill,
Because my places, being but three, contains all his.
I knew the *Organon* to be confused,
And I reduced it into better form;
And this for Aristotle will I say,
That he that despiseth him can ne'er
Be good in logic or philosophy;
And that's because the blockish Sorbonnists   50
Attribute as much unto their works
As to the service of the eternal God.

GUISE

Why suffer you that peasant to declaim?
Stab him, I say, and send him to his friends in hell.

ANJOU

Ne'er was there collier's son so full of pride.
        Kills him.

GUISE

My lord of Anjou, there are a hundred Protestants
Which we have chased into the river Seine
That swim about and so preserve their lives;
How may we do? I fear me they will live.

DUMAINE

Go place some men upon the bridge   60
With bows and darts to shoot at them they see,
And sink them in the river as they swim.

GUISE

'Tis well advised, Dumaine; go see it straight be done.

[*Exit* DUMAINE.]

And, in the meantime, my lord, could we devise

To get those pedants from the King Navarre

That are tutors to him and the prince of Condé –

ANJOU

For that, let me alone; cousin, stay you here,

And when you see me in, then follow hard.

He [ANJOU] *knocketh, and enter the* KING OF NAVARRE *and* [*the*] PRINCE OF CONDÉ, *with their* [*two*] SCHOOL-MASTERS.

How now, my lords, how fare you?

NAVARRE   My lord, they say

70   That all the Protestants are massacred.

ANJOU

Ay, so they are, but yet what remedy?

I have done what I could to stay this broil.

NAVARRE

But yet, my lord, the report doth run

That you were one that made this massacre.

ANJOU

Who, I? You are deceived, I rose but now.

Enter [*to them*] GUISE [*with* GONZAGO, RETES, MOUNT-SORRELL *and* SOLDIERS].

GUISE

Murder the Huguenots, take those pedants hence.

NAVARRE

Thou traitor, Guise, lay off thy bloody hands.

CONDÉ Come, let us go tell the king.

Exeunt [CONDÉ *and* NAVARRE].

GUISE   Come sirs,

I'll whip you to death with my poniard's point.

He kills them [*the* SCHOOLMASTERS].

80   ANJOU Away with them both.

Exit ANJOU [*with* SOLDIERS *carrying the bodies*].

GUISE

And now, sirs, for this night let our fury stay.

Yet will we not that the massacre shall end:
Gonzago, post you to Orleans,
Retes to Dieppe, Mountsorrell unto Rouen,
And spare not one that you suspect of heresy.
And now stay that bell, that to the devil's matins rings.
Now every man put off his burgonet,
And so convey him closely to his bed.

Exeunt.

[*Scene 10*]

Enter ANJOU, *with two* LORDS OF POLAND.

ANJOU

My lords of Poland, I must needs confess
The offer of your Prince Electors far
Beyond the reach of my deserts;
For Poland is, as I have been informed,
A martial people, worthy such a king
As hath sufficient counsel in himself
To lighten doubts and frustrate subtle foes;
And such a king whom practice long hath taught
To please himself with manage of the wars,
The greatest wars within our Christian bounds –   10
I mean our wars against the Muscovites,
And on the other side against the Turk,
Rich princes both, and mighty emperors.
Yet by my brother Charles, our king of France,
And by his grace's council, it is thought
That if I undertake to wear the crown
Of Poland, it may prejudice their hope
Of my inheritance to the crown of France;
For, if th'almighty take my brother hence,
By due descent the regal seat is mine.   20
With Poland, therefore, must I covenant thus:
That if, by death of Charles, the diadem
Of France be cast on me, then with your leaves

I may retire me to my native home.
If your commission serve to warrant this,
I thankfully shall undertake the charge
Of you and yours, and carefully maintain
The wealth and safety of your kingdom's right.

FIRST LORD

All this and more your highness shall command
30   For Poland's crown and kingly diadem.

ANJOU Then come, my lords, let's go.

Exeunt.

[*Scene 11*]

Enter two [SOLDIERS] *with the* ADMIRAL'*s body.*

FIRST SOLDIER Now, sirrah, what shall we do with the
Admiral?

SECOND SOLDIER Why, let us burn him for an heretic.

FIRST SOLDIER O no, his body will infect the fire, and the fire
the air, and so we shall be poisoned with him.

SECOND SOLDIER What shall we do, then?

FIRST SOLDIER Let's throw him into the river.

SECOND SOLDIER O, 'twill corrupt the water, and the water
the fish, and by the fish ourselves when we eat them.

10   FIRST SOLDIER Then throw him into the ditch.

SECOND SOLDIER No, no, to decide all doubts, be ruled by me:
let's hang him here upon this tree.

FIRST SOLDIER Agreed.

They hang him [*and exeunt*].
Enter the DUKE OF GUISE, [CATHERINE *the*] QUEEN-
MOTHER, *and the* CARDINAL [*with* ATTENDANTS].

GUISE

Now, madam, how like you our lusty Admiral?

CATHERINE

Believe me, Guise, he becomes the place so well
As I could long ere this have wished him there.
But come, let's walk aside, th'air's not very sweet.

GUISE

   No, by my faith, madam.
   Sirs, take him away and throw him in some ditch.
             [*The* ATTENDANTS] *carry away the dead body.*
   And now, madam, as I understand,   20
   There are a hundred Huguenots and more
   Which in the woods do hold their synagogue,
   And daily meet about this time of day,
   And thither will I to put them to the sword.

CATHERINE

   Do so, sweet Guise, let us delay no time,
   For if these stragglers gather head again,
   And disperse themselves throughout the realm of France,
   It will be hard for us to work their deaths.
   Be gone, delay no time, sweet Guise.

GUISE   Madam,

   I go as whirlwinds rage before a storm.   30

                                Exit.

CATHERINE

   My lord of Lorraine, have you marked of late
   How Charles, our son, begins for to lament
   For the late night's work which my lord of Guise
   Did make in Paris amongst the Huguenots?

CARDINAL

   Madam, I have heard him solemnly vow
   With the rebellious King of Navarre
   For to revenge their deaths upon us all.

CATHERINE

   Ay, but my lord, let me alone for that,
   For Catherine must have her will in France.
   As I do live, so surely shall he die,   40
   And Henry then shall wear the diadem;
   And if he grudge or cross his mother's will,
   I'll disinherit him and all the rest;
   For I'll rule France, but they shall wear the crown,
   And, if they storm, I then may pull them down.
   Come, my lord, let us go.

                               Exeunt.

[*Scene 12*]

Enter five or six PROTESTANTS *with books, and kneel together. Enter also the* GUISE *and* [*others*].

GUISE

Down with the Huguenots! Murder them!

FIRST PROTESTANT

O *monsieur de Guise*, hear me but speak!

GUISE

No, villain, that tongue of thine

That hath blasphemed the holy Church of Rome,

5   Shall drive no plaints into the Guise's ears

To make the justice of my heart relent.

Tue, tue, tue! Let none escape.

   Kill them.

So, drag them away.

Exeunt.

[*Scene 13*]

Enter the KING OF FRANCE, NAVARRE *and* EPERNOUN *staying him; enter* [CATHERINE *the*] QUEEN-MOTHER *and the* CARDINAL [, PLESHÉ *and* ATTENDANTS].

CHARLES

O, let me stay and rest me here a while,

A griping pain hath seized upon my heart;

A sudden pang, the messenger of death.

CATHERINE

O say not so, thou kill'st thy mother's heart.

CHARLES

I must say so; pain forceth me complain.

NAVARRE

Comfort yourself, my lord, and have no doubt

But God will sure restore you to your health.

CHARLES
    O no, my loving brother of Navarre!
    I have deserved a scourge, I must confess;
    Yet is their patience of another sort   10
    Than to misdo the welfare of their king:
    God grant my nearest friends may prove no worse!
    O hold me up, my sight begins to fail,
    My sinews shrink, my brains turn upside down,
    My heart doth break, I faint and die.
        He dies.

CATHERINE
    What, art thou dead? Sweet son, speak to thy mother!
    O no, his soul is fled from out his breast,
    And he nor hears nor sees us what we do.
    My lords, what resteth there now for to be done,
    But that we presently dispatch ambassadors   20
    To Poland to call Henry back again
    To wear his brother's crown and dignity?
    Epernoun, go see it presently be done,
    And bid him come without delay to us.

EPERNOUN Madam, I will.

                                              Exit.

CATHERINE
    And now, my lords, after these funerals be done,
    We will, with all the speed we can, provide
    For Henry's coronation from Polony.
    Come, let us take his body hence.
                All go out but NAVARRE *and* PLESHÉ.

NAVARRE
    And now, Navarre, whilst that these broils do last,   30
    My opportunity may serve me fit
    To steal from France and hie me to my home,
    For here's no safety in the realm for me;
    And now that Henry is called from Poland,
    It is my due, by just succession;
    And therefore, as speedily as I can perform,
    I'll muster up an army secretly,

For fear that Guise, joined with the King of Spain,
Might seem to cross me in mine enterprise.
40   But God that always doth defend the right
Will show His mercy and preserve us still.
PLESHÉ
The virtues of our true religion
Cannot but march with many graces more,
Whose army shall discomfort all your foes,
And, at the length, in Pampelonia crown,
(In spite of Spain and all the popish power
That holds it from your highness wrongfully)
Your majesty her rightful lord and sovereign.
NAVARRE
Truth, Pleshé; and God so prosper me in all
50   As I intend to labour for the truth
And true profession of His holy word!
Come, Pleshé, let's away whilst time doth serve.

                                                        Exeunt.

[*Scene 14*]

Sound trumpets within, and then all cry 'vive le roi' *two or
three times. Enter* HENRY [ANJOU] *crowned;* [CATHERINE
the*] QUEEN[-MOTHER], CARDINAL, DUKE OF GUISE,
EPERNOUN, *the King's Minions* [JOYEUX *and*
MUGEROUN], *with others, and the* CUTPURSE.
ALL *Vive le roi, vive le roi!*
    (*Sound trumpets.*)
CATHERINE
Welcome from Poland, Henry, once again,
Welcome to France, thy father's royal seat.
Here hast thou a country void of fears,
A warlike people to maintain thy right,
A watchful senate for ordaining laws,
A loving mother to preserve thy state,
And all things that a king may wish besides;

All this and more hath Henry with his crown.

CARDINAL

And long may Henry enjoy all this, and more!   10

ALL *Vive le roi, vive le roi!*
    (*Sound trumpets.*)

HENRY

Thanks to you all. The guider of all crowns
Grant that our deeds may well deserve your loves!
And so they shall, if fortune speed my will,
And yield your thoughts to height of my deserts.
What says our minions? Think they Henry's heart
Will not both harbour love and majesty?
Put off that fear, they are already joined.
No person, place, or time, or circumstance,
Shall slack my love's affection from his bent.   20
As now you are, so shall you still persist,
Removeless from the favours of your king.

MUGEROUN

We know that noble minds change not their thoughts
For wearing of a crown, in that your grace
Hath worn the Poland diadem before
You were invested in the crown of France.

HENRY

I tell thee, Mugeroun, we will be friends,
And fellows too, whatever storms arise.

MUGEROUN

Then may it please your majesty to give me leave
To punish those that do profane this holy feast.   30
    He cuts off the CUTPURSE's *ear, for cutting of the gold
    buttons off his cloak.*

HENRY How mean'st thou that?

CUTPURSE O lord, mine ear!

MUGEROUN

Come, sir, give me my buttons, and here's your ear.

GUISE [*to an* ATTENDANT] Sirrah, take him away.

HENRY [*to* MUGEROUN]

Hands off, good fellow; I will be his bail
For this offence. [*To* CUTPURSE] Go, sirrah, work no more

Till this our coronation-day be past.
And now, our solemn rites of coronation done,
What now remains but for a while to feast
40   And spend some days in barriers, tourney, tilt,
And like disports, such as do fit the court?
Let's go, my lords, our dinner stays for us.
         Go out all but [CATHERINE] *the* QUEEN[-MOTHER] *and*
                                                    the CARDINAL.

CATHERINE
    My Lord Cardinal of Lorraine, tell me,
    How likes your grace my son's pleasantness?
    His mind, you see, runs on his minions,
    And all his heaven is to delight himself;
    And whilst he sleeps securely thus in ease,
    Thy brother Guise and we may now provide
    To plant ourselves with such authority
50 As not a man may live without our leaves.
    Then shall the Catholic faith of Rome
    Flourish in France, and none deny the same.
CARDINAL
    Madam, as in secrecy I was told,
    My brother Guise hath gathered a power of men,
    Which are, he saith, to kill the Puritans;
    But 'tis the house of Bourbon that he means.
    Now, madam, must you insinuate with the king,
    And tell him that 'tis for his country's good,
    And common profit of religion.
CATHERINE
60 Tush, man, let me alone with him,
    To work the way to bring this thing to pass;
    And if he do deny what I do say,
    I'll dispatch him with his brother presently,
    And then shall monsieur wear the diadem,
    Tush, all shall die unless I have my will,
    For, while she lives, Catherine will be queen.
    Come, my lord, let us go seek the Guise
    And then determine of this enterprise.

                                              Exeunt.

[*Scene 15*]

Enter the DUCHESS OF GUISE *and her* MAID.

DUCHESS
Go fetch me pen and ink.

MAID   I will, madam.

                                             Exit MAID.

DUCHESS
That I may write unto my dearest lord.
Sweet Mugeroun, 'tis he that hath my heart,
And Guise usurps it 'cause I am his wife.
Fain would I find some means to speak with him,
But cannot, and therefore am enforced to write
That he may come and meet me in some place
Where we may one enjoy the other's sight.
    Enter the MAID, *with* [*pen,*] *ink, and paper.*
So, set it down and leave me to myself.

                                     [*Exit* MAID.]

    She writes.
O would to God this quill that here doth write   10
Had late been plucked from out fair Cupid's wing,
That it might print these lines within his heart!
    Enter the GUISE.

GUISE
What, all alone, my love, and writing too?
I prithee, say to whom thou writes?

DUCHESS
To such a one, my lord, as when she reads my lines
Will laugh, I fear me, at their good array.

GUISE
I pray thee, let me see.

DUCHESS
O no, my lord, a woman only must
Partake the secrets of my heart.

GUISE
But, madam, I must see.   20
    He takes it.

Are these your secrets that no man must know?

DUCHESS

O pardon me, my lord!

GUISE

Thou trothless and unjust, what lines are these?
Am I grown old, or is thy lust grown young,
Or hath my love been so obscured in thee,
That others needs to comment on my text?
Is all my love forgot which held thee dear,
Ay, dearer than the apple of mine eye?
Is Guise's glory but a cloudy mist,
30   In sight and judgement of thy lustful eye?
Mort dieu! Were't not the fruit within thy womb,
Of whose increase I set some longing hope,
This wrathful hand should strike thee to the heart!
Hence, strumpet, hide thy head for shame,
And fly my presence, if thou look to live.

                                        Exit [DUCHESS].

O wicked sex, perjurèd and unjust,
Now do I see that from the very first
Her eyes and looks sowed seeds of perjury.
But, villain, he to whom these lines should go
40   Shall buy her love even with his dearest blood.

                                                Exit.

[*Scene 16*]

Enter the KING OF NAVARRE, PLESHÉ *and* BARTUS, *and
their train, with drums and trumpets.*

NAVARRE

My lords, sith in a quarrel just and right
We undertake to manage these our wars
Against the proud disturbers of the faith,
I mean the Guise, the Pope, and King of Spain,
Who set themselves to tread us under foot,

And rent our true religion from this land;
But for you know our quarrel is no more
But to defend their strange inventions,
Which they will put us to with sword and fire;
We must with resolute minds resolve to fight,   10
In honour of our God and country's good.
Spain is the council-chamber of the Pope,
Spain is the place where he makes peace and war:
And Guise for Spain hath now incensed the king
To send his power to meet us in the field.

BARTUS

Then in this bloody brunt they may behold
The sole endeavour of your princely care,
To plant the true succession of the faith
In spite of Spain and all his heresies.

NAVARRE

The power of vengeance now encamps itself   20
Upon the haughty mountains of my breast,
Plays with her gory colours of revenge,
Whom I respect as leaves of boasting green
That change their colour when the winter comes,
When I shall vaunt as victor in revenge.
    Enter a MESSENGER.
How now, sirrah, what news?

MESSENGER

My lord, as by our scouts we understand,
A mighty army comes from France with speed,
Which are already mustered in the land,
And means to meet your highness in the field.   30

NAVARRE

In God's name, let them come!
This is the Guise that hath incensed the king
To levy arms and make these civil broils.
But canst thou tell who is their general?

MESSENGER

Not yet, my lord, for thereon do they stay;
But, as report doth go, the duke of Joyeux

Hath made great suit unto the king therefore.

NAVARRE

It will not countervail his pains, I hope.
I would the Guise in his stead might have come,
40   But he doth lurk within his drowsy couch
And makes his footstool on security;
So he be safe, he cares not what becomes
Of king or country – no, not for them both.
But come, my lords, let us away with speed
And place ourselves in order for the fight.

Exeunt.

[*Scene 17*]

Enter the KING OF FRANCE, DUKE OF GUISE, EPERNOUN
and DUKE JOYEUX.

HENRY

My sweet Joyeux, I make thee general
Of all my army, now in readiness
To march against the rebellious King Navarre.
At thy request I am content thou go,
Although my love to thee can hardly suffer't,
Regarding still the danger of thy life.

JOYEUX

Thanks to your majesty, and so I take my leave.
Farewell to my lord of Guise and Epernoun.

GUISE

Health and hearty farewell to my lord Joyeux.

Exit JOYEUX.

HENRY

10   So kindly, cousin of Guise, you and your wife
Do both salute our lovely minions.
Remember you the letter, gentle sir,
Which your wife writ to my dear minion
And her chosen friend?

He makes horns at the GUISE.

GUISE

How now, my lord? Faith, this is more than need.
Am I thus to be jested at and scorned?
'Tis more than kingly or imperious;
And sure, if all the proudest kings in Christendom
Should bear me such derision, they should
Know how I scorned them and their mocks.   20
I love your minions? Dote on them yourself!
I know none else but holds them in disgrace.
And here by all the saints in heaven I swear,
That villain for whom I bear this deep disgrace –
Even for your words that have incensed me so –
Shall buy that strumpet's favour with his blood,
Whether he have dishonoured me or no!
Par la mort Dieu, il mourra!

                                            Exit.

HENRY

Believe me, this jest bites sore.

EPERNOUN

My lord, 'twere good to make them friends,   30
For his oaths are seldom spent in vain.

    Enter MUGEROUN.

HENRY How now, Mugeroun? Met'st thou not the Guise at the
door?

MUGEROUN Not I, my lord; what if I had?

HENRY

Marry, if thou hadst, thou mightst have had the stab,
For he hath solemnly sworn thy death.

MUGEROUN

I may be stabbed and live till he be dead.
But wherefore bears he me such deadly hate?

HENRY

Because his wife bears thee such kindly love.

MUGEROUN

If that be all, the next time that I meet her   40
I'll make her shake off love with her heels.

But which way is he gone? I'll go make a walk
On purpose from the court to meet with him.

Exit.

HENRY
I like not this. Come, Epernoun,
Let's go seek the duke and make them friends.

Exeunt.

[*Scene 18*]

Alarums, within. The DUKE JOYEUX *slain. Enter the* KING
OF NAVARRE, [*with* BARTUS,] *and his train.*

NAVARRE
The duke is slain and all his power dispersed,
And we are graced with wreaths of victory.
Thus God, we see, doth ever guide the right
To make his glory great upon the earth.

BARTUS
The terror of this happy victory,
I hope will make the king surcease his hate,
And either never manage army more,
Or else employ them in some better cause.

NAVARRE
How many noble men have lost their lives
10   In prosecution of these cruel arms,
Is ruth and almost death to call to mind.
But God, we know, will always put them down
That lift themselves against the perfect truth,
Which I'll maintain so long as life doth last,
And with the Queen of England join my force
To beat the papal monarch from our lands,
And keep those relics from our countries' coasts.
Come, my lords, now that this storm is overpast,
Let us away with triumph to our tents.

Exeunt.

[Scene 19]

Enter a SOLDIER [*with a musket*].

SOLDIER Sir, to you, sir, that dares make the duke a cuckold,
and use a counterfeit key to his privy-chamber door; and
although you take out nothing but your own, yet you put in
that which displeaseth him, and so forestall his market and
set up your standing where you should not; and whereas he
is your landlord, you will take upon you to be his, and till the
ground that he himself should occupy, which is his own free
land – if it be not too free, there's the question. And though I
come not to take possession (as I would I might), yet I mean
to keep you out, which I will, if this gear hold. What, are ye   10
come so soon? Have at ye, sir!

Enter MUGEROUN. *He shoots at him and kills him. Enter
the* GUISE [*and* ATTENDANTS].

GUISE
Hold thee, tall soldier, take thee this and fly.

Exit SOLDIER.

Lie there, the king's delight and Guise's scorn.
Revenge it, Henry, as thou list or dare,
I did it only in despite of thee.

[ATTENDANTS] *take him away.*

Enter the KING [HENRY] *and* EPERNOUN.

HENRY
My lord of Guise, we understand that you
Have gathered a power of men:
What your intent is yet we cannot learn,
But we presume it is not for our good.

GUISE
Why, I am no traitor to the crown of France;   20
What I have done, 'tis for the Gospel sake.

EPERNOUN
Nay, for the Pope's sake, and thine own benefit.
What peer in France but thou, aspiring Guise,
Durst be in arms without the king's consent?
I challenge thee for treason in the cause.

GUISE

    Ah, base Epernoun, were not his highness here,
    Thou shouldst perceive the duke of Guise is moved.

HENRY

    Be patient, Guise, and threat not Epernoun,
    Lest thou perceive the King of France be moved.

GUISE

30   Why, I am a prince of the Valois' line,
    Therefore an enemy to the Bourbonites;
    I am a juror in the Holy League,
    And therefore hated of the Protestants.
    What should I do but stand upon my guard?
    And, being able, I'll keep a host in pay.

EPERNOUN

    Thou able to maintain a host in pay,
    That livest by foreign exhibition!
    The Pope and King of Spain are thy good friends,
    Else all France knows how poor a duke thou art.

HENRY

40   Ay, those are they that feed him with their gold,
    To countermand our will and check our friends.

GUISE

    My lord, to speak more plainly, thus it is:
    Being animated by religious zeal,
    I mean to muster all the power I can,
    To overthrow those sectious Puritans.
    And know, my lord, the Pope will sell his triple crown,
    Ay, and the catholic Philip, King of Spain,
    Ere I shall want, will cause his Indians
    To rip the golden bowels of America.

50   Navarre, that cloaks them underneath his wings,
    Shall feel the house of Lorraine is his foe.
    Your highness needs not fear mine army's force;
    'Tis for your safety, and your enemies' wrack.

HENRY

    Guise, wear our crown, and be thou King of France,
    And as dictator make or war or peace,
    Whilst I cry '*placet*' like a senator.

I cannot brook thy haughty insolence:
Dismiss thy camp, or else by our edict
Be thou proclaimed a traitor throughout France.
GUISE [*aside*]
  The choice is hard, I must dissemble.   60
    [*To* KING HENRY]
  My lord, in token of my true humility,
  And simple meaning to your majesty,
  I kiss your grace's hand and take my leave,
  Intending to dislodge my camp with speed.
HENRY
  Then farewell, Guise, the king and thou are friends.

                               Exit GUISE.

EPERNOUN
  But trust him not, my lord, for had your highness
  Seen with what a pomp he entered Paris,
  And how the citizens with gifts and shows
  Did entertain him,
  And promised to be at his command –   70
  Nay, they feared not to speak in the streets
  That the Guise durst stand in arms against the king
  For not effecting of His Holiness' will.
HENRY
  Did they of Paris entertain him so?
  Then means he present treason to our state.
  Well, let me alone. Who's within there?
    Enter one with a pen and ink.
  Make a discharge of all my council straight,
  And I'll subscribe my name and seal it straight.
  My head shall be my council, they are false;
  And, Epernoun, I will be ruled by thee.   80
EPERNOUN
  My lord, I think for safety of your royal person,
  It would be good the Guise were made away,
  And so to quite your grace of all suspect.
HENRY
  First, let us set our hand and seal to this,
  And then I'll tell thee what I mean to do.

He writes.

So, convey this to the council presently;

Exit one.

And Epernoun, though I seem mild and calm,
Think not but I am tragical within.
I'll secretly convey me unto Blois;
90   For, now that Paris takes the Guise's part,
Here is no staying for the King of France,
Unless he mean to be betrayed and die.
But, as I live, so sure the Guise shall die.

Exeunt.

[*Scene 20*]

Enter the KING OF NAVARRE, *reading of a letter, and*
BARTUS.

NAVARRE

My lord, I am advertisèd from France
That the Guise hath taken arms against the king,
And that Paris is revolted from his grace.

BARTUS

Then hath your grace fit opportunity
To show your love unto the King of France,
Offering him aid against his enemies,
Which cannot but be thankfully received.

NAVARRE

Bartus, it shall be so; post then to France,
And there salute his highness in our name;
10   Assure him all the aid we can provide
Against the Guisians and their complices.
Bartus, be gone; commend me to his grace,
And tell him, ere it be long, I'll visit him.

BARTUS

I will, my lord.

Exit.

NAVARRE [*calling out*]
                    Pleshé!
        Enter PLESHÉ.
PLESHÉ   My lord.
NAVARRE
    Pleshé, go muster up our men with speed,
    And let them march away to France amain,
    For we must aid the king against the Guise.
    Be gone, I say, 'tis time that we were there.
PLESHÉ I go, my lord.

                                        [*Exit* PLESHÉ.]

NAVARRE
    That wicked Guise, I fear me much, will be   20
    The ruin of that famous realm of France,
    For his aspiring thoughts aim at the crown,
    And takes his vantage on religion
    To plant the Pope and popelings in the realm
    And bind it wholly to the see of Rome.
    But if that God do prosper mine attempts,
    And send us safely to arrive in France,
    We'll beat him back and drive him to his death
    That basely seeks the ruin of his realm.

                                        Exit.

                    [*Scene 21*]

        Enter the CAPTAIN OF THE GUARD, *and three* MUR-
            DERERS.
CAPTAIN
    Come on, sirs. What, are you resolutely bent,
    Hating the life and honour of the Guise?
    What, will you not fear, when you see him come?
FIRST MURDERER Fear him, said you? Tush, were he here, we
    would kill him presently.
SECOND MURDERER O that his heart were leaping in my hand!

THIRD MURDERER But when will he come, that we may murder
    him?

CAPTAIN Well, then, I see you are resolute.

10 FIRST MURDERER Let us alone, I warrant you.

CAPTAIN Then, sirs, take your standings within this chamber,
    for anon the Guise will come.

ALL THREE MURDERERS You will give us our money?

CAPTAIN
    Ay, ay, fear not. Stand close. So, be resolute.
      [*The* MURDERERS *hide.*]
    Now falls the star whose influence governs France,
    Whose light was deadly to the Protestants.
    Now must he fall and perish in his height.
      Enter the KING [HENRY] *and* EPERNOUN.

HENRY Now, captain of my guard, are these murderers ready?

CAPTAIN They be, my good lord.

HENRY
20   But are they resolute and armed to kill,
    Hating the life and honour of the Guise?

CAPTAIN I warrant ye, my lord.

HENRY
    Then come, proud Guise, and here disgorge thy breast
    Surcharged with surfeit of ambitious thoughts;
    Breathe out that life wherein my death was hid,
    And end thy endless treasons with thy death.
      Enter the GUISE [*within*] *and knocketh.*

GUISE
    Holà, varlet, hé! [EPERNOUN *goes to the door.*]
                   Epernoun, where is the king?

EPERNOUN
    Mounted his royal cabinet.

GUISE [*within*]
    I prithee tell him that the Guise is here.

EPERNOUN
30   An please your grace, the duke of Guise doth crave
    Access unto your highness.

HENRY   Let him come in.

[*Aside*]

Come, Guise, and see thy traitorous guile outreached,
And perish in the pit thou mad'st for me.

The GUISE *comes to the* KING.

GUISE

Good morrow to your majesty.

HENRY

Good morrow to my loving cousin of Guise.
How fares it this morning with your excellence?

GUISE

I heard your majesty was scarcely pleased
That in the court I bare so great a train.

HENRY

They were to blame that said I was displeased,
And you, good cousin, to imagine it.   40
'Twere hard with me if I should doubt my kin,
Or be suspicious of my dearest friends.
Cousin, assure you I am resolute –
Whatsoever any whisper in mine ears –
Not to suspect disloyalty in thee,
And so, sweet coz, farewell.

Exit KING [*with* EPERNOUN *and* CAPTAIN OF THE
GUARD].

GUISE

So, now sues the king for favour to the Guise,
And all his minions stoop when I command.
Why, this 'tis to have an army in the field.
Now by the holy sacrament I swear,   50
As ancient Romans over their captive lords,
So will I triumph over this wanton king
And he shall follow my proud chariot's wheels.
Now do I but begin to look about,
And all my former time was spent in vain.
Hold, sword, for in thee is the duke of Guise's hope.

Enter one of the MURDERERS.

Villain, why dost thou look so ghastly? Speak!

THIRD MURDERER O pardon me, my lord of Guise!

GUISE Pardon thee? Why, what hast thou done?

60 THIRD MURDERER O my lord, I am one of them that is set to
    murder you.

GUISE To murder me, villain?

THIRD MURDERER Ay, my lord; the rest have ta'en their stand-
    ings in the next room; therefore, good my lord, go not forth.

GUISE
    Yet Caesar shall go forth.
    Let mean conceits and baser men fear death:
    Tut, they are peasants, I am duke of Guise;
    And princes with their looks engender fear.

        [*Enter two* MURDERERS.]

FIRST MURDERER [*within*] Stand close, he is coming; I know
70   him by his voice.

GUISE As pale as ashes! Nay, then 'tis time to look about.

ALL Down with him, down with him!

        They stab him.

GUISE O, I have my death's wound! Give me leave to speak.

SECOND MURDERER Then pray to God, and ask forgiveness of
    the king.

GUISE
    Trouble me not, I ne'er offended him,
    Nor will I ask forgiveness of the king.
    O, that I have not power to stay my life,
    Nor immortality to be revenged!
80 To die by peasants, what a grief is this!
    Ah, Sixtus, be revenged upon the king;
    Philip and Parma, I am slain for you.
    Pope, excommunicate, Philip, depose
    The wicked branch of cursed Valois his line.
    Vive la messe! Perish Huguenots!
    Thus Caesar did go forth, and thus he died.

        He dies.

        Enter CAPTAIN OF THE GUARD.

CAPTAIN What, have you done? Then stay a while, and I'll go
    call the king. But see where he comes.

        [*Enter the* KING, EPERNOUN, *and* ATTENDANTS.]

    My lord, see where the Guise is slain.

HENRY

Ah, this sweet sight is physic to my soul.   90
Go fetch his son for to behold his death.
> [*Exit an* ATTENDANT.]
Surcharged with guilt of thousand massacres,
Monsieur of Lorraine, sink away to hell!
And in remembrance of those bloody broils
To which thou didst allure me, being alive,
And here in presence of you all, I swear
I ne'er was King of France until this hour.
This is the traitor that hath spent my gold
In making foreign wars and civil broils.
Did he not draw a sort of English priests   100
From Douai to the seminary at Rheims
To hatch forth treason 'gainst their natural queen?
Did he not cause the King of Spain's huge fleet
To threaten England and to menace me?
Did he not injure monsieur that's deceased?
Hath he not made me in the Pope's defence
To spend the treasure that should strength my land
In civil broils between Navarre and me?
Tush, to be short, he meant to make me monk,
Or else to murder me, and so be king.   110
Let Christian princes that shall hear of this
(As all the world shall know our Guise is dead)
Rest satisfied with this: that here I swear,
Ne'er was there king of France so yoked as I.

EPERNOUN

My lord, here is his son.
> *Enter the* GUISE'S SON.

HENRY

Boy, look where your father lies.

GUISE'S SON

My father slain! Who hath done this deed?

HENRY

Sirrah, 'twas I that slew him, and will slay
Thee too an thou prove such a traitor.

GUISE'S SON

120   Art thou king and hast done this bloody deed?
      I'll be revenged!
        He offereth to throw his dagger.

HENRY

      Away to prison with him! I'll clip his wings
      Or e'er he pass my hands. Away with him!
                             Exit BOY [*guarded*].
      But what availeth that this traitor's dead,
      When Duke Dumaine, his brother, is alive,
      And that young cardinal that is grown so proud?
        [*To the* CAPTAIN OF THE GUARD]
      Go to the Governor of Orleans,
      And will him, in my name, to kill the duke.
                 ·   [*Exit* CAPTAIN OF THE GUARD.]
      [*To the* MURDERERS]
      Get you away, and strangle the Cardinal.
                  [*Exeunt the* MURDERERS.]
130   These two will make one entire duke of Guise,
      Especially with our old mother's help.

EPERNOUN

      My lord, see where she comes, as if she drooped
      To hear these news.
        Enter [CATHERINE *the*] QUEEN-MOTHER.

HENRY

      And let her droop, my heart is light enough.
      Mother, how like you this device of mine?
      I slew the Guise because I would be king.

CATHERINE

      King? Why, so thou wert before;
      Pray God thou be a king now this is done!

HENRY

      Nay, he was king and countermanded me,
140   But now I will be king and rule myself
      And make the Guisians stoop that are alive.

CATHERINE

      I cannot speak for grief. When thou wast born,
      I would that I had murdered thee, my son!

My son? Thou art a changeling, not my son.
I curse thee and exclaim thee miscreant,
Traitor to God and to the realm of France!

HENRY

Cry out, exclaim, howl till thy throat be hoarse.
The Guise is slain and I rejoice therefore!
And now will I to arms; come, Epernoun,
And let her grieve her heart out, if she will.   150

                    Exeunt the KING *and* EPERNOUN.

CATHERINE Away, leave me alone to meditate.

          [*Exeunt* ATTENDANTS *with the body of the* GUISE.]

Sweet Guise, would he had died, so thou wert here!
To whom shall I bewray my secrets now,
Or who will help to build religion?
The Protestants will glory and insult,
Wicked Navarre will get the crown of France,
The popedom cannot stand, all goes to wrack,
And all for thee, my Guise! What may I do?
But sorrow seize upon my toiling soul,
For since the Guise is dead, I will not live.   160

                                                    Exit.

                          [*Scene 22*]

     Enter two [MURDERERS] *dragging in the* CARDINAL.

CARDINAL Murder me not, I am a cardinal.

FIRST MURDERER Wert thou the Pope, thou mightst not 'scape
     from us.

CARDINAL What, will you file your hands with churchmen's
     blood?

SECOND MURDERER Shed your blood? O lord, no, for we
     intend to strangle you.

CARDINAL Then there is no remedy but I must die?

FIRST MURDERER No remedy, therefore prepare yourself.

CARDINAL
     Yet lives my brother Duke Dumaine, and many moe   10

To revenge our deaths upon that cursed king,
Upon whose heart may all the Furies gripe,
And with their paws drench his black soul in hell!
FIRST MURDERER Yours, my Lord Cardinal, you should have
said.
  Now they strangle him.
So, pluck amain; he is hard-hearted, therefore pull with viol-
ence. Come, take him away.
                            Exeunt [with the body].

[Scene 23]

Enter DUKE DUMAINE, *reading of a letter, with others.*
DUMAINE
My noble brother murdered by the king!
O, what may I do for to revenge thy death?
The king's alone, it cannot satisfy.
Sweet duke of Guise, our prop to lean upon,
Now thou art dead, here is no stay for us.
I am thy brother, and I'll revenge thy death,
And root Valois his line from forth of France,
And beat proud Bourbon to his native home,
That basely seeks to join with such a king,
10 Whose murderous thoughts will be his overthrow.
He willed the Governor of Orleans, in his name,
That I with speed should have been put to death;
But that's prevented, for to end his life,
And all those traitors to the Church of Rome
That durst attempt to murder noble Guise.
  Enter the FRIAR.
FRIAR My lord, I come to bring you news that your brother,
the Cardinal of Lorraine, by the king's consent is lately
strangled unto death.
DUMAINE
My brother Cardinal slain, and I alive?
20 O words of power to kill a thousand men!

Come, let us away and levy men;
'Tis war that must assuage this tyrant's pride.

FRIAR My lord, hear me but speak. I am a friar of the order of
the Jacobins, that for my conscience sake will kill the king.

DUMAINE But what doth move thee above the rest to do the
deed?

FRIAR O my lord, I have been a great sinner in my days, and
the deed is meritorious.

DUMAINE But how wilt thou get opportunity?

FRIAR Tush, my lord, let me alone for that.   30

DUMAINE Friar, come with me, we will go talk more of this
within.

                                                      Exeunt.

[*Scene 24*]

Sound drum and trumpets, and enter the KING OF FRANCE,
and NAVARRE, EPERNOUN, BARTUS, PLESHÉ [*and*
ATTENDANTS] *and* SOLDIERS.

HENRY
Brother of Navarre, I sorrow much
That ever I was proved your enemy,
And that the sweet and princely mind you bear
Was ever troubled with injurious wars.
I vow, as I am lawful King of France,
To recompense your reconcilèd love
With all the honours and affections
That ever I vouchsafed my dearest friends.

NAVARRE
It is enough if that Navarre may be
Esteemèd faithful to the King of France,   10
Whose service he may still command till death.

HENRY
Thanks to my kingly brother of Navarre.
Then here we'll lie before Lutetia walls,
Girting this strumpet city with our siege,

Till, surfeiting with our afflicting arms,
She cast her hateful stomach to the earth.
   Enter a MESSENGER.
MESSENGER An it please your majesty, here is a friar of the
order of the Jacobins sent from the President of Paris, that
craves access unto your grace.
HENRY
20   Let him come in.

                                  [*Exit* MESSENGER.]

   Enter FRIAR, *with a letter.*
EPERNOUN [*aside to* KING HENRY]
   I like not this friar's look,
   'Twere not amiss, my lord, if he were searched.
HENRY
   Sweet Epernoun, our friars are holy men
   And will not offer violence to their king
   For all the wealth and treasure of the world.
   Friar, thou dost acknowledge me thy king?
FRIAR
   Ay, my good lord, and will die therein.
HENRY
   Then come thou near, and tell what news thou bring'st.
FRIAR My lord, the President of Paris greets your grace, and
30   sends his duty by these speedy lines, humbly craving your
gracious reply.
   [*Gives letter.*]
HENRY
   I'll read them, friar, and then I'll answer thee.
FRIAR *Sancte Jacobus*, now have mercy upon me!
   He stabs the KING *with a knife as he readeth the letter, and
   then the* KING *getteth the knife and kills him.*
EPERNOUN O my lord, let him live a while!
HENRY
   No, let the villain die, and feel in hell
   Just torments for his treachery.
NAVARRE What, is your highness hurt?
HENRY
   Yes, Navarre, but not to death I hope.

NAVARRE

    God shield your grace from such a sudden death!

    Go call a surgeon hither straight.   40

                                 [*Exit an* ATTENDANT.]

HENRY

    What irreligious pagans' parts be these

    Of such as hold them of the holy church?

    Take hence that damnèd villain from my sight.

                    [SOLDIERS *remove the* FRIAR's *body*.]

EPERNOUN

    Ah, had your highness let him live,

    We might have punished him to his deserts!

HENRY

    Sweet Epernoun, all rebels under heaven

    Shall take example by his punishment

    How they bear arms against their sovereign.

    Go call the English agent hither straight.

                                 [*Exit* SOLDIER.]

    I'll send my sister England news of this,   50

    And give her warning of her treacherous foes.

      [*Enter a* SURGEON.]

NAVARRE

    Pleaseth your grace to let the surgeon search your wound?

HENRY

    The wound, I warrant ye, is deep, my lord.

    Search, surgeon, and resolve me what thou see'st.

      The SURGEON *searcheth* [*the wound*].

      Enter the ENGLISH AGENT.

    Agent for England, send thy mistress word

    What this detested Jacobin hath done.

    Tell her, for all this, that I hope to live;

    Which if I do, the papal monarch goes

    To wrack and antichristian kingdom falls.

    These bloody hands shall tear his triple crown,   60

    And fire accursèd Rome about his ears.

    I'll fire his crazèd buildings and incense

    The papal towers to kiss the holy earth.

    Navarre, give me thy hand: I here do swear

To ruinate that wicked church of Rome
That hatcheth up such bloody practices,
And here protest eternal love to thee,
And to the Queen of England specially,
Whom God hath blessed for hating papistry.

NAVARRE

70   These words revive my thoughts, and comforts me
To see your highness in this virtuous mind.

HENRY Tell me, surgeon, shall I live?

SURGEON

Alas, my lord, the wound is dangerous,
For you are stricken with a poisoned knife.

HENRY

A poisoned knife! What, shall the French king die
Wounded and poisoned both at once?

EPERNOUN

O that that damned villain were alive again,
That we might torture him with some new-found death!

BARTUS He died a death too good; the devil of hell torture his
80   wicked soul!

HENRY

Ah, curse him not sith he is dead.
O, the fatal poison works within my breast.
Tell me, surgeon, and flatter not, may I live?

SURGEON

Alas, my lord, your highness cannot live.

NAVARRE

Surgeon, why say'st thou so? The king may live.

HENRY

O no, Navarre, thou must be King of France.

NAVARRE

Long may you live, and still be King of France.

EPERNOUN Or else die Epernoun.

HENRY

Sweet Epernoun, thy king must die.
90   My lords, fight in the quarrel of this valiant prince,
For he is your lawful king and my next heir;
Valois' line ends in my tragedy.

Now let the house of Bourbon wear the crown,
And may it never end in blood, as mine hath done!
Weep not, sweet Navarre, but revenge my death.
Ah, Epernoun, is this thy love to me?
Henry thy king wipes off these childish tears,
And bids thee whet thy sword on Sixtus' bones,
That it may keenly slice the Catholics.
He loves me not that sheds most tears,   100
But he that makes most lavish of his blood.
Fire Paris, where these treacherous rebels lurk.
I die, Navarre, come bear me to my sepulchre.
Salute the Queen of England in my name,
And tell her, Henry dies her faithful friend.
   He dies.

NAVARRE

Come, lords, take up the body of the king,
That we may see it honourably interred.
And then I vow for to revenge his death
As Rome and all those popish prelates there
Shall curse the time that e'er Navarre was king,   110
And ruled in France by Henry's fatal death!
     They march out, with the body of the KING *lying on*
       four men's shoulders, with a dead march,
         drawing weapons on the ground.

Appendix: *The Massacre at Paris*, Scene 19 (Folger MS.J.b.8)

*Enter A souldier w*th *a Muskett*

Now ser to you y^t dares make a dvke a Cuckolde
and vse a Counterfeyt key to his privye Chamber

SOULDIER

thoughe you take out none but yor owne treasure
yett you putt in y^t displeases him / And fill vp his rome y^t
he shold occupie. Herein ser you forestalle the markett
and sett vpe yor standinge where you shold not: But you will
saye you leave him rome enoughe besides: thats no answere
hes to have the Choyce of his owne freeland / yf it be
not to free theres the questione / now ser where he is
your landlorde. you take vpon you to be his / and will needs
enter by defaulte / whatt thoughe you were once in possession
yett Comminge vpon you once vnawares he frayde you
out againe. therefore your entrye is mere Intrvsione
this is againste the lawe ser: And thoughe I Come not
to keep possessione as I wold I mighte yet I come to
keepe you out ser. yow are wellcome ser have at you

Enter minion

He Kills him

MINION

Trayterouse guise ah thow hast mvrthered me

Enter guise

GUISE

Hold thee tale soldier take the this and flye

Exit

thus fall Imperfett exhalatione
wch our great sonn of fraunce Cold not effecte

a fyery meteor in the fermament
lye there the Kinges delyght and guises scorne
revenge it henry yf thow liste or darst
I did it onely in dispight of thee
fondlie hast thow in Censte the guises sowle
y^t of it self was hote enoughe to worke

GUISE

thy Iust degestione wt extreamest shame
the armye I have gathered now shall ayme
more at thie end then exterpatione
and when thow thinkst I have foregotten this
and y^t thow most reposest one my faythe
then will I wake thee from thie folishe dreame
and lett thee see thie self my prysoner

Exeunt

Notes

ABBREVIATIONS

A A-text (*Doctor Faustus*, 1604)
A2 second quarto (*Doctor Faustus*, 1609)
B B-text (*Doctor Faustus*, 1616)
G Glossary
N List of Mythological, Historical and Geographical Names
O octavo
OED *Oxford English Dictionary*
Q quarto
Q2 second quarto (*Edward the Second*, 1598)
SD stage direction
SP speech prefix
Tilley M. P. Tilley, *A Dictionary of the Proverbs in England in the Sixteenth and Seventeenth Centuries* (Ann Arbor, Michigan, 1950)

Biblical references are to the Geneva Bible (1560), except when the Latin text of the Vulgate is cited. Translations are by Frank Romany unless otherwise stated. Bibliographic references are by author/date where full details are given in the Further Reading.

DIDO, QUEEN OF CARTHAGE

Usually dated 1585–6, *Dido* was first published in a quarto of 1594 which provides the copy-text for this edition. Its title-page tells us the play was performed by the Children of the Chapel, and its style and dramaturgy match the conventions of other plays for boys' companies: sophisticated, ironic and faintly scandalous. Staging, too, probably reflected the style of the private theatres: scholars have conjectured that different locales were indicated by 'houses' or even full sets, between which, for instance, Venus walks as she descends from Olympus to the shores of Carthage in the first scene. The play requires a 'discovery-space', whose curtains open at the beginning of the action, and elaborate props, including a statue of Priam (2.1). More problematically, the title-page also claims that the play was co-written with Thomas Nashe. Some traces of Nashe's vocabulary have been found in the play (though there are more of Marlowe's), but no one has yet succeeded in dividing the text between them.

Dido is closely modelled on Virgil's *Aeneid*, Acts 1 and 2 deriving, respectively, from Books I and II of the poem, Acts 3–5 from Book IV. But Marlowe's imitation of Virgil is a curiously irreverent act of cultural piety. Although the famous incidents of the epic recur in the play, they are transformed by Marlowe's compressions, transpositions and additions. In Virgil, the love of Dido and Aeneas is a tragic episode in tension with the larger narrative of the founding of Rome – one which importantly qualifies the poem's celebration of Aeneas. It is the origin of the long enmity of Rome and Carthage. Events are numinous, presided over by gods who are the agents of a complex historical fate. Marlowe's ironic love-tragedy is more narrowly focused, and its gods, from the first, invented scene between Jupiter and Ganymede, are debased, spiteful and petty. Marlowe's Jupiter is more interested in Ganymede than in the fate of the Trojan exiles; Juno's jealousy is manifested in clouting Ganymede round the head and plotting to murder another child, the sleeping Ascanius, later in the play. The most important god is Cupid. In Virgil, he is substituted for Ascanius for one night; Marlowe leaves him in Carthage, where his continued presence suggests the dependence of human fates on irresponsible, childlike divinities.

With Love thus literally at the centre of the action, it is appropriate that there are more lovers: Marlowe expands the role of Iarbas to make him a sometimes comic rival to Aeneas, and has Anna hopelessly in love with him. The infatuated nurse is also invented. Marlowe shows much more of the principals' interaction than does Virgil. Dido veers between giving operatically excessive expression to her passion and being tongue-tied. Aeneas is at first dumbly insensitive, later perfidious and unreliable (perhaps a reflection of the medieval tradition of Aeneas' treachery). Unlike Virgil's, Marlowe's Aeneas swears to stay with Dido, and then changes his mind. (Marlowe delays the *appearance* of Mercury so that Aeneas' decision to abandon Dido looks more sudden and vacillating.) When she catches him out, he lies to her, but is quickly won over by her ever-more extravagant gifts. Just to be sure, Dido takes the supposed

Ascanius hostage and disables Aeneas' fleet by reclaiming the luxury ship's fittings she has given him. After Mercury's embassy (it takes two visitations to drive Marlowe's Aeneas away), the lovers' parting is shifted more climactically towards the end of the action, and Aeneas skulks away from her in silence. In Virgil, Dido dies by the sword on the burnt reminders, including the bed, of their affair; Marlowe has her burn to death on a pyre of love-tokens – uttering, nonetheless, her most solemn Virgilian lines as she does so – and has Iarbas and Anna commit suicide with perhaps comically indecent haste.

The prominence of the bonfire of love-tokens is in keeping with the rest of the play. Itself a luxury object, encrusted with verbal riches, *Dido* is also full of expensive material objects, many of them love-gifts: Juno's jewellery given to Ganymede, the robes, sails and crown Dido showers on Aeneas. No doubt this reflects the high production values of the Chapel Children. But it also bespeaks an imaginative materialism in the play. In Virgil, when Venus appears to Aeneas, she is suddenly *there*; in Marlowe, she steps out of a bush. When his companions fail at first to notice Virgil's Aeneas, it is because he is invisible, not, as here, because he is too wretchedly dressed to be recognized. In these moments, and in the play as a whole, staging the supernatural epic exposes it to laughter.

ACT 1

Scene 1

0.1 SD *the curtains draw*: The curtains belong either to a concealed discovery-space at the back of the stage or (if the staging followed the conventions of court performance) to one of the 'mansions' or 'houses' constructed on the stage. See Smith 1977.

0.2 SD *dandling*: Bouncing a child up and down on one's knee, but with connotations of erotic play.

SD *MERCURY*: (N) The messenger-god is sometimes given his Greek name, Hermes.

5–8 *Today . . . mine ears*: Ganymede supplanted Hebe, the daughter of Juno, as Jupiter's cup-bearer.

6 *pleasance*: (i) Fine linen, (ii) joy, pleasure.

10 *By Saturn's soul*: Jupiter swears by his father's soul (N), and by his own *hair* (amended from Q's *aire*, in the light of line 11: see Ovid, *Metamorphoses* 1, 179–80).

13–14 *To hang her . . . cords*: Cf. the punishment of Hera (the Greek Juno) in *Iliad* XV.

17 *Helen's brother*: Like Ganymede, Castor and Pollux were originally mortals, to whom the gods granted an immortality which alternated

between them. The association of one of them here with their
sister, Helen of Troy, perhaps adds to the frivolity of Ganymede's
laughter.

20   *walled-in . . . wings*: Ganymede was taken to Mount Olympus by
Jupiter's eagle, or by the god himself in that guise.

23   *wag*: A term of endearment (normally applied to a mischievous
boy).

25   *exhaled*: Inflamed. Ganymede's look acts on Jupiter like the sun
turning a substance to a fiery vapour or 'exhalation', such as a
meteor. There is a pun on 'haled' (27) = dragged.

26   *driven back . . . night*: Perhaps the 'meteoric' Jupiter has lit up the
night. The phrasing recalls Ovid, *Amores* I.xiii.40 (*lente currite
noctis equi*), which famously reappears in *Doctor Faustus* 14.71.

28   *thy content*: Whatever you please.

32   *Vulcan*: He was lame.

33   *nine daughters*: The Muses.

34   *Juno's bird*: The peacock.

50–108   *Ay, this is it . . . attempts*: Closely modelled on *Aeneid* I, 223–
301. Oliver 1968 notes, however, that 'Marlowe's Venus addresses
Jupiter in a tone of greater scorn and anger than Virgil considered
appropriate'.

54–61   *Juno . . . all his train*: See (N). Juno asks the god of the winds
(Aeolus) for a storm.

63   *Aeolia*: Aeolus' floating island home.

64–73   *Poor Troy . . . Astraeus' tents*: See (N). The storm at sea repli-
cates the destruction of Troy.

65   *envious*: Malicious.

66–7   *Epeus' horse . . . walls*: The rocks of Mount Etna threaten to
smash the ships' hulls, taking the place of the wooden horse constructed by Epeus which was used to broach the walls of Troy.

68   *sounds*: Commands (like a trumpet sounding an order).

70–73   *See how . . . Astraeus' tents*: See (N). The night overtakes the
day like Ulysses capturing the Trojan spy Dolon. (Having learned
the password from his captive, Ulysses entered the Trojan camp
and stole away the horses of Rhesus in order to avert a prophecy
which said that Troy would not fall if the horses fed or drank in
Trojan territory.) The stars appear suddenly, like the horses, as
though snatched from the tent of their father Astraeus.

75   *our crystal world*: I.e. the bright (crystalline) heavens, now menaced
by the waves below.

85   *fair walls*: The walls of Aeneas' future city.

86   *in blood . . . bud*: Blood can be used as a fertilizer.

87 *Turnus' town*: Ardea. Turnus (N) led his people, the Italian race of the Rutuli ('Rutiles', line 89), against the Trojan exiles in Latium until Aeneas killed him.

88 *her*: I.e. Fortune.

96–103 *bright Ascanius ... fame*: Ascanius will reign in heaven, even having his name engraved on its gates.

104 *Hector's race*: The Trojan royal line.

106 *princess-priest*: I.e. Rhea Silvia (also called Ilia), the Vestal Virgin and daughter of Numitor, king of Alba Longa, who became pregnant by Mars, bearing Romulus and Remus, the twin founders of Rome.

108 *eternise ... attempts*: Preserve the eternal fame of Troy by their exploits.

111–12 *Phoebus ... Tyrrhene main*: In the stormy dark, the sun seems to be avoiding the Mediterranean as it avoids the waters of the underworld ('Stygian pools').

112 *taint his tresses*: Dirty his hair, i.e. Phoebus refuses to shine upon.

115 *Whereas*: Where.
   wind-god ... fate: Aeolus (singular subject of a plural verb) is defying the will of fate in attacking Aeneas.

116 *offspring ... kingly loins*: Aeneas, a descendant of Dardanus, son of Jupiter and Electra.

125 *conceived with*: Heavy, pregnant, with.

128–9 *issued from ... froth*: Venus was born of the foam of the sea.

130 *Triton ... with Troy*: The merman Triton commanded the waves and winds by blowing through a conch; the line seems to associate Triton's trumpet with that of Fame, and to mean that he has made the Trojans' suffering well known.

132 *Thetis ... Cymodoce*: See (N). 'Cymodoce' is emended from Q's *Cimodoae*.

146–7 *barking Scylla ... Ceraunia's seat*: The locations of famous dangers for epic voyagers. See (N).
   Cyclops' shelves: The shores of Sicily, home of the Cyclopes.

151 *Pergama did vaunt*: Troy boasted of.

153 *virtues ... annoy*: Powers ... suffering, injury.

154 *coming*: For Q's *cunning*.

158 *rest the map*: Are still the very picture.

159 *hair*: For Q's *aire*. Cf. lines 10, 111–12.

169 *See ... finds out*: Proverbial (Tilley N61, P527).

170 *How near ... art thou driven*: Into what straits, what extremities, you are forced.

179 *society's supports*: The necessities of a community.

193   *the sun's bright sister*: The moon-goddess Diana (or Phoebe, sister of Phoebus).
196   *lighten our extremes*: Alleviate the extremity we are suffering.
202   *milk-white*: The colour of the most highly prized sacrificial animals.
203   *affect*: (i) Aspire to, (ii) delight in.
204   *Tyrian*: (For Q's *Turen*) the Carthaginians came from Tyre in Phoenicia.
206   *suit . . . in purple*: Tyre was famed for the production of red-purple dye.
      for the nonce: Specifically for the purpose.
210   *Punic kingdom*: Carthage.
213   *Sidonian*: Of Sidon, another city in Phoenicia.
220   *Phrygian*: Trojan (from Phrygia in Asia Minor).
224   *tilts*: Pitches, slops; moves unsteadily up and down.
233   *A' God's name on*: Carry on, in the name of God.
244   *in these shades*: In such deceptive shapes as this (of the huntress).
248   *discoursive*: (i) Articulated in words, (ii) protracted.

Scene 2

4   *envièd*: (Accented on second syllable) hated, loathed.
11   *household lares*: The Lares were the Roman (and hence Trojan) hearth-gods, tutelary spirits of the household.
15   *weal, of victory forsook*: State, having no hope of victory.
22   *fertile . . . wealth*: Rich in corn; for Ceres, see (N).
23   *of his name*: Italia supposedly derived its name from the Arcadian Italus whose tribe, the Oenotrians, once lived there.
25   *Thither made we*: An imitation of a Virgilian half-line.
26   *Orion*: The winter constellation associated with storms.
28   *brackish*: (i) Partly fresh, partly salt (usually of water), (ii) wet.
33   *knows*: Knows how.
34   *barbarous sort*: The multitude, commoners.
37   *first earth interdict our feet*: Forbid us to land on the shore.
41   *Baucis' house*: Despite being disguised, Jupiter and Mercury were kindly entertained in the humble ('silly') house of Baucis and Philemon, who therefore became bywords for hospitality. Q's *Vausis* is nonsense.
47   *As shall surpass . . . speech*: 'As it will be beyond our power to describe in words' (Oliver 1968).

ACT 2

Scene 1

1–9   *Where am I . . . I die*: Aeneas is 'amazed' (line 2) at a statue (in Virgil, a painting) of Priam. Niobe (N) is perhaps remembered because, like the king, she lost many children, or because, in her grief, she was turned to stone.

7–8   *Ida's hill . . . Xanthus' stream*: Mount Ida near Troy, from which the river Xanthus flowed down to the Hellespont.

10   *humour*: Mood, disposition.

13–14   *saving air, / Is nothing here*: There is nothing here but air.

38.1   SD *Enter CLOANTHUS . . . others*: The Trojans do not recognize each other because Ilioneus' party is dressed in rich Carthaginian clothes, and Aeneas' in rags. (In Virgil, Aeneas is invisible.)

40   *vouchsafe of ruth*: Grant out of pity.

51   *names*: For Q's *meanes*.

79–85   *base robes . . . Irus ware*: The emphasis on clothes is Marlowe's. It is probably ironic that Aeneas, as badly dressed as the beggarly suitor of faithful Penelope, is offered the garment of Dido's former husband. See (N).

87   *wait*: Stand in attendance.

99–100   *your grace . . . thou*: Aeneas uses the deferential plural form ('your grace'); Dido insists on the more intimate 'thou'.

110–11   *Antenor . . . Sinon*: See (N). Virgil's version, repeated later in this scene, held Sinon responsible; medieval tradition blamed the treachery of Antenor (and sometimes of Aeneas).

114–288   *A woeful tale . . . sacrificed*: Adapted from Aeneas' narrative in *Aeneid* II.

115   *stony mace*: Cf. John Milton, *Paradise Lost* (X.294): 'Death with his mace petrific'.

121–3   *Achilles' tongue . . . Myrmidons' harsh ears*: Aeneas needs the strength of Achilles to tell his story; his hearers will need the legendary hardheartedness of Achilles' companions, the Myrmidons, to listen to it.

129   *Atrides*: The Greek commander, Agamemnon, son of Atreus.

134   *Gave up their voices*: Shouted their decision.

135   *Tenedos*: An island off the Trojan coast, but here apparently treated as part of the mainland.

145–6   *Hermes' pipe . . . sleep*: To reach Io, Hermes lulled asleep the hundred-eyed guard, Argus, who had been set to watch over her, and killed him.

162 *him*: Priam.

165 *his*: The wooden horse's.

187 *pride of Asia*: I.e. Troy.

188 *camp*: I.e. army.

193–9 *Young infants . . . brains*: The atrocities are not in Virgil.

198 *a Greekish lad*: I.e. Pyrrhus (but 'dashed' [199] seems to need a plural subject).

215 *Priam's youngest son*: The death of Polites is mentioned in Virgil, but not the mutilation of his body.

217 *balls of wildfire*: Handheld fire-bombs.

221 *jealous of*: Protective of, anxious for.

222 *crooked*: (i) Shaped, curved, (ii) underhand, crafty.

230 *Megaera*: One of the Furies (N), she is a personification of violence and revenge (Pyrrhus was avenging the death of his father).

235 *turned*: Altered.

244–54 *the frantic queen . . . fell down*: Not in Virgil. Hecuba's 'howling' (248) may be an anticipation of her eventual transformation into a dog.

254 *wind*: The received emendation of Q's *wound* emphasizes Priam's frailty.

264 *Ilion*: The Greek form of Ilium (N).

274–5 *Cassandra . . . Ajax*: See (N); Virgil mentions the attempted rescue, but not the rape, of Priam's daughter.

275 *Diana's fane*: Diana's temple (Q's *Fawne* may be merely a variant spelling).

281–8 *Polyxena . . . sacrificed*: Marlowe took Pyrrhus' murder of Polyxena, another of Priam and Hecuba's children, from Ovid (*Metamorphoses* XIII, 441–80) rather than Virgil.

289 *leave*: Cease.

298 *Alexander*: An alternative name for Paris.

322 *Cytherea's*: For Q's *Citheidas*.

334 *nephew*: Grandson.

ACT 3

Scene 1

2 *thy brother's*: Aeneas' (like Cupid, Venus' son).

50 *feed . . . my love*: Indulge my beloved's whim *or* indulge in my own passion.

57 *love*: Q's *Ioue* (Jove) may be correct, especially in the light of 'shrined', but is probably only an example of 'foul case', an 'I' having been mistakenly dropped into the case of 'l' type.

73   *gross eye-beams*: Since the eye was believed to emit a beam, it was conceivable that one could be tainted by being looked at by common eyes.

81   *dull-conceited*: Unimaginative, slow-witted.

96   *Achates . . . your lord*: Dido pretends not to have noticed Aeneas.

106   *oars*: Apparently disyllabic, as also at line 117.

108   *stern*: (Here) rudder.

116   *odoriferous trees*: The scent of the spice-trees would be communicated to the tackle.

122   *pyramides*: (Four syllables) obelisks.

123   *wrought*: (Here) embroidered.

127   *manly*: Q's *meanly* could be correct if used ironically, but the sense is strained.

131   *Thetis . . . Apollo's neck*: See (N). 'The comparison is with the glories of the sun (Apollo) setting in the sea' (Oliver 1968).

132   *So that*: Provided that.

146   *disputed*: Took part in an academic disputation.

154–64   *This was an orator . . . The rest*: Dido's suitors are free inventions on figures of classical myth.

Scene 2

1–20   *Here lies . . . Rhamnus town*: Juno's opening speech (a Marlovian invention) is notable for a number of textual cruces, see notes to lines 3, 11 and 16 below.

3   *Fame . . . Fates*: Q reads *furie . . . the face*.

4   *imp*: Child (sometimes used pejoratively: an imp could be the offspring of the devil).

7   *raze*: Erase. Juno intends to alter the book of fate which has decreed Ascanius' future glory.

11   *let-out life*: The life-blood she will let out (for Q's *left-out*).

12–13   *Paris . . . Ascanius die*: Juno intends the murder of Ascanius as revenge for Venus' triumph over her in the Judgement of Paris. The prize (an apple) was inscribed 'for the most beautiful'.

14–15   *O no . . . down told*: Spoken ironically: 'I am so helpless that I can neither wait for the proper time for action nor immediately do two good deeds in return for one' (Oliver 1968).
    double fee: Twice the stake.

16   *mind*: For Q's *made*.

18   *adulterous child*: Venus, famously unfaithful to Vulcan.

20   *Juno . . . Rhamnus town*: Juno identifies herself with Nemesis, the goddess of vengeance, who was worshipped in her temple at Rhamnus in Greece.

21   *doves*: See 2.1.320.

22   *prest at hand*: (i) Close at hand (of the danger), (ii) readily (of the doves).

57   *to a sceptre*: As an emblem of his new association with Juno, the queen of the gods.

58   *Fancy and modesty*: I.e. the eroticism of Venus and the matronly decorum of Juno.

60   *desire is thine*: Whatever you desire is yours (because Venus *is* desire).

68   *motion*: (Here) proposal.

76   *casualty of sea*: An accident at sea (Juno disavows her part in raising the storm).

84   *Darts forth her light . . . shore*: Looks forward to the shore of Lavinium (where Lavinia, his future wife, awaits). The soul was usually thought of as feminine, and vision was supposed to involve light being directed from the eye to its object.

85   *divorce*: Dissolve, put an end to (as a divorce ends a marriage).

86   *weary . . . thoughts*: As the following lines suggest, Juno intends to wear out Aeneas' thoughts of Lavinia and his promised kingdom as his body is tired by the hunt and by love-making.

91   *Silvanus' dwellings*: The forests (home of the wood-god).

96   *savour of*: Have some of the characteristics of, 'have a smack of'.

97   *have it*: Absent from Q, 'it' seems necessary to grammar and metre.

99   *Ida*: (Here, apparently) Venus' groves near Idalium in Cyprus.

100 *Adonis' purple down*: Probably a bed of the purple anemones which sprang from the blood of Adonis.

Scene 3

4   *Diana's shrouds*: Hunting clothes.

5   *All fellows*: All equals (proverbial, Tilley F182–3).

24   *otherwhile . . . out of joint*: He is sometimes not his normal self.

26   *man of men*: Any man, however great.

29   *given . . . in gage*: Wagered, i.e. risked.

30   *pitch . . . toils*: Set snares.

45   *And dead . . . brought me up*: (Perhaps) and dead to the honour on which my life has been based.

59   *a winter's tale*: An adventure story suitable for long winter evenings.

61   *soil*: Marshy area where wild animals wallow.

64   *forfeit to*: For Q's *far fet to*.

77   *very*: Mere.

79   *fancy's shapes*: Objects of desire.

84   *That resteth . . . pain*: Which my rival presently enjoys, in contrast
      with my pain.

Scene 4

0.1   SD *The storm*: Probably the occasion for spectacular sound-effects,
      see 4.1.1–13.
0.1–0.2 SD *at several times*: I.e. they enter separately.
4   *in a net*: Vulcan caught Venus and Mars in a net as they made love.
      where: Whereas.
19   *butts his beams*: Casts his rays.
20–21 *Prometheus . . . burning arms*: Dido's burning passion is so
      intense that it is as though the fire-bringer Prometheus (N) had
      disguised himself as the god of love. There is an echo of the myth
      of Semele, who was consumed in the flames when she requested
      that her lover, Jupiter, should appear before her in his true form.
35   *Whose . . . content*: Who, being both royal and desirable, could
      match my desire and royalty.
37   *for me*: Instead of me.
38   *to Sirens' eyes*: Aeneas prefers to be at sea, where he can be admired
      by the alluring but dangerous Sirens (N); 'to' is omitted in Q.
45   *Paphos*: A town in Cyprus, the home of Aeneas' mother Venus.
51   *Delian*: From Delos, the birthplace of Apollo, the god of music.
55   *made disdain . . . fancy's lap*: Made coldness turn (for childlike
      comfort, or adult love) to love's own lap.

ACT 4
Scene 1

11   *Apollo's axle-tree*: The axis on which the sphere carrying the sun
      was thought to revolve *or* the axle of the sun-god's chariot.
12   *Atlas' . . . out of joint*: Such an injury to Atlas (N) would shake the
      heavens.
19   *Typhoeus' den*: Mount Etna in Sicily, under which Typhoeus was
      imprisoned. Q's *Tiphous* may be a compositor's error for Mar-
      lowe's usual spelling Typhon (N).
24   *sporting*: (Here) copulating.
35   *cares*: Oliver 1968 justifies Q's *eares* as a reference to Iarbas'
      eavesdropping. But Iarbas has not known Dido's whereabouts.

Scene 2

1–22 *Come . . . eyes*: Modelled on Iarbas' reaction in Virgil to the
      rumour of Dido's liaison with Aeneas (*Aeneid* IV, 198–218). Mar-

lowe adds the sacrificial ritual (compare 5.1) and the dialogue with Anna.

2–3   *gloomy Jove . . . ills*: Iarbas supposes that Jupiter is punishing him for neglecting to worship him.

10   *Eliza*: Dido was also called Elissa. The spelling here may indicate a compliment to Queen Elizabeth, but the reminiscence which some detect here to Spenser's *Epithalamion* (composed for his wedding on 11 June 1594, more than a year after Marlowe's death) is chronologically impossible unless the line is post-Marlovian.

13   *hide of ground*: When Dido arrived in Africa, Iarbas offered her as much land as could be covered by an ox-hide. She cut a hide into strips and marked out the boundary for a city which became Carthage. A 'hide' was also an Old English measure (approximately one hundred acres) of land.

27   *partake*: Share, hence impart, communicate.

32   *coloured*: (Here) specious.

39   *numbers*: (i) Quantity, (ii) songs (cf. line 45).

44   *In this . . . pensiveness*: 'Luxuriating in this swooning ['dying'] self-pity' (Oliver 1968).

56   *dishevelled hair*: (Q's spelling *discheveld* is etymological) emblematic of emotional disturbance.

Scene 3

6   *my Phoenissa*: Dido (the Virgilian epithet *Phoenissa* means 'Phoenician').

8   *clogged*: Burdened, weighted down.

9–11   *immortal house . . . glassy fields*: Fame and honour are given allegorical dwellings, the sea is thought of as land to be worked.

18   *realms*: For Q's *beames*.

22–4   *slice the sea . . . the deep*: The black ('sable') ships will move so fast that the winds will follow after them like servants.

31   *Banish . . . your mouth*: Achates reacts punningly to the erotic extravagance of line 29.

32   *follow . . . stars*: Navigate by the stars in which your future is written.

50   *accustom*: Customarily do.

55   *dure this female drudgery*: Endure this enslavement to a woman, *or* stand these laborious female contrivances (tears, kisses, etc.).

Scene 4

6   *drift*: Purpose, with a pun on the ships' motion.

11   *Circe*: See (N). The suggestion of an association between the

enchantress and Dido's late husband seems to be Marlowe's invention.

13   *how might I . . . chide?*: What can I do to chide them?

19   *How haps . . . not*: How happens Achates not to bid me . . .

29–30 *Hath not . . . leave him here*: Either Aeneas was prepared to abandon Ascanius, or this is bare-faced bluff.

50   *clouds . . . thou fled'st*: Various myths describe Aeneas being hidden by a cloud sent by a god, but not his fleeing in one.
     fled'st: Q's *fleest* may be merely a variant form of the past tense.

57   *Destinies*: Fates.

62   *Moors*: Dido's north African subjects.

64   *make experience of*: Test, demonstrate.

68   *my guard*: Probably a guard of honour, but the hint of preventing another attempted escape is not uncharacteristic of the play.

92   *fire proud Lacedaemon*: Burn Sparta (in revenge for the burning of Troy).

104 *prevent*: Forestall, act first.

105 *take young Ascanius*: Dido's plan to keep Ascanius (here, of course, Cupid) hostage is Marlowe's invention.

127 *Packed*: (i) Conspired, compacted, (ii) hoisted full sail.

151 *not . . . base tackling*: Nothing, not even so humble a thing as these ropes.

157 *to chastise shipboys*: The knotted ropes (155) could serve as whips.

159 *favours*: Ribbons given as love-tokens (and useless as sails).

Scene 5

This comic scene, with his first pastiche of 'The Passionate Shepherd to his Love', is entirely Marlowe's invention.

5   *services*: (Here) a type of pear.

6   *Dewberries*: Blackberries or gooseberries.

20   *twigger*: (Affectionately) a good breeder, a rake.

28   *our*: Emended from Q's *your*, but her pronouns are becoming confused in her excitement.

36–7 *Well . . . say him nay*: The Nurse remembers a rejected suitor, who would succeed ('speed') better now.

ACT 5
Scene 1

11–15 *The sun . . . her fumes*: Like bees bearing the sweet honey of Hybla (N), the sun's beams will carry the perfumes of the east, and shed them on the new town. 'Wherewith' (12) is syntactically ambiguous.

38–9   *Ascanius' prophecy . . . thousand years*: 'The prophecy was that Ascanius would found Alba Longa, and that he and his descendants (Iulus was the son of Ascanius, born in Lavinium) would rule the empire for centuries to come' (Gill 1977). Virgil treats Iulus and Ascanius as identical, using both names to refer to the son of Aeneas. Cf. 1.1.96–108.

89   *road*: Roadstead, sheltered water just beyond the harbour.

106   *use to quit*: Make a practice of leaving.

110   *'Let me go . . . hence'*: Q gives this line to Aeneas, but Dido is echoing his words, as in line 124.

114   *chained*: Q's *chaungd* is possible but weak.

116   *for grief of thee*: Caused by my grieving over you.

117   *thy*: For Q's *my*.

136–8   *Si bene . . . mentem*: 'If I have deserved anything from you, or anything about me has been dear to you, take pity on a falling house; and I beg this – if there is still [*adhuc* for Q's *ad haec*] any place for prayers – abandon this purpose', *Aeneid* IV, 317–19.

139–40   *Desine . . . sequor*: 'Stop inflaming both of us with your laments. Against my will, I must go to Italy', *Aeneid* IV, 360–61.

156–9   *Thy mother . . . gave thee suck*: Close to *Aeneid* IV, 365–7. The mountains of the Caucasus were famed for their harshness, as were the tigers of Hercynia in Persia for their ferocious cruelty.

162   *fisher swain*: Poor fisherman.

165–8   *O serpent . . . thee*: An elaboration on the almost proverbial dangers of nurturing a serpent in one's bosom.

171   *at large*: Fully.

201   *mermaid's eye*: Mermaids allured sailors with their looks, as sirens did with their voices.

202   *Aulis' gulf*: Where the Greek fleet assembled before it sailed for Troy.

215   *fairies*: Fairies were said to spirit away human children, and replace them with changelings (which, like Cupid, might then disappear).

234   *heart's of adamant*: (Aeneas') heart is made of impenetrable stone (Q's *heart* leaves the sentence without a main verb).

247   *Triton's niece*: Marlowe confuses the sea-monster Scylla (N), a relative of Triton (N), with Scylla the daughter of King Nisus, who swam after her lover Minos' boat.

248   *Arion's harp*: The musician Arion (N) was robbed and thrown overboard by pirates, but rescued by a dolphin which had been

charmed by his music (Q's *Orions* is a confusion with the mythological hunter and his constellation).

268 *my*: For Q's *thy*.

271 *straight*: Straightaway, very soon.

274–7 *Not far . . . relics*: In *Aeneid* IV, 478–502, Dido's invented
sorceress is an Ethiopian priestess of the Hesperides (N).

275 *arts*: Magical skills.

277 *ticing relics*: The love-tokens Aeneas has left behind.

306 *a conqueror*: I.e. Hannibal, the Carthaginian general who invaded
Italy and nearly defeated Rome in the Second Punic War, imagined
as a phoenix rising from Dido's ashes.

308 *his*: Aeneas'.

310–11 *Litora . . . nepotes*: 'I pray that coasts may fight opposing
coasts, waves fight waves, arms fight arms; may they and their
descendants go on fighting', *Aeneid* IV, 628–9.

313 *Sic . . . umbras*: 'Thus, thus I rejoice to go down into the shadows',
Aeneid IV, 660.

314–28 *O help . . . to thee*: Marlowe's addition to Virgil.

317 *tires upon*: Feeds on, consumes.

319 *prevail*: (Here) avail.

TAMBURLAINE THE GREAT

Marlowe did not invent Tamburlaine. The historical Timur (1336–
1405) was widely known in the West as the conqueror of Baghdad (1401)
and Damascus (1403); his defeat and capture of Beyazit I (Marlowe's
Bajazeth) in 1402 at the battle of Angora (modern Ankara) made him
especially famous as the humbler of the proudest of monarchs, and – since
this victory relieved for a time the Ottoman pressure on Christendom –
led to the belief that he was the scourge of God. Marlowe draws particularly on the accounts of the Spaniard Pedro Mexía's *Silva de Varia Lección*
(1542), as translated both in Thomas Fortescue's *The Forest or Collection
of Histories* (1571) and in George Whetstone's *The English Mirror*
(1586); and of Petrus Perondinus, *Magni Tamerlanis Scythiarum Impera-
toris Vita* (1553), which he seems to have read in Latin. Nonetheless,
when Part One, *The Conquests of Tamburlaine the Scythian Shepherd*,
was first staged in 1587 by the Lord Admiral's Men, it was a startlingly
innovatory play, an aggressively learned celebration of power radically
different from the normal repertoire of the popular theatre. There were
other plays about eastern conquerors, but their protagonists were usually
assimilated to familiar Elizabethan paradigms: Thomas Preston's

Cambises (*c.* 1561) is a Morality play whose 'hero' exemplifies the evils and suffers the fate of a tyrant; the anonymous *Wars of Cyrus* (late 1580s) transforms the king of Persia into a model of romance chivalry and magnanimity, 'A prince . . . most mild and merciful' (sig. F^r). Tamburlaine is different – so different that he seems to stand outside merely human categories:

> Some powers divine, or else infernal, mixed
> Their angry seeds at his conception;
> For he was never sprung of human race. (2.6.9–11)

The excitement the play originally caused can be difficult to recapture today. In performance, however, it can still be exhilarating.

Like its hero, its poetry tends to disrupt familiar categorizations. Tamburlaine's first appearance is a surprise (1.2). We have been led to expect a brigand (Scythia was virtually synonymous with barbarism); instead, he is an Errol Flynn swashbuckler who, however, overwhelms Zenocrate not with erotic charisma but with 'high astounding terms' (Prologue, 5):

> With milk-white harts upon an ivory sled
> Thou shalt be drawn amidst the frozen pools
> And scale the icy mountains' lofty tops,
> Which with thy beauty will be soon resolved. (1.2.98–101)

Everything is in the future tense ('For "will" and "shall" best fitteth Tamburlaine', 3.3.41), as indefinite as the strange journey he envisages through high, cold places. The ivory sled drawn through the snow by white harts is literally dazzling. At one level, it evokes a delight in material riches, revelling in the luxury of being drawn along, as in the triumphs to which the play frequently returns. But this is also a fantasy of being transported in another, more transcendent sense: the imagined wealth is fabulous, it shades into the exoticism of romance, as, later, will Dr Faustus' dream of spirits 'Like Almain rutters with their horsemen's staves, / Or Lapland giants, trotting by our sides' (1.127–8). Zenocrate too is both an invaluable prize ('more worth to Tamburlaine / Than the possession of the Persian crown', 1.2.90–91) and a more-than-mortal being whose radiant beauty can melt ('resolve', 101) the snow.

There is a comparably exalted materialism in Tamburlaine's lines when he seizes the crown (2.6). One reason the speech compels attention is that, like much of the play's most memorable poetry, it is the hero's own articulation of his complex, almost superhuman ambition. Another is that the lines condense and draw into themselves many of the verbal motifs we have already heard, and so seem naturally climactic. The defeated Cosroe had earlier supposed Tamburlaine's rebellion to be against the hierarchy of nature, 'With such a giantly presumption' (2.6.2) like that of the Titans against Jupiter. But here Tamburlaine propounds a new cosmology: ambition is a bodily need, 'The thirst of reign' only to be satisfied by the 'sweetness of a crown' (52); and it is a drive that permeates the universe from Jupiter down through the warring elements that make up the body and the rest of 'The wondrous architecture of the world' (62) and crosses the divide between matter and spirit to enter our 'aspiring minds' (60). The world teaches, wills us to aspire. 'Our souls' become grammatically confused with the 'wand'ring planet[s]' and 'restless spheres' they contemplate, all borne along by the perpetually continuing present participles 'climbing', 'moving' (61–5). Some readers have felt that the object of all this aspiring, 'The sweet fruition of an earthly crown' (69), is oddly anti-climactic. But the whole speech centres on the crown Tamburlaine holds in his hand, and is designed to confound the usual hierarchy of spirit and matter: Jupiter's mother, the goddess of earthly wealth whose name in Latin means 'riches', is here called 'heavenly Ops' (53), and 'th'empyreal heaven' (55) turns the empyrean into an empire. Like a great aria, the speech returns in its last line to its opening theme of sensual pleasure, the 'fruition', enjoyment almost sexually fruity, of the crown's earthly sweetness.

Tamburlaine's poetry is dominated by excess, by hyperbole and insistent comparatives and superlatives. Like the play's hero, it strives to outdo, to overgo. At its peaks, it turns its own rhetorical power back on itself, declaring that it cannot express its inexpressibility. Thus, when Tamburlaine ponders Zenocrate's beauty (5.1), his words dwell on their own inadequacy ('Fair is too foul an epithet for thee', 136) and climax in the claim that even a super-poem on beauty distilled from all the poets would leave something unsaid:

> Yet should there hover in their restless heads,
> One thought, one grace, one wonder at the least,
> Which into words no virtue can digest. (171–3)

The verse enacts this unspeakable beauty in its own huge, almost unspeakable sentences, and confounds together the subject and its expression in imagery that fuses Zenocrate's face with the metaphors that describe it:

> ... thy shining face
> Where Beauty, mother to the Muses, sits
> And comments volumes with her ivory pen,
> Taking instructions from thy flowing eyes –
> Eyes, when that Ebena steps to heaven
> In silence of thy solemn evening's walk,
> Making the mantle of the richest night,
> The moon, the planets, and the meteors, light. (143–50)

But *Tamburlaine*'s words are not separable from its theatrical action. Words are weapons to be 'manage[d]' (3.3.131) in verbal duels, part of the play's expression of power. The action itself combines static, symmetrical tableaux with relentless forward movement, as though enacting the tension between the end-stopped single line and the larger verse-paragraph. Tamburlaine is constantly breaking the rules, defying conventions, yet he turns his defiance into ceremonies, rituals, of conflict. The effect is to render the audience's reactions excitedly uncertain. Marlowe tightens the dramatic structure by interweaving the siege of Damascus with the tormenting of Bajazeth, and both with the reactions of Zenocrate (whose part is almost entirely an invention). Tamburlaine's victories are both glamorous and repellant.

The Second Part of the Bloody Conquests of Mighty Tamburlaine (1588) is a sequel, and is generally felt to be a weaker play. Marlowe had used up most of the historical materials in Part One and had little interest in the real Timur's comfortable old age in Samarkand. Part Two was therefore assembled from a variety of sources, and tellingly little of the new material directly concerns Tamburlaine himself. The hero is no longer so securely at the centre of things; he is slightly displaced by all the new characters and is caught in a wider history just as he moves in a wider geography (taken from the 1570 atlas of Abraham Ortelius). The perfidy and subsequent defeat of the Christians is an adaptation of the events leading up to the later battle of Varna (1444), as reported, for instance, in Antonius Bonifinius, *Rerum Ungaricarum Decades* (1543). Olympia's ruse to escape the attentions of Theridamas is borrowed from Canto 29 of Ariosto's *Orlando Furioso* (1516). (Other, smaller borrowings are recorded in the Notes.) The little Olympia sub-plot has certain obvious resonances with the main action: Olympia's devotion to her dead husband is like and unlike Tamburlaine's to the dead Zenocrate, as her murder of her son is like and unlike Tamburlaine's murder of Calyphas. When she contrives to be stabbed in the throat, her death is oddly reminiscent of Tamburlaine stabbing his arm. Yet the action remains disconnected from the main plot. The play has greater thematic coherence than dramatic unity.

Its organizing theme is death, and its distinctive poetry is funereal. Zenocrate's death reverses the language of Part One ('Black is the beauty of the brightest day', 2.4.1), and Tamburlaine's finest words are his great lament, with its solemn refrain:

> Now walk the angels on the walls of heaven,
> As sentinels to warn th'immortal souls
> To entertain divine Zenocrate. (15–17)

Tamburlaine can still rise to hymning himself, even recalling (4.1) the earlier speech on the aspiring mind in Part One, but he does so as he kills his own son. And we recognize the play's distinctive leitmotif of mortality when it returns in his captains' choric threnody for Tamburlaine himself at the beginning of the play's last scene.

The dramatic rhythm is slow, gradually arraying the forces of Tamburlaine against those of his enemies, cataloguing the armies and the vast distance of their marches, and finally harnessing them to its central dramatic symbol, Tamburlaine's chariot. In the opening dumb show of George Gascoigne and Francis Kinwelmarsh's *Jocasta* (1566),

> there came in upon the stage a king with an imperial crown upon his head, very richly apparelled . . . sitting in a chariot very richly furnished, drawn in by four kings in their doublets and hosen, with crowns also upon their heads, representing unto us Ambition, by the history of Sesostris, king of Egypt.

In *Tamburlaine*, the emblem of ambition is staged in all its grim cruelty, an extraordinary realization of the persistent language of triumph. Yet it is as though, without knowing it, Tamburlaine is also taking part in the greater triumph of Death. The historical Timur did return to Samarkand, as Tamburlaine here plans to; but 'death cuts off the progress of his pomp / And murd'rous Fates throws all his triumphs down' (Prologue, 4–5). The chariot becomes the symbol of his limitation as well as of his triumph.

Part Two is a more ideologically self-conscious play. Tamburlaine seems now to be caught inside a more traditional representation of the smallness of human ambition in the face of death. Traditionally, mortal thoughts led to a sober contemplation of religion, normally Christianity. But Marlowe withholds any unambiguous reassurances from his audi-

ence: Orcanes attributes his victory over the Christians to divine punishment, but his henchman is sceptical: ''Tis but the fortune of the wars,
my lord, / Whose power is often proved a miracle' (2.3.31–2). It is
also disturbing that Tamburlaine is so ready to excuse his atrocities by
embracing the description of him as 'the scourge of God' which had
traditionally been used to explain him away.

Both Parts of *Tamburlaine* were published together in an anonymous
octavo edition of 1590 (the basis for the text printed here); and their
popularity is attested by further quarto editions of 1592 and 1605. They
were much imitated.

TAMBURLAINE THE GREAT, PART ONE

TO THE GENTLEMEN READERS AND OTHERS THAT TAKE PLEASURE IN READING HISTORIES

9   *fond . . . jestures*: Foolish . . . comic action.
14   *graced*: Favoured (by popular audiences).
24   *degree*: Rank.
26   *R. J.*: Richard Jones, the publisher responsible for both parts of
      Tamburlaine.

PROLOGUE

1   *jigging veins*: The doggerel styles of the comic 'jigs' which were
      performed after plays.
      rhyming: Unlike *Tamburlaine*'s heroic blank verse.
      mother-wits: Mere natural wits. The opening line makes two con-
      temptuous references to Elizabethan popular theatre.
2   *such conceits . . . pay*: *Either* the kind of wit that earns a living
      from clowning, *or* such tricks as pay the clowns' wages.
7   *glass*: Mirror.

ACT 1
Scene 1

11   *freezing . . . cold*: Snow and ice.
      meteors: Meteorological phenomena.
13–15 *At whose birthday . . . brain*: Mycetes was born under the

conjunction of the changeable Moon (Cynthia) and dull Saturn, and without the benign influences of Jupiter (greatness), the Sun (majesty) and Mercury (wisdom, eloquence).

15 *their*: For O's *his*, a mistaken anticipation of the use of the pronoun later in the line.

19 *through your planets*: Mycetes understands Cosroe's astrological lore.

33 *pull my plumes*: Like his 'flocks' of travellers (32), Mycetes will be easy pickings (like domestic fowl for a fox).

36–8 *Scythian thief . . . Isles*: From Scythia (a traditionally barbarous region in central Asia, north of the Black Sea), Tamburlaine intercepts the overland trade route from the capital of Persia to Britain and Ireland. *Trading* (38) is the reading of the second octavo; other early texts read *Treading*.

39 *confines*: Borders, hence territories.

41 *dreaming prophecies*: Prophetic dreams, or perhaps prophecies as meaningless as dreams.

45 *vagrant ensign*: Nomadic banner.

50 *Damon*: A byword for friendship. See (N).

63 *gall*: Bile, rancour. The antecedent of 'Whose' is unclear; the line perhaps conflates the horses with their riders, but they are an odd subject for 'Have sworn' (64).

66 *the Grecian dame*: Helen of Troy.

67–8 *Time . . . today*: Like the rhyme, the proverbs (Tilley T323, 327) are banal.

69 *borrowed*: From the sun.

87 *task*: Necessary to metre and sense, but missing from all early texts.

89 *Assyria*: This emendation of O's *Affrica* seems necessary to both geography and metre. Cf. line 164. Babylon once formed part of the Assyrian empire.

98 *kiss it*: One would sometimes kiss an object (e.g. the Bible) on which one swore an oath. Cosroe may also be punning on 'seat' (= arse) in response to Mycetes's reference to his throne (97).

99 *Embossed*: Richly decorated.

107 *mated*: (Here) daunted.

109 *pass*: (Here) care.

111 *Median*: From Media, the north-eastern part of the Persian empire.

118 *resolve*: Melt, dissolve.

119 *equinoctial line*: The equator (apparently indicating people from much farther west; or perhaps an error for the northern tropic).

130 *Cyrus*: Cyrus the Great of Persia (N) overran the Ionian Greek cities of Asia Minor. Though the armies of his son Darius I invaded

Greece, only *his* son Xerxes led his own forces into Europe in 480 BC.

131–2   *forces . . . Christendom*: Perhaps referring to the Byzantine empire.

135.1   SD CENEUS: O's *Conerus* is a phantom character, produced by a misreading of this name.

137   *states*: (Here) peers, noblemen.

153–4   *Macedonians . . . host*: Alexander the Great of Macedon (N) defeated Darius III in 333 and 331 BC.

159   *them shall malice*: Those who will resent.

166   *late-discovered isles*: The West Indies or islands in the eastern oceans.

182   *too exasperate*: So exasperated as.

Scene 2

8   *mean*: Low-born.

10   *silly*: (Here) defenceless.

15   *privy signet*: Document of authorization, with the royal seal.
hand: Signature.

16   *thorough Africa*: I.e. to Egypt. In some medieval traditions, 'Africa' designated the Turkish empire. See Seaton 1924:20.

18   *the puissant Cham*: The Great Khan, ruler of Mongolia and Tartary.

28   *prizes . . . precinct*: Treasure out of my hands.

29   *For . . . my state*: I.e. he needs booty to feed his infant power.

33   *for . . . import*: I.e. he acts like a lord.

41   *Lie . . . weeds*: His change of clothes marks symbolically his transition from shepherd to conqueror.

45   *success . . . unvaluèd*: Outcome and incalculable loss.

50–51   *exhalations . . . earth*: Earthquakes were attributed to winds trying to escape from beneath the earth's surface.
tilt: Joust, battle.

57   *Spurning*: (i) Kicking, (ii) treating disdainfully.

61   *our estimates*: The reputations we give ourselves.

64   *conceit*: (Here) imagination.

88   *Rhodope*: For O's *Rhodolfe*. See (N). The Thracian mountain, famous for its silver mines, may be recalled because it was supposedly named after a queen of Thrace who claimed to be lovelier than Juno.

103   *fifty-headed Volga*: The river Volga with its fifty tributaries.

104   *Shall all we offer*: All of these we shall offer.

118   *Such hope . . . horse*: The Persian horsemen hope so too, but they will themselves be captured.

129 *play the orator*: Tamburlaine mocks the tradition of big speeches before battles. His enemies' wealth will be an adequate stimulus for his troops.

133 *top*: The quarto's reading, correcting O's *foot* in the light of line 135.

134 *alarm*: Alarum, battle-cry.

144 *possession*: (Four syllables) winnings.

147 *chain*: Chain of office.

160 *Avernus' darksome vaults*: Hell (N).

161 *triple-headed dog*: Cerberus (N). (One of the labours of Hercules was to drag him up from the underworld.)

163 *outward habit judge*: Appearance (or clothing) reveals.

169 *characters graven . . . brows*: Signs indelibly written in your face ('characters' is accented on the second syllable).

170 *stout aspect*: Valiant appearance ('aspect' is accented on the second syllable).

187 *portly*: (Here) stately.

189 *conduct*: Guidance (accented on the second syllable).

194 *merchants*: Merchant ships.
stems: Timber prows.

199–200 *Jove . . . heavens*: Because Jupiter usurped the throne of heaven and, coincidentally, sometimes disguised himself ('maskèd') as a shepherd, Tamburlaine takes him as a precedent for his own aspirations. There may also be the suggestion that the gods began as human beings.

215 *Should . . . state*: Should offer to aggrandize us with dukedoms right now.

216 *We think . . . exchange*: We would think that a poor exchange.

225 *resolvèd noble Scythians*: Theridamas is surprised to find barbarians with these qualities.

243 *Pylades and Orestes*: See (N). When captured by the Taurians of Scythia, who wished to make a human sacrifice, the friends offered to die in each other's place.

250 *Shall want . . . pierced*: I.e. I would gladly have my heart pierced.

258 *For you . . . doubt*: Tamburlaine is sure that Zenocrate too must have been won over.

ACT 2

Scene 1

1 *Thus far*: Cosroe has heard of Theridamas's and Tamburlaine's alliance (35–9) and is advancing to meet them at the 'river Araris' (63 and note).

8   *lift*: Lifted.

12   *A pearl*: I.e. his head.

15–17 *fiery circles . . . throne*: His eyes are like the heavenly spheres and bear the stars propitious to his fortune.

21   *in folds . . . figure*: When furrowed . . . prefigure.

27   *sinewy*: O's *snowy* is probably an error for *sinowy*, a variant spelling.

29–30 *the man / Should*: The man who is destined to.

31   *terms of life*: Lively terms.

33   *Nature . . . his stars*: His natural gifts, his fortune and the influence of his stars all compete.

42   *strait . . . port*: Narrow . . . gate. Cf. Matthew 7:14: 'Strait is the gate and narrow is the way which leadeth unto life.'

43   *palace*: The image seems to be dictated by the topographical metaphor (and alliteration) of lines 40–44.

44   *Proud . . . if*: He will be very lucky if.

63   *river Araris*: Probably a mistake for the river Araxes in Persia, caused by an apparent reference to a river Araris in Virgil, *Eclogue* I, 61–2.

Scene 2

3–4 *On . . . of*: Both mean 'because of'.

10   *Aurora*: See (N). Mycetes threatens quick vengeance, at first light.

27   *false*: (Here) betray.

31   *Albania*: In Ortelius's atlas, a province to the west of the Caspian Sea.

40   *champian*: Variant form of 'champaign', flat open country.

42   *Which*: I.e. the observers on horseback.

47–8 *cruel brothers . . . dragons*: In Greek mythology, when Cadmus sowed the earth with dragon's teeth, armed warriors sprang up and then started to fight each other.

59–71 *to entrap . . . Persia*: A device recommended by sixteenth-century strategists. Cf. Tamburlaine's use of his gold in 1.2.

Scene 3

2   *approvèd*: Proven (by experience).

5   *I take . . . satisfaction*: I am satisfied by your judgement.

7   *oracles of heaven*: Early texts omit *of*.

11–12 *sway . . . in*: Exercise some command over.

15–16 *The host of Xerxes . . . Araris*: The huge armies of Xerxes (see (N) and 1.1.130n) drank rivers, including the Araxes, dry. See Herodotus, *Histories* VII.21.

21   *Cyclopian wars*: The Cyclopes (N) who forged Jupiter's thunder-bolts are confused with the giants or Titans, both of whom made war on the Olympian gods.

25   *working*: (i) Moving, (ii) effective.

26   *top*: In all early texts, *stop* is nonsense.

33   *and*: The reading of the quarto, against O's *not*.

37   *she*: Nemesis, the personification of divine vengeance for human presumption, whose temple was located at Rhamnus in Attica.

57   *wings*: I.e. the cross-piece of the cutlass ('curtle-axe', 55).

59–60   *sure . . . assure*: Apparently a disyllable and a trisyllable.

Scene 4

0.2   SD *offering*: Attempting

3   *those were*: Those who were.

9   *the pin*: It held the clout in place; to 'cleave' it was to hit the bull's-eye.

11   *close*: Secretly.

12   *far from*: Uncharacteristic of.

18   *give the lie*: I.e. accuse me of lying.

22   *witty*: Wise.

25   *when I see my time*: When the occasion arises. Mycetes is trying to sound 'witty' (22).

41.1   SD *Sound . . . battle*: Give the signal to resume the battle.

Scene 5

0.4   SD *presenting . . . crown*: Having refused to take Mycetes's crown in the previous scene, Tamburlaine now apparently presents it to Cosroe, who already has the one he acquired in 1.1.

20   *embassage*: A message by ambassador.

27   *take Meander's course*: Do as Meander has done, i.e. change sides.

30   *gratify . . . good*: Repay your service.

33   *And sought . . . deserved*: And sought to honour your rank as it deserved.

37   *Better replies*: I.e. better rewards than mere words.

42   *witless brother . . . lost*: Cf. 1.1.119–21.

43   *with fame and usury*: For our glory and profit.

51   *brave*: Grand, glorious.

73   *in greatest novelty*: 'No matter how new and rare' (Jump 1967).

74   *rest attemptless*: Not make the attempt.

83   *they*: I.e. Techelles and Usumcasane.

85–6   *the Turk . . . apace*: The submission of the Sultan of the Turkish empire, the Pope (who presides over Western Christendom), the

Sultan of Egypt (who rules Africa) and the Byzantine Emperor would, in effect, give Tamburlaine world domination.

89   *before his room be hot*: Before he has warmed up his throne.

92   *purchase*: (i) Undertaking, (ii) cost, (iii) advantage gained, plunder.

96   *lose more labour*: Cost us more labour.

100   *turn him*: For O's *turn his*.

103   *more warriors*: The opportunity to gather more troops.

105   *for me*: As far as I am concerned.

Scene 6

2–6   *giantly presumption . . . jaws*: After the giants' unsuccessful war against the gods, during which they piled mountains on top of one another in an attempt to reach the heavens, Jupiter imprisoned one of them (Enceladus or Typhon (N)) under Mount Etna (whence, supposedly, its volcanic fires).

13   *doubtlessly resolve of*: Fearlessly resolve to.

14   *by profession*: (i) Avowedly, (ii) as a vocation.

15   *What*: Whatsoever.

17   *mould*: (i) Earth, (ii) mould.
        mettle: (i) Substance, (ii) metal.

19   *Let us . . . minds*: Let us adopt fit attitudes to encounter him.

25   *sucked*: Breathed (but like a baby suckling).

26–7   *same proportion . . . Resolve*: I.e. when we die, we will melt into the four elements whence we first came.

36–7   *make . . . life*: Determine the hateful end of my life.

40.2   SD *Enter [the armies]*: Some editors begin a new scene here, but the action is continuous. O's *Enter* indicates that Cosroe and his forces leave the stage to fight the battle, and he returns in defeat with his conqueror.

52–69   *The thirst . . . earthly crown*: For a discussion of this speech see Headnote.

53   *son of . . . Ops*: Jupiter. Ops (N), his mother, was the goddess of *earthly* riches.

55   *empyreal*: (i) Empyrean (the highest heaven), (ii) imperial.

57   *precedent*: Perhaps with a pun on *president* (O's spelling), one who presides, sits on the throne.

65   *restless spheres*: The constantly moving carriers of the heavenly bodies in Ptolemaic astronomy.

69   *fruition*: Enjoyment.

71   *he*: Anyone.

77   *Neptune and Dis*: Jupiter's brothers. See (N).

82–90 *bloodless body . . . life*: According to ancient physiology, the removal of blood (heat and moisture) would cause a devastating imbalance of the bodily humours, leaving only cold and dryness.

90 *tires on*: Tears at (in falconry), alluding to the talons of the harpy (N).

ACT 3
Scene 1

0.1 SD *BAJAZETH*: Based on Beyazit I.

1 *Barbary*: The north coast of Africa, ruled by the 'bassoes' (pashas or bashaws) of Fez, Morocco and Algiers.

4 *Presume a bickering with*: Dare to attack.

10 *ocean . . . Terrene*: Atlantic . . . Mediterranean.

11–12 *the moon . . . horns*: I.e. at the full moon, when the tides are high.

13–14 *Yet would . . . yield*: Though confident that he could defeat them, Bajazeth is unwilling to engage an external enemy who would distract him from the siege of Constantinople.

25 *coal-black sea*: The Black Sea.

29 *colours*: Banners.

38–9 *take . . . reclaimed*: If the basso has not returned by the dawn of the fourth day, Bajazeth will take this as a sign of determined revolt by Tamburlaine.

46 *stir your siege*: (i) Lift the siege you are conducting, (ii) disturb your throne.

60 *Carnon*: Not identified. Perhaps 'a confusion of the famous aqueduct of Constantinople with its equally famous Golden Horn, seeing that Carnon represents adequately the Turkish for horn' (Seaton 1924).

63 *countermand*: (i) Control, (ii) forbid (the approach by sea).

65 *Orcus' gulf*: Hell.

Scene 2

6 *rape*: Seizure.

11 *queen of heaven*: I.e. Juno.

13 *since*: Since then.

15 *dyes . . . as they are*: Gives me this lifeless pallor.

16 *if . . . events*: If my worst imaginings came true.

19 *all . . . eye*: 'All that the moon beholds' (Jump 1967).

27 *despite*: (Here) defiance.

30 *but for necessity*: Beyond a necessary pretence.

31   *So*: Provided that.

35   *Agydas*: The name is missing from all early texts.

40   *fancy*: Love.

45   *facts*: Deeds, crimes.

50–51   *Muses' song . . . Pierides*: The Muses (goddesses of poetry and music) sang their finest song when challenged to a contest by the Pierides (N).

52   *Minerva . . . Neptune*: Athene (Minerva, goddess of wisdom) and Poseidon (Neptune, god of the sea) competed in their gifts to Attica to become the patron gods of the Athenians. Athene won and gave her name to the city. This contest is linked to that of the Muses with the Pierides in Ovid, *Metamorphoses* V, 302ff.

53   *estimate*: Sense of my own worth.

57   *the young Arabian*: Alcidamus, the King of Arabia, to whom Zenocrate was previously betrothed.

74   *comets*: Regarded as portents of impending doom.

76–87   *As when . . . overthrow*: An imitation of an epic simile.

77   *Cimmerian*: Black (the Cimmerians, in classical legend, lived in perpetual darkness in the far north).

80   *enforcing thunderclaps*: Thunder was sometimes attributed to the clashing of the winds.

82   *sounds the main*: Measures the depth of the ocean.

87.1 SD *naked*: Unsheathed.

99   *stay*: Await.

101   *prolongèd fates*: Longer life.

Scene 3

1   *by this*: By now.

2   *Bithynia*: See (N). Tamburlaine takes his stand in Asia Minor to await Bajazeth's arrival from Constantinople.

3   *See . . . comes*: Spoken ironically. Tamburlaine contrasts Bajazeth's 'brags' (3) with the non-appearance of his army.

5   *He . . . hence*: Does he think he can fight me and rescue you?

15   *janizaries*: An élite division of the Turkish infantry, but here imagined as cavalry.

16   *Mauritanian*: The province in north-west Africa was renowned for its horses.

20   *expedition*: 'Speedy waging' (Jump 1967).

38   *rouse him . . . Europe*: Drive Bajazeth out of Europe.

44   *scourge . . . of God*: Tamburlaine proleptically assumes the title he won for defeating the Turks. Note that it is associated with divine punishment for the Turks' cruelties to Christians.

55 *pirates of Argier*: The cruelty of the Turks to their galley slaves causes them to be identified with the Barbary pirates who terrorized the Mediterranean.

58 *make quick havoc*: (i) Quickly devastate, (ii) make carnage of the living ('quick') bodies.

76 *Alcoran*: The Koran (al-Qur'ān).

104–5 *Hercules ... serpents*: The infant Hercules first displayed his strength by strangling the serpents sent by Juno to kill him in the cradle.

109 *y-sprung*: The Middle English prefix to this past participle is rare in Marlowe. Cf. *Tamburlaine*, Part Two, 4.3.119 (a borrowing from Spenser).

119 *paragon*: (i) Paramour, consort, (ii) equal.

142 *they*: Bajazeth's soldiers.

148 *marshal*: Direct (Marlowe may be comparing the swords to a marshal's rod of office).

154 *Pharsalia*: The climactic battle of Pharsalus (48 BC) in which Pompey the Great was defeated by Julius Caesar. Marlowe's spelling recalls the title of Lucan's poem on the war, the first book of which he translated.

158 *air*: O's *lure* seems impossible, but the emendation is awkward. Perhaps *wound[ing] the senseless air*, usually an emblem of futility, is here an index of Tamburlaine's extraordinary powers. Some editors also emend *our* to *your*.

160–61 *Victory ... tent*: Victory flies to Tamburlaine's colours.

175 *advocates*: Attracted into the plural by association with Bajazeth and Zabina.

188.1 SD *They sound ... stay*: I.e. trumpets sound offstage for the start of the battle, and then stop.

194 *issue conqueror*: Come out the winner.

213 *soil*: Ground on which the battle was fought. O's *foile* is a misreading of long 's'.

215 *strew*: Are strewn over.

222 *gat the best*: Have got the upper hand.

229 *terms*: (i) Names, (ii) statuary busts mounted on pillars.

236 *miscreants*: The 'infidels' of Christian Europe.

248 *pilling brigantines*: Pirate ships used in plundering.

251–59 *Asant ... British shore*: For the geographical details see (N). While the Turkish fleet waits at Zacynthus ('Asant') in the Mediterranean, the Persian fleet will circumnavigate the globe. Joining forces at Gibraltar, they will dominate the Atlantic seaboard of Europe.

273 *Triumph*: (i) Rejoice, (ii) hold a triumphal procession (see Introduction, pp. xvii–xviii).

ACT 4

Scene 1

1–3 *Awake . . . down*: The Sultan imagines that the sounds of the siege of Damascus which Tamburlaine is now conducting in Syria should be audible in Memphis in Egypt.

4   *rogue of Volga*: Tamburlaine, here identified with the area north and west of the Caspian Sea.

18   *monstrous*: Trisyllabic.
     Gorgon: See (N); 'prince of hell' suggests this is not merely one of the classical gorgons (such as Medusa), but the devil Demogorgon (cf. *Doctor Faustus*, 3.19).

26–7 *Environing . . . wood*: The weapons of the men surrounding their banner ('standard') create the appearance of a thicket bristling with thorns.

51   *spangled white*: Decorated with silver spangles (?). We are asked to imagine an intenser flash of *snowy white*.

61   *jetty*: Jet-black.

68   *See*: See to it that.

71   *fresh warning . . . us*: Renewed notice to join us in war.

Scene 2

3–4 *sacrificing . . . blood*: Perhaps a misunderstanding of Shi'ite Muslim penitential practices commemorating the murder of al-Hussein, grandson of the prophet, by the oppressive rulers of his day. Seaton (1929) found a possible source in François de Belleforest, *Cosmographie Universelle* (1575), II, 597.

5–6 *every fixèd star . . . fens*: The sun and stars were thought to draw up infectious vapours from bogs and fenland.

7   *glorious*: Boastful.

8–9 *God . . . lamps*: God, the prime mover, sets in motion the *primum mobile*, which in turn imparts its motion to the other heavenly spheres (see Aristotle, *Metaphysics* 12.6), including here spcifically that of the fixed stars.

27   *god of hell*: Pluto.

30   *triple region of the air*: The air was traditionally divided into three parts: the highest region heated by the sphere of fire and the movement of the heavenly spheres, the middle region cold, the

lowest region heated by the reflection of the sun's rays against the earth. Tamburlaine asks for all three to be translucent.

37   *aspect*: (i) Appearance, (ii) position and influence (of a heavenly body).

38   *meridian line*: The highest point of noon.

43–6 *As when . . . earth*: The traditional explanation of lightning.

49   *Clymene's brainsick son*: The story ('fame') of Phaethon (N), son of Apollo and Clymene, is Tamburlaine's climactic instance of fire in heaven.

50   *brent*: Burnt.
      the axletree of heaven: The axis which was supposed to run through the centre of the earth and around which the heavenly bodies revolved.

52   *fiery meteors*: The weapons whizzing through the air will become blazing comets (portents of impending doom).

82   *in again*: Back into the cage.

96   *Plato's wondrous year*: Plato's *Timaeus* (39d) predicts a time when the planets will return to their original positions, and the present phase of the world will end.

103–4 *Like . . . Memphian fields*: I.e. like copies ('shadows') of the obelisks ('Pyramides': four syllables) of Memphis.

105   *statue*: A legendary golden statue of an eagle in Damascus (mentioned in the medieval romance *Bevis of Hampton*), or perhaps of the ibis, the sacred bird of Egypt (cf. 4.3.37).

108   *mask*: (Here) dress (richly, as in a masque).

120   *their*: The streamers'.

Scene 3

1–6   *Methinks . . . Aonian fields*: See (N). The Sultan compares his march against Tamburlaine with the feats of classical hunters. Meleager, with help from the warriors of the Argolid in Greece, slew the monstrous Calydonian boar (but himself died as a consequence); Cephalus hunted the uncatchable Teumessian fox (rather than 'wolf'), sent by Themis to punish the Thebans ('Aonian' = Greek) for the death of the Sphinx.

22   *brave*: (Here) defy.

37   *Ibis*: Sacred bird of the Egyptians, perhaps linked to 4.2.105. A mistake for Isis?

49   *partial*: Biased (in his favour).

Scene 4

0.2 SD *all in scarlet*: Philip Henslowe records payments for 'Tamerlane's breeches of crimson velvet' (Henslowe's *Diary*, ed. R. A. Foakes and R. T. Rickert (Cambridge, 1961), p. 322).

10 *stomach*: (i) Hunger, (ii) anger.

17–22 *Ye Furies ... dish*: See (N). Bajazeth asks the goddesses of vengeance for a poison from Hell ('Avernus' pool'), or for the venom of the snakes from the Lernean swamp.

17 *mask*: (Here) hide.

24 *Procne*: She fed her son to her husband. See (N).

31 *proper*: Own.

44 *brawns ... carbonadoes*: Muscles ... grilled strips of meat.

59 *while*: Until.

63–4 *consort of music*: (i) Musical harmony, (ii) group of musicians.

79 *triple region*: I.e. Africa, Asia and Europe.

80 *trace*: (i) Travel, traverse, (ii) chart.

81 *pen*: I.e. sword.

reduce them to: (i) Transform them into, (ii) subjugate them.

85 *the perpendicular*: In the old 'T-in-O' maps – so called because their division of the world into three regions (Asia in the upper part of the circle, Africa in the lower left-hand part, and Europe in the lower right) formed a 'T' inside an 'O' – the T's downstroke passed through Jerusalem, the centre of the world. Or 'perpendicular' = first meridian of longitude.

88 *still*: Forever.

91 *friends*: Kinsmen.

98 *bloody humours*: Traditional physiology maintained that health depended on the balance of the four bodily fluids, or 'humours' (blood, phlegm, choler, bile). Here, Bajazeth's need for food is so severe that his stomach feeds on his own blood; paradoxically, the body's attempt to preserve itself actually hastens death.

102–3 *looking ... enlarge us*: Hoping some kindly force will pity us and set us free.

107 *Soft*: Stay, wait.

108 *surfeit*: Become ill from over-eating.

110.1 SD *second course of crowns*: Either real crowns, or sweetmeats in the shape of them.

127–9 *As far ... torrid zone*: From the frozen north to the far east, and then to the tropics.

127 *plage*: Region (emended from O's *place*: cf. Part Two 1.1.68).

128 *bower*: O reads *hower*, corrected in later octavos and quarto.

131   *valour*: Emending O's *value*.
134   *they ... she investeth*: Those are worthy whom she (virtue or honour) makes.
135   *so well vouchsafed*: So graciously granted (them).
137   *states*: Ranks.
142   *underneath our feet*: In the southern hemisphere.

ACT 5

Scene 1

0.2   SD *branches of laurel*: The 'signs of victory' of line 55.
13   *I fear ... sword*: I fear that his personal practice in war.
14   *parcel*: An essential part.
20   *unspotted*: Virginal.
21   *blubbered ... hearty*: Tear-stained ... heart-felt.
25–6 *tears ... and hearts*: I.e. the Virgins wept tears of blood in their earlier petitions to the Governor. Cf. line 85.
27   *made*: I.e. being.
30   *only danger*: The threat (as distinct from the present certainty) of disaster.
31   *warrants*: Assurances (referring to the black banners).
40   *in that*: Considering that.
45   *overweighing*: Overruling (continuing the imagery of the 'balance', lines 41–42).
46   *qualify*: Mitigate, moderate.
49   *holy patrons*: Divine protectors.
54   *Convey events ... heart*: Suggest to him the idea of a merciful resolution.
55   *signs of victory*: I.e. the laurel branches they are holding.
58   *shadow*: Conceal.
64   *turtles*: Turtle-doves.
65   *be first*: Be the first who.
68–70 *when first ... eyes*: A main verb must be understood, e.g. 'when first my milk-white flags *appeared*'.
77   *the holy Graces*: Deities of gracious kindness.
87   *Whose ... with conceit*: Whose cheeks and hearts, so pained by the thought. In the extraordinarily suspended syntax of this speech, the 'cheeks and hearts' govern 'wax' (91).
88   *never-stayèd arm*: To stay one's arm = to spare.
89–90 *prevent ... bear*: Deprive their souls of heavens of comfort which they might still enjoy in old age.

100 *prostrate service*: Offer of service, delivered in a state of prostration (perhaps literally prostrating themselves).

102 *of rule*: In a position of authority.

103–5 *And wished . . . diadem*: And wished that they might have the opportunity, as worthy subjects, to invest you with the crown of Egypt.

111–12 *For . . . slicing edge*: Death has jurisdiction (like a judge on his 'circuit') wherever Tamburlaine swings his sword.

115 *fleshless body*: Death is usually represented as a skeleton.

117 *charge*: Charge at, with a cruel pun on 'charge' = order (116).

118 *scarlet*: (i) The robes of a judge, (ii) blood.

122 *observations*: Observances, rituals.

123 *Gihon*: The river Gihon, in Eden (Genesis 2:13), identified with the Nile. Its 'golden waves' (also mentioned by Spenser, *Faerie Queene* I.vii.43) perhaps arise from confusion with the gold of the river Pison (Genesis 2:11–12).

125 *god of arms*: Mars, Venus' lover.

127 *peremptory*: (Stressed on the first and third syllables) absolute.

133 *Thessalian*: Thessaly was renowned as a place of magic and drugs. *mithridate*: An antidote; here used in the sense of 'poison'.

135–90 *Ah, fair Zenocrate . . . nobility*: On the language of this speech, see Headnote, pp. 579–80.

137 *passion*: (Here) sorrow, compassion.

142 *resolvèd pearl*: I.e. the dew.

144–5 *Beauty . . . ivory pen*: I.e. Zenocrate is so beautiful that Beauty herself (here substituted for Memory as the origin of poetry) is reduced to the role of commentator on the poem of her face.

146–50 *Taking instructions . . . light*: I.e. Zenocrate's eyes illuminate the night skies (but the construction is very loose).

147 *Ebena*: Night (literally, 'the ebony one'), Marlowe's coinage.

151–9 *There angels . . . Zenocrate*: Tamburlaine is tempted to spare his victims by the angelic beauty of Zenocrate, whose power to defeat him he fears more than any of his earlier enemies.

158 *conceit of foil*: The thought of defeat.

160 *What is beauty . . . then?*: My suffering demands, 'What is beauty (that it can cause such suffering)?'

162 *fed the feeling*: Described precisely (?). Writing about one's emotion increases the feeling it describes (perhaps with a pun on the 'feeding' of a pen with ink).

165 *still*: Distil.

169 *period*: (i) Sentence, (ii) end, goal.

173 *Which . . . can digest*: Which no power can reduce to words.

179 *whose instinct*: The instinct for which.

182 *beat on his conceits*: Hammer on his thoughts.

183 *conceiving and subduing, both*: Both experiencing and resisting these thoughts.

184–90 *That which . . . nobility*: Love has caused the gods to become shepherds, and though Tamburlaine feels it, he is determined by overcoming it to show that though born a shepherd he possesses a higher nobility.

184 *stopped the tempest*: Some editors emend to *stooped the topmost*.

187 *strewèd weeds*: Herbs and rushes scattered on the floor.

201 *no way but one*: The proverbial phrase (Tilley W148) implies, 'nothing but disaster', but Tamburlaine (202) turns the phrase to his own account: If there can be only one outcome, let us be the winners.

218 *Furies . . . Cocytus*: See (N). Cf. 4.4.17–18.

226 *proper rooms*: Natural places.

234 *Cimmerian Styx*: An oath by the Styx, the principal river of Hades, bound even the gods.

236–7 *aye / Griping*: Constantly clawing: the 'thoughts' are imagined as curled talons. The sentence lacks a main verb.

240 *fiend*: Infernal spirit to whom we might pray for help.

241 *infamous*: Stressed on the second syllable. Cf. lines 391 and 404.

244 *Erebus*: Usually, the darkness of Hell; here associated with the river Styx (see next note).

246 *ferryman*: Charon, who conveyed the souls of the dead across the river Styx to the underworld, which included the Elysian fields (247).

249 *build up nests*: Build false hopes.

256 *noisome parbreak*: Offensive vomit.

257 *standing*: Stagnant.

259 *engines*: I.e. eyes.

270–74 *Accursèd Bajazeth . . . break*: Bajazeth would wish to condole with Zabina, but hunger gnaws at the source of his feelings.

277 *date*: I.e. life.

282 *expressless, banned inflictions*: The inexpressible, cursed things inflicted on.

300 *resolved . . . air*: Melted into transparent, bright air.
     air: O's *ay* is nonsense.

311 *wildfire*: Inflammable substance used as a weapon of war.

332 *charged*: (Here) levelled.

333 *check*: Stamp, paw.

337 *Whose*: The Virgins'.

347 *entrails*: Perhaps trisyllabic.

349 *Shake . . . grief*: Zenocrate calls for an earthquake to mark their deaths.

358 *in conduct*: Under the guidance.

365 *Of . . . pity*: 'For the inevitable turn of Fortune's wheel and for considerations of pity' (Bevington and Rasmussen 1995).

368 *In*: As in the case of (or, on account of?).

380 *Turnus . . . Aeneas*: See (N). Aeneas killed his rival for the hand of Lavinia. Cf. lines 392–4.

387 *racked*: Tormented, pulled apart (by her divided loyalties).

390 *change I use*: My inconstancy.

393 *Prevented*: Deprived.

394 *fatally*: (i) By decree of fate, (ii) disastrously (to Turnus).

395–9 *So . . . my hope*: Similarly, to end my sorrows and reconcile my nation with my beloved, Tamburlaine must, through the irresistible power of the gods, grant honourable terms to the losers.

397 *by . . . powers*: Referring to 'the gods' (392).

400–402 *Then . . . fair Arabia*: Zenocrate prays that the King of Arabia may be saved, as well as her father.

412 *for such love*: For one so unworthy of that love.

414 *Whose fortunes . . . griefs*: Whose good fortune has never overcome her sorrow.

424–5 *sweet accidents . . . merits*: Happy events such as you deserve which have befallen you.

438 *had ere this*: Would by now have.

449 *confirmed*: Established firmly, or was confirmed by.

454 *the Fatal Sisters*: The three Fates (N); see 1.2.174.

459–62 *swelling clouds . . . drinks*: Tamburlaine has killed so many people that their blood, drawn up by the sun, has fallen like a portentous rain on the earth.

466 *foughten fields*: Battle fields (an archaic poetic formula).

474 *of power to*: Able to.

487 *record*: Call to witness.

488 *find . . . time*: Wait no longer.

497 *her love*: Your love for her.

504 *work us rest*: Cause us to stop the work of conquest.

510–11 *the giants . . . Jove*: On Zeus' triumph over the giants, see 2.3.21 and 2.6.5–6.

512 *shadowing*: (i) Depicting, (ii) bearing.

514 *Latona's daughter*: Diana, whom Marlowe here seems to conflate with Minerva (Athena); she played a prominent role in the war of the gods against the giants.

528   *Alcides' post*: The door-post of the temple of Hercules, *or* the Pillars of Hercules, which marked the end of the known world.

TAMBURLAINE THE GREAT, PART TWO

PROLOGUE

8   *sad*: For O's *said*.

ACT 1

Scene 1

2   *Placed by the issue*: Appointed by (or to a place close to) the offspring (his son Callapine).

6–10 *Now ... a truce*: They have marched from Anatolia to the Danube, where Christian and Muslim worlds met.

17   *Guyron*: Marlowe seems to give the name of this town on the upper Euphrates, north-east of Aleppo, to a river.

20   *Besides*: Apparently hypermetrical (i.e. the line has six feet instead of the pentameter's five).

22   *Slavonians*: Slavs.
      Almains, rutters: German cavalry.
      Muffs: An abusive name for the Swiss or Germans.

24   *hazard that*: Endanger what.

25   SP *ORCANES*: Omitted in all early texts.

25   *shortest northern parallel*: The most northerly (and shortest) line of latitude.

26–8 *Vast Gruntland ... Polypheme*: Greenland was legendarily populated by giants, here compared to the Cyclops of the *Odyssey*. See (N).

29   *cut the Arctic line*: Cross the Arctic Circle.

32   *champian mead*: Open plain.

33–41 *Danubius' stream ... argosies*: Marlowe 'sees the waters of the Danube sweeping from the river mouths in two strong currents, one racing across the Black Sea to Trebizond, the other swirling southward to the Bosporus, and so onward to the Hellespont and the Aegean. Both currents bear the slaughtered bodies of Christian soldiers, the one to bring proof of victory to the great Turkish town, the other to strike terror to the Italian merchants cruising round the Isles of Greece' (Seaton 1924:33).

42   *Europe . . . bull*: The continent is identified with Europa, abducted
        by Jupiter in the form of a bull.

55–6   *My realm . . . overthrown*: 'Natolia' is larger than modern Ana-
        tolia, occupying most of Asia Minor.

59   *Fear not . . . Tamburlaine*: [They] do not frighten me, but great
        Tamburlaine does.

61   *Albanese*: Albanians.

62   *Sicilians*: O's *Cicilians* may be an error for Cilicians, from Ana-
        tolia.

63   *Sorians*: Syrians (in Part Two, Soria is treated as distinct from
        Egypt). Alternatively, the name may designate inhabitants of Zor,
        i.e. Tyre.

68   *oriental plage*: Eastern region.

73–5   *Even from . . . Archipelago*: All of Africa, from the northern
        Tropic of Cancer to Amazonia (near the southern Tropic of Capri-
        corn in Marlowe's maps), and as far north as the islands of the
        Aegean archipelago.

81   *as the Romans used*: As was the custom of the Romans.

88   *the continent*: (Here) the ground.

90   *axletree of heaven*: See Part One, 4.2.50n. Orcanes compares the
        force of his cannon to earthquakes which shake the globe on its
        axis.

92   *powdered shot . . . steel*: Gunshot and arrows.

93   *blink-eyed burghers*: Citizens shutting their eyes in fear, wincing.

94   *County Palatine*: Count enjoying territorial autonomy under the
        Holy Roman Emperor.

95   *Austric*: Austrian.

100   *princely fowl*: The eagle, emblem of the Holy Roman Empire.

122   *So prest are we*: We too are ready for action.

123   *stand not upon terms*: Does not insist on unreasonable conditions.

161   *chief*: Most.

163   *stay*: Await.

Scene 2

3   *the western world*: The Turkish Empire, from an oriental point of
        view. Orcanes's ambitions may also stretch to the rest of Europe.

12–18 *Not for . . . of this*: Almeda's jokey prose, with its puns on
        'move' and 'run', perhaps gives a hint of the kind of comedy cut by
        the printer.

12   *move*: Urge.

20   *Darote's streams*: Ortelius's atlas shows a town of this name (pro-
        nounced with three syllables) in the Nile delta.

33 *Straits*: Straits of Gibraltar.

44 *cloth of arras*: Rich tapestry (originally manufactured in Arras, France).

48 *goest*: Take a walk.

50–52 *fair veil . . . Antipodes*: The veil of starlight, after the sun has set.

71 *haughty*: Lofty.

77 *Even straight*: Immediately.

Scene 3

23 *Water . . . in one*: The combination of the moist cold phlegmatic humour (associated with water) with the moist hot humour of blood (associated with air).

39 *Trotting the ring*: Riding around a circular enclosure for training horses.

41 *reined . . . curvet*: Raising the forelegs of a horse and exercising a leap with the back ones alone.

44 *Armour of proof*: Armour tested for strength.

46 *harmless*: Unharmed.

79 *superficies*: Surface (for O's *superfluities*).

80 *purple*: (Blood-)red.

103 *channel*: Throat, or perhaps shoulder (channel-bone = collar-bone).

133–4 *From Azamor . . . unpeopled*: The people of North Africa ('Barbary'), from Azimur in Morocco as far east as Tunis, have all been conscripted.

143 *infernal Jove*: Pluto.

144 *thee . . . these*: For O's *them . . . this*.

152 *Makes me . . . joy*: Overjoys me at the thought of future delight.

165 *lavish*: Profligate spilling.

166 *his wingèd messenger*: Mercury.

169 *Thetis'*: I.e. the sea's (N).

170 *Boötes*: Boötes (N), a ploughman, drove oxen.

174–215 *My lord . . . th'inhabitants*: The journeys of Tamburlaine's henchmen are all derived from Ortelius. See (N).

176 *lain in leaguer*: Encamped for besieging.

182 *recreate*: Rest, spend time in recreation.

188 *John the Great*: Prester John, the legendary Christian priest-king who ruled Abyssinia.

189 *triple mitre*: Papal tiara.

192 *Amazonians*: Amazons.

193 *vouchsafed a league*: Granted an alliance.

194 *Zanzibar*: Not the island, but part of the mainland.

196 *Ethiopian sea*: (Apparently) the southern Atlantic.

198–201 *Therefore ... to Cubar*: See (N). Techelles travelled up through west Africa.

202 *Nubia*: An area between the Red Sea and the Nile, with its capital at 'Borno' (203).

209–15 *Tyros ... Mare Maggiore*: 'The river Tyros (the Dniester) acts as a southern boundary of the province of Podalia; Stoko is on it, and Codemia lies to the north-east on another stream. Partly separating Codemia from Olbia, and thus perhaps suggesting an otherwise unnecessary sea-journey, is the thick, green, hollow square of Nigra Silva [see next note]' (Seaton 1924:29).

212 *Nigra Silva ... devils dance*: The 'Black Forest' designates the Hercynian wilderness, legendarily populated by evil spirits.

215 *Mare Maggiore*: (The greater sea) the Black Sea.

216 *period*: (Here) stop.

221 *Lachryma Christi*: (Christ's tears) a sweet wine from southern Italy.

224 *orient*: Lustrous (for O's *orientall*).

225 *the whiles*: Until then.

ACT 2

Scene 1

2   *motion*: (Here) impulse, purpose.

8   *Varna*: The city in north-east Bulgaria, apparently mistaken for a region.

16   *Natolia*: I.e. Orcanes.

18–20 *Cutheia ... Caesaria*: See (N). The towns are in Anatolia, Mount Horminius in Bithynia.

21   *Soria*: See 1.1.63n.

31   *should*: Would.

32   *profession*: Oath.

35   *those accomplishments*: Fulfilments of oaths.

37–9 *But as ... ourselves*: Just as no rules of statecraft bind us to put our trust in the oath ('faith') they make in their own profane religion.

47   *consummate*: Consummated, fulfilled (for O's *consinuate*).

50   *dispensive faith*: An oath which can be put aside by special Church dispensation (or simply dispensed with).

54   *Saul*: Cf. I Samuel 15, where Saul spared Agag, and so failed to enact God's command to destroy the Amalekites.
     Balaam: Cf. Numbers 22–3, where Balaam *obeyed* God's instruction that the children of Israel should not be cursed.

Scene 2

11 *by scores . . . arms*: Challenge him twenty at a time.
41 *Jove*: Euphemism for 'God'.
45 *these papers*: The 'scroll' of 1.1.144.
47 *shining veil of Cynthia*: The moonlit sky (cf. 1.2.50–52n).
50 *in one . . . circumscriptible*: Is bound to one locality.
51 *continent*: (i) Space, (ii) land-mass.

Scene 3

8   *wherein . . . I die*: With which (death) my sins end.
18 *Tartarian*: Of Hell (Tartarus).
20–23 *That Zoacum . . . fiends*: In the Koran (37:60–64), the Zaqqūm-tree stands in the nethermost region of Hell, bearing fruits shaped like devil's heads which are eaten by those who are perpetually damned.
32 *Whose power . . . miracle*: I.e. the fortunes of war often seem like miracles.
38 *We will . . . trunk*: We decree that a guard keep watch over his body.
40 *give it . . . charge*: Give the order to do it immediately.
43 *brother*: Fellow monarch.
47 *his angry fate*: The vengeance that has fallen on Sigismond.

Scene 4

0.1 SD *The arras is drawn*: The curtain in front of the discovery-space, drawn to reveal a bedridden Zenocrate.
0.3 SD *tempering*: Mixing, blending.
9   *ivory bowers*: Eye-sockets, or eye-lids.
10 *tempered . . . heat*: Tamburlaine attributes to Zenocrate's eyes the sun's power to balance the humoral *temperature* (= mixture) of living bodies.
12 *jealousy . . . mate*: The heavens are too jealous to share the heavenly Zenocrate with a human husband.
13 *latest*: Last.
14 *dazzled*: Blinded (usually by excessive light).
17 *entertain*: Welcome.
24 *trièd*: Refined, purified.
52–4 *As when . . . train*: I.e. as during a lunar eclipse (occurring at points in the celestial map at which the moon's orbit intersects with the ecliptic, known as the serpent's head and tail).

58–60   *And sooner . . . majesty*: Zenocrate would rather that the sphere of fire (the *elementum ignis*) be put out to make room for Tamburlaine's glory than see it obscured in the grave.

61   *suspect . . . by mine*: (i) Suspect that you might die for grief at my death, (ii) suspect, from the evidence of my death, that you too are mortal.

68   *second life*: Afterlife.

74   *latest memory*: Recollection as I die.

81   *spheres*: Her eyes, like heavenly spheres.

87–8   *Helen . . . a thousand ships*: Cf. *Doctor Faustus*, 13.90–92.

90   *Her*: Zenocrate's.

99   *the Fatal Sisters*: The Fates (N).

100   *triple moat of hell*: The rivers Lethe, Styx and Phlegethon.

114   *Janus' temple doors*: Opened in time of war. See (N).

129   *thou*: Zenocrate's body.

131   *lapped in lead*: Placed in a lead coffin.

140   *stature*: Statue (the spelling may represent the common variant 'statua').

ACT 3

Scene 1

1   *Callapinus . . . Cybelius*: The names (or possibly titles) are taken from Lonicerus (Seaton 1929:388).

19–20   *blot our dignities . . . infamies*: Remove our exalted names from the book of lowly shame.

27–32   *We shall . . . encounter*: Callapine is confident that Fortune, despite her favours to Tamburlaine, will revert to her usual inconstancy, and favour the Turks in the coming battle.

40–42   *Some that . . . sufficient*: Some who, having overcome the superior numbers of Sigismond's army, think they are sufficient.

46   *Scalonia's*: For O's *Scalonians*, the inhabitants of Ascalon.

49   *neighbour*: Next.

50–53   *from Trebizond . . . towns*: 'For the king of Trebizond, Marlowe's finger traces from west to east the northern seaboard of Asia Minor: Chia, Famastro, Riso, Santina' (Seaton 1924:30).

52   *Mare-Major sea*: The Black Sea.

59–60   *Aleppo . . . Damasco*: 'For the king of Soria, [Marlowe] passes from Aleppo south-westward to the sea-coast near Cyprus, and chooses Soldino and Tripoli, and so inland again to Damasco' (Seaton 1924:30).

64   *battle*: Forces (whose disposition is described in the following lines).

Scene 2

0.4 SD *the town*: Larissa.

3 *exhalations*: Fiery vapours.

6 *zenith*: Highest point of the sun's, or any star's, course and influence. Tamburlaine wishes a comet ('blazing star'), traditionally a portent of disaster, to predominate over his fortunes.

15–18 *This pillar . . . again*: In Marlowe's loose rhetorical grammar, 'this pillar' seems to govern 'forbids'.

20 *Wrought*: Embroidered.

29–33 *the stars . . . Zenocrate*: The stars of the southern hemisphere ('arc'), usually invisible above the equator ('the centre's latitude'), will travel, like pilgrims, into the northern hemisphere to gaze on Zenocrate's beauty.

34 *Thou*: Zenocrate's likeness. Tamburlaine appears to change his mind about hanging her picture on the pillar.

39 *Those*: O's *Whose* is possible but grammatically strained.

58 *thirst*: For O's *cold*.

61 *caper*: Dance, leap (because they have been blown up).

62–90 *Then next . . . place*: The display of military technique is taken from Paul Ive's *Practise of Fortification* (1589); see Paul Kocher, 'Marlowe's Art of War', *Studies in Philology* 39 (1942), pp. 207–25.

65–7 *the corners . . . desperate*: The arrangement of the fortifications in the shape of a star or pentagon ('quinque-angle', 64) is not suitable for flat open ('champian', 63) country, but for uneven ground, where its stronger and weaker sections can be disposed at the points of greater and less vulnerability. For other military terms in this passage, see (G).

74 *secret issuings*: Small doorways which allowed defensive sallies.

75 *covered ways*: Protected passages.

79 *ordnance*: (Here) ammunition.

80 *scour*: (Here) rake with gun-shot.

81 *Dismount . . . part*: Dislodge the enemy's cannon.

85 *mount*: Rise (through the use of dams).

98 *peal of ordnance*: Cannonshot.

99 *A ring . . . horse*: A ring of soldiers with pikes supported by infantrymen and cavalry.

101 *sunny motes*: Dust particles in the sunlight.

107–8 *Filling . . . blood*: Digested wine supposedly replenished lost blood.

124 *the Afric potentate*: Bajazeth.

126   *search*: A technical term for the probing of a wound.
136   *bravely*: Well.
153   *at a bay*: At bay (like hunted animals).
158   *puissance*: Power, might (here, three syllables).

Scene 3

3   *Balsera*: Probably Marlowe's misreading of Ortelius's Passera, a town close to the Natolian border.
      hold: Stronghold.
7   *Filling . . . breach*: Rubble from the breach in the enemy's walls will be used to fill in their defensive ditches.
11   *drum*: Addressed to a drummer.
14.2 SD *above*: They enter on the gallery over the stage.
26   *his ruin*: The falling rubble.
33   *any*: Omitted in all early texts.
39   *that can*: That you can.
53   *full point-blank*: With direct aim; all the way.
54   *see*: See to.
56   *gabions*: Defensive emplacements made of earth held together by a cylinder of stakes (for O's *Galions*).
62   *alarum*: Sound the attack.

Scene 4

9   *orifex*: Orifice; the wound to his liver and veins.
21   *the wheel*: An instrument of torture; victims were pinned to it and their limbs broken.
33.1 SD *burns the bodies*: Necessary in the light of lines 36 and 71–2.
48–50 *from . . . Cynthia sits*: I.e. from the circle of fire at the edge of the universe (the empyrean), which forms the under-surface of heaven, down to the sphere of the moon.
51   *Like lovely Thetis*: The moon in her sphere is associated with a nymph of the sea (N).
57   *Rhamnusia*: Nemesis (N).
64–5 *straight line . . . heaven*: I.e. the axletree of heaven.
75   *frame*: Framing, making.
79   *No remedy*: (There is) no alternative.
81   *fatal*: Fated.

Scene 5

3   *Here at Aleppo*: Callapine and his army appear not in fact to be in Syria (indicated by its capital city), but in southern Natolia.

6   *Ida's forest*: Mount Ida, near Troy, is imagined with a royal forest in which the sultan of Turkey hunts.

8   *Natolia's*: I.e. the king's.

14   *play the men*: Act like men.

34   *showed*: Displayed before.

36   *metropolis*: Babylon, rebuilt by Semiramis (N).

40   *Asia the Less*: Asia Minor.

46   *from Halla is repaired*: Have come from Halla (a town south-east of Aleppo).

58   *knot*: Cluster.

65–8 *Hector . . . his fame*: This chivalric incident comes not from the *Iliad*, but from the post-Homeric tradition, retold, for example, in John Lydgate's *Troy Book* (fifteenth century). The scene is largely concerned with honour and chivalry.

74   *my glove*: The gauntlet thrown down as a challenge to combat.

75–6 *Now . . . person fight*: Now that you doubt your army's power, you seek victory through single combat.

80–82 *Heaven . . . world*: Tamburlaine's birth, though humble, was favoured by a conjunction of stars uniquely propitious to a conqueror and never to be repeated.

87   *That villain*: Almeda.

95   *his ancient trade*: Robbery.

100–101 *clog . . . for*: A heavy weight . . . to prevent.

115 *journey you*: Drive you hard (like horses).

137 *make up . . . dozen*: Tamburlaine is scornful of the number of petty kings Callapine has crowned.

138 *give arms*: (i) Display a coat of arms, (ii) fight.

ACT 4

Scene 1

26   *flesh our taintless swords*: Give our unstained swords their first taste of blood.

32   *house*: Family, race.

34   *toward*: (i) Promising, (ii) willing.

39   *lay*: I.e. lay dead.

51.1 SD *run in*: Amyras and Celebinus leave the stage for the battle, not to the tent; Calyphas remains on stage.

68   *taratantaras*: Trumpet calls.

69   *net of gold*: Fine veil of gold thread.
     and: And who.

76 *stoops*: Humiliate. 'Children' is treated as singular.

87 *fresh supplies*: I.e. new enemies.

95 *may*: Which may.

100 *argument of arms*: Code of military conduct.

104 *jealousy*: Zeal, ardour.

108 *Jaertis' stream*: The river Jaxartes, here supposed to flow through, or around, Samarkand.

112–15 *A form ... consists*: Calyphas's soul ('form') is unworthy of its living connection with Tamburlaine's flesh, which is animated by a spirit like that of Jove himself. (The Aristotelian categories of matter and spirit are confused.)

117 *thy*: Jove's.

123 *massy dregs*: Densest and least valued parts (the metaphor continued in the next line is from the fermentation of wine).

128 *he*: An unspecified Titan.

129 *the burden*: I.e. the heavens.

131 *for being seen*: To avoid being seen.

132 *cankered curs*: Worm-ridden dogs.

137 *Approve*: (i) Demonstrate, (ii) experience.

157 *resist in*: For O's *resisting*.

188 *Cimbrian*: The Cimbri were a Teutonic tribe who, in the second century BC, overpowered several Roman armies. Marlowe is imitating Spenser, *Faerie Queene* I.viii.11: 'As great a noyse, as when in Cymbrian plaine / An heard of Bulles, whom kindly rage doth sting, / Do for the milkie mothers want complaine'.

189 *the females' miss*: For the loss of their females.

190 *their following*: Following them.

198 *For hot ... pride*: For the burning of his country's cities and palaces (193–4).

Scene 2

0.1 SD: Olympia may emerge from a tent, like that of Calyphas in the previous scene.

11 *Contagious smells ... infect*: Foul air was considered the source of infectious disease.

13 *invention*: (Here) scheme, device.

30 *Cynthia's ... wilderness*: The moon's effect on the tides of the sea.

55 *And, will you*: And if you will.

61–3 *simplest extracts ... metaphysical*: Olympia claims that the alchemist has distilled the pure essence (the hardness) of marble, worked into an ointment by supernatural ('metaphysical') knowledge.

86   *theoria of*: Contemplation, survey of (only instance in *OED*).

Scene 3

1   *jades*: Horses (contemptuous). Marlowe borrows from Golding's Ovid (IX, 238): 'pampered jades of Thrace'.

5   *Asphaltis*: See (N); the bituminous lake near Babylon is now retro-spectively identified as the site of Orcanes's defeat.

10   *governor*: Apollo, who drove the horses of the sun.

12–15   *headstrong jades . . . divine*: The flesh-eating horses belonged to Diomedes of Thrace. Marlowe perhaps confused their owner with King Augeas, whose stables Hercules ('Alcides') had to clean in one of his labours.

21   *racking clouds*: Clouds driven before the wind.

24   *right*: Indeed.

25   *figure*: Emblem (perhaps his whip).

32–42   *O thou . . . hell!*: An invocation of Pluto (N).

41   *once*: Once and for all.

46   *hedges*: I.e. their teeth. 'Hedge of teeth' is, perhaps coincidentally, a formulaic phrase in Homer.

49   *their kicking colts*: Their unruly tongues.

61–2   *Raise me . . . heaven*: Classical heroes were frequently stellified when they died, as Tamburlaine imagines he may be raised to join 'Aldebaran' (N) in the constellation Taurus.
        threefold astracism: A cluster of three stars also in Taurus, *or* the tripartite division of the universe into earth, planets and stars.

63   *triple world*: Europe, Asia and Africa.

65   *prefer*: Promote (ironic).

70–71   *queens . . . queens*: Punning on 'queans' (= whores).

73   *let . . . your turns*: I.e. take turns raping them.

75   *Brawl not . . . lechery*: Tamburlaine warns the soldiers against fighting over the concubines.

86   *'Twere but time*: It's a bit late for that (spoken ironically).

89   *jesting pageants*: Laughable spectacles.

104 *Sinus Arabicus*: The Red Sea (*sinus* = gulf).

119–24   *Like . . . is blown*: Adapted from Spenser's *Faerie Queene*, I.vii.32. For details of the Sicilian place-names, see (N).

125 *Saturn's royal son*: Jupiter.

126 *Mounted*: Mounted on.

127 *the path*: The Milky Way, as in line 132.

ACT 5

Scene 1

0.1   SD *upon the walls*: In the gallery over the stage.

14   *As . . . conceit*: As anything you esteem valuable.

15   *for all*: Despite.

17–19   *famous lake . . . stream*: The bituminous lake (seemingly identi-fied with the 'Asphaltis' of 4.3.5) petrifies anything that falls into it, making fresh defences.

33   *Will*: Who will (the omission of the pronoun makes the verb emphatic).

34   *environèd*: Surrounded (like a city under siege).

54   *I turn . . . throat*: I return the word 'traitor' back down your own throat.

64–5   *lofty pillars . . . the deep*: In reality Babylon was 100 miles from the sea.

66   *Being carried thither*: Blown all the way to Limnasphaltis.

69   *Belus, Ninus . . . Alexander*: For Tamburlaine's predecessors in Babylon, see (N).

72   *Drawn with*: Drawn by.

75   *trod the measures*: Danced.

87–90   *the region . . . earth*: Exhalations were believed to catch fire in the region below the circle of fire, and, as comets, to shed disastrous influences from their tails ('trains').

93   *quailed*: Made to quail.

98   *black Jove*: Pluto.

104   *the anger . . . Highest*: I.e. the scourge of God.

126   *something quail*: Be somewhat daunted.

158   *like Baghdad's governor*: As beseems the governor of Baghdad (here identified with Babylon): explained in lines 159–60.

165   *Assyria*: For O's *Affrica* (cf. Part One 1.1.89n).

196   *abstracts*: Summaries, digests (i.e. the Koran).

214   *be removed the walls*: From the walls.

217   *distempered*: Unwell.

Scene 2

9   *full from Babylon*: I.e. back to full strength after the siege (cf. 58).

19   *record*: (Here) remember.

58   *Or that*: Before.

Scene 3

19   *retain . . . holiness*: Still deserve to be worshipped.

22   *Bear . . . burden*: Do not join in the chorus ('burden' = refrain).

34   *they think . . . out*: The devils think their allotted time of suffering is over.

38   *note*: Mark, sign.

41.1–3   SD This entrance could instead be placed at the beginning of the scene.

44   *a man*: A mere mortal.

58   *charge*: Level.
        his: Atlas'.

62   *Apollo*: Here as god of healing.

82   *hypostasis*: Sediment (for O's *Hipostates*).

84   *accidental*: Abnormal.

86   *humidum . . . calor*: Moisture . . . natural heat.

91   *critical*: Astrologically unfavourable (but also linked to 'crisis' (92): the day of the turning-point of an illness).

96   *organons*: Organs (or fluids: the 'animal spirits') acting as instruments of the soul.

97   *by argument of art*: According to medical diagnosis.

111   *endure*: Harden, strengthen.

116   *vanished*: Dispelled.

125   *all my wants*: All the conquests I leave incomplete.

145–9   *Look here . . . Antipodes*: Tamburlaine imagines conquering the western hemisphere, from the point (near the Canary Islands) where the Greenwich meridian intersects the Tropic of Cancer, to the far east, where the sun rises on the other side of the world.

149   *Antipodes*: Those who live on the other side of the globe.

151   *here*: I.e. in the Americas.

154–5   *from th'Antarctic . . . descried*: The still-undiscovered Australasia (*terra incognita* in the maps).

164–5   *Your soul . . . flesh*: Your soul animates our bodies, whose substance is derived from your flesh. Cf. 4.1.112–15.

168   *this subject*: This substance (my body).

170   *Must part . . . impressions*: Must depart, leaving behind its traces.

185–90   *With what . . . dignity!*: How hard-hearted I would have to be to enjoy the burden of my life, and if my body, all made up of pain, could still put into action the feelings of a heart that felt joy at a worldly honour!

195–8   *How should . . . sovereignty?*: How could I stir against the

promptings of my heart, living only with the wish to die, and with
only an unwelcome crown to cite as an argument?

203   *steelèd stomachs*: Tough spirits.

207   *damnèd*: Doomed, wretched.

208   *send*: May heaven send to.

211   *my fatal chair*: The throne in which I am fated to die, *or* the chariot.

216–17   *The monarch . . . monster*: Death.

225   *And when . . . sight*: And when my soul enjoys its spiritual sight.

237   *Phyteus*: Apollo, the sun (continuing the thought of lines 230–33
and picked up in lines 242–4).

238–41   *The nature . . . clifts*: Combining the proverb 'Take occasion
(or time) by the forelock' (Tilley T311) with the fate of Hippolytus
(N), the anger of whose great father Theseus caused his chariot to
be dragged on to rocks where he was torn apart.

250   *earth . . . fruit*: Earth has exhausted the finest thing she has borne.

252   *timeless*: Untimely.

THE JEW OF MALTA

The play dates from *c.* 1590: Machevil's prologue alludes to the death
of the duke of Guise (23 December 1588), and the play's first recorded
performance was on 26 February 1592 by Lord Strange's Men, at the
Rose. It was immensely popular: thirty-six performances are recorded
by June 1596; its title-role was one of Edward Alleyn's great parts; and
its influence on Ben Jonson (*Volpone*) and Shakespeare (*The Merchant
of Venice, Othello*) was profound. It was further revived in 1601 and, at
an uncertain date, for Caroline audiences at court and at the Cockpit
theatre. No text survives earlier than a quarto edition of 1633. This has
a dedication, prologue and epilogue by Thomas Heywood, but there
seems little reason to think that he interfered with the text, and it forms
the basis for the present edition.

The play's action has a teasingly uncertain relation to historical fact.
No narrative source has been found for its plot, and its events are
apparently fictional. Yet it is persuasively set in the Mediterranean world
of the later sixteenth century, and, in a way, Fernand Braudel's great
history *The Mediterranean and the Mediterranean World in the Age of
Philip II* (1949, tr. 1972–3) is the best guide to the complex and ambiguous relations between races, nations and cultures the play evokes. Malta
was repeatedly besieged by the Turks, most notably in 1565, though its
Christian occupiers, the Knights of the Order of St John, never in fact
compounded with their Ottoman enemies. There were historical Jews

whose lives may have provided prototypes for the career of Barabas. The favourite candidate is Joseph Mendez Nassi (also known in his native Portugal as Joao Miques), who led an exodus from Christian persecution to Constantinople in 1547. A fabulously wealthy merchant and 'diplomat', he rose to become an adviser to Süleyman the Magnificent's son Selim. Created duke of Naxos on Selim's succession in 1566, he was reputed to have persuaded the Sultan to attack Venetian-held Cyprus in 1570, and was treated as a notorious enemy by European chroniclers and diplomatic agents.

But Barabas is not copied from a specific historical person. He is, rather, derived from the collective fantasy of 'the Jew' – the focus not only of continuing medieval anti-Semitism, but also, by the sixteenth century, the object of a more specific fear: the few, converted, Jews living in western Europe were commonly suspected of being covert allies of 'the Turk', a fifth column whose conversion to Christianity and commitment to the security of Christendom were merely nominal, not to be trusted. (It is hard to say whether this was fear or paranoia: disquietingly, the converted Jews living in London were, apparently, much involved in conspiracies against the Elizabethan regime. See David S. Katz, *The Jews in the History of England 1485–1850* (Oxford, 1994), ch. 2, 'The Jewish Conspirators of Elizabethan England'.) It would, however, be dull-witted to complain about our uncertainty over the play's links with reality, since such uncertainties are exactly what *The Jew of Malta* is about.

The uncertainties begin with its vertiginously ironic prologue. Machevil speaks like the Presenter of a Morality play, but instead of instruction he offers the beginnings of a 'lecture' (29) (almost, at this date, a sermon) on atheism. Seemingly an immortal soul, he 'count[s] religion but a childish toy' (14). One of the Presenter's functions was to gain a hospitable reception for the players – an essentially reciprocal entertainment (cf. 34) – and Machevil too comes to 'frolic with his friends' (4). If we react with horror to his amorality, we are caught in his paradoxical trap:

> To some perhaps my name is odious,
> But such as love me guard me from their tongues,
> . . .
> Admired I am of those that hate me most. (5–6, 9)

Critics have debated how far the play reflects first-hand knowledge of Machiavelli's writings, how far the common stereotype of 'the murderous Machiavel'. The answer appears to be, 'Both.' Barabas may be a poisoner, but he is conspicuously less Machiavellian than the canny and unscrupulous Christians.

His first appearance leads us to expect a Morality about the evils of avarice, but the 'desire of gold' (3.5.4) is a universal in the play, and Barabas himself is soon less interested in riches than in revenge. His name associates him with the thief who was released instead of Christ, but it is the Christians who steal Barabas's wealth in 1.2. Ferneze's opportune production of 'the articles of our decrees' (67) and the appearance of the soldiers who have already seized Barabas's goods suggest that he is the victim of a preconcerted trick. When he makes the point – 'Is theft the ground of your religion?' – he is answered:

> No, Jew, we take particularly thine
> To save the ruin of a multitude;
> And better one want for a common good
> Than many perish for a private man. (96, 97–100)

Ferneze's words are uncomfortably close to the sentiments of Caiaphas plotting the death of Christ (John 11:50). G. K. Hunter (1964) argues that the persistent biblical allusions imply the play's conformity with traditional theological anti-Semitism. They seem rather to highlight the gap between reality and 'counterfeit profession' (291).

Similarly, Barabas casts himself as Job later in the scene, only to reveal that he has provided a further hoard against such a calamity (under a board mockingly marked with a cross). Like the Morality-play Vice, he is protean and unpredictable. Audiences delight in his ambiguities, which frequently occur on the fault line between the material and the spiritual, traditionally the distinction between Judaism and Christianity:

LODOWICK
> This is thy diamond. Tell me, shall I have it?

BARABAS
> Win it and wear it. It is yet unfoiled.
> O, but I know your lordship would disdain
> To marry with the daughter of a Jew;
> And yet I'll give her many a golden cross,
> With Christian posies round about the ring. (2.3.295–300)

The crosses here are pointedly secular, stamped onto the coins of the dowry, and the posies fit equally the mottoes on coins and wedding-rings. And, of course, the promise is false. Barabas is a deceiver, and neither characters nor audience can be sure what can be taken for granted, what is stereotypical 'Jewish' custom and what malicious improvisation (Barabas turning into the air, Abigall's 'modesty').

Structurally, the play is built out of the double deceits Barabas calls 'crossbiting' (4.3.13). He sets Lodowick against Mathias, Friar Jacomo against Friar Barnadine, just as the Knights try to play Spain off against the Turks. Barabas poisons the nuns with what looks like a charitable offering, killing his own daughter with a biblically ambivalent mess of pottage (for which Esau sold his birthright to the deceiver Jacob, Genesis 25). He deceives Ithamore with the promise of making him his heir ('I'll pay thee with a vengeance, Ithamore', 3.4.117); Ithamore turns against him, gulled in his turn by Bellamira and Pilia-Borza. Barabas poisons them all with flowers, and then, in a crowning deception, fakes his own death. The discrepancy between the frenzied intrigue and the strange, unsettling reflections it implies about Christianity and its inheritance from Judaism is marked. In the end Barabas is caught in his own trap, caught out by the subtler 'policy' of the Christians.

DRAMATIS PERSONAE

BARABAS (accented on the first syllable) In the New Testament, Barabbas was a murderer (Mark 15:7, Luke 23:19), and a thief (John 18:40) who was released by Pilate instead of Jesus.

ABIGALL In the Geneva Bible, the catalogue of proper names translates Abigail as 'the father's joy', but the spelling here hints at the way her actions gall her father. Hunter 1964 argues that the Old Testament Abigail (I Samuel 25) was regarded as an archetype of a Jew who converted to Christianity.

ITHAMORE Perhaps recalling Ithamar, the son of Aaron (Exodus 6:23).

FERNEZE Grand Master of the Knights of Malta, perhaps recalling the aristocratic Italian Farnese family.

CALYMATH Also called Selim Calymath, probably in allusion to Selim, the son of Süleyman the Magnificent (ruled 1520–66) who was Sultan of Turkey during the siege of Malta in 1565.

PILIA-BORZA From the Italian *pigliaborza*, 'pick-purse'.

THE DEDICATORY EPISTLE

0.1 *Thomas Hammon*: Probably the Thomas Hammon who was born *c.* 1592, and matriculated at Christ's College, Cambridge, in 1608; he entered Gray's Inn in 1611, to become a barrister in 1617. Thomas Heywood had previously dedicated two of his own plays, *The Fair Maid of the West* (part two, 1631) and *The Iron Age* (part one, 1632), to him.

3   *Master Alleyn*: Edward Alleyn (1566–1626), the famous tragedian
     who also played the parts of Tamburlaine, Faustus and Barabas.
5   *Cock-pit*: The private Drury Lane theatre, also known as 'The
     Phoenix'.
19   *Tuissimus*: Latin, your very own.

THE PROLOGUE SPOKEN AT COURT

8   *a sound Machevill*: A true Machiavel.

THE PROLOGUE TO THE STAGE,
AT THE COCK-PIT

5   *Hero and Leander*: Marlowe's narrative poem, which was pub-
     lished with a continuation by George Chapman in 1598.
12   *Perkins*: Richard Perkins (d. 1650), the Jacobean and Caroline
     actor who played Barabas for the play's revival.
14   *condition*: (i) Temperament, (ii) status, birth.

PROLOGUE

1   SP *MACHEVIL*: I.e. Machiavelli, but so spelt as almost to turn him
     into a Morality character. He was popularly depicted by Eliza-
     bethans as an unscrupulous atheist.
3   *the Guise*: Henri de Lorraine, the third duke of Guise, who oversaw
     the slaughter of French Protestants (Huguenots) at the Massacre of
     St Bartholomew in 1572. He was killed on 23 December 1588 by
     order of the French king, Henri III. The villain of *The Massacre at
     Paris*.
4   *this land*: I.e. England.
6   *guard me from . . . tongues*: I.e. don't refer to me openly. In the
     Morality-play *Respublica* (1.1.12–15), Avarice remarks on his fol-
     lowers' reluctance to acknowledge him by name.
8   *weigh*: (Here) esteem.
12   *Peter's chair*: I.e. the papacy.
16   *Birds . . . murders past*: Possibly an allusion to the Greek poet
     Ibycus, whose murder was revealed by a flight of cranes. Machevil
     scoffs at the notion that murders cannot remain hidden.
19   *Caesar*: Machiavelli contended that Julius Caesar was a tyrant
     because he acquired power by violence rather than by legal right
     (*Discourses* I.29).

21 *the Draco's*: The laws of Draco (for Q's *Drancus*) were notoriously severe. See (N).

22 *citadel*: Machiavelli expressed divers views regarding the use of citadels: in *The Art of War* (VII) he gave instructions on building them; in *The Prince* (XX), he maintained that citadels provided limited protection for a ruler when confronted with civil disobedience, but are inadequate against foreign intruders; in *Discourses* (II.24) their use is categorically denounced. Bawcutt 1978 notes, however, that the anti-Machiavellian tradition treats them as a standard device of the Machiavellian tyrant.

24–6 *Phalaris ... envy*: The Sicilian tyrant Phalaris' reputation for a love of literature depended on the false attribution to him of a book of letters. He was overthrown not, as Machevil implies, through 'great ones' envy', but in a popular rising at Agrigentum, and was burned alive in the bronze bull which he had used to dispatch his own victims – a fate which perhaps anticipates Barabas's (N).

26 *Of*: Because of.
petty wights: Common people.

27 *Let ... pitièd*: Proverbial. 'It is better to be envied than pitied' (Tilley E177).

29 *Britainy*: This common Elizabethan variant spelling is metrically preferable to Q's *Britaine*.

33 *grace*: Honour, favour.

35 *favours*: (i) Resembles, (ii) takes my part, is on my side. Proverbially paired with 'grace'.

ACT 1

Scene 1

0.1–0.2 SD It is likely that Barabas's counting-house occupies a discovery-space, concealed by a curtain which is drawn by Machevil as he leaves the stage.

1–3 *So that ... satisfied*: Barabas takes great satisfaction in the huge profits from his most recent financial venture.

3 *summed and satisfied*: Tallied up and settled.

4 *Samnites*: Emended from Q's *Samintes*. Mentioning the Samnites (N), an ancient central Italian tribe, in the same line as the biblical 'men of Uz' (N), emphasizes the extent of Barabas's commercial empire.

8 *Well fare*: May they fare well.

11 *Tell*: Count.

13   *Would make ... coin*: Would think such a sum of money miraculous.

21–32 *The wealthy ... captivity*: The delight in precious stones may be a traditional feature of the caricature stage Jew, as in the late-medieval Croxton *Play of the Sacrament*.

21   *eastern rocks*: The mountains of India, famed for their precious minerals.

29   *indifferently rated*: Impartially valued.

34–5 *frame ... from*: Arrange in a way which is distinct from.

36–7 *enclose ... little room*: Perhaps a parody of the traditional conception of Christ within the womb of the Virgin.

39   *peers*: Points.
      halcyon's bill: Stuffed halcyons (a species of kingfisher) were used as weathervanes.

49   *riding ... road*: Riding at anchor in the roadstead.

52   *custom them*: Pay the customs duties.

57   *as I*: As if I.

62   *The very custom barely*: 'Even the customs duties alone' (Bawcutt 1978).

68   *there's somewhat come*: 'At least something has arrived safely' (Bawcutt 1978).

74   *Where Nilus ... main*: Where the Nile flows into (contributes its waters to) the sea.

79   *crazèd*: (Here) unseaworthy.

80   *they are wise*: They think they know best.

82   *loading*: Bill of lading.

90–91 *they coasted ... businesses*: They sailed by Crete ('Candy') for oils and other goods.

93   *Without ... conduct*: I.e. without an escort (which protected against pirates).

94   *wafted*: Escorted.

103–4 *the blessings ... happiness*: An allusion to the covenant between God and Abraham (Genesis 17:1–22). See also Exodus 6:1–8 and Galatians 3:16.

109   *substance*: Wealth (cargo).
      successful blasts: Propitious winds.

110   *happiness*: Good fortune.

114   *fruits ... faith*: The fruits of faith are a New Testament commonplace, e.g. Matthew 7:16–20.

116   *profession*: Professed religion.

117   *Haply*: Perhaps.
      hapless: (i) Unfortunate, (ii) poor.

119   *scattered nation*: The diaspora was seen as a consequence of the curse in Deuteronomy 28:25.

120   *scambled up*: (i) Competed fiercely, (ii) sought money rapaciously.

122   *Kirriah Jairim*: The name of an Old Testament city (I Chronicles 2:50–53), here given to a person.

123   *Obed*: The name of the son of Boaz and Ruth (Ruth 4:17–22).
        Bairseth: An unclear reference; possibly a variation of Baaseiah (I Chronicles 6:40) (Bawcutt 1978).
        Nones: Probably alluding to Hector Nuñez (1521–91), the Portuguese physician, merchant and head of the Marrano (Jewish convert) community in London.

134   *charge*: Expenses.

138   *of policy*: As a matter of expediency.

146   *they*: I.e. the Maltese governors.

162   *With whom*: Against whom.
        attempted: Launched attacks.

169   *Provide him*: Prepare himself.
        fashion: Fashion's.

170   *state*: Condition.

174   *Zaareth . . . Temainte*: Possibly reminiscent of Zophar the Naamathite, and Eliphaz the Temanite, two of Job's comforters (Job 2:11).

187   *Ego . . . proximus*: I am always closest to myself (adapted from Terence, *Andria* 4.1.12).

Scene 2

0.1   SD *Governor*: Q's reading, *Governors* (also at lines 10, 17, 27, 32 and 129), is most likely attributable to compositorial error, but may indicate that Marlowe did not originally give Ferneze the prominence he has later in the play.

0.2   SD *BASHAWS*: Pashas, or Turkish army officers. The form *Basso[es]* is used interchangeably.

2   *Knights of Malta*: The Knights of St John of Jerusalem who were based in Malta from 1530 onward.

9   *consider*: Show consideration for.

11   *my father's cause*: I.e. the Sultan of Turkey's business.

13   *leave*: Permission (to talk privately amongst themselves).

15   *send*: Give orders.

22   *That's more . . . commission*: That is more than we are authorized to do.

23   *Callapine*: The Bashaw appears to share the name of Bajazeth's son in *Tamburlaine* Part Two.

25–6 *'tis more ... constraint*: Proverbial. 'It is better to obtain by love than force' (Tilley L487).

45 *there's more ... so*: There's more to it than that.

47 *cast*: Calculated.
cannot compass it: Cannot manage it.

64 *Who ... heaven*: Christian anti-Semitism was based on the belief that the Jews had accepted responsibility for the death of Christ and in consequence were an accursed race (cf. Matthew 27:25).

91 *Corpo di Dio!*: Italian, body of God!

97–8 *particularly thine ... multitude*: An echo of John 11:50: 'it is expedient for us, that one man die for the people, and that the whole nation perish not' (Geneva Bible).

105 *Of naught ... made*: Proverbial (Tilley N285).

108 *your first curse*: See line 64n. above.

117 *The man ... live*: Cf. Proverbs 10:2 and 12:28.

121 *profession*: (i) Barabas's Jewish faith, (ii) his commercial activities.

136 *other*: Other Jews.

137 *take order ... residue*: Make arrangements about the rest.

152 *And therefore ... wrong*: And so don't try to make fine distinctions between equally evil acts.

159 *if ... day*: If we fail to pay the tribute on time.

160 *simple policy*: The strategy of a simpleton.

161 *policy*: Trickery (playing on the previous line).

162 *simplicity*: Honesty (picking up on 'simple' in line 160).

163 *plagues of Egypt*: Cf. Exodus 7–12.

165 *Primus Motor*: Latin, Prime Mover, God.

182–6 *I wot ... She-asses*: Cf. Job 1:3: 'His substance also was seven thousand sheep, and three thousand camels, and five hundred yoke of oxen, and five hundred she asses' (Geneva Bible).

187 *indifferent rate*: Fair price.

193–6 *Thy fatal ... eyes*: Cf. Job 3:1–10, 'Afterward Job opened his mouth, and cursed his day. And Job cried out, and said, Let the day perish, wherein I was born, and the night when it was said, There is a man-child conceived. Let that day be darkness, let not God regard it from above, neither let the light shine upon it, but let darkness, and the shadow of death stain it, let the cloud remain upon it, and let them make it fearful as a bitter day ... Because it shut not up the doors of my mother's womb: nor hid sorrow from mine eyes' (Geneva Bible).

197–9 *For only ... me*: Cf. Job 7:3: 'So have I had as an inheritance the months of vanity, and painful nights have been appointed unto me' (Geneva Bible).

208   *'Tis in ... I speak*: Cf. Job, 7:11: 'Therefore I will not spare my
      mouth, but will speak in the trouble of my spirit, and muse in the
      bitterness of my mind' (Geneva Bible).

216   *for*: Because.

220   *mould*: (i) Mould, (ii) earth, clay.

222   *A reaching thought*: I.e. one who has foresight.

223   *cast*: Forecast.

237–8   *things past recovery ... exclamations*: Proverbial (Tilley C921).

239   *sufferance breeds ease*: Proverbial (Tilley S955).

240–41   *And time ... turn*: 'And time, which cannot help us in this
      sudden crisis, may give us an opportunity to do something later on'
      (Bawcutt 1978).

267   *put me ... shifts*: Leave me to my own devices.

283   *precise*: Strict in religious observance.

285   *Entreat 'em fair*: Be civil to them.

289–90   *As good ... dissemble it*: It makes no difference whether you
      dissemble from the start or only later when you have lost your
      faith.

291–2   *A counterfeit ... hypocrisy*: I.e. a Jew's false profession of
      Christianity is better than the secret hypocrisy of Christians. Bar-
      abas does not entertain the possibility that any religious faith could
      be sincere.

309   *waters*: Water supply; perhaps Barabas's house has ponds and
      fountains.

312   *you, happy virgins' guide*: Although the text does not specify,
      Abigall perhaps addresses the First Friar, who is guiding the nuns.

315   *The hopeless daughter ... Jew*: Cf. Kyd, *The Spanish Tragedy*:
      'The hopeless father of a hapless son' (4.4.84).

324   *labouring*: Troubled, distraught.

325   *proceedeth ... spirit*: Comes about through the agency of the Holy
      Ghost.

326   *moving spirit*: The friar puns on the previous line, implying that
      Abigall is sexually alluring.

333   *profit*: In both spiritual and economic senses.

336   *What mak'st thou*: What are you doing?

339   *mortified herself*: Become dead to worldly values.

347, 353   *markèd thus*: The obelus (†) printed in Q after 'thus' indicates
      that Barabas ironically makes a gesture resembling the sign of the
      cross.

Scene 3

9   *in a dump*: Despondent, depressed.

16   *metamorphized nun*: Turned into a nun.

21   *countermured*: Fortified with a double wall. The emendation of Q's *countermin'd* is supported by the 'walls of brass'. Cf. 5.3.8n.

27   *or it shall go hard*: Unless really bad luck prevents me.

ACT 2

Scene 1

0.1 SD *with a light*: Indicating a nocturnal scene.

1   *presaging raven*: Ravens were believed to be omens of death.

2   *passport*: Permit allowing one to pass from life to death.

12–13 *O Thou . . . shades*: Cf. Exodus 13:21–2.

19.1 SD *above*: I.e. on the balcony.

25   *wealth*: Days of prosperity.
     winter's tales: Fantastic tales.

31   *Now that*: Now would that.

39   *Bueno . . . no era*: Spanish, my gain was not good for everybody.

47–54 *O my girl . . . bliss*: Cf. the report of Shylock's passion over the loss of his gold and his daughter in *The Merchant of Venice* (2.8.15–22).

53   *practise thy enlargement*: Devise your freedom.

61   *for*: In place of.

64   *Hermoso . . . dineros*: Spanish, beautiful pleasure of money.

Scene 2

7   *Catholic king*: The King of Spain.

11   *Turkish*: Q's *Spanish* is clearly erroneous.

14   *luffed and tacked*: Del Bosco's ship outmanoeuvred the Turkish galleys by sailing against the wind ('luffed') and zig-zagging ('tacked'). Dyce's emendation makes nautical sense of Q's *left, and tooke*.

15   *fired*: Destroyed by fire.

23   *tributary league*: A truce requiring the payment of tribute.

27   *he*: The Turk.

31–2 *The Christian . . . here*: The Knights of St John were removed from Rhodes in 1522 by Süleyman the Magnificent, but later settled in Malta in 1530 by order of Charles V.

38   *them*: Q's *you* makes a threat of Del Bosco's reassurance.

Scene 3

6   *present money*: Ready cash.

16   *Ferneze's hand*: Perhaps Barabas has either a written assurance from Ferneze or one confirmed by a handshake.

18   *the tribe of Levi*: Marlowe is probably recalling Joshua 20–21, where the Levites held jurisdication over the cities of refuge.

23   *Florence*: The home of Machiavelli.

25   *duck*: Bow.

26   *stall*: Shop benches used to display goods were often used by vagrants at night as places to sleep.

27   *be gathered for*: Have a collection taken for them.

33   *insinuate*: Ingratiate myself.

36–7   *show myself . . . dove*: I.e. be more cunning than innocent (taken from Matthew 10:16).

41   *his father too*: (Perhaps) Barabas wishes that Lodowick's future son will also become Governor.

42–3   *hog's cheek new singed*: I.e. Lodowick has just shaved.

45–7   *custom . . . purge ourselves*: Not a Jewish custom, but a parodic allusion to the anti-Semitic myth that Jews had a distinct smell (the *foetor Judaicus*).

48   *the promise*: God's promise (cf. 1.1.103–4n.).

53   *I'll sacrifice . . . wood*: This echoes Genesis 22, where Abraham is prepared to sacrifice his son, Isaac, as a burnt offering to God.

54   *poison of the city*: This is not convincingly explained.

55   *white leprosy*: White scales on the skin are a symptom of leprosy.

56   *a foil*: 'A thin leaf of some metal placed under a precious stone to increase its brilliancy' (*OED* 5).

57   *foiled*: I.e. set by a jeweller.

58   *foiled*: Defiled, dishonoured (punning on the previous line).

60   *pointed*: Referring to how the diamond was cut.

61   *Pointed*: Appointed (punning on the previous line).
      it: (i) The diamond, (ii) Abigall, (iii) Barabas's vengeance.

74   *in catechizing sort*: In the manner of the catechism.

84–5   *doing . . . fruit*: The *fruit* Barabas has in mind are the offspring of nuns' and friars' illicit sexual activity.

87   *glance not at*: Don't make slighting remarks about.

91   *have a saying to*: Have something to say to.

93   *no price . . . part*: (i) We won't quarrel over the price, (ii) you won't get out alive.

103   *new trick . . . purse*: New method of stealing a purse.

105–6 *So . . . the gallows*: If he is bought, he could steal the city's seal, and issue pardons for himself under it.

107–8 *The sessions . . . purged*: To thieves, the day of the trial is like the day of crisis in a disease – fatal for most of them.
being purged: (Metaphorically) executed.

113–14 *philosopher's stone*: In alchemy, a stone that would turn base metals to gold.

116 *shaver*: (i) Chap, fellow, (ii) swindler, trickster.

118 *youth . . . Lady Vanity*: Two characters from the Morality-play tradition.

121 *colour*: Pretence.

125–6 *an't be*: If it be.

133 *for my turn*: For my purposes.

135 *mark*: Brand.

136 *mark*: Observe.

157 *comment on . . . Maccabees*: The two apocryphal books of Maccabees which recount the emancipation of the Jewish people from the Syrians in the second century BC. No Renaissance commentary on them is known.

167 *condition*: Status.

171 *teach thee that*: Q omits *thee*.

176 *your nose*: Barabas may have worn a large false nose.

179 *poison wells*: Jews were often caricatured as well-poisoners.

180–83 *cherish . . . my door*: I.e. Barabas lets Christian thieves steal from him for the pleasure of seeing them punished.

187 *in ure*: In practice.

190–91 *wars . . . Charles the Fifth*: Alluding to the conflict between Francis I of France and the Holy Roman Emperor, Charles V, which was initiated in 1519 and continued until 1558.

194 *forfeiting*: 'Exacting a fine or forfeit because a borrower of money has been unable to fulfil his obligations' (Bawcutt 1978).

195 *brokery*: Financial broking; here, commercial malpractice is implied.

197 *And with . . . hospitals*: And supplied the almshouses with orphans.

198 *moon*: Month (the moon was thought to produce lunacy).

199 *one hang*: I.e. caused one to hang.

201 *with interest*: I.e. interest charged at usurious rates.

214 *a-good*: Heartily.

223 *walk in with me*: Barabas and Ithamore have arrived at Barabas's house in the course of their conversation.

231 *Philistine*: Biblical adversaries of the Jews.

239 *made sure*: Betrothed.

243 *factor's hand*: Agent's handwriting.
245 *The account is made*: I.e. settled, reckoned (with pun on the previous line).
251 *manna*: The food which fell upon the Jews from heaven (cf. Exodus 16).
272 *rouse*: Drive out (like an animal from hiding).
293 *hold my mind*: Conceal my thoughts and feelings.
299 *golden cross*: Gold coin stamped with a cross.
300 *Christian posies*: Pious maxims engraved onto contemporary coins and rings.
304 *offspring of Cain*: I.e. Lodowick is a wicked descendant of Cain, the first person to commit murder in the Old Testament.
Jebusite: The tribe of Canaanites who were expelled from Jerusalem by King David in II Samuel 5.
305 *Passover*: The Jewish observance which celebrates the liberation of the Jews from Egypt in Exodus 12.
306 *Canaan*: The land promised to the Jews as part of their covenant with God in Genesis 17:8.
307 *Messias*: Messiah.
308 *gentle*: Punning on 'gentile'. 'Gentle' was also the common name for a maggot.
338 *made thee sure to*: Assured you of your engagement to.
365 *put her in*: Make her enter the house.
385 *spirit*: Demon, devil.

ACT 3
Scene 1

3 *ducats*: Venetian gold coins.
8 *liberal*: (i) Well-educated, (ii) generous.
16 *go hard*: See 1.3.27n.
21 *hooks*: Gear used by thieves to snatch valuables from windows, or to scale walls.
28 *by her attire*: I.e. by the red taffeta dress commonly worn by prostitutes.

Scene 2

2.1 SD *reading*: Lodowick is reading the challenge from Mathias delivered to him by Ithamore. This is inconsistent with 2.3.72–86 and 3.3.19–21.
5 *home*: Mortally.
7 *tall*: Brave (said sardonically).

18   *lively*: Life-giving.
34   *reveal*: Supplied to correct the absence of a verb in Q.

Scene 3

3   *held in hand*: Tricked.
     flatly: Completely.
10   *bottle-nosed*: Big-nosed.
     to: For.
20   *imprimis*: Latin, first of all (a comic misuse by Ithamore).
22–3 *And then ... days*: The archaic-sounding couplet parodies the
     ending of an old 'story'.
22   *and*: Omitted in Q.
31   *Saint Jacques*: I.e. the Dominican friars, who had their headquarters
     in the Church of St Jacques, Paris. Cf. 3.4.76n.
35   *feeling*: Earnest (punning on the idea of sexual groping).
     sport: I.e. sexual intercourse.
37   *sirrah sauce*: Impudent (saucy) fellow.
43   *sire*: For Q's *sinne*.
53   *Virgo, salve!*: Latin, Greetings, maiden!
54   *When, duck you?*: Perhaps Ithamore expresses surprise at Abigall's
     reverence to the friar.
68   *Son*: Son of God, with a pun on 'sun'.
74   *heavy*: Grievous.

Scene 4

6   *Spurca!*: Latin, filthy!
     pretendeth: Portends.
15   *self*: Q's *life* is probably a corruption from the previous line.
31   *within my gates*: Cf. Exodus 20:10, and Deuteronomy 14:21.
33   *Like Cain by Adam*: Barabas adapts Genesis 4 (where Cain was, in
     fact, cursed by God, and not Adam, for murdering his brother) to
     his own situation.
37   *'less*: Unless.
51   *hold*: Bet.
55   *husht*: Shush.
59–60 *the proverb ... spoon*: Cf. Tilley S771.
65–6 *mess of rice porridge*: Recalls Genesis 25 in which Esau sells his
     birthright for a mess of pottage (mess = helping).
70   *an Italian*: The Elizabethans considered Italians accomplished
     poisoners.
71   *bind*: Cause constipation.
76   *This even they use*: The custom on this evening is. This observance

of a vigil for the saint's day (25 July) seems to be invented. The Elizabethan liturgy for the day following St James's includes a reference to 'a boiling pot' from Jeremiah 1:13, which may be relevant both to the pot of porridge and to the cauldron in which Barabas dies (5.5). One tradition recalled that the besieged Knights of Malta expected relief (which did not come) on St James's day (Bonnie Blackburn and Leofranc Holford-Strevens, *The Oxford Companion to the Year* (1999), p. 306). In *The Massacre at Paris*, 'a friar of the order of the Jacobins' (23.23–4) invokes the saint as he murders King Henry (24.33).

85   *pot*: For Q's *plot*.

92   *'tis better . . . spared*: It's better to do this than to spare (them).

93   *by the eye*: 'In unlimited quantity' (*OED* 4b).

98   *great Alexander . . . died*: According to Plutarch, Alexander the Great was poisoned.

99   *Borgia's wine*: It was commonly thought that Pope Alexander VI was poisoned by his son, Cesare Borgia, in 1503.

101   *In few*: In short.

103   *Stygian pool*: The Styx, one of the rivers of the underworld.

104   *fiery kingdom*: I.e. hell.

112–13   *Flanders mares*: Belgian horses; also, a euphemism for promiscuous women, which Ithamore directs at the nuns.
         with a powder: Quickly, at once (punning on the poisoned powder).

114   *horse-pestilence*: (?) A horse disease.

Scene 5

11   *shalt*: Thou shalt.

32   *profitably*: (i) For a good cause, (ii) for financial gain.

Scene 6

5   *fair Maria*: A 'ghost' character whose introduction hints at the friars' lasciviousness.

12   *ghostly father*: Spiritual confessor.

18   *desperate*: I.e. have no hope of salvation.

22   *contract*: Betroth.

29   *Set down at large*: Written down in full.

31   *work my peace*: Obtain absolution.

35   *degraded*: Defrocked.

36   *sent to the fire*: The prospect of being burnt alive for transgressing canon law is an elaboration invented by Marlowe (Bawcutt 1978).

42   *exclaim on*: Denounce.

49   *crucified a child*: An example of the anti-Semitic myth that Jews

crucified Christian children as part of a ceremony which derided the crucifixion.

50   *in shrift*: In confession.

ACT 4
Scene 1

1   *to*: Compared with.
6   *swell*: I.e. become pregnant.
14   *royal*: Splendid.
21   *Cazzo, diabole*: Two Italian oaths, meaning 'penis' and 'devil'.
22–3   *caterpillars*: I.e. parasites.
25   *God-a-mercy, nose!*: Ithamore is ironically impressed by Barabas's sense of smell.
30–46   *Barabas ... Lodowick*: Barabas keeps interrupting the friars until they hint at the murder of Mathias and Lodowick.
58   *A hundred ... ta'en*: I.e. I have charged 100 per cent interest on a loan.
61   *lost*: Damned.
78   *banco*: I.e. bank. The Italian form suggests the institution was still exotic.
99   *rogue*: Q's *goe* is plausible, but the emendation seems necessary in light of the next line.
115 *the Turk*: I.e. Ithamore.
123 *turned*: Converted.
138 *order*: Religious practice.
144 *see him ... heels*: I.e. see him hanged.
146 *girdle*: A friar's rope belt.
150 *Confess ... hanged*: Tilley C587.
152 *have*: For Q's *save*.
155 *print*: Marking (caused by the noose).
165 *proceed*: Prosper.
182 *on's*: Of his.
208 *particular*: Detail.

Scene 2

7   *man of another world*: Ghost.
14   *critical aspect*: Malign influence, as of a star.
16   *freehold*: I.e. pitch (where Pilia-Borza picks pockets).
17   *conning*: Memorizing.
     neck-verse: One could escape hanging by claiming 'benefit of

      clergy', which involved the reading of a verse from the Vulgate
      Bible (usually Psalm 51).

17–18 *friar's execution*: I.e. Jacomo's.

18   *hempen*: Alluding to the hangman's noose.

19   *Hodie . . . mihi*: Latin, today your turn, tomorrow mine.

20   *exercise*: Act of devotion, at the execution.

23–4 *hempen tippet*: An ironic allusion to the priest's stole, i.e. the rope.

25   *cure*: Parish.

39   *Turk of tenpence*: A poor Turk (apparently Marlowe's coinage).

44   *family*: Household.
       stand or fall: Here used with sexual innuendo.

47   *foully*: Punning on the sense 'dirty', not 'clean'.

59   *partridges . . . eggs*: Cf. Pliny, *Historia Naturalis* X, 100.

83   *use him in his kind*: Treat him according to his nature; also meaning,
      'to treat harshly', from the proverb, to 'use someone like a Jew'
      (Tilley J52).

91–101 *Content . . . my love*: A parodic invitation to love, ending with
      a quotation of Marlowe's own lyric, 'The Passionate Shepherd to
      his Love'.

94   *painted carpets*: Bright flowers (the metaphor is comically lit-
      eralized).

108   *beard*: Q's *sterd* looks like a corruption from *stared*, line 107.

118   *grey groat*: Small silver coin worth about fourpence.

119   *ream*: Approximately 500 sheets of paper (punning on 'realm,
      kingdom').

133   *runs division of*: I.e. Bellamira is well practised in kissing; here,
      'division' refers to the exquisite musical variations created by divid-
      ing the long notes into short ones.

Scene 3

5   *coupe de gorge*: French; i.e. I'll cut his throat.

12   *catzerie*: Cheating, trickery (apparently Marlowe's coinage from
      cazzo: cf. 4.1.21n).

14   *husband*: I.e. a pimp.

19   *want'st . . . thy tale?*: Is anything missing from the sum you
      demanded?

28   *what . . . for you*: I.e. the 100 crowns that Ithamore has demanded
      (4.2.123) for the bearer of the letter.

31   *make . . . away*: Kill him.

51   *as unknown*: As befits one to whom I have not been introduced
      (ironic politeness).

63   *demand*: Not in Q.

Scene 4

1   *pledge thee*: Drink to you.

4   *Of*: On.

5   *Nay . . . none*: Q ascribes the line to Pilia-Borza.

10 *Rivo Castiliano!*: Italian, River of Castile!; possibly used here as a
    drinker's cry, calling out for Spanish wine.
    A man's a man: Proverbial (Tilley M243).

23 *snickle hand too fast*: Since a snickle is a snare or noose, this
    difficult phrase seems to mean 'with the quick hand of a poacher
    (or hangman)'.

30 *Love . . . long*: Proverbial (Tilley L559).

31 *incony*: Fine, delicate, sweet (with a bawdy pun on 'cunny' = female
    genitalia).

40 *A vôtre commandement*: French, at your command.

46 *cat's guts*: Lute strings.

48 *Pardonnez-moi*: French, pardon me.

49 *now all be in*: All the strings are now in tune.

54 *fingers very well*: Plays the lute with skill (punning on 'filching').

56 *runs*: Plays a rapid sweep of notes.

73–4 *the elder . . . hanged himself*: Judas reputedly hanged himself from
    an elder tree.

75–6 *Great Cham*: The Great Khan, the title applied both to the ruler
    of the Tartars and Mongols, and to the emperor of China.

77 *masty*: (?) Fattened on mast (pig food).

87 *The meaning . . . meaning*: Ithamore is drunkenly knowing.

ACT 5

Scene 1

4   *hovered here*: I.e. Calymath's ships are anchored offshore.

20 *cannot out-run . . . constable*: Proverbial (Tilley C615).

29 *he*: Not in Q.

41 *I'll*: Q reads *I*, which fails to emphasize Barabas's continuing
    defiance.

49 *passed*: Passed judgement.

61 *Well fare, sleepy drink*: Barabas gives thanks to the effectiveness of
    the sleeping potion.

80 *poppy . . . mandrake*: Soporific drugs (cf. Shakespeare, *Othello*
    3.3.334–7).

86 *sluice*: The island's drainage sewers; Q's *truce* is clearly incorrect.

91 *vault*: I.e. the underground drainage system.

Scene 2

0.1   SD *Alarms*: Sounds of battle, trumpet calls.

22   *entrance*: The first step.

33   *Whenas*: Seeing that.

40–42   *ass . . . thistle tops*: Not from the *Fables* of Aesop (N), but from the emblem tradition, where it symbolizes the rich man who does not benefit from his riches.

42   *snap*: Feed.

44   *Occasion's bald behind*: In Renaissance iconography, Occasion or Opportunity was depicted as a bald-headed woman with a long forelock of hair which one had to seize as she passed by.

63   *for me*: As far as I am concerned.

68   *got my goods*: Acquired my wealth.

73   *remediless*: In a hopeless state (qualifying 'Malta').

81   *outhouse . . . city*: Building outside the city walls.

84   *pretendest*: Intend, offer.

96   *cast it*: I.e. formulate a plan.

106   *Ottoman*: Turkey.

107   *about this coin*: Undertake to collect this money.

121   *My policy . . . prevention*: 'I hate to have my cunning plots revealed in advance' (Bawcutt 1978).

Scene 3

8   *countermured*: For Q's *countermin'd*. Cf. 1.3.21.

9   *toward Calabria . . . Sicily*: I.e., Sicily protects the eastern approach to Malta.

10   *Where*: For Q's *When*.
      Dionysius: (N) Here recalled as another island tyrant.

11   *Two lofty turrets*: Probably the forts of St Angelo and St Elmo which stood at the entrance of the harbour of Valletta.

16   *great Ottoman*: The Sultan.

Scene 4

3–4   *culverin . . . kindled thus*: The Governor lights the taper ('linstock') which will fire the signal cannon ('culverin').

9   *adventure*: Risk.

Scene 5

3   *levelled . . . mind*: (i) Designed to achieve my purpose, (ii) smoothly finished to my specifications.

9   *die*: This may be a simple curse urging the carpenters to drink themselves to death; or Barabas may have poisoned the wine.
10   *so*: Provided that.
38   *blithely set*: Cheerfully seated.
39   *warning-piece*: A gun fired as a signal.
49   *Now tell me, worldlings*: Barabas adopts the guise of the medieval stage-villain and Morality Vice, directly addressing the audience and appealing to their own sense of mischief.
62   *charge*: Trumpet-call to signal an attack.
62.1–2 SD The Governor cuts the rope securing the trapdoor from the gallery and Barabas falls into the hot cauldron which is simultaneously revealed in the discovery-space.
77   *breathe forth . . . fate*: 'Breathe out the last moments of life allotted to you by fate' (Bawcutt 1978).
90   *train*: Trap.
98   *all's one*: It would make no difference.
115   *meditate*: 'to arrange by thought and discussion' (Bawcutt 1978).
118   *come all the world*: I.e., if you summon all the world.

EPILOGUE SPOKEN AT COURT

1   *dread sovereign*: Charles I.
4   *Thus low dejected*: I.e. bowing.

EPILOGUE

4   *outgo*: Surpass.
5   *prize was played*: Match was contested (a fencing term).

DOCTOR FAUSTUS

Many of the questions we ask about *Doctor Faustus* – questions of date, text and interpretation – cannot be answered with certainty. The play can be variously dated 1588–9 and 1591–2. Two early versions of it (known as the A- and B-texts) survive, but there is general agreement that neither text represents exactly what was first performed. Both show signs of theatrical adaptation. Many have suspected that someone else (Thomas Nashe?) wrote at least some of the clowning scenes. So complex are the textual problems that they are discussed in a separate note below. The text of this edition is based on the A-text.

Nor is there agreement about the interpretation of the play, which seems unquestionably orthodox to some and questioningly heterodox to others. For some it is learned and theologically subtle, for others a populist, even subversive, barnstormer. No interpretation which positively excludes any of these possibilities can hope to be complete. The play's dramatic mode lurches from solemn terror to proverbial, folksy comedy from scene to scene, even from line to line, as when Lucifer tells Faustus, 'Thou shouldst not think of God. Think of the devil, / And of his dame, too' (7.92–3). The disconcerting mixture of register is quintessentially Marlovian.

Quintessentially, but not exclusively. Legends of the magician Johann Faust who sold his soul to the devil developed in sixteenth-century Germany, and were collected and published by Johann Spies in the German Faustbook of 1587. Marlowe's play depends for its detail on an English translation (by one 'P. F.'), *The Historie of the Damnable Life and Deserved Death of Doctor John Faustus*. The earliest extant edition of this book dates from 1592, which might seem to make the case for the later dating of the play, but there are grounds for thinking that Marlowe knew an earlier, now lost, printing: the arguments are intricately discussed in J. H. Jones's critical edition, *The English Faust Book* (1994). As well as supplying the incidents, the Faustbook also probably contributed its 'solemnly edifying and crudely jocular' (Levin 1954) tone to the play – a tone also found in such influential sixteenth-century books on magic as Agrippa's *De Occulta Philosophia*. But there are differences. Despite its geographical expansiveness, the world of the Faustbook is domestic, *bürgerlich*. Faust is a trickster who shares a homely thieves' kitchen with Wagner his servant and a 'familiar' Mephostophiles 'that ever was diligent at Faustus' command, going about the house, clothed like a friar, with a little bell in his hand, seen of none but Faustus' (Jones 1994:100–101); Helen of Troy lives with him for a year and bears him a son. Marlowe sharpens the focus on Faustus' academic environment, and winnows out many of the more trivial everyday bits of sorcery. The play occupies the less naturalistically defined, more abstract world of the Morality play: in the Faustbook, the old man is simply a concerned neighbour who invites the magician in for dinner and edification; in the play, his appearances are as abrupt and unexplained as those of the Good Angel, whose role, indeed, he seems to take over. By the same token, Faustus himself is sometimes (especially in soliloquy) a distinctive, credible personality, at other times merely an exemplary figure. His habit of talking about himself in the third person may reflect an acute self-consciousness – or a Morality-actor's tendency to name himself for the convenience of his audience. His subjectivity fades in and out.

Marlowe's focus on learning is much sharper. The Faustbook deals cursorily with its protagonist's education in its first chapter:

> But Doctor Faustus within short time after he had obtained his degree, fell into such fantasies and deep cogitations that he was marked of many, and of the most part of the students was called the Speculator; and sometimes he would throw the Scriptures from him as though he had no care of his former profession: so that he began a very ungodly life . . . (Jones 1994:92)

The author is suspicious of learning in general, and he can explain Faustus' interest in magic only as the product of 'a naughty mind'. By contrast, the play's opening scene takes us inside Faustus' thoughts, and we sense the tedium of the study, the dissatisfaction of knowledge. And Marlowe's Faustus actually cites his texts. 'The play itself is almost macaronic in its frequent scholarly lapses into Latinity' (Levin 1954:137). (Macaronic texts are learned games which mingle Latin with the vernacular – a nice parallel to the play.) But how good was the Latin of its first audiences? And if they understood the words, did they also spot Faustus' mistakes, his mis-citations and partial quotes? Or is the language of learning (standing out in italic type in the early black-letter quartos) a blind – verbal pyrotechnics to match the fireworks onstage? The Latin formula to summon the devil with which Marlowe furnishes Faustus sounds worryingly like the real thing; and Mephistopheles responds with scholastic precision: 'That was the cause, but yet *per accidens*' (3.47). At a performance one feels that something dangerous is happening.

Both the doctor and the devil are more precisely defined than in the Faustbook. There, Faustus is reluctant to give the devil the soul he demands; here, he offers it in exchange for twenty-four years of life. He seems driven by a terrible curiosity, yet he learns nothing new. Mephistopheles hides nothing, but he is playing a cat-and-mouse game: in the Faustbook, Faustus melts for himself the congealed blood which Mephistopheles here brings fire from hell to unclot, and his asides ('O, what will not I do to obtain his soul?', 5.73) are a glimpse into that unseen abyss. Somewhat later in the Faustbook, the devil torments the already damned Faustus with the thought of hell. Marlowe's Mephistopheles is himself tormented by his own knowledge of hell, the only knowledge he has to offer. Faustus hopes that forbidden knowledge will bring him power ('All things that move between the quiet poles / Shall be at my command', 1.58–9), and imagines that power in terms of unlimited spatial extension ('his dominion that exceeds in this / Stretcheth as far as doth the mind of man', 1.62–3). Instead he finds himself on the brink of an unthinkable infinity: 'Why, this is hell, nor am I out of it'

(3.78). 'Hell hath no limits, nor is circumscribed / In one self place, for where we are is hell, / And where hell is must we ever be' (5.123–5). In these scenes, the small space of the stage seems to open onto the depths. They are the most darkly compelling in Elizabethan drama.

The play's middle scenes are disappointing, a loose concatenation of episodes. Hell, significantly, is much less frequently mentioned. At one level, this structural weakness is thoroughly appropriate: Faustus' adventures are crude and demeaning because he is wasting the powers, and the time, he has secured. The Knight's insulting observation rings true: 'I'faith, he looks much like a conjurer' (10.11). The comedy of the clowns' scenes, too, though their authenticity is doubtful, may also be functional, parodying the mindlessness of Faustus' own actions. Still, it seems unlikely that Marlowe was wholly responsible for their execution, and what relevance and coherence they have is thematic rather than theatrical. They treat as comic the very fears that haunt the main plot.

Those fears return in the closing scenes, and with them the intensity of the writing. No other play so deftly exploits the audience's consciousness of the approaching end. Faustus' end (the word pervades the play) is predictable, inevitable; he has bargained for it; yet the mind reels trying to comprehend exactly what is happening: 'no end is limited to damnèd souls' (14.101). Faustus' pleasures become more extreme, more sensual and more desperate as he attempts to 'extinguish' (13.85) the thought of damnation. But he cannot escape the knowledge that he is literally a *lost* soul: 'Where art thou, Faustus? Wretch, what hast thou done? / Damned art thou, Faustus, damned! Despair and die!' (13.47–8). We are acutely aware at this point of the overdetermination of the play's theology and its action. Faustus' despair is both a psychological condition and a divine punishment, at once the cause and the consequence of his damnation, and in the play's closing sequence supernatural intervention is indistinguishable from the working of his own mind. 'Hell strives with grace for conquest in my breast' (13.64): space bends in the line, as does time in the running hour of his final soliloquy. (The Faustbook provided the merest hint: 'Time ran away with Faustus as the hour-glass', Jones 1994:174.) Watching his 'hellish fall', we are enjoined '[o]nly to wonder' (Epilogue, 4, 6).

Doctor Faustus was highly successful, mutating but remaining in the repertoire even after the Restoration. A persistent early tradition associated performances of the play with the appearance of real devils. It is a testimony to its black theatrical magic.

The A- and B-Texts

The A-text first appeared in print in a black-letter quarto of 1604 (having been entered in the Stationers' Register in 1601), with subsequent editions in 1609 and 1611. This is not a perfect text: it is short for a Renaissance play; the comic scenes in particular seem sketchy; and scene 6 is apparently misplaced. Scholars once thought that it was a memorial reconstruction, but modern opinion tends to the view that the text was set from the authorial 'foul papers' of Marlowe and the collaborator to whom the central scenes of the play were entrusted.

The B-text was first printed in a quarto of 1616, and reprinted six times between 1619 and 1663. This lacks some 36 lines of the A-text, but adds 676 lines of new material, and makes in addition thousands of smaller verbal changes (a few of these offer better readings than the A-text, and have been adopted in this edition). The additional scenes are probably those for which Philip Henslowe paid William Birde and Samuel Rowley £4 in 1602. They augment the action of the A-text with new incidents, and amplify the supernatural spectacle and anti-Catholic sentiment. In Rome, Faustus becomes involved with an anti-pope whom he spirits away to the imperial court. Here he comes into conflict with Benvolio (based on the A-text's anonymous Knight) and eventually tricks him with a false head (apparently drawing on the use of the false leg in A). The plot against the Horse-Courser is expanded to provide further comic action for the A-text's Clowns. It is apparent that the new scenes develop and interweave materials from the A-text. Possibly the most significant changes come at the end of the play, where now the action occurs under the gaze of the devils who remain above in the gallery (a stage space not used in the A-text); and Faustus is dismembered in view of the audience. The B-text thus tends to display literally what is only menacingly suggested in A.

Ultimately a preference for one text over the other cannot be based solely on bibliographical evidence, but rests on an understanding of what the two versions of the play are. Older scholarship viewed the A-text as a mangled version of the fuller B-text. Like most modern editors, we regard the B-text as an interesting theatrical adaptation and the A-text as the more authentic version of the play.

PROLOGUE

0.1 SD The Chorus, apparently for the first time on the English stage, is a single speaker.

1–2 The Carthaginians defeated the Romans near Lake Trasimeno in

217 BC; but since 'mate' must mean 'overcome', Marlowe seems to attribute the victory to the Romans and their god of war. Some gloss 'mate' as 'side with, ally himself with' (*OED* 4); but since its primary sense refers to sexual coupling, it could also be the equivalent to 'screw'. Such ambiguities are frequent in this speech.

6   *muse*: Poet.
     vaunt: B's reading. A's *daunt* looks like a compositor's error ('d' and 'v' are easily confused in black-letter), and both sense and alliteration are against it.

9   *To patient ... plaud*: We appeal (the case of) our applause to patient 'judgements' (with a pun), as to a higher court.

13   *Wittenberg*: For A's *Wertenberg*.The university of Luther and of the Faustbook's Faustus is probably meant; the more theologically radical university of Tübingen in Württemberg is possible but less likely.

15–17 *So soon ... name*: Faustus' studies in theology, the fertile ground of sanctified ('graced') learning, led quickly to his being graced (a technical academic term) with the title of Doctor.

21–2 *waxen wings ... overthrow*: An allusion to the flight and fall of Icarus. See (N).

Scene 1

0.1   SD The study may have been represented by filling the discovery-space at the back of the stage with books, which were then used as props.

2   *profess*: (i) Claim expertise in, (ii) teach.

3   *commenced*: (i) Begun, (ii) taken a degree (as at Cambridge).

7   *Bene disserere ... logices*: (Translated from Latin in line 8) not from Aristotle's treatises on logic, the *Prior* and *Posterior Analytics* (A's *Analutikes* (6) follows the Greek pronunciation), but the opening definition of the *Dialectic* of Ramus (N).
     logices: Greek genitive, for A's *logicis*.

12   *On kai me on*: Greek, 'being and non-being', a topic in metaphysics.

13   *ubi ... medicus*: Where the philosopher leaves off, there the doctor begins. Not from Galen (N), but from Aristotle, *On Sense and Sense-Perception*, I.436a.

16   *Summum ... sanitas*: (Translated in line 17) adapted from Aristotle, *Nicomachean Ethics* 1094a8.

19   *aphorisms*: Principles of medicine, like the *Aphorisms* attributed to Hippocrates.

28–9 *Si una ... rei*: If one and the same thing be left to two people, one (is entitled to) the thing, the other to the value of the thing (*legatur* for A's *legatus*). Very loosely based on Justinian (N), *Institutes* II.xx.8.

31 *Exhaereditare . . . nisi*: A father cannot disinherit (*exhaereditare* for A's *ex haereditari*) his son unless . . . Reminiscent of Justinian, *Institutes* II.xiii.

33 *law*: A's *Church* could be defended since Justinian's *Institutes* were central to Canon Law, but B's *law* gives them their rightful place in the *corpus juris* ('body of the law') and makes better sense.

34 *His*: Of this.

36 *Too servile*: B's reading; A's *The devill* is nonsense.

38 *Jerome's Bible*: St Jerome (N), here pronounced with three syllables, was responsible for the standard Latin translation of the Bible, the Vulgate.

39 *Stipendium . . . est*: Romans 6:23 (translated in line 41). Neither this nor lines 42–3 are quotations from the Vulgate text.

42–3 *Si peccasse . . . veritas*: 1 John 1:8 (translated in lines 44–5).

49 *Che serà, serà*: Italian proverb, translated in line 50.

53 *Lines . . . characters*: The illustrations of line 52's 'necromantic books'.
     schemes: Accepted emendation of A's *sceanes*: diagrams.
     characters: Symbols.

58 *quiet poles*: Motionless poles of the (Ptolemaic) universe.

78 *Jove*: Classicizing euphemism for God.

80 *glutted with conceit*: (i) Filled with hungry longing by the thought, (ii) filled only with imagined anticipation.

92 *public schools*: Universities.
     silk: For A's *skill*.

95 *the Prince of Parma*: Spanish governor-general of the Netherlands, 1579–92.

98 *fiery keel . . . bridge*: Parma's bridge over the Scheldt at Antwerp was destroyed by a Dutch fire-ship on 4 April 1585.

114–15 *with . . . syllogisms / Gravelled*: Confounded with succinct logical arguments.

117 *problems*: Questions posed for scholastic disputation.

119 *Agrippa*: (N) was famed for raising the phantoms ('shadows', 120) of the dead.

124 *subjects*: Servants, spirits taking material form. B's *spirits* is the easier reading.

127 *Almain rutters*: German cavalry.

131 *Queen of Love*: Venus.

133–4 *from America . . . treasury*: The American gold which supplied

the wealth of Philip II of Spain is compared to the Golden Fleece
carried to Greece by Jason in the Argo.

140 *in*: Supplied from A2.

141 *tongues*: Languages.
    well seen: Well versed.

145 *the Delphian oracle*: The oracle of Apollo at Delphi. A's *Dolphian*
is corrected from A2.

157 *Hebrew Psalter . . . New Testament*: The Psalms and the opening
of St John's Gospel were used in conjuring.

Scene 2

2 *sic probo*: Thus I prove it (to cap an argument).

11–12 *That follows . . . upon't*: Graduates ('licentiate[s]') like you
shouldn't fall into such a *non sequitur*. Wagner parodies the style
of scholastic disputation, punning on the physical and logical senses
of 'follows' and 'stand upon'.

17 *Ask . . . a thief*: I.e. your witness is as unreliable as one thief's
testimony in support of another.

20–21 *corpus naturale . . . mobile*: A natural body . . . capable of
movement.

22–5 *But that . . . execution*: Wagner claims that only his good nature
makes it safe for them to approach so dangerous a place (or perhaps
that they can't get near his standard of wit), then adds that he
expects to see them hanged soon anyway.

28–32 *Truly . . . dear brethren*: A parody of the verbal style, as well as
the pious expression, of a puritan ('precisian').

37 *Rector*: Head of the university.

Scene 3

1–4 *gloomy shadow . . . breath*: Night, the shadow of the earth in
Ptolemaic cosmology, rises into the sky from the south towards the
constellation of Orion, the winter rising of which was associated
with cloud and rain (Virgil's *nimbosus Orion, Aeneid* I, 535).

9 *anagrammatized*: B's reading; A has *and Agramathist*.

10 *breviated*: The *abbreviated* form puns on the breviary, the Catholic
office-book, which included readings from the lives of the saints.

11–12 *Figures . . . stars*: Representations of everything pertaining to
the skies, and symbols of the signs of the Zodiac and the planets.

16–23 *Sint . . . Mephistopheles*: May the gods of Acheron (Hell) be
propitious to me; let the threefold godhead of Jehovah be gone (*or*
be powerful); hail, spirits of fire, air and water [*aquatici* for A's
Aquatani]; prince of the east, Beelzebub, monarch of burning Hell,

and Demogorgon, we ask your favour, that Mephistopheles may appear [*appareat* for A's *apariat*] and rise. Why do you delay [*quid tu moraris* for A's *quod tumeraris*]? By Jehovah, Hell, the consecrated water which I now scatter, by the sign of the cross which I now make, and by our prayers, may Mephistopheles himself now rise to us on our commands [*dicatis* for A's *dicaetis*].

35   *Quin redis . . . imagine!*: Why don't you return, Mephistopheles, in the guise of a friar!

47   *per accidens*: As a secondary cause (Mephistopheles too speaks the language of scholarship). A's *accident* may indicate Anglicization, or student argot.

61   *confounds hell . . . Elysium*: Faustus refuses to distinguish Hell from the pagan Elysian fields.

89   *these*: B's reading; A's *those* is probably a corruption from line 88.

109–10 *I'll join . . . Spain*: Faustus imagines closing the Straits of Gibraltar.

115   *speculation*: Contemplation, study.

Scene 4

3   *pickedevants*: Pointed beards (French *pic à devant*).
      quotha: Indeed, forsooth (used sarcastically).

4   *comings in*: Income, with a bawdy quibble.

5   *goings out*: (i) Expenditure, (ii) holes in clothes. There are similar 'misunderstandings' throughout the clown's lines.
      else: If you don't believe me.

15   *Qui mihi discipulus*: '[You] who [are] my pupil', the opening of William Lily's *Carmen de Moribus*, a didactic poem used as a school textbook.

17   *beaten silk . . . stavesacre*: Embroidered silk and delousing powder (with puns on the ache of a servant beaten with staves and (18) acres of land).

33   *Gridirons*: Robin's misunderstanding of 'guilders' (32). The association of gridirons with torture by fire may suggest the pains of hell.

34–6 *French crowns . . . English counters*: The clown implies that French *écus* are as worthless as 'counterfeit' English coins. 'French crowns' were associated with the baldness caused by syphilis ('the French disease'), and 'counter' may pun on 'cunt'.

46   *Balioll and Belcher*: (N) The devils are summoned with comic variants on their names.

49–51 *Do ye . . . over*: The clown imagines himself with the costume ('the round slop' (G)) and reputation of a daredevil.

50   *tall*: Brave.

51   *Kill devil*: Perhaps also the name of a strong drink.
55–6 *horns . . . clefts*: (i) The horns and cloven feet of devils, (ii) the
      penis (or cuckold's horns) and vulva.
59   *Banios*: Punning on *bagno* (Italian) = brothel.
66   *plackets*: Slits in petticoats; hence, in the bodies beneath.
72–3 *quasi . . . insistere*: As though to follow in our (= my) footprints
      (the irregular Latin in A may reflect Wagner's ignorance).
74   *fustian*: Originally a cloth; hence, 'nonsense' (cf. 'bombast').
75   *that's flat*: That's for sure.

Scene 5

29   *Veni . . . Mephistophile!*: Come, come, Mephistopheles!
31   *he lives*: B's reading gives better sense than A's *I live*.
35   *a deed of gift*: Mephistopheles insists on a legally binding document.
42   *Solamen . . . doloris*: It is a comfort to the miserable to have had
      companions in sorrow.
74   *Consummatum est*: It is finished (Christ's last words on the cross,
      in the Latin of the Vulgate, John 19:30).
77   *Homo fuge!*: Flee, man! (1 Timothy 6:11).
105   *by these presents*: Not 'gifts', but 'documents' (a legal formula).
153   *think no more*: The 'no' is supplied from A2.

Scene 6

This scene is inserted at this point by modern editors. In A, the action is
continuous from the end of Scene 5 to the start of Scene 7.

3   *circles*: (i) Magic circles, (ii) vaginas.
8   *chafing*: (i) Quarrel, (ii) rubbing.
16   *he for . . . study*: He will wear the cuckold's horns; her 'private
      study' hints at her 'privates'.
17   *to bear with*: (i) Put up with, (ii) support my weight (during inter-
      course), (iii) bear my child.
27   *turn . . . wind her*: (Like meat on a spit.) Both verbs sometimes have
      sexual connotations.
32   *of free cost*: For nothing.

Scene 7

27   *Alexander*: I.e. Paris, who deserted Oenone (N) for Helen.
28   *he . . . Thebes*: The walls of Thebes were magically raised by the
      music of Amphion.
35–43 *Tell me . . . erring stars*: Faustus asks how many spheres there
      are above that of the moon (though 'heavens' crosses from cos-
      mology to divinity), and/or whether the heavenly bodies all form a

single sphere, with the earth at the centre. Mephistopheles replies that, like the four elements (arranged in concentric spheres of earth, water, air and fire), the spheres too are concentrically arranged round a single great axis, the farthest point of which ('terminine') is the pole of the universe. Each of the planets has its own sphere. The questions are provocative, the replies orthodox.

44–5   *both situ . . . tempore*: Both in position and in time. Faustus asks whether the spheres all move in the same direction and complete their rotations of the earth at the same intervals.

51–7   *Who knows . . . intelligentia*: Faustus demonstrates his familiarity with the rotations of the planets relative to the background stars (the figures are approximations, sometimes inaccurate). The planetary spheres were traditionally under the guidance of angelic 'intelligences' (*intelligentiae*). 'Dominion' (celestial influence) may here be confused with 'domination', one of the hierarchies of angels.

61   *empyreal*: Both 'imperial' and 'empyrean' (the fiery heaven).

63   *conjunctions . . . aspects*: Stars in conjunction appear close together; in opposition, to be opposite each other in the heavens; aspects are their relative positions.

65   *Per . . . totius*: Through unequal motion (of the planets) in respect to the whole.

92–3   *the devil . . . his dame*: The devil and his dam (mother) were a proverbial comic pairing.

111   *Ovid's flea*: The subject of the pseudo-Ovidian erotic *Elegia de Pulice*. The joke is repeated from 4.64–6.

115   *cloth of arras*: Luxurious tapestry from Arras in Flanders.

118   *leathern bag*: A money-bag.

130–31 *chimney-sweeper . . . oyster-wife*: Emblematic of dirt and poverty.

139   *the devil a penny*: Not a damned penny.
      pension: Payment for a child's board and lodging (hence payment of any kind).

144   *Martlemas-beef*: Beef killed on St Martin's day (11 November) and salted.

147   *March-beer*: Strong beer brewed in March.
      progeny: (Here) parentage, progenitors.

159–60   *I am . . . stockfish*: Lechery prefers an inch of 'raw mutton' (slang for 'food for lust': cf. 4.10–11) to a lot (an ell = 45 inches) of dried cod ('stockfish').

160–61   *ell . . . letter . . . Lechery*: Lechery puns on the name and sound of the letter, presumably to make lewd gestures with her tongue in pronouncing it.

Chorus 2

6   *yoky*: Yoked (B's reading).

7   *to prove cosmography*: To test the accuracy of the geographers' maps.

Scene 8

12   *Quarters . . . equivalents*: Divide the town into four equal parts.

13–15 *Maro's . . . tomb . . . space*: Virgil was buried outside Naples, where he was reputed to have created a long tunnel by magic. The phrasing is very close to that of the Faustbook.

17   *sumptuous temple*: Presumably St Mark's in Venice.

27–8 *be bold . . . cheer*: Make free with his hospitality.

31–43 *this city . . . Africa*: The local detail (including the inaccurate positioning of the Castel Sant'Angelo on the bridge) is from the Faustbook.

33–4 *Just through . . . parts*: Supplied from B.

42   *pyramides*: (Four syllables) obelisks from Egypt.

51   *And take . . . feast*: And play a part in the feast ('meal' and 'feast-day') of St Peter.

52   *bald-pate*: Tonsured.

53   *summum bonum*: Highest good (scholastic term for the goodness of God).

73–4 *ghost . . . pardon*: The sale of papal indulgences for the souls of the dead in Purgatory had provoked the start of the Reformation.

75   *dirge*: Mass for the dead; from its Latin key word, *dirige* = 'direct (my soul, O Lord)'.

82–3 *cursed . . . candle*: Excommunicated in a ritual in which the bell is rung, the book (the Bible) closed, and the candle put out. As in the Faustbook, the rite is here confused with that of exorcism.

90   *Maledicat Dominus*: May the Lord curse (him).

99   *Et omnes sancti*: And all the saints.

Scene 9

2   *Ecce signum!*: Behold the sign! (a reminiscence of the mass).

2–3 *a simple . . . horse-keepers*: An impressive haul for two stable-boys.

3   *eat no hay*: Be unusually well fed.

11   *etc.*: *Et cetera* may be a euphemism, or Latin bombast, or a signal to the actor to improvise. The grooms pass the cup between them as they are frisked.

20   *scour you*: Knock you about (punning on scouring, polishing a drinking-vessel).

26–8   *Sanctobulorum . . . Mephistopheles!*: Robin's invocation sounds like bits of Latin and Greek, but is nonsense. Yet Mephistopheles comes (perhaps at the mention of his name).
       tickle: (Used ironically) thump.

28.1 SD–35   *Enter MEPHISTOPHELES . . . enterprise*: Since Mephistopheles dismisses the grooms again in lines 45–7, and there threatens different transformations, these lines are sometimes treated as an undeleted first version of the end of the scene, and omitted. But the Vintner may be included in the first curse, but then left out of the second, because Mephistopheles spares him (he could exit at line 35.1). And the grooms' initial failure to be transformed seems consistent with their sauciness.

29–32   *O, nomine . . . nobis!*: The scraps of Latin (*nomine Domine* (for *Domini*): 'name of the Lord'; *Peccatum peccatorum*: 'sin of sins'; *Misericordia pro nobis*: 'pity for us') recall phrases from the Catholic liturgy (*in nomine Domini*: 'in the name of the Lord'; *in remissionem peccatorum*: 'for the remission of sins'; *miserere nobis*: 'have mercy on us').

Chorus 3

3   *stayed his course*: Ended his journey.

Scene 10

11   *conjurer*: I.e. one who does ordinary magic tricks.

28   *Chief . . . pre-eminence*: Most admired of those who have been pre-eminent in the world.

31   *motion*: Mention.

36   *his beauteous paramour*: Probably Alexander's Persian wife, Roxana; or perhaps the courtesan Thais.

45   *if it like your grace*: If your grace pleases. Faustus' polite formulation disguises his anxiety that the Emperor might be displeased by his inability to bring on the 'true substantial bodies' (46).

50   *lively resemble*: Imitate to the life.

59   *Actaeon*: For his presumption Actaeon (N) was transformed into a stag and killed by his own hounds. Faustus' reply puns on the cuckold's horns, which are literalized later in the scene.

64–5   *this lady . . . neck*: This legend has not been traced.

81   *no haste but good*: Proverbial. 'No haste but good (speed)' (Tilley H199).

Scene 11

There is no break in the action at the end of Scene 10; leaving the Emperor's court, Faustus and Mephistopheles walk into a new episode.

0.1   SD *HORSE-COURSER*: Horse-dealers were proverbially disreputable. Faustus cons this one with a device beyond the usual tricks of the trade.

2   *Fustian*: (G) The slip identifies Faustus as one who deceives with verbal trickery.

Mass: By the mass; a Catholic oath surviving in Elizabethan English.

10–12   *I pray . . . child*: Spoken ironically; the Horse-courser spends a lot ('has a great charge'), even without the expense of a family.

15   *water*: Water traditionally dispels enchantment.

16   *will he . . . waters?*: 'Isn't he ready for anything?' (Proverbial: R. W. Dent, *Shakespeare's Proverbial Language: An Index* (Berkeley, 1981): W131.11).

21   *forty*: I.e. 'dollars'.

22   *hey, ding, ding*: A song-refrain, often a euphemism for sexual intercourse. If the horse were not a gelding, the Horse-courser might 'make a brave living' from stud-fees (his slick buttock was a sign of potency).

25   *water*: Urine.

33–4   *Christ . . . in conceit*: Faustus comforts himself with the prime example of a sinner being saved at the last minute, and promptly falls asleep as a sign of his complacency. Christ promised salvation to the repentant thief crucified with him (Luke 23:40–43).

34.2   SD *crying*: Lamenting loudly, but perhaps also weeping.

36–7   *Doctor Lopus . . . purgation*: Doctor Faustus' medicine (the 'purgation') is even worse than that of Lopus, the notorious doctor-poisoner (N). Since he was executed in 1594 (i.e. after Marlowe's death) the line is probably not Marlovian and may cast doubt on the authenticity of the scene.

36   *H'as*: He has, like modern 'he's'.

46–7   *O, yonder . . . master*: Mistaking Mephistopheles for a servant, the Horse-courser addresses him contemptuously (*snipper-snapper*: whipper-snapper; *hey-pass*: a magician's catch-phrase (cf. 'hey presto'), hence a trickster).

63   *So-ho*: A hunter's cry.

83   *niggard . . . cunning*: Miser with my skills.

Scene 12

0.1   SD: A's stage-directions here are slightly inconsistent with those at the end of Scene 11. The action is probably still continuous, but a scene may be missing.

5   *great-bellied*: Pregnant.

21–4 *the year ... East*: Faustus confuses seasonal differences between northern and southern hemispheres with climatic variation between western and eastern countries. 'Saba' (biblical Sheba) is modern Yemen.

30   *let us in*: Let us go in.

34   *beholding*: Beholden.

Scene 13

1–8   These lines are sometimes printed as a separate Chorus; but, though Wagner's function is choric, his speech is assimilated to the action of the scene.

24.1 SD *passeth over the stage*: The formula indicates a processional entrance and exit.

39–46 *Break heart ... guilt*: The Old Man talks of Faustus' spiritual state in terms of bodily suffering; and he can be saved only by Christ's blood.

40   *heaviness*: Sadness.

50.1 SD *dagger*: The dagger is a temptation to suicide, and Faustus seems about to kill himself in line 51.

75   *age*: Old man.

91   *topless*: Immeasurably high.

93–4 *Her lips ... again*: The soul was believed to rise to the mouth in a kiss (in line 94, Faustus asks for a second). Succubi took human souls through sexual contact.

95   *be*: Probably just a variant for 'is'; but perhaps optative ('Let heaven be ...').

105–8 *Brighter ... azured arms*: Semele's disastrous request to Jupiter to appear in his full divine form was well known (N). The nymph Arethusa was pursued by the river-god Alpheus, and was transformed into a fountain to escape him. Some commentators described him as a descendant of Apollo, but 'monarch of the sky' suggests the sun-god himself. See (N) and Introduction, pp. xiii–xiv.

112.1 SD *Enter the* DEVILS: They come to torment the old man's flesh.

113   *sift*: Make trial of, as in Luke 22:31: 'Satan hath earnestly desired to sift you as wheat' (Bishops' Bible).

Scene 14

10   *surfeit*: A disease of over-eating.

48   *save*: Supplied from B.

71   *O lente . . . equi!*: Oh, run slowly, slowly, horses of the night! Slightly adapted from Ovid, *Amores* I.xiii.40 (which Marlowe translated), where it is a call to prolong the night for love.

81–2   *Mountains . . . God*: Recalling Hosea 10:8: 'and they shall say to the mountains, "Cover us," and to the hills, "Fall on us"', and Revelation 6:16, 'And said to the mountains and rocks, "Fall on us, and hide us from the presence of him that sitteth on the throne, and from the wrath of the Lamb."'

86–92   *You stars . . . heaven*: Faustus asks the stars which predominated at his birth, and whose 'influence' (astrological power) has determined his fate, to draw him up, like moisture, into a thundercloud, and destroy his body when its lightning erupts, so long as his soul may go on up to heaven. In Renaissance meteorology, lightning was produced by the pressure of exhalations on their enclosing clouds.

92.1   SD *The watch*: The 'clock' of 61.2SD.

104   *Pythagoras' metempsychosis*: The doctrine of the transmigration of souls, attributed to Pythagoras (N). Though A's *metem su cossis* suggests a compositor's confusion, it seems also to preserve a learned Greek pronunciation.

120   *I'll burn my books*: A traditional gesture of renouncing magic.

EPILOGUE

2   *Apollo's laurel bough*: An emblem of poetic, and other intellectual, achievement.

9   *Terminat . . . opus*: 'The hour ends the day, the author ends his work.' Not apparently part of the foregoing speech, this line, for which no source has been found, and which may be a printer's addition, reads like a motto on the whole play. It occurs also at the end of the manuscript play *Charlemagne* in BL MS Egerton 1994.

EDWARD THE SECOND

The play was probably completed in 1592 and was first performed by Pembroke's Men. Its first printing was in a quarto-size octavo of 1594, which forms the basis of this edition. Later quartos of 1598, 1612 and

1622 (which refers on its title-page to a revival of the play by Queen Anne's Men at the Red Bull) attest its continuing popularity.

Like other Elizabethan history-plays, *Edward the Second* is about the conflict between a king and his nobles, and shows the clear influence of Shakespeare's treatment of the theme in his *Henry VI* plays. But it differs from them in a number of ways: its characters are unconcerned with dynastic issues and show little interest in the larger shape of history; there is no trace of a providential design and no sense of the sanctity of monarchy (all are important issues in Shakespeare's other comparable play, *Richard II*). *Edward the Second* is a play about power, pure and simple. 'Essentially,' writes J. B. Altman, 'the conflict remains one between willful, mean-minded peers determined to preserve their own ancient prerogatives and a willful king jealous of his right to feed his fantasies, at whatever cost to others' (*The Tudor Play of Mind: Rhetorical Inquiry and the Development of Elizabethan Drama* (Berkeley, 1978), pp. 363–4).

With the exception of a few details from the chronicles of Richard Grafton (1569) and John Stow (1580), events are drawn from Holinshed's *Chronicles* (probably from its second edition, 1587). But they are drastically reshaped. Holinshed's narrative of Edward's twenty-year reign is a long annalistic account cluttered with the detailed circumstances of the conflict with the barons, interwoven with full descriptions of Edward's equally disastrous relations with Scotland, Ireland and France. Marlowe leaves out the complexities and aggregates events together so that the play is dominated by the intense desires and fierce hostilities of its protagonists, especially Gaveston and Mortimer. He personalizes the action. Gaveston's relationship with the king is virtually the only issue between Edward and the barons. Marlowe eroticizes their love much more explicitly than does Holinshed, and extends Gaveston's life to keep him at the centre of contention. The younger Spencer, who had, historically, little connection with Gaveston, becomes first his dependant and later his substitute in the king's affections. Marlowe, and some members of his early audiences, would have known of at least two contemporary kings whose homosexuality supposedly made them susceptible to the influence of favourites (or minions) – Henri III of France, who figures in *The Massacre at Paris*, and James VI of Scotland, the future king of England. Gaveston's sexual behaviour, in the play, matters less than his opportunism and casual cruelty, the exultation he feels when he first arrives and its rapid development into his vengeful humiliation of the bishop of Coventry. Mortimer too is given greater prominence. In the chronicles he scarcely figures until the end of the reign, but here he is present from the first as an antagonist of Gaveston and ally of the queen, later becoming her lover (as Holinshed only belatedly hints) and sole deviser of the plot to murder the king. Unlike the heroes of Marlowe's other plays, who dominate the action, Edward is thus surrounded by personalities more powerful than himself.

A further consequence of the aggregation of events is a remarkable tightening of the chain of historical causation. *Edward the Second* is Marlowe's best-constructed play. Actions lead directly to their consequences, as when Edward's ill-timed and provocative exaltation of Gaveston goads the barons to switch tactics from legally banishing to kidnapping him (scene 4: this edition preserves the octavo's fluid division into scenes only, rather than adopting the five act divisions favoured by some modern editors). Many of the causal linkages are made to feel like pointedly ironic reversals: Gaveston's murder leads to Edward's one victory in avenging it; his cruelty in exploiting his success provokes Kent's desertion and leads to Mortimer's fatal alliance with Isabella against the king. These reversals complicate the play's characterization: proud Mortimer starts out like Hotspur and ends up a Machiavellian, while Isabella changes from wronged wife to practised hypocrite. Are these inconsistently used stereotypes or subtly ironic modulations? When Isabella sounds formulaic and insincere, she may be meant to – to sound as though she is half-consciously using a false language.

The question is linked to the problem of the play's verbal style. Its language is generally bare and tense. Big speeches are frequently punctured by colloquially plain counterstatements. Single lines are heavy with hidden meaning. Apparently polite formulae are used as insults (compare the taunting heraldic devices in scene 6); Edward's murder is ordered in one ambiguous sentence. The language keeps checking itself, its switches of idiom reflecting the larger reversals of the action.

All these reversals are framed by Edward's own 'strange exchange' (21.35), his decline from kingship to abjection. Structural and verbal patterns converge in the closing scenes, where Edward's laments are juxtaposed with the callous double-talk of Mortimer and Isabella. Details of the king's torment emphasize the reversal: the shaving in sewer-water is taken from Stow (see note on 23.36.1–2SD below) and 'rhymed' with the treatment of the bishop of Coventry in scene 1; and in the murder itself there surfaces a ghastly fusion of cruelty and sexuality long latent in the play. The idiom remains grimly ironic: one of the horrors of Marlowe's invented murderer Lightborne is that he sounds so menacingly comforting.

Scene 1

7   *France*: Gaveston had been banished to his native Gascony by
       Edward I.

14   *die*: (i) Swoon, (ii) reach orgasm.

16–17 *What ... night*: Since Gaveston enjoys the king's sun-like
       favour, he has no need for the goodwill of lesser lights, such as the
       nobles, and least of all for the 'sparks' (20) of the common people.

22   *Tanti!*: Italian, so much for that!
       fawn: For Q's *fanne*.

25   *your worship's service*: To serve your worship.

31   *lies*: Travellers' tales.

33   *against the Scot*: In Edward I's military campaign against Robert
       Bruce.

39   *porcupine*: It was believed that porcupines would shoot their quills
       in self-defence, on the authority of Pliny's *Historia Naturalis*
       (VIII.xxxv).

54   *masques*: Extravagant court entertainments of Italian origin, some-
       times involving the use of lavish costumes and sets, were popular
       in Tudor and early-Stuart England.

56–71 *And in ... lord*: As the speech unfolds, it becomes apparent that
       Gaveston plans to stage the myth of Diana and Actaeon (N).

57   *sylvan nymphs*: Wood-nymphs.

89   *Mort Dieu!*: God's death! (punning on Mortimer's name).

94   *these knees ... stiff*: I.e. too stiff to kneel.

107   *to the proof*: Irrefutably.

110   *Mowbray*: Q's spelling *Mowberie* suggests the name is trisyllabic.

117   *Preach upon poles*: Traitors' heads were placed upon poles and
       mounted above the gates of city walls as a warning to others.

126   *Wiltshire*: Because the Mortimers had no historical connections
       with Wiltshire, Roma Gill argues strongly against Q's reading,
       maintaining that the compositor may well have misread 'Welshrye',
       i.e. the people of Wales, the power-base of the family. See 'Morti-
       mer's Men', *N&Q*, n.s. 27 (1980), p. 159.

127–8 *All Warwickshire ... many friends*: Both lines are spoken
       ironically.

132   *minion*: (i) Favourite, (ii) darling boy (from French *mignon*). The
       nobles perhaps use the word in the latter sense as a term of homo-
       phobic contempt.

142   *Thy friend, thy self*: Proverbial (Tilley F696).

149   *high-minded*: Proud, arrogant.

155   *King and Lord of Man*: The lords of the Isle of Man were also

known as kings because of the sovereign rights they possessed. There may also be a sexual quibble.

167   *seal*: If this is the Great Seal of the realm, Edward confers near-regal power on Gaveston.

185   *Saving your reverence*: Polite formula, used derisively, with a pun on 'Sir reverence', a euphemism for faeces, which might well be found in a 'channel' (= sewer: 187).

197   *Tower . . . Fleet*: The Tower of London and the debtors' prison.

200   *True, true*: A rueful comment on the aptness of 'Convey' (= steal: 199).

206   *prison . . . holiness*: A prison would suit the austere life of a priest (imprisonment was one of the sufferings of the early Christians).

Scene 2

6   *timeless sepulchre*: Early grave.

11   *villain*: Villain, with a pun on 'villein', serf.

75   *the New Temple*: Home of the Knights Templar, and later part of the Inns of Court.

78   *Lambeth*: Site of the Archbishop of Canterbury's official residence.

Scene 3

The shortness of this scene has led to suspicions of textual corruption. But it further establishes Gaveston's brusque confidence, despite his knowledge of the forces ranged against him.

Scene 4

0.1 SD *NOBLES*: Q is sometimes unspecific about which nobles are required.

1   *form*: Formal articles.

7   *declined from*: Less inclined towards.

8   *sits here*: Edward grants Gaveston the Queen's place next to himself, probably on a throne.

13   *Quam male conveniunt!*: How badly they suit each other! (based on Ovid, *Metamorphoses* II, 846–7: 'Majesty and love do not suit each other, and do not remain long in one seat').

19   *faced and overpeered*: Insolently outfaced and looked down on (with a pun on 'peer').

26   *pay them home*: I.e. punish them fully for their treason.

51   *legate to*: Representative of.

54   *Curse*: Excommunicate.

61–2 *discharge . . . allegiance*: Pope Pius V excommunicated Elizabeth

I in 1570, thus supposedly absolving her subjects of obedience to her.

68   *President of the North*: Cf. John Cowell, *The Interpreter* (1607), 'President . . . is used in common law for the king's lieutenant in any province or function, as: President of Wales, of York, of Berwick' (Gill 1967).

97–105   *Proud Rome . . . live*: Such vehement anti-papalism might well appeal to Elizabethan Protestants; but Edward's obvious pique and murderousness might be more disturbing.

102   *make*: For Q's *may*.

168   *repealed*: Recalled from exile.

175   *those arms*: I.e. Edward's arms (embracing Isabella).

178   *frantic Juno*: From Ovid, *Metamorphoses* X, 155–61.

189   *ill entreated her*: Treated her badly.

191   *long of*: Because of.

195   *Cry quittance*: (i) Get even, (ii) quit him, (iii) give up the marriage bond, declare yourself free of marital obligations.

199   *wanton humour*: Amorous mood (Forker 1994).

211   *tend'rest*: Care for.

216   *him*: I.e. Mortimer Senior.

223   *torpedo*: The electric ray, which can deliver a numbing shock.

224   *floats*: Sails, but with the implication of a drowned corpse floating.

247   *make white . . . day*: Proverbial (Tilley B440).

255   *play the sophister*: I.e. deceive by false arguments.

261   *whereas*: While.

269   *in the chronicle*: In the year-by-year annals of the reign. Mortimer is thinking of how history will judge Gaveston's hypothetical killer.

284   *night-grown mushroom*: Because mushrooms grow overnight, this metaphor was proverbially used to describe the unprecedented rise of an upstart (cf. Tilley M1319).

318   *Diablo!*: Italian, devil!

327   *golden tongue*: There is some evidence of medieval jewels in the form of metal tongues.

330   *these*: Edward's arms.

341   *sovereign's*: For Q's *soveraigne*.

350   *bear the sword*: The sword was a symbol of state power, usually carried before the monarch during processions.

358   *Chirk*: Mortimer Senior's estate which bordered Shropshire and Wales.

374   *Against*: In preparation for the time when.

377   *made him sure*: Betrothed.

378   *Gloucester's heir*: I.e. Lady Margaret de Clare.

381 *triumph*: I.e. the jousting tournament (cf. 375).

390–96 *mightiest kings . . . Alcibiades*: Mortimer Senior tries to placate his nephew by citing classical examples of homoerotic love. See (N).

392 *Hercules*: Q's *Hector* mangles the myth.

406 *He wears . . . his back*: Proverbial (Tilley L452).

407–8 *Midas-like . . . heels*: He struts around in court decked in gold, with a train of low-born foreign rascals (literally, 'testicles').

415 *other*: Others.

Scene 5

14 *preferred . . . to*: (i) Put me forward for promotion, (ii) liked me more than.

20 *our lady*: Margaret de Clare.

30 *read unto her*: Tutored her.

32 *court it*: Behave like a courtier.

33–4 *black coat . . . serge*: Baldock wears the modest, and cheap, clothes of a scholar.
band: collar.
serge: A cheap material.

38 *making low legs*: Bowing obsequiously.

44 *formal toys*: Trivial politenesses.

53 *propterea quod*: Because. Baldock satirizes the Latinate rhetoric of scholarship.

54 *quandoquidem*: Because. The joke is unclear.

55 *form*: Conjugate.

71 *coach*: Coaches were not widely used in England until the 1560s.

Scene 6

11 *device*: An emblematic painting and motto which decorated a shield.

20 *Aeque tandem*: Equal at last.

28 *Undique mors est*: Death is on all sides.

35 *my brother*: I.e. Gaveston.

40 *jesses*: For Q's *gresses*.

42 *Britainy*: Britain.

62 *painted*: Decorated with flowers.

73 *Return . . . throats*: Defy them.

74 *Base leaden earls*: 'Spurious nobles (like coin of alloy rather than of true metal)' (Forker 1994).

75 *eat . . . beef*: I.e. the nobles are beef-witted (stupid) and parasitic.

81 *Here, here*: Pembroke points at Gaveston.

122   *gather head*: Raise an army.
146   *the broad seal*: Letters patent under the Great Seal, which gave the bearer the right to collect money for a special purpose without fear of being prosecuted for begging.
158   *treasure*: Treasury.
159   *The murmuring ... hath*: And has overtaxed the discontented common people.
163   *O'Neill*: Irish clan-leader during Edward II's reign.
164   *the English pale*: English settlement around Dublin.
165   *made road*: Made raid.
167   *narrow seas*: English Channel.
171   *Valois*: Philip of Valois, King of France.
186   *women's favours*: Love-tokens given to knights and often worn in combat.
189–94   *Maids...rumbelow*: From Robert Fabyan's *Chronicle* (1559).
190   *Bannocksbourn*: Edward's forces were famously crushed by the Scots at the Battle of Bannockburn (24 June 1314).
194   *rumbelow*: A meaningless refrain.
195   *Wigmore shall fly*: I.e. Mortimer Junior's Herefordshire estate, Wigmore Castle, shall be sold.
202–3   *cockerels...lion*: Traditionally, lions feared the cock's crowing.
225   *him*: I.e. Mortimer Junior.
241   *arms*: Coat of arms.
242–3   *gentry...Oxford*: An MA degree conferred gentlemanly status.
248   *well allied*: Of good stock.
264   *Have at*: (Imperative) let us attack.

Scene 7

5   *of policy*: As an act of politic deception.
20   *give the onset*: Begin the attack.
23   *the name of Mortimer*: Historically, the family took its name from Mortemer in Normandy, but Mortimer prefers the association with the Dead Sea (*Mortuum Mare*) and the Crusades.

Scene 8

4   *hold*: Fortress.
46   *Flemish hoy*: Small fishing vessels used in the North Sea by the Flemish.

Scene 9

4   *unsurprised*: Uncaptured.
5   *malgrado*: Italian, in spite of.

14   *welter in thy gore*: Be soaked in your own blood.
15   *the Greekish strumpet*: Helen of Troy.
27–8 *But . . . our hands*: Gaveston is to be beheaded, a privileged form
     of execution reserved for the nobility.
62–3 *seize . . . possess*: Get hold of . . . keep.
64   *in keep*: In custody.
67   *for*: Because.
69   *To make . . . thief*: To kill a man of honour who has stood hostage
     for a dishonest man.
72   *Question . . . thy mates*: Bandy arguments with your equals.
84   *had-I-wist*: (Literally) had I known (proverbial; Tilley H8). War-
     wick is reluctant to let Gaveston escape, only to repent of it later.
85   *over-woo*: Plead excessively to.
88   *in this*: In this matter.

Scene 10

1   *wrong thy friend*: I.e. betray Pembroke.
5   *Centre . . . bliss*: ?Applied to the king.
13   *watched it well*: I.e. kept a vigilant guard over Gaveston.
14   *shadow*: Ghost.

Scene 11

13   *braves*: Insults.
14   *beard me*: Pluck my beard (i.e. defy me).
20   *preach on poles*: Cf. 1.117n.
27   *We'll steel . . . tops*: We'll sharpen our swords against their helmets
     and cut off ('poll') their heads.
29   *affection*: Desire.
31.2 SD *truncheon*: A staff which symbolized authority.
36   *bowmen . . . pikes*: Lances with sharp metal tips at both ends were
     driven into the ground just in front of the archers to protect them
     in battle (Wiggins and Lindsey 1997).
37   *Brown bills*: Soldiers carrying halberds (covered in bronze to pre-
     vent rusting).
42   *in him*: In his person, to the advantage of his family.
43–4 *an it . . . pours*: If it please your grace, one who pours . . .
53   *Lord Bruce . . . land*: Holinshed reports that when William de
     Bruce offered to sell some of his land in the Welsh Marches to the
     Mortimers to pay his debts, they were outbid, with the king's help,
     by Spencer Junior.
54   *in hand withal*: Are negotiating for it.

57   *Soldiers, a largess*: Edward promises the soldiers a generous gift of money for their loyalty.
66   *Sib*: Kinswoman (i.e. wife), or a contraction of her name.
76–7 *heaven's . . . shoulder*: Atlas (N) is here imagined supporting the roof-beams of the heavens.
79   *towardness*: Boldness.
87   *once*: Once and for all.
121   *part*: Action.
127   *fire . . . starting-holes*: Smoke them out of their lairs (like animals).
129   *moving orbs*: The heavenly spheres which, according to Ptolemaic cosmology, moved in their concentric orbits around the earth.
145   *merely*: Purely.
152   *iwis*: I know.
158   *plainer*: Complainant (who brings an allegation).
163   *deads*: Deadens.
      royal vine: Edward's crown was in fact adorned with strawberry leaves, but the association of the vine with royalty was traditional.

Scene 12

0.1   SD *excursions*: Soldiers rush across the stage, emulating the confusion of battle.
9   *retire*: Retreat.
18   *Thou'd best . . . them . . . trains*: You had better quickly abandon them and their intrigues. Q reads *Th'ad . . . thee*.
20   *on thy face*: Apparently a variant of the more usual riposte 'in thy face'.
23   *trow ye*: Think you.
35   *Saint George*: Established as the patron saint of England during Edward III's reign.

Scene 13

3   *hang the heads*: As in French, Elizabethan English could use the definite article where modern English uses a possessive.
4   *advance*: Raise their heads on poles (punning on 'advance' = to promote).
22   *but temporal*: I.e. Edward can only inflict physical torment, and not spiritual suffering.
25   *my lord of Winchester*: Spencer Senior, earl of Wiltshire.
45   *Bestow . . . France*: Spencer Junior employs Levune to bribe the French lords, and thus prevent Isabella from receiving aid in France.
47–8 *Jove to . . . Danaë*: The shower of gold in which Jupiter reached Danaë (N) was sometimes interpreted as a bribe.

53 *levelled*: For Q's *levied*.
54 *lay their heads*: Punning on the sense 'conspire'.
55 *clean*: Absolutely.
56 *clap so close*: (For Q's *claps close*) shake hands (to strike a deal) in secret.

Scene 14

10 *stay*: Await.
11 *Stand . . . device*: Kent calls upon the darkness of night to assist Mortimer Junior's escape.
14 *But . . . so happily?*: Did your sleeping potion work successfully on the warders?

Scene 15

1-2 *Ah, boy . . . unkind*: Levune's mission has been successful.
4 *a fig*: An obscene gesture involving the thumb being thrust between two fingers.
5 *my uncle's*: Kent's.
7 *'A*: He (unstressed form).
9-10 *tuned . . . jar*: The metaphors are from music.
10 *jar too far*: (i) Quarrel too much, (ii) have become out of tune.
13 *Hainault*: A Flemish county in the Low Countries adjacent to France.
20 *shake off*: Cast off. The emendation *share of* is attractive.
24 *staff*: Quarter-staff used in combat.
32 *marquis*: William, Count of Hainault, brother to Sir John.
41 *thraldom*: (Here) captivity, bondage.
47 *Monsieur le Grand*: A fictional character invented by Marlowe.
49 *king*: I.e. the King of France.
50-51 *right . . . weapons want*: Mortimer means that right can find an opportunity even without weapons, but his words can also mean that right must cede place if it lacks power.
52 *made away*: Murdered.
55 *cast up caps*: Throw caps into the air with joy.
56 *appointed for*: Armed for battle.
66 *to bid . . . base*: Alluding to the children's game in which players could be caught by opponents when running between two bases.
67 *match*: Game.
74 *brother*: I.e. brother-in-law.
75 *motion*: Proposal.
76 *forward in arms*: Eager to fight.

Scene 16

8   *note*: Official list.

11.1   SD *SPENCER reads their names*: Q does not provide details of those
        nobles who were executed. However, the following passage (from
        Holinshed, *Chronicles of England, Scotland, and Ireland* (1587),
        vol. 3, p. 331) could be adapted for performance purposes:

> the lord William Tuchet, the lord William Fitz William, the lord
> Warren de L'Isle, the lord Henry Bradbourne, and the lord William
> Chenie barons, with John Page an esquire, were drawn and hanged
> at Pomfret aforesaid, and then shortly after, Roger lord Clifford,
> John lord Mowbraie, and sir Gosein d'Eevill barons, were drawn
> and hanged at York. At Bristow in the like manner were executed
> sir Henrie de Willington, and sir Henrie Montfort baronets; and at
> Gloucester, the lord John Gifford, and sir William Elmebridge
> knight; and at London, the lord Henry Teies baron; at Winchelsea,
> sir Thomas Culpepper knight; at Windsor, the lord Francis de
> Aldham baron; and at Canterbury, the lord Bartholomew de Badelis-
> mere, and the lord Bartholomew de Ashbornham, barons. Also at
> Cardiff in Wales, sir William Fleming knight was executed: divers
> were executed in their countries, as sir Thomas Mandit and
> others . . .

12   *barked apace*: (i) Barked rapidly like dogs, (ii) embarked swiftly
        (upon their treasons) (Forker 1994).

20   *'A will be had*: He will be caught.

28   *promised*: Levune begins formulaically with a reminder of the
        dutiful promises he has made. Many editors emend to 'premised'.

38   *Your honour's . . . service*: At your honour's disposal for anything
        you want to do.

41   *lead the round*: Lead the dance.

42   *a'*: In.

43   *rout*: Band of followers.

52   *equal*: Able.

Scene 17

3   *Belgia*: The Netherlands.

4   *cope with*: (i) Engage with, (ii) embrace. Lines 3–9 all reflect this
        ambiguity.

26   *havocs*: Causes havoc in (i.e. plunders). Havocking was the indis-
        criminate slaughter of game.

Scene 18

0.1–0.2 SD *flying about*: Cf. the 'fly' of line 1.

6   *r'enforce*: Once more encourage.

7   *bed of honour*: The ground on which the soldiers will die honourably, and be buried.

Scene 19

16–17   *Bristol . . . false*: I.e. the Mayor of Bristol has betrayed Edward I's son.

17   *Be . . . suspect*: Don't be found alone for it arouses suspicion.

43   *A goodly chancellor*. This is spoken sarcastically.

45.1 SD *RICE ap HOWELL*: A Welshman (Rice = Rhys) employed to arrest Edward.

48   *this presence*: The royal presence (with a pun in the next line).

60   *started thence*: Driven from their place of refuge.

63   *in a muse*: Perplexed.

70   *Your lordship . . . head*: Your recently acquired status may save you from hanging, but not beheading.

75   *Being of countenance*: Having authority.

Scene 20

18   *nurseries of arts*: I.e. universities.

20   *life contemplative*: The *vita contemplativa*, the monks' life of religious devotion.

29   *gloomy fellow*: The Mower who appears at line 45.

35   *fall on shore*: Run aground.

44–5   *drowsiness . . . no good*: Sleepiness was sometimes considered an evil omen.

45.1 SD *Welsh hooks*: Long-handled hedging bills resembling a scythe.

53–4   *Quem . . . iacentem*: 'He whom the coming day [dawn] saw in his pride, the passing day [dusk] has seen laid low' (from Seneca's *Thyestes*, 613–14).

56   *by no other names*: Leicester denies the titles which Edward has conferred upon Spencer Junior and Baldock.

58   *Stand not on titles*: Do not depend upon the privileges of noble status.

61–2   *O day . . . stars*: A recollection of Gaveston's lament, 10.4–5.

67   *in rescue of*: As payment for the release from custody of.

81   *Killingworth*: A common variant of 'Kenilworth', but the associations of the name darken as the play proceeds.

85   *As good . . . benighted*: I.e. it would be best to leave for Killingworth
      before nightfall (Wiggins and Lindsey 1997).
89   *hags*: Hellish spirits.
90   *these, and these*: Edward probably indicates the monks of Neath
      Abbey, Spencer Junior and Baldock.
96   *feignèd weeds*: False clothes (i.e. the disguises they are wearing).
98   *Life . . . friends*: Now that his friends have been sent to their deaths,
      his life has become meaningless.
101   *Rend, sphere . . . orb*: Let heaven be torn apart, and let the fire
      burst from its sphere (which surrounded the world in Ptolemaic
      cosmology).
113   *the place appointed*: I.e. the gallows.
115   *remember me*: I.e. remunerate me.

Scene 21

3   *lay . . . a space*: Resided a while here for pleasure.
9–10 *forest deer . . . herb . . . wounds*: It was believed that the herb
      dittany could heal wounds. Cf. Pliny, *Historia Naturalis* VII.xli.97.
      being struck: I.e. shot with an arrow.
13   *And*: Missing from all early texts.
18   *pent and mewed*: Penned and caged (like a bird in a 'mew' or cage).
27   *perfect*: Mere (Rowland 1994).
35   *exchange*: Change of circumstances.
43–4 *this crown . . . fire*: Medea gave Creusa (for whom Jason had left
      her) a crown which burst into flames when it was worn.
47   *vine*: An emblem of royal lineage. See also 11.163n.
66   *watches of the element*: I.e. stars and planets.
67   *rest . . . stay*: Remain motionless.
71   *tiger's milk*: Tigers were emblematic of cruelty.
85.1 SD *The* KING *rageth*: In the Coventry *Pageant of the Shearmen and
      Taylors* (Late fourteenth-century mystery play), 'Erode [Herod]
      ragis in the pagond and in the strete also' (783–4).
88   *install*: Invest (a person) to a position of authority.
109   *for aye*: For ever.
115   *protect*: Be Lord Protector to.
130   *to . . . breast*: Edward offers 'himself as to a murderer's dagger'
      (Gill 1967).
149   *estate*: Condition.
153   *I . . . once*: Proverbial (Tilley M219).

Scene 22

2   *light-brained*: Frivolous.

8   *slip*: Escape.

9   *And grip . . . himself*: And bite more fiercely for having been captured himself. 'Grip' is not clearly distinguished at this date from *gripe* (Q's reading), used of an animal seizing its prey (cf. 23.57).

10 *that imports us much*: That (it) is most important for us.
    us: For Q's *as*.

11 *erect*: Establish on the throne.

13–14   *For . . . under writ*: I.e. Mortimer Junior and Isabella will enjoy greater power when they can act in the name of the new king.

17 *so*: Provided that.

30 *or this . . . sealed*: Before ('or') Edward's letter of abdication was sealed.

31 *he*: Edward.

33 *no more but so*: Without more ado (Forker 1994).

37 *privy seal*: Royal seal.

39 *To dash . . . drift*: To frustrate the stupid Edmund's plan.

48 *resign*: Hand over.

57 *casts . . . liberty*: Is contriving to free him.

110 *'sdain'st thou so*: Are you so disdainful?

114 *nearer*: Closer in blood to Prince Edward.

115 *charge*: Responsibility.
    Redeem him: Give him back.

Scene 23

6–7   *nightly bird . . . fowls*: The owl, which other birds will mob if it appears in daylight. Because it was thought to foul its own nest, it was traditionally a dirty bird, which may explain Edward's identification with it.

10 *unbowel*: Open up.

12 *mark*: Target.

17 *air of life*: Breath.

22 *closet*: Chamber.

26 *excrements*: (Here) faeces.

27 *channel water*: Sewer-water.

28 *Sit . . . your grace*: Matrevis plays upon the alternative sense of 'excrements' (26), which could also mean 'hairs'.

36.1–2   SD *They wash . . . away*: The incident is taken from John Stow's *Chronicles of England* (1580).

52   *Thrust in*: I.e. into Killingworth Castle. Marlowe is thinking of the doors at the back of the stage; cf. *Jew of Malta* 2.3.365.

Scene 24

8, 11   *Edwardum . . . est*: The two interpretations of the Latin are given in the succeeding lines.

13   *Unpointed*: Unpunctuated.

14   *being dead*: I.e. when Edward is dead.

16   *quit*: Exonerated.

21   *Lightborne*: An anglicization of 'Lucifer' (= light-bearer), this is also the name of a devil in the late fifteenth-century Chester cycle of mystery plays.

26   *use much*: Am much accustomed.

31   *lawn*: Strip of linen, here stuffed down a victim's throat to cause suffocation.

41   *At every . . . horse*: Fresh horses have been stationed for him at intervals of ten miles.

42   *Take this*: I.e. the secret token used at 25.19.

50   *seal*: Authorize with the royal seal.

51   *Feared . . . feared*: Reminiscent of Machiavelli, *The Prince*, ch. 17: 'because hardly can [love and fear] subsist both together, it is much safer to be feared, than to be loved' (trans. Edward Dacres (1640), p. 130).

53–4   *Aristarchus' eyes . . . boy*: I.e. the prince fears Mortimer as much as his pupils feared the Greek scholar Aristarchus (N), whose very looks were like a whipping ('breeching').

59   *imbecility*: (Here) incapacity, weakness.

60   *onus quam gravissimum*: A very heavy burden. Like the tag in line 62, part of the legal formula for the installation of a Roman governor.

62   *Suscepi . . . provinciam*: I have undertaken that office.

68   *Maior . . . nocere*: I am greater than one Fortune can harm (i.e. too great for Fortune to harm me), from Ovid, *Metamorphoses* VI, 195.

71.2   SD *CHAMPION*: One who, in a formal coronation ceremony, offers to fight any who challenge the claim of the new king to his crown.

79   *here's to thee*: The king customarily drank the champion's health from a silver-gilt cup, which was then presented to him as his fee.

81   *blades and bills*: Swords and halberds.

106   *none of both them*: I.e. neither of them (Q2's reading; Q has *none of both, then*).

Scene 25

9   *savour*: Stench.

16   *for the nonce*: Purposely.

24   *Pereat iste*: Let this man perish. The instruction may be included in the unpunctuated letter or inscribed on the token. It is in Latin so that Lightborne cannot understand it.

25   *lake*: (Here) dungeon, cell.

33   *featherbed*: Feather mattress.

41   *Foh*: An expression of disgust at a bad smell.

     with all my heart: 'I must say' (Bevington and Rasmussen 1995).

41.1 SD *Enter KING EDWARD*: Because Q provides no stage directions, Edward's entrance is unclear. He may enter from beneath the stage via a trap door, or he could be 'discovered' (i.e. revealed) from behind a curtain drawn by Lightborne.

48   *used*: I.e. being treated.

54   *Caucasus*: See (N). The mountains were a byword for hardness.

69   *ran at tilt*: Jousted.

77   *That, even*: Q's *That, and even* is just possible but strained and hypermetrical.

92   *You're overwatched*: You are exhausted (from having little sleep), perhaps punning on the sense, 'under my eye'.

113.1 SD *EDWARD dies*: Q is unspecific about the murder, but the details were notorious. In Holinshed's words:

> they came suddenly one night into the chamber where he lay in bed fast asleep, and with heavy featherbeds or a table (as some write) being cast upon him, they kept him down and withall put into his fundament an horn, and through the same they thrust up into his body an hot spit, or (as other have) through the pipe of a trumpet a plumber's instrument of iron made very hot, the which passing up into his entrails, and being rolled to and fro, burnt the same, but so as no appearance of any wound or hurt outwardly might be once perceived. His cry did move many within the castle and town of Berkeley to compassion . . .
>
>   (*Chronicles of England, Scotland, and Ireland* (1587),
>   vol. 3, p. 341)

Scene 26

4   *ghostly father*: Priest (administering the last rites to one about to die), i.e. here a murderer.

9   *Fly ... savages*: Take flight beyond civilization.
11   *Jove's huge tree*: The oak.
24   SP *FIRST LORD*: Though Q attributes speeches in this scene to a
       collectivity of LORDS, it is likely that they were apportioned to
       individuals in performance (as at 93).
52   *hurdle*: The frame or sledge used to drag criminals through the
       streets on the way to the place of execution.
53   *Hang him ... quarters up*: Mortimer Junior is to be hanged, drawn
       and quartered – the traditional punishment for treason.
80   *trial*: Investigation.
101   *distilling*: Falling.

THE MASSACRE AT PARIS

The Massacre at Paris probably dates from 1592. It must post-date the
assassination of Henri III (2 August 1589), and is generally supposed to
have been the play whose first performance, under the title 'The Tragedy
of the Guise', by Lord Strange's Men at the Rose in January 1593, is
recorded in Philip Henslowe's Diary. That play was a great success,
and continued in the repertoire. But the only early publication of *The
Massacre* was in an undated octavo usually assigned on bibliographical
evidence to 1602, and from the difficulties presented by this text (the
basis of this edition) spring most of the problems which beset the understanding of the play. It seems to have been assembled from the memories
of actors, and perhaps as much as half the play Marlowe wrote is missing.
A single manuscript leaf, now in the Folger Shakespeare Library in
Washington, DC, preserves a significantly fuller version of the opening
of scene 19, and hints tantalizingly at the original verbal texture of the
play (see Appendix).

The action of the first half of the play, dealing with the
St Bartholomew's Day Massacre (1572), derives from François Hotman's
De Furoribus Gallicis, published under the pseudonym 'Ernest Vara-
mund', translated in 1573 as *A True and Plain Report of the Furious
Outrages in France* and reprinted in 1574 without acknowledgement as
Book 10 of Jean de Serres, *The Three Parts of the Commentaries ... of
the Civil Wars in France*. Some details of the planning of the massacre
may be taken from Simon Goulart's collection of *Mémoires de l'état de
France* (1576–7). The killing of Ramus comes from the anonymous
Tocsin contre les massacreurs (1579). This clearly touched a chord for
Marlowe: Guise, impugning Ramus's scholarship for 'never sound[ing]
anything to the depth' (9.25), recalls (or anticipates) Faustus' resolution

to 'sound the depth' of his 'profess[ion]' (1.2). Sources for the latter half of the play, which treats events of seventeen years with distorting compression, cannot be so clearly determined. There are innumerable hostile accounts of the reign of Henri III (his interests in magic and *mignons* were especially execrated in Guisard polemics); and Marlowe need not have been confined to written sources of information: events were within living memory, English soldiers were fighting in France in the early 1590s, and Marlowe may have been there twice in person.

One of the play's nineteenth-century editors thought it beneath criticism:

> the language seldom rises above mediocrity, the characters are drawn with the indistinct faintness of shadows, and the plot is contemptible: events in themselves full of horror and such as should strike the soul with awe, become ludicrous in the extreme by injudicious management; The whole is in fact not so much a tragedy as a burlesque upon tragedy . . .
>
> (William Oxberry, quoted in Oliver 1968:1)

Its stock has risen since then (Judith Weil argues that its concerns are central to the understanding of all Marlowe's work), but the key issues remain the play's historical accuracy and the interpretation of its black humour. Earlier scholars thought its historical vision corrupted by the Protestant propaganda of its sources. More recently, its bloodthirsty comedy has been seen to reflect the vicious sacrilegious humour which characterized the atrocities of the French wars of religion, 'the rites of violence'. However, the anthropologically minded historian who coined the term (Natalie Zemon Davis, in *Society and Culture in Early Modern France*, 1975) was explicitly concerned with *popular* violence. Marlowe's is a sixteenth-century 'Machiavellian' interpretation of the massacre as a conspiracy engineered by the Catholic nobility. He gives far greater prominence than his sources to his villainous duke of Guise, and, as Guise's big soliloquy (2.34ff.) makes clear, his motivation is not religion but the distinctly Marlovian ambition for a crown, 'the diadem of France' (44). 'For this,' the speech insists, are all his actions shaped, including a hypocritical show of religion:

> For this, have I a largess from the Pope,
> A pension and a dispensation too;
> And by that privilege to work upon,
> My policy hath framed religion.
> Religion: O *Diabole!*

> Fie, I am ashamed, how ever that I seem,
> To think a word of such a simple sound,
> Of so great matter should be made the ground. (2.62–69)

As in Shakespeare's early histories, *Henry VI, Parts Two and Three* (1591–2), with which the play shares a number of lines, popular violence is the tool of aristocratic ambition.

In the fast-moving second half, as in the Shakespeare histories, civil war is treated as a revenge-drama played out by the nobility (the conspirators speak of the Massacre itself as a bloody piece of theatre). The Guise is caught up in a lethal court intrigue, and the massacre he engineers in the first half is ironically recalled in the slaughter of the second. The text is full of ironic symmetries, though we cannot be quite sure of their import: are Queen Catherine's casually murderous speeches about her two royal sons in scenes 11 and 14 so similar because they depict the terrible repetitive mechanism of civil war (as in *Henry VI*), or because the reporter mixed up the original speeches? Similarly, is Anjou apparently so different once he becomes Henry III because ideological confusion in Marlowe's treatment of him makes the character 'wellnigh unintelligible' (Kocher 1941), or because Marlowe intended to disconcert his audiences, or, as Potter suggests, because the historical king really was so enigmatic? The problem is acute in the final scene, when the dying king has an unexpected attack of pro-Elizabethan sentiment and violent anti-Catholicism (especially since his anti-papal speech seems to have got tangled up with Edward II's equally uncharacteristic outburst on the same theme). Can the lines in which Henry gives the Protestant Navarre his blessing be Marlowe's? If so, was Marlowe being serious? And what would the lines have meant to audiences who saw the play after the new king, Henri IV, converted to Catholicism in 1593?

Scene 1

1   *brother*: Brother-in-law (he has just married Charles's sister Margaret).

3   *religious league*: Between the Catholics and Protestants.

8   *fuelled*: Perpetuated, continuing the imagery of lines 6–7.

12 *queen-mother*: Catherine de' Medici, who retained many of the powers of a regent.

49 *house of Bourbon*: The Bourbon family, rulers of Navarre, now allied to the royal family of Valois.

52 *beats his brains*: Racks his brains.

53 *pitched . . . toil*: Set . . . snare.

Scene 2

1–2 *Hymen . . . lights*: The frown of the god of marriage and the dim candles on his altars would be unpropitious to the wedding-day.

11 *prove and guerdon*: Test and reward.

31 *perform*: Bring about, execute (with a suggestion of his 'tragic part' (28)).

32 *crowns*: Coins (the French '*écues*' of 61).

34–5 *deep-engendered thoughts . . . flames*: Plans conceived in secret to reveal themselves in all their violence.

37 *levelled*: Guessed, speculated ('level at' = take aim at).

38 *peril . . . happiness*: Proverbial (Tilley D28, 35).

41 *hangs*: Like easily picked fruit.

43 *pyramides*: (Four syllables) pyramids, high spires or obelisks.

49 *attendance*: 'Waiting the leisure, convenience, or decision of a superior' (*OED* 4).

63 *dispensation*: A licence to break ecclesiastical law without punishment.

64–5 *And by . . . religion*: And with that privilege (the dispensation) to work with, I have shaped religion to suit political expediency. Proverbial: Tilley R63.

66 *Diabole*: (Mixed French and Italian) the Devil.

74 *So that . . . name*: So that in effect he is king in name only.

81 *As*: Such as.

84 *of my knowledge . . . keeps*: To my knowledge in one monastery there live . . .

86 *comprised*: (i) Contained, (ii) comprehended, imagined.

98 *As Caesar*: Guise likens himself to Julius Caesar throughout the play, especially because of his unscrupulous acquisition of power (see *The Jew of Malta*, Prologue 19).

106 *against*: I.e. into.

Scene 3

13 *late suspicion of*: Recent suspicions entertained about.

18 *passion*: (Here) malady, affliction.

28 *fresh supply*: I.e. of grief.

Scene 4

2 *fatal*: Fated, doomed. The Huguenots are spoken of as trapped animals.

7–8 *under safety . . . protection*: Apparently the king has given the

Huguenot nobles his personal assurance of their safety ('challenge' = claim).

24   *nephew*: Kinsman.

34   *ordinance*: Artillery (a metrically more suitable form of *ordnance*).

35   *set*: Beset (as with a net).

36   *watchword*: Signal.

50.2 SD *Enter*: Presumably Charles's walk upstage to the discovery-space to find the Admiral indicated a change of location.

64   *Cossin*: Emended from O's *Cosin* to distinguish the name of the captain of the guard (cf. 5.19) from 'cousin' applied generically to a kinsman.

Scene 5

12   *entrance*: First part, beginning.

23.1 SD *the ADMIRAL's house*: Line 32 indicates that the murder of the Admiral occurs in the stage gallery.

37   *missed him near*: Just failed to kill him.

38   *Shatillian*: Châtillon, one of Admiral Coligny's titles.

40   *despite*: Contempt.

45   *Mount Faucon*: Montfaucon, where hanged corpses were left to decompose.

47   *thereon*: I.e. on the cross of a gibbet.

51   *partial*: (i) Unfair, (ii) incomplete (in massacring the Huguenots).

Scene 6

1   *Tue, tue, tue*: Kill, kill, kill.

Scene 7

1   *follow Loreine*: Punning on 'follow Lorraine', the war-cry of the Guise faction.

5   '*Dearly beloved brother*': Guise mimics the words of a Protestant preacher.

6   *Stay . . . psalm*: Anjou continues Guise's joke, mocking the singing of psalms at Protestant services.

Scene 8

6   *ha't*: Have it (O's *hate* may indicate its pronunciation).

7   *O . . . death*: The line is identical with Shakespeare, *3 Henry VI*, 1.3.35.

10–11 *Christ . . . saint*: Protestants objected to the Catholic practice of prayer to the saints. Mountsorrell parodically refuses to let Seroune pray to God.

12   *Sanctus Jacobus*: Saint James. Cf. 24.33 and *The Jew of Malta* 3.4.76n.

Scene 9

0.1   SD *in his study*: Probably the discovery-space, filled with books.

1   *Seine*: For O's *Rene*, as at line 57.

24   *smack in*: Smattering of.

26   *scoff'dst the Organon*: Scoffed at Aristotle's dissertations on logic, collectively known as the Organon (= instrument).

28   *flat dichotomist*: Outright dichotomizer. In logic, dichotomy was a method (rejected by Aristotle) for dividing a class or genus into two component classes or genera.

29   *seen in . . . epitomes*: Well versed only in abridgements. (Ramus shortened and simplified Aristotelian logic.)

31   *preach in Germany*: Apparently a reference to the distrust of traditional scholastic logic (upon which much Catholic orthodoxy was founded) in the doctrinal expositions of Lutheran preachers.

32   *Excepting . . . axioms*: Raising objections to the axioms (for O's *actions*) of the Doctors of the Church.

33   *ipse dixi*: I myself have said, i.e. citing oneself as an authority for an argument.
      quiddity: Quibble (from *quidditas*, the scholastic term for the essence of a thing).

34   *Argumentum . . . inartificiale*: An argument from testimony is inadequate, i.e. an argument is not proven by the authority of the person who makes it. Guise ironically disproves this argument in the next lines.

36   *nego argumentum*: I deny the argument.

41   *purge myself*: Clear myself (of an imputation).

43   *Scheckius*: O's *Shekins* highlights the obscurity of Ramus's opponent. See (N).

44   *my places . . . his*: Ramus claimed to have successfully reduced the *loci* or 'topics' ('places') of Aristotelian logic to three categories.

46   *reduced*: Compressed, 'digested'.

50   *Sorbonnists*: (For O's *thorbonest*) scholars from the Sorbonne, the theology faculty of the University of Paris.

55   *collier's son*: Despite aristocratic descent, Ramus's father made money by producing and selling charcoal.

65   *pedants*: Schoolmasters.

72   *stay this broil*: Stop this violence.

75   *rose*: Got up (from bed).

79   *whip you*: Like a schoolmaster whipping his pupils.

86 *the devil's matins*: Since the massacre began at dawn, the bell which signalled its beginning was like a diabolical parody of the bell which sounded to morning service.

88 *convey him closely*: Steal secretly.

Scene 10

This scene inserts into the action events that occurred a year later, probably for the sake of ironic juxtaposition.

2   *Prince Electors*: Princes who possessed the right to elect a monarch.

11 *Muscovites*: The forces of Muscovy in Russia, led by Ivan the Terrible.

Scene 11

4–5 *his body . . . him*: Infectious diseases were believed to be communicated by foul air.

22 *synagogue*: Hebrew terminology was sometimes applied (sardonically, by their enemies) to the Puritans.

26 *gather head again*: Regroup their forces.

38 *let me alone for that*: Leave that to me.

45 *storm . . . down*: Complain . . . overthrow them.

Scene 13

Charles died in 1574 (by poison, Marlowe's sources suggested); the Queen-Mother's conduct here, coming after her last speech in scene 11, hints strongly at her responsibility for his death.

2   *griping*: (Here) agonizing.

9–12 *I have . . . no worse*: Admitting that he has deserved divine vengeance ('a scourge') for his complicity in the massacre of the Huguenots, Charles nonetheless exonerates them in their patient suffering ('patience') of any part in his death, and prays that his 'nearest friends' are similarly innocent.

28 *Polony*: Poland (from Latin *Polonia*, which may be the pronunciation here).

35 *It . . . just succession*: Navarre is next in line to the French throne (ignoring Anjou's historical younger brother: cf. 14.63–4 and 21.105).

43 *march with*: (i) Be associated with, (ii) be joined to the host of.

46–7 *In spite . . . wrongfully*: Parenthetically inserted into the promise to crown him king in Pamplona, the capital of Navarre.

Scene 14

0.1   SD *vive le roi*: May the king live.

0.4   SD *Minions*: (i) Favourites, (ii) homosexual lovers.

15   *And yield . . . deserts*: And grant that your intentions towards me
      are as good as I deserve.

20   *his bent*: Its natural inclination (Oliver 1968); 'slack' suggests a
      metaphorical application of the stringing of a bow in archery.

30.1–2 SD *He cuts . . . his cloak*: No historical source for this incident
      is known.

40   *barriers*: Combats between two men on foot armed with short
      swords, conducted inside barriers or 'lists'.
      tourney: Tournaments fought in groups.
      tilt: Combat on horseback with lance or spear.

54   *power*: Force.

55   *are*: For O's *as*.

56   *house of Bourbon*: I.e. the royal house of Navarre.

63–4 *I'll dispatch . . . diadem*: I'll send him the way of his elder brother,
      and then his younger brother (known as 'monsieur') will be king.

67   *lord*: O's *Lords* must be wrong in the light of 42.1–2SD.

Scene 15

3   *Mugeroun*: His role is conflated with that of the duchess's historical
      lover Saint-Mégrin.

16   *good array*: I.e. bad handwriting (ironically, and to stop Guise
      looking).

23   *trothless and unjust*: Disloyal and false.

25–6 *Or hath . . . text?*: Is my love for you so inadequate that it needs
      to be supplemented by others, as an obscure text demands the
      attentions of commentators?

31   *Mort dieu! Were't not*: God's death! Were it not for.

Scene 16

8   *defend . . . inventions*: Defend ourselves against their plots.

16   *brunt*: (Here) conflict.

19   *Spain*: I.e. the king of Spain.

20–5 *The power . . . revenge*: Obscure, perhaps because of faulty
      reporting. Navarre seems to be saying that his breast is now occu-
      pied with bloody thoughts, as by an army ('power') with its menac-
      ing red banners; but that his desire for revenge will be altered (to a
      more benign disposition), like leaves changing colour, once he
      has defeated his enemies. Alternatively, though he is currently

compelled to meet violence with violence, he does not expect his
enemies to live up to their menacing show once he has defeated
them.

35 *thereon do they stay*: They are waiting for the appointment of a
general.

38 *countervail*: (Here) repay, be worth.

41 *And makes ... security*: And takes his ease in his over-confidence
of safety.

Scene 17

5   *suffer't*: (For O's *suffer*) endure it.
14.1 SD *makes horns*: The sign of the cuckold.
28 *Par ... mourra!*: By God's death, he shall die!
37 *I may ... dead*: I.e. He will not be the man to kill me.
41 *shake off ... heels*: (i) Stop her loving me, but (ii) while heels are
raised in lovemaking.

Scene 18

0.1 SD *The DUKE JOYEUX slain*: Oliver 1968 treats this as an offstage
cry, rather than an indication of stage-action.

17 *relics*: A jibe at Catholic reverence for the relics of saints and
martyrs.

Scene 19

For the fuller version of the opening of this scene preserved in a manuscript in the Folger Shakespeare Library, see Appendix.

2   *counterfeit ... door*: A bawdy reference to the affair between
Mugeroun and the duchess of Guise.

4–5 *forestall ... should not*: I.e. he steals the Guise's trade ('market')
and sets up a stall ('standing', with a pun on 'erection') in a forbidden place (the duchess).

6–8 *landlord ... land*: Mugeroun exercises rights of ownership over
the duchess.

7   *occupy*: With the sense of sexual 'possession'.

10 *gear*: (i) Plan, (ii) weapon.

12 *this*: Money.

25 *in the cause*: In the matter.

30 *I am ... Valois' line*: Guise claims alliance with the French royal
family.

31 *Bourbonites*: Navarre's lineage.

32 *juror ... Holy League*: One who has sworn allegiance to the Holy

Christian League (established in 1576 to promote the interests of the Catholic Church in France).

35   *able*: (Here) sufficiently wealthy.

37   *foreign exhibition*: A pension from abroad.

45   *sectious*: Sectarian, factious (for O's *sexious*).

50   *them*: The 'Puritans' (45).

55–6 *dictator . . . senator*: In times of crisis, the Roman republic elected a single leader (*dictator*) to exercise the powers usually vested in the Senate.

     placet: Latin, it pleases (me), a form of giving assent in an assembly.

62   *simple meaning*: Innocent intentions.

73   *His Holiness'*: The Pope's.

83   *And so . . . suspect*: 'And in such a way as to clear you from all suspicion' (Oliver 1968) or, and so rid you of any further anxiety (about Guise).

88   *tragical*: Disposed to create a tragedy.

Scene 20

23   *vantage*: Vantage-ground (a military term).

Scene 21

1   *bent*: Determined.

27   *Holà, varlet, hé*: Guise calls for a page (French *varlet*).

28   *Mounted . . . cabinet*: Gone up into his private apartments.

65   *Yet Caesar . . . forth*: Julius Caesar ignored portents of his impending murder. This line recurs in Shakespeare's *Julius Caesar* (2.2.28).

71   *As pale as ashes*: Possibly Guise inspects his 'looks' (68) in a mirror, or the phrase may refer to an intensification of the third murderer's 'ghastly' look (57).

     look about: Be on one's guard.

81   *Sixtus*: Pope Sixtus V. See (N).

82   *Philip and Parma*: King Philip II of Spain and his general (N). Cf. *Doctor Faustus* 1.95n.

85   *Vive la messe!*: Long live the mass!

101 *Douai . . . Rheims*: Under the patronage of the duke of Guise, a number of students who had been expelled from the seminary at Douai were resettled at Rheims. The Elizabethan authorities were deeply fearful of the seminary at Rheims which was often used to harbour Catholic converts from England (see Introduction, p. xi).

103 *Spain's huge fleet*: I.e. the Spanish Armada.

105   *monsieur that's deceased*: The duke of Alençon, whose death in
      1584 left Navarre the heir to the throne. Cf. 14.63–4n.
109   *make me monk*: Subject me to a life of monastic austerity.
114   *yoked*: Restrained (as by a yoke).
126   *that ... cardinal*: The Cardinal of Lorraine, whom Marlowe has
      already made partly responsible for the massacre of 1572.
130   *These two ... Guise*: Together these two are as dangerous as one
      duke of Guise.
144   *changeling*: Unnatural children were sometimes supposed to be
      substitutes left by fairies who stole the real child from its cradle.
145   *exclaim thee miscreant*: Proclaim you an evildoer (infidel).
155   *insult*: Exult (over the Catholics).
158   *all for thee*: All as a result of your death.

Scene 22

13   *drench*: Drown.
16   *pluck amain*: Pull with full force.

Scene 23

3   *The king's alone ... satisfy*: The King's death alone is not enough
      (to avenge the death of my brother).
5   *stay*: Support.
11   *He*: I.e. King Henry.
13–14 *But that's ... Rome*: Syntax and punctuation are unclear (and
      O repeats *His life* at the beginning of line 14). Dumaine can forestall
      ('prevent') the plot against him by killing the king and the other
      enemies of the Church.
15   *durst*: Dared.
23–4, 27–8 *I am ... meritorious*: Religious orders were regarded with
      deep suspicion by Protestants in England, who believed that the
      Catholic Church sanctioned the murder of Protestant monarchs
      (such as Elizabeth).
24   *Jacobins*: Dominicans (from the church of St Jacques in Paris).

Scene 24

13   *lie before Lutetia walls*: Besiege Paris, here given its Latin name
      (for O's *Lucrecia*).
14   *strumpet*: Disloyal (Paris supported the Guisards).
16   *cast*: (i) Vomit up, (ii) throw down.
      stomach: (i) Stomach-contents, (ii) courage.
18   *President of Paris*: The chief officer of the *parlement* (local
      assembly) of Paris.

30 *speedy*: Hastily written.

33 *Sancte Jacobus*: Inconsistently inflected Latin vocatives.

41 *pagans' parts*: Unchristian actions.

42 *hold them of*: Claim to belong to.

47 *his*: Emended from O's *their*.

52 *search*: Examine with a probe.

60-63 *These bloody hands . . . holy earth*: These lines are a mangled recollection of *Edward the Second*, 4.99–101.

62 *crazèd*: Unsound.

66 *practices*: Plots.

78 *new-found death*: Newly devised method of killing.

98 *whet . . . Sixtus' bones*: Sharpen your sword on the Pope's bones (i.e. if Sixtus V is, as he was at the time of Henri III's murder in 1589, still alive, kill him).

109-10 *As Rome . . . king*: For the unintended historical irony, see headnote to this play.

Glossary

(M) = Marlowe's coinage; *n* noun, *v* verb, *adj* adjective, *adv* adverb, *imp* imperative.

abject (*v*) lower, degrade
abortive useless, imperfect; as produced by abortion
abstract epitome
aby pay for
accidental abnormal
accomplishment fulfilment of vows
adamant magnet, proverbially hard stone
admire wonder, marvel at
adventure risk
advertised informed
affect (*n*, *v*) love, desire
affecter lover
affection emotion
against in preparation for
airy (i) thin, light, (ii) lofty, ethereal
alarm, alarum call to arms
Alcoran the Koran
Almain German
alongst parallel to
amain at full speed or power
ambergris an aromatic
an if
anagrammatized made into anagrams

annoy (*n*) injury, (*v*) injure
anon soon
antic hay grotesque rustic dance
arbitrament control, judgement
argent silvery-white
argin earthwork to protect infantry
argosy large trading vessel
armado warship
arras cloth curtain
artier artery
artisan practitioner
assafoetida strong smelling resinous gum, used in medicine
asseize possess by force
astonied astounded
astracism stars (? bright stars near Aldebaran)
attemptless without attempting (M)
avail (*n*) advantage
avaunt (*imp*) begone
avouch prove
aware (*v*) beware
aweful awe-inspiring
axletree axis

balk neglect
balsamum medicinal balm
ban curse
bands bonds
bandy exchange blows (from tennis)
bane poison
banquet (i) banquet, meal of many dishes, (ii) snacks
bark boat
barrier armed combat
basilisk (i) fabulous serpent whose breath or looks could kill, (ii) large cannon
bastone cudgel
batten grow fat
beard confront
beaten embroidered
behoof benefit
belike in all likelihood, perhaps
benighted overtaken by darkness
beseem become, accord with one's position
betimes in good time, quickly
bever snack
bewray reveal
bickering skirmish, fight
bill (i) prescription, advertisement, (ii) weapon, a halberd, (iii) deed
bind gird
bolt fetter
bombard a kind of cannon which fired large stones
boot give advantage, help
bootless useless
boss fat woman
bottle bundle
bottle-nosed big-nosed
brain-pan skull
brake (*n*) thicket, bush
brave (*adj*) excellent, splendidly

dressed, (*v*) (i) challenge, (ii) flout
brawn muscle
breeching beating
brent burnt
brigantine pirate ship
broil battle
brook tolerate
brown bill foot soldier with bronzed spear
brunt attack
buckled grappled, fought
buckler shield
bug bugbear
bulk trunk, body
bulwark projecting earthwork at right angles to fort
burgonet light, visored helmet
buzz murmur
by'r Lady by our Lady (the Virgin Mary)

cabinet study, private room
calor natural heat
camp army
canker parasitic worm (hence, corruption)
canonize celebrate (as with a saint)
canvass discuss, consider
carbonado cooked strip of meat
case (i) a pair, (ii) vagina
casemate underground chamber
cassia fragrant shrub
cast (*v*) (i) conjecture, plan, (ii) vomit
cates exotic food
cavaliero high earthwork forming fortification for cannon
cazzo diabole (Italian) vulgar oath of contempt (cock devil)
censure criticism, judgement

centric central
certify inform
chafer portable grate
challenge (*v*) claim
champian level, open
changeling fairy child
channel (i) gutter, sewer, (ii) neck,
   throat
chaplet garland
characters (i) writing, description,
   (ii) magic symbols
charge (*v*) command
charming spell-casting
chary carefully
chitterlings pig's intestines, used
   for sausages
chop jowl
circuit judicial circuit
clang sound, note
clap pat, stroke
clean completely
cleft (i) vulva, (ii) cloven foot
clift cliff
clog heavy weight that impedes
   motion
close (*adj*) secret
closet chamber
clout centre of a target in archery
coil tumult, fuss
coll embrace, hug
colour (i) pretext, (ii) military
   banner
comfit sweet
commence graduate
compact (*v*) made, composed
compass (*n*) range, (*v*) reach,
   achieve, win
competitor partner
complice confederate
comprise comprehend
concave cavity
concealed occult

conceit imagination, intellect,
   thought, conception
conceive register in the mind
concoct digest
conduct (i) leadership, (ii) escort
conference conversation
congé (French) deferential bow
conster construe
consummate (*adj*) (i) perfect, (ii)
   continued without cessation
contemn despise
content agreed
continent (*n*) space, ground, (*adj*)
   connected, bordering
contributory tributary
control (i) challenge, (ii) rebuke,
   (iii) govern
controlment rebuke
corpo di dio (Italian) God's body
corse corpse, body
counterbuff rebuff
counterfeit (*n*) imitation
counterfort brace strengthening
   wall from within
countermand revoke by a
   contrary command
countermine (i) deep
   underground tunnel, (ii)
   counterplot
countermure make impregnable
   by wall within fortification
counterscarp wall of fortification
   ditch
countervail equal
coz kinsman
cozen cheat, deceive
crazed cracked, rotten
crest helmet
crisis critical day of an illness
cross (*n*) coin with a cross on it,
   (*v*) obstruct, thwart
crossbiting swindling

crownet bracelet
cull pick, select
cullion rascal
culverin long cannon
curious exquisitely crafted or
    embellished
curse excommunicate
curst virulent, harsh
curtain wall connecting
    fortifications
curtle-axe cutlass
cutpurse pick-pocket

dalliance idle delay, sexual play
damp mist, vapour
date period of time
dated having a predetermined end
daunt control
dazzle blind
declined turned away
defy formally renounce allegiance
descried charted
despite scorn, contempt
device handiwork
devoir duty
diadem crown
diametarily diametrically
digested endured, got over
dirge mass for the dead
discomfit defeat, rout
discoursive protracted,
    wide-ranging
dismissed redeployed
dismount throw down from a
    gun-carriage
dispensive subject to dispensation
    (M?)
disport pastime, entertainment
disposition planetary situation
disquiet (adj) unquiet, restless
dissever shatter, blow up
distain stain

distained dishonoured
distempered troubled, disturbed
dollar large silver coin
dolour misery
doom (n) judgement, (v) judge,
    sentence
doubt (v) fear
doubtful perplexing, ambiguous
drave drove
drench (n) dose, draught, (v)
    drown
drift purpose
droop be miserable
ducat Venetian gold coin
dumps melancholy thoughts
dusky dim, obscure
Dutch fustian gibberish

earn grieve
ebon black
ecstasy frenzy
écu French crown coin
effect meaning, gist
egregious distinguished
ell 45 inches
emboss decorate
empale encircle
empery empire, rule
empyreal empyrean
enamelled richly painted
enchased adorned
engine (i) instrument, (ii) siege
    weapon
engineer maker of military
    hardware
English counter worthless coin,
    token
enlarge free
enow enough
entertain receive, take into
    service, welcome
enthral enslave

entreat persuade
entreated treated
envy (*n*) hatred, malice, (*v*) hate
epitome summary
erect elevate (to the throne)
erst before, formerly
essay try, attempt
estate rank, station
eternize immortalize
events outcomes
exclaim (*n*) exclamation
excruciate torment
exequies funerals
exhaled turned into a fiery vapour
exhibition stipend
exigent exigency, extremity
expedition speed
expert experienced
exquisite excruciating

faced (i) outfaced, derided, (ii)
   trimmed
fact action, crime
factious seditious
factor agent
faggot bundle of wood
faint faint-hearted
falchion sword
falconet small cannon
false (*v*) betray, violate
familiar evil spirit, attendant
fancy (*v*) love
fatal fated, fateful
favour (i) face, (ii) love-token
favourless without beauty
fear (*v*) frighten
feeling (*adj*) (i) sincere, (ii) sensual
fell cruel
fence (*v*) protect, defend
field-piece field-gun
figure likeness, image
file defile

flagitious wicked
fleer jeer
fleet drift, float
flout mock
foil (*n*) metal placed behind a
   jewel to accentuate its
   brilliance, (*v*) (i) defile, (ii)
   defeat
follower servant, retainer
fond foolish
forslow waste
forward (*adj*) eager, precocious
fraught freight, cargo
fray (*v*) frighten
French crown (i) coin of the reign
   of Henri III, (ii) the pox
frolic (*v*) play, (*adj*) frolicsome
front confront
fruition enjoyment
full restored to full strength
furniture armour, weapons
furtherer helper, abetter
fustian (i) flax cloth, (ii) nonsense

gat got
gear business
gentry rank of gentleman
glaive broadsword
glass mirror
glass-windows spectacles
glorious boastful
gloze flatter, dissimulate
gramercy thank you
gratulate salute, welcome
gravel perplex, confound
graving sculpture
grief pain, suffering
gripe seize tenaciously
groat coin of small value (4d)
groom menial, servant
guerdon reward
guilder Dutch coin

gull trick

gum aromatic resin (in perfume and sacrifice)

halberd long-handled weapon

halcyon kingfisher

hale drag, draw

hap fortune

hapless unfortunate

haply perhaps

happy fortunate

haught haughty, lofty

haughty high-minded, heroic

headed beheaded

heavy sad

hebon ebony, the juice of which was considered poisonous

hempen (i) of a noose of hemp rope, (ii) made of hempen cloth, homespun

hest behest

hippocras spiced wine

hogshead 63-gallon cask

hoise hoist

hold (i) bet, wager, (ii) stronghold

horse-bread horse feed

horse-courser horse-dealer

hospital almshouse

hostry hostelry, inn

hoy small trading boat

hugy huge

humidum moisture

humour bodily fluid responsible for health, hence mood

hurdle sledge (to carry condemned to execution)

hurly-burly confusion, commotion

illustrate shed light on

imbecility feeble-mindedness, weakness

imperial imperious

import imply, signify

imprecation prayer

incense incite, set on fire

incontinent immediate, (*adv*) immediately

incony sweet

Indian Moor American Indian

indifferent impartial

influence (astrological) power

insinuate ingratiate

insult exult

interdict forbid

intolerable incomparable

invention plot, plan

investion investiture

issue (*n*) offspring, (*v*) come out, turn out

iterating repetition

iwis indeed

jack upstart

Jacob's staff surveying instrument, used for range-finding

janizary Turkish infantry-man

jar fight, quarrel

jealous (i) anxious for someone's well-being, (ii) suspicious

jennet small Spanish horse

jesses leather thongs used to restrain hunting birds

jesture (i) gesture, (ii) jest

jet strut

jig (i) song and dance, (ii) scurrilous ballad

keel ship

kern peasant fighter

kind (*adj*) (i) kind, (ii) natural

label strip of ribbon for attaching
    seals to documents
Lachryma Christi red wine of
    southern Italy
lake dungeon
lance slit open
larded encrusted
lares Roman household gods
largess largesse, generous reward
latest last
latter last
laund glade, open space
lavish (*n*) prodigious spilling,
    (*adj*) insolent, unrestrained
lawn piece of fine linen
leager state of besieging
league (i) unit of distance: 3 miles,
    (ii) alliance
leman sweetheart
lenity pity
let hinder, prevent
level (*v*) (i) aim, (ii) deduce, guess
    at
libel subversive pamphlet
liberal (i) well-educated, (ii)
    generous
licentiate graduate
liefest dearest
linstock stick for holding spill to
    light cannon
list (i) desire, (ii) listen
litter vehicle for one person
    carried by two servants
loadstar, lodestar guiding light
looseness sexual incontinence
lour frown
lown rogue (Scottish or northern
    dialect form)
lure imitation bird made of
    feathers and leather
lusty pleasant

magnanimity courage in battle
mail bag containing treasure
main overpowering
malgrado (Spanish) in defiance of
manage (*n*) conduct, (*v*) tame,
    control
mark (i) brand, (ii) watch,
    observe
marry by Mary (an oath)
mask lurk in darkness, hide
massy solid, weighty
masty fattened on pig food
mate companion, (*v*) daunt
maximé maxim
measures stately dances
meat food
meed merit, reward
meet (*adj*) appropriate
members people
mends amends, reward
meteor atmospheric phenomenon
mettle strength, material
mew capture
mickle much
minion (i) small cannon, (ii)
    sycophant, (iii) lover,
    favourite
minx slut
miscreants heretics, unbelievers
miss (*n*) lack of
mistrust suspect
mithridate (usually) antidote to
    poison
moe more
monument record of achievement
motion (i) movement, (ii)
    suggestion, (iii) desire
mought might
mount earthwork used for
    fortification
Muff derogatory term for the
    Swiss (M?)

muscadel, muscadine, muscatel
  strong sweet wine
mustacho moustache
mystery secret art

native natural
noisome stinking, offensive
nonce purpose; for the nonce
  purposely, expressly
nonplus state of bewilderment
nosegay posy
noted stigmatized, branded

occupy possess, have sex with
offencious causing offence
organon (i) bodily organs or
  fluids, (ii) philosophical works
  of Aristotle (*Organon*)
orient (*adj*) (i) eastern, (ii)
  brilliant (of gems)
orifex orifice, wound
orison prayers
ostler stable-man
ostry hostelry, inn
otherways otherwise
overdare surpass in daring (M)
overthwart across
overwatched (i) tired through
  constant vigilance, (ii) spied
  upon

painted colourful
pale boundary, fence
paragon consort
paramour lover
parcel essential part
parley debate, dispute
partial (i) unfair, (ii) incomplete
pash smash to pieces
pass care
passenger traveller
passing surpassingly

pate head
pathetical emotive, persuasive
patience suffering
paw claw
pedant schoolmaster
pelf money
pensiveness melancholy
perfecter more skilled
perforce (i) by violence, (ii)
  necessarily
pericranion skull (technically, the
  membrane around it)
period (i) end, conclusion, (ii)
  sentence
physic medicine
pickadevant short, pointed beard
pickle-herring (i) pickled herring,
  (ii) an idiot
pill (*v*) plunder
pin nail which secures a clout
  (*q.v.*) in archery
pined tormented
pioners sappers, those who dig
  mines
pitch breadth of shoulders
pitchy pitch-black
places topics
placket (i) (slit in) a skirt or
  petticoat, (ii) vulva
plage region
plain (*v*) complain
plainer plaintiff
plate piece of silver
platform ground-plan
plaud applause
pleasant jocular
pleasantness facetiousness
pledge drink toast
pole-axe halberd
policy cunning
poniard dagger
port gate

portague Portuguese gold coin

portend prophesy, suggest,
  foresee

portly stately

post (n) messenger, (v) ride fast

posy pious motto

pottage (i) porridge, (ii) stew,
  soup, broth

power army

preachment sermonizing

precinct area of secure authority

precise puritanical

precisian puritan, radical
  protestant

present(ly) immediate(ly)

prest ready for action

pretty (i) admirable, (ii) amusing

prevent anticipate, forestall

principality princely
  government

problem scholastic disputation

prolocutor herald, spokesman

proper own

prorex viceroy

protest swear, profess

prove test, experience

provender fodder

puissant powerful

purchase win

purgation an emetic

pyramid obelisk

qualify mitigate

quenchless unquenchable

quick alive

quicksilver mercury

quiddity (i) the essence (of
  something), (ii) quibble

quinque-angle five-pointed,
  star-shaped

quite (i) repay, acquit, (ii) requite

quittance quits

rack tear apart, violate

racking driven before the
  wind

ragged rugged

rampire (n) inner rampart, (v)
  fortify with ramparts

range (v) roam

rankle fester

rape abduction

rapine theft

raze (i) erase, destroy, (ii) graze

reave take away

rebated blunted

reclaim reform

recreant traitor

rector a university principal

recure cure

redoubted fearsome

reflex shine

refluence flowing back

refreshing refreshment, food

regiment power, authority

regreet greet anew (M)

remorseful compassionate

renied apostate

rent rend, tear

repair imminent arrival

repeal recall (from banishment)

repine complain

repute understand by

reserve preserve

resolve (i) determine to achieve,
  (ii) satisfy, (iii) melt

respect particular circumstances

rest remain

resteth remains to be done

retire strategic withdrawal from
  battle

retorqued turned back on
  themselves (M)

reverberate beaten back

rivelled twisted, plaited

road (i) roadstead, harbour, (ii) raid
room position, office
round slop baggy trousers
roundly (i) with complete success, (ii) briskly
rout mob
royalize crown, make celebrated
rub polish
ruin falling
runagate renegade, runaway, vagabond
ruth suffering, pity
rutter knight, cavalry

sack dry Spanish white wine
sakar, saker small cannon
salute greet
sarell seraglio, harem
sauce (*v*) season, flavour
savour (*n*) smell
scald contemptible
scamble compete fiercely for money
scathe harm
scholarism scholarship
scour beat, punish
scutcheon escutcheon, heraldic shield
sectious factious, sectarian
seignory governorship
sennet trumpet call
serge cheap woollen fabric
servitor servant
several separate
shag-rag ragged, rascally
shape (i) appearance, (ii) costume
shaver swindler, rogue
shrewdly with conviction, zealously
shrift confession
signs zodiacal signs

silly feeble, simple
silverling silver coin
sink cesspool
sith since
slack neglect
snipper snapper whipper-snapper
society community
soil marsh
sollar loft, store-room
sometime formerly
sophister specious reasoner
sort pack
sound (*v*) (i) blow (of trumpet), (ii) resound, echo, (iii) measure (depth)
spials spies
splendant bright, resplendent
spoil plunder
spurca (Latin) filthy, base
spurn kick, disdain
squib firework
stand upon understand
standing (*n*) position, (*adj*) stagnant
starting holes refuges for hunted animals
state (i) government, (ii) pomp, ceremony, (iii) throne, (iv) condition
stature statue
staying supporting
steel (*v*) sharpen
stern rudder
still constantly, continuously
stilts crutches
stomach (*v*) resent
stoop humiliate
straggle wander, (of a soldier) desert
straggler vagabond
straight immediately

strait strict
stranger foreigner
strangle choke
style title
suffer allow, permit
superficies surface, outer crust
superfluities that which floats on
   the surface
surcease cease, bring to an end
surcharge overburden
sure secure, safe
surprise capture
suspect suspicion
Switzers Swiss mercenaries
'swounds by God's wounds
symbolize mix

table memorial tablet
tainted hit (technical term from
   tilting)
talents talons
tall brave, valiant
targeteers footsoldiers with small
   shields (targets)
tartar scum left after fermentation
tax censure
tempered refreshed, enlivened
term statuary bust on top of a
   pillar
terminine boundary
theoria contemplation, survey
   (only instance in *OED*)
throughly thoroughly
tice entice
tickle chastise
tilt fight on horseback
timeless (i) eternal, (ii) untimely
tippet scarf, hence noose
tire (*v*) feed, eat ferociously
toil snare
topless exceedingly high,
   immeasurable

torpedo electric ray
tottered tattered
tourney tournament
toy trifle, jest
trace track, traverse
train retinue
trained enticed
trapped adorned
trencher plate
trick decorate, adorn
tried purified
troll flow
trothless disloyal, faithless
troublous disordered, disturbed
trow believe, trust
trull whore
trustless untrustworthy,
   treacherous
tun barrel
turtle turtle-dove
twigger scoundrel, good breeder

unacquainted unexampled
uncontrolled unrebuked, without
   restraint
uncouth strange, unpleasant
unfoiled (i) not set against a metal
   background, (ii) undefiled
unhappy miserable, unfortunate
unkind unnatural
unresisted irresistible
ure use
use (*n*) custom, (*v*) exhibit

vail salute by lowering a sail
vailing taking off, with a flourish
valurous valuable (M)
vaunt boast
vex torment
victuals food
villeiness bondwoman, slave
virtue power, force

wag naughty child
wanton naughty, skittish
wants lacks
watches units of time (usually three hours)
wedge ingot
weeds clothes
weigh care for, value
welkin sky
welter toss about, overwhelm
whilom formerly
whisk whisper, flutter
whist silent, hushed
will decree that

withal with
wont, wonted accustomed
wot know
wrack ruin, shipwreck
wreak exact vengeance
wreckful causing shipwreck

yoke (i) constrain, (ii) couple
yoky joined by a yoke
youngling brat

zenith highest point
zounds by God's wounds

List of Mythological, Historical and Geographical Names

Abraham biblical patriarch, originally named Abram until God chose him as the progenitor of Israel and gave the land of Canaan to him and his descendants.

Acantha town in Asia Minor.

Acheron one of the rivers of the underworld.

Achilles legendary Greek warrior. His mother Thetis immersed him (all except the heel by which she held him) in the river Styx to render him invulnerable. After killing the Trojan hero Hector, in revenge for the death of his beloved Patroclus, he was slain by Paris, who exploited his only weakness by shooting an arrow through his heel.

Actaeon the hunter who was torn to pieces by his own hounds after being turned into a stag by Diana, the wood-goddess, when he espied her bathing naked in the forest.

Adonis legendarily beautiful youth, with whom Venus fell in love; he was killed by a boar while hunting but restored to life by Proserpina, with whom he lived in the underworld for half the year, spending the remaining months with Venus.

Aeacus grandfather of Achilles; a judge in the underworld.

Aegeus king of Athens and father of Theseus. He killed himself, thinking his son dead, when Theseus, returning from Crete, failed to signal his escape from the Minotaur. Marlowe confuses him with Diomedes of Thrace, who owned savage horses which he fed on human flesh; Hercules killed him and tamed the horses by feeding him to them.

Aeneas Trojan warrior and founder of Rome; the hero of Virgil's *Aeneid*, he also features in *Dido, Queen of Carthage*.

Aeolus god of the winds.

Aesop legendary Greek author of a collection of fables.

Aetolia a region of Greece.

Agamemnon king of Argos in Greece; son of Atreus, hence also called Atrides. He was required to sacrifice his daughter Iphigenia to secure a favourable wind for the Greeks' voyage to Troy; on his return he was murdered by his wife Clytemnestra and her lover.

Agenor king of Phoenicia and ancestor of Dido.

Agrippa Henry Cornelius Agrippa von Nettesheim (1486–1535), Renaissance magician and sceptical philosopher. He was reputed to have raised the spirits of the dead.

Ajax (i) Greek hero, son of Telamon, who fought at Troy. When he failed to be awarded the armour of the dead Achilles, he went mad and slew a flock of sheep, thinking them Greek warriors, and when he discovered his mistake killed himself. (ii) Another Greek warrior at Troy, son of Oileus. He attempted to rape Cassandra, for which Athene killed him in a shipwreck on his way home.

Albania in Ortelius's atlas, a province to the west of the Caspian Sea.

Albanus Pietro d'Abano (c. 1250–1316), Italian philosopher and physician who dabbled in the black arts.

Alcibiades late 5th-century BC Athenian general and statesman, who eventually had to seek refuge with the Persians; the beloved of Socrates.

Alcides see Hercules.

Aldebaran bright red star in the constellation of Taurus.

Aleppo city close to the border between Syria and Turkey.

Alexander (i) the Great of Macedon (356–323 BC), king and military commander who conquered the Persian empire in 331 BC; (ii) in Homer, the name of Paris, the son of the Trojan king Priam.

Amasia province in northern Asia Minor.

Amazons legendary female warriors.

Ancona Adriatic port with significant Jewish population until expelled by Pope Paul IV in 1556.

Antenor Trojan elder; in medieval tradition, he betrayed the city to the Greeks.

Antipodes the southern hemisphere; hence, its inhabitants.

Aonian Greek.

Apelles 4th-century BC painter, favoured with commissions by Alexander the Great.

Apollo son of Jupiter and Latona (Leto), god of the sun and of the arts; also known as Phoebus. His oracle was at Delphi in Greece.

Aquilon the north-east wind.

Araris probably the river Araxes which flowed through Armenia to the Caspian Sea; Herodotus suggested that the army of Xerxes drank it dry.

Archipelago the Aegean Islands.

Arethusa a nymph who was turned into a fountain by the goddess

Artemis, having aroused the lust of the river-god Alpheus when she bathed in his stream.

Argier Algiers.

Argolian from Argos and its territory (the Argolid) in Greece.

Ariadan small town on the Red Sea, near Mecca.

Arion musician from Lesbos, who was rescued by a dolphin when pirates threw him into the sea.

Aristarchus an Alexandrian scholar of the 2nd century BC whose rigorous methodology made his name synonymous with severity.

Asant Zacynthus, island off the western coast of Greece.

Ascanius son of Aeneas, he appears in *Dido, Queen of Carthage*.

Asphaltis invented site of a battle, perhaps identified with Limnasphaltis.

Assyria middle-eastern empire.

Astraeus husband of Aurora and father of the stars.

Atlas a Titan sentenced by Jupiter to bear the vault of the sky on his shoulders as punishment for making war on the gods; sometimes identified with a mountain in North Africa.

Atrides see Agamemnon.

Aulis assembly-place of the Greek fleet which sailed to Troy.

Aurora goddess of the dawn and morning.

Auster the south wind.

Avernus lake near Naples, adjacent to the cave of the Cumaean Sibyl through which Aeneas descended to the underworld, and henceforth associated with the realms of the dead. Sometimes a synonym for Hell.

Azamor Azimur, town on the Atlantic coast of Morocco.

Bacchus god of wine and ecstasy, also known as Dionysus.

Bacon Roger Bacon (*c.* 1212–92), the Franciscan philosopher at Oxford who reputedly practised magic.

Balaam a Canaanite who was preparing, against God's instructions, to curse the insurgent children of Israel, when God made his ass speak to warn him of his danger, whereupon he blessed them and prophesied a great future for them (Numbers 22–3).

Balioll comic misnomer for Belial, a devil.

Balsera probably Passera, a town in Asia Minor.

Barbary the north coast of Africa.

Baucis Phrygian woman who, along with her husband Philemon, won the gratitude of Jupiter and Mercury for the hospitality of their poor house when the gods visited them in disguise.

Beelzebub 'the lord of the flies', high-ranking devil, second in command to Satan.

Belcher comic name of an otherwise unknown devil.

Belgasar town in Asia Minor.

Belgia the Netherlands.

Bellona Roman goddess of war.

Belus son of Neptune and the founder of Babylon.

Biledull district of northern Africa.

Bithynia province of north-west Asia Minor.

Blois French town, the site of a royal château.

Boötes northern constellation, identified as the driver of the Plough; also known as Arcturus the Bear.

Boreas the north wind.

Borno chief town of Nubia; the same name applies to the nearby Lake Chad.

Buda region of Hungary including modern Budapest.

Byather probably Biafra, west African province.

Byron town close to Babylon.

Caesar, Julius Roman general and politician (100–44 BC), whose dictatorship finally ended on the Ides (15th) of March when he was assassinated by a number of conspirators, amongst whom were Cassius and Brutus.

Cain first-born son of Adam and Eve; he murdered his brother, Abel, for which he was cursed by God.

Caire, Cairon Cairo in Egypt.

Calabria area in southern Italy.

Campania in the 16th century a district of Italy near Naples.

Canarea Canary Islands.

Candy Crete.

Capys paternal grandfather of Aeneas.

Carmonia Carmania, province on the borders of Syria and Asia Minor.

Carolus the Fifth Charles V of Spain, and Holy Roman Emperor (1519–56).

Caspia the Caspian Sea.

Cassandra daughter of Priam, inspired with prophecy but fated not to be believed.

Catiline Lucius Sergius Catilina (d. 62 BC), Roman politician, conspirator and enemy of Cicero, who composed diatribes against him.

Caucasus barren and harsh mountain range between the Black and Caspian Seas.

Cazates town near the source of the Nile. In Ortelius's atlas the home of the Amazons.

Cephalus famed hunter, beloved of Aurora. He accidentally killed his wife Procris while hunting, and took part in the hunt for the Teumessian fox with his hound Lailaps.

Ceraunia dangerous promontory in north-west Greece.

Cerberus three-headed dog which guarded the entrance to the underworld.

Ceres goddess of corn and harvests, mother of Proserpina by Jupiter, and closely associated with Sicily where annual sacrifices to her were performed.

Cham title (khan) of the emperors of Tartary, fabled for their wealth.

Charon ferryman who transported the souls of the dead over the river Styx into the underworld.

Chio Chia, on the Black Sea coast of Asia Minor.

Cimmerians race believed to live in a sunless land at the edge of the world, and thus associated with the perpetual darkness of the underworld.

Circe enchantress who transformed her rival Scylla into a monster, and humans she seduced into animals. She tried to detain Odysseus on his journey home.

Clymene beloved of the sun-god Apollo and mother of Phaethon, who died attempting to drive his father's chariot.

Cocytus river of the underworld.

Codemia town on the river Dniester.

Colchis country on the east of the Black Sea, home of the Golden Fleece.

Corinna the name Ovid gave to the woman who is the focus of his erotic poetry, much of which Marlowe translated.

Creusa daughter of the Trojan king, Priam, and his wife, Hecuba; wife to Aeneas and mother of Ascanius. She died during the escape from Troy following its siege by the Greeks.

Cubar Gubar, chief town of Biafra.

Cutheia town in Asia Minor (modern Kütahya).

Cyclopes (plural of Cyclops) one-eyed monsters who forged thunderbolts for Jupiter.

Cymbrian Teutonic.

Cymodoce a sea-nymph.

Cynthia Diana, the goddess of the moon, named after her birthplace, Mount Cynthus on Delos.

Cyrus 6th-century BC King of Persia, conqueror of Babylon, sometimes regarded by the Greeks as an ideal ruler.

Cytherea Venus, named after Cythera, her favourite island.

Damon philosopher from Syracuse, famed for his friendship with Pythias; his offer to be executed in place of his friend so impressed the tyrant Dionysius that he pardoned both of them.

Danaë the daughter of Acrisius, the king of Argos, who was imprisoned in a bronze tower when an oracle predicted that her son would murder her father. While she was incarcerated, Jupiter visited her in a shower of gold and she later bore his son Perseus.

Dardania Troy.

Dardanus founder of Troy.

Darius Darius III, 4th-century BC Persian king, defeated in battle by Alexander the Great, who took from him a jewelled chest in which he allegedly kept the works of Homer.

Darote town of the Nile delta.

Deiphobus successor to Paris as lover of Helen.

Deucalion when Zeus flooded the earth, Deucalion and his wife, Pyrrha, were the only human survivors; they threw stones which metamorphosed into the men and women who were to re-people the world.

Diana goddess of the moon, chastity, woodland and hunting.

Dido daughter of a king of Tyre (whom Virgil names as Belus). Following the murder of her husband Sychaeus by her brother Pygmalion, she fled to Libya where she founded Carthage.

Dionysius Tyrant of Syracuse (405–367 BC).

Dis alternative name for Pluto.

Dolon Trojan spy captured by the Greeks.

Draco 7th-century BC Athenian legislator, whose 'draconian' laws were said to be written in blood and frequently involved the death penalty.

Ebena Night (from Latin, *hebenus*).

Edward Longshanks Edward I (1239–1307), King of England, nicknamed for his long legs.

Eleanor of Spain wife of Edward I.

Elysium that part of the underworld where heroes enjoyed a blissful afterlife.

Emden an important trading port on the German North Sea coastline.

Epeus builder of the Trojan Horse.

Erebus primeval darkness, often associated with the underworld.

Erycina Venus, named after her temple on Mount Eryx in Sicily.

Europa a Phoenician princess whom Jupiter seduced by assuming the shape of a beautiful bull.

Euxine the Black Sea.

Famastro in Ortelius's atlas, a town on the Black Sea coast of Asia Minor.

Fates Clotho, Lachesis and Atropos, daughters of Jupiter, who (respectively) spin, measure and cut the thread of life.

Fez town in North Africa.

Flora Roman goddess of flowers and fertility.

Furies Roman demons of the underworld, identified with the Greek Erinyes, spirits of vengeance.

Gaetulia Morocco.

Galen Greek physician (*c.* AD 129–99) whose medical knowledge was still respected in the sixteenth century.

Ganymede beautiful son of Tros, king of Troy, who was carried away by Jupiter to become his cup-bearer; he is usually regarded as an icon of homoerotic desire.

Gihon biblical name for a river flowing out of Eden, identified with the Nile.

Gorgon (i) Demogorgon, supposedly a primeval god (actually a post-classical invention), later a devil; (ii) the gorgon Medusa.

Graces three goddesses of gracious kindness.

Gruntland Greenland.

Guallatia Gualata, a town and province of western Libya.

Guyron town on the upper Euphrates, possibly a border outpost of Natolia.

Hainault county of Flanders near France.

Halla town to the south-east of Aleppo.

Harpies monsters with the faces of women but the bodies of vultures.

Hebe daughter of Zeus and Hera, the Greek goddess of youth and her father's cup-bearer.

Hector most illustrious of all Trojan warriors, eventually killed by Achilles.

Hecuba wife of Priam and queen of Troy. The mother of many children; when her beloved son Polydorus was treacherously killed by Polymestor, she blinded the murderer and slew his children. In her inconsolable grief, she was transformed into a howling dog.

Helen (of Troy or Greece) the wife of Menelaus, king of Sparta; reputedly the most beautiful woman in the world, her adultery with the Trojan Paris became the pretext for the Trojan War.

Hephaestion soldier, lover and adviser to Alexander the Great.

Hercules son of Jupiter and Alcmene, the greatest of mythic heroes, famed for physical strength, obedience to his father, and for performing the Labours (including the cleaning of the Augean stables) set him by King Eurystheus. Sometimes called Alcides, after his grandfather Alceus.

Hercynia wilderness in Persia. See Nigra Silva.

Hermes see Mercury.

Hesperia 'the western land', Italy.

Hesperides the daughters of Hesperus, nymphs of the setting sun who guarded the golden apples in the far west.

Hippolytus son of Theseus. When he rejected the advances of his stepmother Phaedra, she accused him of attempting to rape her, causing Theseus to call on Poseidon (Neptune) to destroy him. The god sent a monster to terrify his chariot-horses, which dragged him to his death.

Homer Greek epic poet, reputedly blind, and who composed the *Iliad* and the *Odyssey*.

Hyades daughters of Atlas who were turned into seven stars in the constellation of Taurus and who were believed to cause bad weather.

Hybla town in Sicily famous for its honey.

Hydra many-headed monster which lived in the Lernean swamp near Argos; each of its heads would be replaced by two more if cut off, but it was eventually killed by Hercules.

Hylas a beautiful boy kidnapped by water-nymphs from the expedition of the Argonauts; loved and lamented by Hercules.

Hymen Greek god of marriage, conventionally portrayed as a veiled young man bearing a flaming torch.

Iarbas son of Jupiter and Garamantis, king of Gaetulia.

Ibis sacred bird of Egyptian religion.

Icarus the son of Daedalus; he escaped from captivity with his father on a pair of wings held together with wax, but he flew too near the sun, the wax melted and he fell into the sea.

Ida (i) Mount Ida, near Troy, birthplace of Aeneas and site of the Judgement of Paris; (ii) Idalium in Cyprus.

Ilion, Ilium Troy.

Illyrians inhabitants of Illyria, on the eastern shore of the Adriatic.

Inde India or the West Indies.

Io a priestess of Juno, desired by Jupiter; for a time she was metamorphosed into a beautiful cow and then back to the human form in which she bore Jupiter a son, Epaphus.

Iphigen Iphigenia, the daughter of Agamemnon, who sacrificed her at Aulis to gain a favourable wind to sail for Troy.

Iris winged messenger of Juno.

Irus a beggar; one of the suitors of Penelope.

Jaertis the river Jaxartes which runs from Tartary into the Caspian Sea.

Janus Roman god of beginnings, doors and gates; the gates of his temple in the Forum stood open in times of war and closed in the rare interludes of peace.

Jason Greek hero who led the Argonauts in the quest for the Golden Fleece of Colchis.

Jebusite Canaanite tribe who were dispossessed of Jerusalem by David; the word became an abusive term for Jesuits.

Jerome St Jerome, 4th-century AD theologian, whose highly influential translation of the Bible into Latin (the Vulgate) was the standard text of the scriptures until the Reformation.

Jubalter Gibraltar.

Juno goddess of marriage, wife of the incessantly promiscuous Jupiter. She defended the sanctity of marriage by seeking the destruction of those who were implicated in his adultery. Saturnia was a cult name for Juno.

Jupiter most powerful of all the gods. The son of Saturn, who attempted to eat him in his infancy, he was protected by his mother Ops, and overthrew his father; famed for his use of thunderbolts to resolve disputes both human and divine, and his wide-ranging and insatiable sexual appetites; also frequently called Jove.

Justinian Flavius Petrus Justinianus (*c.* AD 482–565), Roman emperor at Constantinople who codified Roman law in his *Corpus juris civilis*.

Lacedaemon Sparta.

Lantchidol the Indian Ocean.

Laocoön Trojan priest who tried to prevent his countrymen from accepting the Trojan Horse, but who was killed with his sons by a monstrous sea-snake.

Larissa coastal town on the border between Syria and Egypt.

Latona beloved of Jupiter, mother to both Diana and Apollo.

Lavinia princess of Latium in Virgil's *Aeneid*; she was destined to marry Aeneas, the destroyer of her betrothed, Turnus.

Leander the hero of Marlowe's poem *Hero and Leander*, he swam the Hellespont to meet his beloved Hero, but died trying to swim home.

Lerna site of a swamp in Greece, home of the monstrous Hydra which Hercules killed.

Lesbia the woman addressed in the erotic poetry of Catullus.

Lethe one of the three rivers of the underworld; its waters induced forgetfulness.

Limnasphaltis bituminous lake near Babylon; its fumes supposedly killed birds which flew over it.

Lopus, Doctor Dr Roderigo Lopez, Elizabeth I's physician, who was hanged in 1594 for his alleged involvement in a plot to poison the queen.

Machda Abyssinian town, capital of the legendary Christian king of Ethiopia, Prester John.

Machevil Niccolò Machiavelli (1469–1527), Italian historian and political thinker; reviled in Elizabethan England for supposed atheism and for the advocacy of ruthlessness in his manual for rulers, *The Prince*.

Manico Manicongo, an African province.

Mare Maggiore the Black Sea.

Mare Rosso the Red Sea.

Maro see Virgil.

Mars god of war and lover of Venus.

Mauritania province of north-west Africa.

Mausolus 4th-century BC king of Caria in Asia Minor, whose tomb, the Mausoleum, was one of the seven wonders of the ancient world.

Media province of the Persian empire.

Megaera one of the Furies.

Meleager a prince of Calydon, who heroically killed the wild boar Diana sent to ravage his land.

Memphis former capital of Egypt and site of the Pyramids.

Menelaus the king of Sparta, married to Helen, who was carried off by the Trojan prince Paris, thus precipitating the Trojan War. In Elizabethan literature he was commonly associated with ineffectualness and cuckoldry.

Mercury messenger of the gods, and god of travellers, lawyers and thieves.

Midas king of Phrygia, whose touch turned all things to gold (including, unfortunately, his food). He judged the music of the satyr Marsyas superior to that of Apollo, for which misjudgement the god made asses' ears grow on his head.

Minerva goddess of war, wisdom and handicrafts; her shield bore the head of the gorgon Medusa, who was killed by Perseus with her assistance.

Morpheus god of dreams.

Musaeus legendary poet whom Aeneas meets in his journey through the underworld in Virgil's *Aeneid* (VI, 666–7).

Myrmidons the bodyguard of Achilles.

Natolia Anatolia, the entire promontory of Asia Minor. Marlowe sometimes uses it as the name of a town in the region.

Neoptolemus the son of Achilles; also called Pyrrhus.

Neptune god of all waters, including the sea; he shared the dominion of the world with Jupiter and Pluto.

Nigra Silva the 'Black Forest' of Hercynia, held to be highly dangerous in the 16th century.

Nilus the river Nile.

Ninus the first Assyrian king, founder of Nineveh; his queen was Semiramis.

Niobe in Greek myth, she boasted that her seven children made her superior to Leto (Latona), the mother of Apollo and Artemis; in revenge, these two killed all her children with their arrows. Niobe wept until she was turned to a pillar of stone, which continued to weep.

Nubia north African province between the Red Sea and the Nile.

Oblia Olbia, area near the Black Forest.

Oceanus god of the ocean.

Octavius (63 BC–AD 14), nephew of Julius Caesar; later known as Augustus; ruler of Rome.

Oenone a nymph of Mount Ida, who stabbed herself when her former lover, Paris, died at her feet during the Trojan War.

Olympus the highest mountain in Greece, reputedly the habitation of the twelve gods, as well as the birthplace and home of the Muses.

O'Neill Irish clan leader in the reign of Edward II.

Ops goddess of the earth, fecundity and riches, wife of Saturn, and mother of Jupiter, who eventually usurped Saturn's throne.

Orcus Roman name for Hades, god of the underworld.

Orestes son of Agamemnon and Clytemnestra; he killed his mother in revenge for her murder of his father, and was subsequently pursued by the Eumenides (the Furies) but aided by his loyal friend Pylades and his sister Electra.

Orion a giant blind huntsman, transformed after his death into the constellation bearing his name, which is predominant in winter.

Orminius Mount Horminius, in Natolia (Asia Minor).

Ormus prosperous trading city in the Persian Gulf.

Padua north Italian town, famous for its university.

Paean cult-name of Apollo as god of healing.

Pampelonia Pamplona, capital of Navarre.

Paphos town in Cyprus.

Paris son of Priam and Hecuba. The most beautiful man in the world, he was chosen to decide which goddess should be awarded a golden apple inscribed 'for the most beautiful'. Offered greatness by Juno, conquest by Minerva and the gift of the most beautiful woman in the world (Helen, the wife of Menelaus) by Venus, he gave the apple to Venus. He deserted his lover Oenone and abducted Helen, precipitating the Trojan War.

Parma, Prince of Tyrannical Spanish governor-general of the Netherlands (1579–92), who was a byword for Catholic cruelty.

Parthia Asian kingdom, south-east of the Caspian Sea.

Patroclus friend and possibly lover of Achilles.

Pegasus winged horse, associated with Mount Helicon, home of the Muses.

Penelope wife of Odysseus and archetype of marital fidelity who frustrated her many suitors by insisting that she would not remarry until she had completed a shroud for her father-in-law. During her husband's absence she spent each night unravelling the shroud to ensure that it would never be finished.

Pergama (Pergamum) Troy.

Persepolis capital of Persia.

Phaethon 'the shining one', son of Apollo, the sun-god, who ignored warnings not to ride his father's chariot. When he lost control, he burnt a scar in the sky (the Milky Way) and plummeted to earth; Jupiter destroyed him with a thunderbolt during his descent, and thus prevented the destruction of the earth.

Phalaris 6th-century BC tyrant of Acragas (Agrigento) in Sicily. He roasted his enemies to death in a brazen bull, which was later used to kill him. A series of improbably humane letters were attributed to him.

Pharsalus site of the most savage battle of the Roman civil wars, at which Julius Caesar defeated Pompey (48 BC). It gave its title to Lucan's epic poem *Pharsalia*, of which Marlowe translated the opening book.

Philip Philip II, King of Spain 1556–98, briefly husband to 'Bloody' Mary Tudor, and the monarch responsible for the almost successful invasion of England by his Armada in 1588.

Phlegethon a river of fire, a boundary to the underworld.

Phoebe Diana, goddess of the moon.

Phoebus Apollo, god of the sun.

Phoenissa see Dido.

Phrygia the region of Troy in western Asia Minor.

Phyteus rare name for Apollo, i.e. the sun.

Pierides the daughters of King Pierus of Thessaly; they challenged the Muses to a song contest and were turned into magpies for their presumption.

Pliny Caius Plinius Secundus (AD 23–79), 'the Elder'; Roman writer, compiler of an encyclopaedic *Natural History*.

Pluto the god who ruled the underworld; he abducted Proserpina, the daughter of Ceres, from Sicily, and made her his queen.

Podalia in the southern part of Russia, close to Romania.

Polony Poland.

Polyphemus Cyclops who ate people until his single eye was blinded by Ulysses.

Polyxena daughter of Priam and Hecuba; she was sacrificed by Neoptolemus on the tomb of Achilles.

Portingale, Bay of Bay of Biscay.

Priam king of Troy and father (in Homer) of fifty sons and many daughters.

Procne wife of the Thracian king Tereus; when he raped her sister Philomela she served up her own son Itys to him in a stew.

Prometheus Titan who stole fire from the gods and gave it to humans.

Proserpina daughter of Jupiter and Ceres, Proserpina (Greek Persephone) was abducted by Pluto, who made her queen of the underworld; her distraught mother persuaded Jupiter to allow Proserpina to live half the year with her (summer) and half with Pluto (winter).

Proteus omniscient sea-god who could change shape.

Pygmalion a king of Cyprus who created a statue with which he fell in love; at his entreaty Venus brought the statue to life.

Pylades devoted friend of Orestes.

Pyrrhus son of Achilles (also called Neoptolemus).

Pythagoras 6th-century BC Greek philosopher, ascetic and mathematician, who originated the doctrine of metempsychosis, the transmigration of souls.

Ramus Pierre de la Ramée (1515–72); French humanist and philosopher who advocated a simplification of Aristotelian logic and rhetoric; killed in the St Bartholomew's Day Massacre.

Rhadamanthus son of Zeus, whose just life was posthumously acknowledged by his being made a judge of the dead.

Rhamnus site of the temple of Nemesis in Attica.

Rhamnusia Nemesis, goddess of fate and retribution, whose temple stood at Rhamnus in Attica.

Rhesus Thracian ally of the Greeks at Troy.

Rhode Stadtroda, in eastern Germany.

Rhodope (i) mountain in Thrace, famed as the site of Orpheus' dismemberment and for its silver mines; (ii) queen of Thrace; (iii) Greek courtesan.

Riso town on the Black Sea coast of Asia Minor.

Roscius celebrated actor in 1st-century BC Rome.

Rutiles Italian tribe ruled by Turnus.

Saba in the Old Testament, Sheba, whose queen challenged Solomon with 'hard questions' (1 Kings 10:1).

Samarcanda Samarkand, central Asian town, south-east of the Aral Sea.

Samnites an ancient people of central Italy.

Sancina town on the Black Sea coast of Asia Minor.

Saturn god of time and leader of the Titans; father of Pluto, Neptune, Juno and Jupiter, the last of whom overthrew him and ended the Golden Age.

Saturnia see Juno.

Saul king of Israel; God ordered him to destroy the Amalekites completely, but he spared King Agag and the best of the flocks, until rebuked by Samuel for his disobedience (1 Samuel 15).

Scalonia Ascalon, usually called Scalonia on ancient maps, a Philistine city on the coast of Palestine.

Scheckius Jacob Shegk (1511–87); German logician, opponent of Ramus in a famous philosophical dispute over the value of Aristotle.

Scylla a monster from whose lower body grew the heads of barking dogs. She menaced ships in the Straits of Messina, opposite the whirlpool Charybdis.

Selinus Sicilian town, site of a temple to Jupiter.

Semele one of Jupiter's lovers, who was consumed by lightning when she demanded that he should appear to her in his true form.

Semiramis legendarily beautiful Assyrian queen, wife of Ninus, she refortified Babylon and built its hanging gardens.

Shatillian Elizabethan spelling of Châtillon, town in France and the name of the prominent family of the Coligny.

Sichaeus (Sychaeus) Dido's husband, whose murder at the hands of her brother Pygmalion drove her to flee to Africa.

Sidon city in Phoenicia.

Silvanus Roman god of the woods.

Sinon Greek agent who deceived the Trojans into taking the Wooden Horse into Troy.

Sinus Arabicus the Red Sea.

Sirens female sea-deities who lured sailors to their deaths with their song.

Sixtus Pope Sixtus V, pontiff 1585–90, who revolutionized and centralized the power of papal administration and virtually rebuilt Rome in the process; he also began the overtures to Henry of Navarre which eventually prompted his conversion to Catholicism.

Socrates philosopher and teacher in 5th-century BC Athens, eventually executed for allegedly corrupting the morals of Athenian youth.

Soldino coastal town opposite Cyprus.

Soria (i) Syria; (ii) Zor, i.e. Tyre.

Stoka Stoko, a town on the Dniester.

Styx the principal river of the underworld.

Tanaïs the river Don, the boundary of Europe and Asia.

Tenedos an island off the coast of Troy.

Terrene Sea the Mediterranean.

Tesella area south of Oran in North Africa.

Thebes Greek city in the province of Boeotia. The stones of its walls rose to the music of Amphion.

Themis goddess of rights and customs, who sent an uncatchable fox to ravage Thebes in revenge for the death of the Sphinx; both the fox and the invincible hunting hound of Cephalus which pursued it were turned to stone by Zeus.

Thessaly region of Greece famous for its drugs and witches.

Thetis a sea-nymph, goddess and the mother of Achilles.

Tisiphone snake-haired Fury; perpetrators of crimes within the family were particularly vulnerable to her persecutions.

Titus Roman emperor AD 79–81, conqueror of Jerusalem (AD 70).

Trasimene battlefield near Lake Trasimeno, north of Rome, where the Carthaginian commander Hannibal conquered the Romans in 217 BC.

Trebizond town in northern Turkey (modern Trabzon).

Trier town in western Germany.

Triton sea-god, sometimes half-human and half-fish.

Tully Marcus Tullius Cicero (106–43 BC), Roman orator and statesman.

Turnus king of Ardea in Italy, heroic antagonist in Virgil's *Aeneid*; he violently opposed the prophesied marriage between his betrothed, Lavinia, and Aeneas, but the latter killed him in single combat.

Typhon (Typhoeus) formidable monster with a hundred serpentine heads; his offspring included the three-headed dog Cerberus, the Hydra, the Chimaera and the Sphinx.

Tyre city in Phoenicia.

Tyros the river Dniester, which runs through southern Russia.

Ulysses (Odysseus) wily Greek hero who assisted in the fall of Troy. His adventures in returning home to his faithful wife, Penelope, are recounted in Homer's *Odyssey*.

Uz biblical homeland of Job, bordering Palestine.

Vanholt Anhalt in central Germany.

Venus goddess of erotic love, notoriously unfaithful wife of Vulcan, sometime lover of Mars, and would-be seducer of Adonis.

Verna Bulgarian seaport.

Vespasian Titus Flavius Vespasianus, Roman emperor (AD 69–79), he subdued a rebellion in Judaea, but failed to capture Jerusalem.

Virgil Publius Vergilius Maro (70–19 BC), Roman poet of the *Eclogues*, the *Georgics* and the *Aeneid*; buried just outside Naples; he later acquired the reputation of being an adept magician.

Volga the river Volga; the maps of Ortelius which Marlowe used clearly showed its many tributaries.

Vulcan Roman god of fire and metalwork, he forged the arms of the gods. He was married to the unfaithful Venus, whom he caught in a net as she made love with Mars. He was lame.

Xanthus river near Troy.

Xerxes Persian king (d. 465 BC) who was said by Herodotus to have assembled the greatest army ever known in ancient times for his disastrous invasion of Greece in 480 BC.

Zanzibar in Ortelius's atlas, a south-western province of Africa.

Zona Mundi ('the girdle of the world') mountain range in the northern regions of Tartary in central Asia.

Zula city to the north of the river Danube.

PENGUIN ⟨●⟩ CLASSICS

The Classics Publisher

'Penguin Classics, one of the world's greatest series' JOHN KEEGAN

'I have never been disappointed with the Penguin Classics. All I have read is a model of academic seriousness and provides the essential information to fully enjoy the master works that appear in its catalogue' MARIO VARGAS LLOSA

'Penguin and Classics are words that go together like horse and carriage or Mercedes and Benz. When I was a university teacher I always prescribed Penguin editions of classic novels for my courses: they have the best introductions, the most reliable notes, and the most carefully edited texts' DAVID LODGE

'Growing up in Bombay, expensive hardback books were beyond my means, but I could indulge my passion for reading at the roadside bookstalls that were well stocked with all the Penguin paperbacks . . . Sometimes I would choose a book just because I was attracted by the cover, but so reliable was the Penguin imprimatur that I was never once disappointed by the contents.

Such access certainly broadened the scope of my reading, and perhaps it's no coincidence that so many Merchant Ivory films have been adapted from great novels, or that those novels are published by Penguin' ISMAIL MERCHANT

'You can't write, read, or live fully in the present without knowing the literature of the past. Penguin Classics opens the door to a treasure house of pure pleasure, books that have never been bettered, which are read again and again with increased delight' JOHN MORTIMER

CLICK ON A CLASSIC
www.penguinclassics.com
The world's greatest literature at your fingertips

Constantly updated information on over 1600 titles, from Icelandic sagas to ancient Indian epics, Russian drama to Italian romance, American greats to African masterpieces

•

The latest news on recent additions to the list, updated editions and specially commissioned translations

•

Original scholarly essays by leading writers: Elaine Showalter on Zola, Laurie R. King on Arthur Conan Doyle, Frank Kermode on Shakespeare, Lisa Appignanesi on Tolstoy

•

A wealth of background material, including biographies of every classic author from Aristotle to Zamyatin, plot synopses, readers' and teachers' guides, useful web links

•

Online desk and examination copy assistance for academics

•

Trivia quizzes, competitions, giveaways, news on forthcoming screen adaptations

•

eBooks available to download

READ MORE IN PENGUIN

In every corner of the world, on every subject under the sun, Penguin represents quality and variety – the very best in publishing today.

For complete information about books available from Penguin – including Puffins and Penguin Classics – and how to order them, write to us at the appropriate address below. Please note that for copyright reasons the selection of books varies from country to country.

In the United Kingdom: *Please write to* Dept EP, Penguin Books Ltd, Bath Road, Harmondsworth, West Drayton, Middlesex UB7 0DA

In the United States: *Please write to* Consumer Services, Penguin Putnam Inc., 405 Murray Hill Parkway, East Rutherford, New Jersey 07073-2136. *VISA and MasterCard holders call 1-800-631-8571 to order Penguin titles*

In Canada: *Please write to* Penguin Books Canada Ltd, 10 Alcorn Avenue, Suite 300, Toronto, Ontario M4V 3B2

In Australia: *Please write to* Penguin Books Australia Ltd, 487 Maroondah Highway, Ringwood, Victoria 3134

In New Zealand: *Please write to* Penguin Books (NZ) Ltd, Private Bag 102902, North Shore Mail Centre, Auckland 10

In India: *Please write to* Penguin Books India Pvt Ltd, 11, Community Centre, Panchsheel Park, New Delhi 110017

In the Netherlands: *Please write to* Penguin Books Netherlands bv, Postbus 3507, NL-1001 AH Amsterdam

In Germany: *Please write to* Penguin Books Deutschland GmbH, Metzlerstrasse 26, 60594 Frankfurt am Main

In Spain: *Please write to* Penguin Books S. A., Bravo Murillo 19, 1°B, 28015 Madrid

In Italy: *Please write to* Penguin Italia s.r.l., Via Vittoria Emanuele 45ia, 20094 Corsico, Milano

In France: *Please write to* Penguin France, 12, Rue Prosper Ferradou, 31700 Blagnac

In Japan: *Please write to* Penguin Books Japan Ltd, Iidabashi KM-Bldg, 2-23-9 Koraku, Bunkyo-Ku, Tokyo 112-0004

In South Africa: *Please write to* Penguin Books South Africa (Pty) Ltd, P.O. Box 751093, Gardenview, 2047 Johannesburg